ARTHURIAN STUDIES LXXXIV

THE MANUSCRIPT AND MEANING OF
MALORY'S *MORTE DARTHUR*

ARTHURIAN STUDIES

ISSN 0261-9814

General Editor: Norris J. Lacy

Previously published volumes in the series
are listed at the back of this book

THE MANUSCRIPT AND MEANING OF MALORY'S *MORTE DARTHUR*

RUBRICATION, COMMEMORATION, MEMORIALIZATION

K. S. Whetter

D. S. BREWER

© K. S. Whetter 2017

All rights reserved. Except as permitted under current legislation no part of this work may be photocopied, stored in a retrieval system, published, performed in public, adapted, broadcast,transmitted, recorded or reproduced in any form or by any means, without the prior permission of the copyright owner

The right of K. S. Whetter to be identified as the author of this work has been asserted in accordance with sections 77 and 78 of the Copyright, Designs and Patents Act 1988

First published 2017
Paperback edition 2020

D. S. Brewer, Cambridge

ISBN 978 1 84384 453 2 hardback
ISBN 978 1 84384 563 8 paperback

D. S. Brewer is an imprint of Boydell & Brewer Ltd
PO Box 9, Woodbridge, Suffolk, IP12 3DF, UK
and of Boydell & Brewer Inc.
668 Mount Hope Ave, Rochester, NY 14620–2731, USA
website: www.boydellandbrewer.com

The publisher has no responsibility for the continued existence or accuracy of URLs for external or third-party internet websites referred to in this book, and does not guarantee that any content on such websites is, or will remain, accurate or appropriate

A CIP catalogue record for this book is available
from the British Library

For Eleanor and Hadley

Contents

List of Plates	viii
Acknowledgements	x
Abbreviations	xii
A Note on the Text	xiv
A Textual Introduction	1
1 The Unusual Nature of Winchester's Rubrication	23
2 Tracing Winchester's Rubrication and Marginalia	54
Appendix I: Classifications of Rubrication	92
Appendix II: Rubrication Errors or Departures from the Usual Pattern	94
3 Malory's Sacralized Secularity	105
4 Rubricated Elegy	159
Conclusion: The Red and the Black	199
Bibliography	215
Manuscripts	215
Primary Sources	216
Secondary Sources	218
Index	235
Addenda to the Paperback Edition	243

Plates

Between pages 34 and 35

Plate I: The close of Tale II and opening of Tale III as it appears in the Winchester-manuscript text of *Morte Darthur*, London, British Library, Additional MS 59678, fol. 96^r. ©The British Library Board, Add. 59678, fol. 96^r.

Plate II: The opening of *Generides*, Morgan Library, MS M.876, fol. 103^v. The Pierpont Morgan Library, New York. MS M.876, fol. 103^v. Photographic credit: The Pierpont Morgan Library, New York.

Plate III: The partial rubrication of *Generides*, Morgan Library, MS M.876, fol. 109^r. The Pierpont Morgan Library, New York. MS M.876, fol. 109^r. Photographic credit: The Pierpont Morgan Library, New York.

Plate IV: Partial rubrication of names in *Generides*, Morgan Library, MS M.876, fol. 110^r. The Pierpont Morgan Library, New York. MS M.876, fol. 110^r. Photographic credit: The Pierpont Morgan Library, New York.

Plate V: Occasional rubrication of rulers' names in *Brut* MSS: in this case, Oxford, Bodleian Library MS Laud Miscellany 733, fol. 19^v. The Bodleian Libraries, The University of Oxford, MS Laud Miscellany 733, fol. 19^v.

Plate VI: Erratic red underlining of names as illustrated by *Brut* manuscript Oxford, Bodleian Library MS Bodley 840, fol. 1^r. The Bodleian Libraries, The University of Oxford, MS Bodley 840, fol. 1^r.

Plate VII: Erratic red underlining of names as illustrated by *Brut* manuscript Oxford, Bodleian Library MS Laud Miscellany 550, fol. 24^r. The Bodleian Libraries, The University of Oxford, MS Laud Miscellany 550, fol. 24^r.

Plate VIII: Partial name rubrication in the first version of Hardyng's *Chronicle*, London, British Library, Lansdowne MS 204, fol. 34^r. ©The British Library Board, Lans. 204, fol. 34^r.

Plate IX: Rubricated initials of new Round Table knights, Hardyng's first *Chronicle*, British Library Lansdowne MS 204, fol. 70^r. ©The British Library Board, Lans. 204, fol. 70^r.

Plate X: Decorative emphasis on Round Table knights, Hardyng's first *Chronicle*, British Library Lansdowne MS 204, fol. 83^r. ©The British Library Board, Lans. 204, fol. 83^r.

Plate XI: Rubricated glosses emphasizing Arthur's reign: Hardyng's *Chronicle*, Oxford, Bodleian Library, MS Arch. Selden B.10, fol. 52^v. The Bodleian Libraries, The University of Oxford, MS Arch. Selden B.10, fol. 52^v.

Plate XII: Typical rubricated caption titles in the *Lancelot-Graal* Cycle: from London, British Library, Additional MS 10294, fol. 53^r. ©The British Library Board, Add. 10294, fol. 53^r.

Between pages 162 and 163

Plate XIII: The Tale VII *explicit*–Tale VIII *incipit* as it appears in the Winchester-manuscript text of *Morte Darthur*, London, British Library, Additional MS 59678, fol. 449^r. ©The British Library Board, Add. 59678, fol. 449^r.

Plate XIV: Marginalium recording the death of Lott and the rebels and memorializing Arthur's victory, as it appears in the Winchester-manuscript text of *Morte Darthur*, London, British Library, Additional MS 59678, fol. 28^v. ©The British Library Board, Add. 59678, fol. 28^v.

Plate XV: The beginning of the great catalogue of knights who attempt the healing of Sir Urry, as it appears in the Winchester-manuscript text of *Morte Darthur*, London, British Library, Additional MS 59678, fol. 446^r. ©The British Library Board, Add. 59678, fol. 446^r.

Plate XVI: The middle section of the great Urry catalogue, as it appears in the Winchester-manuscript text of *Morte Darthur*, London, British Library, Additional MS 59678, fol. 447^r. ©The British Library Board, Add. 59678, fol. 447^r.

The author and publishers are grateful to all the institutions and individuals listed for permission to reproduce the materials in which they hold copyright. Every effort has been made to trace the copyright holders; apologies are offered for any omission, and the publishers will be pleased to add any necessary acknowledgement in subsequent editions.

Acknowledgements

This book has been a long time coming and I have accumulated quite a few debts to family, friends, and other scholars along the road to completion. My central thesis here has also bled into several other publications over the years. The core of Chapter One first appeared in slightly different guise as 'Malory, Hardyng, and the Winchester Manuscript: Some Preliminary Conclusions', *Arthuriana* 22.4 (2012): 167–89. The new version includes substantial revision and additional material, but I am indebted to Dorsey Armstrong and *Arthuriana* for allowing me to reproduce my previous argument. Parts of Chapter Three first appeared in 'Malory's Secular Arthuriad', in *Malory and Christianity: Essays on Sir Thomas Malory's Morte Darthur*, ed. D. Thomas Hanks, Jr, and Janet Jesmok (Kalamazoo, 2013), pp. 157–79, to which due credit is here given. Other aspects of 'Secular Arthuriad' are reworked in Chapter Four. Chapter Four also reprints some material and expands ideas from my 'Weeping, Wounds and *Worshyp* in Malory's *Morte Darthur*', *Arthurian Literature* 31 (2014): 61–82. I am indebted to the presses and editors where each of these essays first appeared for allowing me to reproduce the relevant materials. I hope in each case that the new incarnation is sufficiently expanded to warrant the occasional repetition.

For permission to access special materials, I owe a great deal of thanks to the manuscript reading room supervisors and staff at the British Library, the Bodleian Library, Cambridge University Library, Cambridge Trinity College Wren Library (especially Sub-Librarian Sandy Paul), Fitzwilliam Museum and the Pierpont Morgan Library. The manuscript research for this book was enabled through a series of grants from the Acadia University Research Fund, to which I am deeply grateful. I am especially indebted to Drs Andrea Clarke and Julian Harrison of the British Library for granting me permission to examine BL Add. MS 59678 (Winchester) first-hand.

Other debts are less legal but no less binding. Boydell & Brewer's readers provided invaluable feedback. Dorsey Armstrong, Fiona Tolhurst and R. A. McDonald each read lengthy draft chapters, and I benefitted considerably from their comments and corrections. Michael W. Twomey supported the study from its inception, whilst also offering much encouragement and scholarly advice. Thomas Crofts, David Johnson, Amy Kaufman, Megan Leitch, Samantha Rayner, Robert Rouse, Cory Rushton and a host of others have listened to my ideas at length and offered much wisdom, counsel, challenges and corrective criticism. Keith Busby, Carol Chase, A. S. G. Edwards, John Finlayson, Helen Cooper and Don Kennedy have all kindly allowed me to pester them with questions, and I have benefitted from their expertise about manuscript study, the material contexts of the *Morte Darthur* and its sources, or both. Bits and pieces of the book were aired at various conferences, notably Kalamazoo, the Atlantic Medieval

Association and the International Arthurian Congress, and here, too, I benefitted from many valuable comments, challenges, or encouragement. I also explored a number of my ideas in several upper-level seminars at Acadia, and am especially grateful to former students Myles, Jesse, Robert, and Reese, Marc, Ceileigh, Elisabet, Danielle and Ian for their enthusiasm and discussion. Caroline Palmer, as always, has been a joy to work with.

Finally, and most importantly, I am considerably indebted to Ann, Eleanor and Hadley, to my mother and grandmother, and to my brother, for their unfailing love and support.

Abbreviations

Add.	Additional (for manuscript shelf marks)
Aspects	*Aspects of Malory*, ed. Toshiyuki Takamiya and Derek Brewer (Cambridge and Totowa, 1981)
BL	British Library, London
Bodl.	Bodleian Library, Oxford
C	*Le Morte d'Arthur: Printed by William Caxton 1485*, Intro. Paul Needham (London, 1976). (This style occurs exclusively in quotation citations or footnotes.)
the Caxton	refers to Caxton's 1485 print of Malory's *Morte Darthur*
Companion	*A Companion to Malory*, ed. Elizabeth Archibald and A. S. G. Edwards (Cambridge, 1996)
CUL	Cambridge University Library, Cambridge
Debate	*The Malory Debate: Essays on the Texts of Le Morte Darthur*, ed. Bonnie Wheeler, Robert L. Kindrick and Michael N. Salda (Cambridge, 2000)
EETS	Early English Text Society
	ES Extra Series
	OS Original Series
	SS Supplementary Series
Essays	*Essays on Malory*, ed. J. A. W. Bennett (Oxford, 1963)
Field	Field's Introduction, Apparatus, or Commentary to Sir Thomas Malory, *Le Morte Darthur*, ed. P. J. C. Field (Cambridge, 2013)
MD	The text of the *Morte Darthur*, from Field's edition
MS	Manuscript
MSS	Manuscripts
O^1	The 1st edition of *Works* (1947). (This is used only in footnotes.)
O^2	The 2nd edition of *Works* (1967). (Again, this style occurs exclusively in footnotes.)
O^3	The 3rd edition of *Works* (1990). (Again, this style occurs exclusively in footnotes.)

Originality	*Malory's Originality: A Critical Study of Le Morte Darthur*, ed. R. M. Lumiansky (Baltimore, 1964)
Studies	*Studies in Malory*, ed. James W. Spisak (Kalamazoo, 1985)
Tale I	The first narrative section or tale of the *Morte Darthur*: Caxton's Books I–IV; Vinaver's 'Tale of King Arthur'; Field's 'King Uther and King Arthur'. Winchester's *explicit* reads 'Fro the Maryage of Kynge Uther unto Kyng Arthure that Regned Aftir Hym and ded Many Batayles'
Tale II	Malory's second tale, called 'The Tale of the Noble Kynge Arthure that was Emperoure Hymself Thorow Dygnyté of His Hondys' at the beginning of its Winchester *explicit*, but also called 'The Noble Tale betwyxt Kynge Arthure and Lucius the Emperour of Rome' in the final lines of the same *explicit*. Caxton's Book V; Field's 'King Arthur and the Emperor Lucius'
Tale III	The third of Malory's component tales, 'The Noble Tale of Sir Launcelot'. Caxton's Book VI; Field's 'Sir Launcelot du Lake'
Tale IV	Malory's fourth tale, 'The Tale of Sir Gareth of Orkeney'. Caxton's Book VII; Field's 'Sir Gareth of Orkney'
Tale V	Malory's fifth tale, 'The Boke off Syr Trystram'. Caxton's Books VIII–XII; Field's 'Sir Tristram de Lyones: The First Book' and 'Sir Tristram de Lyones: The Second Book'
Tale VI	Malory's 'Tale of the Sankgreal'. Caxton's Books XIII–XVII; Field's 'The Sankgreal'
Tale VII	Long known by Vinaver's editorial title 'The Book of Sir Launcelot and Queen Guinevere'; renamed by Field 'Sir Launcelot and Queen Guenivere'. Caxton's Books XVIII–XIX
Tale VIII	The final component tale of Malory's narrative, the 'Morte Arthure' proper. Caxton's Books XX–XXI. This tale is sometimes called 'The Death of Arthur' by modern scholars.
Texts and Sources	P. J. C. Field, *Malory: Texts and Sources* (Cambridge, 1998)
Vinaver	Vinaver's Introduction and Apparatus to the 3rd edition of *Works* (below)
Winchester	The Winchester manuscript, now London, British Library, Additional Manuscript 59678. In some citations, this is further abbreviated to W.
Works	Sir Thomas Malory, *The Works of Sir Thomas Malory*, ed. Eugène Vinaver, 3rd edn, rev. P. J. C. Field (Oxford, 1990)

Note on the Text

All references to Malory's *Morte Darthur* are to Field's edition: *Le Morte Darthur*, ed. P. J. C. Field, 2 vols (Cambridge: D. S. Brewer, 2013). I am grateful to Boydell & Brewer for allowing me to quote at length. References to other texts are detailed in the notes and bibliography. In quotations from the primary texts, I have silently reproduced all editorial emendations *without* copying or indicating editorial italics and brackets. In usual scholarly practice, any square brackets remaining within quotations denote my own modifications.

NB: In my Malory quotations I regularly depart from Field's text in two ways. First, I have not adopted Field's uniform italicization of the *explicits*. Second, I print all quoted names in bold. The bold text is an attempt to mimic the rubrication of names in Winchester. Since Vinaver's edition was the scholarly standard for two generations, and in order to facilitate cross-references to it or other editions, all Malory quotations will give the Winchester folio number, followed by Field's page number (e.g. 70^r; 143.1–3). At the beginning and end of the *Morte*, where Winchester is wanting, I give Caxton's book and chapter numbers, followed by the Field citation (e.g. C XXI.13; 940.21).

In other citations, I do not include subtitles in footnotes: such information is included in the bibliography.

A Textual Introduction

Late mediaeval aristocratic culture valued visual spectacle. As Nigel Saul puts it, 'In the Middle Ages, when literacy was limited, it was through visual display that messages about status were communicated.'[1] London, British Library Additional MS 59678, otherwise known as the Winchester manuscript of Sir Thomas Malory's *Le Morte Darthur*, despite its lack of miniatures is a visually striking artefact.[2] It is also an artefact in which spectacle and meaning coalesce. It is my contention that the spectacular nature of the Winchester manuscript engages with and reflects the principal themes and characters of the *Morte Darthur* in ways unprecedented by other secular literary texts and their manuscripts in the Middle Ages. That is, with the *Morte Darthur* and its manuscript there is a marked and unique correlation between the physical layout of the manuscript text and the major narrative and thematic concerns of the lexical text. Winchester's physical layout, especially its rubrication of each and every character's name, creates a visual exaltation of the glory and splendour of earthly Arthurian chivalry. This close connection between manuscript and narrative is so marked and so unusual that it is much more likely to be authorial than scribal in origin.

Sir Thomas Malory's fifteenth-century *Le Morte Darthur* is the last major Arthurian work of the Middle Ages and the first and only Arthurian text in Middle English to recount the entire legend of Arthur from his birth to his death.[3]

---

[1] Nigel Saul, *For Honour and Fame* (London, 2011), p. 53.

[2] Some scholars refer to the manuscript as the 'Malory Manuscript', but I shall employ the more traditional 'Winchester' title, derived from the college where the MS was discovered in 1934. On this discovery, see W. F. Oakeshott, 'The Finding of the Manuscript', in *Essays*, pp. 1–6. For professional descriptions of Winchester, see the introduction to the black-and-white facsimile: *The Winchester Malory*, intro. N. R. Ker, EETS SS 4 (London, 1976), pp. ix–xxii; also Hilton Kelliher, 'The Early History of the Malory Manuscript', in *Aspects*, pp. 143–58 (pp. 143–7). The *Index of English Literary Manuscripts, Volume 1: 1450–1625*, compiled Peter Beal (London and New York, 1980), 1(ii): 323–4, lists two Malory manuscripts: Add. 59678, and a second manuscript, but this second MS is, as Beal makes clear, an incomplete 'index' or 'compilation of the principal deeds of King Arthur and the Knights of the Round Table'. This compilation was made by John Grinken in the late sixteenth century. It is an interesting response to the *Morte*, and further proof of Malory's early readership, but it is not a textual witness. Grinken's MS is privately owned by Toshiyuki Takamiya, and is currently held by the Beinecke Library.

[3] Unless otherwise noted, all references to the *Morte* throughout this book will be by page and line number to *Le Morte Darthur*, ed. P. J. C. Field, 2 vols (Cambridge, 2013). References to the text (Volume I) will be parenthetical, with Field's Introduction and Apparatus (the latter in Volume II) being cited in footnotes. Because of my focus on the manuscript, and in order to facilitate cross-references to other editions, each quotation also includes the Winchester folio reference or, where these are missing, a Caxton book and chapter reference.

R. M. Lumiansky styles it 'the outstanding English book of the fifteenth century',[4] and the *Morte*'s interest for modern scholars and influence upon modern authors and film-makers is sufficient to bear this out. Indeed, Malory's *Morte* has proven to be the most influential of all mediaeval treatments of the story of Arthur, inspiring a vast array of post-mediaeval authors and film-makers, including Edmund Spenser, Alfred Lord Tennyson, Mark Twain, T. H. White, John Steinbeck, Naomi Mitchison, John Boorman and Peter Ackroyd. Malory himself tells us that his 'book was ended the ninth yere of the reygne of Kyng Edward the Fourth' (C XXI.13; 940.26–7): that is, 4 March 1469–3 March 1470. The *Morte* was interesting enough in its day, and seemingly also popular enough, that William Caxton printed a version, and Caxton's successor Wynkyn de Worde printed two further editions. Both Caxton and de Worde would have expected to recoup their publication costs, yet Malory's story remained current enough that de Worde went so far as to commission twenty special woodcuts for his 1498 *Morte* incunable, most of which he reused in his 1529 reprint. The *Morte* was still popular enough in court that even in the reign of Elizabeth I Roger Ascham could famously complain about people reading the *Morte* instead of the Bible.[5]

However many copies of the text were extant in the Middle Ages and Renaissance, Malory's *Morte Darthur* survives today in only two textual witnesses: a late fifteenth-century manuscript now in the British Library and designated 'British Library Additional Manuscript 59678' but still commonly referred to as the 'Winchester manuscript' due to its discovery in Winchester College in 1934, and an incunabulum or early printed book published by William Caxton, commonly styled 'the Caxton', printed – a little later than Winchester – in the year 1485.[6] The manuscript is unique but imperfect, missing the opening and closing gatherings (of eight folios each), and three other folios. The Caxton survives in two copies: one perfect copy in the Pierpont Morgan Library, New York, and one, lacking eleven leaves, in the John Rylands Library, Manchester.

The *Morte*'s literary importance should be matched by its material pedigree since the text stands at a watershed moment in England's transition from a manuscript culture to a print culture, with one textual witness existing in manuscript and the other as an incunabulum produced by England's first printer. The ways in which the *Morte* literally embodies the movement from script to print, however, are all too often ignored. Malory wrote his presumably rather messy holograph in prison in the late 1460s, during the Wars of the Roses. This handwritten manuscript was itself copied into at least one and maybe two further manuscripts between the holograph and Winchester. Winchester itself (as we shall see below) may well have been planned and was certainly in production not long after Caxton set up his shop in London in late 1475 or early 1476. Caxton (as

---

[4] R. M. Lumiansky, 'Introduction', in *Originality*, pp. 1–7 (p. 1).
[5] Roger Ascham, *The Scholemaster*, in *The English Works of Roger Ascham*, ed. William Aldis Wright (Cambridge, 1904), pp. 230–1.
[6] Both the manuscript and the incunabulum are available in monochrome facsimile: see, respectively, *The Winchester Malory*; and *Le Morte D'Arthur Printed by William Caxton 1485*, intro. Paul Needham (London, 1976). At the time of going to press, a colour facsimile of Winchester, and selected pages of the Caxton, are available through Takako Kato's Malory Project at www.maloryproject.com[.]

we shall also see below) had Winchester and one other manuscript of Malory's Arthurian book in his printing house in the 1480s, but the version of the text read by nearly everyone who came after Wynkyn de Worde was a print copy, not a manuscript. Malory's book thus started life as a manuscript but quickly became – and became widely known as – a printed text.

Despite the ways in which the *Morte Darthur* encapsulates the evolution from manuscript to print, and despite a long and distinguished tradition of scholarly study of English literary manuscripts, neither manuscripts in general nor the *Morte* in particular have been much embraced by the modern scholarly juggernaut that is book history. As Alexandra Gillespie remarks in her survey of the discipline, scholarship 'on medieval books apparently has no place in the history of the book', which by and large foregrounds instead 'print' and 'print culture' 'at the expense of the manuscript'.[7] Equally surprisingly, with a handful of notable exceptions who will appear frequently later in my study, even manuscript scholars tend to ignore Malory and Winchester. A. I. Doyle and M. B. Parkes devoted their considerable expertise to manuscripts of Chaucer and Gower; A. S. G. Edwards and Derek Pearsall expanded but further entrenched this poetic focus; even Pearsall's survey of textual criticism and fifteenth-century studies, including noting the increased availability of modern facsimiles of fifteenth-century manuscripts, was remarkably silent about Winchester, despite the fact that Pearsall does discuss popular romance.[8] Partly these silences testify to the understandable casualties of scholarly specialization or the limits of what can be done in a scholarly article (or both). Partly, too, they foreground certain mediaeval poets over prose writers, and partly, it appears, they (again silently) endorse the view carried over from the Victorians that the *Morte Darthur* is not the product of a great author. The *Morte*, by this prejudicial assumption, is great despite rather than because of Malory's artistry. It would follow that manuscripts of Chaucer, Gower and *Piers Plowman* deserve study, but not manuscripts of English prose Arthuriana. All of these scholarly assumptions deserve to be reassessed.

Given the continuities and cooperation between manuscript and print culture throughout the fifteenth century, I share Gillespie's puzzlement over the lack of coordination amongst modern devotees of the manuscript and book. *Pace* Ralph Hanna or even (in part) Gillespie, however, I am not convinced that manuscript study axiomatically needs to change its methodology or goals, or needs to undergo a 'cultural move' that would make it more relevant or acceptable

---

[7] Alexandra Gillespie, 'The History of the Book', *New Medieval Literatures* 9 (2007): 245–86 (260–2). On the lack of respect granted the codicologist and palaeographer, and a host of reasons why manuscript study is important, see further Derek Pearsall, 'Texts, Textual Criticism, and Fifteenth Century Manuscript Production', in *Fifteenth-Century Studies*, ed. Robert F. Yeager (Hamden, Conn., 1984), pp. 121–36 (p. 122).

[8] A. I. Doyle and M. B. Parkes, 'The Production of Copies of the *Canterbury Tales* and the *Confessio Amantis* in the Early Fifteenth Century', in *Medieval Scribes, Manuscripts and Libraries*, ed. M. B. Parkes and Andrew G. Watson (London, 1978), pp. 163–210; A. S. G. Edwards and Derek Pearsall, 'The Manuscripts of the Major English Poetic Texts', in *Book Production and Publishing in Britain 1375–1475*, ed. Jeremy Griffiths and Derek Pearsall (Cambridge, 1989), pp. 257–78; and Pearsall, 'Textual Criticism, and Manuscript Production', in *Fifteenth-Century Studies*, pp. 121–36.

– particularly if we do so merely to emulate early modern book history.[9] After all, a good many scholars advocate embracing the *variance* of manuscripts and manuscript study; by this account, there is no reason why codicology and palaeography need necessarily valorize human readers and purposes. Both approaches and disciplines should be valid, whether we acquire knowledge of a single book or artist or author in relative isolation, or use our knowledge of the manuscript book as a window to access its broader cultural milieu. We should not be forced to pursue cultural studies, but neither need we eschew human contexts. The disciplinary problems are no doubt exacerbated by the comparative lack of details surrounding the pre-modern book: as Lotte Hellinga observes, notwithstanding 'four centuries of incunabula studies surprisingly little is known of the early book trade'. Despite the certainty that the majority of extant incunables must have been 'sold through the book trade', we generally possess 'only a vague notion of how [or even to whom] they were sold'.[10] This lack of identifiable sales and customers and patrons is equally true of a good many manuscripts. Certainly the enigma regarding for whom the extant witnesses of Malory's *Morte Darthur* were produced is unsolved. Caxton famously evokes a vague set of gentlemen behind his print of the *Morte*, but we lack specific identities. We know even less about Winchester's production and patron and circulation.

For these and other reasons, if the methods of the modern historian can be likened to that of one's favourite literary or cinematic detective, the task of the scholar investigating manuscripts and early books might fruitfully be compared to that of an archaeologist.[11] The study of the physical or material remains of past cultures is valuable both for the sake of the material objects and for what those remains might tell us about the peoples and cultures who produced them. The archaeology of the book, moreover, allows literary scholars to flesh out the unseen ghosts that stand behind the modern edition.[12] Unusually for a mediaeval manuscript, the human ghosts of Winchester are quite stunningly foregrounded by its rubrication of names. Winchester's rubrication provides an hermeneutic key foregrounding the people, places and things that Malory wants his audience – his culture – to valorize. As Gillespie advocates, building upon D. F. McKenzie, a book's form, including or perhaps especially a manuscript book's form, helps to create meaning, 'including authorial meaning, the reader's new meaning, the meaning generated by the work of the print shop, the bookseller, the librarian'.[13] With Malory's *Morte Darthur*, however, it is especially the manuscript form that emphasizes – and visually enacts – meaning.

---

[9] Ralph Hanna, 'Middle English Manuscripts and the Study of Literature', *New Medieval Literatures* 4 (2001): 243–63 (248 and 255); Gillespie, 'History', 256–61.

[10] Lotte Hellinga, 'Sale Advertisements for Books Printed in the Fifteenth Century', in *Books for Sale*, ed. Robin Myers, Michael Harris and Giles Mandelbrote (New Castle, Del., and London, 2009), pp. 1–25 (at p. 1).

[11] See, respectively, Robin W. Winks, ed., *The Historian as Detective* (New York, 1968); Pearsall, 'Textual Criticism, and Manuscript Production', in *Fifteenth-Century Studies*, pp. 121 and 128; Lotte Hellinga, *Caxton in Focus* (London, 1982), pp. 17–18.

[12] I adopt this metaphor from John Scattergood, *Manuscripts and Ghosts* (Dublin, 2006).

[13] Gillespie, 'History', 273–5. See also D. F. McKenzie, *Bibliography and the Sociology of Texts* (Cambridge, 1999), pp. 10–13.

When the Winchester manuscript was discovered in the old safe of the college Warden in 1934 there were three major consequences, one immediate, and two following from that. The immediate consequence was that Eugène Vinaver determined to base his new critical edition on the Winchester text rather than the Caxton. In a move the boldness of which is difficult to imagine in these days when scholarly success is measured by publication count, Vinaver abandoned his in-progress edition of a Caxton-based critical edition of *Le Morte Darthur* to embark instead upon a manuscript-based text. (When news of the discovery of the manuscript was announced, Lawrence of Arabia also desired to edit the manuscript: for all of his own learning, Lawrence lacked Vinaver's mastery of the French sources, and Malory studies today would be a vastly poorer field had Lawrence won out over Vinaver!) Based on his examination of Winchester, Vinaver concluded that Malory had written, not one unified story, but rather 'a series of [eight] separate romances'.[14] Accordingly, when Vinaver's Winchester-based edition was first published – some thirteen years later – under the contentious title *The Works of Sir Thomas Malory*, Vinaver instigated a decades-long debate over the unity of Malory's text. This Unity Debate was the second major consequence of Winchester's discovery. The third consequence, slightly later again, was that William Matthews and a handful of other prominent scholars eventually but forcefully disputed Vinaver's claims for the textual superiority of the Winchester version of the *Morte* and whether Caxton or Malory was responsible for the most drastic difference between the two versions. It is one of my conclusions in this book that the visual manner in which the *ordinatio* of Winchester continually engages with the narrative text of the *Morte Darthur* provides further support for the superiority of a manuscript-based critical edition.[15] More radically, I am also suggesting that the unusually close interaction of lexical and bibliographic texts (the words on the modern page and the mediaeval manuscript that preserves them) means that the physical layout of Winchester must derive from Malory himself. It is first necessary, however, to summarize the textual debate.

For obvious reasons it has traditionally been the words, the text of Winchester, not its physical layout, that figure in these textual-critical deliberations. The two witnesses to the *Morte Darthur*, the Winchester manuscript and the Caxton incunabulum, agree on the words about 90 per cent of the time, but in the remaining cases they differ in several important respects. Sally Shaw, for instance, praised the relative accuracy of Caxton's edition of the *Morte* when compared to Winchester, and William Matthews agreed with her, adding that Caxton's *Morte*

---

[14] Eugène Vinaver, ed., *The Works of Sir Thomas Malory* (Oxford, 1947), pp. vi and xxix–xxxv. This claim was repeated in the second and third editions: Vinaver, ed., *Works*, 2nd edn (Oxford, 1967), pp. xxxv–xli (p. xxxix); Vinaver, ed., *Works*, 3rd edn (Oxford, 1990), pp. ix and xxxv–xli (p. xxxix).

[15] *Ordinatio* is a term used by codicologists (scholars who study manuscripts) to denote theories of page design, layout, division and decoration, as distinct from *compilatio*, or theories by which the manuscript book is compiled, shaped or ordered. For further explanation of these terms, see especially M. B. Parkes, 'The Influence of the Concepts of *Ordinatio* and *Compilatio* on the Development of the Book', in *Medieval Learning and Literature*, ed. J. J. G. Alexander and M. T. Gibson (Oxford, 1976), pp. 115–41; also the very accessible discussion relating form in literature and science in Janine Rogers, *Unified Fields* (Montreal and Kingston, 2014), pp. 10–14, 24–9.

is typical of the printer's overall output since *all* of Caxton's incunables are textually sound and what we might call Caxton's editorial principles, the changes he does make to those texts, are reasonably transparent in the printer's various prologues and epilogues.[16] This is equally true, it was maintained, of the Caxton *Morte Darthur*. Matthews further argued not only for the unity of the *Morte* (a view shared by almost all Malory scholars today), but for the validity and superiority of a Caxton-based edition (a much more contentious conclusion).[17]

Leaving aside for the moment Matthews's views on a base text for a critical edition, there is no disputing the essential similarity of the two witnesses in a great many cases. In this sense Bonnie Wheeler and Michael N. Salda no doubt represent the feelings of many readers when they say of the textual differences between Winchester and the Caxton that, 'in thousands of cases of variation spread over hundred[s] of pages there is no "better" [reading], there is merely "different," and these differences do not significantly affect meaning one way or another'.[18] This assessment of the textual variations is, on the whole, quite defensible. Yet literary texts are not self-generating autonomous entities, and in this and other ways Vinaver, P. J. C. Field and even Matthews (amongst others) are correct to say that we have sufficient textual-critical and source evidence to deduce Malory's words rather than those of his scribes or printers. The question is thus which witness to those words is the more accurate and authorial. Whilst Winchester and the Caxton certainly agree on major matters much of the time, in the remaining cases they differ in several important respects. The issue becomes much more important and problematic when we recall that in the Roman War story in Malory's second tale (Caxton's fifth book), 'The Tale of the Noble Kynge Arthure that was Emperoure Hymself thorow Dygnyté of his Hondys', the differences between the Winchester and the Caxton texts are quite extreme: most significantly, the Caxton text is drastically shorter, being less than half the length of that in Winchester. There are also considerable differences in the style and language of the two versions in this (and other) sections of *Morte Darthur*.

Vinaver argued on textual-critical grounds in the first edition of *Works* in 1947 that the scribal errors in the Winchester manuscript were easier to identify and correct than similar errors in the Caxton, the latter of which might be further contaminated by Caxton's conscious editorial changes. Vinaver also argued that Caxton was responsible for the radical abridgement of the Roman War. For all of these reasons, he concluded, the Winchester text 'brings us nearer to what Malory really wrote'.[19] Vinaver's argument was repeated in the second and third

---

[16] Sally Shaw, 'Caxton and Malory', in *Essays*, pp. 114–45 (p. 143); William Matthews, 'The Besieged Printer', in *Debate*, pp. 35–64 (p. 38 for the Shaw approval).

[17] See especially William Matthews, 'A Question of Texts', in *Debate*, pp. 65–107. This edition eventually appeared as *Caxton's Malory*, ed. James W. Spisak, based on work by William Matthews, 2 vols (Berkeley, 1983).

[18] Bonnie Wheeler and Michael N. Salda, 'Introduction', in *Debate*, pp. ix–xiii (p. x). Moorman posits more than twenty thousand differences between the two witnesses: Charles Moorman, 'Caxton's *Morte Darthur*', *Fifteenth-Century Studies* 12 (1987): 99–113 (101, 108, 110).

[19] See Vinaver, ed., *Works* (1947), p. vi; O^2, pp. viii, xxx, c–cxx; and O^3, pp. ix, xxx, c–cxx. These claims are repeated and explicated at various points in Vinaver's Commentary. Henceforth all references to Vinaver's apparatus in his Introduction or Commentary will be to the third edition, abbreviated as 'Vinaver'.

editions as well as by various members of what might be termed the Vinaverian camp, each of whom offered his or her own addenda to Vinaver's original argument. In 1963, in the first collection of essays devoted to Malory's (and Vinaver's) text, C. S. Lewis felt that perhaps the version of the Roman War that had for long been the only known version, that is, the version printed by Caxton, was preferable to the version preserved in Winchester and printed by Vinaver; but although he disagreed with Vinaver in the interpretation of various literary matters, Lewis did not dispute that Caxton was responsible for these textual changes. Far from it: Lewis argued that Caxton's version of the Roman War is, ironically, actually 'much more Malorian, more like the best and most typical parts of Malory' than Malory's own version as revealed by Winchester.[20] Lewis particularly lamented that Caxton had not pruned even more diligently, especially in the alliteration Malory carried over from his principal source for the tale, the alliterative *Morte Arthure*. Shaw likewise agreed that Caxton is responsible for several minor and, in the Roman War, some major textual changes, stating at the outset of her study that 'it seems likely that in spite of numerous blemishes the Winchester text represents the closer approximation to what Malory actually wrote'.[21] Hence Field's observation that, notwithstanding frequent interpretative disagreements with the literary-critical aspects of Vinaver's arguments, the general validity of Vinaver's 'textual-critical conclusions were' for long 'universally accepted'.[22]

All of this scholarly understanding and agreement potentially changed radically in 1975, when Matthews's argument that Malory himself was the reviser of the Roman War story was delivered posthumously at the Triennial Congress of the International Arthurian Society held in Exeter; Matthews's paper subsequently circulated privately through select elements of the Arthurian scholarly community for nearly two decades in two different versions, before finally being published in 1997.[23] Meanwhile, various scholars in the Matthews camp

---

[20] C. S. Lewis, 'The English Prose *Morte*', in *Essays*, pp. 7–28 (p. 26).

[21] Shaw, 'Caxton and Malory', in *Essays*, p. 114. Shaw, like Lewis, also favoured the Caxton version of the Roman War: 'Caxton and Malory', p. 142.

[22] P. J. C. Field, 'The Earliest Texts of Malory's *Morte Darthur*', in his *Texts and Sources* (Cambridge, 1998), pp. 1–13 (p. 2).

[23] As Matthews, 'A Question of Texts', *Arthuriana* 7.1 (Spring 1997): 93–133. This was a special issue of *Arthuriana* devoted to Matthews's unpublished papers, including the longer version of his 1975 congress paper. Field, 'Caxton's Roman War', in *Debate*, pp. 127–67 (pp. 127–9), implies that both versions were drafts, albeit close to completion; Charles Moorman, 'Desperately Defending Winchester', also in *Debate*, pp. 109–15 (p. 110), claims that both versions were 'obviously finished' excepting a few footnotes. Regardless, neither version appeared in print till 1997, when 'Question of Texts' was edited by Robert L. Kindrick to appear in *Arthuriana*. These essays of Matthews were subsequently reprinted as the opening chapters of *Debate*. For the early history and non-published circulation of Matthews's reviser argument post-1975, see Field, 'Caxton's Roman War', pp. 127–9. Surprisingly, Kindrick offers little detailed explanation or explication of the history of the two versions, though he does call them both 'incomplete drafts', thereby confirming Field's assessment: see his 'Introduction' to Matthews's papers in *Debate*, pp. xv–xxxii. Kindrick is an ardent supporter of Matthews, unhesitatingly dismissing 'the widely accepted revisionism of Eugène Vinaver', whose conclusions are labelled 'condemnatory'. Field's 'Roman War' essay first appeared in *Arthuriana* 5.2 (Summer 1995): 31–73, was revised and reprinted in his *Texts and Sources*, pp. 126–61, and slightly revised again for the reprint in *Debate*. All references to Field's paper are accordingly to the final version in *Debate*, though Field's principal argument is the same throughout its own textual history.

furthered his beliefs, arguing that Winchester was not Caxton's copy-text (which is true), but rather an early draft of Malory's Arthuriad, revised and thus superseded by Malory himself (which is, as we shall see, far from true).[24] For Matthews and his followers, it was Malory's revised manuscript, with its vastly shorter account of the Roman War, which became Caxton's more authoritative copy-text for printing *Le Morte Darthur*. Because Caxton's track record with various incunabula is to announce and admit any changes he makes, because what changes there are in his edition of Malory are generally orthographic, and most especially because – it is claimed – only the author with access to and knowledge of his sources could have made the changes to the Roman War that differentiate the two *Morte Darthur* witnesses, Matthews and his followers argue that Malory himself revised and reduced the Roman War narrative in this (now lost) manuscript. For Moorman and Lumiansky, Malory is in fact responsible for almost all of the other changes from Winchester to Caxton *throughout* the *Morte Darthur*.[25] Thus Caxton preserved but did not create the revised version of the Arthuriad, including the abbreviated Roman War story. As Field observes, if this contention were correct, then 'the standard edition of Malory would have been based on a text that Malory had rejected'.[26] The natural corollary of this, though neither camp explicitly says so, is that all scholarship based on Vinaver's edition would be potentially misleading – or at least misled – in places.[27]

There is some logic in Matthews's claims, and some indisputable facts. After all, Vinaver himself concluded that Winchester is two stages removed from Malory's holograph (M-X-Y-W), that the Caxton is likewise two stages removed (M-X-Z-C), and that Winchester and the Caxton stand in collateral rather than linear relation to one another:[28]

```
         Malory
           X
      Y         Z
      W         C
```

In the 1990s Field postulated that there was only one intermediary copy (manuscript X) between Malory and Caxton, but that there may well be another intermediary manuscript (Vinaver's Y) between this common archetype and Winchester;

---

[24] Matthews, 'Besieged Printer', in *Debate*, p. 50; Matthews, 'Question of Texts', in *Debate*, especially pp. 91–101; R. M. Lumiansky, 'Sir Thomas Malory's Le Morte Darthur, 1947–1987', *Speculum* 62.4 (1987): 878–97 (especially 887–97); Moorman, 'Caxton's *Morte Darthur*', 99–113; idem, 'Desperately Defending', in *Debate*, pp. 109–15. Also, by definition, Spisak, ed., *Caxton's Malory*, but see especially Vol. 2, pp. 616–20.

[25] Moorman, 'Caxton's *Morte Darthur*', 99–113; Lumiansky, 'Malory's *Morte Darthur*', 895–6.

[26] Field, 'Earliest Texts', in his *Texts and Sources*, p. 2. Cf. Field, 'Caxton's Roman War', in *Debate*, pp. 127–8.

[27] It turns out that Clarendon was aware of some of Matthews's complaints as far back as 1962, and took care to ensure that the forthcoming O^2 was still justified, even if no longer universally accepted: see Samantha Rayner, 'The Case of the "curious document"', *JIAS* 3.1 (2015): 120–38. Rayner adds to what is now known about the Exeter presentation that no one in the audience made any public comment (124 and n. 17).

[28] Vinaver, pp. c–cxxvi, especially pp. cii–cvi. In this stemma, M = Malory, W = Winchester, C = the Caxton print, and X, Y, Z = lost intermediary copies.

but Field always confirmed Vinaver's collateral view.[29] Helen Cooper argues on different evidence for a shorter collateral stemma of only one step between Malory and Winchester as well as between Malory and Caxton.[30] Field's most recent opinion, based on his re-examination of some fifty passages in both witnesses, confirms Vinaver's position about there being at least two intermediary copies between Malory and each of Winchester and the Caxton.[31] But for all of this disagreement, no one has convincingly argued that Winchester is the holograph or its immediate descendant.[32]

Lotte Hellinga's discovery of traces of printer's ink offsets on sixty-six folios scattered throughout Winchester further muddied the waters by revealing that Winchester was in Caxton's shop from at least 1480 to 1483, the years in which the typefaces causing the ink marks in question were in use.[33] Hellinga also established on the basis of the printer's waste used to repair folio 243 that Winchester remained with Caxton till at least 1489. Winchester was thus in Caxton's printing house and obviously predates the 1485 incunabulum by at least a few years, but it was not the copy-text for the *Morte Darthur* since it contains no compositor's marks. In an attempt to explain Winchester's presence in Caxton's printing house, and Caxton's ink in Winchester, Hellinga tentatively suggests that Caxton (or someone in his shop) copied Winchester to create a copy-text.[34] This argument has not generally been accepted because the textual-critical evidence strongly speaks against Winchester or a copy based on it being the copy-text: there are simply too many passages that appear only in Winchester or only in the Caxton that are clearly genuine on the basis of narrative sense and comparable readings in the sources, but which have no counterpart in the other witness.[35] Winchester

---

[29] See especially Field, 'Earliest Texts', in his *Texts and Sources*, pp. 1–13, and Field, 'The Choice of Texts for Malory's *Morte Darthur*', in his *Texts and Sources*, pp. 14–26.

[30] Helen Cooper, 'Opening Up the Malory Manuscript', in *Debate*, pp. 255–84 (pp. 265 and 277). Cooper's claims are at least partially supported by Field's evidence in 'Earliest Texts', in his *Texts and Sources*.

[31] See Field, I: xi and xvii, and Commentary (Vol. II) on 23.28, 119.35–120.1 and 206.13–14.

[32] Griffith suggests that Caxton's copy-text may have been a fair copy of the holograph, but neither this nor Griffith's accompanying suggestion that the Malory who wrote *Morte Darthur* was from Papworth St Agnes rather than Warwickshire have been widely accepted: see Richard R. Griffith, 'Caxton's Copy-Text for *Le Morte Darthur*', in *Traditions and Innovations*, ed. David G. Allen and Robert A. White (Newark, 1990), pp. 75–87 (pp. 76–7 and 81). Blake goes even further, arguing that both Winchester and the Caxton are direct copies of Malory's holograph, and that Caxton was responsible for producing each: see N. F. Blake, 'Caxton at Work', in *Debate*, pp. 233–53 (pp. 238–42). Blake in his stemma follows Ingrid Tieken-Boon van Ostade, *The Two Versions of Malory's Morte Darthur* (Cambridge, 1995), pp. 4–5, 10–14, 87–97. Takako Kato, *Caxton's Morte Darthur* (Oxford, 2002), p. 67, argues from the likely messiness of Caxton's copy-text that the copy-text was based on Malory's holograph. Malory himself commissioned this copy whilst he was writing, claims Kato, but his finances were such that he could not afford an especially professional scribe. The result was rather an untidy copy than a fair copy.

[33] Lotte Hellinga, 'The Malory Manuscript and Caxton', in *Aspects*, pp. 127–41 (pp. 127–34). Hellinga's findings were first published in 1977, and revised for *Aspects*.

[34] Hellinga, 'The Malory Manuscript and Caxton', in *Aspects*, pp. 135–8. Tieken-Boon van Ostade, *Two Versions*, attempts to support this hypothesis, but her claims for undermining Vinaver's stemma are unsubstantiated.

[35] See Vinaver, pp. cii–ciii and Commentary; and Field, 'Caxton's Roman War', in *Debate*, pp. 129–30. Further and 'decisive proof' that the Caxton 'could not be descended from' Winchester comes in Cooper's explication of eye-skip errors: 'Opening Up', in *Debate*, pp. 265–6.

and the Caxton do indeed stand in a parallel, not linear, relation, and clearly the printer did work from another manuscript. Indeed, as Matthews claims was the case, Caxton seems to have taken some care with his Malory project, using Winchester as a secondary back-up text to check or correct difficult or illegible passages in his source manuscript.[36]

Thus far Matthews's case is sound, and it is equally true (as Matthews accuses) that Vinaver's justification for adopting Winchester rather than the Caxton for his base-text is partly subjective when Vinaver says that choosing 'the less well known of the two versions, which is at least as reliable as the other, is as fair as any choice can be'.[37] As Thomas H. Crofts puts it, Vinaver's justification of his edition, *by these remarks*, actually 'make[s] very little claim for W's greater authenticity'.[38] Vinaver's *textual-critical* justifications for the superiority of Winchester, however, are much less subjective and harder to critique. Harder, but not impossible, for further complaints of modern research, especially by Murray J. Evans, Kevin T. Grimm and Helen Cooper, have revealed ways in which Vinaver did not always follow his own editorial principles,[39] probably because he was led astray by his conviction that Malory's narrative was an unconnected series of tales instead of a unified whole.

Regardless of how or why, Vinaver does occasionally misrepresent Winchester's version of events, and frequently misrepresents the manuscript's physical layout. In *Works*, for instance, each of the *explicits* is printed throughout in small capitals, but as Evans points out, the manuscript support for this is at best inconsistent.[40] Thus, where Vinaver prints 'HERE ENDYTH THIS TALE, AS THE FREYNSHE BOOKE SEYTH, FRO THE MARYAGE OF KYNGE UTHER UNTO KYNG ARTHURE', Winchester has only occasional capitalization: 'Here endyth thys tale as þe Freynshe booke seyth, fro the maryage of kynge **Uther** unto kyng **Arthure**' (*Works*, 180.15–16; Winchester, folio 70ᵛ). Obviously a modern text requires more capitals than a mediaeval one, but Vinaver's universal capitalization of every word of the *explicits* is certainly excessive. Having said this, some sort of distinction needs to be made between the wording of the colophons and the text proper. Field accordingly normalizes the capitalization of the *explicits* in his edition, but he does place them entirely in italics and in full justification on the page, thereby drawing attention to the wording. Vinaver also titles the adventures celebrating Arthur and Gwenyvere's wedding 'Torre and Pellinore', presumably because of the revelation of their familial relationship and their role, together with Gawayne, in the wedding adventures and the later family feud. This makes decent narrative sense, but Winchester gives a

---

[36] On Winchester as a consultation copy, which is the only logical remaining explanation for the ink offsets, see Griffith, 'Caxton's Copy-Text', in *Traditions and Innovations*, p. 76, and Field, 'Earliest Texts', in *Texts and Sources*, pp. 4–5.

[37] Vinaver, p. cxxi; Matthews, 'Question of Texts', in *Debate*, p. 65. Kevin T. Grimm, 'Editing Malory', *Arthuriana* 5.2 (Summer 1995): 5–14 (13–14, n. 11), similarly claims that such a statement might well support the superiority of the Caxton text. It might, but only if we ignore the textual-critical and homoeoteleuton evidence.

[38] Thomas H. Crofts, *Malory's Contemporary Audience* (Cambridge, 2006), p. 26.

[39] Murray J. Evans, 'The Explicits and Narrative Division in the Winchester MS', *Philological Quarterly* 58.3 (1979): 263–81; Grimm, 'Editing Malory'; Cooper, 'Opening Up', in *Debate*.

[40] Evans, 'Explicits', 263–81. As Evans says earlier, in terms of denoting major textual divisions, 'Vinaver's capitals seem to "protest too much"' (264).

clear title in the closing phrase, '**Explicit the Weddyng of Kyng Arthur**' (folio 44ᵛ).⁴¹ As Evans, Grimm and Cooper all point out, Vinaver also badly misrepresents a couple of section breaks in Winchester, including the transition from the 'Tale of Sir Launcelot' to the 'Tale of Sir Gareth', where the 'Explicit' on folio 113ʳ serves both as conclusion *and* introduction: 'Explicit a Noble Tale of Sir **Lancelot du Lake**. Here folowyth Sir **Garethis** Tale of **Orkeney** þat was callyd **Bewmaynes** by Sir **Kay**'. Here and elsewhere, Vinaver's splitting of the colophon into two phrases, separated by a title page and the relevant Caxtonian chapter rubrics, completely obscures the fact that many of the 'colophons ... constitute less an announcement of "The End" than "Watch out for the next thrilling instalment!"'⁴²

Even the number of major textual divisions and tales in the Winchester text of *Morte Darthur* is open to debate: Vinaver has seven distinct divisions and eight *unconnected* tales; Evans posits four major divisions and five unified tales; Carol M. Meale argues for three major manuscript breaks and four main unified narrative sections; and Cooper suggests four or five unified divisions, depending on whether one privileges Winchester's closing colophons that are coupled with blank page breaks as visible divisions, or follows the manuscript's major coloured initials.⁴³ Most recently, David Eugene Clark makes an interesting but ultimately overly rigid distinction between visual and aural manuscript divisions within the *Morte*, creating a hierarchy of three kinds of narrative breaks within each of his division types.⁴⁴ Evans, Meale and Cooper each argue further that Vinaver also obscures the *explicits* at the end of the 'Tale of Balyn' and 'The Weddyng' (fols 34ʳ and 44ᵛ), where Vinaver has merely subsections or smaller episodes in the larger opening 'Tale of King Arthur', but where Winchester has *explicits* followed by large red initials.⁴⁵ There is much less agreement, however, on what to do with these two early *explicits*. Evans, for instance, concludes that they denote only subsections of the larger opening unit devoted to Arthur's early kingship: the same story as Vinaver's Tale I, though with fewer subsections (Winchester folios 9–70). Meale similarly critiques Vinaver for ignoring these *explicits* and 'subsuming these episodes within his larger narrative units', but like Evans (or Vinaver, for that matter) she likewise divides the *Morte* into sundry *major* narrative sections or tales, most of which are comprised of one or more subsections or minor divisions. Thus Meale's opening narrative section is – like Vinaver's and like Evans's – devoted to the establishment of Arthur's reign and Round

---

⁴¹ Field accordingly retitled this section in his revision of *Works* (O³), and he rightly maintains this section title in his own edition.

⁴² Cooper, 'Opening Up', in *Debate*, p. 259. See also Evans, 'Explicits', 279, who concludes that several of the colophons are links, and Robert H. Wilson, 'How Many Books Did Malory Write', *Studies in English* 30 (1951): 1–23 (3). On Vinaver's sundering of the 'Launcelot'–'Gareth' colophon see also Evans, 'Explicits', 271, and Grimm, 'Editing Malory', 6–7.

⁴³ Evans, 'Explicits', 263–81, and Murray J. Evans, 'The Two Scribes in the Winchester MS', *Manuscripta* 27 (1983): 38–44; Carol M. Meale, '"The Hoole Book"', in *Companion*, pp. 3–17 (pp. 8 and 13–14); Cooper, 'Opening Up', in *Debate*, pp. 258–9. See also Field, I: xxiv–xxix.

⁴⁴ David Eugene Clark, 'Hearing and Reading Narrative Divisions in the *Morte Darthur*', *Arthuriana* 24.2 (2014): 92–125. As Field perceptively argues, 'Some two and three-line initial capitals in W ... appear to be used as marks of emphasis', not division breaks: Field, I: xxviii.

⁴⁵ Evans, 'Explicits', 263–9; Meale, '"The Hoole Book"', in *Companion*, p. 15 n. 38; and Cooper, 'Opening Up', in *Debate*, pp. 258–9.

Table (Winchester folios 9–70); but whilst she considers the 'Balyn' *explicit* as a significant subdivision of this opening section, and whilst she notes Vinaver's obscuring of the 'Weddyng' *explicit*, she herself makes no subdivision after the 'Weddyng'. Cooper, on the other hand, argues that the divisions after 'Balyn' and the 'Weddyng' have 'the same force' as the manuscript's more major divisions. Broadly speaking, I believe that the narrative divisions adopted by Vinaver and Field are mostly correct and textually and codicologically justified, but as D. Thomas Hanks Jr rightly puts it, 'the question of textual divisions [in Winchester and the *Morte*] remains vexed'.[46]

Certainly these two early *explicits* are important. The closing lines or end title of the 'Tale of Balyn' on folio 34^r, 'Thus endeth the tale of **Balyn** and **Balan** ... **Explicit**', is in dark brown ink except for the rubricated names and '**Explicit**'.[47] This combination of dark brown text and rubricated names is the typical layout for most of the *explicits* throughout Winchester, as it is for the text and names in the narrative proper throughout the manuscript. Thus the lack of colour in the majority of the 'Balyn' *explicit* renders Vinaver's layout defensible, though his tale divisions are, as Evans and Cooper note, much more intrusive than almost all of those in Winchester. At the same time, even the largely brown-ink 'Here endeth' or 'Explicit' colophons are offset by a blank line or two at the end of Vinaver's Tale III (folio 113^r) and Tale IV (folio 148^r), while the 'Explicit' closing 'Balyn' is in red, offset in the middle of the line at the bottom of a page; there then follows a blank page at 34^v, before a large red initial opens the next narrative episode at the top of 35^r. The close of Tale I as a whole is similar to 'Balyn', with a mid-line rubricated '**Explicit**' appearing at the bottom of folio 70^v. All of these narrative breaks, then, have considerable authority, and Tales V and VI (respectively folios 346^v and 409^r) use the typical dark brown text, red name ink patterns, but leave two-thirds of a blank page after their colophons.[48] Some sort of textual division is justifiably called for in these cases as well. The remaining *explicits* vary these patterns, but still denote significant narrative breaks – though not necessarily divisions into separate works. Thus '**Explicit the Weddyng of King Arthur**', near the top of folio 44^v, is all in red, prefaced by a line break and followed by most of a blank page before a large, three-line red initial begins the next section of narrative on folio 45^r. The end of Tale II at folio 96^r has two closing titles for the Roman War, with very different wording, the first in brown ink which does not stand out from the surrounding brown text, but a second which is entirely rubricated and offset by a (nearly double) blank line both before and after. The next tale, 'The Noble Tale of Sir Launcelot', does start on the same folio, but it is prefaced by the preceding post-*explicit* blank line and a two-line large red initial and is thus probably meant to form a new tale, especially given its concluding *explicit*-cum-*incipit* language, mentioned above.[49] (See Plate I: Winchester fol. 96^r.)

---

[46] D. Thomas Hanks Jr, 'Textual Harassment', in *Re-Viewing Le Morte Darthur*, ed. K. S. Whetter and Raluca L. Radulescu (Cambridge, 2005), pp. 27–47 (pp. 32–3). Hanks himself argues for 'six, more probably seven ... major divisions'.

[47] Rubrication is represented in my quotations by bold type.

[48] The 'Tale of the Sankgreal' (Tale VI) *explicit* at 409^r also has a rubricated prayer, which I shall discuss in Chapter Three, below.

[49] *Pace* Evans, 'Explicits', 270, and Cooper, 'Opening Up', in *Debate*, p. 259 and n. 15.

Thus the contentiousness of the precise number of narrative divisions in *Le Morte Darthur* is nicely illustrated by the 'Balyn' and 'Weddyng' *explicits* in Winchester. In each case, the possible weight of the rubricated 'Explicits', followed by one completely blank and one mostly blank page and new initials for the subsequent tales, has to be balanced against the fact that there is some confusion of scribal labour in the stories that follow each *explicit*. In contrast to the usual scribal practice of each scribe copying different folios in separate tales, both scribes work on folios 35^r and 45^r. It is probable, then, that what look like potential marks of major division at these two points – the *explicits*, opening initials and especially the blank pages – represent merely missteps in the shared transcription process.[50] The likelihood of quiring or paper-estimation error due to confusions in the shared copying is to my mind confirmed by the three stubs that exist between folios 44^v and 45^r, meaning three folios had to be removed to splice the shared sections back together in their proper textual and codicological cohesion.[51]

It should also be recalled that such confusion regarding manuscript narrative division or even page representation is hardly unique to Winchester: similar debate has been raised about modern versus mediaeval fitt divisions in a wide array of verse romances, including *Sir Gawain and the Green Knight*.[52] Nevertheless, in our current understanding of the *Morte Darthur* and its textual witnesses some sort of minor division is necessary in these two subsections, and Field's new layout helps mitigate the divisiveness of Vinaver's edition whilst maintaining the more justified episode breaks.

Even Winchester's 111 extant coloured initials cannot on their own be taken as reliable *a priori* narrative divisions, major or minor. On at least two occasions, for instance, these two- or three-line initials are misleading. The division between the two parts of 'The Boke of Syr Trystram' is marked in Winchester by a third of a blank line and then a three-line initial (fol. 229^{r-v}), but this seeming break is premature, falling in the middle of a sentence. Similarly, towards the end of the final tale, on folio 483^r, another large, three-line red initial stands prominently on the page just after we read of the death of Arthur and Gwenyvere's retreat to an abbey. The capital initial is given even greater prominence because it is preceded by a line-and-a-half of blank space: line six stops about two-thirds of the way across the page, with a rubricated **Launcelot du Lake**, the rest of line six is blank, all of the next line is blank, and then the next line after that begins with the large red capital **T**. Looking only at the *mise-en-page*, there would seem to be

---

[50] A similar conclusion is reached by Evans about the break at folios 44–5: Evans, 'The Two Scribes', 39. David Eugene Clark, 'Scribal Modifications to Concluding Formulae in the Winchester Manuscript', *Arthurian Literature* 32 (2015): 123–54 (at 139–45), attempts to argue that the 'Weddyng' *explicit* and division at fols 44–5 is purely scribal.

[51] Ker, Intro. to *Winchester*, p. xiii, notes two leaves between 44 and 45, as does Kelliher, 'Early History', in *Aspects*, p. 145. Consulting Winchester directly, however, allowed me to discern that there are manifestly three stubs. My heartfelt thanks to Andrea Clarke and Julian Harrison of the British Library for allowing me to examine the manuscript.

[52] See especially Phillipa Hardman, 'Fitt Divisions in Middle English Romances', *Yearbook of English Studies* 22 (1992): 63–82, and A. S. G. Edwards, 'The Manuscript', in *A Companion to the Gawain-Poet*, ed. Derek Brewer and Jonathan Gibson (Cambridge, 1997), pp. 197–219 (pp. 200–2).

at least a minor textual division here, corresponding to a modern chapter break or at least some sort of narrative subdivision. But when the words and story are actually read and taken into account, it is immediately obvious not merely that no break is called for, but that no break is allowable. Not only does this blank line and red capital interrupt Malory's standard narrative transition formula of 'now turn we', but they occur in the middle of one of the principal clauses of the sentence: 'now turne we from her and speke we of Sir **Launcelot du Lake**, That whan he harde in hys contrey that Sir **Mordred** was crowned kynge …' (see *MD* 930.3–5). Only by ignoring the word 'that' can one make this a sensible division, and this is what Cooper does in her edition.[53] But ignoring the word 'that' means ignoring the red capital **T** at the start of the word, and if we cut the capital initial then we are not justified in adopting it as a break. As Field judiciously notes in his Commentary, Winchester's presentation conflicts with its wording on this occasion.[54] Hence Vinaver is correct to place his subdivision where he does here. Significantly – and equally justifiably – Field makes the same subdivision.

Thus the textual critical evidence, the literary critical evidence, and the codicological evidence all support one another. As Robert H. Wilson compellingly remarks of Tale I, the *Morte Darthur*'s 'shorter units are not separate compositions, or we should have to conclude that Malory wrote, not eight tales or books, but dozens. … Malory apparently wrote [the "Tale of King Arthur"] continuously, all from the same source; and the *explicit* indicates that he thought of a reader going straight through it as one story, "fro the maryage of kynge Uther" to its end'.[55] In this light it significant that, for all the differences in their conception of manuscript division, Vinaver, Evans and Meale each conceptualize the same large opening narrative devoted to Arthur's early reign. After this tale, both Evans and Meale place various subsections in many of the same places as Vinaver, even when they treat many of his major tales as but subsections of their larger units. Thus Evans's second major unit comprises Vinaver's tales of 'Arthur and Lucius' (Tale II), 'Launcelot' (Tale III) and 'Gareth' (Tale IV), whereas Meale's second major unit comprises all of these tales plus the 'Trystram' (Tale V). But all three scholars agree on some sort of division between each of these major narrative blocks. All in all, then, Vinaver's eight-tale layout is sensible, provided we consider the eight tales as parts of a larger unified whole, and provided we accept that each tale may well have sundry episodic subsections like the Balyn narrative or the story of Alexander the Orphan. After all, notwithstanding his unravelling of the interlaced threads of his French sources, 'Malory had not [entirely] abandoned the general tradition of a complex narrative in which separate and often entirely episodic accounts are yet, in a way, parts of a larger whole.'[56] Such a narrative and codicological arrangement of parts and whole would be easily recognizable to mediaeval readers. After all, Chaucer's Criseyde and her friends

---

[53] Malory, *Le Morte Darthur*, ed. Cooper, p. 517.
[54] Field, Commentary on 930.2–5.
[55] Wilson, 'How Many Books', 7. This conclusion is partly supported by Evans, 'Explicits', 263–9.
[56] Wilson, 'How Many Books', 7. On Malory's penchant for avoiding interlace and the sundry ways in which he generally unravels his French sources, see especially Vinaver, pp. xlvi–li, lx–lxxiii.

take a break from reading 'This romaunce ... of Thebes' when they reach a logical narrative division marked by 'thise lettres rede': rubricated letters that obviously demarcate a subsection of the larger story, not a new romance.[57]

The fact that Vinaver sometimes ignores Winchester's layout or fails to edit as faithfully as his principles espouse, moreover, does not invalidate either his monumental achievement or the debt modern Malory studies continues to owe him. More importantly for my present purposes, Vinaver's occasional textual lapses do not invalidate his general textual-critical conclusions. Even Homer nods, it is said. And while it is clear that further textual work might still fruitfully be done,[58] none of the arguments surveyed here invalidate the idea of using Winchester as the base-text for modern (critical) editions of Malory's Arthuriad: necessary corrections are not the same as cancellation. Hence Field is entirely justified to base his new edition of the *Morte Darthur* on Winchester; indeed, partly as a means of rectifying some of these textual inadequacies, Field treats the manuscript merely as the most important of the surviving witnesses, one which he frequently emends.[59] But even in Field's interventionist edition, Winchester remains a primary witness.

As for the claim of Matthews and his followers that Malory himself revised and replaced Winchester, it is simply not tenable. For one thing, time itself is against it. By all accounts it took Malory nearly two years to write the *Morte Darthur*, and he is unlikely to have had time to revise it or have it revised before his death.[60] My timeline here accepts the argument that the Sir Thomas Malory who penned the *Morte Darthur* was the Warwickshire Malory.[61] Although the precise date of the manuscript is uncertain, its likely date of composition, based on the watermarks, is the late 1470s.[62] As Yuji Nakao rightly objects, the Warwickshire Malory died in 1471, and since Matthews argues that the reviser used Malory's sources *as well as Winchester itself*, Malory was almost certainly quite dead before Winchester came into being. He cannot therefore have revised Winchester,[63] and is unlikely even to have had time to revise one of the posited earlier lost manuscripts such as Vinaver's X or Y.

Notwithstanding Matthews's or Lumiansky's scepticism of the Warwickshire Malory as the likely author,[64] Field's biography of Malory's life, activities and

---

[57] Geoffrey Chaucer, *Troilus and Criseyde*, in *The Riverside Chaucer*, ed. Larry D. Benson, 3rd edn (Boston, 1987), II.100–3.
[58] See e.g. Shunichi Noguchi, 'The Winchester Malory', in *Debate*, pp. 117–25 (pp. 122–3); Ralph Norris, 'Errors in the Malory Archetype', *Studies in Bibliography* 60 (2017), and idem, 'Once Again King Arthur and the Ambassadors', *JIAS* 3.1 (2015): 102–19.
[59] See Field's Introduction (I: xi–xliii) for details.
[60] Vinaver, p. xx, implies considerably longer than one year; William Matthews, *The Ill-Framed Knight* (Berkeley and Los Angeles, 1966), p. 139, claims probably two years or a little less; P. J. C. Field, *The Life and Times of Sir Thomas Malory* (Cambridge, 1993), p. 131, says two years.
[61] The most detailed account of the Warwickshire case is Field, *Life and Times*, though Christina Hardyment's admittedly more speculative biography confirms Field's findings: *Malory* (London, 2005).
[62] See Kelliher, 'Early History', in *Aspects*, pp. 144–5.
[63] Yuji Nakao, 'Musings on the Reviser of Book V in Caxton's Malory', in *Debate*, pp. 191–216 (pp. 206–8). Cf. Kelliher, 'Early History', in *Aspects*, pp. 143–4. Nakao further and rightfully points out that the Cambridgeshire Malory died even earlier, in 1469, so we cannot use the reviser argument to resuscitate the possibility of that Malory authoring the *Morte*.
[64] Matthews, *The Ill-Framed Knight*; Lumiansky, 'Malory's Morte Darthur', 879–83.

imprisonment, and thus his detailed case for the Warwickshire Malory as the only candidate for authorship, is compelling. Although the recent biography by Christina Hardyment is, by Hardyment's own admission, partly biography and partly speculative historical fiction, she did undertake considerable research, none of which contradicts Field's conclusions.[65] Compelling new evidence is needed if Field's account of things is to be undermined. Anne F. Sutton claims to have unearthed precisely such evidence in her discovery of a document of 20 April 1469 in which Malory acts as one of twenty-one men bearing witness to a certain Thomas Mynton, a gentleman prisoner dying in Newgate gaol.[66] Sutton concludes from this witness that Malory himself was also a prisoner in Newgate, not (*contra* Field) the Tower, and that as such he was guilty of crimes of misdemeanour, including violence and debt, but not felony or treason. Although Sutton makes a persuasive case, her conclusions are contradictory, particularly in her differing accounts of Malory's finances, which alternately have him in debtors' prison but simultaneously possessed of enough surplus income to rent or buy a vast range of source manuscripts and writing materials for the composition of his lengthy Arthuriad. Malory's witnessing of the document in Newgate in April 1469, moreover, does not mean that he was not brought from the Tower as an armigerous and therefore reasonably high-ranking witness. Or he may only temporarily have been in Newgate; he was frequently moved from one prison to the next during his eight-year incarceration in the 1450s.[67] Many of these movements were legally sanctioned, some seem politically motivated and a few were due to Malory's own escape efforts. Finally, even if Malory were imprisoned in Newgate instead of the Tower, this does not invalidate the length of time taken to compose a narrative the better part of 400,000 words in length.[68]

Furthermore, against Matthews and his camp stand a host of equally impressive scholars. As noted, Matthews was disputing Vinaver's claim that Caxton had revised the Roman War, an argument which continued and still continues to carry conviction even after Matthews's views were announced. Shaw, too, arguing before Matthews made his case, stated categorically that her comparison of the Caxton and Winchester texts revealed Caxton himself to be the 'deliberate' reviser of the Roman War episode and the source of a great many other editorial changes.[69] Shaw did conclude, as Matthews said, that Caxton's text is reasonably accurate, but this is not the same thing as being a more authoritative text than Winchester. Admittedly Winchester actually contains a greater number of scribal errors (eye-skip, end-of-word errors, omission, *difficilior lectio*, etc.), but these are easier, on textual-critical grounds, to identify and correct than the editorial tinkering of Caxton. And *contra* Matthews, Caxton seems to have modified his text a great deal. Field's careful examination of Vinaver's textual-critical reasoning

---

[65] Hardyment, *Malory*; and Field, *Life and Times*.
[66] Anne F. Sutton, 'Malory in Newgate', *The Library* 7th series 1.3 (2000): 243–62.
[67] Field, *Life and Times*, pp. 105–25.
[68] 340,000, to be precise. I follow Field's arithmetic in 'Note to the Third Edition', *Works*, p. 1748, and his 'Earliest Texts', in *Texts and Sources*, p. 2.
[69] Shaw, 'Caxton and Malory', in *Essays*, pp. 114–15. Some of these changes are linguistic or dialectic. In addition to Shaw's arguments, see Jeremy J. Smith, 'Some Spellings in Caxton's Malory', *Poetica* 24 (1986): 58–63; Yuji Nakao, 'Does Malory Really Revise His Vocabulary?', *Poetica* 25–6 (1987): 93–109, and idem, 'Musings on the Reviser', in *Debate*.

and the two witnesses reveals that the printer was in fact quite prepared 'to alter Malory's words', and that he did so on a regular basis.[70] Just how much minor tinkering Caxton or his compositors did has been established beyond doubt by Takako Kato, whose careful study of Caxton's printing and editorial practices for the 1485 *Morte Darthur* demonstrates, amongst other things, that Caxton and his printers made many substantial changes to the wording of their manuscript source towards the bottom of the page to compensate for casting-off mistakes.[71] Such modifications are hardly authorial. For all of these reasons I agree with Field's conclusion that Vinaver 'seriously understated the value of the Winchester text of the *Morte Darthur*': obviously the Caxton is needed to supply Winchester's lacunae, and to help correct error, but Winchester is superior, not merely easier to correct than the Caxton print, 'but a better text as it stands'.[72]

There remains, however, the problem of the Roman War. A possible solution is offered by Meg Roland, who argues that we should print the Caxton and Winchester versions in tandem.[73] A parallel text, argues Roland, privileges diversity and debate and maximizes interpretation, especially regarding how the textual differences between Winchester and the Caxton affect narrative and meaning. Such an approach, however, neatly (and deliberately) side-steps the issue of whether or not one text is more authoritative than the other. Accepting that one version of the *Morte Darthur* is closer to what Malory wrote than the other does not mean we cannot still fruitfully explore the literary and cultural history of the *Morte* and its reception. Furthermore, the view that all versions of or witnesses to a text are equally valid is a theoretical position that not all readers agree with, just as not all readers agree with the best text theory of editing espoused by Vinaver and his teachers. Roland also fails to address the fact that a good part of the critical controversy over which text of the Roman War is more authoritative rests precisely on questions of narrative and meaning. For myself, I agree with Vinaver, Field and Cooper that Winchester is closer, or can more accurately and justifiably be corrected to be closer, to what Malory wrote, meaning that the Caxton is interesting and important, but not the same as Malory's own words, even when those words are based on textual-critical reconstruction.

That conclusion brings us back to the question of revision. The crux of Matthews's argument that Malory himself revised the Roman War hinges on three suppositions: (i) that only the author would have sufficient knowledge of the sources to make the revisions that we see in the Caxton text; (ii) that the language of the tale is more like Malory's than Caxton's; and (iii) that the revisions are generically more akin to the *Morte Darthur*'s predominant overall kind, more romance than the epic-heroic genre of the alliterative *Morte Arthure* that stands

---

[70] Field, 'Choice of Texts', in *Texts and Sources*, pp. 14–26 (quoting p. 16); see also P. J. C. Field, 'Malory and His Scribes', *Arthuriana* 14.1 (2004): 31–42. For further evidence of the changes made by Caxton or his printers, see Tieken-Boon van Ostade, *Two Versions*.
[71] Kato, *Caxton's Morte Darthur*, esp. pp. 34–47. See also Toshiyuki Takamiya, 'Editor/Compositor at Work', in *Arthurian and Other Studies Presented to Shunichi Noguchi*, ed. Takashi Suzuki and Tsuyoshi Mukai (Cambridge, 1993), pp. 143–51.
[72] Field, 'Choice of Texts', in *Texts and Sources*, p. 24.
[73] Meg Roland, 'Malory's Roman War Episode', in *Debate*, pp. 315–21, and eadem, '"Alas! Who may truste thys world"', in *The Book Unbound*, ed. Siân Echard and Stephen Partridge (Toronto, 2004), pp. 37–57.

as the major generic source for the episode. Appropriately enough, given the modern controversy over this section of the *Morte*, Winchester records *two* titles in its final colophon for the tale, styling the story both 'The Tale of the Noble Kynge Arthure that was Emperoure Hymself thorow Dygnyté of his Hondys', and 'The Noble Tale betwyxt Kynge Arthur and Lucius the Emperour of Rome' (W folio 96ʳ; *MD* 189.18–22).[74]

The first belief, that only Malory could have made the changes, has been seriously and to my mind effectively rebutted by Field. Field explicates and challenges Matthews's argument in detail, but he agrees with Matthews that 'the three main sources of the Roman War story in W' – that is, the alliterative *Morte Arthure*, the French Vulgate *Suite de Merlin* and Hardyng's *Chronicle* – 'did influence C' (the Caxton text). But, says Field, it is more likely that such material is there by inheritance rather than because the reviser put it there after consulting the sources. Second, 'C cannot derive from W', partly because, as Matthews himself points out, 'Malory's way of selecting and rephrasing his sources was such that it is unlikely that even he could have found his way again through the maze. Such material must have been in the original' – that is, adds Field, in the archetype(s) standing behind both Winchester and the Caxton.[75] Matthews's insistence that Caxton did not have the source knowledge necessary to make the changes and additions found in the incunabulum version of the Roman War is further undermined by the evidence that such material could well be derived from the well-known Prose *Brut*, a popular text twice published by Caxton under the title *The Chronicles of England* in 1480 and 1482.[76] The textual-critical evidence, then, convincingly attests that Caxton himself must be responsible for the revisions.

The language point is perhaps more subjective. Matthews and Moorman claim that the revised Roman War is more Malorian in style, syntax and diction than the version in the Winchester manuscript; in contrast, Noguchi, Smith and others argue that the language in the revised text is more typical of Caxton as seen by comparison with other of Caxton's works.[77] Although no less an authority than Moorman disputes such linguistic evidence as being too reliant upon 'accidentals', no less an authority than Edward Donald Kennedy accepts such evidence

---

[74] Vinaver's Tale II or Caxton's Book V. Caxton's title of 'The Conquest of Lucius th'Emperour' (C 3ᵛ) does not exactly reproduce either of the titles from W here, but his own *explicit* clearly echoes the 'Dygnyté of his Hondys' version because Caxton closes this section of the *Morte* by noting, 'Thus Endeth the Fyfthe book, of the *Conqueste* that Kynge Arthur hadde ageynste Lucius the Emperoure of Rome' (my emphasis and capitalization).

[75] Field, 'Caxton's Roman War', in *Debate*, pp. 141–2, quoting what he calls the 'Long Version' of Matthews's conference paper; this text is now available as Matthews, 'Question of Texts', in *Debate*, p. 101.

[76] See especially John Withrington, 'Caxton, Malory, and the Roman War in the *Morte Darthur*', *Studies in Philology* 89.3 (1992): 350–66; Masako Takagi and Toshiyuki Takamiya, 'Caxton Edits the Roman War Episode', in *Debate*, pp. 169–90 (especially pp. 179–84); Edward Donald Kennedy, 'Caxton, Malory, and the "Noble Tale of King Arthur and the Emperor Lucius"', in *Debate*, pp. 217–32 (pp. 222–3).

[77] Matthews, 'Question of Texts', in *Debate*; Moorman, 'Caxton's *Morte Darthur*'; Shaw, 'Caxton and Malory', in *Essays*; Terence McCarthy, 'Caxton and the Text of Malory's Book 2', *Modern Philology* 71 (1973): 144–52; Shunichi Noguchi, 'Caxton's Malory', *Poetica* 8 (1977): 72–84, and idem, 'Caxton's Malory Again', *Poetica* 24 (1986): 33–8; Smith, 'Some Spellings in Caxton's Malory'; and Nakao, 'Does Malory Really Revise His Vocabulary?'

as compelling and conclusive.[78] Noguchi also argues that the Winchester version of the War offers a more dramatic narrative, and that the Caxton version is accordingly less effective.[79] Since Malory does know what is he is doing as an author, Winchester's greater narrative power further argues against the Caxton version representing a superior text revised by the author. Thus, although the stylistic and linguistic case is perhaps not as certain a rebuttal as the issue of the reviser's handling of the sources, it is sufficient to undermine the idea that only Malory could be responsible for such changes. We are, moreover, once again on firmer ground with genre.

Matthews argues in part that the Caxton version of the Roman War reveals Malory further revising his sources towards romance and away from the epic-heroic genre and values of the alliterative *Morte Arthure*. As I argue at length in another study, however, Malory is not actually writing a typical romance, either in the Roman War episode or elsewhere.[80] Granted Malory's *Morte Darthur* is not predominantly an epic-heroic piece like the alliterative *Morte Arthure*, but neither is it exclusively or even predominantly romance. Rather, throughout his Arthuriad Malory consistently combines romance with epic-heroic and tragic generic features to create a generic hybrid best styled – and no doubt recognized in its day as – a *tragic-romance*. Significantly for the present debate, the tragic features of the *Morte*, as well as the clear indications of its generic mixture, often come precisely in those kinds of scenes which Matthews claims Malory revised away: scenes of violence, vengeance and bloodshed.

Malory makes it quite clear throughout the *Morte* that combat is both a theatre in which knights can win that all-important Malorian trait of *worshyp*, but equally one in which knights are very likely to be laid 'to the colde erthe' in injury or death (as at 86ᵛ; 172.34–5 or 479ᵛ; 922.30).[81] Each of Malory's knights who undertakes adventure is aware of this paradox, and each accepts it in order to win renown. Hence Balyn's recognition that 'That [horn] blast … is blowen for me, for I am the pryse, and yet am I not dede' (C II.17; 70.30–1), or Launcelot's quoting of the 'olde-seyde sawe' that 'there ys harde batayle thereas kynne and frendys doth batayle ayther ayenst other, for there may be no mercy, but mortall warre' (425ᵛ; 820.35–821.2). In accepting the paradox, the knights also accept the potential for tragedy. Nor is it true that the tragedy in either Malory or the alliterative *Morte* is the result of sinful moral failure. On the contrary, as I shall argue in Chapters Three and Four, the tragedy is all the greater precisely because it is the same traits that make knights great – Launcelot's love of Gwenyvere or Balyn's

---

[78] Moorman, 'Desperately Defending', in *Debate*, pp. 110–11; Kennedy, 'Caxton, Malory, and the "Noble Tale"', in *Debate*, p. 217.
[79] Noguchi, 'Winchester Malory', in *Debate*, p. 121.
[80] K. S. Whetter, *Understanding Genre and Medieval Romance* (Aldershot, 2008), pp. 99–149.
[81] As Rushton pithily observes, being so laid to the ground is 'never good for one's health in Malory': Cory James Rushton, '"Layde to the Colde Erthe"', in *The Arthurian Way of Death*, ed. Karen Cherewatuk and K. S. Whetter (Cambridge, 2009), pp. 151–66 (p. 155). For a fuller explication of the good and bad consequences of violence in the *Morte*, see my 'Warfare and Combat in Le Morte Darthur', in *Writing War*, ed. Corinne Saunders, Françoise Le Saux and Neil Thomas (Cambridge, 2004), pp. 169–86, and 'Weeping, Wounds and Worshyp in Malory's *Morte Darthur*', *Arthurian Literature* 31 (2014): 61–82.

and Gawayne's senses of honour – that also ultimately secure the destruction of the Round Table.

In these and other ways Malory retains more of the generic spirit of the alliterative *Morte Arthure* than Matthews allows. Genre, in other words, actually argues firmly *against* Malory being the reviser, further supporting the textual superiority of Winchester. The textual themes of the Winchester version of the Roman War, moreover, are visually reinforced by the manuscript's rubrication and marginalia, since both forms of *ordinatio* serve to glorify Arthurian heroes by supplying exactly the sort of public fame and memorialization which Matthews claims is wrongfully present in the alliterative *Morte* and rightly removed from the revised Roman War in the Caxton text of Malory's Arthuriad.[82]

The arguments of Matthews and his followers that the revisions to the Roman War story bring the narrative more in line with both the genre and style of the rest of the *Morte Darthur*, then, do not stand up. Nor do the changes in the Caxton text necessarily help to unify the overall story, as is claimed. In fact, John Withrington convincingly maintains that 'comparison of the opening sentences of the two versions ... reveals that ... the Caxton edition seems to be more concerned with emphasizing its *separate* nature from the other tales in the *Morte Darthur*'.[83] The Winchester account of the Roman War, for instance, links the tale back to the close of the preceding 'Tale of King Arthur' by invoking the wedding of Arthur and Gwenyvere, the vanquishing of 'the moste party of [Arthur's] enemyes', and the arrivals of Launcelot and Trystram to court (W 71ʳ; *MD* 145.1–6). This wording succinctly summarizes the second half of the opening tale, but the reference to Launcelot and Trystram coming to court is a distinct echo of the same statement in the manuscript colophon to Tale I (W 70v; *MD* 143.29–32). Caxton thoroughly obscures this link between tales in his expurgation of Tale I's *explicit*, as well as in his omission of the summary of the events preceding the Roman War, including omitting the reference to Launcelot and Trystram. Not only does the Caxton text thus lack Winchester's unity, but its narrative and tone are, in the opening lines, actually more belligerent than in Winchester. The Caxton text here is accordingly actually closer to the alliterative *Morte*.[84]

The poem opens with a summary of Arthur's fame and conquests, immediately establishing his credentials as conqueror king and heroic warrior:[85]

> Qwen that the Kynge Arthur, by conqueste hade wonnyn
> Castells and kyngdoms   and contreez many,
> ....
> Qwenn he thes dedes had don, he doubbyd hys knyghtez
> Dyuysyde dowcherys and delte   in dyuerse remmes.

---

[82] See William Matthews, *The Tragedy of Arthur* (Berkeley and Los Angeles, 1960), especially p. 174, and idem, 'Question of Texts', in *Debate*, pp. 67–78.

[83] Withrington, 'Caxton, Malory, and The Roman War', 352–3; my emphasis.

[84] All of which adds literary critical support to Field's textual-critical argument, noted below, that Malory's version of the opening of the Roman War can be best reconstructed by briefly interweaving both witnesses: see Field, 'Caxton's Roman War', in *Debate*, pp. 144–8 and Appendix II. Field's theory is now actualized in his edition.

[85] *Morte Arthure*, ed. Mary Hamel (New York and London, 1984), vv. 26–49.

The Caxton version of Malory's War is similar, recalling not the fledgling days of Arthur's court and knights, as in Winchester's account of the vanquishing of merely *most* of Arthur's enemies, but rather the 'longe werre' which precedes the Roman embassy's arrival (*Works* 185.C1). The 'implication is that Arthur has already proven triumphant'.[86] Similarly, Cador's response to the Roman embassy in the Caxton *Morte Darthur* is straight from the poem: in the alliterative *Morte* Cador laughingly exclaims, 'Þe lettres of sir Lucius   lyghttys myn herte: / We hafe as losels liffyde   many longe daye' (251–2). In the Winchester text, as in the poem, Cador greets the Roman threat as an opportunity for winning worship, but it is the Caxton text that echoes 'losels liffyde' by having Cador lament the idleness of the court (*Works* 187.18–21 and 187.C17–20). At least in the beginning, then, the Caxton text is more, not less, like the alliterative poem that the revisions to the Winchester *Morte* were supposedly hiding.

All told, the literary, thematic, generic and textual-critical evidence is firmly against the Matthews camp for Malory being the reviser of the Roman War story as printed by Caxton. But we can go further than this in reclaiming the 'auctorysed' (C XXI.13; *MD* 940.10) version of Malory's narrative and words. After a meticulous comparison of the Winchester and Caxton texts and the relevant sources, Field offers the compelling solution of *combining* both Winchester and the Caxton's wording to fill in gaps in the other witness, thereby bringing us to a version of the Arthuriad more in line with Malory's probable intentions, and thus more complete and authoritative than any thus far printed or suggested. As all parties agree, each of the *Morte Darthur*'s exemplars has its merits in places, especially where the readings in one or the other version are supported by the sources against its fellow. Field's solution again builds upon a suggestion of Matthews himself. Gaps and faulty readings in the Roman War narrative in Winchester reveal that Tale II even in the manuscript 'must be a shortened and revised version of Malory's original', especially since there is no codicological evidence for missing gatherings in these locations.[87] In fact, says Field, 'at the *beginning* of Malory's Roman War story, the two surviving texts apparently *drastically but alternately abbreviate* their original', so that in the opening section, 'each text in turn gives a fuller narrative (supported by one or more sources) that the other abbreviates or cuts out'.[88] To my mind Field's reconstructed text is convincing and sound. It is supported not only by the sources and some of Matthews's own reasoning, but also by Withrington's observation about the differences in the way each version begins. Field is thus amply justified to produce such a combined and reconstructed text in his new edition.

There is, however, one further point to be made about Malory's *Morte Darthur* and its manuscript. As important as Winchester is for establishing what Malory wrote, it seems to me that the manuscript's value extends beyond the textual. A striking feature of Winchester is the care that went into its *ordinatio*, including the

---

[86] Withrington, 'Caxton, Malory, and The Roman War', 353.
[87] Field, 'Caxton's Roman War', in *Debate*, pp. 144–6, following Matthews, 'Question of Texts', also in *Debate*, p. 84.
[88] Field, 'Caxton's Roman War', in *Debate*, p. 147 and App. II (my emphases). For a qualification to Field's proposal see Norris, 'Once Again King Arthur', 112, where Norris proposes not alternate abbreviations, but 'independent mutations of a common original'.

wide, clean margins and relative lack of decoration. The clean margins and lack of marginal scrolls or leaves so common in many other late mediaeval manuscripts make the other features of Winchester's layout stand out all the more: the rubrication of names and the marginalia. Neither of these features is employed in its usual fashion in Winchester. Equally tellingly, both features foreground Malory's principal textual themes and interests. These themes are human and chivalric more often than they are sacred or ethical. In subsequent chapters I will argue that Winchester's layout is deliberate and unique, and that there is a profound and meaningful correlation between the lexical text of the *Morte Darthur* and its codicological context. Such a close interaction of matter and meaning, I will suggest further, is in all probability authorial.

1
The Unusual Nature of Winchester's Rubrication

Prolegomena: Malory's Red and Black

For the better part of five and a half centuries, the story known today as *Le Morte Darthur* existed in only one version: that printed by William Caxton in 1485. According to Caxton, this English *Morte Darthur* was modelled 'after a copye unto me delyverd, whyche copye Syr Thomas Malorye dyd take oute of certeyn bookes of Frensshe and reduced ... into Englysshe'.[1] Richard R. Griffith takes Caxton's delivery statement quite literally, speculating that Caxton's copy-text may well have been a reasonably 'fair' but far from elaborate authorial manuscript, not nearly as decorated as Winchester, and thus more easily marked up and taken apart for printing purposes.[2] Griffith's argument is part of his larger case for the author of the *Morte Darthur* being the Papworth St Agnes Malory, from Cambridgeshire. This view has not found wide acceptance amongst Malory scholars, and Griffith's account of Caxton's copy-text, though highly interesting, is quite speculative. The question of where Caxton acquired his copy-text, however, once again raises the issue of Winchester's relation to the Caxton print. Textual errors in the early print history of Malory's work reveal that, whatever Caxton's copy-text manuscript looked like, it was quickly lost to later printers. Instead of being printed from the manuscript, almost all versions of the *Morte* printed after Caxton were based on a Caxton incunable.[3] Or rather, they were based on copies of Caxton. Wynkyn de Worde, Caxton's apprentice and successor, seems to have had access to Caxton's copy-text as well as Caxton's incunabula, and to have used the original copy-text to make some corrections for his reprinting of the *Morte Darthur* in 1498,[4] but apart from de Worde's first edition, the early texts of *Morte Darthur* were Caxton texts. In fact, by the mid-sixteenth century they were not even that; the print tradition had quickly degraded, with new printings being based on copies of previous copies rather than the Caxton. It was not until the nineteenth century that Robert Southey with William Upcott (1817), and then Sir Edward Strachey (1868), went back to the Caxton directly in an attempt to create a more accurate text; even then Upcott had to fill in several

---

[1] Caxton's Prologue to *Le Morte Darthur*, from C, fol. 3ʳ. Cf. Field, II: 856.3–5.
[2] Richard R. Griffith, 'Caxton's Copy-Text for *Le Morte Darthur*', in *Traditions and Innovations*, ed. David G. Allen and Robert A. White (Newark, 1990), pp. 75–87 (pp. 76–7 and 81).
[3] Broadly speaking this is true of the print history of Chaucer's *Canterbury Tales* as well. See Derek Pearsall, *The Canterbury Tales* (London, 1985), p. 8, and Appendix (B) Principal Editions of The Canterbury Tales (p. 325).
[4] Tsuyoshi Mukai, 'De Worde's 1498 *Morte Darthur* and Caxton's Copy-Text', *Review of English Studies* n.s. 51 (2000): 24–40. See also Field, I: xv–xvi.

lacunae in his copy-text, and Strachey partly modernized his text. It was not until H. Oskar Sommer's edition (1889–91) that a reasonably scholarly text and apparatus appeared. Throughout this half-millennium, excepting Caxton's original copy-text manuscript, a manuscript inherited by de Worde but otherwise quickly lost to later generations, the only textual witnesses to Malory's *Morte Darthur* were the Caxton incunabula, and even these were not used as copy-texts again for the better part of four hundred years.

All of this changed radically in June 1934 with the remarkable discovery of an untitled manuscript version of *Le Morte Darthur*. Walter F. Oakeshott, Librarian of the Moberly Library at Winchester College, was preparing an exhibition on early books and recalled that his quest for knowledge about mediaeval manuscript bindings had, 'some weeks' earlier, led him to a large prose Arthurian manuscript in the Fellows' Library.[5] What Oakeshott determined when subsequently preparing the exhibition was that this prose Arthurian codex was actually an unknown version of Malory's *Morte Darthur*. This manuscript version, moreover, was different in some crucial regards from the established Caxton text. Suddenly there were two possible witnesses to Malory's text and two very different versions of his Roman War story. For obvious reasons, this manuscript became known as the Winchester manuscript. Now the property of the British Library and catalogued British Library Additional Manuscrip. 59678, this manuscript text of Malory's *Morte* is styled by some scholars 'the Malory manuscript', but is still commonly referred to as 'the Winchester manuscript' – the title I employed in my Introduction and which I shall continue to use throughout this study.[6]

The Winchester manuscript is not Malory's autograph but a copy one or two stages removed from Malory. Although there are several lacunae in Winchester which must be filled by supplying the relevant portions of the Caxton text, Eugène Vinaver established that the Winchester text was the more authoritative of the two witnesses, partly because it could on textual-critical grounds more easily and accurately be corrected to bring us closer to what Malory wrote. He accordingly based his influential critical edition of the *Morte Darthur* on the Winchester text. Although Vinaver's textual-critical arguments were eventually hotly contested – especially by William Matthews, Charles Moorman and James Spisak – two generations of scholarship, dominated by Vinaver and P. J. C. Field, have established that the Winchester manuscript, whilst not Malory's own holograph-copy, is the closest we have to Malory himself and the text he actually wrote. Indeed, Field concludes that Winchester is in fact an even 'better text' than Vinaver realized, both as a base-text and on its own terms; Field's new edition of Malory is accordingly also based on Winchester, albeit with considerable emendation from the other witnesses and sources to reclaim 'what Malory

---

[5] W. F. Oakeshott, 'The Finding of the Manuscript', in *Essays*, pp. 1–6. P. J. C. Field characterizes Oakeshott's discovery as nothing less than the 'critical moment in the modern understanding of the *Morte Darthur*': see Field, 'Introduction', in *Re-Viewing Le Morte Darthur*, ed. K. S. Whetter and Raluca L. Radulescu (Cambridge, 2005), pp. 1–7 (p. 1).

[6] For an account of the controversial sale and the manuscript's removal (in a 'knapsack'!) from the College to London, see Paul Yeats-Edwards, 'The Winchester Malory Manuscript', in *Debate*, pp. 367–89 (pp. 380–1).

intended to write'.[7] The possible exception to this conclusion is the two versions of Malory's Roman War narrative. I discuss in my Introduction why the case for Malory himself revising and reducing the story, thereby creating the major difference between the Winchester and Caxton texts of *Le Morte Darthur*, is at best ambiguous.[8] Consequently, for those readers and critics who believe that literary texts are not self-generating but rather author-derived artefacts, modern critical editions of the *Morte*, and at least one form of modern critical inquiry, must accordingly be based on the Winchester version of the text as the copy that most closely resembles Malory's own.

Although the Winchester manuscript is not a *de luxe* production, it does possess one especially striking decorative feature: the main text of the manuscript is in dark brown ink, but the names of all of the characters are consistently rubricated in red ink and drawn in a slightly different script; some object and many place names are likewise rubricated.[9] This rubrication, moreover, was done consecutively with the brown script, not with the scribe or rubricator adding the red after the fact, as was usually the case for decoration in manuscripts. And it is done in red alone, not red traced over brown (or black), a technique which is still effective but naturally duller than the effect produced in Winchester. N. R. Ker adduces that the 'distinguishing of personal names [in Winchester] was evidently a matter of great consequence to the scribes', all the more so considering that the task of repeatedly changing pens and inks must have been 'very laborious'.[10] Laborious, but effective: the visual impression is vivid, amplified all the more by the relative paucity of other decorative features and by Winchester's wide, clean margins. In Thomas H. Crofts's inimitable phrase, 'in turning from this manuscript back to the typographical text, one feels as if the lights had gone out'.[11] Decoration was a common feature of manuscript production throughout the Middle Ages; in *de luxe* manuscripts this decoration can be quite elaborate, with gold engraving, marginal illustrations or commentary, and miniature or even full-sized colour illustrations. At other times the decoration is more modest, consisting mostly of larger, blue or red flourished initials at the start of the text and beginning of paragraphs. Still other manuscripts have practically no decoration at all. Rubrication, as I shall outline below, was likewise used in a wide array of fashions in different manuscripts and contexts. One 'notable use of red is in liturgical books, where the directions for action are in red, the words actually to be spoken in black; the same distinction can be found in texts of drama'.[12] In all cases, though, the *consistent* red rubrication of each and every character's name is relatively rare: indeed, one of my principal arguments in this book is that this

---

[7] See P. J. C. Field, 'The Choice of Texts for Malory's *Morte Darthur*', in his *Texts and Sources*, pp. 14–26 (p. 24); and Field, I: xi–xviii (quoting xviii).

[8] See pp. 15–21, supra.

[9] For examples see Plates I and XIII–XVI of the present study. At the time of going to press, the entire manuscript can be viewed in colour online, one page at a time, via the Malory Project: www.maloryproject.com[.]

[10] N. R. Ker, Introduction, *Winchester Malory*, p. xiv.

[11] Thomas H. Crofts, *Malory's Contemporary Audience* (Cambridge, 2006), p. 66. Cf. Helen Cooper, 'Opening Up the Malory Manuscript', in *Debate*, pp. 255–84 (p. 273).

[12] J. P. Gumbert, '"Typography" in the Manuscript Book', *Journal of the Printing Historical Society* 22 (1993): 5–28.

ubiquitous red writing (and reading) of names is, at least amongst Arthurian and romance manuscripts, unique to Winchester. A number of critics have previously commented on the striking effect of the rubrication, and Carol M. Meale, Andrew Lynch, Helen Cooper and Thomas H. Crofts have all rightly but briefly noted that its most immediate effect is to create a roll-call of named knights and knightly worship.[13] The *significance* of the rubrication and its effects, however, is something that no critic adequately addresses, not even Cooper or Meale in their otherwise perspicacious accounts of the manuscript.

According to Meale, the rubrication acts a sort of signpost or lectoral aid. Meale argues further that the kind of rubrication of names found in Winchester is typical of fifteenth-century romance manuscript 'detailing', but the only example she offers as support for this claim is the Pierpont Morgan copy of *Generides*.[14] New York, Pierpont Morgan Library MS M.876 (formerly the Helmingham Tollemache MS), is a fifteenth-century composite containing an incomplete copy of Lydgate's *Troy Book* (fols 1–102^v) and the unique couplet version of the anonymous Middle English romance *Generides* (fols 103–52^v). The manuscript was written and decorated in England, and the same scribe and artist are responsible for the layout of both texts. Morgan 876 is usually dated AD/CE 1450 or earlier, but Meale makes a convincing case for a 1460 compilation date on the basis of the presentation of armour and clothing in the illustrations.[15] Although its decoration programme is incomplete, Morgan 876 was clearly designed to be a sumptuous product throughout, with numerous larger red and black capitals heading most columns of both texts, occasionally shifting to black and gold capital headings in *Generides*. There are also blue and red paragraph marks in the *Troy Book*, and seven miniatures in varying degrees of completion across both texts, with spaces left for many more illustrations. Folios 1^v–3^r even contain a few gold paragraph marks. The *Troy Book* also possesses rubricated book headers (such, for example, as 'Librum prim') and *explicits*.

Most pertinent to the present discussion is the fact that Meale's argument about Morgan 876's detailing is seemingly supported by Guddat-Figge. Guddat-Figge claims that 'Chapter headings and names in the text of *Generides* [are] in red, [but] from f. 111b [these are] mostly blanks'.[16] Both Meale and Guddat-Figge, however, overstate the evidence: 'from f. 111b' constitutes most of the text. *Generides* opens, after a blank half-page for an unexecuted illustration, with a rubricated prose summary-cum-introduction. The summary is notable for my purposes because in it the names of Generides (three times), his mother Sereyne

---

[13] See Carol M. Meale, '"The Hoole Book"', in *Companion*, pp. 3–17 (p. 10); Andrew Lynch, *Malory's Book of Arms* (Cambridge, 1997), pp. 3–4; Cooper, 'Opening Up', in *Debate*, pp. 273–4; and Crofts, *Malory's Contemporary Audience*, pp. 66–71.

[14] Meale, '"The Hoole Book"', in *Companion*, p. 10 and n. 21.

[15] For the date and description of the manuscript, including its decoration programme, see Henry Bergen, ed., *Lydgate's Troy Book*, Vol. IV, EETS ES 126 (London, 1935), pp. 21–5; Gisela Guddat-Figge, *Catalogue of Manuscripts Containing Middle English Romances* (Munich, 1976), pp. 243–4; Carol M. Meale, 'The Morgan Library Copy of *Generides*', in *Romance in Medieval England*, ed. Maldwyn Mills, Jennifer Fellows and Carol M. Meale (Cambridge, 1991), pp. 89–104; and Martha W. Driver, 'Medievalizing the Classical Past in Pierpont Morgan MS M 876', in *Middle English Poetry*, ed. A. J. Minnis (York, 2001), pp. 211–39.

[16] Guddat-Figge, *Catalogue*, p. 243.

(twice) and his lover Clarionas (once) are written in black instead of red, thereby providing a sort of reverse rubricated emphasis. Significantly, however, other names in the introduction, including both the hero's father and the chief villain, are not rubricated. Something similar occurs in the rubricated captions for the illustrations in this part of the manuscript, where Generides's name is always written in black against the red ink of those captions which mention him (e.g. fols 106^v, 113^r, 121^v, 127^r, 133^r, 140^v, 142^v, 147^r, and three name blanks in the rubric at 149^v). Other caption names, however, are usually left in red, undistinguished from the rest of the caption, and not all captions mention Generides (e.g. fol. 119^{r-v}). Likewise some of the rubricated chapter headings write Generides's name in black instead of red (115^v, 139^v), but not all chapter headings do this (e.g. 146^r or 148^v–149^r). As for the opening of the poem proper rather than its *mise-en-page*, here again there is no rubrication of any sort, either of names or of chapters (see fol. 103^v in Plate II). In point of fact, rubrication of names within the story itself does not begin till folio 107^b, several folios into the text, with the birth and baptism of Generides himself. Hereafter the hero's name is steadily rubricated for several folios, and the name 'Clarionas' is likewise rubricated from 110^v; but only these two names of all of the characters in the story are rubricated or, more commonly, left blank for subsequent rubrication. The more typical manuscript rubrication of chapter titles and illustration captions appears in several locations throughout, and in some of the captions 'Generides' is in black ink instead of red.[17] (See Plate III.) In contrast to what Guddat-Figge implies in her description, there are large stretches of text where the two names are left blank, but the rubrication of 'Generides' and 'Clarionas' does recur sporadically throughout the entire poem; there are several name blanks for several pages from folio 111 verso, but the two names are rubricated again on folios 127^v–128^r, 135^r, 145^v–148^r and 151^r. And Generides's name is similarly emphasized frequently in the chapter rubrics or illustration captions; indeed, to the best of my knowledge this distinction of names by changing colour in rubrics is all but unique to this manuscript.

Despite some initial and seemingly striking resemblances (see Plate IV of folio 110^r), then, there are actually considerable differences between the *ordinatio* of Winchester and Morgan 876, the most important being the *de luxe* nature of Morgan versus Winchester's lack of illustration, the fact that what decoration we have in Winchester is complete whilst that in Morgan is not, and that Morgan's rubrication of names is done in the usual method of leaving blank spaces to be rubricated later. Indeed, whilst Winchester's scribes changed pen and ink at each and every name, occasionally forgetting to change immediately back to brown once a name was written in red, the Morgan scribe quickly abandoned the consistent rubrication of even two names for a later moment, and never completed the project: some of the name-gaps were eventually filled in (in black) by a later reader who sometimes got the name wrong (e.g. fols 123^v, 124^v). Most significant of all, apart from the black ink for the hero's mother in the opening rubricated summary of the text, the rubrication of names that does appear in Morgan 876

---

[17] New York, Pierpont Morgan Library MS M.876, folios 106^v, 113^r, 119^{r-v}, 121^v, 127^r, 133^r, 140^v, 142^v, 147^r, 149^v (for illustration captions), and 109^r, 112^d, 121^a, 129^a, 139^c, 146^b, and 148^v–149^r for chapter rubrics. Folio 109^r is reproduced as Plate III.

is confined exclusively to the hero and heroine. Such is the case on folio 121ᵛ, in the important battle between Generides and Amalek, a major scene in the romance, warranting one of the text's fully executed half-page illustrations and accompanying captions. As is typical of manuscript decoration in general, the caption is rubricated (except for 'Generides'), and the name **Generides** is rubricated in column b of the text, but 'Amalek' a few lines above 'Generides' is not rubricated.[18]

In other words, although the rubrication of names in Winchester and the Morgan *Generides* is unusual enough to make the two manuscripts cognate in modern codicological analyses, two manuscripts alone are insufficient evidence for Meale's pattern of fifteenth-century 'detailing' of names, especially when Morgan 876 is in other respects so much more elaborate than Winchester. There is also the question of why the names were to be rubricated in *Generides* but not the *Troy Book*, especially since the same scribe copied both texts in Morgan and since, in other respects, the *ordinatio* of the two texts remains the same throughout. Crucially, and in marked contrast to Winchester's rubrication of each and every character's name and some place names, only two names are rubricated or, more commonly, left blank for rubrication, in Morgan 876. Two swallows, we might say, hardly make a spring.

The copy of the stanzaic *Generides* in Cambridge, Trinity College MS O.5.2 (c. 1470), is again paired with Lydgate's *Troy Book*, but the Trinity manuscript version is much less richly decorated than its Morgan counterpart.[19] The stanzas in the Trinity O.5.2 *Generides* are marked by flourished initials of two or three lines, in varying colours, and the opening folio has a floral spray border around the left and top margin, but there are no illustrations in the Trinity *Generides* and no rubrication of any sort. The only exception is the rubricated *explicit* (fol. 37ᵛ), which is obviously a different kind than that under discussion. The Lydgate *Troy Book* that follows is by the same scribe, but is much more *de luxe*, beginning with a large, eleven-line, column-wide illustration in many colours, extending to a full-page border. Many folios will then have no decoration, but similarly elaborate decoration recurs at various pages throughout. There is, however, no rubrication in the *Troy Book*. In contrast, no illustrations occur in, or (on the basis of a lack of empty spaces) were even intended for, Trinity's *Generides*. The final item, the *Siege of Thebes*, has rubrication, but of the usual glosses, headers and titles, not of characters' names (see fols 191ʳ–211ᵛ). We thus need to look elsewhere for the origin of Winchester's rubrication than Meale's notion of a generalized fifteenth-century tradition. Indeed, in terms of manuscript layout, the consistent rubrication of all names that so distinguishes *Le Morte Darthur* in its manuscript

---

[18] Morgan MS M.876, fol. 121ᵛ. Again, 'Generides' is written in black in the rubricated caption, but 'Amalek' is in red with the remainder of the caption. For a black-and-white reproduction, see Driver, 'Medievalizing the Classical Past', p. 225, Plate 8.

[19] Guddat-Figge, *Catalogue*, p. 87 is helpful but somewhat misleading. My own examination of the manuscript suggests it is elaborate, but less *de luxe* than the Morgan copy, particularly in *Generides*. Nor does there appear to be any rubrication of names in the fifteenth-century fragments of the stanzaic *Generides* discovered and reproduced by Frank Stubbings, 'A New Manuscript of *Generydes*', *Transactions of the Cambridge Bibliographical Society* 10 (1993): 317–40. Cambridge, Trinity College MS O.5.2 is now widely available via the college's Wren Digital Library.

context is all but unique to Winchester amongst French and English romance manuscripts, and *is* unique amongst Arthurian manuscripts.

Even more important than the provenance or rarity of the rubrication in Winchester is the *effect* of this decoration scheme. It seems to me that the most significant result of Winchester's rubrication of personal names is not merely that it draws attention to Malory's principal characters, but rather that it does so in order to aggrandize and memorialize Arthur and his knights in ways which emphasize key themes of the text. Keith Busby points out that pen-flourished initials in French romance, especially when the flourish occurs near or on the initial of a name, serve to 'reinforc[e] the social setting of the narrative', including the 'absolute respectability' of the protagonists.[20] My central thesis in this study is that the narrative codex and content of Malory's *Morte Darthur* are similarly interrelated, but that Winchester's rubrication goes much further than the French tendency. For more than two generations now the dominant scholarly interpretation of the *Morte Darthur* from a wide array of modern critics with diverse theoretical methodologies dictates that Malory is ultimately interrogating Arthurian chivalry.[21] Vinaver had argued differently, but critics coming in Vinaver's considerable wake often made a name for themselves by disputing his literary-critical findings, even if they accepted his textual-critical conclusions. Even critics who do not explicitly emphasize the failure of chivalry in the *Morte* still emphasize Malory's focus on the religious deaths of Gwenyvere and Launcelot, an interpretation which implicitly supports Malory's supposed abandonment of chivalry or which at least foregrounds a new set of values.[22]

It is my contention that Winchester's rubrication of names emphatically glorifies and memorializes Arthurian characters and deeds in ways which reveal an alternative reading of Malory's Arthuriad. The rubricated names effectively – and, I hope to show, deliberately – turn the entire manuscript into the codicological equivalent of the many tombs and memorials which are erected throughout the *Morte Darthur* to commemorate the deeds or deaths of knights and ladies.[23] The marginalia echo and reinforce this memorializing effect.[24] Readers more interested in those thematic contentions than the physical evidence standing behind

---

[20] Keith Busby, *Codex and Context* (Amsterdam and New York, 2002), I:193.
[21] See, e.g., most of the papers in *Originality*; Elizabeth T. Pochoda, *Arthurian Propaganda* (Chapel Hill, 1971); Kathleen Coyne Kelly, 'Malory's Body Chivalric', *Arthuriana* 6.4 (1996): 52–71 (59); Dorsey Armstrong, *Gender and the Chivalric Community in Malory's Morte d'Arthur* (Gainesville, 2003); eadem, 'Postcolonial Palomides', *Exemplaria* 18 (2006): 175–203; and Christopher Cannon, *Middle English Literature* (Cambridge and Malden, 2008), pp. 25–6 and 38.
[22] See, e.g., Robert L. Kelly, 'Penitence as a Remedy for War in Malory's "Tale of the Death of Arthur",' *Studies in Philology* 91 (1994): 111–35; Karen Cherewatuk, 'The Saint's Life of Sir Launcelot', *Arthuriana* 5.1 (1995): 62–78; Corinne Saunders, 'Religion and Magic', in *The Cambridge Companion to the Arthurian Legend*, ed. Elizabeth Archibald and Ad Putter (Cambridge, 2009), pp. 201–17 (p. 214).
[23] Batt also discusses Malory's concern with commemoration in the *Morte*, but we reach very different conclusions: see Catherine Batt, *Malory's Morte Darthur: Remaking Arthurian Tradition* (Basingstoke and New York, 2002).
[24] Obviously this manuscript-tomb parallel is not exact, since most individual mediaeval tombs in graveyards or churches commemorate only one or two individuals, whereas I am proposing that Winchester commemorates the entire Round Table Fellowship, knights and ladies, king and queen. But the end result, I think, is similar, and equally deliberate.

them may wish to move to Chapters Three and Four, which explore the narrative connections between Winchester and the *Morte* in more literary-critical ways. The remainder of the current chapter is devoted to a comparative codicological survey of the kinds of manuscripts the *Morte Darthur* reveals Malory to have read and been interested in, in order to establish the uniqueness of Winchester's style of rubrication. My codicological examination of Winchester continues in Chapter Two, where I turn to the nature, function and origin of the memorializing rubrication and marginalia.

Rubrication Patterns in the Sources: A Survey

Etymologically, the English noun *rubrication* derives from post-classical Latin *rubricatio*, itself from *rubricare*, and refers to both a 'heading' or 'title', and to the 'act of rubricating'. The English verb *rubricate* has similar origins, going back to the sixth century, and the headword note in the *OED* entry states that 'The use of *rubricae* or passages written in red ink to indicate chapter headings or other significant passages in certain sorts of manuscripts extends back to antiquity.'[25] Often rubrics are used to provide emphasis or clarity; at other times they provide decoration; sometimes they do both. Even though his incunable is black-and-white, Caxton invokes just such a notion in labelling his table of contents to the *Morte Darthur* as 'The table or rubrysshe of the contents'.[26] This long-standing tradition of various uses of red ink is evident in the ubiquitous appearance of manuscript rubrics in a wide variety of texts and fashions throughout the Middle Ages. At about the same time that Sir Thomas Malory, for whatever reasons, embarked upon the remarkable crime spree that secured his first imprisonment, for instance, *The Life of St Cuthbert in English Verse* of circa 1450 records a distinction between 'þis chapiter þe sext' and how 'In þe rubryke is þe texte; / How bosilus bare witnes / In cuthbert cominyng'.[27] A little more than a century after Malory's death, John Foxe similarly entitles one section of his 1583 *Book of Martyrs*, 'The Canon of the Masse, with the rubricke of the same', a remark which serves to illustrate the longevity of rubrication in ecclesiastical uses, including biblical and divine office contexts.[28] These comments also remind us of the usual distinction between rubric and text, reminding us further that rubricated headers, chapter titles and glosses are especially common in a wide variety of religious, political and secular texts. Yet these distinctions between text and rubric also illustrate the highly unusual nature of Winchester's rubrication, which is an integral part of the main text, not an addition, gloss, narrative title or division.

[25] See 'rubrication, n.' and 'rubricate, v.', *Oxford English Dictionary*, 3rd edn, March 2011; online version. Accessed 12 April 2012. See also Christopher de Hamel, *The British Library Guide to Manuscript Illumination: History and Techniques* (London, 2001), pp. 16–17.
[26] Modern editions tend to ignore this statement, but it occurs clearly on fol. 3ᵛ of the Morgan Library Caxton.
[27] *The Life of St Cuthbert in English Verse, c. A.D. 1450*, ed. J. T. Fowler (Durham, 1891), vv. 1317–20.
[28] John Foxe, *The Unabridged Acts and Monuments Online or TAMO*, 1583 edition, Book 10, p. 1423. (HRI Online Publications, Sheffield, 2011). www.johnfoxe.org[.] Accessed 14 June 2014.

Rubrication is common in, but not exclusive to, Bibles and religious texts. Red-ink headings, rubrics or instructions appear frequently in liturgical texts, especially Missals, Breviaries, Calendars and Books of Hours: the phrase 'red-letter day' ultimately reflects the use of red ink in Calendars to denote a particularly important feast or saint's day. Such general rubricated days, names or chapters are closer to Winchester's *ordinatio* than the more elaborate decoration characteristic of *Bibles moralisées*. In this context, the full rubrication of names that we see in Winchester might be thought to have more in common with certain kinds of religious material than with romances or even chronicles, but whilst my own view is that the *Morte Darthur* is not a straightforward romance, it is certainly not in any way a biblical text.[29] It is possible that the Winchester scribes were familiar with biblical and religious rubrication and incorporated that decoration programme into the *Morte Darthur* as they copied the narrative into what is now the Winchester manuscript. Nevertheless, I shall argue in this and the following chapter that the kind of rubrication found in Winchester is so unusual for romance, and that it interacts so cohesively with the major themes and emphases of the *Morte*, that the idea of rubricating all names is more likely to be authorial than scribal. I also wish to reiterate the arguments of Maurice Keen and Richard W. Kaeuper about the many ways in which mediaeval chivalry at times functioned to a significant extent as a form of secular piety, appropriating the rules of the Church for its own ends as much as the Church attempted to appropriate and control chivalry.[30] Some knights, that is, would be deeply pious and consider themselves fighting for God, but others would be less pious and more mercenary or at least earthly in motivation. It is notable in this context that the kind of rubrication of names found in Winchester serves to aggrandize Arthur and Gwenyvere and the Round Table knights and their lady-loves (and opponents) in ways which emphasize this *secular* fellowship. Given my focus on the origin and purpose of the red rubrication of names in the Winchester manuscript, I am obviously concerned in the following discussion with rubrication in the specific sense of red lettering, not with all rubrics per se, nor with all uses of red ink. I will discuss rubricated glosses and headings in my analysis of *Brut* manuscripts below, but I have tried throughout to maintain a distinction between rubrication as red lettering, specifically in names, and a broader sense of rubrication for any sort of header or gloss.

Murray J. Evans argues that romances are more decorated than non-romances,[31] but my own investigations suggest that the most we can say is that the manuscript decoration of different genres seems about equal. The fame of the Auchinleck manuscript (National Library of Scotland MS Advocates' 19.2.1; c. 1330–40) as an anthology containing legendary, devotional and romance texts is well known and much discussed. Of Auchinleck's forty-four extant items, eighteen (or sixteen, for some critics) are romances, eight of which occur uniquely in

---

[29] My views on the genre of the *Morte* are laid out in full in K. S. Whetter, *Understanding Genre and Medieval Romance* (Aldershot, 2008).
[30] See especially Maurice Keen, *Chivalry* (New Haven, 1984), pp. 52–63, and Richard W. Kaeuper, *Chivalry and Violence in Medieval Europe* (Oxford, 1999), pp. 47–51.
[31] Murray J. Evans, *Rereading Middle English Romance* (Montreal and Kingston, 1995), pp. 39–50.

this manuscript, including the stanzaic *Guy* and Middle English *Sir Tristrem*.[32] In terms of its mixed contents, anthologizing romance and chivalric material with religious and didactic matter, Auchinleck is typical of Middle English romance collections; in terms of its decoration scheme and miniatures, however, Auchinleck is far from typical. In the English tradition, at least, most romance manuscripts are actually *not* heavily decorated.[33] This is true enough even of Chaucer manuscripts, for despite the prominence of the Ellesmere manuscript and its pilgrim portraits, even *Canterbury Tales* manuscripts, which have enough romances to warrant extra decoration were Evans's contention accurate, are typically not lavish. *Canterbury Tales* manuscripts also tend to employ the same decoration throughout individual manuscripts; whatever differences there might be in layout between one manuscript or group of manuscripts and another, there are no notable changes in layout between the different genres amongst the *Tales* within the same manuscript apart from the obvious exception of different rhymes and prose or verse writing.[34] In light of the seeming similarity between Winchester and certain biblical manuscripts, it should be noted that the border sprays of several *Canterbury Tales* manuscripts, including Hengwrt, have corresponding spray patterns in certain Bibles, including the 'Great Bible' of MS Royal 1.E.ix, discussed below.[35]

The simple – and unsurprising – fact is that many features of manuscript decoration are found in a wide array of manuscripts and genres amongst both secular and religious items. Even the common practice of having red tracing or pen-strokes in opening initials of letters in certain romance manuscripts is matched by an equally common practice of having little or no decoration in other manuscripts. In this sense the stanzaic *Morte Arthur* in London, British Library Harley MS 2252 stands somewhere in the middle of the range of typical English romance manuscript decoration, for the bulk of the manuscript is plain, with the exceptions noted below. *The Weddynge of Sir Gawen and Dame Ragnelle*, on the other hand, perhaps an early attempt by Malory to try his hand at Arthurian romance, is completely unadorned – at least in the manuscript that has come down to us.[36] None of these English manuscripts employ Winchester's kind of rubrication. *Brut* manuscripts, however, might provide possible parallels.

---

[32] For a digital facsimile, including an authoritative overview of the manuscript, its contents, and history, see *The Auchinleck Manuscript*, ed. David Burnley and Alison Wiggins, http://auchinleck.nls.uk/[.]

[33] On this issue, see further John Finlayson, 'Reading Romances in Their Manuscript', *Anglia* 123.4 (2006): 632–66 (634); and Harriet Hudson, 'Middle English Popular Romances', *Manuscripta* 28 (1984): 67–78.

[34] See further William Matthews, 'Caxton and Chaucer', in *Debate*, pp. 1–34 (p. 8); and especially John M. Manly and Edith Rickert, *The Text of the Canterbury Tales*, Vol. I: *Descriptions of the Manuscripts* (Chicago and London, 1940).

[35] Manly and Rickert, *Text of the Canterbury Tales*, I: 567–8.

[36] Oxford, Bodl. MS Rawlinson C.86, fols 128^v–140^r. The theory that Malory authored the *Weddyng* was first proposed by Field, and has recently been buttressed by Ralph Norris. See, respectively, P. J. C. Field, 'Malory and *The Wedding of Sir Gawain and Dame Ragnell*', in his *Texts and Sources* (Cambridge, 1998 [originally 1982 and revised for this collection]), pp. 284–94; and Ralph Norris, 'Sir Thomas Malory and *The Wedding of Sir Gawain and Dame Ragnell* Reconsidered', *Arthuriana* 19.2 (2009): 82–102.

In broad terms the pan-European story of Arthur even in the late Middle Ages still owes as much to chronicle and *Brut* accounts of the Round Table as to romance. As the title helps to indicate, the *Brut* tradition covers the history of Britain from its mythical foundation by the descendants of Aeneas, the Galfridian history of the early kings and rise and fall of King Arthur, and continues through the eventual supremacy of the Saxons and then Normans; various versions updated events to what were, for mediaeval readers, contemporary times. According to Julia Marvin, 'The anonymous prose *Brut* chronicle was the most popular secular vernacular work, and the most widespread Arthurian work, of the later Middle Ages in England.'[37] According to Edward Donald Kennedy, the *Brut*'s popularity and pervasiveness are such that Malory almost certainly had some sort of familiarity with it,[38] and it is also significant for later marketing and intertextuality purposes that William Caxton twice printed a version of the *Brut* under the title the *Chronicles of England* before turning his attention to Malory's *Morte Darthur*.

Rubricated headings, chapter titles and glosses appear widely in Latin, French and English chronicle and *Brut* manuscripts.[39] Significantly, many *Brut* manuscripts also have red underlining of rulers' names in the text (as opposed to in the header, chapter title or gloss), where the first instance or first few instances of a new ruler's name will be underlined in red whilst the name is written in black or brown ink like the rest of the text. Very occasionally, the first letter of a ruler's name will be traced in red, but this is not the same as the writing of each and every name entirely in red, as in Winchester. Even more occasionally, in *Brut* manuscripts an entire name will be in red, but only once or twice, not in every appearance, as in Winchester, and both *Brut* practices are erratic. (See Plate V.) *Brut* manuscript Oxford, Bodleian Library MS Bodley 840, for instance, has chapter rubrics and some red underlining of names in the text, but the underlining stops at line 5 of folio 117^r, and is inconsistent even on the pages where it is used. (See Plate VI.) Oxford, Bodleian Library MS Laud Misc. 550 is typical of *Brut* manuscripts in rubricating opening lines and headings or chapter glosses, but its red underlining of names is even more occasional and random than in Bodley 840. (See Plate VII.) Similarly erratic in its red underlining is Bodleian Library MS Lyell 34, yet Lyell is notable in other respects for its elaborate opening folio, with a gold and blue and red border, with leaves. A version of the *Brut* in London, British Library Harley MS 53 likewise underlines rulers' names in red throughout, and on a few folios also adds a red downstroke through the opening initial of the ruler's name, but this additional red stroke differs from the underlining in not being done consistently.[40] Neither effect creates the same

---

[37] Julia Marvin, ed. and trans., *The Oldest Anglo-Norman Prose Brut Chronicle* (Woodbridge, 2006), p. 1.

[38] Edward Donald Kennedy, 'Sir Thomas Malory's (French) Romance and (English) Chronicle', in *Arthurian Studies in Honour of P. J. C. Field*, ed. Bonnie Wheeler (Cambridge, 2004), pp. 223–34 (p. 229).

[39] In the discussion that follows I am much indebted to Edward Donald Kennedy and especially to Elizabeth Bryan and Sarah Peverley for sharing their insights about chronicle manuscripts with me.

[40] Red downstrokes appear in Harley 53 at folio 14^r, and on the recto side only at folios 68, 69, 70 and 71; folio 72 has red underlining and the red downstroke on both recto and verso, as does 73. The usual red underlining pattern with no additional red splashing continues

sort of pattern as in Winchester. This occasional red colouring of the opening initials of rulers' names also occurs in the elaborately decorated London, British Library, Royal MS 20.A.ii, a composite manuscript (c. 1307–27) containing Peter of Langtoft's *Chronicle*, the *Lament of Edward II*, and fragments of the Vulgate *Lancelot* and *Queste del Saint Graal*. Despite its elaborate layout and mixed contents, this manuscript, too, has no Winchester-like rubrication of names.

Brut manuscripts and their cognates, then, provide a rough parallel to Winchester, but their scribes do not rubricate names in the text (as opposed to in headings, chapters or glosses) in anything like the same fashion or with the same level of consistency as does Winchester. Red underlining is relatively common for names of rulers, but not for all names, and it is not always done even for the same ruler throughout one reign. In all *Brut* manuscripts the red underlining or colouring of names, where it exists at all, works in conjunction with glosses and chapter titles to add a further indexing function, enabling readers to track a particular ruler or dynasty. This is not at all what happens in Winchester.

The situation is largely the same in the manuscripts of John Hardyng's English metrical *Chronicle*, a text well known to Malory and long recognized by Malory scholars as an important minor source for *Le Morte Darthur*. Hardyng's *Chronicle* exists in two different authorial recensions: a longer and Lancastrian-biased version dating to somewhere between 1440 and 1457, and a considerably revised shorter version of circa 1464, also heavily revised in political tendencies, becoming now quite Yorkist. Both versions offer what Edward Donald Kennedy justly terms 'an idealized and enthusiastic account of King Arthur', but the Arthurian emphasis is arguably greater in the second version because its imperial coronation of Arthur gives him even greater honours than most Arthurian stories, including the first version of Hardyng's own *Chronicle*.[41] Kennedy convincingly argues that Malory read Hardyng early in his literary career and that Hardyng influenced Malory's treatment of his sources and *matière* much more than the actual number of borrowings from the *Chronicle* would seem to indicate.[42] Ralph Norris rightly cautions that the differences between Hardyng and Malory are as great as the similarities, but his careful study of Malory's minor sources confirms Hardyng's influence in a number of important episodes.[43] The *Chronicle* may well be the most significant of Malory's minor sources for his opening tale, for instance, a tale long known as the 'Tale of King Arthur' after Vinaver's edition, but which Field retitles 'King Uther and King Arthur'. Malory also follows Hardyng in having Arthur crowned emperor in Rome at the successful completion of the Roman War rather than being forced to return to England before the imperial coronation, as in most of the chronicles. One of Malory's principal

---

from folio 74ʳ. Charles Lethbridge Kingsford, *English Historical Literature in the Fifteenth Century* (Oxford, 1913), p. 125, places the composition of this version of the *Brut* chronicle to 1436–37, and the transcription of Harley 53 itself to 1452–53. I am indebted to Megan G. Leitch for bringing this manuscript to my attention.

[41] Edward Donald Kennedy, 'Malory's Use of Hardyng's *Chronicle*: A Reconsideration', *West Virginia Philological Papers* 54 (2011): 8–15 (8).

[42] See the series of studies by Kennedy: 'Malory's Use of Hardyng's *Chronicle*', *Notes & Queries* ns 16 (1969): 167–70; 'Malory and His English Sources', in *Aspects*, pp. 27–55 (pp. 42–8); and 'Malory's Use of Hardyng's *Chronicle*: A Reconsideration'.

[43] Ralph Norris, *Malory's Library* (Cambridge, 2008), pp. 15–16.

kynge toke hys leve off þe holy fadir þe Pope and Patryarkys and Cardynalys and Senatours full
ryche and lefste good governaunce in þt noble cite and
all þe contrayes off Rome for to warde and to kepe on
payne off deth þt in no wyse hys comaundement be
brokyn. Thus he passyth thorow þe contreyes off all
ptyes And so kyng Arthure passed ovir þe see vnto
Sandwyche haven. Whan quene Gwenyvere her-
de off hys comynge she mette wt hym at London.
So dud all oþer quenys and noble ladyes for þr was
nevir a solempner metyng in one cite to gedyrs for
all maner off rychesse they brought wt them at þt full.
  Here endyth þe tale off þe noble kynge Arthure
that was Empour hym self thorow dygnyte off hys
hondys. And here folowyth afftir many noble
talys off Sir Launcelot de lake.

Explycit the noble tale be twyxt kynge
Arthure and Lucius the Emperour of Rome.

Sone afftir that kynge Arthure was com frome
Rome in to Ingelonde than all þe knyghtys
off þe Rounde table resorted vnto þe kynge & made
many Jousteys and turnementes. And som þr were þt
were but knyghtes encresed in armys and worshyp
þt passed all oþ of her felowys in prouesse and noble
dedys and þt was well proved on many. But in
especiall hit was pvyd on Sir Launcelot de lake
for in all turnementes Justys & dedys off armys bothe
for lyff and deth he passed all oþer knyghtes and at
no tyme was he ovircom but yff hit were by treson

man that hath litel to doone
Seek he may make him soone
Ne that him nat be idel long
That any werk wil bryng'
Neithur lewd man ne clerk
That he ne may fynd him werk
ffor to syng' or ffor to rede
Or for to speke of sum old dede
That here before hath be wroght
Whiche entorne may be on thoght
Of doughtie men that sum tyme were
howe noble that they bien here
Guy of Warwik' and Tristram also
Beues of Hampton and other moo
Percyuale and curteys Gawein
And other knyghtes as Sir Oweyn
I ne may reken hem all
That worship han goote in boure and hall
And for here ladyes sake to and froo
Suffred grete sorwes and woo
And at the last to here purpos
They gate worship and grete los
Ros of a geste that was sum tyme
That was made in frensh ryme
A clerk it in to latyn booke
Att hertford out of ye booke
These in latyn was it seyeth
As clerkes wele knowen and seeten
Nowe if ye wil listen & stound
like as I haue this tale I found
I shal yow tell in my name
yf it plese yow ffords here

        Worshipful sires a tale I fynde
        That som tyme was a king in pride
        A feir man gentil and wise
        Of noblesse he bare the prise
        Loued he was curies and free
        About him he held a feyr meynee
To god he bare him trewe and mylde
To mysdoers stern and wolde
Anthonye the knyght hight
Sothele he had a ladie bright
The kinges doughter of Assirik
ffeers of heuie were hir sike
Enemyes that ladie hight
Born of noble blode a pight
Entere she was and compenable
But of hert not hevyy stable
Blid denke that was there prive
Or elles a gode ladie was she
Same that she was somdele fell
And that was pite sothlie to tell
ffor to liue she ne soght
In othir wise than she ought
Yit such wifes han often shame

That doon hir husbondes dishonor of name
ffor many a goode man gose it sore
seyeth that name and knoweth not
And Iust were for his wife
That she ne wold for hir life
While he lueth an othir tak
But him that is hir chosen mak
Thus noble lady this ryoall quene
In hir there was no lak I wene
But that she was som what to glad
Of hir bodie to be so bad
The king hir lord had a Stewarde
A bold knyght and neuer cowarde
Riche he was of lond and fee
A grettur man myght no there be
Born he was of noble trude
Of the gretest of all prude
Of all the lond he had his will
They durst noman lowde ne still
him disobey in spache not tene
ffor drede of displesaunce of the Quene
She loued him best I yow ensure
Of any othir liuyng creature
If ye wil knowe his name a right
Sir Amalek hight that knyght
The quene and he a long while
Vsed the kinges treason and gyle
The Stewarde durst no man disaye
So fals he was of conscience
ffor all the lond was in his myght
him durst disobey no maner wyght
All thei held hem in pees
The king him self was rechelees
And had no maner suspecion
To hem of theyr fals treason
It was in may seisan the leues spring
And smale foules merylle song
The king was somdele hevy
And he ne wiste wherfor ne why
Into the forest he wold werde
If god wold him game send
That light myght his hert make
Som of his men he dod w him take
But thre or foure and no moo
In to forest went he tho
Right as he was comen there
Anon he perseiued where
A grete hert passed him beforn
he vncoupled his houndes and blew his horn
All the forest rymed of that blast
Suth horn and crie he folowed fast
No mo than some houndes he had
Al were goode and noon bad
The king of hunting coweth ynogh
Alwey nygh his houndes he rogth

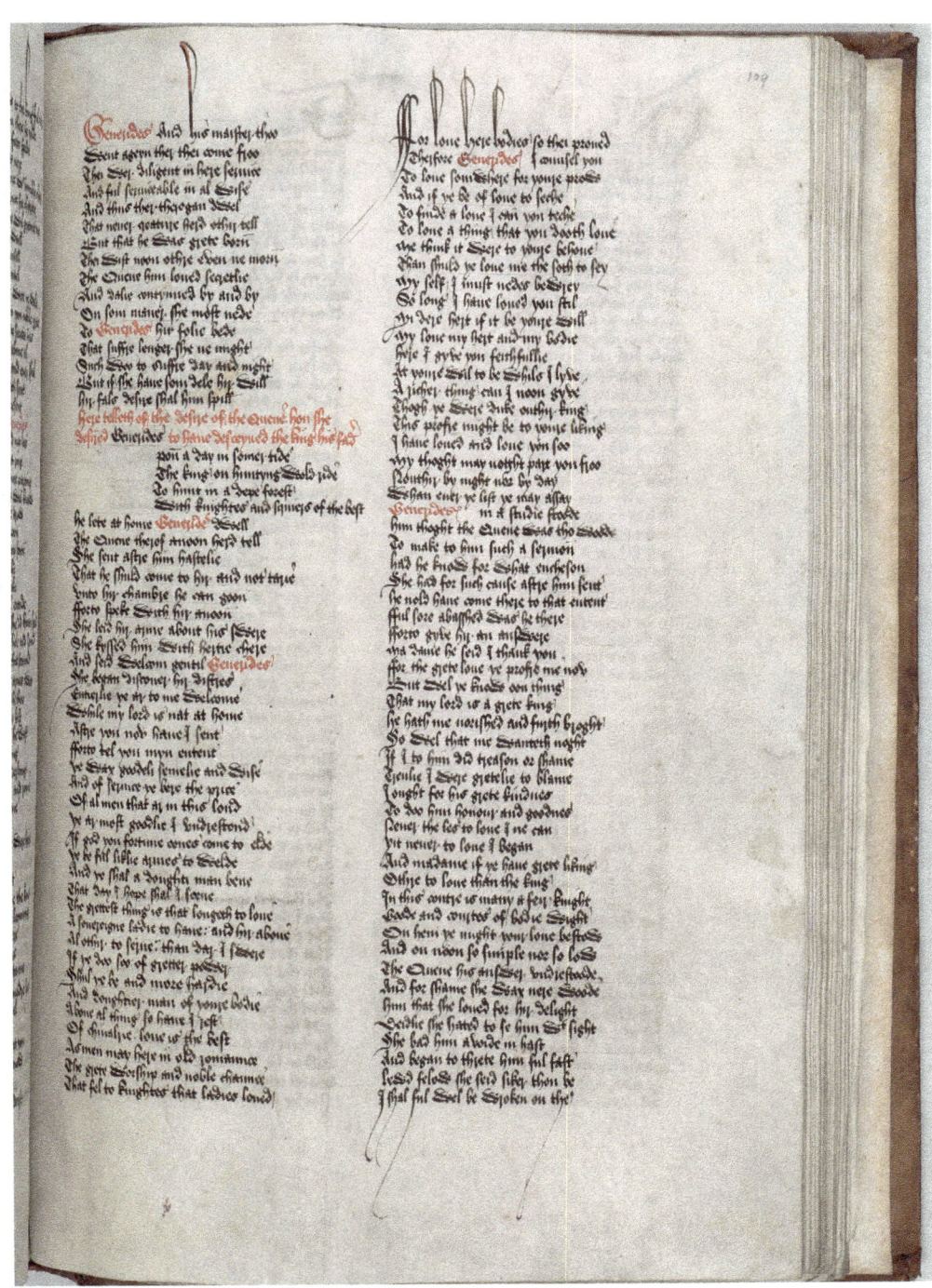

Plate III: Rubrication of illustration caption and the hero's name in *Generides*, including reverse name rubrication in the caption: Morgan Library, MS M.876, fol. 109ʳ.

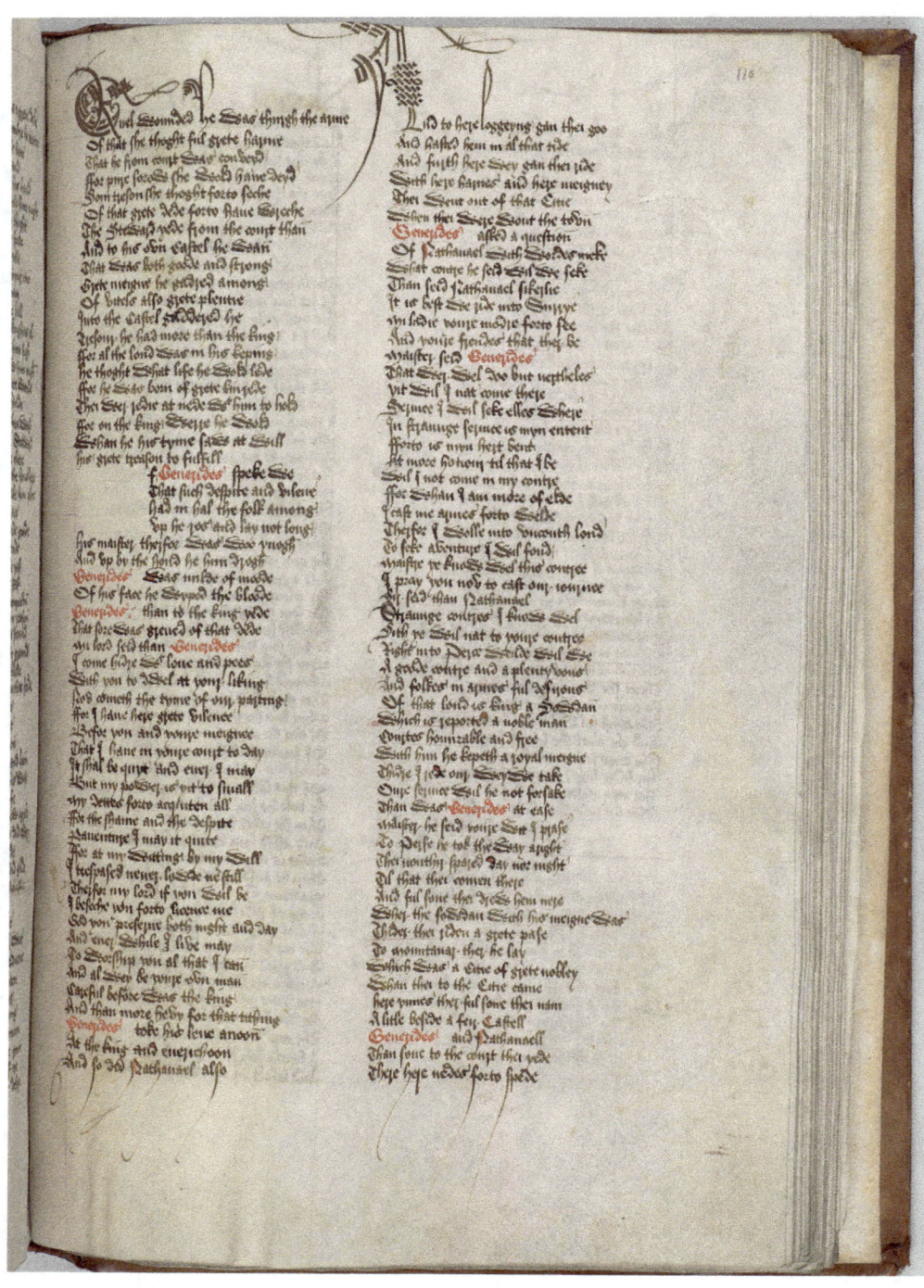

Plate IV: Rubrication restricted to select names in *Generides*: Morgan Library, MS M.876, fol. 110r.

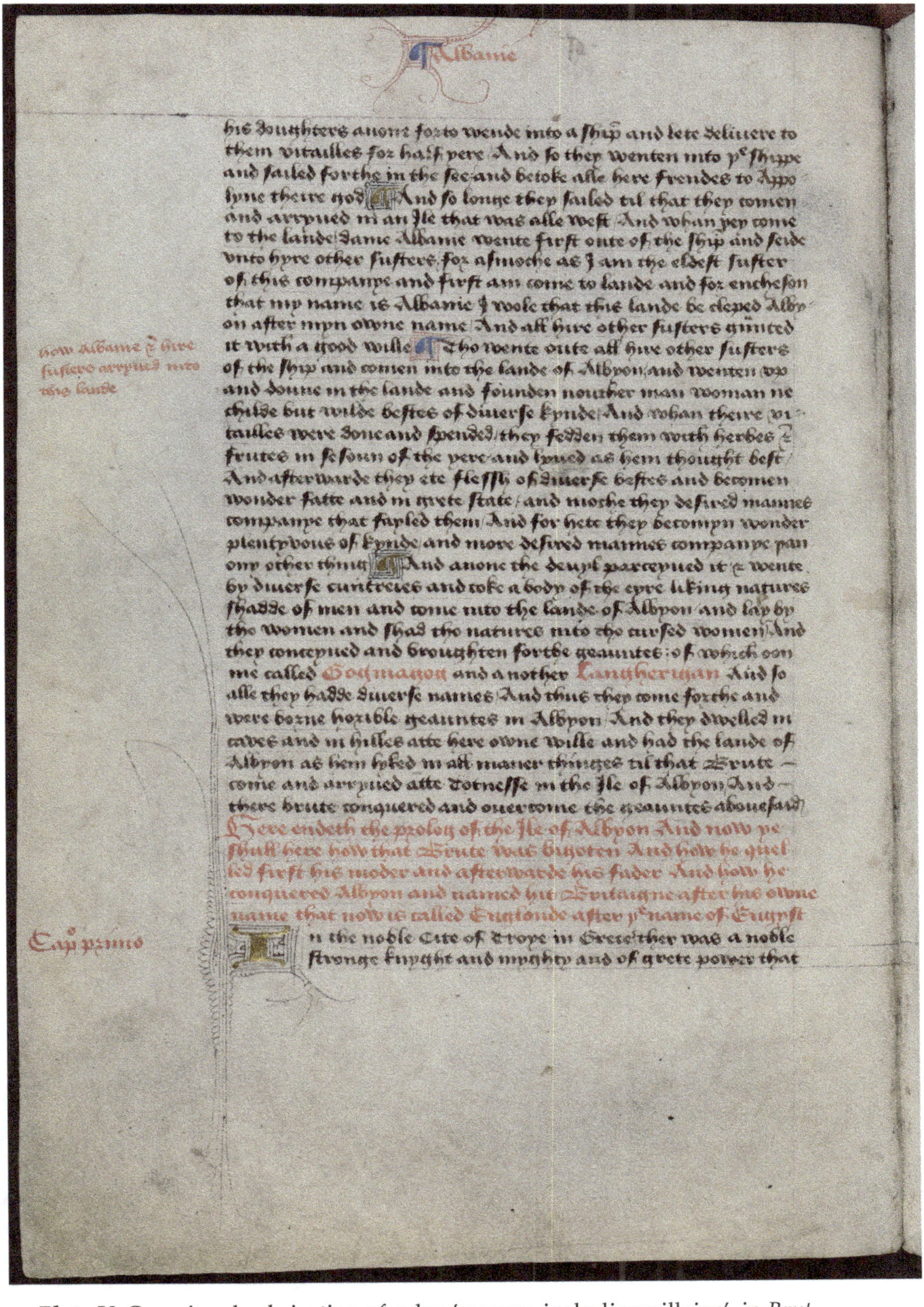

Albanie

his doughters anone for to wende into a ship and lete deliuere to them vitailles for half yere And so they wenten into ye shyppe and sailed forthe in the see and betoke alle here frendes to Appolyne there god And so longe they sailed til that they comen and arryued in an Ile that was alle west And whan they come to the lande dame Albanie wente first oute of the ship and seide vnto hyre other sustres for asmoche as I am the eldest suster of this companye and first am come to lande and for encheson that my name is Albanie I wole that this lande be clepid Albion after myn owne name And all hire other sustres graunted it with a good wille

how Albanie & hire sustres arryued into this lande

Tho wente oute all hire other sustres of the ship and comen into the lande of Albyon and wenten vp and doune in the lande and founden nouther man woman ne childe but wilde bestes of diuerse kynde And whan theire vitailles were done and spended they fedden them with herbes & frutes in sesoun of the yere and lyued as hem thought best And afterwarde they ete flessh of diuerse bestes and becomen wonder fatte and in grete state and mothe they desired mannes companye that fayled them And for hete they becomyn wonder plentyuous of kynde and more desired mannes companye þan ony other thing And anone the deuyl parceyued it & wente by diuerse cuntreyes and toke a body of the eyre likyng natures shadde of men and come into the lande of Albyon and lay by the women and shad tho natures into the cursed women And they conceyued and broughten forthe geauntes of which oon me called **Gogmagog** and another **Langherigan** And so alle they hadde diuerse names And thus they come forthe and were borne horible geauntes in Albyon And they dwelled in caues and in hilles atte here owne wille and had the lande of Albion as hem liked in all maner thinges til that Brute come and arryued atte Totnesse in the Ile of Albyon And there Brute conquered and ouercome the geauntes aboue said

Here endeth the prolog of the Ile of Albyon And now ye shull here how that Brute was bigoten And how he quellid first his moder and afterwarde his fader And how he conquered Albyon and named hit Britaigne after his owne name that now is called Englonde after ye name of Engyst

Cap primo

In the noble cite of Troye in Grece ther was a noble stronge knyght and myghty and of grete power that

Plate V: Occasional rubrication of rulers' names, including villains', in *Brut* MSS: from Bodleian Library MS Laud Misc. 733, fol.19ᵛ.

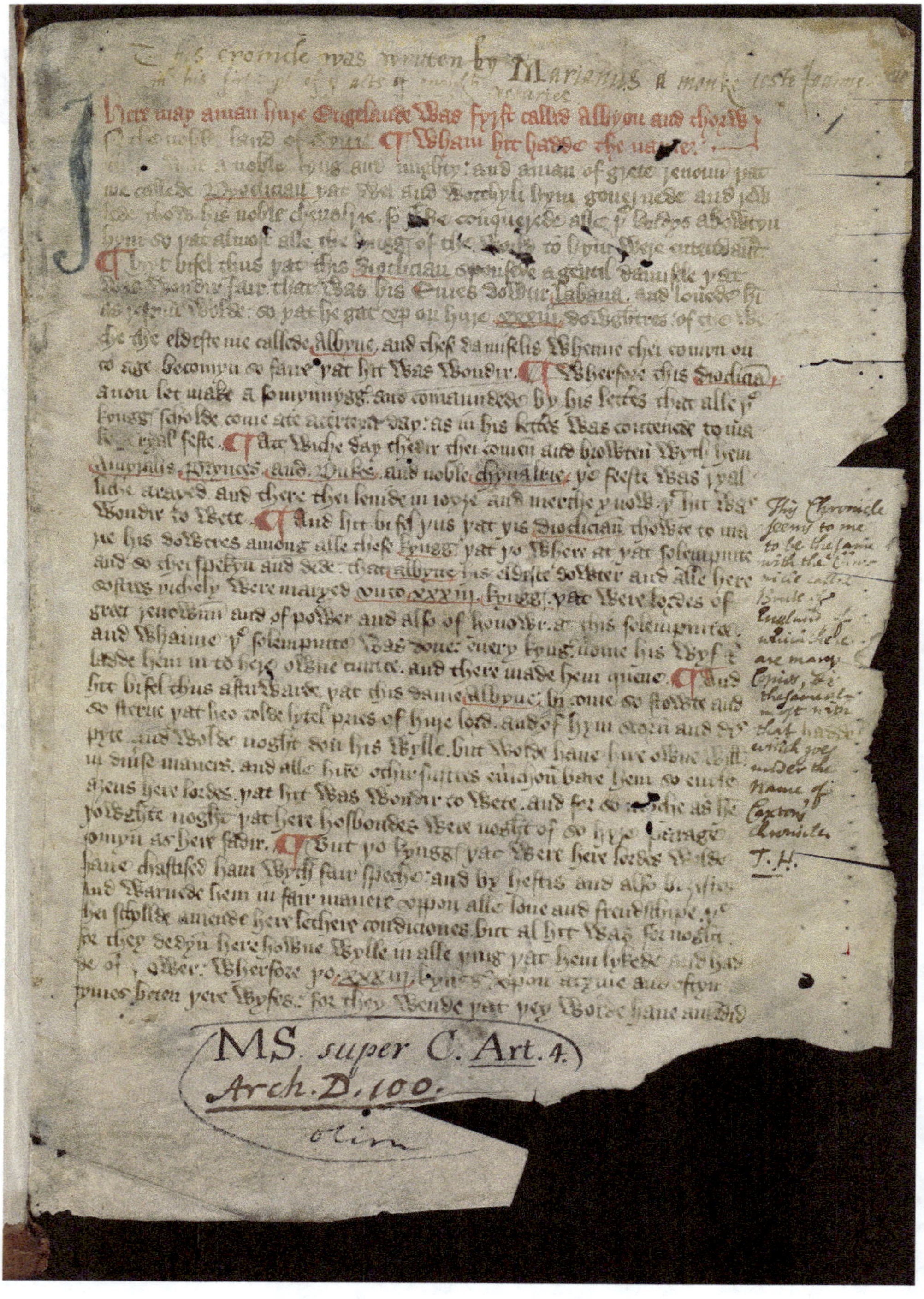

[Middle English manuscript text, Brut chronicle, MS Bodley 840, fol. 1r. Transcription of the Middle English script is not attempted here.]

Marginal note (right side): *This Chronicle seems to me to be the same with that which is called Brute of England, which tells are many Copies, & the same is yet with that hath which goes under the name of Caxtons Chronicle. T.H.*

Lower inscriptions:
MS. super C. Art. 4.
Arch. D. 100.
olim

Plate VI: Erratic red underlining of names as illustrated by *Brut* MS Bodley 840, fol. 1ʳ.

scapid out of prison and wente ayen in to his owne
cuntre and ordeyned a gret power and cam ayen
in to this lond and werrid on kyng Oter/ And for
asmoche as the kyng was seek he ordeyned Aloth his sone in lawe to be capteyn and gouernour of his peple and he with his ost faught with Otta and e-
hym descomfitid and wente fro thennes with his
peple to Werlamchestre put yo was a fair cite
yere seint Albon was marturizid and after it was
destroid be the paynemes and in that cite Otta &
Ossa his brother held ham/ The britons hadde indy-
nacion and scorn of Aloth hir capteyn and wolde
not be rewlid be hym / Wherfore ye kyng was so
attredid and leet put hym in a hors liter al seek
as he was and so he was to Werlamchestre yo
his enemies were and Otta and his brother
cam out and yaf ye kyng a strong bataille and
in that bataille thay were bothe slayn / and yo
that myghte askape fledde in to Scotland and
made on Colgryn hir capteyn and cam ayen
in to this land and ordeyned amonge ham hou
thay myghte empoysen ye kyng/ and ordeyned
a traitour þrto empoysen the welle that ye
kyng drank of for he myghte drynke non oþer
licour but water because of his seeknesse / And
whanne ye kyng drank next þrof he was
empoysned and deide and was buried atte sto-
nehenyns beside Anzel Ambros his brother
the xvj yeer of his Regne Of kyng Artur
and hoo he faught with the saxons

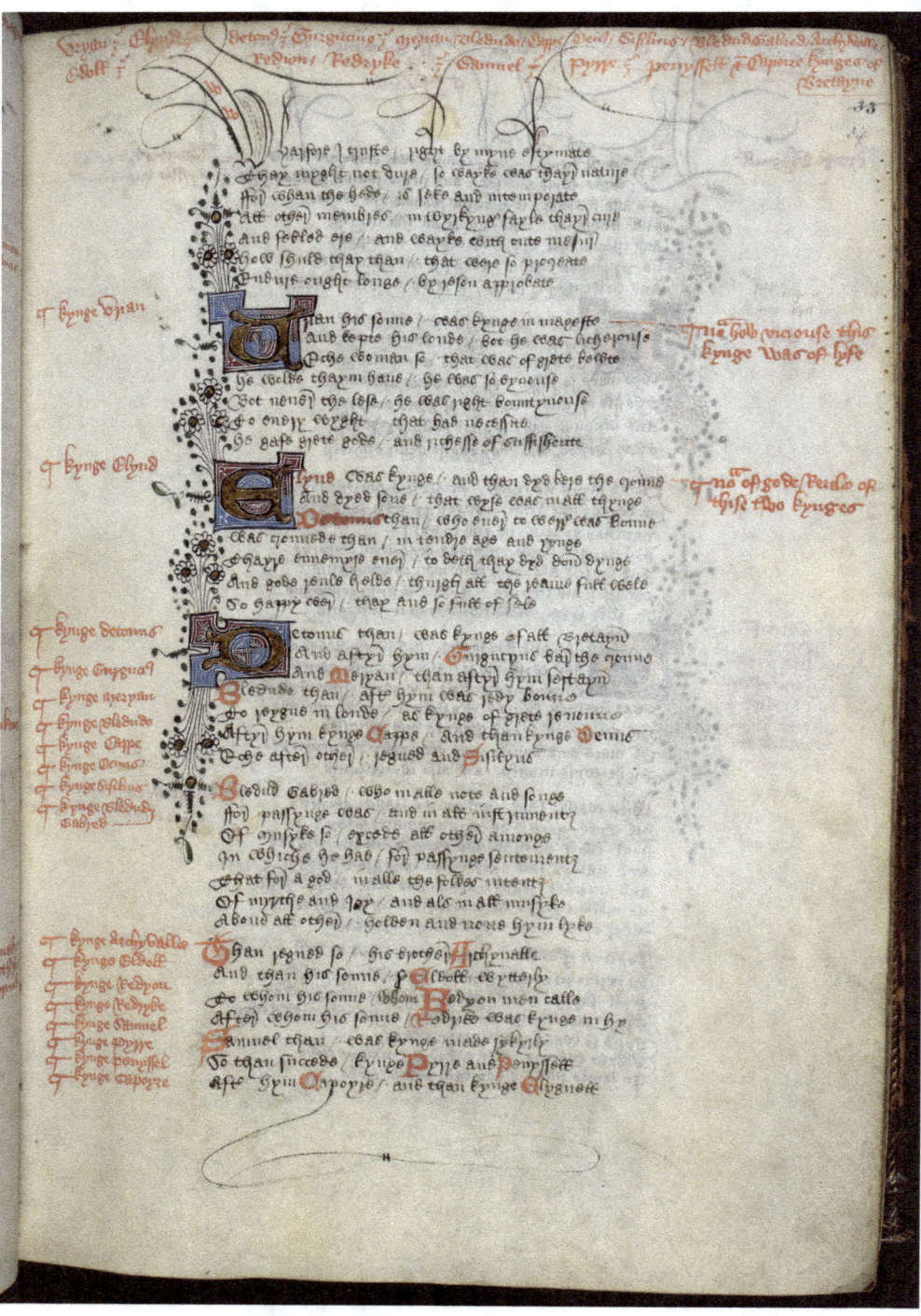

Plate VIII: Partial name rubrication in the first version of Hardyng's *Chronicle*: BL Lansdowne MS 204, fol. 34ʳ.

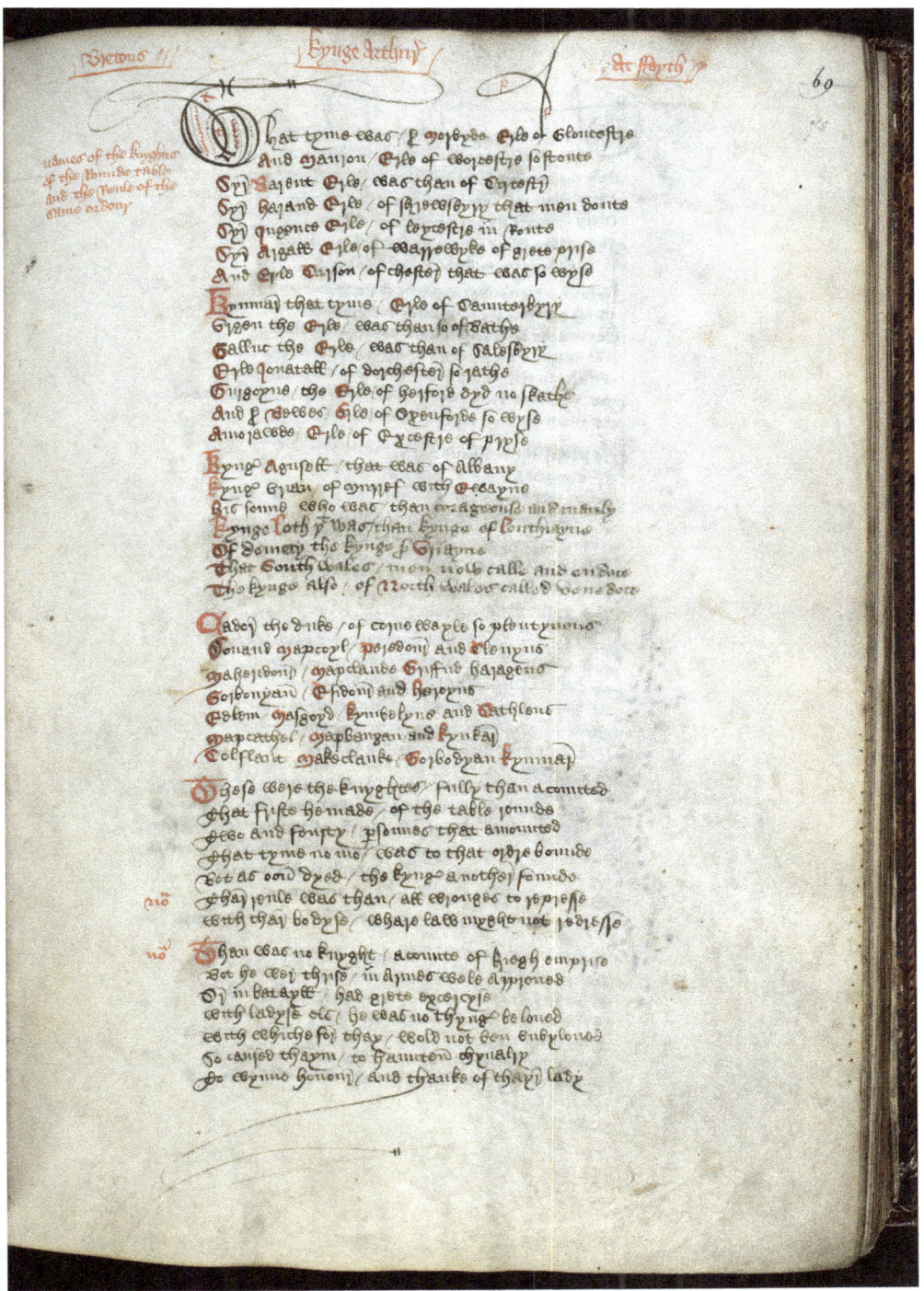

Plate IX: Rubricated initials of new Round Table knights, Hardyng's first *Chronicle*: BL Lansdowne MS 204, fol. 70r.

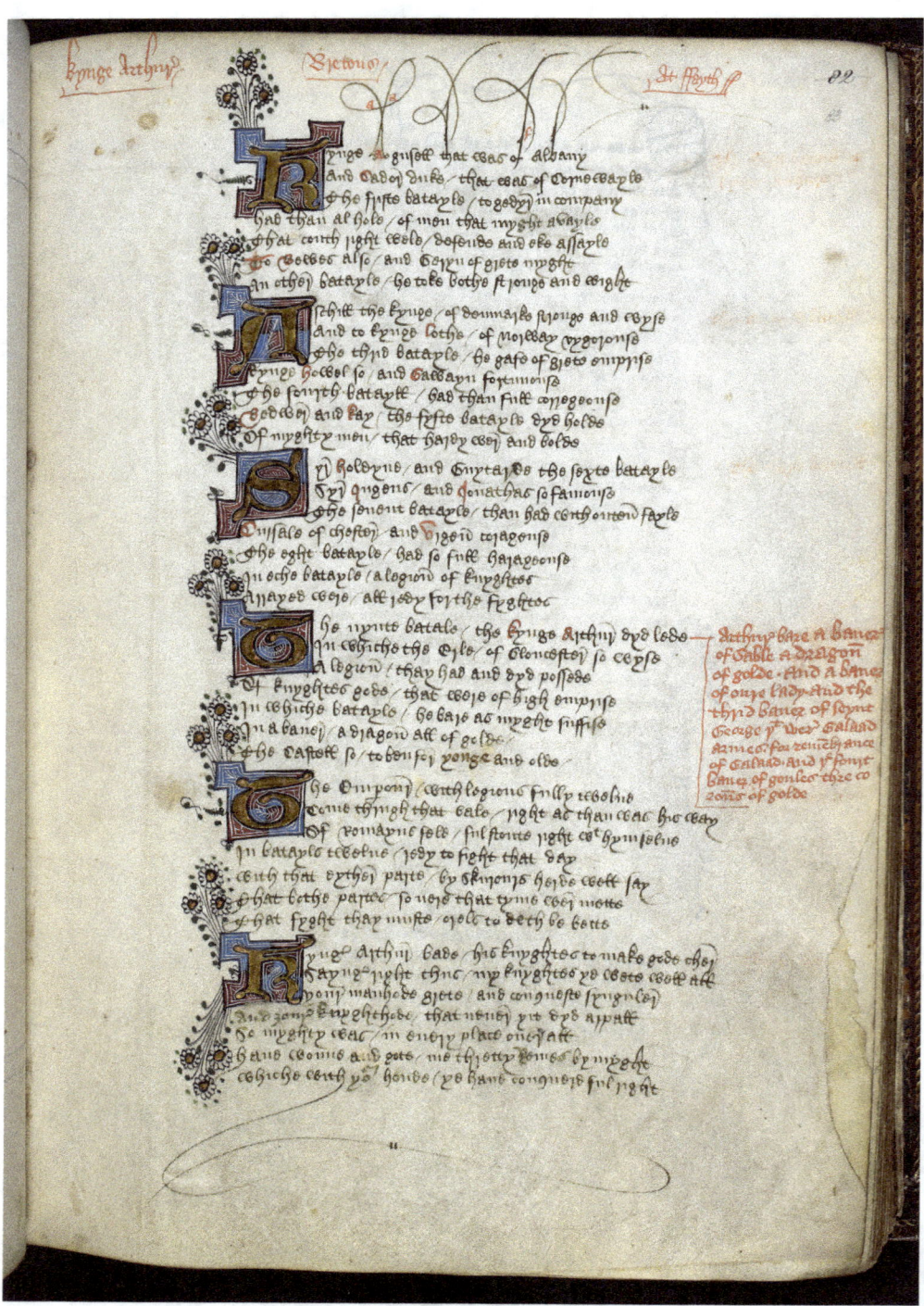

Plate X: Decorative emphasis on Round Table knights, Hardyng's first *Chronicle*: BL Lansdowne MS 204, fol. 83ʳ.

His sister Anne vnto his wife had wedde
On whom he gate ye curtais knyghte Gawayn
In Dunbarre castel his lyfe he ledde
And Achuzel his knyght þat tyme certayne
Of Albany and kyng of Murreffe slayne
The kyng was þan to kyng Arthure ful trewe
His liege men ay þat were of olde and newe

⁊ Nota howe kyng Arthure renewed and
encresed the Table Rounde and helde
it vpstially and the rule of it

Þis kyng Arthure þan wedded to his wife
Gwynour fairest of any creature
That tyme accompte for passyng birthe nature
So moly fair she was of hir figure
More lustielike þan womanysshe nature
In so ferforthe men thoughte þem self wele esed
Hir to beholde so wele alle folke she pleased

The table Rounde of knyghtes honorable.
That tyme vex voide by their Absence
ffor many were þerowith actes mareable
Dispended þan by wyves violence
Wharfore ye kyng þan of his sapience
The worthiest of euery reame aboute
In ye table rounde þan sette withouten doute

The thre kynges foreseid of Scotlond
Thre knyghtes also of Wales ful chiualrouse
Howel ye knyght of lesse britayne londe
And Duke Cador of Cornewaile curtuteouse
And other feel þere rule was wrought to expresse
With youre bodyes where lawe myght nat expresse

Plate XII: Typical rubricated caption titles, with no other name rubrication, in the *Lancelot-Graal* Cycle: from BL, Add. MS 10294, fol. 53ʳ.

sources for the Roman War, the alliterative *Morte Arthure*, employs just this sort of forced return, as does the first version of Hardyng's own *Chronicle*. But Malory here follows Hardyng's revision.

Robert H. Wilson reveals how, in terms of the handling of Arthurian characters and sources, Malory's most consistent variation from his sources, and thus his greatest degree of originality, is evident in the characterization of Arthur himself.[44] Where the Arthur of French romance is often presented as a doddering fool or deserving cuckold, Malory refuses to adopt such a view, and his consistently favourable portrait of Arthur is something which he may have inherited from Hardyng as well as from (parts of) the alliterative *Morte Arthure* and stanzaic *Morte Arthur*. According to Kennedy, 'No one, in fact, could have written of Arthur with more enthusiasm' than does Hardyng.[45]

Certainly Hardyng's Arthur is the peer of kings and knights:

> Was neuer prince so highly gloryfied:
> The rounde table with princes multipled,
> That auentures then sought cotidianly,
> With greate honour, as made is memory.[46]

Arthur plays a key role throughout Hardyng's narrative; even the arrival of the Grail knight Galahad is an opportunity for elevating Arthur. Hardyng is unique amongst chroniclers for incorporating a Grail Quest into the historical *Brut* tradition, but when Galahad does arrive at court and takes his seat at the Siege Perilous, Hardyng remarks in the revised *Chronicle* how:

> none durst sitte [there] afore
> But Ioseph, that was full religious,
> That made it so ere Galaad was bore,
> And kyng Arthure that satte therein [to fore].[47]

Not even Malory, who is generally as enthusiastic as Hardyng in his portrait of Arthur, allows Arthur this partial Grail victory. This same scene in Hardyng's original *Chronicle* is even more favourable to Arthur, for there is no mention of Joseph: only Arthur anticipates Galahad's feat of sitting in the Siege.[48]

It is a commonplace of mediaeval literary and historical narrative to attribute the fall of kings and heroes to divine punishment for sin, but Hardyng clearly refuses to interrogate Arthur's heroic stature. On the contrary, Hardyng uses Arthur's death as an opportunity, marked in several manuscripts with a

---

[44] See Robert Henry Wilson, *Characterization in Malory* (Chicago, 1934), pp. 65–79.
[45] Kennedy, 'Malory and His English Sources', in *Aspects*, p. 44.
[46] John Hardyng, *The Chronicle of John Hardyng ... together with the Continuation by Richard Grafton*, ed. Henry Ellis (London, 1812; rpr. New York, 1974), p. 128. Ellis's edition is of the revised *Chronicle*. The first version of the *Chronicle* is currently unpublished, but an edition by James Simpson and Sarah Peverley is forthcoming with Medieval Institute Publications. For now, see London, BL Lansdowne MS 204, fol. 73ʳ, edited (with the rest of the Arthurian section of the first *Chronicle*) by Christine Marie Harker, 'John Hardyng's Arthur: A Critical Edition', unpublished PhD dissertation, University of California, Riverside, 1996 (lines 1079–82 for this scene).
[47] Hardyng, *The Chronicle*, pp. 131–2. In the last line I have adopted Ellis's more sensible variant reading rather than the 'therfore' which he prints as his base reading.
[48] BL Lansdowne MS 204, fol. 76ʳ; Harker, 'John Hardyng's Arthur', lines 1331–4.

mournful marginal rubric or chapter heading, to extol the king and lament the earthly treachery and misfortune which secure his downfall. Arthur is thus commended as the

> Moste redoubted in erth & moste famous,
> The worthiest and wysest without pere,
> The hardyest man and most coragious,
> In actes marciall moste victorious. . . .
> There was neuer prince of giftes more liberal,
> Of landes geuyng, ne of meate so plenteous,
> Agayn his fooen ... moste imperiall,
> And with his owne subiectes moste bounteous.[49]

Malory's Arthur is equally magnanimous and heroic, but there seems little doubt that Malory's favourable portrait of the king owes much to Hardyng.[50]

What I wish particularly to emphasize is that this enthusiasm for Arthur and Arthurian chivalry is evident in the manuscript *ordinatio* of both Hardyng's *Chronicle* and Malory's *Morte Darthur*. Malory, that is, seems to have been influenced as much by the bibliographic and codicological as the lexical and thematic text of the *Chronicle*. Although no manuscript of either version of Hardyng's *Chronicle* exhibits Winchester's specific rubrication programme, we do find the typical chronicle and *Brut* use of rubricated headings and marginal glosses to draw attention to the birth, reign or momentous deeds of various kings and nobles throughout the *Chronicle*. Such rubrics, Arthurian and otherwise, have both exemplary and indexing functions; but nowhere in Hardyng manuscripts do we find the same kind or even degree of rubrication as in Winchester. Indeed, the partial exception helps to prove the rule. This exception is London, British Library Lansdowne MS 204 (c. 1440–50), the sole surviving manuscript of the first version of Hardyng's *Chronicle*.[51] In Lansdowne 204, the opening capital initial of names on several folios is rubricated, though the remainder of the name is in black. This practice begins suddenly on folio 34^r with a list of mythical kings; these kings change rapidly, so this list includes many such red-initial names, as well as two other names where the original black-ink name has been heavily traced in red, creating quite a striking effect and the closest in style to that encountered in Winchester. (See Lansdowne 204, fol. 34^r in Plate VIII.) Having

---

[49] Hardyng, *The Chronicle*, p. 148. I have removed editorial brackets from the fifth line of the quotation. A rubricated 'compleynt [{and in one MS} lamentacion] of the maker' appears in at least three manuscripts: Lansdowne MS 204 (the first version), fol. 87^r, Oxford, Bodl. MS Douce 345 (second version), fol. 47, which has two such rubrics, one on each side of the page, and London, BL, Egerton MS 1992 (second version), fol. 55^v. New York, Pierpont Morgan MS B.5 (second version) fol.15^r likewise places two different marginal 'compleynts' here, but Morgan B.5 differs from these other *Chronicle* manuscripts in that none of its glosses are rubricated.

[50] I thus disagree with Ruth Lexton's claims for Arthur's tyranny in the *Morte Darthur*: *Contested Language in Malory's Morte Darthur* (Basingstoke and New York, 2014).

[51] At first glance, the foliation of Lansdowne 204 can be confusing. The first twenty-five folios have only one number, but the original foliation missed a page between fols 25 and 26, consequently misnumbering everything that follows, despite the attempt to correct things later by adding a '25*'. Thus, from 25*, each folio has a clear but faulty ink number, and a second and fainter pencil foliation that is actually the correct number. My citations, including in my plates, are to this second, fainter but correct foliation.

said that, this rubrication of the opening initials of names is not done consistently throughout the manuscript, or even consistently within the sections where it does appear.[52] Thus on folio 65^r, 'Gorloyse Duke of Cornwayle' has a rubricated 'G' and 'C', but other names on the same folio, including other instances of 'Gorloyse' as well as 'Igrayne', and several appearances of 'Octa' and 'Offa', are in normal black. Furthermore, even when it does appear, this pattern of what might be termed partial name rubrication is far from the norm for the majority of the *Chronicle* or its manuscript: Lansdowne 204 is 230 folios long, and such partial name rubrication appears on only some names on a mere thirty-three folios. Overall, the rubricated initials and very occasional rubricated names that we get in the first version of Hardyng's *Chronicle* do admittedly look similar to Winchester's names, but as with *Generides* in Morgan Library MS M.876, such names in Lansdowne are notable mostly for being atypical of the manuscript's general layout.

Significantly, such partial name rubrication that we do see in Lansdowne 204 occurs most often in the mythical foundation of Britain, in the Arthurian section, and in later sections of the history where Scottish kings or nobles render homage to the English: that is, in those sections which particularly appealed to Hardyng's personal and political purposes in writing.[53] The importance of Arthur and his knights, for instance, is emphasized in the first version of the *Chronicle* by the sudden increase of rubrication of initials of names in the list of knights who are added to the ranks of the Round Table after Arthure and Gaynore's wedding (see Plate IX: Lansdowne 204, fol. 70^r). Such Round Table promotions are necessary to repair the depletions suffered by the order in the preceding wars. Further new Round Table knights and further rubrication of the opening initials of their names soon follow (see Lansdowne 204, fol. 71^{r-v}). Not all such lists of names are given red colouring, of course, but there is one other quite striking visual change in Lansdowne's *ordinatio* during the Arthurian section, this time in a list of commanders and battles during the Roman War. Suddenly, and for the first in a long time, each stanza in this list begins with a large, three-line, gold Lombard with blue and red borders and floral sprays. Although several of the knights' names, including Arthur's, have rubricated opening initials in these stanzas, the rubricated initials are dwarfed and almost overshadowed by the elaborate capitals opening all six stanzas of the folio. (See Plate X: Lansdowne 204, fol. 83^r.)

This layout is certainly striking and unusual, but not without precedent in the manuscript.[54] Such gold capitals typically begin each new king's reign, or sometimes mark a new section in a king's reign, but they can appear serially in rapid succession when several kings rule closely together. To take a few examples: this

---

[52] In addition to Plate VIII, see folios 35^r, 41^v, 44^v, 46^r, 65^r, 70^r, 71^r, 71^v, 76^r, 76^v, 83^r, 88^v, 89^r, 94^v, 101^v, 102^v, 109^v, 124^v, 139^r, 141^r, 144^v, 145^{r-v}, 148^r, 154^r, 170^r, 173^r, 223^v, 224^r. Entire names traced in red occur again at folios 99^r, 103^v, 109^v, 127^v and 155^r.

[53] On Hardyng's penchant for Arthur, see the work of E. D. Kennedy, mentioned above, n. 42. On Hardyng's attempts to secure patronage by bolstering English claims against the Scots and alternating praising the Lancastrian or Yorkist king, see especially Richard J. Moll, *Before Malory* (Toronto, 2003), pp. 157–97; and Sarah L. Peverley, 'Dynasty and Division', *Medieval Chronicle* 3 (2004): 149–70, and eadem, 'Political Consciousness and the Literary Mind in Late Medieval England', *Studies in Philology* 105 (Winter 2008): 1–29.

[54] *Contra* Moll, *Before Malory*, p. 305, n. 72.

happens early in the *Chronicle* with the rapid change of kingship on folios 24ᵛ–25ʳ (six kings and six such capitals over eleven stanzas), folios 30ᵛ–31ʳ (with five new kings and five gold capitals over seven stanzas), or especially folios 32ᵛ–35ʳ where practically every new stanza starts with a gold capital and a new king. So the effect in the Arthurian list is not unique. Perhaps more importantly, manuscript *ordinatio* once again serves strikingly to valorize Arthur and his knights on the eve of their defeat of Rome, a crucial moment in their collective career. Indeed, the similarities between this layout and the partial rubrication of mythical kings' names earlier in the *Chronicle* gives Arthur himself a suitably mythical stature. Arthur's continental victories are further significant for Hardyng himself since they provide precedence for, foreshadow and (in the eyes of Hardyng and his royal patrons) justify England's claims to imperial status in the fifteenth century. As Elizabeth J. Bryan reveals, the *ordinatio* of London, BL Cotton MS Otho C.xiii, the Otho Laʒamon, likewise emphasizes Arthur, but in contrast to this mythical portrait of Arthur in Lansdowne 204, Otho C.xiii plays down Arthur's Roman War, the episode of Arthurian history, says Bryan, most questioned in the twelfth and thirteenth centuries.[55]

In terms of rubrication, manuscripts of the second version of Hardyng's *Chronicle* are generally even less like Winchester than is Lansdowne 204. A. S. G. Edwards argues that the various manuscripts of the second version of the *Chronicle* have differing levels of decoration, and that there is considerable variation in textual reliability amongst the different witnesses.[56] My own examination of four of Edwards's five most elaborate second-version *Chronicle* manuscripts (Oxford Bodl. MS Arch. Selden B.10; Bodl. MS Douce 345; Bodl. MS Ashmole 34; and London BL Harley MS 661) confirms the variety of manuscript decoration in broad terms, but does nevertheless reveal a marked similarity in other aspects of layout, where the same chapter rubrics or marginal glosses are used across manuscripts.

Significantly for my purposes, the section devoted to Arthur in several *Chronicle* manuscripts is given especial emphasis by changes to the usual page layout or an increase in glosses. Hardyng or his rubricators – and the *de luxe* nature of the Lansdowne and Selden manuscripts suggests that the decision originates with Hardyng – use manuscript layout to valorize Arthur over and above his fellow monarchs. In Lansdowne 204, for instance, Arthur's reign commences with what is the usual decoration for new monarchs of an opening gold letter (of three to four lines in height), marginal rubric and rubricated header, but Arthur's is one of only three reigns in the *Chronicle* proper further distinguished by a marginal shield; a fourth shield occurs at the end, but this is in praise of Hardyng's patron, and so is slightly different from the kings' shields.[57] Likewise,

---

[55] Elizabeth J. Bryan, *Collaborative Meaning in Medieval Scribal Culture* (Ann Arbor, 1999), pp. 93–5.
[56] A. S. G. Edwards, 'The Manuscripts and Texts of the Second Version of John Hardyng's *Chronicle*', in *England in the Fifteenth Century*, ed. Daniel Williams (Woodbridge, 1987), pp. 75–84.
[57] BL Lansdowne MS 204, fol. 67ᵛ for Arthur's shield. Prior to this, the only other shield is for King Constantyne at fol. 46ᵛ. After Arthur, there are no further shields till King Edward the Confessor at fol. 129ᵛ. Unless a shield was cut from the marginal notes for Henry VI at fol. 217ᵛ, no one else is given a shield apart from Robert Umfraville at fol. 220ʳ, in a passage

although the use of decorated initials is common in stanzas denoting new kings in Lansdowne and several manuscripts of the revised *Chronicle*, in both Selden B.10 and Douce 345 the opening initial of the stanza commencing Arthur's reign is denoted by a three-line decorated initial, whereas the usual practice prior to this point has been to start reigns with a two-line initial.[58]

In Selden B.10, Arthur's importance is further suggested by a marked increase in the number of in-text (as opposed to marginal) titles or glosses: prior to Arthur's reign, the last in-text heading was on folio 11^v, whereas in the Arthur section such rubricated textual markers suddenly appear frequently and in rapid succession at 50^v (Uther fighting from a horse-litter), 51^r (the beginning of Arthur's reign), 51^v (Arthur's war banners) and 52^v (Arthur's establishment of the Round Table). (See Plate XI: Selden B.10, fol. 52^v.) Similarly, several manuscripts employ a new or exaggerated script for the list of Round Table knights created by Arthur or fighting on his behalf, as in the list of Round Table knights at both Selden B.10 folio 52^v and Douce 345 folio 36^v, where the ascenders of the opening lines of each of these two stanzas are noticeably larger and more elaborate than elsewhere in either manuscript.[59] There is very little colour, and no all-red, Winchester-like rubrication of names, nor a series of elaborate gold initials as with the comparable list of commanders in the Roman War in Lansdowne 204. The reader of these manuscripts is nevertheless given a strong visual clue that this section of the narrative and the people involved here (the knights in the list) are more than usually important.[60]

Many of the manuscript headings or glosses found in Selden also occur, with occasional variation in wording or spelling, in Lansdowne 204; several of them are also found as rubricated marginal gloss titles in Harley 661, and as chapter titles in Ellis's modern edition. Although Ellis's text is based on Harley 661, his folio cross-references are wildly inaccurate, and his chapter titles can be misleading, since some of them accurately reproduce rubricated marginal titles from the Harley manuscript, whilst others are expansions of, modifications to or even additions to the base text.[61] But even these changes by Ellis admirably (however coincidentally) reflect the overall manuscript rubric pattern, for although I can find no acknowledgement of the practice in Ellis's introduction or notes, he seems to have taken several of his non-Harleian chapter titles verbatim from

---

explicitly marked by Hardyng in a marginal rubric as praising his master. According to Kingsford, Hardyng spent thirty years in Umfraville's service, so the appearance of the latter's arms is hardly surprising: C. L. Kingsford, 'The First Version of Hardyng's *Chronicle*', *EHR* 27.107 (July 1912): 462–82 (463). It is thus a safe conclusion that Arthur's own shield considerably distinguishes his reign.

[58] Bodl. MS Selden B.10 fol. 51^r; Bodl. MS Douce 345 fol. 35b^r. In Selden the initial is in gold, with a blue and red background and penwork; in Douce it is only blue and red.

[59] See also Lansdowne 204 fols 70^r, 71^r, 71^v, 83^r; and Bodl. MS Ashmole 34, fol. 49^v.

[60] Again there are parallels with Cotton MS Otho C.xiii, the Otho Laȝamon, where much of the rubrication, whether it be marginal gloss or header or red highlighting of letters, concerns 'shifts of political power', Merlin's supernatural power and Arthur's battles. Like other chronicles, the Otho text uses decorated initials to emphasize 'regnal succession', but the greater number of such initials in the Arthur section glorify Arthur: Bryan, *Collaborative Meaning*, pp. 77 and 111–15.

[61] After Arthur's death, e.g., Ellis's title for his Chapter 85 (p. 148) includes a 'compleynte and lamentacion of the … maker', but Harley 661 includes no such gloss at this point (fol. 56^{r-v}). See, however, n. 49, supra.

another second-version *Chronicle* manuscript, London, British Library Egerton MS 1992.[62] Although Egerton is a paper manuscript with considerably less decoration than those *Chronicle* manuscripts discussed thus far, including having no headers and no decorated initials of any sort, it does include regular rubricated in-text or inter-stanza (as opposed to marginal) chapter titles throughout, many of them adopted by Ellis. Edwards also notes Egerton's less elaborate appearance and its (and its fellows') occasional textual lapses, but he concludes that it is still a professional product.[63] I agree, and whatever its textual faults, Egerton in some respects does a better job of recording the more typical Arthurian rubricated glosses or chapter titles than does the more elaborate Harley MS 661. In fact, Egerton 1992's more complete title-rubrics attest to just how widespread was the programme of rubricated glosses and chapter titles amongst manuscripts of Hardyng's *Chronicle*. The programme was quite different from Winchester in terms of physical appearance, but was, I suggest, similar in function and thematic significance.

The Arthurian section of the second-version *Chronicle* preserved in Harvard University, MS Eng 1054, for instance, is imperfect, yet this manuscript, too, contains similar glosses and headings in similar places.[64] The same is true of New York, Pierpont Morgan MS B.5, which is imperfect and plain, but which does contain unrubricated marginal glosses in the usual places in the Arthurian section (now fols 1^r–15^r). At the same time, none of these manuscripts of the second version of Hardyng's *Chronicle* has the same kind of rubrication of all complete names as found in the Winchester manuscript. Bodleian MS Douce 345 sometimes has yellow highlighting of the first letter of a line. This yellow highlighting is, however, inconsistent: sometimes *all* first letters in a stanza are highlighted; at other times, only *some* letters are highlighted, and at other times none. Bodleian MS Ashmole 34 more consistently uses faint yellow highlighting through the opening letter of most lines, but it does not rubricate all names as does Winchester. No such highlighting appears in the more *de luxe* Selden manuscript. Nevertheless, because they employ the same decorative features in different or more frequent ways, the Arthurian sections of several *Chronicle* manuscripts consistently present a subtle *mise-en-page* that emphasizes Arthur and his knights over his fellow kings and conquerors. Manuscript *ordinatio* thus complements and enforces narrative theme, considerably emphasizing Arthur's greatness and worth.

That such manuscript emphasis on Arthur occurs in both the first and second versions of the *Chronicle* strongly suggests that the layout scheme is deliberate and authorial. The likely authorial provenance of the rubrication is all the more probable given that both Lansdowne and Selden may have been presentation copies. It is consequently quite likely that whatever version of Hardyng's *Chronicle* Malory saw, it would have looked something like those discussed here. Some such decorated manuscript(s) of the *Chronicle* may even have been circulating

---

[62] This is especially true in the Arthur section, which is naturally my concern here.
[63] Edwards, 'Manuscripts and Texts of the Second Version', in *England in the Fifteenth Century*, p. 77.
[64] See Harvard University, MS Eng 1054, folios 32^r, 34^r, 34^v.

in Edward IV's court at the time that Richard Barber speculates Malory was in attendance.[65] More certainly, whilst the narrative *text* of Hardyng's *Chronicle* is a significant minor source for Malory's *Morte Darthur*, it seems that the *manuscript layout* of Hardyng's *Chronicle* influenced Malory in equally significant ways, and that he decided to employ (or indicate) a similar scheme in his holograph. I shall return to this possibility later. Given, however, that none of the *Chronicle* or *Brut* manuscripts rubricate names as emphatically or consistently as Winchester, I suggest that Malory took a codicological or bibliographic cue from his source and, as he did so often with his narrative *matière*, made it entirely his own.

To the best of my knowledge, no comparable codicological scheme of valorizing Arthur and his knights exists in manuscripts of other of Malory's sources. Some manuscripts of (part of) the prose *Tristan* have rubricated chapter titles such as 'coment le roi ...', but no rubricated names in the text proper, as is the case in Winchester.[66] Chapter rubrics such as these are actually much more common in Bibles and chronicles than in romances, and other prose *Tristan* manuscripts do not have chapter rubrics at all; this is so whether the manuscript is *de luxe* or plain.[67] More *de luxe Tristan* manuscripts do have rubricated captions accompanying their miniatures, as in New York, Pierpont Morgan MS M.41 (dated 1468) or London, British Library Additional MS 5474 (late thirteenth century), but caption rubrics are obviously not the same as the rubrication of names in the text proper, as in Winchester. Thus, although it is possible that a series of manuscripts whose rubrication looked similar to Winchester's has been lost to us, the general level of similarity amongst various kinds of texts and their manuscripts suggests that we would have at least a few other examples extant were Winchester's sort of rubrication an even quasi-regular practice. This is not the case. I have already suggested that chronicle and *Brut* manuscripts supply some reasonable parallels, but nothing exact. Looking at manuscripts of Malory's other sources we find even fewer and less precise parallels.

Prominent amongst Malory's 'French book' sources are various parts of the Vulgate or *Lancelot-Graal* Cycle, a vast collection of tales written circa 1215–30, originally comprising the prose *Lancelot*, *La Queste del Saint Graal* and *La Mort le roi Artu*, to which were added as prequels *L'Estoire de Saint Graal* and the prose *Merlin*.[68] There are more than one hundred (perhaps as many as 220) extant

---

[65] Richard Barber, 'Malory's *Le Morte Darthur* and Court Culture under Edward IV', *Arthurian Literature* 12 (1993): 133–55.

[66] My example is from London, British Library Additional MS 23929, folio 3ᵛ, which has other such chapter rubrics throughout, though there are no such chapter headings given in the mid third of the manuscript, from folio 21ᵛ till 64ᵛ, at which point they begin again, sometimes two per folio. London, BL, Harley MS 49, another prose *Tristan*, more regularly rubricates its chapter titles and includes rubricated chapter numbers in the appropriate margins.

[67] Neither the frequently illustrated London, BL Royal MS 20.D.ii and BL Add. MS 5474, nor the much plainer London, BL Egerton MS 989 or Oxford, Bodl. MS Douce 189 have anything resembling rubricated names or rubricated name initials unless the name appears with all the other rubricated words in one of Add. 5474's many picture captions.

[68] See further Elspeth Kennedy et al., 'Lancelot with and without the Grail', in *The Arthur of the French*, ed. Glyn S. Burgess and Karen Pratt (Cardiff, 2006), pp. 274–324; Jean Frappier, 'The Vulgate Cycle', in *Arthurian Literature in the Middle Ages*, ed. Roger Sherman Loomis (Oxford, 1959), pp. 295–318.

manuscripts of the sundry parts of this cycle,[69] but as with different versions and manuscripts of Hardyng's *Chronicle*, there are certain basic decoration patterns that emerge as common to a wide range of manuscripts across the Cycle as a whole. From the perspective of basic *ordinatio*, and speaking in very broad terms, manuscript decoration falls into three different categories, ranging from *de luxe* manuscripts with detailed and numerous miniatures and other decorative features at the top of the scale, through manuscripts with frequent decorated initials and perhaps occasional miniatures at the middle level, to manuscripts that are little more than bare text, with little or no decoration beyond an opening coloured initial at the most basic level. In only one of these levels of decoration is rubrication regularly found, and even then only in a limited and specific fashion.

Rubrication of the sort under discussion here is common in *de luxe* manuscripts of the *Lancelot-Graal* Cycle, but only in the much more typical fashion of rubricating caption titles for miniatures. Such is the case, to take one especially notable example, throughout London, British Library Additional MS 10292–4 (which dates to about 1317), but despite the impressive and detailed decoration of this manuscript, rubrication of words is confined to caption titles. Thus, for instance, the miniature at folio 53^b is prefaced by an accompanying rubricated caption, but the remainder of the text, including the close of the *Queste* and the phrase 'Expliciont les auentures del saint Graal', is in the same black ink as the rest of the narrative proper. (See Plate XII.) Given the sumptuous nature of Additional 10292–4, whose 748 illustrations (sic!) are more than double the next most-heavily illustrated *Lancelot-Graal* Cycle manuscript, at least amongst surviving copies,[70] we might expect there to be a corresponding increase in rubrication that extends to colouring names in the text rather than just in coloured caption titles. This is not the case. Throughout the manuscript, names are nowhere rubricated or even partly touched with colour unless they appear in a caption title or with one of the frequent *litterae notabiliores* (Lombard, inhabited or historiated initials) which subdivide the narrative. (Plate XII again provides a typical example.) In richly decorated *Lancelot-Graal* manuscripts, then, names are rubricated only when they appear in a caption rubric for an accompanying illustration. My conclusion here is supported by a valuable study from Carol J. Chase in which Chase traces the pattern and significance of these kinds of caption rubrics with specific reference to MS Bourg-en-Bresse, Médiathèque Vailland 55 (circa 1330s). For Chase, rubrics generally take the form 'Comment …' or 'Ci devise … ', with 'les rubriques décrivent le contenu des illustrations'; occasionally they also anticipate narrative events to follow.[71]

---

[69] On these manuscript numbers see, respectively, Alison Stones, '"Mise en page" in the French *Lancelot-Grail*', in *A Companion to the Lancelot-Grail Cycle*, ed. Carol Dover (Cambridge, 2003), pp. 125–44 (p. 125), and Roger Middleton, 'Manuscripts of the *Lancelot-Grail Cycle* in England and Wales', also in *Companion to the Lancelot-Grail Cycle*, pp. 219–35 (p. 219).

[70] For the manuscript's date and number of illustrations, see Stones, '"Mise en page"', in *Companion to the Lancelot-Grail*, 'Appendix 2. Working List of Manuscripts with Cycles of Illustrations Made in France before 1360', pp. 136–8.

[71] Carol J. Chase, 'Un manuscrit mesconnëu de l'*Estoire del Saint Graal*', *JIAS* 3.1 (2015): 72–101 (especially 87–93).

Other illustrated Cycle manuscripts, such as New York, Pierpont Morgan MSS M.805 and M.806 (c. 1310–15), are given quite detailed miniatures and historiated initials, but no accompanying captions and thus not even collateral rubrication of names – or any other rubrication. In all of these types of decorated manuscripts, in marked contrast to Winchester, names are given no special treatment for their own sake. Unsurprisingly, rubricated names do not appear at all in those manuscripts of the Cycle that do not have illustrations, such as the prose *Lancelot* in London, British Library Royal MS 19.B.vii, or the *Mort Artu* in Oxford, Bodleian Library MS Douce 189, which does have a rubricated *explicit* at folio 64^d but otherwise no special rubrication of names.[72] New York, Pierpont Morgan MS M.807 (fifteenth century) concludes with an *explicit* (fol. 115^b), but neither the text nor the *explicit* are rubricated in this manuscript. Based on the rubrication patterns amongst extant manuscripts, then, it is highly doubtful that Malory found a source for the Winchester-style rubrication of names amongst *Lancelot-Graal* or *Tristan* manuscripts.

It has, however, recently been claimed that Malory took as his codicological model a specific manuscript in the Post-Vulgate tradition. Jonathan Passaro argues that Malory adopted the rubrication of names, as well as key narrative events, thematic concerns and even specific wording from the Cambridge University Library manuscript of the Post-Vulgate *Suite du Merlin*: CUL Additional MS 7071.[73] This *Suite* is an adaptation-cum-continuation of the more popular Vulgate *Merlin*, and forms the central section of the Post-Vulgate Cycle or *Roman du Graal*. Composed probably AD/CE 1235–40, the Post-Vulgate Cycle attempted to unify, elucidate and synthesize the divergent materials and themes inherent in earlier Arthurian traditions, especially within the *Lancelot-Graal* Cycle.[74] Whereas the earlier cycle has come down to us (in whole or part) in well over one hundred manuscripts, the Post-Vulgate Cycle is extant in only three incomplete French manuscripts and various Portuguese and Castilian manuscript redactions or fragments, including two printed editions from 1498 and 1535 that are complete as far as they go, but which do not contain everything in the French. The most complete of the surviving French texts is CUL Additional MS 7071 (fourteenth century). There is an interesting marginal note at the top of CUL Add. MS 7071, fol. 189^r, in which 'an early sixteenth-century' reader familiar with Malory's Arthuriad observes at a certain moment in the *Suite*, 'Ci commence le livre que Sir Thomas Malori chevalier reduce in Engloys et fuist emprente par William Caxton.'[75] The note is fascinating as an indication of Malory's reception and the reading habits of some of his earliest readers, but beyond that little can

---

[72] Douce 189 also includes the death of Tristran from the prose romance.
[73] Jonathan Passaro, 'Malory's Text of the *Suite du Merlin*', *Arthurian Literature* 26 (2009): 39–75; quotations below are from 62 and 60 respectively.
[74] On the Post-Vulgate Cycle see Fanni Bogdanow, *The Romance of the Grail* (Manchester and New York, 1966), and eadem, 'The Post-Vulgate *Roman du Graal*', in *Arthur of the French*, pp. 342–52. On Malory and the *Suite* see especially Vinaver, pp. 1267–82; Norris, *Malory's Library*, pp. 13–52; and P. J. C. Field, 'Malory's Source-Manuscript for the First Tale of *Le Morte Darthur*', *Arthurian Literature* 29 (2012): 111–19.
[75] 'Here begins the book that Sir Thomas Malory, knight, reduced into English, and that William Caxton printed.' The date of the note is Vinaver's, who also reproduces the MS page in question: see Vinaver, p. 1280 and the plate between pp. 1280–1.

(or should) be gleaned from this learned doodle. Nevertheless, the Cambridge *Suite* is further notable, says Passaro, for being not just one version of the French text, but the very manuscript from which Malory worked.

Much of Passaro's argument is textual-critical, based on similarities of phrasing and textual details. Part of his evidence, however, is codicological, based on what he considers to be the 'overall similarities between rubrication in Cam [CUL Add. MS 7071] and W [Winchester]', including that both manuscripts, so it is said, 'share ... the much less common practice (at least in manuscripts of the Vulgate) of rubricating proper names'. The more common practice against which the rubrication is here measured is that of abbreviating Merlin's name to 'M', a policy again shared – albeit inconsistently – by both manuscripts. The practice of abbreviating characters' names is relatively common in French prose romance, though it is by no means universal, and it is common even in the same manuscript to write names in full but also to abbreviate them when necessity or scribal whim dictate.[76] Passaro makes much of the fact that the name *Merlin* is often both abbreviated and rubricated in CUL Add. 7071 and in Winchester, particularly since the Huth *Merlin* (London, British Library Add. MS 38117), the only other major extant French manuscript of the Post-Vulgate *Suite*, regularly abbreviates Merlin's name but does not rubricate any names, Merlin's or otherwise. As in CUL Add. 7071 and Winchester, 'Merlin' is not *always* abbreviated in the Huth manuscript *Suite*, and Passaro does not point out that all other names, such as 'Pendragon', 'Artus', 'Griflet', etc., are regularly written out in full, just as all names are in full in the first item in the manuscript, an *Estoire du Graal* (also called *Joseph* by modern scholars). It should further be added that the Huth manuscript is a *de luxe* production, with approximately seventy miniatures and frequent and elaborate red, blue and gold-leaf *notabiliores*. Merlin's name is the only one that is regularly abbreviated, but no names anywhere in the manuscript are coloured red, not even with the miniatures since the illustrations do not have accompanying captions. Since CUL Add. 7071 is in all respects a much plainer manuscript than Huth, Passaro's claims about the 'Physical similarities between Cam and W', like his conclusions about the textual-critical importance of CUL 7071 as a source text for Malory's narrative, are potentially quite significant.

Unfortunately, the remainder of Passaro's argument, especially the codicological details, is problematic.[77] As we have just seen, the statement that Winchester's rubrication of names is unusual is quite true, and it is equally true, as we have seen, that rubrication of names in Vulgate Cycle manuscripts is – where it appears at all – confined to illustration captions or decorated initials. However, my own comparison of the manuscripts in question suggests that the similarities between Winchester and CUL Add. MS 7071 are far from pronounced. For one

---

[76] Such is the case, for instance, in Oxford, Bodl. MS Douce 199, or Morgan MSS M.805, M.806 and M.807.

[77] I am also unconvinced by the textual-critical aspects of Passaro's argument, for he overlooks the positive portrait of Arthur inherited from English Arthuriana, and does not pay enough attention to formulaic phrasing, Malory's knowledge of French or Malory's method of source conflation. For a detailed textual-critical rebuttal of Passaro which concludes that 'Malory composed his first tale from a lost manuscript that sometimes agreed with Cambridge Additional 7071 against the Huth manuscript, and sometimes' the reverse, see Field, 'Malory's Source-Manuscript'.

thing, the rubrication in CUL Add. 7071 is always after the fact, red traced over black, whereas in Winchester the rubrication is always red ink alone. Passaro acknowledges this, but he still insists that the overall visual 'effect is much the same' in *both* manuscripts, creating a 'striking' visual cue.[78] Such red over black can indeed be nearly as striking as red alone – witness the partial rubrication of names in the Lansdowne 204 copy of Hardyng's *Chronicle* (Plate IX, discussed above). Nevertheless, I believe that Passaro overstates his case, especially regarding the degree of rubrication in the two manuscripts; in my opinion their layout is far from similar.

Taking CUL Add. MS 7071 folio 171^v as an example, and keeping any page of Winchester in mind as a comparison, it is evident after even a cursory glance at the *Suite* manuscript how striking is Winchester's colour and how nearly absent is colour in the Cambridge codex. Careful scrutiny of Add. 7071's folio 171^v reveals that column b, line 2 does contain a trace amount of red in the 'A' of 'Artus', and an abbreviated and coloured 'M' for 'Merlin' occurs twice in the bottom third of the column – though my bold-rubrication is rather more pronounced that the red colouring of the brownish-black initials in the manuscript. But the third-last line of column a has red colouring in the capital 'M' of 'Mais je voil', which is obviously not a name and which is in the middle of a speech, and something similar occurs with the capital 'E' of 'Et quant tu' in column b, line 18. There is also a red paraph mark, a common enough feature in French and English manuscripts, but one which is obviously not a name. This paraph is important to my discussion because it is followed by a red-coloured capital 'E' of 'Einsi parla M' (col. b.28), where 'M' is an abbreviated 'Merlin' but in black ink, and where the red colouring instead goes to the transitional 'Einsi'. Here is another significant contrast to Winchester, for not only is the rubrication in CUL Add. 7071 confined to the opening initials of words whilst Winchester rubricates the entire name, but Add. 7071's partial rubrication is not confined exclusively to names, being also used for the opening initials of conjunctions or new sentences (as with the examples just cited). Even on the same folio a character's name may begin with a red-traced initial on one line, but subsequently be written solely in black later on the same folio. (Again, folio 171 provides an example.)

Admittedly there are a great many abbreviated and red-coloured 'M's from this point on in the Cambridge *Suite*, often appearing during dialogue, but the overall pattern of rubrication such as it is in CUL Add. 7071 is at best erratic. 'M' does regularly get red tracing at least from folio 171^v onwards, and this red occurs sometimes with an abbreviated 'M for Merlin' and sometimes with a full 'Merlin' – but it is far from consistent: not every instance of either the full or abbreviated Merlins get red colouring, and most other names, at least in the early stages of the *Suite*, are not rubricated at all. Folio 183^c, for instance, does give several red-coloured and abbreviated 'M's, as well as a red-coloured 'N' of 'Northumberland'. But the same section also has a perfectly bland, black, non-abbreviated and non-coloured 'Blaise'. Likewise the majority of names during the interaction and dialogue between Ulfin and Ygraine at folio 188^v have no colour. And the red colouring or tracing continues to get used for paraphs as well

---

[78] Passaro, 'Malory's Text of the *Suite*', 61–2.

as for non-name initials for section or sentence demarcation. Even non-abbreviated *Merlin*s start to creep back in later in the manuscript (as at folio 250^b) – albeit these full versions of Merlin's name are often (but not always) still coloured with red in the opening initial. This erratic pattern of sometimes colouring initials of names and sometimes not colouring them is continued throughout the manuscript, and is not dissimilar to what we saw in *Brut* and *Chronicle* manuscripts. Thus neither of the two appearances of 'Artus', nor any of the single appearances of 'Logres', 'Carlion' or 'Loth' at folio 202^d, is even partially rubricated. There is not even consistency on the same folio. To take one example, 208^r has a number of unadorned appearances of 'Ban', as well as several instances of '**B**an' that do get a coloured '**B**'. Likewise, the same folio and same scene feature several unadorned appearances of 'Claudas', and also several of '**C**laudas' where the cap 'C' is coloured with red. Interestingly, and despite Passaro's claim about the Cambridge *Suite* elevating Arthur,[79] in at least one respect CUL Add. 7071's decoration pattern does not reflect this Arthurian focus: 'Merlin' does often get abbreviated and often traced in red, but 'Artus' gets red tracing much less often: thus, for instance, folio 214^b has the phrase '**M** et le roi Artu', where '**M**' has red tracing but 'A' does not. The rubricator's greater focus on Merlin is only natural given Merlin's pronounced role in the *Suite*, but the decoration pattern – such as it is – does offer one more contrast with Winchester, where Arthur's name is as prominent as the rest of his fellows, including Merlin. Merlin's name may occasionally be abbreviated in Winchester as in Add. 7071, but it is rubricated no more often than is Arthur's own name. Indeed, since Merlin disappears from the narrative relatively early in Winchester, his name is inevitably less frequently emphasized than is Arthur's. In all these ways, then, the red colouring that does appear in CUL Add. MS 7071 is far from being similar to, or having the same striking visual effect as, the rubrication of names in Winchester.

Although it is still nowhere as emphatic as in Winchester, a more regular pattern of partial rubrication of names is actually found in a completely different manuscript: London, British Library Royal MS 20.C.vi, a late thirteenth- or early fourteenth-century manuscript containing part of the prose *Lancelot* as well as a *Queste del Saint Graal* and *Mort Artu*. This manuscript has a similar layout to CUL Add. MS 7071 in the tendency to add colour to the opening initials of characters' names as well as transitional words, but the colour is a light yellowish-brown rather than red. Significantly, the effect is still not confined to names, and the pattern of what name or word gets a coloured initial is dictated more by what word starts the sentence than anything else, but the process is much more frequent in Royal 20.C.vi than in CUL Add. 7071. Royal's brownish-yellow colouring is, moreover, applied to initials of words in all three texts from the outset of the manuscript, and is found from start to finish.[80] The partial prose *Lancelot* found

---

[79] Passaro, 'Malory's Text of the *Suite*', 39–75 (especially 39–40, 70–2); this is one of his key pieces of evidence for CUL Add. 7071 being Malory's source text.

[80] This observation is based on my own examination of the manuscript, but at the time of going to press, a handful of folios from Royal 20.C.vi is available online from the BL's digital catalogue. The brownish-yellow colouring of initials is observable on folios 3 and 150: www.bl.uk/catalogues/illuminatedmanuscripts/record.asp?MSID=5838&CollID=16&NStart=20036[.]

in London, British Library Royal MS 20.D.iv (c. 1315) likewise adds a thick red stroke (vertical or horizontal, depending on the letter) to the opening capital letter of *most* (not all) sentences: once again this practice occurs from the outset of the manuscript, and some of these red-stroked capital initials belong to names; the majority do not.[81] A thin red downstroke or light colouring of opening initials of sentences can also be seen in Paris, Bibliothèque nationale de France, fr. 16999, a fourteenth-century manuscript containing the first part of the prose *Lancelot*. BnF fr. 16999 is related to Bourg 55, but the interesting thing (for me) is that the red highlighting of initials in the *Lancelot* in BnF fr. 16999 is itself incomplete, found only on folios 1ʳ to 84ᵛ of 291 extant folios.[82] The lavishly illustrated London, British Library Royal MS 14.E.iii (c. 1315–20), with its 116 miniatures, contains an imperfect French *Estoire*, a *Queste* and an imperfect *Mort Artu*. In places Royal 14.E.iii employs a similar pattern to Royal 20.D.iv, with the opening initials of most sentences of the recto sides of the first several folios of text having red tracing or colouring over the black letters.[83] But some verso folios early in the manuscript have no red tracing of initials, and the emphasis is as much or more on the start of new sentences and transitions as on names. This sort of erratic or incomplete red tracing of initials of sentences regardless of whether the opening word is a name or otherwise thus seems to be a common pattern amongst some *Lancelot-Graal* manuscripts. MS Bourg-en-Bresse, Médiathèque Vailland 55, for instance, containing an *Estoire del Saint Graal*, has red touches of initials on at least folios 1ʳ, 6ᵛ and 21ᵛ; in a few cases (as at fol. 6ᵛ, col. c) the letter so highlighted begins a name (e.g. 'Joseph'), but more often it does not. And the red touching in Bourg 55 seems to stop by folio 28ʳ.[84] Something similar occurs in the prose *Lancelot* copied in London, British Library, Harley MS 6342 (fifteenth century), where the capital letters of some names are occasionally traced or coloured with red, but not consistently. This red tracing, furthermore, may equally often be non-existent, or applied to other words that have nothing to do with identifying characters.[85] Despite the fact that *Lancelot-Graal* manuscripts are more heavily illustrated than any other Arthurian romance,[86] they fail to provide a model for Winchester's full rubrication of each and every name.

In actual fact, then, the sort of red colouring or splashing of red over black in the opening initials of letters that we see sporadically in the Cambridge *Suite du*

---

[81] See, e.g., folios 1ʳ, 102ᵛ, 237ᵛ and throughout. Royal 20.D.iv also includes rubricated illustration captions, as on these three examples.

[82] The MS can be consulted online through Gallica. For connexions between BnF fr. 16999 and Bourg 55, see Chase, 'Un manuscript mesconnëu'.

[83] London, BL Royal MS 14.E.iii, folios 3ʳ, 4ʳ, 6ʳ. I was unable to examine the manuscript directly, so this time my observations are based on the digitized manuscript images available from the BL's digital catalogue: www.bl.uk/catalogues/illuminatedmanuscripts/record.asp?MSID=7793&CollID=16&NStart=140503[.] Attempts have also been made to associate Royal 14.E.iii with Malory, though the argument usually involves the Cambridgeshire candidate: for a cogent rebuttal of this connection see Carol Meale, 'Manuscripts, Readers and Patrons in Fifteenth-Century England', *Arthurian Literature* 4 (1985): 93–126. The entire question of Malory's library remains vexatious.

[84] See the figures supplied by Chase, 'Un manuscript mesconnëu', 79, 81, 84.

[85] E.g. Harley 6342 fols 39ᵃ, 180ᵃ or 198ᶜ.

[86] On the degree of Vulgate Cycle illustration, see Alison Stones, 'The Earliest Illustrated Prose *Lancelot* Manuscript?', *Reading Medieval Studies* 3 (1977): 12–44. The contrast with Winchester is my own.

Merlin, and by which Passaro would link CUL Add. MS 7071 with Winchester and Malory, is a remarkably common occurrence amongst manuscripts in both English and French, prose and verse. Indeed, judging from the available manuscript evidence, it seems that this practice was quite common from quite early in the generic history of both French and English romance. Whatever their other differences, this same sort of physical layout occurs even in some cognate Welsh texts usually classified 'romances', as in the copy of *Owein* or *Chwedyl Iarlles y Ffynnawn* in the late fourteenth-century Red Book, or Llyfr Coch, of Hergest (Oxford, Jesus College MS 111, fols 154ᵛ–161ᵛ).[87] Where the loops of the opening letter are not large enough to be coloured red, or as an alternative decoration scheme, it is equally common to add a vertical red (or sometimes yellow) downstroke over or through the black or brown letter. Such is the case, to take a notable instance, in the fourteenth-century copy of Chrétien's *Chevalier au lion* copied in Paris, Bibliothèque nationale fr. 1433; this manuscript also has ten miniatures.[88] A relevant but curious example in this context is the unique manuscript copy of the stanzaic *Morte Arthur*, London, British Library Harley MS 2252. Excepting a rather staid red capital 'L' at the beginning of the text (fol. 86ʳ), the story throughout is in plain brownish-black script until three folios from the end when, quite suddenly and for no obvious reason, the opening letters of the first one or sometimes two words of each line are brownish-black but coloured in with red.[89] This red staining or doodling is also found in the tale's *explicit* in the loops of 'E' and 'l' of 'Explicit', the 'L' of 'Le' and the 'A' and 'h' of 'Arthur'.

This pattern of red over black is initially more consistent in the unique manuscript copy of alliterative *Morte Arthure*, the well-known Lincoln Thornton manuscript (Lincoln, Cathedral Library MS 91; c. 1430–40), where there is red tracing over the opening black initial of *each* line, even to the point of tracing the regular-sized initial that follows the two larger decorated initials at the top and bottom of the opening folio (53ʳ).[90] The Thornton *Morte Arthure* also presents us with a mid-line rubricated dotted virgule (like so :/) or double virgule (//) to mark alliteration; frequently the initial which follows the mid-line virgule is also traced with red, but there is less consistency colouring this medial initial than with that at the start of the line. As with other French and English romances, moreover, Thornton's red initialization is not confined to names, but is applied to whatever word opens a line (or mid-line break). Although such red-coloured or red-stroked initials *do* stand out from their black or brown fellows, neither instance of colouring is as visually stunning as the writing of the entire name in red, as in Winchester. In further contrast to Winchester there is, in neither of

---

[87] On genre problems with the Welsh romances see Ceridwen Lloyd-Morgan, 'Medieval Welsh Tales or Romances?', *Cambrian Medieval Celtic Studies* 47 (2004): 41–58.

[88] Paris, BnF, fr. 1433, fols 61–118. On this MS, see further Busby, *Codex and Context*, I: p. 329; and Lori Walters, 'The Creation of a "Super Romance"', *Arthurian Yearbook* 1 (1991): 3–25.

[89] London, BL Harley MS 2252, fols 130ᵛ–133ᵛ. The manuscript as a whole is early sixteenth century, but scholars agree that the section containing *Morte Arthur* and *Ipomydon* is older. The red colouring begins part way through Launcelot and Gaynour's final meeting.

[90] I am much indebted to Dr Nicholas Bennett, Vice-Chancellor and Librarian of Lincoln Cathedral Library, for granting me access to the manuscript. Folio 53ʳ does have a rubricated *incipit*-title of *Morte Arthure*, but such rubricated titles are common to a wide array of manuscripts and genres and are obviously not the same as rubricated names.

these Arthurian examples, no special rubrication of names per se. In the Thornton *Morte Arthure*, furthermore, this pattern of tracing opening initials in red, and of marking the alliterative mid-line with red virgules, only occurs from folios 53^r to 69^r. For the remainder of the text, until folio 98^v, there is no rubrication pattern.[91]

This colouring of the opening letter is in fact a common feature of many genres and manuscripts.[92] The opening initial of every line of every item in the Auchinleck manuscript, for instance, is slightly set apart from the rest of the line and touched with red. This is true of the romances and the non-romances alike. Although the opening initials of lines are not spaced off from their fellows, many fifteenth-century manuscripts of Chaucer's *Canterbury Tales* similarly give red tracing or slight red colouring to the opening initial of every line. Such is the case in the copy of *The Canterbury Tales* surviving in New York, Pierpont Morgan Library, MS M.249 (c. 1450–60), in London, British Library Sloane MS 1686 (1480–90), and in Cambridge, Trinity College MS R.3.3 (later fifteenth century).[93] Cambridge, Trinity College MS R.3.15 (later fifteenth century) varies this pattern by giving a faint yellow touch of colour to the opening initial of (generally) every other line, though suddenly for the recto side of folio 54 the colour changes to red and is applied to every line; thereafter the yellow returns. Sloane MS 1686 also sometimes underlines character names or key ideas (*amor vincit Omnia*, e.g. [fol. 2^v]) in red, and Trinity College MS R.3.3 marks each pilgrim portrait in the *General Prologue* with a slightly enlarged but still one-line-high rubricated letter (not just red tracing), though the letter starts the relevant line, not the pilgrim: thus '**A** Knight there was' (fol. 1^a) or '**A** Frere' (2^a) or '**A** Merchant' (2^b). Trinity R.3.3 also sometimes touches the pilgrim's opening initial in red, but not always: of my three previous examples, only 'Merchant' has red splashing in its opening capital. Trinity R.3.3 does however continue this practice of touching name initials, including place names, with red throughout the *Tales*. Cambridge, Fitzwilliam Museum MS McClean 181 likewise places a red stroke through the opening initial of every line for the opening page of text (fol. 2), but thereafter the red splashing is applied only to the opening initial of the opening line (not the name) of each new pilgrim portrait. Cambridge, Trinity College MS R.3.15 uses rubricated initials to mark new pilgrim portraits in the *General Prologue*, and these stand out all the more for being two-lines high, though again these mark the appropriate line or portrait, not names. These patterns are consistent, but other decorative practices across these *Canterbury Tales* manuscripts are inconsistent.

---

[91] Cf. *The Thornton Manuscript*, intro. D. S. Brewer and A. E. B. Owen, rev. edn (London, 1977), p. xv. For a fine account of the manuscript illustrations accompanying the *Morte*, see Thomas Howard Crofts, 'The Occasion of the *Morte Arthure*', *Arthuriana* 20.2 (2010): 5–27.

[92] The practice continued with at least some incunabula, where the habit of hand-decorating early books included touching opening initials of sentences with red: see Margaret M. Smith, 'Patterns of Incomplete Rubrication in Incunables and What They Suggest about Working Methods', in *Medieval Book Production*, ed. Linda L. Brownrigg (Los Altos Hills, Calif., 1990), 133–46.

[93] According to Manly and Rickert, London, Royal College of Physicians, MS 13 (1460–80) employs a similar pattern: see Manly and Rickert, *Text of the Canterbury Tales*, I: 440. Morgan and Trinity are not as consistent as Manly and Rickert's descriptions imply (respectively pp. 373, 523).

Sloane MS 1686's underlining, for instance, is relatively rare and inconsistent, though the red colouring of name initials occurs throughout. Beginning in *The Miller's Tale* and continuing through the tales of the Reeve, Cook and Man of Law, there is in Morgan M.249 an occasional red stroke through the opening initial of names; Trinity College MS R.3.3 more consistently applies this red stroke to the opening initial of names, including place names, but also frequently adds a red splash to the loops of ascenders. As with other examples discussed in this chapter, this red touching of initials of names in Morgan M.249 is not applied throughout the manuscript or its texts as a whole, and even when this red stroke is added, it is not done consistently in any of the relevant tales.[94] Trinity College MS R.3.3 is generally consistent in its red colouring of name and place-name initials, but the effect is still not as emphatic as Winchester's rubrication of the entire name. Likewise a handful of fifteenth-century *Canterbury Tales* manuscripts give some sort of rubric effect for the Pilgrims' names, but not necessarily the names of characters within the individual tales, and not necessarily to the degree that Manly and Rickert claim.[95] Generally such indexical rubrics are in the margins and occur only in the *General Prologue*, but Cambridge, Fitzwilliam Museum MS McClean 181 gives a rubricated Pilgrim header at the top of the relevant pages throughout the *Prologue*. Where the same folio has several portraits, this header can get quite busy, notably at folio 10ᵛ, where it extends over two lines to introduce and index '**A Plowman, A Reve, A Myller, A Sompnor and A Pardoner** [line break] **A Maunciple and Chaucer**'.

Other manuscripts vary this practice. Thus, in London, British Library Royal MS 18.C.ii, the Pilgrims each get a marginal rubric at their first appearance, but no characters are rubricated in either the texts or margins beyond the *Prologue*. In the early tales of Cambridge University Library Ii.3.26, characters' names are given a marginal rubric demarking each character's first appearance in a tale, but the rubricated name appears only once and only in the margin, not in the text proper.[96] Once again such name rubrics are indexical rather than thematic, and once again the practice does not continue through the entire manuscript. The underlining inconsistencies of Sloane MS 1686 have already been noted, and in CUL Ii.3.26 the name decoration stops in the *Man of Law's Tale*, at folio 71 of 237 folios. The inconsistent treatment of names in Chaucer manuscripts is readily apparent in Sloane 1686, where the scribe or designer cannot even decide which header to use for the *Knight's Tale*. Throughout this tale, folios 13ʳ–49ᵛ, some pages have no header-title, some pages use 'Arcite', some pages use 'Palamon', and the opening page, which includes the final line of the *General Prologue*, gives 'Arcite' as the header but an in-text, interlinear title of 'Theseus' near the page bottom, just before the tale begins. The most consistent partial rubrication of

---

[94] The practice in Morgan Library MS M.249 is confined to fols 47ʳ through 83ᵛ. I examined the Morgan MS myself, but it is also mentioned by Manly and Rickert, *Text of the Canterbury Tales*, I: 372–5.

[95] The MSS are: Oxford, Bodl. MS 414; Cambridge, Fitzwilliam Museum MS McClean 181; CUL Ii.3.26; Cambridge, Trinity College MS R.3.15; and London, BL, Royal MS 18.C.ii. For descriptions see Manly and Rickert, *Text of the Canterbury Tales*, I: 58–9, 160–2, 295–6, 485–6, 527–30.

[96] E.g. **Theseus of Thebes** or **Ypolita** (both at fol. 11ʳ).

names that I am aware of in this context occurs in Cambridge, Trinity College R.3.15, which mostly succeeds in underlining all personal, place or title names from the *Prologue* through to the opening of the Reeve (fol. 66ʳ), but then stops its regular appearance and becomes quite random, disappearing for several folios, then recommencing, then stopping again and so on.⁹⁷ The yellow stroke through names does at least continue with some regularity, but it is not confined to names.

Again, however, none of these manuscripts looks precisely like Winchester. Since it is common in fifteenth-century *Canterbury Tales* manuscripts to rubricate headers, *incipits* and *explicits*, the rubrication or underlining of Chaucer manuscripts, whatever forms it takes, seems on the whole to serve the same sort of indexing function that can be observed in some Bible and some *Brut* manuscripts. Most significantly for my purposes, not all Bibles, *Brut* or *Canterbury Tales* manuscripts employ such rubrication, and of those that do, none of them exactly resembles Winchester with its ubiquitous rubrication of each and every character name, many place names and some objects.

As intimated at the beginning of my rubrication discussion, all of the decorative features discussed in this chapter regularly appear as standard decoration in biblical and religious manuscripts, where the *mise-en-page* ranges from full-page illustrations to miniatures to historiated initials, inhabited initials, illuminated initials, marginal glosses, chapter rubrics or underlining (or both), and often extends to smaller pen-stroked or coloured opening initials as well. The touching of opening initials of sentences with red or yellow is especially common in biblical manuscripts, and becomes even more common in the Gospels and Psalms; Gospels and Books of Hours also frequently begin with an entire line in red, but again, this is different from Winchester. A notable example of all of these features, one roughly contemporary to Malory's birth, is the 'Great Bible' of circa 1410–15, now London, British Library Royal MS 1.E.ix, which may have belonged to England's Henry IV (and heirs). In addition to the typical major kinds of decoration, this Bible employs consistent yellow highlighting of initials at the start of sentences. Significantly, there are also some rubricated names at the top of folio 163ᶜ (**Loth, Caph, Nun, Mem, Phe, Sin, Sade**), while folio 166ʳ is dominated by rubricated dialogue markers such as '**Vox Ecclesie**' and '**Vox ecclie ad xpm** [ad Christum]', as well as '**Sponsus ad sponsam**', where the rubricated phrases honour Christ as bridegroom and the Church as his bride.⁹⁸ Likewise in Richard Rolle's commentary on the Psalms (first quarter of the fifteenth century), the bilingual Latin–English Psalms are underlined in red, followed by (and thus distinguished from) the lengthy commentary. A similar layout is employed in a

---

⁹⁷ Trinity College R.3.15 has red-pencil pagination, and dark-ink foliation. I cite the ink numbers. The underlining starts again with a couple of folios in the tales of the *Cook* (74ᵛ–76ʳ); the *Squire* (fols 91ᵛ–92ʳ), the *Merchant* (117ᵛ); the *Wife's Prologue* (129ᵛ–130ʳ); the *Friar* (143ʳ–145ʳ); the *Summoner* (fols 153ᵛ–154ʳ); sporadically through most of the *Clerk* (157ʳ–174ᵛ); again in the *Second Nun* (202ʳ–210ʳ); and parts of the *Physician* (212ᵛ–213ʳ), *Shipman* (fol. 215ᵛ) and *Parson* (fol. 306ʳ). The underlining is fairly regular through the *Melibee* and *Monk* (fols 222ʳ–257ᵛ) and for the titles of Chaucer's works in the *Retraction* (316ᵛ), though the ink here may be later.

⁹⁸ I am much indebted to Fiona Tolhurst for assistance in deciphering the meaning of the rubrication here, and from whom I borrow the idea of honouring the bride and groom.

bilingual Wycliffite Psalter of the fifteenth century, where the Latin text is in red, followed by English translation in brown ink.[99]

Sylvia Huot points out that rubricated names appear widely in *Roman de la Rose* manuscripts 'to identify speakers ... in dialogue sections': **l'Amant** or **l'Aucteur**, for instance; Huot connects this rubrication pattern to 'learned compendia and philosophical dialogues'.[100] New York, Pierpont Morgan MS M.372 (c. 1320) is one type of *Rose* manuscript that rubricates change in speaker throughout, as at 14^c and a rubricated '**Amour respont a lamant**', or 80^b and '**L'aucteur parle**'. New York, Pierpont Morgan MS M.503 is a more elaborate *Rose* manuscript (from later in the fourteenth century) which includes rubricated captions for its twenty-seven gold-leaf miniatures, but it maintains this same pattern of rubricating changes in speakers' names throughout the poem and manuscript. As with other examples under discussion, there are many lines and even many folios in both of these MSS with no rubricated names, so *Rose* manuscripts, too, are only roughly cognate to Winchester. A similar pattern occurs in at least one notable debate poem, for each of the two surviving manuscripts of the early Middle English *The Owl and the Nightingale* typically, though not exclusively, use 'large decorated initials [to] mark the beginnings or ends of speeches'.[101]

Partial rubrication of some character names, some place names, some speeches and some Latin phrases occurs in numerous B-version manuscripts of *Piers Plowman*, including the relatively early fifteenth-century Oxford, Corpus Christi College, MS 201. According to Noelle Phillips, the scribe of Corpus Christi MS 201 rubricates some names and some initial letters of some words in order to emphasize voice and morality, with the rubrication varying in form from colouring an initial to underlining in red to writing the word in red.[102] As with *Canterbury Tales* manuscripts, however, even this partial rubrication does not continue at the same level through the entire manuscript, and neither the appearance or function are quite the same as with the *Morte Darthur*'s manuscript context. The erratic nature of Oxford, Corpus Christi College, MS 201's rubrication typifies the *ordinatio* of *Piers* B-manuscripts. Indeed, C. David Benson highlights inconsistencies both across and within B-version *Piers* manuscripts in terms of what and how things are rubricated, including, in marked contrast to Winchester, the all-important fact that 'Not every important name is emphasized' or even 'consistently rubricated'.[103] Consequently, as with the chronicle and romance manuscripts discussed earlier, Winchester is and is not like any of these other examples; even the Great Bible does not employ this sort of rubrication all the

---

[99] Respectively, London, BL Royal MS 18.C.xxvi; and London, BL Harley MS 1896. Partial images of both manuscripts are available via the BL's digital catalogue: www.bl.uk/catalogues/illuminatedmanuscripts/searchMSNo.asp[.]

[100] Sylvia Huot, '"Ci parle l'aucteur"', *SubStance* 17.2 (1988): 42–8 (44). The Morgan Library manuscript examples are my own.

[101] Bryan, *Collaborative Meaning*, pp. 77 and 78. The MSS are Oxford, Jesus College 29, and London, BL, Cotton Caligula MS A.ix, both dated to the last quarter of the thirteenth century.

[102] Noelle Phillips, 'Seeing Red', *Chaucer Review* 47.4 (2013): 439–64.

[103] C. David Benson and Lynne S. Blanchfield, *The Manuscripts of Piers Plowman* (Cambridge, 1997), pp. 17–18. Benson also notes how rubrication in *Piers* manuscripts helps to index plot and speech, especially in Oxford, Corpus Christi College, MS 201 (pp. 19–20).

way through, and Winchester does not use rubrication only for dialogic voices or only for certain names.

All told, then, Winchester's *ordinatio* does not exactly resemble any other manuscript or genre. The closest parallel, and the one Malory certainly knew, is found in manuscripts of Hardyng's *Chronicle*. Although the codicological design of the *Chronicle* is again not quite like that in Winchester, the likely inspiration for Winchester's rubrication is Hardyng and the *Chronicle*, not Bible manuscripts, not the Cambridge *Suite du Merlin* and not a possible fifteenth-century romance manuscript practice of detailing names as exemplified by late Chaucer manuscripts or the copy of *Generides* in Morgan MS M.876.

Conclusion: Malory as Rubricator

Given the uniqueness of Winchester's *ordinatio*, there is considerable reason for believing that Winchester's layout was carried over from its exemplar and thence back to the authorial holograph. Winchester is a tidy product, with ample and clean margins apart from its eighty marginalia and occasional pointing hands (or *maniculae*). But its rubrication of names is so unusual that it is much more likely to originate with the author than his scribes or patrons or printer. The scribes who copied Winchester may have been experienced enough copyists or readers to recognize the rubrication of names as occurring in some Bibles and having parallels in the *Brut* tradition, but as I have hopefully established, the *Brut* parallels are inexact, and it is most unlikely the scribes would mistake the *Morte Darthur* for the Bible or Psalms. Takako Kato has established that Winchester's scribes were in fact much more than the mere mechanical automata they have traditionally been characterized to be,[104] but their inventiveness would have had to have taken a very confused turn to conflate the conception of Arthur and the Round Table with the Acts of the Apostles or Wisdom of Solomon. Amongst Arthurian manuscripts, the consistent and complete rubrication of each and every name that we see in Winchester (as opposed to underlining or rubricating the opening initial), with the attendant necessity of changing pen and ink on every occasion, is, I hope I have established, a decorative feature unique to Winchester: so unique that it most likely derives from Malory himself.

Further evidence for this authorial rubrication hypothesis is explored in the next chapter, a quest that includes examining the specifics of Winchester's layout in more detail, as well as reopening the issue of Malory's library and the possible patron for the printing of the *Morte Darthur*.

---

[104] Takako Kato, 'Corrected Mistakes in the Winchester Manuscript', in *Re-Viewing Le Morte Darthur*, pp. 9–25.

2
Tracing Winchester's Rubrication and Marginalia

When Mador yields himself unto Launcelot and releases Gwenyvere from the charge of treason at the conclusion of the trial by combat to settle Gwenyvere's innocence in Malory's Poisoned Apple episode, Launcelot qualifies the mercy he will grant Mador: 'I woll nat graunte the thy lyff ... only that thou frely release the quene for ever, *and that no mencion be made uppon Sir Patryseys tombe* that ever Quene Gwenyvere consented to that treson' (415ᵛ; 801.30–3; my emphasis).¹ Launcelot's awareness of the positive and negative memorial potential of monuments in the *Morte Darthur*, especially engraved tombs, is not unique. Many other occasions in the *Morte* record writing on tombs and the memorial and elegiac possibilities of inscribed messages. In this case, however, Launcelot's concern with the memorial force of the written word is original to Malory.² What I hope to reveal in the current book is the extent to which this same memorial and elegiac use of writing occurs not only in Malory's lexical text (the words of the story), but in the manuscript or codicological text as well. The rubrication of knights' and ladies' names throughout the Winchester manuscript, together with the marginalia announcing various deeds, is the codicological equivalent to the many inscribed tombs and chivalric records within Malory's *Morte Darthur* itself. Just as Launcelot is concerned that Gwenyvere not be dishonoured by a false memorial, so Winchester's rubrication and marginalia serve both to memorialize and glorify the knights and deeds and loves of the Round Table. The Winchester-manuscript version of the *Morte*, that is, creates a rubricated testimonial to Arthur and his knights, celebrating the glory and lamenting the tragedy of 'The Hoole Book of Kyng Arthur and of His Noble Knyghtes of the Rounde Table, that whan They were Holé Togyders there was ever an Hondrede and Fyfty' (C XXI.13; *MD* 940.17–19).³

As the Poisoned Apple episode reveals, Malory's narrative style throughout the *Morte Darthur* is largely unobtrusive. The result, as P. J. C. Field convincingly demonstrates, is that the audience's or reader's focus is drawn all the more to those voices we do hear: the characters themselves.⁴ Characterization was, in

---

¹ All Malory citations are to Field's edition, but with an accompanying manuscript folio cross-reference. Where Winchester is missing the relevant page, I give Caxton's Book and chapter.
² On Malory's changes to his sources in this scene, see Vinaver, Commentary on *Works* 1058.1–3 and 1059.26–31; and my 'Weeping, Wounds and Worshyp in Malory's *Morte Darthur'*, *Arthurian Literature* 31 (2014): 61–82 (72). For a similar reading with different conclusions, see Catherine Batt, *Malory's Morte Darthur: Remaking Arthurian Tradition* (New York and Basingstoke, 2002), pp. 175–6.
³ I have made some minor capitalization changes to this quotation.
⁴ P. J. C. Field, *Romance and Chronicle* (London, 1971), pp. 151–8.

fact, an obvious concern of Malory's, for he goes out of his way to people his narrative with a recognizable and familiar cast, even giving names to minor characters who are not named in the sources.[5] Whether or not it is Malory's design, and I believe it is, the decoration pattern of the Winchester manuscript of the *Morte Darthur* likewise foregrounds character because, ignoring a few doodles and the eighty marginalia, the only real decoration scheme employed in the manuscript is the consistent red rubrication of names: most place names, some object names and all characters' names. The marginalia, with their brief episodic summaries such as 'The dethe of Marys de la Roche' (12^v; 23.30–2), or 'How Sir Gawayn wrote a letter to Sir Launcelot at the tyme of his deþe' (477^r; 918.17–23), are obviously not part of the text in the way the characters are. The marginalia may be authorial, scribal, or the whim of some earlier patron or owner, but regardless of provenance, the marginalia, too, are in red ink, and they likewise tend to foreground characters' deeds or deaths.

I shall examine the thematic consequences of the rubrication and marginalia in subsequent chapters. For now, I wish to examine precisely what is and is not rubricated, trying to trace patterns and omissions and possible origins. It may be significant, for instance, that the name **Sankgreal** is usually, but not always, rubricated. Although it is an accident of manuscript survival, the very last word of Winchester as it stands today is in fact a rubricated **Sankgreall** (484^v). The penultimate rubrication, on the fourth-last line of this last surviving page, is also a rubricated **Sankgreall**. A number of other 'Sankgreal' appearances are not rubricated, however, and it is worth noting that both of these final mentions of 'Sankgreal' occur during Launcelot and Gwenyvere's final meeting in the nunnery, a meeting in which the rubricated name **Launcelot** appears four times earlier on the page. It is likewise probably significant that places like **Winchester** or **Sarras** or **Salysbury** are usually (but not always) rubricated. I think it is definitely significant that Arthur's sword **Excalybur** is rubricated, including with a telling rubricated collocation of '**Excalebir, Arthurs** swerde' in the very episode where Morgan has stolen Excalibur and replaced it with a false sword, hoping Arthur will be killed (51^r; 110.3). Most significant of all, however, is the fact that what is most consistently and most obviously rubricated, on every page of the manuscript, are the names of Malory's characters. In an attempt to mimic Winchester's rubrication during quotations in this book, I print all rubricated material in bold. I established in the previous chapter the uniqueness of this sort of rubrication pattern. In the current chapter, I turn first to a study of precisely what is and is not rubricated, including any mistakes and their possible significance. I shall then examine the probable source of the rubrication pattern to further my suggestion (of Chapter One) that the most logical point of origin for such an unusual design is Malory himself. Although Winchester's marginalia are not part of the text of the *Morte Darthur* in the same way as the rubricated names belonging to the narrative, the marginalia nevertheless are a prominent feature of the manuscript's layout, and they are likely authorial. As such, the final question this chapter will

---

[5] See especially the magisterial studies by Robert H. Wilson: *Characterization in Malory* (Chicago, 1934); idem, 'Malory's Naming of Minor Characters', *JEGP* 42 (1943): 364–85; and idem, 'Addenda on Malory's Minor Characters', *JEGP* 55 (1956): 563–87.

address is that of the status of the marginalia, including their provenance and meaning.

Winchester is a good-quality paper manuscript of imprecise date, missing its opening and closing gatherings (of eight leaves each) and three other folios of text at what are now folios 32, 33 and 252.[6] It is copied by two scribes, who did make corrections but who mostly try, successfully, to produce wide margins and extremely clean pages. There are a few blank or nearly blank folios, notably the blank page after the 'Tale of Balyn' (fol. 34^v), the mostly blank page and three folio stubs that close 'The Weddyng of Kyng Arthur' (fol. 44^v), and the two-and-a-half empty folios which conclude 'The Boke off Sys Trystram' and preface 'The Tale of the Sankgreal' (fols 346^v–348^v).[7] These gaps are sometimes thought to represent significant and deliberate textual divisions,[8] but they more likely reflect missteps in the division of scribal labour; accordingly, not much textual weight should be given to these blanks. Of Winchester's 484 extant leaves, only folios 139^v and 279^v have marginal corrections in the scribes' hands, though folios 22^v, 61^r and 215^v have clarifications or corrections in a very light brown or (in Kelliher's phrase) 'greyish ink' from a contemporary hand distinct from the scribes, probably a sporadic supervisor or corrector.[9] (Other marginal notes are discussed below.) Occasionally the scribes use red ink to mark an in-text (as opposed to marginal) correction, crossing out the faulty brown-ink word or phrase with a horizontal red stroke.[10] In contrast to the rubricated names or marginalia, however, the purpose of these red cancellations is immediately obvious and relatively typical.

Winchester has no formal illustrations or scroll-work, but decorates and divides the text with slightly more than one hundred larger coloured capitals and several flourished initials, the latter usually red, sometimes red ornamented with brown and, on one occasion, blue with red. Sometimes the *incipits* and *explicits*

---

[6] For professional descriptions, see Vinaver, pp. ci–cxiv; N. R. Ker, intro., *The Winchester Malory* (London, 1976); Hilton Kelliher, 'The Early History of the Malory Manuscript', in *Aspects*, pp. 143–58 (pp. 143–7); Helen Cooper, 'Opening Up the Malory Manuscript', in *Debate*, pp. 255–84; and P. J. C. Field, 'Malory's Own Marginalia', *Medium Ævum* 70 (2001): 226–39.

[7] Ker, Introduction, p. xiii, says 'there were once two more blank leaves' between folios 44 and 45, but there are plainly three stubs there now, all of which seem to be original and all of which, on the basis of textual content, must have been blank or a miscalculated quire. I am considerably indebted to Andrea Clarke and especially Julian Harrison of the British Library for allowing me to examine BL Add. MS 59678 first-hand rather than in facsimile.

[8] Most recently by Raluca L. Radulescu, *Romance and Its Contexts in Fifteenth-Century England* (Cambridge, 2013), pp. 152–3. Here and throughout I disagree with Radulescu's conclusions, but I agree with her claim that the *Morte*'s manuscript contexts can be a fruitful interpretative aid.

[9] Kelliher, 'Early History', in *Aspects*, pp. 146–7; Field, 'Malory's Own Marginalia', 236. For corrections made in the text rather than margins of Winchester, see Takako Kato, 'Corrected Mistakes in the Winchester Manuscript', in *Re-Viewing Le Morte Darthur*, ed. K. S. Whetter and Raluca L. Radulescu (Cambridge, 2005), pp. 9–25.

[10] Such red negations occur at folios 9^v, 10^r, 12^r, 16^r, 24^r, 36^r, 39^r, 40^r, 55^r, 56^r, 67^r, 72^v, 77^r, 82^r, 87^v, 97^r, 101^{r-v}, 105^r, 108^v, 113^r, 114^r, 127^r, 129^v, 130^v, 132^r, 133^v, 134^v, 135^r, 142^r, 145^r, 146^v, 149^v, 151^r, 152^{r-v}, 157^{r-v}, 165^{r-v}, 170^v, 172^r, 175^r, 177^r, 179^r, 180^{r-v}, 182^r, 183^v, 191^r, 195^r, 233^v, 238^r, 239^r, 246^v, 253^r, 259^r, 262^r, 265^r, 267^r, 269^r, 271^v, 272^r, 276^r, 277^r, 278^r, 279^r, 280^r, 287^v, 288^r, 291^r, 294^v, 296^r, 301^v, 303^{r-v}, 304^r, 306^r, 310^r, 311^{r-v}, 317^r, 319^{r-v}, 322^r, 325^r, 326^r, 327^r, 328^{r-v}, 333^r, 334^r, 336^r, 338^r, 339^r, 341^r, 345^r, 352^r, 380^r (the second of which may be a different shade of red), 415^v, 421^v, 423^v, 425^v, 426^r, 440^v, 443^r and 450^r (though the stroke is almost lost in the name).

are in red ink, as with the phrase '**Hyt befelle whan Kyng Arthur** had wedded Quene **Gwenyvere**' that opens Tale II (71ʳ; 145.1). Some transitional phrases dividing one episode from another, such as '**So levith thys tale and turnyth unto Sir Launcelot**' (371ᵛ; 713.6), are likewise in red. The manuscript's official classification is London, British Library Additional MS 59678, and some scholars use this title when citing the manuscript; others style it 'the Malory manuscript'. But given its discovery in Winchester College and the fact that the manuscript is not the holograph, most Malorians, myself included, continue to refer to the manuscript as 'Winchester'.[11] (On this issue, see further pp. 1, 5, 24.)

Convincing evidence suggests that Winchester postdates Malory, who died in March 1471, but antedates the Caxton, which was printed in July 1485. Based on palaeography, Eugène Vinaver dated the manuscript 'roughly contemporary with Caxton's edition', a position endorsed by N. R. Ker. Peter Beal, in the *Index of English Literary Manuscripts*, hedges his bets, offering a wider range of 'c. 1470–83'; much the same range, '*circa* 1471–83', is listed in the British Library's *Catalogue of Additions*.[12] We can, I think, be a little more precise. Hilton Kelliher dated the paper watermarks and the manuscript's compiling to the years 1477–80, several years after Malory's death.[13] His conclusion is supported by Lotte Hellinga's forensic study of the manuscript, for Hellinga revealed traces of Caxton's printing ink types 4 and 2 on sixty-six folios at various points across the manuscript, allowing her to place Winchester in Caxton's printing-house precisely between 1480 and 1483, the only years use of the two inks overlap.[14] We know from the printer's waste used to repair folio 243 that Winchester remained in Caxton's shop till at least 1489, but we also know from the lack of casting-off marks that Winchester is not Caxton's copy-text. But since Caxton had Winchester from approximately 1480 onwards, the manuscript must have been complete before it arrived in his shop. This pushes us towards the earlier watermark range of the late 1470s for the manuscript's production. The manuscript is obviously not the authorial holograph, but a copy one or two stages removed from Malory.[15]

The main narrative text of Winchester is written in a dark brown ink, punctuated at times with coloured initials, mostly minor, four of them major. The majority of the manuscript's smaller red capitals are two lines tall, but some are three lines in height. At least one, commencing 'The Boke off Syr Trystram', is four lines tall (fol. 148ᵛ).[16] The major flourished initials are the five-line red with brown initial at 71ʳ (the opening of Tale II); the eight-line red initial at 113ᵛ (the

---

[11] The Winchester College classification 'Nº. 13' is still quite visible in a blackish ink at the top of fol. 9ʳ. It is also embossed in gold near the bottom of the spine of the modern binding.

[12] Vinaver, p. cii; Ker, 'Introduction', p. xv; *Index of English Literary Manuscripts*, Volume 1: *1450–1625*, compiled Peter Beal (London and New York, 1980), I(ii): 324; *The British Library Catalogue of Additions to the Manuscripts*, New Series 1976–80 (London, 1995).

[13] Kelliher, 'Early History', in *Aspects*, pp. 144–5. Although I accept the Newbold Revel Malory as the *Morte*'s author, Kelliher's point stands for the Cambridgeshire candidate as well: the latter died even earlier, in 1469.

[14] Lotte Hellinga, 'The Malory Manuscript and Caxton', in *Aspects*, pp. 127–41 (esp. pp. 128–33).

[15] This is another reason to avoid using the classification 'Malory manuscript'. For the most likely manuscript stemmata, see my Introduction, pp. 8–10.

[16] Ker, Introduction, p. xviii, suggests that this is a typical two- or three-line initial, but it is manifestly four, even in the black-and-white facsimile. I am indebted to P. J. C. Field for bringing this error to my attention.

opening of Tale IV); the three-line initial, blue with red flourishing, at 349^r (the opening of Tale VI); the five-line red initial at 409^v (the opening of Tale VII); and the eight-line red initial at 449^r (the opening of Tale VIII).[17] Although Winchester lacks the *de luxe* illustration of some manuscripts of the *Lancelot-Graal* Cycle, its page layout is dominated by the consistent red-ink rubrication of names, mostly of characters, but also of some places and objects. There are also eighty red-ink marginal notes in the scribes' two hands, fourteen pointing fingers or *maniculae*, which are in a different hand and ink from the text and marginalia and are confined to Tale I, a rough cross atop three steps at the bottom of folio 357^v, corresponding to the inscribed directional cross encountered by Galahad and Melyas de Lyle early in the Grail Quest (*MD* 684.1–18), and three other (and perhaps later) annotations: one on folio 23^r about hidden virtue; one on folio 302^r recording an extremely vague '1584' (whether a date or some other number is unclear); and one on folio 464^r seemingly comparing Arthur's near papal indictment to King John's actual one.[18] Carol M. Meale dates the annotation and *manicula* on folio 23 to around 1500, and the very faint note about 'Penes Jhoa*nnem*' on folio 464 may be from the same time period.[19] My own investigation of Winchester leads me to conclude that the *maniculae* are in the same ink and same hand as this anomalous 'vertue & manhode' marginalium (23^r). Since the ink and pen-strokes look to be the same in all instances – *maniculae*, the scribbled marginalium and the corrections – I also believe that the same hand is responsible for the three supervisory annotation-corrections (fols 22^v, 61^r, 215^v), and that these annotations were made at the same time as the manuscript's copying; the three corrections, however, are much neater than the stray marginalium.[20]

More certain is the rubrication, which was obviously executed at the same time as the main brown-ink text was being copied rather than via the usual practice of leaving blank spaces and decorating afterwards. The rubricated names are also in a slightly different script from the main text. The rubrication is obviously simultaneous to the main copying because all of the names fit their spaces perfectly and because occasionally the scribes forgot to switch back to brown ink after the name rubrication, carrying the red over to normal narrative text for a word or two.[21] As Ker observes of the rubrication, besides the names, 'Headings, links, explicits, and colophons and the words on Arthur's tomb (f. 482^v) are also

---

[17] There is also an eight-line red initial (preceded by a blank verso) at the start of 'The Weddyng of Kyng Arthur' at 35^r, and a large three-line red initial (preceded by three-quarters of a blank verso and those three paper stubs) at 45^r announcing the various post-wedding adventures that begin with Merlin's entombment and the war with the five kings. These are major in terms of appearance, but minor for textual purposes.

[18] Crofts offers a detailed account of Winchester's *maniculae*, as well as a stimulating interpretation of manuscript layout in the 'Tale of Balyn': Thomas H. Crofts, *Malory's Contemporary Audience* (Cambridge, 2006), pp. 61–93. My own reading of Winchester is partly inspired by Crofts, both from his monograph and in conversation.

[19] Carol M. Meale, '"The Hoole Book"', in *Companion*, pp. 3–17 (p. 9 and n. 19). Meale lists only six pointing hands. I follow Kelliher's reconstruction of the Jhoannem annotation: 'Early History', in *Aspects*, p. 146.

[20] For a fuller account of the hands at work in Winchester and an attempt at explaining the *maniculae*, see my 'Inks and Hands and Fingers in the Manuscript of Malory's *Morte Darthur*', forthcoming in *Speculum* (2017).

[21] I list all of the rubrication errors in Appendix II of this chapter.

in this script and ink, as are the side-notes which the scribes wrote[.] ... The distinguishing of personal names was evidently a matter of great consequence to the scribes. Whatever their failings in other matters they are consistent and almost faultless in this one, even to writing names in catchwords in red and names in the red-ink link, f. 364ᵛ/18, in black.'[22] It is obvious from the ubiquity of the rubrication that it would have started at the beginning of the narrative and continued to the end, but as Winchester survives today, the first folio of the manuscript is 9ʳ, which falls part way into the opening civil wars Arthur must fight to establish his kingdom in the opening tale, a tale titled 'Fro the Maryage of Kynge Uther unto Kyng Arthure that Regned Aftir Hym and ded Many Batayles' in Malory's *explicit* (W, fol. 70ᵛ), simplified to 'The Tale of King Arthur' by Vinaver, and 'King Uther and King Arthur' by Field.[23]

There is an unintentional irony in the fact that a tale revolving around rival claimants to Arthur's throne should have rival titles in modern editions, but there is no doubt about what is rubricated here or anywhere else in the manuscript: Winchester's first folio typifies the text's entire layout, for it is dominated by twenty-nine red names, immediately foregrounding Arthur, Merlin, and their allies and enemies. The name **Arthur** occurs at the top of the folio and four further times; **Claudas** appears three times; **Merlyon** occurs once; **Ulphius** and **Brastias** appear together five times, usually with a rubricated conjunction; and **Ban** and **Bors** likewise appear twice each. The very minor characters **Lyonses** and **Pharyaunce** each make one rubricated appearance. There are also two rubricated places, **Benwyk**, which appears twice, and a single **Bayarne**.

The rubrication of all character names that we see on Winchester's first extant folio creates a striking visual impression, one that continues throughout the entire manuscript and narrative to create a unique visual design. Also evident from this opening folio is the rubrication of place names, sometimes on their own, as (to take new examples) **Wynchestir**, **Salysbiry** or **Sarras**, but sometimes as a character epithet or appellation, as in **Clarivaunce of Northehumbirlonde** or **Launcelot du Lake**. Later in the manuscript, some objects are also rubricated, notably **Excaliber** and **Sankgreal**, though there is less consistency with places and objects than with rubricated individuals.[24] Character names, in contrast, are always rubricated. Apart from the odd error, details of which are outlined in an appendix below, the only exception to the full rubrication of each and every character name is the name *Merlin*. Beginning on folio 10ʳ Merlin's name, variously spelled **Merlyon**, **Merlyn** or **Marylon**, is sometimes written in full, and sometimes abbreviated to '**M**'.[25] Merlin's name is the only name abbreviated to an initial in Winchester, though some name endings are shortened at times: '**Gwenyv~**', for instance. Such abbreviation of names to initials is common in

---

[22] Ker, Introduction, pp. xiv–xv.
[23] Cooper and Shepherd follow Malory: Cooper gives 'From the Marriage of King Uther unto King Arthur' (Helen Cooper, ed., *Le Morte Darthur* (Oxford, 1998), p. 3); Shepherd gives the fuller 'Fro the Maryage of Kynge Uther unto Kyng Arthure that Regned Aftir Hym and ded Many Batayles' (Stephen H. A. Shepherd, ed., *Le Morte Darthur* (New York, 2004), also p. 3).
[24] I have tried to chart precisely who, where and what is rubricated in Appendix I.
[25] Merlin's name is abbreviated to 'M' at folios 10ʳ; 15ᵛ; 17ᵛ; 18ʳ⁻ᵛ; 20ʳ⁻ᵛ; 21ʳ; 26ᵛ; 27ʳ⁻ᵛ; 28ʳ⁻ᵛ; 34ʳ; 35ᵛ; 36ᵛ; 37ʳ⁻ᵛ; 39ᵛ; 41ᵛ; 44ʳ; 45ʳ⁻ᵛ; 49ʳ.

French romance manuscripts, but not in Winchester. Abbreviated or full, however, **Merlin**'s name or initial are still always rubricated.

Stepping back from this opening folio to an overview of the entire manuscript, it is evident that the rubrication was difficult and that the scribes regularly made errors, but considering the rarity of this scheme of rubrication what is surprising is not the errors in the pattern but that there are not as many errors as one might expect.[26] The scribes were indeed professional, but they were also extremely careful in copying manuscript layout. The rubrication also confirms the textual-critical evidence that neither scribe shared Malory's specialized martial vocabulary, nor his knowledge of French. Hence the rubrication of **gesseraunte** or **basnet** or **genytrottys** during Arthur's battle with the Giant of Seynte Mychael's Mounte (fols 76^v and 77^v). In each of these cases the scribes may not have recognized the word and so rubricated in the mistaken belief that it was a name.[27] Rather more likely, though, is that Malory rubricated (or made indications for the rubrication of) these terms because of his interest in fighting and French, and because of the significance of the scene in which these words occur for Arthur's heroic reputation. Certainly the overall pattern of rubrication across the manuscript reveals that some of the rubrication changes are emphatic: neither 'Pope' nor 'Senatours' is typically rubricated, but both are suddenly written in red ink when Arthur is crowned Emperor of Rome (fols 95^r and 96^r), thereby visually enforcing the narrative significance of this plot episode, as well as Arthur's heroic stature.

Looking at possible patterns in and explanations for Merlin's abbreviated appearances, Helen Cooper notes that where Merlin appears as himself, his name is generally given in full, but when he appears in disguise, his name is abbreviated.[28] The manuscript abbreviation thus enhances the narrative effect of Merlin's magic and disguises. Usually the name is given in full when Merlin first appears in a scene, or 'when he has not been mentioned for some time', just as sometimes the abbreviation seems to be a scribal convenience. Cooper posits further – and justifiably – that since both scribes are consistent in this practice of sometimes abbreviating Merlin and sometimes not, they are likely following the exemplar; accordingly, Malory himself is the person who initiated the abbreviation. Cooper is largely compelling, except for the convenience theory. Abbreviating for scribal ease is perfectly plausible except for the fact that no other name is so abbreviated in Winchester, and the sheer number of names cries out for further abbreviation if convenience were the decisive factor. The mere fact of the rubrication and the accompanying necessity of constantly switching pens and inks also indicates that the scribes were not concerned with making the transcription process easier in this text. There may, however, be one more thing to add to Cooper's position. Malory has not traditionally been granted much

---

[26] For an overview of what is rubricated, a list of rubrication errors and the evidence behind my conclusions in this paragraph, see the two appendixes to the current chapter.

[27] In reality, 'gesseraunte' derives from Old French and refers to a 'light coat of armour'; 'basnet' derives from Old French and refers to a light helmet; and 'genytrottys' derives from Anglo-Norman and means 'genitals'. See *Oxford English Dictionary* online, respectively 'jazerant | jesserant, n'; 'basinet | basnet, n.'; 'genitory, n.'

[28] Helen Cooper, 'M for Merlin', in *Medieval Heritage*, ed. Masahiko Kanno et al. (Tokyo, 1997), pp. 93–107 (esp. p. 97); also 'Opening Up', in *Debate*, pp. 274–7.

respect as a skilled artist. Granted that he kills off some characters who reappear alive and well later in the Arthuriad, and granted that he makes other mistakes. At the same time, he is much more than a mere translator of French Arthuriana, and the originality of his narrative and the accompanying power and longevity of the *Morte Darthur* should be sufficient evidence of Malory's artistry. Although Malory is nowhere as self-referential or self-conscious an author as Chaucer, the uniqueness of the 'M' abbreviation might just mean that 'M' stands for 'Malory' as well as 'Merlin', an authorial self-awareness and self-stamping of his narrative which has heretofore been largely unacknowledged.[29]

Both with **Merlin** and other characters, places and objects, the fact of the rubrication is considerably more apparent than its provenance or significance. In his Introduction to the Winchester facsimile, for instance, N. R. Ker notes the care and labour necessary to produce the rubrication, but he says nothing about its possible origins; he does posit that the marginalia 'were presumably taken over from the exemplar'.[30] Kelliher concludes that Winchester's pointing fingers are later additions, and that the marginalia were 'transferred rather mechanically from the exemplars', but he says nothing about the rubrication's provenance beyond noting the unlikelihood of Malory either commissioning or supervising Winchester's copying.[31] Caroline D. Eckhardt, in her brief but cogent remarks on the text and its manuscript, takes the opposite approach: she says nothing of the marginalia, but suggests that the scribes rubricated names at the behest of the architect or designer who planned Winchester's layout.[32] Cooper argues convincingly that Winchester's layout, excepting the marginalia but including the rubrication, was carried over from the exemplar, 'and ... that it may be Malory's own'.[33] I think Cooper's observation entirely plausible, and I think it can be elaborated upon. Likewise Eckhardt rightly emphasizes that Malory's text is dominated by human character and action, adding that the rubrication of names 'call[s] attention to' Malory's focus on Arthurian agency and character. This, too, is entirely accurate and compelling. I believe, however, that the way in which Winchester's rubrication of names mirrors Malory's narrative focus on character is significant, so significant as to originate not with an extremely sympathetic or coincidental reader response, but with the author. The ways in which the rubrication of names draws attention to characters and their deeds, thereby complementing Malory's principal narrative themes, likewise suggests an authorial design.

Before proceeding with an investigation of Malory as the originator of Winchester's *mise-en-page* it is best to consider the other possibilities, partly for interpretative honesty and partly because ruling these options out strengthens

---

[29] The exceptions are (once again) Cooper, 'Opening Up', in *Debate*, p. 277, and Alan J. Fletcher, *The Presence of Medieval English Literature* (Turnhout, 2012). pp. 255–8. In both cases, my reasoning and arguments ultimately differ. See also Joanna Summers, *Late-Medieval Prison Writing and the Politics of Autobiography* (Oxford, 2004), pp. 170–86. Summers examines the *Morte*'s colophons for what they may say about 'autocitation'.

[30] Ker, Introduction, pp. xiv and xvii.

[31] Kelliher, 'Early History', in *Aspects*, pp. 146–7 and 143–4.

[32] Caroline D. Eckhardt, 'Reconsidering Malory', in *The Fortunes of King Arthur*, ed. Norris J. Lacy (Cambridge, 2005), pp. 195–208 (pp. 200–1 and n. 25)

[33] Cooper, 'Opening Up', in *Debate*, pp. 263–74.

the case for Malory's hand. The other options are that the layout and decoration originated through ownership or production, or via scribal invention. Printers and purchasers of manuscripts or incunabula might well make decoration decisions or modifications to inherited decoration models based on personal taste or customer fancy, especially since early book production even after print remained partly a bespoke trade. If, however, Caxton created Winchester's rubrication pattern, it follows that he would employ a similar scheme in at least a few other manuscripts or incunables, especially since 'the period from about 1482 to 1485 was one of experimentation in [his] workshop'.[34] Strikingly, this is not the case: nothing else associated with Caxton remotely resembles Winchester, not even those of his incunables with coloured initials. Julia Boffey notes Caxton's interactions with scribes and artists, justifiably advancing the likelihood 'that even once established at Westminster [Caxton] remained involved in the production, sale, and binding of manuscript books'.[35] Printing, however, was still expensive, and manuscript production even more so. Caxton also remained a mercer and successful business person; his ability to rubricate a manuscript is not the same thing as his willingness to do so on speculation. It also seems from the watermarks and ink evidence that Winchester was not produced in Caxton's shop. Even if it were, Caxton's commercial interests, his need to make money to offset expenses, make it most unlikely that he or his supervisors or compositors would add to the expense of Winchester's layout by rubricating a non-prestige book by what was at the time a distinctly non-prestige author.

According to Curt F. Bühler, while booksellers regularly took a hand in the decoration of their incunables, they did not in fact normally instigate manuscript decoration.[36] Owners could dictate manuscript decoration, but the unique nature of Winchester's layout and the close correlation between rubrication and theme make it unlikely to be the whim of a purchaser or owner. If even a small portion of those readers comprising the late mediaeval book-buying market wanted manuscript books with every single name rubricated, it follows that at least a few such decorated texts would be extant. This is not the case: no other late mediaeval manuscript looks quite like Winchester. It is thus well to remember that manuscript patrons or purchasers need not be involved in decoration beyond expecting or rejecting it. Owners are also more likely to commission decoration in the form of coats of arms or portraits of family members, not unusual rubrication schemes.[37] Even patrons of *de luxe* manuscripts might not have anything to do with the layout of their books. The Bohun family, for instance, kept a complete stable of their own bookmakers, but the magnificent Psalter and Hours named after the family, compiled somewhere in the 1360s to 1380s and now catalogued British Library Egerton MS 3277, 'was designed and executed by artists in the employ of the Bohun family', not by the Bohuns themselves, who had nothing

---

[34] N. F. Blake, 'Caxton at Work', in *Debate*, pp. 233–53 (p. 251).
[35] Julia Boffey, *Manuscript and Print in London c. 1475–1530* (London, 2012), pp. 46–7.
[36] Curt F. Bühler, *The Fifteenth-Century Book* (Philadelphia, 1960), p. 69.
[37] On the (self-)identification of manuscript owners, see Kathleen Scott, '*Caveat Lector*', *English Manuscript Studies 1100–1700* 1 (1989): 19–63.

to do with the manuscript's layout.[38] The fifteenth-century Ireland manuscript (now Princeton, University Library, MS Taylor 9), the first half of which includes the romances *The Avowynge of Arthur*, *Sir Amadace* and *The Awntyrs off Arthure*, was likewise organized and designed by its compiler, though Ireland is a much plainer manuscript than Bohun.[39] Neither of these manuscripts, though, looks like Winchester. It is of course possible that a patron with unique tastes commissioned Winchester's unique rubrication, and that this rubrication just happened to mirror Malory's major narrative concerns; but given the thematic significance of the rubrication, it is simpler to accept a deliberate correlation between layout and text, and to attribute this correlation to the author rather than an accidental by-product of an otherwise unprecedented decoration whim. Printers or owners or buyers are consequently unlikely to be responsible for Winchester's *ordinatio*.

Likewise Winchester's *ordinatio* or page layout could conceivably be a scribal innovation, but if this were so, the scribes were both incredibly ambitious and sympathetic to their work, and unusually willing to undertake the considerable extra labour and expense of constantly having two inks and two different pens on the go at the same time.[40] Both the uniqueness and difficulty of Winchester's style of rubrication can be measured against the Pierpont Morgan manuscript of *Generides* or late mediaeval Chaucer manuscripts, where rubrication was executed after the main text and brown or black ink.[41] In *Generides*, moreover, the rubrication of even two names proved to be too much. Even with Chaucer manuscripts, which might be expected to have enough prestige to warrant extra decoration efforts and extra labour, the indexical marginal rubrication of even the first appearance of a name or partial red colouring of opening name initials is almost never carried all the way through the few manuscripts in which such partial patterns do appear. These factors alone make it highly improbable that the scribes designed Winchester's rubrication.

A. I. Doyle and M. B. Parkes conclude that late Middle English manuscripts, especially of Chaucer and Gower, have similar layout because professional scribes working in urban production centres could 'draw on each other's skills and imitate each other's products'.[42] Such scribal collaboration or mutual professional awareness should mean that at least a few other manuscripts would share Winchester's rubrication scheme if its layout were scribal in origin. Instead, as we saw in Chapter One, Winchester's physical design is all but unique. Michael Johnston argues that scribes of rural gentry manuscripts lack the experience and knowledge of their professional London counterparts, with the result that gentry romance manuscripts such as the Findern manuscript (Cambridge, University Library, MS Ff.1.6) or the Lincoln Thornton manuscript (Lincoln Cathedral

---

[38] Lucy Freeman Sandler, *Illuminators and Patrons in Fourteenth-Century England* (London and Toronto, 2014), pp. 3, 14–19 and 84 (quoting p. 3).

[39] Phillipa Hardman, 'The Unity of the Ireland Manuscript', *Reading Medieval Studies* 2 (1976): 45–62. For Hardman, the compiler's modifications to these texts emphasize proper moral and knightly behaviour.

[40] I am indebted to Stephen C. B. Atkinson for helping me clarify my thinking here.

[41] See my previous chapter.

[42] A. I. Doyle and M. B. Parkes, 'The Production of Copies of the *Canterbury Tales* and the *Confessio Amantis* in the Early Fifteenth Century', in *Medieval Scribes, Manuscripts and Libraries*, ed. M. B. Parkes and Andrew G. Watson (London, 1978), pp. 163–210 (pp. 199–203).

Library MS 91) reveal considerable 'inconsistency in the[ir] *mise-en-page*'.⁴³ But even here, with these supposedly more unusual manuscripts, nothing looks precisely like Winchester. The codicological and scribal evidence thus make it most doubtful that Winchester's *mise-en-page* was a scribal concoction.

Alternatively, if the scribes did not initiate the rubrication pattern themselves, then perhaps they, or Scribe A as the more senior scribe, may have been acting in concert with Malory's widow or son, cooking up the rubrication scheme as a way of creating a somewhat embellished presentation copy of the *Morte*, perhaps in order to gain the favour of a noble patron, perhaps even Anthony Wydeville himself (1440/42–83).

Wydeville (or Woodville) was after all King Edward IV's brother-in-law, a notable chivalric enthusiast and redoubtable jouster, and Caxton's known patron for other publications. Nigel Saul even claims that one can see affinities between Wydeville and Malory's Gawayne or Launcelot.⁴⁴ For all of these reasons, Wydeville is a favourite candidate amongst modern scholars for being Caxton's possible patron for printing the *Morte*, the figure alluded to in Caxton's Prologue as the particular 'one in specyal' of the 'noble and dyvers gentylmen' who requested a book about Arthur.⁴⁵ Wydeville is thought to have had an excellent library, he certainly had interests in controlling the Tower of London, where Malory almost definitely penned the *Morte*, and, from 1473, he was also charged with educating Edward, Prince of Wales.⁴⁶ Equally certainly, Malory's interests in knighthood and combat overlapped with Wydeville's own. As a book about chivalry, including fighting wars to secure and stabilize one's royal inheritance and to win knightly renown, the *Morte* might well have made a good inclusion in the prince's didactic entertainment. Kelliher even speculates that Wydeville knew the Malory family, and that he acquired Winchester through the author's cousins, a manuscript initially procured for the edification of the prince and subsequently delivered to Caxton for printing.⁴⁷ N. F. Blake modifies Kelliher's argument to suggest that Caxton received his copy-text directly from Malory's widow Elizabeth or their son Robert.⁴⁸ This is certainly not impossible, but if Elizabeth or Robert Malory were capable of successfully pitching Malory's English prose Arthuriad to England's first printer, it is equally possible that one or both of them might seek out instead a more aristocratic patron such as Wydeville.

This issue of Malory's possible patron is tied to larger issues of sources and authorship. Much ink has been spilled on the question of Malory's library, of where or how he acquired the manuscripts necessary to provide him with the sources for his Arthuriad, particularly the many romances that comprise Malory's

---

⁴³ Michael Johnston, *Romance and Gentry in Late Medieval England* (Oxford, 2014), *passim* (quoting p. 11).
⁴⁴ Nigel Saul, *For Honour and Fame* (London, 2011), p. 335.
⁴⁵ C, fols 2ᵛ and 2ʳ respectively; or see *MD* II: 855 and 854.
⁴⁶ For Anthony Wydeville and the Tower, see P. J. C. Field, *The Life and Times of Sir Thomas Malory* (Cambridge, 1993), App. IV, p. 206.
⁴⁷ Kelliher, 'Early History', in *Aspects*, pp. 153–5. Kelliher's position is cautiously supported by Field, *Life and Times*, pp. 4 and 145.
⁴⁸ Blake, 'Caxton at Work', in *Debate*, pp. 247–9.

much-invoked 'French book'.[49] Of necessity the question of sources is tied to the question of authorship, for the major players in the authorship controversy all agree in thinking that whichever Malory authored the *Morte Darthur*, he could only have done so with access to an incredibly well-stocked library. Arguments about where such a library might be and how a particular authorship candidate – the Cambridgeshire, Warwickshire or Yorkshire Malory – might access it are accordingly central to many of the claims made about which Malory penned *Le Morte Darthur*. Hence, in part, the potential involvement of Anthony Wydeville. Despite the considerable learning and reasoned conclusions of those scholars hunting for this library, however, its necessity seems to be a false assumption. The same is true of the need for a patron.

In the argument that instigated the debate about the identity of the *Morte Darthur*'s author, William Matthews claimed that no such library, private or public, existed on English soil.[50] Matthews looked instead to France, arguing that the only library containing all of the relevant French sources for the *Morte* was that of Jacques d'Armagnac (1433–77), Duke of Nemours. Matthews tentatively suggested that the Yorkshire Malory accessed this library as a prisoner of war in the late 1460s. Richard R. Griffith also argues for a French library, but favours instead the one-time royal library acquired by the Duke of Bedford in 1425, a library eventually passing through marriage to Bedford's young widow Jacquetta, who subsequently married Sir Richard Wydeville, later the first Earl Rivers.[51] This library was in turn inherited by Anthony Wydeville, Lord Scales and second Earl Rivers. Establishing connections between Wydeville and the Cambridgeshire Malory, Griffith uses this library – 'the one library in England containing the books essential for [Malory's] work' – as key evidence for the Papworth St Agnes Malory's authorship of the *Morte*. Wydeville and a Thomas Malory, moreover, would likely have met at the siege of Alnwick castle in the 1462 Yorkist campaign, making it all the more likely that Wydeville knew the author and supplied his library. But as Field convincingly points out, neither the Yorkshire nor Cambridgeshire Malorys were knights, and since Malory in the *Morte* repeatedly identifies himself as author, prisoner and knight, neither of these other individuals can be the author of *Le Morte Darthur*: that leaves us with Sir Thomas Malory of Newbold Revel, Warwickshire, as the author and the 1462 campaigner.[52]

Earlier in the twentieth century Edward Hicks, who like all modern scholars prior to Matthews accepted the Warwickshire Malory's authorship, postulated an alternate library. In Hicks's account of Malory's imprisonment, Malory

---

[49] Invoked seventy times, by Wilson's account: Robert H. Wilson, 'Malory's "French Book" Again', *Comparative Literature* 2 (1950): 172–81 (173).
[50] William Matthews, *The Ill-Framed Knight* (Berkeley and Los Angeles, 1966), pp. 139–50.
[51] Richard R. Griffith, 'The Authorship Question Reconsidered', in *Aspects*, pp. 159–77 (pp. 171–3). For further details, but without citations, see Griffith's 'Arthur's Author', *Ventures in Research* 1 (1972): 7–43.
[52] Field, *Life and Times*, pp. 1–35. This was also the prevailing view prior to Matthews, and Field's account has, justifiably to my mind, won wide – albeit not universal – acceptance. Christina Hardyment, *Malory* (London, 2005), p. 486, unnumbered note to 'Page 11, closer examination', adds to Field's research that the Cambridgeshire Malory actually 'took out a distraint of knighthood in 1465', further establishing his non-knightly status.

served a lengthy stint in Newgate gaol; Hicks argued that Malory accordingly had access to the library of the Greyfriars Abbey, across the street.[53] Anne F. Sutton also puts Malory in Newgate, a theory supported partly by Malory's signature on a Newgate document she discovered, and partly by Malory's burial in Greyfriars Church.[54] Sutton accepts Matthews's claim that the Greyfriars library did not hold the requisite sources for the *Morte Darthur*, but draws attention instead to the proximity of Newgate to 'the booksellers' shops of Paternoster Row', speculating that Malory could have 'borrowed' the sources he could not acquire elsewhere 'from a stationer', perhaps in exchange for publication rights of the in-progress English Arthuriad.[55] Over the course of the fifteenth century, Paternoster Row and its immediate environs around St Paul's Cathedral became the epicentre of the growing English book trade in London – a literary and bookselling pre-eminence that the Row would hold until the time of Dickens. Partly the associations between the Row and the book trade were due to its proximity to such major purchasers as the numerous nearby schools, convents, abbeys – including Greyfriars – and lawyers.[56] In addition to purely economic benefits, the closeness of book-related shops, crafts and artisans also enabled various producers of manuscript books to collaborate more easily.[57]

In light of all this Paternoster book activity and Sutton's argument that Malory was in Newgate, it is easy to suppose that Malory might well have acquired writing supplies from a Row stationer. One might speculate further that perhaps Caxton was associated even at this stage with some unknown Row bookman. Caxton was Governor of the English Merchant Adventurers in Bruges from around 1463 or 1465 to 1469 or 1470, but perhaps by the late 1460s he was already anticipating his move to publishing. According to Nellie Slayton Aurner, the Mercers traded not only in wool, but in other fineries, including manuscripts.[58] The Burgundian ducal court was one of the greatest in Europe: Bruges's docks were crowded with all kinds of trade goods from across Europe and the Orient, and the dukes and their nobles were considerable patrons of the arts. As a result of his own and his forefathers' efforts, Philip the Good (died 1467) possessed what was even in his day heralded as a wonderful library, and Caxton had long-standing literary interests even before he set up his press in Westminster. Duke Philip's court was well known for its appetite for prose epic and romance, and although Burgundian subjects were obviously in high favour, the duke's collection of tapestries included at least one King Arthur.[59] The Burgundian court also shared the aristocratic pastime common across Europe of recreating literary tournaments and Arthurian round tables. England's ties to Bruges became even stronger when Edward IV's sister Margaret of York married Duke Charles

---

[53] Edward Hicks, *Sir Thomas Malory* (Cambridge, Mass., 1928), pp. 65–9.
[54] Anne F. Sutton, 'Malory in Newgate', *The Library* 7th series 1.3 (2000): 243–62.
[55] Sutton, 'Malory in Newgate', 253–4. For Matthews's rejection, on various grounds, of the Greyfriars library, see *Ill-Framed Knight*, pp. 51–7.
[56] C. Paul Christianson, 'The Rise of London's Book-Trade', in *The Cambridge History of the Book in Britain*, ed. Lotte Hellinga and J. B. Trapp (Cambridge, 1999), III: 128–47 (pp. 128–30).
[57] See further Doyle and Parkes, 'Production of Copies', in *Medieval Scribes*, pp. 196–203.
[58] Nellie Slayton Aurner, *Caxton Mirror of Fifteenth-Century Letters* (1926; New York, 1965), p. 21.
[59] Richard Vaughan, *Valois Burgundy* (London, 1975), pp. 163–4.

the Bold in July 1468. Duchess Margaret was herself a noted benefactress of the arts, including of Caxton himself, who seems to have entered her service – or at least claimed her as patroness – almost immediately upon her arrival at the Burgundian court.

It is thus plausible that by the late 1460s Caxton was on the lookout for literary prospects beyond the works of Raoul Lefèvre that he started translating in 1468. Perhaps he even had contacts, direct or second-hand, with some of Paternoster Row's booksellers. Maybe he had heard of an in-progress English Arthuriad and merely had to bide his time before printing it, meanwhile encouraging these Paternoster contacts to keep Malory well supplied with paper, pen and ink, and even – where necessary – sources. There are a lot of suppositions in my advancement of Sutton's hypothetical Malory–book trade and book contacts scenario, especially with my addition of Caxton to the mix; but the overall image is not impossible. Certainly there is no doubting Caxton's mercantile and publishing ambitions and successes. Proof, however, is considerably wanting, and neither Caxton's successes nor the presence of Paternoster Row's book suppliers necessarily mean Malory acquired sources and materials in the fashion just outlined. The whole scenario of early associations between Malory and the book trade is further complicated by the fact that the English book industry in the late 1460s was obviously still manuscript-based, and manuscript books were produced and sold primarily on a bespoke basis. Consequently, it is far from self-evident that Malory would be able to arrange some sort of pre-publication deal with one of these Paternoster booksellers, with or without Caxton's influential interests.

The whole scenario is further undermined by Sutton's contradictory account of Malory's finances, for she portrays Malory as alternately imprisoned for debt or solvent enough to buy and rent numerous source materials and writing supplies. She also asks much of this unknown Row stationer. Part of Caxton's prestige as England's first printer is simple economics: he flourished when so many of his early contemporaries failed into obscurity.[60] Early printers and booksellers had to be commercially shrewd to survive, and Malory's name as either author or prisoner must have looked particularly unpromising in the late 1460s, regardless of whether or not the prominence of vernacular books amongst producers of insular incunables meant there was a growing demand for native English Arthuriana. Greyfriars Church, moreover, was highly fashionable, and its graves housed churchmen, a few royals, numerous nobles and respectable citizens, not (or not just) debtors and misdemeanour gentry criminals from the local prison, which is how Sutton envisages Malory. Furthermore, Malory was buried under a marble tombstone in a prestigious and no doubt expensive location in the Chapel of St Francis, so his financial and political fortunes must have risen considerably at the end of his life. Field's notion of imprisonment primarily in the Tower consequently remains compelling for having fewer holes in the argument. Malory in the late 1460s could still have been moved from place to place – as he certainly was in the 1450s – either on occasion as it suited his gaolers or political oppo-

---

[60] For an overview, see Tamara Atkin and A. S. G. Edwards, 'Printers, Publishers and Promoters to 1558', in *A Companion to the Early Printed Book in Britain 1476–1558*, ed. Vincent Gillespie and Susan Powell (Cambridge, 2014), pp. 27–44.

nents, or due to civil unrest, or specifically to witness legal documents before returning to the Tower. But none of these accounts of Malory's imprisonment adequately answers the question of where or how he accessed his many sources.

Accordingly, Field draws attention to a library in the Tower itself.[61] Although this Tower library is not attested until Henry VII's day, it may well have been in place sooner than the records indicate, and it may have contained the requisite sources. Even if the library wasn't there, so the reasoning goes, Wydeville was. Since both Wydeville and Malory were active in or around Edward IV's court and shared considerable chivalric interests, Field justifiably accepts Wydeville as the patron providing Malory's sources, but modifies Griffith's argument to have Wydeville share his excellent library with the Warwickshire Malory rather than the Cambridgeshire candidate.[62] If Wydeville had indeed supplied some of Malory's library in the late 1460s, then he would presumably be all the more open to the idea of patronizing Caxton's printing of the Arthuriad nearly two decades later, especially if Malory's family presented him with the Winchester manuscript. By this account, Wydeville could conceivably have been the person responsible for designing Winchester's unique rubrication pattern. This is not, however, the only or even most likely scenario.

Although the question of Malory's library and where and how he accessed his many sources looms large, it is somewhat misleading. Source study reveals that Malory worked closely with his sources, sometimes translating word for word; but Malory also adapted his sources freely at times, and he need not always have had a source manuscript open in front of him, especially since memory in an oral culture, as the late Middle Ages still partly was, would be better than memory in a modern print or electronic culture. Carol Meale also raises the not inconsiderable objection that Wydeville's mother Jacquetta, former wife of the Duke of Bedford and the person from whom Wydeville supposedly inherited Bedford's French library, was still alive when the *Morte Darthur* was being written: the Cambridgeshire Malory died in 1469, the Warwickshire Malory died in 1471 and Jacquetta died in 1472, two or three years after the *Morte*'s completion in 1469–70.[63] Wydeville might still have borrowed the sources from his mother to lend to our author, but the duchess is not known for her generosity, and Meale's timeline definitely complicates things. The issue of whether or not Anthony Wydeville was free to loan the library is, moreover, not the only complication.

Meale knows more than most about book ownership in fifteenth-century England, and she further points out, against Matthews and his adherents, that books are often not listed in wills, meaning it is difficult to ascertain whether a suitable library did or did not exist in England in Malory's day. It is also hard to determine how much or little of the French royal library actually made it to England or into Wydeville's hands. Nor did Malory need *de luxe* versions of the source-texts: he could well have found most of his principal sources in a handful of plainer romance anthologies, one or two of which he may have owned

---

[61] Field, *Life and Times*, p. 132, n. 33.
[62] Field, *Life and Times*, pp. 144–5.
[63] Carol M. Meale, 'Manuscripts, Readers and Patrons in Fifteenth-Century England', *Arthurian Literature* 4 (1985): 93–126 (97 and n. 11).

himself, and the remainder of which he could easily have borrowed.[64] Roger Middleton's authoritative survey of ownership of French Arthurian manuscripts leads to a similar observation and Middleton's endorsement of Meale's position. The common assumption that Malory must have required access to a large library or large number of expensive manuscripts to pen the *Morte Darthur* is, argues Middleton, 'a misconception. All the French texts that Malory used could be contained in two or three volumes at most, and there is no need for any of them to have been expensive.'[65] This is equally true, I would add, of Malory's English sources, for it is likely that many more copies of the alliterative and stanzaic *Morte* existed in Malory's day than the unique surviving manuscript copies known to the modern world.[66]

Although Meale's composite example of Royal MS 14.E.iii is an elaborate manuscript of 116 illustrations and so rather beyond Malory's means, it is significant that Royal 14.E.iii is described by an early owner as a 'grete booke', for Karen Cherewatuk convincingly locates Malory and his Arthuriad and its audience precisely in the context of the chivalric anthologies found in such 'grete bookes', particularly those copies owned and made by the gentry.[67] Royal 14.E.iii also contains a copy of the Vulgate *Estoire, Queste* and *Mort Artu*. Similar if plainer manuscript anthologies may well have been within Malory's finances or personal friendships, whether through Wydeville or even another gentry member of the court. As Cherewatuk reveals, the *Morte Darthur* is similar in terms of its portrait of various kinds of knighthood to various 'grete bookes' or chivalric anthologies assembled by John Astley and John Paston. Such chivalric anthologies, with varying levels of decoration, were much 'in the air' at the time Malory was writing. The point is, Malory need not have been dependent on a particular patron or library for his French sources, and this literary independence further reduces the possibility that Winchester's composition and design necessarily reflect the tastes of a patron rather the author himself.

Thus, whilst any one of these possible relationships between Wydeville and Malory, Malory's heirs and Wydeville, or Wydeville and Caxton is plausible, they are also all rather complicated and hypothetical. Kelliher also never tries to reconcile his originary theory of Wydeville acquiring Winchester with Winchester's lack of casting-off marks: would Wydeville or Caxton have had the time or inclination to copy Winchester into the copy-text Caxton eventually printed from? The fifteen-year gap between the *Morte*'s completion in 1469–70 and publication in 1485 theoretically supplies this extra copying time, and Field

---

[64] Meale, 'Manuscripts, Readers and Patrons', 101–8. For the temporary acquisition of manuscripts by gentry readers and copyists from libraries, religious houses and friends, see the account of Robert Thornton's reading by Johnston, *Romance and Gentry*, pp. 167–72.

[65] Roger Middleton, 'The Manuscripts', in *The Arthur of the French*, ed. Glyn S. Burgess and Karen Pratt (Cardiff, 2006), pp. 8–92 (p. 47).

[66] The alliterative *Morte Arthure* survives only in Lincoln Cathedral Manuscript 91 (Thornton). The stanzaic *Morte Arthur* is known only from London, British Library MS Harley 2252.

[67] Meale, 'Manuscripts, Readers and Patrons', 103; Karen Cherewatuk, '"Gentyl" Audiences and "Grete Bookes"', *Arthurian Literature* 15 (1997): 205–16, and her 'Sir Thomas Malory's "Grete Booke"', in *The Social and Literary Contexts of Malory's Morte Darthur*, ed. D. Thomas Hanks Jr and Jessica Gentry Brogdon (Cambridge, 2000), pp. 42–67 (quoting p. 52). Interestingly, Royal 14.E.iii was owned at one point by Elizabeth Wydeville.

wonders if Wydeville supplied Caxton with both Winchester and the copy-text. At first glance, such speculation is contradicted by those scholars who argue that Caxton copied (directly or by proxy) Winchester from the copy-text.[68] It is, however, highly unlikely that a busy and successful entrepreneur such as Caxton would take time to copy a superfluous manuscript of nearly half a million words.[69] Winchester's presence in Caxton's workshop, and the printer's ink offsets present in Winchester, make it almost certain that Caxton used the manuscript as a consultation copy rather than creating it himself.

Meale, moreover, raises a number of further problems with the idea of Malory working with a patron: if there were such a figure, then there should be some mention of the patron in the *Morte*'s *explicits*, especially since as they stand these contain biographical information about the author that is unrelated to the plot and, from a material distribution point of view, less important than aristocratic approval.[70] For Meale, Winchester's 'competent' but relatively unelaborate decoration scheme and paper rather than vellum pages likewise belie the notion of an aristocratic patron. I would add that, as with Malory himself revising the Roman War section of the *Morte*, time starts to work against this theory of Malory's heirs dictating the rubrication to win patronage.[71] Winchester, as noted, is best dated 1477–80. If early, Malory's widow or son might be involved, but Elizabeth (née Walsh) Malory was dead by September or October 1479, and Robert died a month or so later, by early November 1479; Lady Elizabeth was succeeded by her thirteen-year-old grandson, Nicholas.[72] I think it improbable that the young Nicholas had anything to do with the *Morte*'s publication or manuscript layout and distribution. If Elizabeth or Robert were involved in Winchester's creation and layout, they needed to have acted quickly. Perhaps they did, but even if this were true, they may not have had exactly the same artistic and thematic conception of the *Morte* as Malory himself, a conception that the rubrication and marginalia visually represent and enhance. There are, then, considerable grounds for doubting that the rubrication and marginalia in Winchester were created by Malory's heirs or patron or printer – unless, of course, one or more of these groups was following Malory's directives.

There are also political complications that buttress these codicological and literary objections to Wydeville's patronage of Malory's Arthuriad. Field records how, in August 1469, Sir Thomas's son Robert was accused, with various other men, of murdering one of the queen's brothers, together with Richard Wydeville (first) Earl Rivers, father to the queen and to Anthony Lord Scales.[73] The accusation was made by Rivers's widow, Jacquetta Duchess of Bedford, not by Anthony Lord Scales, or by Queen Elizabeth (Wydeville), and top of the list of ill-doers is Richard Neville Earl of Warwick. But the name 'Robert Malory' occurs in the

---

[68] See, e.g., Hellinga, 'Malory Manuscript and Caxton', in *Aspects*, pp. 134–8; Sue Ellen Holbrook, 'On the Attractions of the Malory Incunable and the Malory Manuscript', in *Debate*, pp. 323–65 (p. 355).
[69] Cf. Takako Kato, *Caxton's Morte Darthur* (Oxford, 2002), pp. 18 and 21.
[70] Meale, 'Manuscripts, Readers and Patrons', 108–10 and 114–17.
[71] On Malory and the revision of the Roman War, see my Introduction, pp. 5–8, 15–21.
[72] Field, *Life and Times*, pp. 127 and 190.
[73] Field, *Life and Times*, pp. 151–61.

same list. The murders typify both the violence of the Wars of the Roses and the factional affinities dominating late mediaeval English politics, especially in Warwickshire. Not unreasonably for the times, Robert Malory seems to have been acting loyally towards the Earl of Warwick, and Warwick and his followers – including the younger Malory – acting violently against the Wydevilles and the king, but neither of these commonalities was likely to endear the Malorys to the unforgiving Wydevilles. Thus Robert's role in the murders, however much it reveals his factional loyalty (and some of his father's ability for being both desired and denied by those in power), also illustrates the unlikelihood of Malory's heirs going anywhere near Lord Scales, or Scales's willingness to patronize Sir Thomas's work. Anthony Wydeville was admittedly a man of contradictions,[74] but it seems doubtful that his sense of chivalric splendour or political realism would countenance the deaths of two close family members.

Certainly there is circumstantial evidence of a long-lasting Wydeville grudge. With the partial exception of Anthony Lord Scales himself, the Wydevilles of Edward's reign are seen as a 'greedy and grasping' lot; nevertheless, there may well be a personal motive beyond mere greed in their role in attempting to defraud Malory's heir.[75] In 1486, seven months after Caxton printed the *Morte Darthur*, a certain Ralph Wolseley successfully claimed feoffee ownership of some of the Malory estates outside Newbold Revel, apparently in order to return them to Nicholas Malory, which happened two years later, 'in May 1488'. During Nicholas's minority he had been given over to Margaret Kelem, an associate of Queen Elizabeth (Wydeville). Margaret seems to have done right by Nicholas in most matters, but to have been party to a Wydeville fraud in the events leading up to this land settlement. It is possible that this whole settlement issue was partly revenge for the deaths of (the first) Earl Rivers and his son some years earlier. Perhaps Anthony Wydeville, who was executed by Richard of York shortly before the latter's coronation, was uninvolved in the land dispute. Perhaps by the very early 1480s, a dozen or so years after the murders, he might just have been willing to instigate or sponsor Caxton's edition, especially if it aided his education of the prince and if Caxton's long-term possession of Winchester meant that Malory's heirs would not benefit from the printing or the seeming patronage. In this sense, there may be further personal and political reasons that explain why Caxton expunged so many of Malory's biographical *explicits* when he printed the *Morte*. But Anthony Wydeville was executed in June 1483, and the *Morte* completely printed by July 1485, so he may not have been involved at all.[76] All told, there are simply too many reasons for Malory's heirs to steer clear of the Wydevilles in the 1470s and 1480s. It is therefore improbable that Winchester was a presentation copy whose unusual rubrication pattern was designed to win

---

[74] See Charles Ross, *Edward IV* (Berkeley and Los Angeles, 1974), pp. 97–8.
[75] For Wydeville greed, see Ross, *Edward IV*, p. 97. For their possible role in attempting to defraud Nicholas Malory, see Field, *Life and Times*, pp. 127–9 and 133–7. The 1488 quotation that follows is from Field, p. 128.
[76] In a palinode of his earlier position, N. F. Blake, 'Caxton Prepares His Edition of the *Morte Darthur*', *Journal of Librarianship* 8.4 (1976): 272–85, argues that Caxton did not have any patron for the *Morte Darthur*.

Anthony Wydeville's favour. It is equally doubtful, for reasons outlined above, that Winchester's layout was dictated by Malory's scribes or printer.

Thus a simpler explanation, one amply supported by the uniqueness of Winchester's kind of rubrication and its thematic connections to the narrative text, is to posit an authorial origin for the rubrication.[77] Although the visual effect of Winchester's rubrication has been remarked by several leading scholars, no one has examined in detail the textual significance of this *ordinatio*, the complex and continual manner in which Winchester's rubrication elucidates key themes of the *Morte Darthur*. I will explore these thematic connections and consequences in detail in subsequent chapters. At the moment, one point bears emphasis: the uniqueness of Winchester's decoration scheme makes it much more likely that the rubrication and the attendant interconnection between manuscript structure and narrative *sens* are authorial inventions rather than scribal innovation. Certainly Malory had time on his hands, albeit not sufficient time to draft and then recopy the entire *Morte Darthur*. Equally certainly, Gower, Chaucer and Hoccleve amongst other late mediaeval English authors were taking some interest in the manuscript appearance of their works.[78] So Malory would not be unique in his awareness of the potential material aspects of his *Hoole Book*.

Malory's holograph was no doubt much messier than is Winchester, but it could have had directions as to what its clean copy should look like; the names may have been rubricated in full as in Winchester, or perhaps, for ease of composition, underlined in red, as occurs occasionally in *Brut* manuscripts, with instructions to make them entirely red.[79] Such authorial rubrication or rubric-instructions would be rare, but then, the whole point of Winchester's rubrication is that it, too, is rare. It is not known exactly how Winchester came to be, or how it arrived in Caxton's printing-house. It has even been suggested that Caxton printed from the holograph. Griffith takes Caxton's statements about printing the 'Englysshe' *Morte Darthur* 'after a copye unto me delyverd' and 'accordyng to my copye' quite literally.[80] This copy, speculates Griffith, was Malory's holograph, delivered by a mutual friend of both author and printer, and a copy that was rough enough that Caxton had no compunctions about marking it up as his copy-text. As a corollary to the theory, mentioned above, that Caxton received his copy-text from Lady Malory, Blake has Caxton copying or commissioning both Winchester and the Caxton incunable directly from Malory's unbound holograph.[81] We must, however, be wary of Caxton making more copies of such a lengthy book than absolutely required. The textual-critical evidence also

---

[77] As we shall see below, Winchester's marginalia are also most likely authorial.

[78] See A. S. G. Edwards and Derek Pearsall, 'The Manuscripts of the Major English Poetic Texts', in *Book Production and Publishing in Britain 1375–1475*, ed. Jeremy Griffiths and Derek Pearsall (Cambridge, 1989), pp. 257–78 (pp. 258–60); Stephen Partridge, '"The Makere of this Boke"', in *Author, Reader, Book*, ed. Stephen Partridge and Erik Kwakkel (Toronto, 2012), pp. 106–53.

[79] There is one underlined name in Winchester – a Torre – on folio 40^v, where Scribe A on one occasion forgot to change pens and inks.

[80] Richard R. Griffith, 'Caxton's Copy-Text for *Le Morte Darthur*', in *Traditions and Innovations*, ed. David G. Allen and Robert A. White (Newark, 1990), pp. 75–87 (pp. 76–7 and 81); and C, sig. 3^r.

[81] Blake, 'Caxton at Work', in *Debate*, pp. 242–9.

undermines the notion of Winchester and the Caxton both being immediately descended from the holograph, for if they were, there should be fewer variants between the two witnesses.

Attempting to explain both the differences and similarities between Winchester and the Caxton, Takako Kato argues forcefully that the copy-text was not produced by Caxton, and that compositor's and printer's errors in the Caxton print reveal the copy-text to have been quite messy.[82] Textual details in the Caxton cause Kato to speculate further that the copy-text is the same as Vinaver's lost archetype X, the first post-Malory manuscript in the line of transmission between both Malory and Winchester and Malory and Caxton:

Vinaver's Stemma		Kato's Shorter Stemma	
M		M	
X		X	
Y	Z	Y	C
W	C	W	

For Kato, this archetype-cum-copy-text was a rough fair copy commissioned by Malory himself. But because Malory could not afford a more distinguished scribe, the fair copy was rather messy and unclear at times, possibly even copied onto different sizes of paper or vellum. Nonetheless, Vinaver's theory of two copying stages between Malory and Winchester still stands on textual-critical grounds. Although Kato's shorter stemma between Malory and the Caxton is supported by earlier research by Field and Cooper, each of whom points out weaknesses in this branch of Vinaver's stemma, Field recently discovered textual-critical evidence confirming the two steps between author and printer.[83]

Kato's theory about archetype X being an author-commissioned but messy fair copy, however, remains as compelling as anything else. My thesis that Malory is responsible for the *ordinatio* we see today in Winchester is certainly strengthened if Malory himself were also responsible for having the first (now lost) archetype manuscript before Winchester copied. The tradition of copied manuscripts would thus begin with the author's wishes, for Malory could ensure that the copied manuscript, however messy, nonetheless be decorated to his design. Kato's theory about X's scribe being less than stellar also provides one explanation for how the marginalia got copied into the manuscripts between Malory and Winchester: the scribe copying X failed to recognize the distinction between Malory's marginal comments and more traditional glosses explaining sources or meaning. Alternatively, Malory himself may have written the marginalia into the archetype. Regardless of which theory one favours, Malory himself is the most plausible and convincing source for Winchester's rubrication and marginalia.

---

[82] Kato, *Caxton's Morte Darthur, passim*. For her stemma and copying argument, see esp. pp. 63–7.
[83] For stemmata and bibliographic details, see my Introduction, pp. 8–9, esp. nn. 29–30.

Whether Winchester is one or two stages removed from Malory, there is no *a priori* reason why its rubrication pattern could not be carried through one or more layers of transmission, just as the text itself was. After all, as Doyle and Parkes make clear, scribes and artists, although often introducing variation or error, were equally as prone to copy faithfully the *mise-en-page* as well as the narrative text of their exemplars.[84] In the Lincoln Thornton manuscript (Lincoln, Cathedral Library, MS 91; c. 1430–40), for instance, Robert Thornton employed a different *mise-en-page* for some of his romances than others, suggesting not just different exemplars for his book, but faithful reproduction of the different layout of the different exemplars:[85] *Octavian, Isumbras* and *The Earl of Tolous* are all laid out in the same double column, and all begin with a formal 'Here begynnith' statement. In each romance, moreover, the tail-rhyme is part of the normal column of text, with no special bracketing or layout. In *Sir Degrevant*, in contrast, the tail-rhymes run into the margins of each column; the rhymes are also bracketed, as is common with this layout in general, but cramped and at odds with Thornton's ruling in this particular manuscript.[86] Thornton's *Degrevant* also lacks a formal opening *incipit* or title, again making its appearance different from its fellow romances in the Lincoln manuscript. All of this suggests a different exemplar, and Thornton's copying of both text and *mise-en-page*. Another example of the scribal copying of text and *ordinatio* relevant both in content and time to Malory occurs with John Paston's 'grete booke' or chivalric anthology, mentioned above. Parts of Paston's book of chivalric materials, now British Library Lansdowne MS 285 (compiled 1468–69), were copied from the similar book of John Astley, now New York, Pierpont Morgan Library MS 775 (compiled 1450–60). Astley's manuscript is the more elegant, vellum, with several illustrations, three of which depict Astley himself in combat. Significantly, however, Paston's scribe copied not just texts from Astley's book to Paston's, but distinct features of 'identical layout, such as paragraphing', and even, in one item, 'the duplication of a meaningless gap of half a line'.[87] Since each of Winchester's two scribes faithfully rubricates, since the kind and extent of rubrication is highly unusual throughout the manuscript, and since each scribe records marginalia, both features of Winchester's layout were accordingly carried over from the exemplar, and thence back to the author.

For all of these reasons, I fully support Cooper's hypothesis that the very consistency of Winchester's rubrication strongly indicates that it derives from the exemplar, not the scribes; Cooper adds that the strenuous concentration required to maintain the rubrication might well result in the preponderance of homoeoteleuton errors in Winchester.[88] Given the unusual nature of Winchester's

---

[84] Doyle and Parkes, 'Production of Copies', in *Medieval Scribes*, p. 165. See also Stephen Partridge, 'Designing the Page', in *The Production of Books in England 1350–1500*, ed. Alexandra Gillespie and Daniel Wakelin (Cambridge, 2011), pp. 79–103 (pp. 80–4 and 92).

[85] See Johnston, *Romance and Gentry*, pp. 177–81; *The Thornton Manuscript (Lincoln Cathedral MS. 91)*, intro D. S. Brewer and A. E. B. Owen, rev. edn (London, 1977), fols 98ᵛ–122ᵛ and 130ʳ–138ʳ.

[86] Purdie coins the apt term 'graphic tail-rhyme' to describe this sort of bracketed layout: see Rhiannon Purdie, *Anglicising Romance* (Cambridge, 2008), esp. pp. 66–78.

[87] G. A. Lester, *Sir John Paston's 'Grete Boke'* (Cambridge and Totowa, 1984), pp. 33–4.

[88] Cooper, 'Opening Up', in *Debate*, p. 273. Homoeoteleuton is an eye-skip error caused by similarities in the endings of words causing scribes to skip from one word to the other,

rubrication and the scribes' general competence, the scribes must surely have recognized this threat themselves, again making it less likely that they initiated the rubrication pattern given their obvious concern to produce a clean manuscript book.[89] Field suggests that Winchester 'may have been a presentation copy' and that Caxton's copy-text, in contrast, might have been 'a more workaday product', though not in the sense argued by Griffith.[90] Matthews justifiably claims that Caxton may well have viewed print not so much as a revolution as 'simply an extension of the *scriptoria*, a device that could produce *copies that looked something like manuscript* but did not cost [quite] so much'.[91] In that sense it is probable that the copy-text shared some of Winchester's more important designs. Furthermore, Winchester's physical appearance may well help explain why the manuscript was in Caxton's printing-house in the first place: far from being produced in-house by Caxton or someone copying at his behest, as has sometimes been suggested, Winchester seems instead to have been employed as a correction copy and a model for textual divisions and certain aspects of layout. Certainly the printer's inks offsets and watermarks mean that Winchester was created before Caxton printed the *Morte Darthur* in 1485. Equally certainly, a notable feature of the Caxton is how often it does resemble Winchester, although obviously the Caxton is black-ink only, with no rubrication of any sort.

Significantly, this lack of rubrication in the Caxton *Morte Darthur* was not a given. Many early incunables were explicitly designed to resemble manuscripts, with early printers often employing 'a *Scriver*, or *Rubrisher*, to insert the initial letters at the beginning of chapters, and to make paragraph marks in appropriate places'.[92] This practice of imposing red into incunables no doubt echoes the common manuscript practice of colouring opening initials and paragraph marks in red or blue ink, discussed in my previous chapter. The use of colour by early printers was especially common on the Continent, but it also occurs in English incunables produced by Caxton and his contemporaries in the 1480s. A prime example is Caxton's *Golden Legend*, printed at Westminster in 1483–84, though Caxton had inserted at least some coloured initials or paragraph marks into his *Recueil des histories de Troie*, printed on the Continent in 1474 or 1475. A contemporary but non-Caxtonian example is *The Boke of St Albans*, 'the first printed English treatise on hawking and hunting', and 'the first example of colour-printed

---

omitting the intervening material (varying from a single word or phrase to entire sentences).

[89] For detailed explications of the scribes being better than their reputation, see Kato, 'Corrected Mistakes in the Winchester Manuscript', in *Re-Viewing Le Morte Darthur*, pp. 9–25; and P. J. C. Field, 'Malory and His Scribes', *Arthuriana* 14.1 (2004): 31–42.

[90] P. J. C. Field, 'The Earliest Texts of Malory's *Morte Darthur*', in his *Texts and Sources*, pp. 1–13 (p. 12); Griffith, 'Caxton's Copy-Text', in *Traditions and Innovations*, p. 76. Such views of the copy-text are supported by Kato's conclusions in her *Caxton's Morte Darthur*.

[91] William Matthews, 'Caxton and Chaucer', in *Debate*, pp. 1–34 (p. 9; my emphasis). Matthews is following Murray F. Markland, 'The Role of William Caxton', *Research Studies* 28.2 (1960): 47–60. For detailed refinements of the relationship between manuscript and print culture, see Bühler, *The Fifteenth-Century Book*; William Kuskin, *Symbolic Caxton* (Notre Dame, Ind., 2008), pp. 16–21.

[92] William Blades, *The Life and Typography of William Caxton, England's First Printer* (London, 1863), II: liii; quoted with approval by A. S. G. Edwards, 'Decorated Caxtons', in *Incunabla*, ed. Martin Davies (London, 1999), pp. 493–506 (p. 493 and n. 4).

woodcut illustration known in England'.[93] Printed in 1486, the St Albans book gives red paragraph marks and, even more striking, red initials at the beginning of most section titles and most new paragraphs. The 1486 St Albans *Chronicles of England* also imposes red type for decorative purposes. In a few places in *The Boke of St Albans*, the paragraph marks and occasional capital are blue, not red.[94] In a few places in the hunting section, the names of animals are printed in red, whilst elsewhere, in what looks like an echo of the manuscript use of red for dialogic purposes, the various calls and expressions used during the hunt are printed in red.[95]

In his survey of the fifteenth-century book, Bühler provides considerable evidence and examples of black-ink incunables being augmented with red, blue and sometimes even gold colour. Sometimes these colours were set by print – occasionally only just fitting in the proper place – and sometimes they were applied by hand by a rubricator or artist, but in either case we see evidence of the ways in which early printers often mimicked manuscript tradition.[96] English printers soon stopped using colour, though even the Caxton black-letter *Morte Darthur* resembles Winchester's layout in other ways.[97] But the lack of colour in Caxton's *Morte*, together with the ways in which it resembles Winchester in other aspects of layout, make it highly unlikely that Caxton designed Winchester or its rubrication scheme. He seems, however, to have recognized the rarity of Winchester's appearance: Caxton's detailed 'Table or *Rubrysshe* of the Contente of Chapytres' to his *Morte Darthur* is, appropriately enough given the uniqueness of Winchester's rubrication scheme, the only occasion in all of his prefaces and books that Caxton employs such a descriptive rubric.[98] For Blake, this contents-rubric is purely a marketing gimmick. Nonetheless, given Caxton's success as a printer, it seems fair to credit him with some recognition of Winchester's unusual appearance, one he acknowledged with his own different but – for Caxton – equally unusual rubric.

Significantly, there is broad agreement amongst scholars on both sides of the divide over whether Winchester or the Caxton best represents Malory's final intentions for the text of the *Morte Darthur* that Caxton's copy-text manuscript reproduced Winchester's decorative features and layout, even if it modified the text in places.[99] Caxton thus used Winchester not only for the odd bit of proof-

---

[93] Rachel Hands, ed., *English Hunting and Hawking in The Boke of St. Albans* (Oxford, 1975), p. v. Hands notes further (p. xviii) the presence in the heraldic section, which is not reproduced in her facsimile, of a three-coloured coat of arms: 'black, red, and blue'. I am indebted to P. J. C. Field for this example.

[94] *Boke of St. Albans*, c2^r, c3^r, c6^v, c7^v.

[95] Respectively *Boke of St. Albans*, e1^r, e3^v and e5^v–e6^v.

[96] Bühler, *Fifteenth-Century Book, passim*, esp. pp. 72–87.

[97] On physical similarities (and textual differences) between Winchester and the Caxton, see further D. Thomas Hanks Jr, 'Textual Harassment', in *Re-Viewing Le Morte Darthur*, pp. 27–47 (esp. pp. 33–5 and 40); and Helen Cooper, 'The Book of Sir Tristram de Lyones', in *Companion*, pp. 183–201 (pp. 199–201).

[98] C, sig. 4^v (pencilled folio 3^v in the Morgan copy); Blake, 'Caxton Prepares His Edition', 273–4 and 279–80.

[99] In his attack on Matthews's opponents, Moorman castigates this supposition that the copy-text and Winchester were comparable, seemingly overlooking the fact that Matthews himself accepted the similarity: respectively, Charles Moorman, 'Desperately Defending

ing or correction of the words of the text, but also for guidance on where and how to divide the narrative of the *Morte*. Caxton's copy-text manuscript may not have mirrored Winchester's rubrication scheme, though I think it probably did given the similarities between Winchester and the Caxton and the small number of intermediary copying stages; but the copy-text almost certainly did share Winchester's use of coloured red (and one blue) Lombard initials for major paragraph and section breaks. Critics disagree as to whether there are 106, 108 or 111 of these initials extant in Winchester. My own count is 111, but beyond simple pedantic accuracy, what is important in the initial count is that Caxton regularly transferred the manuscript's decorated initials into his own narrative divisions in the incunable. Indeed, all of his twenty-one book divisions, and a good many chapter divisions, correspond to a decorated initial in Winchester.

In making this claim I assume that Malory's opening tale in Winchester and any antecedent manuscripts would have commenced with a decorated initial. We are missing this opening folio and initial in Winchester as it survives, but the manuscript was likely complete when Caxton had it, and since all of the other major tale divisions-cum-openings in Winchester have such an initial, and since decorated initials (*litterae notabiliores*) were a commonplace opening in a wide variety of mediaeval genres and manuscripts, including French and English romance, I think the presence of such an initial at this point in Winchester is a safe assumption. Caxton's surviving opening of the *Morte Darthur* thus corresponds to Malory's and Winchester's presumed opening in both textual content and bibliographic layout. Broadly speaking, the same is true of the Roman War story comprising Winchester's (and Vinaver's and Field's) Tale II and Caxton's Book V. Despite the markedly different narrative text of each witness for this portion of the *Morte Darthur*, Winchester's version opens with a large, five-line flourished red initial, and Caxton's book division, despite its different wording, occurs at the same place and with a similar large initial. The opening of the 'Tale of Sir Gareth of Orkeney', 'The Boke off Syr Trystram' and the story of La Cote Male Tayle, Caxton's Books VII, VIII and IX, likewise all have slightly different initials and wording than their counterparts in Winchester, but all three books begin where there is a decorated initial in the manuscript. All of Caxton's remaining book divisions correspond exactly to an initial in Winchester.

At times, moreover, not only the placement but even the wording in these divisions is modelled, sometimes loosely sometimes more closely, on Malory's various *explicits*. Caxton's fourth book, for instance, ends with 'Explicit liber quartus / Incipt liber quintus', in the same place, albeit without the same wording, as Malory's more detailed *explicit* to Tale I; but Malory's 'Explicit a Noble Tale of Sir Launcelot du Lake' (Tale III) becomes Caxton's 'Explicit the noble tale of syr Launcelot du Lake which is the vi book'; likewise even Malory's and Winchester's 'Here endyth the secunde boke off Syr Trystram de Lyones, whyche drawyn was oute of Freynshe by Sir Thomas Malleoré, knyght, ... But here folowyth the noble tale off the Sankegreall . . .', becomes 'Here endeth the second book of syr Tristram that was drawen oute of Frensshe in to Englysshe.

Winchester', in *Debate*, pp. 109–15 (p. 111); and William Matthews, 'The Besieged Printer', also in *Debate*, pp. 35–64 (pp. 50–61).

... And here foloweth the noble tale of the Sancgreal . . .'.[100] All of Malory's and Winchester's major narrative divisions, the *explicits* and subsequent decorated initials that close and open each major division of the *Morte*, are in fact adopted by Caxton as book divisions, even when, as in the division between Books IV and V noted above, he does not precisely follow the manuscript wording of the *explicit*. Again, even Caxton's Roman War tale begins and ends in the same location and with the same sort of narrative divisions as in the manuscript. Caxton even adapts the more textually contentious blank pages and subsequent decorated initials that close the 'Tale of Balyn' and 'Weddyng of Kyng Arthur', placing his divisions for his Books III and IV at places corresponding to folios 34^r–35^r and 44^v–45^r.[101] The most logical conclusion is that Winchester and the copy-text resembled one another closely, or else that the copy-text was more cramped than Winchester, and Caxton turned to Winchester when it came to dividing up the narrative content of Malory's Arthuriad. In either scenario, Winchester's visual layout is important and influential at both the major and minor levels of division.

Matthews makes the interesting observation that the majority of Caxton's book-division titles 'relate almost exclusively to action'.[102] For instance: 'The fourth book, how Merlyn was assotted, and of warre maad to Kyng Arthur . . .'; 'The syxthe book treateth of Syr Launcelot and Syr Lyonel and mervayllous adventures . . .'; or 'The xx book treateth of the pyteous deth of Arthur . . .'. As Meale observes, there is another close correlation between Winchester and the Caxton print here, for there are at least twenty-eight occasions where Caxton's chapter breaks are closely modelled on a marginal gloss in the manuscript, and numerous other breaks that offer rough correlation to a manuscript gloss.[103] To take just a few representative examples: Caxton's Book I contains twenty-seven chapter divisions; although the corresponding section of Winchester (fols 9^r–22^r) contains only four marginalia, Caxton seems to have been inspired by three of them for the location or wording (or both) of his divisions, even when he expands on the wording. Thus in the opening civil war to defend Arthur's right to the throne, the location of Caxton's chapter break at Book I, chapter 15 seems cued by Winchester's marginalium recording 'The dethe of Marys de la Roche' (fol. 12^v), though Caxton's title is different. Likewise in the 'Tale of Balyn', Caxton's Book II, chapter 5's location is triggered by one of Winchester's two-line red initials at the top of 25^r, even though the chapter title adapts the marginalium about Balyn slaying Launceor on the verso. Then, the location of Caxton's Book II, chapter 6, seems cued by the location of the Launceor marginalium, while Winchester's 'How the lady Columbe slew hir selfe for the deth of Launceor' marginalium at folio 26^v gets reworked into Caxton's chapter 6 title, 'How a damoysel which was loue to Launceor slewe hyrself ... '. In 'The Noble Tale of Sir Launcelot', Caxton's Book VI, chapter 9 is modelled in its wording on the marginalium about

---

[100] Winchester fols 70^v, 113^r, 346^v; Caxton's *Morte*, sigs h7^v, m1^v, N1^r. Matthews, 'Besieged Printer', in *Debate*, pp. 50–5 lists all major correlations between the two witnesses' divisions.

[101] On the relative lack of merit of these blank folios as major textual divisions, see my Introduction, pp. 11–13; see also p. 56 above.

[102] Matthews, 'Besieged Printer', in *Debate*, p. 64, n. 48. My examples of Caxton's chapter rubrics are taken from the end of Caxton's Prologue in C, fols 3^v–4^r.

[103] Meale, '"The Hoole Book"', in *Companion*, p. 9. The examples are my own.

'The deth of Terquyn' at 103^v, whilst chapter 11's 'How Syr Launcelot slewe two geauntes and made a castel free' paraphrases the marginalium at Winchester 105^v. Both the break and the wording of Caxton's Book VIII, chapter 26, 'How Syr Trystram faught wyth Syr Breunor and atte laste smote of his hede', are modelled on Winchester's marginalium '[How] Sir Trystra[mys] slew sir [Bre]wnor & [hys] wyff of [cast]el pleu[re]' (171^v). These parallels of location and wording continue throughout, though obviously Caxton's chapter divisions are much more numerous than the eighty marginalia.

I draw attention to the physical similarities in layout between Winchester and the Caxton not, like Matthews and others, to rehabilitate Caxton's reputation as editor and thus defend the supposed textual superiority of Caxton's version of the *Morte Darthur*, but rather to attempt to recreate the layout of Caxton's exemplar in certain respects and thereby help to trace Winchester's layout, notably the rubrication and marginalia, back to their source or sources. One conclusion to be drawn from the rough correlation between Winchester's marginalia and Caxton's chapter titles, as Matthews himself makes clear, is 'that similar [marginal] rubrics in [Caxton's] own copy must have confirmed him in adding his own more systematic indications of subject'.[104] A corresponding conclusion is that the common archetype had the same layout.

In point of fact, nearly all of Winchester's two- and three-line decorated initials are adopted as book or chapter divisions by Caxton. The few manuscript divisions that Caxton does not adopt, moreover, are all in the Roman War story in his Book V (Vinaver's and Field's Tale II), the section of the text that he reduced by nearly half. There remain of course Caxton's other four hundred-odd chapter divisions, but the marked correlation between Winchester's sectioning initials and his own sectional divisions does strongly suggest either that he was following Winchester's lead where possible, even if he then attempted to improve upon it, or else that Caxton's copy-text shared the same layout as Winchester. My argument here is partly supported by Kato's findings in her careful elucidation of Caxton's printing procedures for the *Morte Darthur*. Kato confirms that 'most of the coloured initial letters in Winchester coincide with Caxton's book and chapter divisions', and she further acknowledges that this correspondence suggests that at least 'some book or chapter divisions in the Caxton were prompted by features in the archetype'.[105]

Where Kato and I disagree is over the issue of what happened next. Kato insists that 'Caxton introduced about five times as many divisions as those found in Winchester', which is true, and that Caxton and his compositors introduced these divisions at their own discretion, independent of anything in the manuscript, which is more subjective. For Kato, these additional breaks, especially of sections of text rather than books or chapters, very often result from Caxton or the compositors trying to make up for casting-off mistakes. Kato likewise argues that many of Winchester's two- and three-line decorated initials were created

---

[104] Matthews, 'Besieged Printer', in *Debate*, p. 55, supported with specific examples.
[105] Kato, *Caxton's Morte Darthur*, esp. pp. 23–38, 46–50, 58, 69.

and inserted by the scribes during copying.¹⁰⁶ My own investigation of the two witnesses, however, suggests otherwise; I would therefore modify Kato's findings to say that Caxton did add many breaks both large and small, but that he was building on the model presented by Winchester.

After all, even when Caxton's narrative divisions do not follow one of the manuscript's two- or three-line coloured initials, the majority of the extra Caxton divisions in the incunable are matched by a double slash (or *virgule suspensiva*, like this //) in Winchester. Such a mark, as Kato herself points out, was often used in manuscripts to show the rubricator where to insert a paragraph mark; significantly, however, the double virgule could function as a paragraph marker in its own right.¹⁰⁷ As Cooper notes about Winchester, after the decorated initials, the double virgule is in fact 'the strongest punctuation mark used within the text, ... a mark approximately equivalent to a modern paragraph break'.¹⁰⁸ Such is the case, to take two random examples, at Winchester 108ᵛ and the beginning of Caxton's Book VI, chapter 14, or Winchester 230ᵛ and the beginning of Caxton's Book X, chapter 2. Thus, I contend, Caxton is still following Winchester's lead in his extra narrative divisions. The similarities between Caxton's divisions and those in Winchester, moreover, are close enough and numerous enough to support the notion that the copy-text looked like Winchester. Indeed, as Cooper rightly argues in her perspicacious study of Winchester, this similarity means that the manuscript layout quite probably derives from Malory himself, though she is not discussing rubrication or marginalia at this point in her argument.¹⁰⁹

This textual similarity and codicological conclusion also mean that Winchester's coloured initials need not be scribal inventions. Kato claims that errors such as that at folio 64ᵛ (becoming Caxton's Book IV, chapter 23), where Winchester reads 'ye shall nat fayle to have þe love of hir and there', followed by a three-line red capital 'A' for a second 'And there ... ', can only occur because the archetype lacked a large initial, Winchester's editor inserted instruction marks for the initial, and the scribe copying the text at first missed the instruction. It is, however, equally as probable that we have a different kind of scribal error, not misreading instructions so much as a combination of dittography and what might be termed rubrication overload: the scribe read and copied the proper words, but forgot that the final 'and there' should start with a large red capital. Certainly the unusual amount of red ink in Winchester, together with the usual perils of scribal copying and contamination, could easily increase the chances of a scribe almost missing the layout of the exemplar. In copying manuscripts, scribes or their supervisors could dictate textual division and layout, but they could also imitate both the text and the layout of their archetypes. It is only natural that a manuscript the size of the *Morte Darthur* will have the occasional layout error to match its many textual errors; both kinds of error can best be attributed to scribal contamination. It also seems as if Winchester's rubrication scheme is the most successfully realized

---

¹⁰⁶ Kato, *Caxton's Morte Darthur*, pp. 69–73. David Eugene Clark, 'Scribal Modifications to Concluding Formulae in the Winchester Manuscript', *Arthurian Literature* 32 (2015): 123–54, builds upon Kato's arguments to attribute several features of W's layout to the scribes.
¹⁰⁷ Kato, *Caxton's Morte Darthur*, p. 25.
¹⁰⁸ Cooper, 'Opening Up', in *Debate*, p. 264.
¹⁰⁹ Cooper, 'Opening Up', in *Debate*, pp. 263–5.

feature of its *ordinatio*, trumping even the *litterae notabiliores*. It is definitely true, as Field argues, that certain of Winchester's decorated initials 'appear to be used as marks of emphasis, even in the middle of speeches', rather than as accurate textual divisions.[110] Such textual emphasis is most likely authorial, particularly since the care and professionalism displayed by Winchester's two scribes make it unlikely that they would create faulty initials.[111] They might attempt to correct what they thought was textually wrong, but creating 111 superfluous and misleading initials is less characteristic of their work habits. Consequently, since Caxton followed Winchester's lead here by placing a chapter break at the initial, it seems more likely that both Winchester and the copy-text shared the same layout, and that both witnesses were in turn mimicking their common exemplar.

What particularly interests me, however, is the strong likelihood that, since the narrative divisions of Winchester and its and Caxton's exemplar almost certainly go back to Malory, then so too is Malory likely responsible for the rubrication idea. The rarity of Winchester's kind of rubrication makes it much more likely to be an authorial innovation than the whim of Malory's scribes, printer or possible patron, especially given the thematic significance of the rubrication for Malory's artistry and meaning in *Le Morte Darthur*, the ways in which manuscript rubrication reinforces the thematic and narrative unity of Malory's text. The same is true, *mutatis mutandis*, of the marginalia. I shall explore these thematic consequences in more detail in the next two chapters. In Chapter One and the current chapter I have hopefully established the uniqueness of Winchester's rubrication. Working on the principle of economy and simplicity of hypotheses, if Winchester's rubrication is rare enough that it is unlikely to originate with scribe, printer or patron, it is also unlikely to derive from an earlier owner of a manuscript anterior to Winchester – assuming such an owner even existed. If manuscript patrons and owners were dictating this sort of *ordinatio*, even if they only did so in chivalric manuscripts, then there should be some surviving evidence. But there is only Winchester, and the easiest explanation for so unique a decoration scheme is to attribute it to the author. There is, however, one final feature of Winchester's layout that must be discussed: the marginalia.

It is well to clarify that I am not concerned with the non-scribal marginalia, of which there are four main instances. There are, as noted above, fourteen pointing fingers scattered through Tale I. There is the non-scribal marginal note exclaiming 'Vertue & manhode ys [hydde] wyth in the bodye', at folio 23^r. There are several doodles: various letters drawn in the top, bottom and right-hand margins of folio 90^r and the bottom of folios 189^r and 254^v; a possible name at the bottom of folio 259^v and 303^r; '1584' as a random number or date written in the outer margin on folio 302^r; what Kelliher reconstructs as 'Penes Jhoannem' scribbled faintly in the top corner of 464^r;[112] some small circles scribbled in the bottom right corner of 473^r; and four pen-strokes in the bottom right corner of 481^r and 482^r. There are also two or three later readers or owners who wrote their names in Winchester:

---

[110] Field, I: xxviii.
[111] On the scribes' care with their product, see above, n. 89.
[112] Kelliher, 'Early History', in *Aspects*, p. 146. My 'watermark' quotation in the next sentence comes from Kelliher, p. 147.

a 'Wim3er Casell' at the bottom of folio 166^v, a possible name or doodle at the bottom of folio 344^r, and a 'Richard Followell', who scribbled three signatures and traced the 'armorial watermark' on the otherwise blank folio 348^r, between Tales V and VI.

More significant are the three marginal corrections made by a contemporary (late mediaeval) hand, likely that of a supervisor, who wrote one-word corrections in the margins of folios 22^v, 61^r and 215^v. Based on my examination of Winchester, I believe that these corrections are in the same hand and ink as the pointing fingers and 'vertue & manhode' marginalium mentioned above. Yet another hand supplies a correct missing word in the inner margin of 218^v. The scribes themselves likewise made a handful of marginal corrections at 139^v, 279^v, 318^v, 341^r and 389^r. Ker seems correct that the scribes also made 'pen trials' or transcription reminders in the corners of folios 35^r and 38^r, but these latter marks are only visible in the manuscript, not in the EETS facsimile.[113]

Corrections, annotations and doodles such as these are typical codicological detritus, appearing in a wide variety of genres and manuscripts. For the sort of specific manuscript–narrative interrelation I am tracing in this project, I am concerned only with the eighty marginalia proper, copied in equal numbers by Winchester's two main scribes, and appearing throughout the manuscript. As Ker, Cooper and Field each observe, the format of these marginalia is varied: some are written in blocks of text of roughly equal line lengths, some are written in blocks of decreasing line length and some are encased in rough shield-like shapes. The style, as these critics likewise remark, is also varied: a single Latin tag of 'Sompnus' for the first marginalium; sundry 'Here' or 'How' annotations such as 'Here Sir Launcelot slew Perys de Forest Saueage' (104^v), or 'How Sir Trystram had a falle' (300^v); and simple statements such as 'The dethe of the Lady of the Lake' (24^r), or 'The deth of Sir Percevalls Syster' (398^v).

As with the rubrication, there are three obvious potential origins for these principal marginalia: (i) that the marginalia, even though they are not part of the *Morte* proper, nonetheless derive from the author; (ii) that the marginalia are a response to the *Morte* by the scribes; (iii) that the marginalia are a response to the *Morte* by an early reader or owner of Winchester.

Until recently, these aspects of Winchester's design have received comparatively little scholarly attention. As noted above, Ker's introductory remarks to the Winchester facsimile (in 1976) drew attention to the scribal care and labour necessary to produce the rubrication, but Ker said little about the rubrication's possible origin; he did conclude that the marginalia 'were presumably taken over from the exemplar'.[114] Kelliher (in 1977, revised 1981) likewise argued that the marginalia were 'rather mechanically' copied from the exemplar.[115] Meale (in 1996) also endorsed Ker's view on the marginalia, adding only that the exemplar (or the scribes) may have 'lacked consistency' in its (or their) deployment of such reading aids.[116] None of these scholars hinted that the exemplar might in

---

[113] Ker, Introduction, p. xvii.
[114] Ker, Introduction, pp. xiv and xvii.
[115] Kelliher, 'Early History', in *Aspects*, pp. 143–58 (p. 146).
[116] Meale, '"The Hoole Book"', in *Companion*, p. 9.

turn mimic Malory's holograph, but neither did any of them explicitly deny this possibility. Thus the matter stood till the turn of the century and Cooper's study of the manuscript (2000), whereupon Cooper suddenly turned this small but significant critical consensus on its head by arguing – amongst much else – that the marginalia originated with Winchester's scribes as the earliest recorded reader response to the *Morte Darthur*.[117]

Cooper's position has proven influential, but Field protests that the marginalia are at odds with the scribes' obvious preference for clean margins, and that the seeming disparity of marginal subject that Cooper detected in the scribes' reading preferences is actually a reflection of the relative narrative content of the *Morte* each scribe is copying at those particular moments.[118] Most significantly, the marginalia sometimes include information or wording unlikely to be known by the scribes or early readers, but which is entirely consonant with Malory's handling of his sources. The slightly torn note recording 'How Sir Launcelot slew kyng Carados of þe dolerous towre' (fol. 173^v) provides a compelling case in point, for the title 'of the dolerous towre' does not occur on this folio. In fact, the last time Carados was so styled was folio 138^v: scribes or readers are unlikely to remember this minor detail, especially across so much intervening prose, but it is consistent with Malory's habit of naming characters and peopling his Arthuriad with a recognizable cast. For reasons such as these, Field concludes, convincingly, I think, that the marginalia are most likely authorial, not scribal.

Winchester's marginalia, though less unique than its kind of rubrication, are still not entirely typical. They do not function as traditional glosses explaining sources or meaning, and they do not work as engaged responses to the text since they mostly summarize rather than explicate events. Nor do they function as subject headers or titles or even straightforward indexes, as is the case with glosses elsewhere, including (to take a relevant example) in many *Brut* manuscripts. Obviously Winchester's marginalia are verbal rather than pictorial, but it may be helpful to recall that many religious or devotional manuscripts have marginal illustrations whose secular or even ribald subject matter is markedly at odds with the sacred images and texts that fall within the margins. Such grotesque or carnal marginal images in manuscripts like the Bohun Psalter illustrate the mediaeval juxtaposition of high and low, sacred and secular. But these supposedly othered images often, claims Lucy Freeman Sandler, have a didactic function, helping by contrast to illuminate doctrinal belief.[119] This is not what happens in Winchester, but there is, I suggest, a similar correspondence between marginalia and text in the *Morte Darthur*. Notwithstanding their opposing theses regarding the provenance of the Winchester marginalia, Cooper and Field reach similar conclusions about the marginalia's supposed lack of consistency. Where two such authoritative scholars agree, the dissident must tread lightly indeed; nevertheless, it seems

---

[117] Cooper, 'Opening Up', in *Debate*, esp. pp. 268–71. Cooper's position is accepted and elaborated upon by both Nicole Eddy and James Wade. See Eddy, 'Annotating the Winchester Malory', *Viator* 42.2 (2011): 283–305 (285–6); James Wade, 'Malory's Marginalia Reconsidered', *Arthuriana* 21.3 (2011): 70–86.

[118] Field, 'Malory's Own Marginalia', 226–39. Wade, 'Malory's Marginalia' attempts to disprove Field's position; I rebut Wade's argument in more detail in Chapter Four.

[119] Sandler, *Illuminators and Patrons*, pp. 73–84.

to me that Winchester's marginalia are closely related to textual events, even if the events they emphasize are random or fail to address such key points as Arthur's drawing of the sword-from-the-stone or death.

I have established how the Caxton incunable physically resembles Winchester in many key respects, including in the crucial issue of building on existing narrative divisions. One conclusion that can safely be drawn from the bibliographic correlations between the two witnesses to the *Morte*, especially given the ways in which the manuscript's marginalia seem to have cued some of the printer's chapter rubrics, is that Caxton's copy-text contained not only the same text and narrative divisions as currently recorded in Winchester, but also the same marginalia. This duplication of marginalia is not a conclusion that Cooper herself allows, but it is a logical inference from her own evidence prior to the marginalia discussion about the similarities between Winchester and the Caxton and about Malory himself being responsible for other aspects of Winchester's layout. Sue Ellen Holbrook purportedly 'buttresses ... Cooper's [scribal] proposal' by questioning the marginalia's presence in any text prior to Winchester, arguing that if marginalia were in Caxton's copy-text, he would have printed them.[120] We saw in Chapter One how rubricated glosses in *Brut* manuscripts sometimes function as the equivalent of modern section titles or indexing aids; Caxton seems to have read Winchester's marginalia in much the same fashion. Certainly the contiguity of manuscript marginalia and incunable chapter titles reveals how Caxton produced an equivalent to the marginalia, albeit in a slightly different guise. To take one clear and early example, Winchester's first surviving marginalium is a simple 'Sompnus' (fol. 11^r) marking a dream of the King of the Hundred Knights, one of the eleven kings who refuse to acknowledge the young Arthur's sovereignty (*MD* 20.27–31). Significantly, the dream denotes Arthur's victory in the coming battle, and Caxton seems to have taken the dream and its marginalium and transformed them into his chapter rubric for Book I, chapter 13: 'Of a dreme of the Kyng wyth the Hondred Knyghtes' (C, 4^v). This bibliographic and textual connection between Winchester and the Caxton both strengthens (if further proof were needed) the case for a collateral stemma between the *Morte*'s textual witnesses, and also makes it all the more likely that Winchester's marginalia do in fact derive from someone other than the scribes. Nicole Eddy is thus correct to insist that 'the marginal notes found in the Winchester manuscript' evince 'one medieval reading of the text ... that is ... fully in sympathy with many of Malory's own apparent priorities and concerns'.[121] Eddy does not, however, pursue this observation to its logical conclusion, that the marginalia accordingly derive from Malory himself.

Placing the event each marginalium annotates into the context of the overall narrative of the *Morte Darthur* in its entirety, Eddy concludes that the marginalia that annotate the Winchester manuscript both do and do not have a unifying or explicatory function. For Eddy, any 'points of connection' attendant upon the marginalia, such as the importance of Gareth's battles with the coloured knights,

---

[120] Holbrook, 'On the Attractions of the Malory Incunable and the Malory Manuscript', in *Debate*, p. 344. See also Cooper, 'Opening Up', in *Debate*, pp. 268–9 and 271.

[121] Eddy, 'Annotating the Winchester Malory', 283.

are generally opportunistic rather than systemic.[122] To my mind, this selective nature of the marginalia makes it all the more likely that they, too, derive from Malory rather than a scribe or reader. Malory would not require the marginalia as indexes or explanatory glosses, but he could well be expected to highlight certain key themes and events, not unlike some modern university students or even professors who occasionally write comments, questions or the odd lecture note in the margins of their texts.[123] My contention about the thematic highlighting or emphasis provided by the marginalia both supports and is supported by Field's argument about the marginalia reflecting Malory's characteristic handling of his sources.

Like Caxton's chapter headings, many of Winchester's marginalia denote action or important events, which is no doubt what initially caused Caxton to imitate certain marginalia in his chapter headings. Winchester's marginalia are notably prone to recording especially significant deeds by the major knights of the Round Table, including memorializing the achievement of major adventures and the deaths of their enemies, as well as a few friends. Taken as a whole, in fact, the marginalia become primarily a record and memorialization of names, deeds and death. Field acknowledges the recurrence of death in the marginalia, but is sceptical of any overall pattern; Thomas H. Crofts, in contrast, convincingly argues that the marginalia in the 'Tale of Balyn' memorialize death, and his comments might fruitfully be applied to the manuscript and narrative as a whole.[124] There are, for instance, a handful of marginal references to the Grail or its principals (fols 31^r; 349^v; 351^r; 351^v; 357^r; 381^r), but even these include 'The deth of Sir Percevalls Syster' (398^v) and Lyonell's attempts to kill Bors (386^v and 387^v), thereby emphasizing character motive, action or death. Back in the 'Tale of Balyn', there is a twofold marginal record of the Lady of the Lake seeking Balyn's head and losing her own (respectively fols 21^r and 24^r), another event dominated by character, action and death. Two marginalia record respectively the death of Launceor (25^v) and the suicide of Columbe (26^v), two more events problematically associated with Balyn. Two other figures whose deaths Balyn cannot prevent are Harleuse and Peryne, figures whose fame as very minor characters rests on the fact that Malory introduces them into the 'Balyn' story only to kill them off (*MD* 63.5–65.4) before unwittingly resuscitating them in the story of Alexander the Orphan (*MD* 512.28–513.23).[125] The deaths of first Harleuse and then Peryne at the hands of the invisible and dastardly Garlonde are also marked with marginalia (both at 29^v), as is Garlonde's own death at Balyn's hands (30^v). We can

---

[122] Eddy, 'Annotating the Winchester Malory', 283–305 (quoting 296).
[123] For a spectacular example of such pedagogic notes, see C. S. Lewis's highly detailed marginalia to his edition of *Sir Gawain and the Green Knight* vv. 555ff: preserved as Oxford, Bodleian Library, Arch. H e.55, and handily reproduced in Nicholas Perkins and Alison Wiggins, *The Romance of the Middle Ages* (Oxford, 2012), p. 164, fig. 75.
[124] Field, 'Malory's Own Marginalia'; Crofts, *Malory's Contemporary Audience*, pp. 61–93. In his Introduction to *Winchester Malory*, p. xvii, Ker also notes the preponderance of death in the marginalia. Much of the argument in this paragraph draws upon my 'Characterization in Malory and Bonnie', *Arthuriana* 19.3 (2009): 123–35 (124–5).
[125] On the thematic and generic consequences of these deaths, see further Thomas H. Crofts, 'Death in the Margins', in *The Arthurian Way of Death*, ed Karen Cherewatuk and K. S. Whetter (Cambridge, 2009), pp. 115–23.

expect Balyn's death similarly to be marked and lamented by a marginalium, but appropriately enough given the nonsensical nature of his fate, the pages in the manuscript that recount Balyn's death are missing.[126]

The full degree to which the marginalia focus on death and character is thus revealed by close scrutiny of Winchester. Surprisingly, only a few marginalia are devoted directly to Arthur, but these include notes about the deaths of Lott and the rebel kings (28^v) and – later – Emperor Lucius (86^v), arguably Arthur's fiercest human foes, and the biggest threats to his kingship before Mordred's rebellion. The threat posed by Mordred is itself symbolized by the dream Arthur has after Mordred's conception, a dream likewise marked by a marginalium (17^r). Appropriately enough given Malory's focus on 'The Hoole Book of Kyng Arthur and of His Noble Knyghtes of the Rounde Table', whilst some of the marginalia highlight some key events in Arthur's own career, the marginalia as a whole are devoted to his companions. Thus the overwhelming number of marginalia concern those paragons of Malorian chivalry, Launcelot (16 marginalia), Trystram (12 marginalia), Gawayne (9 or 10 marginalia, depending on how much weight is given to Chastelayne's recorded death affecting Gawayne, who is Chastelayne's guardian) and Gareth (10 marginalia), as well as the paragon of Malorian inscrutability, Balyn (7 by the scribes, plus 1 in the non-scribal marginalium on fol. 23^r).[127]

Marginalia celebrate – and in retrospect, help elegize – Launcelot's defeat of Tarquyn, one of his greatest foes (fol. 103^v), his rescue of Kay, another important member of the Arthurian community (fol. 106^v), and his overcoming with one 'joyous' spear his friend Gawayne and his three fellows (fol. 108^v; 'joy' comes from the text, not the marginalium). Further Launcelot marginalia record his defeat of Carados and by association the friendship between Launcelot and Gawayne, who is here rescued from Carados (173^v); other Launcelot glosses celebrate his partial vision of the Grail (401^v) and his rescue of no less a figure than Gwenyvere from death (414^v). Marginalia similarly celebrate Gareth's achievement of chivalric pre-eminence by memorializing — and, in retrospect, elegizing — his defeat of each of the various coloured knights (fols 119^r; 120^r; 121^v; 124^r; 129^r), as well as by recording his marriage (147^r). In the tale of 'Sir Gareth of Orkney', at least, the marginalia become something of a scoreboard, marking each of Gareth's many and increasingly more significant knightly achievements. The marginalia thus chart his chivalric worth and development. Something similar occurs with the marginalia devoted to Trystram, since these consistently draw attention to Trystram's two most famous qualities: his chivalric prowess and his fame as a lover. The gaze can cut both ways, though modern critical theorists have only recently acknowledged this, and it is noteworthy that the first marginalium in 'The Boke of Syr Trstram de Lyones' is the note about the gift of a brachet from the French princess (152^r). This gift observation and the later companion

---

[126] Cf. Crofts, *Malory's Contemporary Audience*, p. 93.
[127] A few marginalia, such as the final one recording Gawayne's letter to Launcelot, mention more than one knight. In these cases, I count the marginalia as emphasizing each knight. Although Malory's Gawayne often gets short shrift from critics, it is noteworthy that, by the ranking system of number of marginal glosses, Gawayne comes tied at third amongst the Round Table knights, a (lexical and visual) testament to his importance in the *Morte*.

marginalium about the brachet identifying the mad Trystram (205ᵛ) have a unifying function and indicate the important role women play in Trystram's identity – and vice versa, at least in select cases. The brachet may enter the story as a symbol of Trystram's attempted reshaping by women, but it quickly becomes something more: as Jill Mann illustrates, the brachet symbolizes the 'wholeness' and intensity of Trystram's and Isode's love for one another. At the same time, it also symbolizes the distance between the lovers since the brachet helps Isode recognize the mad Trystram just in time for Trystram to be recognized and exiled by Mark (394.13–396.14).[128] Equally importantly, the second marginalium in 'The Boke of Syr Trystram' memorializes Marhalte's death and emphasizes the fact that he is killed by Trystram, thus marking Trystram's first great knightly deed (154ᵛ). Marhalte, too, was a worshipful knight and the marginalium recognizes this fact; but the key issue is the identification of Trystram as both lover and knight. Significantly, Trystram's heroic stature is thus foregrounded by both narrative and codicological means.

The Trystram marginalia consequently emphasize key themes of the *Morte*, including human tragedy, relations between men and women, and chivalric identity. The thematic potential and meaning of the marginalia are more likely to be recognized by Malory than by his scribes or early readers or manuscript owners, especially given the marginalia's seemingly haphazard arrangement. Trystram is marked as a great knight and lover, but the record of the princess dying from unrequited love reminds mediaeval and modern audiences that not all love affairs end happily. In this sense, the princess's fate presages Trystram and Isode's own unhappy ends, just as Trystram and Isode's fate in turn parallels and presages the unhappy ending of Launcelot and Gwenyvere's love. Even the Galahad marginalia record predominantly secular knightly concerns and deeds such as Galahad's knighting (fol. 349ᵛ), drawing of the sword from the floating stone (fol. 351ᵛ), or his wounding of Gawayne and this wounding's prediction by Launcelot (fol. 389ʳ).[129] Nor are Arthur's own achievements ignored; as noted above, one marginalium records 'þe dethe of', and thus Arthur's victory over, 'Kynge Lot & þe xij kyngis' (28ᵛ), whilst a later marginalium celebrates 'How Kyng Arthure slew þe Emperour of Rome Sir Lucyus' (86ᵛ). Individually and collectively, then, the Winchester marginalia foreground knights and knightly adventure, including female members of the knightly class, and including, by association, all of the chivalric themes Malory's knights carry with them on their adventures. With the partial exception of Galahad, moreover, the adventures and knights so recorded are almost exclusively secular, charting the earthly glory and successes of Arthurian knighthood and the deaths of their foes.

In this sense it is important to recall that the title by which readers have known Malory's text for over half a century is Caxton's title. Malory himself called his Arthuriad 'The Hoole Book of Kyng Arthur and of His Noble Knyghtes of the Rounde Table, that whan they were holé togyders there was ever an Hondred

---

[128] Jill Mann, 'The Narrative of Distance, The Distance of Narrative in Malory's *Morte d'Arthur*', in her *Life in Words* (Toronto, 2014), pp. 275–311 (pp. 285–7).

[129] On ways in which Malory's changes to his narrative *matière* emphasize Galahad's stature as Arthurian knight as much as religious symbol, see Murray J. Evans, '*Ordinatio* and Narrative Links', in *Studies*, pp. 29–52 (pp. 36–8).

and Fyfty' (C XXI.13; 940.17–19), and the noteworthy thing about Malory's title is that it emphasizes the rise and fall of the entire fellowship, not just Arthur or Launcelot.[130] Narrative events and interest in the *Morte* in both its codicological and its textual forms are thus dominated by chivalric character, and the presentation of character, as Robert H. Wilson long ago revealed in a series of masterful studies, is one of those places where Malory is at his best and most original.[131] Indeed, Malory is obviously and consistently attempting to people his narrative with recurring characters, 'not mere names for new characters, but names of knights whom one already expected to be prominent', thereby rendering the *Morte* 'more interesting by increasing the amount of *personal* action'.[132] What I hope to reveal in the current monograph is just how significantly manuscript layout reinforces and reflects Malory's interest in human character.[133]

Precisely because of the notable correlation between marginalia and narrative and theme, it makes much less sense to posit one or more early readers or scribes who may have shared these same authorial priorities – as, in one way or another, do Eddy, James Wade and even Cooper – when the *Morte* and its modern critics have clearly established Malory's love of knightly worship and the whole fellowship of the Round Table. Malory's priorities, moreover, his focus on individual and collective knightly character and deed and tragedy, are emphatically announced and reinforced by the marginalia and rubrication of Winchester, as well as by the lexical-textual narrative of the *Morte Darthur* proper. I am also, for reasons noted above, convinced by Field, who takes the original exemplar argument to its logical conclusion, re-establishing not merely that the marginalia derive from Winchester's exemplar, but that they ultimately derive from Malory himself.[134]

Although the ways in which the marginalia emphasize key characters, events and themes of the *Morte* do not, in themselves, indicate origin – scribal, authorial or otherwise – the collective evidence is such as to weigh most heavily towards an authorial provenance. The same can also be said, I suggest, of the rubrication, which is so unusual and which so emphatically reinforces major themes of the *Morte* that it is much more likely to be authorial than scribal. The strong likelihood that Malory himself designed the layout of Winchester and the close correlation between manuscript and text underlies my suggestion that perhaps the abbreviated 'M' in Winchester also stands for 'Malory'. The abbreviations of

---

[130] Ironically given the importance of the Round Table Fellowship, the only complete witness for this part of the text, the Pierpont Morgan copy of the Caxton, here reads 140 knights. This is clearly an error. I depart from Field in capitalizing Hondred and Fyfty.

[131] Wilson, *Characterization in Malory*; 'Malory's Naming of Minor Characters'; and 'Addenda'.

[132] I quote Wilson, 'Addenda' 571–2 and 573–4. Alastair Fowler, *Literary Names* (Oxford 2012), rightly draws attention to the importance of names in the Renaissance, but Malory, I contend, is equally concerned with individual identity, even if his individuals are defined partly by their position in or against the larger communal Fellowship.

[133] A similar but undeveloped observation about character and rubrication is made by Eckhardt, 'Reconsidering Malory', in *Fortunes of King Arthur*, pp. 200–1. On manuscript and name, see further Dhira B. Mahoney, 'Narrative Treatment of Name in Malory's *Morte D'Arthur*', *ELH* 47.4 (1980): 646–56.

[134] Field, 'Malory's Own Marginalia', 226–35. Field's view is also endorsed by Shepherd, ed., *Le Morte Darthur*, p. xliii; and Fletcher, *Presence of Medieval English Literature*, pp. 16 and 257–8.

'M' for Merlin when the mage is in disguise or when he appears unannounced certainly enhance Merlin's mystery and magic in ways which reveal a close understanding and appreciation of the text. Such a scheme, Cooper concludes, most likely derives from Malory's invention rather than that of his scribes.[135]

Cooper's findings support my contention about the manuscript rubrication, reinforcing the likelihood of Winchester's layout reflecting an authorial provenance and authorial engagement with the narrative. Obviously Merlin's appearances in the *Morte*, abbreviated or otherwise, are confined to the opening tale, but Malory arguably draws attention to the possibility of 'M' denoting both the mage and the author by placing one of the sequences where Merlin's name is abbreviated immediately after the scene in which Merlin visits Blaise to have Blaise record 'how Arthure and the too kynges had spedde at the grete batayle' against the eleven rebel kings (30.23–34). Merlin tells Blaise 'the namys of every kynge and knyght of worship that was there', just as Malory himself has done by constructing this aspect of the *Morte* and rubricating the names of all the worshipful kings and knights involved in the battle (W, fol. 15^v). It is, I believe, significant that the recording and the rubrication continue throughout the narrative and the manuscript, for 'all the batayles that were done in Arthurs dayes, Merlion dud hys mayster Bloyse wryte them. Also he dud wryte all the batayles that every worthy knyght ded of Arthurs courte.' We are reminded of the official recording of the deeds of Arthur's knights again at the conclusion to the Grail Quest, when 'the kynge made grete clerkes to com before hym, for cause they shulde cronycle of the hyghe adventures of the good knyghtes' (408^v; 788.28–30). Cherewatuk points out that this compiling of 'grete bookes' of Arthurian Grail adventures to be 'put up in almeryes ['libraries'] at Salysbury' (408^v–409^r; 788.35) is 'the only place [in the *Morte Darthur*] where Malory describes a scene of book production', though she rightly notes that Bloyse's recordings are similar.[136] Given these two instances of recorded adventure, it is possible that the telling of deeds in the parallel quests by Gawayne, Torre and Pellynore, and Gawayne, Ywayne and Marhalte, are likewise written down as well as spoken aloud. Certainly Merlin is the person who again insists that Arthur have Gawayne and Torre 'telle of hys adventures' (W, fols 39^v and 41^v; *MD* 86.33–4 and 91.28–9), and he is present as well to explicate Pellynore's deeds (44^r; 96.34–97.20). Likewise in all three recountings of the knights' wedding adventures, Merlin appears at least once in abbreviated form. Merlin is not present for the second set of quest retellings by Gawayne, Ywayne and Marhalte, but given the concern with memorializing Arthurian deeds that we see both within the *Morte* and in its manuscript context, it is possible that the 'booke' upon which the knights swear 'to telle [Arthur] all theire adventures' (70^r; 143.1–2) is the book in which these Arthurian adventures are recorded, not merely a religious book to ensure faithfulness in their testimonials. In Malory and his sources, the self-reflexive recording of narrative deeds reveals an awareness of the written word and history and memory. There is also an awareness by author and characters that reputation, in the *Morte*

---

[135] Cooper, 'M for Merlin', in *Medieval Heritage*, pp. 93–107, and eadem, 'Opening Up', in *Debate*, pp. 274–7.
[136] Cherewatuk, 'Malory's "Grete Booke"', in *Social and Literary Contexts*, p. 42 and n. 2.

Darthur, is arguably more public than private; appropriately enough, we see in these accounts of recorded adventure that chivalric deeds in the *Morte Darthur* occasionally have a lexical as well as physical component. Malory's concern with memorializing Arthur's knights is also, I suggest, more secular than his sources.

In this light it is noteworthy that it is not Galahad's or Percyval's vision of the Holy Grail that is marked by one of Winchester's marginalia, but Launcelot's (401^v; 773–4). Eddy suggests that the 'reason for this privileging of Lancelot's incomplete achievement over Galahad's perfect one must remain uncertain', and postulates that it reflects Launcelot's greatness outside the Grail Quest.[137] Certainly, when taken in context of the *Morte* as a whole, Launcelot's partial glimpse of the Grail is worthy of being noted with a marginalium as being one more indication of his human and chivalric greatness. After all, Malory, as is frequently remarked, allows Launcelot to get much closer to the Grail than either the sources or the affair with Gwenyvere should allow, so it makes sense to note this partial success. E. K. Chambers's complaint that 'Malory is not very lucid ... in distinguishing between Lancelot's imperfect vision of the Grail and the more complete one vouchsafed to Galahad' consequently misses the point.[138] Launcelot's vision is merely one more episode in the *Morte* that emphasizes his innate earthly *worshyp*. More specifically, this scene is one of many which helps to emphasize the essentially secular nature of Malory's version of the Arthurian story. Eamon Duffy notes how 'faith in the "vertu" of the Holy Name was particularly strong in the late Middle Ages'.[139] It is, therefore, significant that the names given visual and decorative prestige in Winchester are secular, not sacred. Winchester's consistent rubrication of knights' names, as opposed to God's or Christ's or Jesus', reinforces Malory's predominantly secular outlook, consistently drawing attention to the earthly persons and deeds and *worshyp* of Arthur's knights.

The same is true of Winchester's marginalia, even in their most random moments: most randomly, the two marginalia devoted to Trystram's brachet, at Winchester folios 152^r and 205^v: 'How þe Kynge of Fraunces doughter sente to Sir Trystrames a fayre brachette' (152^r; 296.4–7); and 'How þe brachet of La Beall Isod discreved Sir Trystramys' (205^v; 395.7–10).[140] At first glance these observations are curious in their choice of subject matter or obvious significance, especially given the fifty-odd folio gap which separates them. When read together with one another and with the narrative as a whole, however, the initial gift of the brachet and its marginalia 'emerg[e] as more vital to the plan and execution of the text than is immediately apparent', revealing a possible cross-referencing function for at least some of Winchester's marginalia.[141] I would add that, in this case, the seemingly unconnected and random Trystram marginalia actually emphasize

---

[137] Eddy, 'Annotating the Winchester Malory', 296, n. 64.
[138] E. K. Chambers, *English Literature at the Close of the Middle Ages* (Oxford, 1945), p. 193.
[139] Eamon Duffy, *The Stripping of the Altars*, 2nd edn (New Haven and London, 2005), p. 285.
[140] I have silently expanded abbreviations and normalized the capitalization of names and titles.
[141] Eddy, 'Annotating the Winchester Malory', 296–7. Batt, *Remaking Arthurian Tradition*, p. 103, also argues that the marginalia in 'The Book of Sir Trystram' offer a sort of allusive system of categorization.

important character features, notably Trystram's relations with women (both Isode and the French princess), as well as his identity, since in the second brachet scene Trystram is mad and unrecognized, having been living wild in the woods. The two marginalia also reveal Malory's subtlety and artistry as author, for the second scene, of the brachet's recognition of the incapacitated hero, is considerably expanded from a single terse remark in the source and constitutes Malory's 'longest addition to the Tristan romance' and a scene that 'adds [tragic] poignancy to Isode's farewell monologue'.[142] Such connections between two episodes in the *Morte* and two different marginalia, both of which are separated by a large amount of prose, is one further reason for concluding that Winchester's marginalia are authorial rather than scribal.[143]

Ultimately, my argument about the narrative and thematic significance of Winchester's *ordinatio* should still stand whether Winchester's physical layout was designed by Malory or someone else. But I hope I have illustrated in the previous and current chapter both the uniqueness of Winchester's kind of rubrication, and the likelihood that both rubrication and marginalia derive from Malory. This is, I think, the best and simplest hypothesis for the origin of Winchester's layout, even if it means that the layout was copied, or based on authorial instructions to be copied, into any intermediary manuscripts between Malory and Winchester and Malory and Caxton's copy-text. Typically, as Doyle and Parkes observe, 'writing and illuminating were separate stages in [manuscript] production'.[144] Winchester's rubrication, which was copied and inserted simultaneously with the main narrative text, is thus unusual in appearance and assembly, as well as in the consistency with which it is employed throughout the text. This triple departure from normal practice requires special circumstances or explanation, and authorial provenance provides just such a reason. Admittedly Winchester's layout is no more perfect than its text: as we have seen, some Lombard initials and blank pages are misleading or in the wrong location, though the number of layout errors is almost non-existent in comparison to the number of textual errors. Interestingly, however, there are relatively few errors in the rubrication of names. The very consistency of rubrication, as Cooper perceptively notes, explains the frequency of eye-skip errors in Winchester.[145] The strenuous concentration needed for nearly 1,000 pages of unusual layout probably also explains these errors in features of *mise-en-page*, the places where the scribes do make rubrication errors. At least some of the blank pages are also explained by difficulty in reconciling and assembling the disparate portions of scribal copying.

Needless to say, scribal errors in manuscript decoration and assembly of pages no more negate Malory's responsibility for Winchester's *ordinatio* than the many errors of transcription negate his authorship of the lexical or narrative text of the *Morte Darthur*. Just as there are various kinds of textual scribal error,[146] so too is scribal error likely the cause of the contentious blank folios and couple of

---

[142] Vinaver, Commentary on *Works* 501.14–502.31.
[143] One is tempted to suggest further that perhaps Malory was as fond of hunting dogs as he was of hunting and fighting.
[144] Doyle and Parkes, 'Production of Copies', in *Medieval Scribes*, p. 197.
[145] See above, n. 88.
[146] The errors of the Winchester scribes are outlined in Field, I: xxxii–xxxviii.

two- or three-line initials whose narrative significance vex textual scholars. Field is thus quite correct to label the blank folios (fols 347–8) between 'The Boke off Syr Trystram' and 'Tale of the Sankgreal' as mistakes in paper estimation, 'a permanent reminder of [Scribe B's] limitations'.[147] Since scribes, however, regularly copied their exemplars' layout along with text, there is equally sound explanation for how the rubrication and marginalia could be transmitted from Malory's copy (or instructions) through another stage or two to Winchester and the copy-text. The textual and codicological evidence thus suggests that just as Malory was capable of adapting his authorized French and English books to produce a highly original retelling of the traditional Arthurian *matière*, so too was he capable of envisioning a highly original manuscript layout with which to enshrine that narrative and its characters and their actions.

It remains now to examine the narrative significance of Winchester's layout, elucidating the complex ways in which Winchester's rubrication and marginalia function as elegiac memorials of the type so often erected within the early parts of the Arthuriad by Merlin.

APPENDIX I
CLASSIFICATIONS OF RUBRICATION

It may be useful to consider what exactly is rubricated in the Winchester-manuscript text of Malory's *Morte Darthur*. Personal or character names are consistently rubricated: clearly all names were meant to be highlighted by red, although there are some errors. Even when Trystram is disguised as Tramtryste, the disguised name is rubricated, and both **Trystram** and **Tramtryste** are rubricated when Malory or the scribe distinguishes Trystram's true identity (fols 155^v–157^r). Such consistency might be further evidence that the rubrication is authorial in provenance.

The rubricated names can be divided into three main categories of knights, ladies and other. Place names should be self-evident, and require no further categorization beyond being listed when rubricated. The final main category involves other things that are rubricated. This category requires various subcategories to be in any way useful. For ease of use I list only general patterns, not every example of every rubricated word; otherwise, these appendixes would quickly become unwieldy.

For my purposes, it is significant that the names 'God', 'Jesu' and 'Trynyte' are never rubricated.

Personal Names
King's Names (though usually it is the name or cognomen that is rubricated, not the title).

---

[147] Field, I: xix.

Queen's Names (again, usually it is the name or cognomen that is rubricated, not the title).
Knights' Names.
Ladies' Names.
NB In the substitution *name-doublet* 'Percyval's Sister', only the first half is rubricated: '**Percivalis** sister'.
Select commoners or non-noble characters:
–**Aryes** the Cowherd, whose name is rubricated, but whose cognomen is not rubricated at 36^r, but is with the variant **le Vaysshere** at 240^r. The **wydow** Arthur meets on Seynte **Mychaels Mounte** is rubricated, which is technically not a name but a description of staus. The rubrication signals her narrative importance as symbol of the giant's victims, a suspenseful warning to Arthur and an announcement of adventure.

Other Title Names
–Damesel of the Lake or Lady of the Lake is not rubricated, but **Lyle of Avilion** is, as is **Nynyve**.
–**Phylosopher** is rubricated at 75^v.
–**Dowse leperys** are rubricated at 79^r (a misspelling or faulty recollection of 'Dozen Peers': see Field, Commentary on 159.15).
–'Pope' is inconsistent:
  –Usually 'Pope' is not rubricated, as at 72^r, 112^v (twice), 278^{r-v} (four times), 279^r, 463^v (four times), 464^r–465^r (six times), 467^r.
  –'**Pope**' is, however, twice rubricated, at 95^r and 96^r.
–(Arch)bishop is likewise usually not rubricated: e.g. 'archebysshop of **Cantebury**' (9^v) or 'Bysshop of Canterbury', with neither name nor place rubricated (482^r).
–Names for God, Christ or the Trinity are almost never rubricated. The exception is noted below.
–**Michael** is rubricated in the battle with the giant (77^v–78^v).
–Some title names are not rubricated: Quene of North Galys (322^v). Sometimes the name is rubricated, but the epithet or toponym is not; at other times the reverse, and sometimes both: thus '**Arthure**, Kynge of Ingelonde' (9^r); **Morgause of Orkeney** (198^{r-v}); Joseph of **Aramathy** (323^r), **Bromell la Pleche** (325^r), or **Joseph** of **Aramathy** (351^r or 373^v) or **Joseph of Aramathy** (366^r).
–Nicknames or disguises also are not always rubricated: **Shyvalere Mafete** is rubricated at 342^v, but not on an earlier instance (325^r). **Tramtryste**, as noted, is consistently rubricated. So is all of **La Cote Male Tayle**, except for 193^v, when 'Tayle' is accidently omitted by the scribe. **La Beall Isode** or knights' epithets or toponyms are sometimes rubricated and sometimes not, seemingly at random.
–'King with a Hundred Knights' is usually not rubricated, suggesting the scribes did not recognize this title as a name.

Place Names: are frequently but not always rubricated. Even Inglonde, Logrys, Camelot, Gaule, Salysbury, Sandwyche, Sarras and Winchester are not always rubricated. Castle names are frequently rubricated, but it is the name or title,

not 'castle', that is red. E.g.: 'Castell of **Bedgrayne**' (15ᵛ); 'castell **Wandesborow**' (16ᵛ); **Plewre** (170ʳ); **Joyus Garde** (280ʳ); **Gooth** (365ᵛ); **Carbonek** (365ᵛ).
Likewise **Mychaels Mounte** is rubricated, but not the qualifying 'Seynte' (76ᵛ).

Other

Feast Days – Pentecost, Palme Sonday, Candylmasse – are not usually rubricated, but **Whytsontyde** and **Whytsonday** are both rubricated at 115ʳ as harbingers of Gareth's adventures.

Syege Perelous is not usually rubricated, but is twice at 351ʳ, once in the text and again in the accompanying marginalium. The rubrication emphasizes the importance of this seat and the significance of Galahad's sitting there at the beginning of the Quest.

Dragon is rubricated (75ʳ), as is **Beare** (75ʳ) and **Gyaunte** (75ʳ) in Arthur's dream. It seems that Malory liked beasts as well as hunting and hawking.

Swords: **Excaliber** is always rubricated (24ʳ, 28ᵛ–29ʳ, 51ʳ–52ʳ, 53ᵛ, 55ᵛ, 56ᵛ, 85ᵛ–86ʳ, 480ᵛ–481ʳ).

Gawayne's sword **Galantyne** is also rubricated on two of its three named appearances (80ʳ, 89ʳ).

Sankgreal: is frequently rubricated, but not always. The exceptions are noted in Appendix II.

Arthur's epitaph is rubricated.

The *incipits* and *explicits* and tale titles are usually at least partly rubricated.

Tale transitions are often rubricated:
Here folowyth the dreme of Kynge Arthure (75ʳ) or
Here levith the tale of Sir Launcelot **and begynnyth of Sir** Percyval de Galis (364ᵛ).

APPENDIX II
RUBRICATION ERRORS OR
DEPARTURES FROM THE USUAL PATTERN

It is especially common in Winchester's opening folios for characters to appear in pairs; often such pairs are presented with a rubricated conjunction. In the interests of space, I note only the first few instances of such rubricated conjunctions. Overall, the rubrication errors further confirm the scribal care and consistency necessary to create Winchester's kind of rubrication. Unsurprisingly, many of the same types of errors that occur in copying the text also occur in copying the rubrication of names.[148] Given the number of names in the *Morte*, it is actually surprising that there are not more errors: again the evidence suggests that the rubrication was being copied from an exemplar whose rubrication pattern in turn goes back to the author.

---

[148] On types of error in W, see Field I: xxxii–xxxviii.

Scribe A
- 9ʳ⁻ᵛ the pairing **Ulphius** and **Brastias** always appear together, so much so that sometimes on this folio (and others) the conjunction 'and' is also rubricated. The same is true for the pairing of **Ban and Bors** and even **Benwycke and Gaule** (9ᵛ).
- 10ʳ likewise has a rubricated conjunction between two minor knights' names: **Ladynas and Grascian**. Other conjunctions joining names are also rubricated, including an **Ulphuns, Brascias and Merlion**. We also get rubrication of names and place designations in **Ban of Benwyke** and **Bors of Gaule**. Finally, this page marks the beginning of the common but inconsistent practice in Winchester of abbreviating but still rubricating Merlin's name as **M**. (The remaining abbreviations are noted in the following list.)
- 10ᵛ continues the rubricated joining, also seen on the recto, of the minor knights **Grascian and Placidas**. 'Bedgrayne' is rubricated once and unrubricated twice. There is also a red run-on or hangover after **Merlion** resulting in **Merlion to Arthure**.
- 12ʳ likewise has a red carry-over after a name, resulting in **Cradilmente on foote**. This is thematically apt since so many knights are unhorsed and horsed again in this battle, but incorrect in terms of the rubrication pattern.
- 12ᵛ **Lucas the Butler** is missing the rubrication of the opening 'L', and the bottom of the page witnesses a red run-on between names in the phrase **Kay with Sir Gryfflet**.
- 13ʳ sees the habit of rubricated conjunctions in some doubling of knights continue, most emphatically in **Banne and Bors and Lionse and Phariaunce**.
- 13ᵛ has a red run-on into the first stroke of 'w' in '**Ban** was wood'. There is the usual non-rubricated 'Kynge with the Hondred Knyghtes', but also a non-rubricated 'Carados', the latter of whom, at least, usually is rubricated, including elsewhere on this page.
- 14ʳ has a red hangover after **Ban**, resulting in **Ban stondynge**.
- 14ᵛ sees Scribe A write 'seyde kynge', realize his error, cross out 'kynge' in brown ink, insert a red caret mark after 'kynge' and correct with a red-ink 'Lott' at the inner margin, but then carry the red over into the opening of Lott's speech: '**Lordis ye muste** do othirwyse'.
- 15ʳ likewise has red carry-over after **Merlyon**, resulting in **Merlyon bade h** (also noted by Ker, xiv); the conjunction linking **Ban and Bors** is still frequently rubricated.
- 15ᵛ has several appearances of **Merlion** in full, and several abbreviated but rubricated **M**s.
- 16ᵛ sees Scribe A forgetting to rubricate King 'Royens', but instead using red for the next three words after the name: 'Royens **he hath ynow** ado ...'. This mistake shows both the difficulty of constantly rubricating names at the same time as copying brown-ink text, but also suggests how, even at this early stage of the manuscript, the scribes were getting used to switching inks: Scribe A here missed rubricating the name, but seems after the fact to have switched ink: rubrication was starting to become habitual, if not yet entirely accurate.
- 17ᵛ has an abbreviated but rubricated **M** for Merlin, as well as two Merlins written and rubricated in full. The difficulty of sometimes abbreviating Merlin's

name and sometimes writing it in full is suggested by the fact that the last instance of the name on this page (nine lines from the bottom) is in full but is not rubricated.

–18^{r–v} has several abbreviated but rubricated instances of **M**.

–18^v reveals Scribe A forgetting to rubricate one instance of 'Gryfflet'; all other instances of 'Gryfflet' on this page are rubricated.

–19^r likewise has one instance of a non-rubricated 'Gryfflet'; all other instances of 'Gryfflet' on this page are rubricated.

–20^r one abbreviated but rubricated **M**.

–20^v has four rubricated and full appearances of **Merlion**, two abbreviated Ms, and (at line 5), a condensed and erroneously non-rubricated 'Mlion': probably because Scribe A was trying to squeeze words onto the line and realized he was running out of space. At line 18 Pellynore's sons Percyvalle and Lamorak are both mentioned, but neither name is rubricated, no doubt partly because this is the first mention of each knight and Scribe A did not yet recognize the names, but also due to the difficulty of constantly rubricating. There is a second non-rubricated 'Merlion' at the bottom of the page.

–21^r abbreviated but rubricated **M**.

–21^v has a post-name rubrication run-on: 'seyde **Arthure thou haste** seyde …'.

–22^r sees Scribe A begin to rubricate a bit too soon in the phrase 'as hit rehersith aftir in the booke **of Balyn le Saueage**'.

–24^v has a post-name rubrication run-on: 'in Kynge **Arthurs courte** …' (line 7). At line 16, having written 'kynge', Scribe A switched inks but repeated himself before writing the name, giving an unusual rubrication of title and name: 'kynge **kynge Arthure** …'.

–26^v abbreviated but rubricated **M**, and the continuation of the habit of rubricating conjunctions between names, as in Merlin's prophecy concerning '**Launcelot du Lake and Trystrams**'.

–27^{r–v} abbreviated but rubricated **M**: eight on the recto; twice on the verso.

–28^{r–v} abbreviated but rubricated **M**: three times on the recto; twice on the verso.

–28^v: the first mention of 'Sankgreal' in the *Morte* is not rubricated. But Scribe A does rubricate **Sangreal** at fol. 30.

–29^r has a non-rubricated 'Arthur' on the second line.

–34^r has several abbreviated but rubricated instances of **M**.

–34^r 'Sankgreal' is not rubricated in the phrase 'Booke of the Sankgreall'.

–35^{r–v} abbreviated but rubricated **M**: once on the recto and twice verso.

This folio is unusual for having Scribe A start the recto side, but Scribe B finish the recto before A takes over again on the verso.

–36^v has several abbreviated but rubricated instances of **M**.

–37^{r–v} abbreviated but rubricated **M**. 37^r also has a carry-over rubrication after Pellynore's name of '**Pellinor by the** honde' (also noted by Ker, xiv).

–39^v abbreviated but rubricated **M**.

–40^v sees Scribe A underline in red a brown-ink <u>Torre</u> for which he on this one occasion forgot to change pens and inks.

–41^v abbreviated but rubricated **M**.

–43^v has a stray rubricated **So** after **Arthure** and before Kynge **Pellynor**.

–44^r witnesses a rubrication carry-over to 'son' in '**Torre** kynge **Pellynors son**'; also an abbreviated but rubricated **M**.
–44^v atypically rubricates **Pentecoste**, presumably as a significant occasion marking the Round Table Oath and Arthur and Gwenyvere's wedding.
–45^{r-v} has an abbreviated but rubricated **M** (four and five times on each side). This folio is unusual for having Scribe A start the recto side, but Scribe B finish it.

Scribe B
–46^r sees Scribe B falsely anticipate rubrication with a stray rubricated **pt** [that] immediately before a rubricated **Arthure: pt Arthure**.
–49^r has another abbreviated but rubricated **M**.
–49^v has a post-name rubrication run-on after Arthur: '**Arthure wente**'.
–51^r has a stray rubricated **marbil** in the phrase 'stone of **marbil**'. This occurs in a scene and folio where Morgan plays a key role, and the scribe (B) may have been fooled by the opening letter 'm', a sort of rubricated pen-skip or substitution error.
–72^r presents the only exceptions to the lack of divine rubrication: **Mary** and **Jhesu Cryste** are rubricated once each, together, in an heroic vow of vengeance against the Romans. It seems likely that it was the potential list effect 'Mary and ...' that caused the departure from the usual pattern of not rubricating divine names.
–76^r and 77^r both rubricate **Crystmasse** once each, but other appearances of the word are not rubricated, so the rubrication here, just before Arthur's battle with the giant, is probably meant to indicate the importance of the event and the Arthurian day, not the Christian day. This rubricated emphasis on days or events or things important to Arthur's heroic career is consistent with some of Winchester's larger decorated initials being used for emphasis rather than logical narrative divisions.
–76^v has a rubricated **gesseraunte** and **basnet** where Scribe B clearly failed to recognize what Malory knew to be terms for (respectively) a coat of armour and a helmet. Scribe B may have guessed at the meaning and mistakenly rubricated, or (more likely) Malory may have indicated rubrication because, as a warrior, he knew armour to be important and this battle of Arthur's is especially significant. Named swords are generally rubricated throughout Winchester, but armour only on a few occasions here in Tale II, only with these specialized terms. It is therefore probable that Malory highlighted these terms here to denote Arthur's achievements leading up to being crowned Emperor.
–77^v sees a rubricated **coronal**, and again the implication is that Scribe B does not share Malory's martial vocabulary and knowledge, but that, once again, the rubrication emphasizes the deadly significance of Arthur's combat in the events leading up to his defeat of Rome.
–The rubrication of **Genytrottys** (77^v), on the other hand, may well be a joke on Malory's part to relieve the tension of this deadly battle, or another indication that the scribes did not share Malory's vocabulary, this time his knowledge of French. As the *OED* notes, 'genytrottys' is a Middle English variant of an 'Anglo-Norman and Middle French' term for 'genitals' (*OED*, s.v. 'genitory, n. etymology').

- 79^r has premature rubrication of **Sir** before **Bedwere**.
- 80^v: Scribe B fails to rubricate the second of three named and otherwise rubricated appearances of Gawayne's sword **Galantyne**. See 80^r and 89^r.
- 95^r sees atypical rubrication of **Senatours**, **Cardynalls** and **Poopys** (in 'Poopys hondis'). These terms, too, are not usually rubricated, and their red highlighting here at the moment of Arthur's being crowned Emperor seems designed to add visual grandeur to Arthur's heroic stature.
- 96^r: Scribe B rubricates **Pope** and **Patryarkys**, but not 'cardynalys and senatoures'. 'Pope' is not usually rubricated except for here and 95^r, and the same significance applies here as above.
- 103^v has a rubricated **Pentecoste**, anticipating the reunion of Launcelot and Gaherys and the other Round Table knights Launcelot rescues from Terquyn in the midst of other adventures.
- 127^v sees Scribe B falsely rubricate '**sygamoure** tre', probably due to the similarity of the word to several knights' names, including 'Gryngamoure', Lyonesse's brother.
- 128^v is unusual for having only one rubricated name: a **Bewmaynes**. Most pages rubricate more than one name.
- 135^r sees rubrication of **Pentecoste** as an important occasion on which the coloured knights defeated by Gareth arrive at Arthur's court, thereby confirming both Arthur's – and especially Gareth's – heroic stature.
- 138^v sees Scribe B mistakenly split the minor character Grummor Grummorson into two people, and mistakenly rubricate the conjunction: '**Grummor and Grummorson**'. Cf. 446, infra.

Scribe A

- 191^v has a rubricated eye-skip and substitution error where Scribe A mistakenly wrote in red '**Maledysaunte**', realized his error, negated it, and then wrote in red the proper name **Pendragon**. It looks like the scribe skipped from 'La Cote' to 'damesel' to the damsel's name, no doubt due to the association of La Cote Male Tayle with Maledysaunte.
- 192^v sees Scribe A mistakenly rubricate **Launcelot**, realize his mistake, cross out everything after **La** and then write the proper name in red: **Cote Male Tayle**. This is an easy and obvious error in a scene where both of these knights appear.
- 195^v has a rubrication hangover where Scribe A did not immediately switch back to brown, writing '**Trystram called** unto hym …'. Since the line before has an appearance of the complete rubricated version of **Isode le Blaunche Maynys**, it may be that the scribe here thought that this would be one of those occasions where Trystram's name appeared in full as well.
- 199^r has a rubrication hangover where Scribe A did not immediately switch back to brown, writing '**Brandiles com** to …'.
- 203^v sees Scribe A fail to rubricate one appearance of 'Dagonet', no doubt because Dagonet is a relatively minor character who has only recently reappeared in the story at this point, meaning the name was unfamiliar.
- 207^r sees the scribe mistakenly write another rubricated **Bleoberys**, but immediately cancel it and write (correctly) a rubricated **Trystram**.

–208^v sees Scribe A repeat the tendency from the early folios to rubricate a conjunction joining two knights (**Palomydes and Sir Gaherys**), but unusually also rubricates a **Sir** for '**Sir Dynadan**' in the next line.

–209^r likewise has a premature rubricated 'Sir' before **Sir Collgrevaunce**.

–209^v has a rubricated run-on of 'Sir **Trystram** smote Sir **Kay down** and …'. The next line has a faulty red letter at the beginning of 'rcde' where the opening 'r' and half of the 'o' are rubricated.

–210^r has another premature rubricated 'Sir' before **Sir Gawayne**: clearly the scribes were now comfortable with the rubrication and were anticipating names. They sometimes anticipate wrongly, as A does here, but they are anticipating the rubrication pattern nonetheless.

–210^v has a rubricated dittography: 'Sir **Gawayne** and Sir ~~Gaw~~ **Trystram** …'.

–213^v, 214^v and 221^v each have one instance where the red ink from a character's name is carried over into part of the opening stroke of the next word, which should not be rubricated.

–217^r has another premature rubricated 'Sir' before **Sir Trystram**.

–219^v has another premature rubricated 'Sir' before **Sir Persides**, perhaps here not so much a reflection of rubrication anticipation as an unfamiliar name.

–221^v has a rubrication run-on of '**Trystram was** wroth …'.

–222^v likewise has a rubrication run-on of '**Trystram endu**red …' as well as '**Gaherys what tydyngs**'. There is also a rubricated echo error where initially Scribe A wrote a red **Palomydes**, immediately corrected it and wrote the correct name in red: **Gaherys** (which carries over to the next folio).

–223^v has a rubrication run-on of '**Gaherys ashamed** and …'.

–229^r shows Scribe A being confused by the reappearance of Uwayne, making both textual and rubrication errors in the phrase 'Kyng **Arthure** and Sir **Sir Uwayn** dressed …', where 'Sir' is repeated and once rubricated, and where the opening 'U' is not rubricated.

Scribe B

–242^r has a rubricated eye-skip or echo error where **Dynadan** is mistakenly copied at the end of the line (as it appears at the beginning) before Scribe B immediately realized his error, negated it and wrote a red **Mordrede** instead.

–266^v sees Scribe B fail to rubricate the first of two appearances on this page of 'Aunsyrus', a very minor character who appears only in this scene and on this folio. The second instance is rubricated.

–278^r sees Scribe B fail to rubricate an appearance by Mark.

–279^v sees Scribe B fail to rubricate the last two appearances of Isode.

–280^v shows Scribe B again failing to rubricate an appearance by Isode. Although it may just be simple unconscious error, it is possible that these several errors with this name stem from the fact that sometimes Isode's name is rubricated in full (**La Bealle Isode**) and sometimes it is only her name proper (**Isode**).

–283^v has no rubrication of Mary. Cf. 397^r, infra and 72^r, supra.

–285^v has three non-rubricated instances of 'Isode', although several other appearances on this folio are rubricated.

–290^r again sees Scribe B fail to rubricate two instances of 'Isode'.

–299^r again sees Scribe B fail to rubricate one instance of 'Isode', though others on this folio are in red. Part of the problem may be that much of the action here and at 290 involves fighting and tourneying, and so Isode, as a female non-combatant, is not at the centre of the scribe's attention.

–301^v again sees Scribe B fail to rubricate one appearance of 'Isode', again in the midst of much fighting.

–310 again sees the scribe fail to rubricate two instances of 'Isode' on each side of the folio.

–311^v sees Scribe B fail to rubricate two instances of 'Isode'.

–313^r sees Scribe B fail to rubricate one instance of 'Isode'.

–314^v sees Scribe B fail to rubricate two appearances of 'Isode'.

–315^r sees Scribe B fail to rubricate one instance of 'Isode'.

–318^r is dominated by a dozen rubricated appearances of **Launcelot**, most in the first three-quarters of the page. This seems to have created a substitution or echo error where on one occasion Scribe B mistakenly wrote **Launcelot**, immediately negated it and wrote the proper name, **Palomydes**.

–319 sees Scribe B fail to rubricate one instance of 'Isode' at the bottom of each folio side.

–320^r sees Scribe B fail to rubricate all four instances of 'Isode'. I am unable to explain why Isode's name should not be rubricated more than any other major character unless it is an indication of Scribe B's greater carelessness.

–'Sankgreal' is not rubricated at 322^r.

–324^v has one instance of 'Elayne' that Scribe B failed to rubricate.

–328^v again sees Scribe B failing to rubricate one instance of 'Elayne' and then, in the next line, falsely rubricating **Elayne** before immediately cancelling it and correctly rubricating **Brusen**. Both errors are understandable given the number of times each name appears in this scene.

–331^v sees Scribe B commit a rubricated eye-skip or echo error where **Gawayne** is mistakenly copied and rubricated at the end of the line (as it appears at the beginning) before the scribe immediately realized his error, negated it and correctly wrote a red **Gaherys** instead.

–332^v has a rubricated contamination or miswriting echo error where Scribe B first wrote **Percyvale** before immediately realizing his error, negating it and writing a correct **Persydes** instead. The greater prominence of Percyvale, both in general and on this page, explains the error.

–333^r repeats this ~~Percyvale~~–Persydes error.

–342^v sees rubrication of **Pentecoste**, anticipating Galahad's knighting and his heroic stature.

–343^r likewise sees rubrication of **Pentecoste**, marking the feast that follows Launcelot's recovery from madness and the heroic stature of Trystram, who 'bare the brewte and renowne' whilst Launcelot was incapacitated.

–343^r also sees Scribe B fail to rubricate all but the final appearance of '(La Beale) Isode' on this page.

–334^v is one of those places where 'Sankgreal' is not rubricated (*MD* 643.6).

–344^v has no rubrication of Mary. Cf. 397^r, infra.

Scribe A
- 349^r reveals (for the second-last time) a rubricated **Pentecoste** on the eve of the quest for the Holy Grail, highlighting the importance of the Grail but also of Arthur's court, where the Grail appears and whence the Quest begins.
- 349^v reveals Scribe A being slow to switch inks, missing the opening of Launcelot's name but then catching himself: 'Than seyde Sir La**uncelot**'.
- 351^v has a run-on rubrication with 'cam Kynge **Arthur unto** Sir **Galahad**'. None of the three appearances of 'Sankgreal' at 351^v (*MD* 670.22–671.12) is rubricated.
- 352^v sees Scribe A incorrectly rubricate **aftir** because of a textual error (later corrected) which falsely inserted 'of kynge': 'unto the courte of kyng aftir thys departynge'. Clearly Scribe A thought he was writing 'courte of kyng Arthur' and rubricated accordingly – but erroneously.
- 353^r sees scribal inconsistency in rubricating the Grail: the first appearance of 'Holy Grayle' is not rubricated, but other appearances of **Grayle** or **Sankgreall** are rubricated. Since feast days are inconsistently rubricated in W, it is the significance of the Grail's appearance before Arthur's court that presumably prompts Scribe A to rubricate **Pentecoste** on this folio.
- 353^v does not rubricate 'Sankgreal'.
- 356^v sees Scribe A prematurely rubricate '**Than Joseph** seyde …'.
- 358^v has the first instance of **Sankgreal** missing rubrication in its opening letter.
- 364^v again shows the inconsistent treatment of 'Holy Grayle', which is not rubricated here.
- 365^v has one rubricated and one non-rubricated 'Sankgreal'.
- 365^v also has one **P**ercivale where the opening initial 'P' is not rubricated but the remainder of his name is.
- 366^v sees Scribe A commit not only a line-break error of omission (as Field notes in his Commentary to 703.3), but also a rubrication run-on error of '**Percyvale they** [asked] **hym** . . .'.
- 370^v is unusual for having only one rubricated name, a **Percyvale** about halfway down the page.
- 376^r has an echo or substitution error in its rubricated episodic divisional phrase where the last word should be **Gawayne** but is instead **Launce~**, struck through in what seems to be a thinner stroke and black rather than brown ink (i.e. by a later reader; cf. Field, Commentary to 722.22–3).
- 379^v sees Scribe A twice prematurely rubricate 'Sir' as well as 'Gawayne': **Sir Gawayne**.
- 380^v likewise prematurely rubricates **Sir Prydam le Noyre**: rubrication for 'Sir' as well as the name is atypical.
- 382^r sees the scribe commit a rubrication hangover error, rubricating noun and verb in '**Bors gaffe** hym … '.
- 382^v has no rubrication of Seynte Mary. Cf. 397^r, infra.
- 385^r sees Scribe A repeat this rubrication hangover error, rubricating noun and verb in '**Bors salewede** hym … '. 'Sankgreal' is not rubricated in its first appearance at line 11 of 385^r, but then is rubricated twice near the bottom of the page.
- 386^v sees a premature and run-on rubrication error respectively with '**Sir Lyonell**' and '**Bors kepe** the … '.

–389^r sees the scribe commit a line-break dittography error of 'the/the', but also a rubrication carry-over of '**Galahad þe** / the … '.
–389^v sees a premature rubrication error with '**Sir Galahad**'.
–393^v has no rubrication of 'Virgyne Mary'. Cf. 397^r, infra.
–394^r sees Scribe A fail to rubricate 'Kyng Davith', probably because he is such a minor character in the *Morte*, appearing only in this scene of the Grail Ship and Solomon's bed and sword.
–394^v seemingly interrupts the tale of Solomon and his wife and her preparations of the Grail Ship with an in-text rubricated header or announcement '**Now here ys a wondir tale of kyng Salamon and of hys wyff**'. This phrase is not one of the eighty marginalia proper, nor does it entirely fit on textual-critical grounds, since the Solomon story is largely complete by this point. Field, 'Malory's Own Marginalia', 230, may well be correct that the header was a marginalium-cum-correction in Malory's (messy) holograph that was misinterpreted by the scribes. The Caxton, as Field notes, adopts this header both in the text and as a chapter heading, increasing the likelihood that its exemplar resembled W, or of W's influence on C, or both.
–396^r sees Scribe A commit another post-name rubrication hangover error: **Arthurs courte**.
–397^r again has no rubrication for 'Maydyn Mary' or (several lines later) 'Blyssed Virgyne Mary', partly no doubt because she is not a proper character in the *Morte*, and partly because of the typical lack of rubrication for divine names.
–398^v has no rubrication for 'holy grayle'.
–399^r has a rubricated transitional phrase '**Now turne we to Sir Galahad and to Sir Percivall**' where the knights' names may be a scribal addition, partly for aesthetics in having a fuller red line (see Field, Commentary to 769.10). There is also a missed name towards the bottom of the page, where 'Percivale' should be rubricated.
–400^r sees the scribe commit a dittography error due to premature rubrication, writing 'Sir **Se [Sir] Launcelot du Lake**'. Due to the folio's torn bottom corner, it is impossible to tell whether or not 'Sankgreal' is rubricated on this page.
–400^v has **Sankgreal** missing its rubrication in its opening letter.
–401^v witnesses a premature rubrication error with '**Sir Launcelot**'.
–403^v has a rubricated conjunction in the list of '**Ector, Gawayne and Lyonell**'.
–404^r shows the scribe belatedly changing inks when he fails to rubricate the opening letter of '**Jospeh of Aramathy**'.
–406^r witnesses a stray rubricated conjunction and 'sir' between '**Percivale and Sir Bors**'.
–407^r has another non-rubricated 'Sankgreal'.
–407^v sees 'Sankgreal' not rubricated in its first appearance, but rubricated a few lines later.
–408^r suffers from what might be termed eye-skip rubrication error where the first of two Josephs in the same clause fail to get rubricated: 'I am Joseph, the sonne of **Jospeh of Aramathy**'. This eye-skip mistake may also represent scribal confusion of the two Joseph characters: often 'Joseph of Aramathy' receives inconsistent rubrication, where only the toponym is rubricated, but in

- 410^v has a rubrication hangover error of '**Bors ye**'.
- 411^v has partial scribal error where the first two letters of the final appearance of 'Mador' on this page are not rubricated: 'Ma**dore**'.
- 416^r sees Scribe A fail to rubricate one appearance of 'Pynell', probably because he is a very minor character appearing only three times in the entire *Morte Darthur*, and because many other more recognizable names are rubricated here.
- 418^r has a rubrication hangover or run-on error of '**Lancelot was**'.
- 418^v has the scribe seemingly confused by the toponym of a minor character and uncertain what to rubricate. The result is '**Melyot de** Logrys'.
- 419^{r-v} has a rubricated hangover caused by a scene with many catalogues of knights and a transposition error between 'Lyonell' and 'and': '**Ector de Marys Sir** [page break] **Lyonell** and'.
- 422^v has a premature rubrication error of '**Sir Gawayne**'.
- 423^r has a rubricated hangover of '**Bors was** com'.
- 435^r is unusual for having only one rubricated name: **Arthurs**.
- 435^v sees Scribe A confused about whether or not to rubricate Kay's epithet, so that there is inconsistent rubrication: '**Kay le Senesc**iall'.
- 440^v sees Scribe A correct himself: he starts to write a rubricated '**Mell**' (for 'Mellyagaunt'), realizes his mistake after four letters, crosses these out and copies the correct rubricated name, **Launcelot**.
- 441^r has a premature rubrication error of '**Sir Launcelot**'.
- 441^v witnesses delayed rubrication with a 'La**uncelot**' where the first two letters of the name are not rubricated.
- 443^r sees Scribe A correct himself: he accidentally wrote a rubricated '**Launcelot**', when it should have been **Lavayne**, immediately realized his mistake, cancelled it and inserted the correct rubricated name.
- 445^v again witnesses some confusion over toponyms, with the scribe rubricating '**Urre of** the'.
- 446^v sees Scribe A – or a scribal predecessor – confused by the identity of the very minor Grummor Grummorson and trying to split him into two different knights, mistakenly rubricating the conjunction: '**Grummor and Grummorson**'. Since Scribe B made the same error at 138^v, the confusion was most likely introduced in the manuscript(s) between M and W. See further Field, Commentary to 864.1.
- 447^r has 'La Beall Isode' mistakenly not rubricated in her first appearance in the Urry Catalogue, probably because Scribe A was concentrating on the 103 knights' names in this list.
- 452^v has a delayed rubrication where the first letter of the name is missed: '**Coll**grevance'.
- 462^v witnesses a very small rubrication hangover with the red carried through to opening initial of the following word: '**Lyonell t**horowoute'.
- 465^v witnesses an eye-skip or substitution error in the exchange between Gawayne and Launcelot upon Gwenyvere's return, so Scribe A writes **Gawayne**, negates it and immediately writes the correct name, **Launcelot**.

–480ʳ in the **Mordred-Arthur** dance of death on Salisbury Plain, Mordred's final offbeat name as he falls to the ground is not actually rubricated. There is rubricated hangover error a few lines later, with '**Lucan dep**arted'.

3
Malory's Sacralized Secularity

My overarching thesis in this study is that there is a marked correlation between the central narrative themes of Sir Thomas Malory's *Le Morte Darthur* and the physical layout of that text in its manuscript context in the Winchester manuscript, that Winchester's rubrication pattern is unique, and that the most likely source for Winchester's layout is Malory himself rather than a scribe, patron, reader or printer. Winchester's consistent rubrication of names and its marginalia recording seemingly random knightly deeds all reinforce Malory's predominant focus on the earthly values of knighthood, love and fellowship, and *worshyp*. Even in the 'Tale of the Sankgreal' Malory sacralizes secular chivalry.

My reading of the *Morte Darthur* runs counter to those many critics who argue that Malory eventually castigates chivalry, or that his true focus is religion. D. Thomas Hanks Jr, for instance, claims that Malory and his Arthuriad are deeply religious and that this religiosity is announced by 'six of the more noticeable section breaks' in the *Morte*, intrusive passages where Malory 'emphasize[s] his Christian understanding of the world'.[1] I will examine these breaks and other prayers below, but it is worth pausing for a moment to compare this aspect of *Morte Darthur* to the *Canterbury Tales* and Chaucer's Retraction. Although modern critics are divided on the sincerity and purpose of the Retraction, it is noteworthy that Chaucer explicitly laments his 'unkonnynge', announces his intended 'penitence, confessioun and satisfaccioun', and issues his revocation and retraction of a good many of his works, especially those of his tales 'that sownen into synne'.[2] Malory, in marked contrast, takes nothing back in his *explicits*: he merely asks for release. Religion is present at times in the *Morte*, but knighthood is omnipresent; and Malory never denounces his subject or narrative as sinful.

There are certainly many uses of the word *pray* in Malory's Arthuriad, and many of these uses are religious. Several prominent prayers in the *Morte* are concerned with death and the soul, as with Uther's deathbed announcement that Arthur is his heir and accompanying request that Arthur 'pray for my soule, and … clayme the croune' (C I.3–5; 6.17–23), Balyn and Balan's request that they be

---

[1] See D. Thomas Hanks, Jr, 'Back to the Past', in *Debate*, pp. 285–300 (p. 296); idem, 'Textual Harassment', in *Re-Viewing Le Morte Darthur*, ed. K. S. Whetter and Raluca L. Radulescu (Cambridge, 2005), pp. 27–47 (pp. 28–9); and especially his '"All maner of good love comyth of God"', in *Malory and Christianity*, ed. D. Thomas Hanks Jr and Janet Jesmok (Kalamazoo, 2013), pp. 9–28 (pp. 10–12), which I quote. Hanks's argument is echoed by one of his students, who argues, amongst other things, that Winchester's visual layout emphasizes spiritual concerns: see David Eugene Clark, 'Hearing and Reading Narrative Divisions in the *Morte Darthur*', *Arthuriana* 24.2 (2014): 92–125.

[2] Geoffrey Chaucer, *The Parson's Tale* [and Retraction], in *The Riverside Chaucer*, ed. Larry D. Benson, 3rd edn (Boston, 1987), pp. 288–328 (X.1081–92).

buried together with a memorial to the manner of their deaths on their tomb so that good knights will 'pray for [their] soules' (C II.18; 73.12–27), or Trystram's mother's request that her ladies 'pray [her husband] to be frende to [her] soule' (149^r; 290.21–2). The Fair Maid of Ascolat likewise entreats Launcelot – and Arthur's court, to whom her death-barge letter is publicly read – to 'pray for [her] soule' (429^r; 829.26). After Arthur's death, Bedwere (482^r; 927.28–928.4), Gwenyvere (482^v–483^r; 928.33–929.5), and Launcelot (C XXI.10; 934.21–5) all adopt a life of religion and prayer, both for their own sakes and for Arthur's. Since these episodes all reveal a concern with the welfare of the departed's soul, Karen Cherewatuk is justified to conclude that Malory seems to subscribe to the doctrinal view regarding 'the immortality of the soul and the efficacy of prayer for speeding that soul through the pains of purgatory to heaven'.[3] On the other hand, none of Malory's other characters shares Galahad's unique prayer that 'he myght passe oute of this worlde' (407^r; 785.9–11): Galahad's request is an unusual case because it occurs in the Grail Quest, where typical Arthurian rules do not always apply, and even more so because it comes from Galahad, who is in a special category in both the *Morte Darthur* and its source.

Other prayers in the *Morte* are both sacred and chivalric, as when Percyval prays 'devoutely unto Allmyghty Jesu' after he and Ector fight and wound each other nigh unto death, whereupon they are healed by the Grail (334^{r-v}; 642.12–643.11), or Galahad 'kneled before [an olde] awter and besought God of good counceyle' only to be instructed to seek 'the Castell of **Madyns**, and there do ... away the wycked customes!' (359^r; 687.4–9): told, that is, to undertake chivalric adventure. God or Christ are not infrequently evoked for martial purposes, as when Sir Sadoke says to King Mark, who had earlier killed Alysaundir's father, 'I pray Allmyghty Jesu sende **Alysaundir** myght and power to be revenged uppon the' (263^r; 505.18–19). Less vengeful but no less martial is Bors's and Percyval's entreaty to Galahad: 'in the name of Jesu Cryste, we pray you to gurde you with thys swerde which hath bene desyred so much in the realme of **Logrys**' (395^r; 761.12–14). In all of these cases, the names of Malory's characters are consistently rubricated, his earthly place names are frequently rubricated, and God and Christ are never rubricated.

By far the majority of uses of *pray* in the *Morte*, however, mark more prosaic and perfunctory purposes: requests by characters for physical assistance, or that some unknown knight reveal his identity, or that someone grant someone else the right to pursue an adventure. La Cote Male Tayle provides a representative example when he says to Launcelot, 'I pray you lat me put my body in that adventure' (193^v; 372.3–4). In cases like this – and there are numerous parallels across the Arthuriad as a whole – the prayer is formulaic rather than pious.[4] Perhaps because *pray* more often occurs in secular than spiritual contexts, there are accordingly few instances of *amen* in the *Morte*. Of those relatively few

---

[3] Karen Cherewatuk, 'Christian Rituals in Malory', in *Malory and Christianity*, pp. 77–91 (p. 79).

[4] For other formulaic occurrences of 'pray' see Tomomi Kato, ed., *A Concordance to the Works of Sir Thomas Malory* (Tokyo, 1974), s.v. 'pray', 'prayd', 'prayde', 'praye' and 'prayed'.

appearances of *amen* that do exist, not one in itself denotes a full-scale turn from chivalry to religion on Malory's part.

The first instance of 'Amen', as well as the first authorial prayer for release, is found in the *explicit* to the opening tale (Vinaver's 'Tale of King Arthur'). There is less division here between the close of the plot and the end of this section of narrative than on some other occasions in Malory's Arthuriad, but there is nonetheless a clear close and prayer:

> Here endyth this tale, as the Freynshe booke seyth, fro the maryage of Kynge **Uther** unto Kyng **Arthure** that regned aftir hym and ded many batayles. And this booke endyth whereas Sir **Launcelot** and Sir **Trystrams** com to courte. Who that woll make ony more lette hym seke other bookis of Kynge **Arthure** or of Sir **Launcelot** or Sir **Trystrams**; for this was drawyn by a knyght presoner, Sir **Thomas Malleorré**, that God sende hym good recover. Amen.
> **Explicit** (70ᵛ; 143.29–144.5)

This conclusion clearly asks for Malory's recovery from prison, but equally clearly, especially with the emphasis provided by the rubrication (which occurs in red ink in the manuscript and bold type in my quotations), foregrounds the characters, author and, as a result of the red 'Explicit', the story itself. Neither 'God' nor 'Amen' is so highlighted.

The next 'Amen' is found at the close of 'The Tale of Sir Gareth', together with another prayer for release: 'And I pray you all that redyth this tale to pray for hym that this wrote, that God sende hym good delyveraunce sone and hastely. Amen' (148ʳ; 288.10–12). This prayer, including 'God', is not rubricated. In Winchester, the prayer is followed (after a blank line) by the closing *explicit* 'Here endyth the tale of Sir **Gareth of Orkeney**'. This *explicit* further pushes the prayer to the background by using rubrication to foreground the character, and thus the tale, of Gareth. P. J. C. Field emends the wording of the ending, arguing that a scribal error rearranged the order of the *explicit* and Malory's personal interjection, and that the latter should come last.[5] Significantly, however, whether we follow Winchester's or Field's arrangement of the text, the rest of the conclusion to the tale highlights human character and agency, not divinity, reminding readers and listeners how this section of the narrative closes when 'Sir **Gareth of Orkeney** ... wedded Dame **Lyonesse** ... And ... Sir **Gaheris** wedded ... Dame **Lyonette**, ... and Sir **Aggravayne** wedded Dame **Lawrell**' (148ʳ; 288.3–6). No part of the prayer proper is rubricated.

The same is true of the opening of Tale V at the top of the verso page, where the rubrication emphasizes Trystram and his principal foe: 'Here begynnyth the Fyrste Boke of Syr **Trystrams de Lyones**, ... and how he was made knyght of Kynge **Marke of Cornuayle**' (148ᵛ; 289.2–5). There is no *amen* in this 'Trystram' *incipit*, but Malory does later interrupt his narrative to praise Trystram as the fount of 'all the good termys of venery and of huntynge', exhorting 'all maner jantylmen ... to prayse Sir **Trystram** and to pray for his soule. Amen, sayde Sir **Thomas Malleorré**' (280ᵛ; 538.34–539.9).[6] Although the prayer for Trystram's

---

[5] Commentary to 288.1–3.
[6] The idea of Trystram establishing hunting terms was clearly important to Malory, for he makes a similar claim earlier in Tale V (293.12–25). Both statements are original. See further

soul sounds genuine, so too is Malory's general praise for Trystram's earthly *worshyp* and the joys of the hunt; no mention is made of God's worship or the joys of religion. Once again, the rubrication foregrounds both Trystram and Malory, the human, not divine.

There are two further *amens* at the close of Tale V (346ᵛ; 664.9–18). The first is in the *explicit* 'Here endyth the Secunde Boke off Syr **Trystram de Lyones**, whyche drawyn was oute of Freynshe by Sir **Thomas Malleorré**, knyght, as Jesu be hys helpe. Amen.' The second is when the *explicit* immediately transitions to an announcement-cum-*incipit* of what is to follow: 'But here ys no rehersall of the Thirde Booke. But here folowyth the noble tale off the **Sankegreall** ... and the sygnyfycacion of the Blyssed Bloode off Oure Lorde Jesu Cryste, whyche was brought into thys londe by **Joseph off Aramathye**. Therefore on all synfull, Blyssed Lorde, have on thy knyght mercy. Amen.' The twofold prayer is striking, though whether it is genuine piety or merely a formulaic reflection of the length of the 'Trystram', which occupies 198 of Winchester's 484 surviving folios, is harder to determine. The rubricated emphasis of **Trystram**, **Malleorré**, **Sankegreall** and **Joseph** may well indicate the way in which humanity, for Malory, will bridge chivalry and religion in the upcoming Grail tale (Tale VI). Although the associations between the Grail and Christ warrant the second prayer in the 'Trystram' *explicit*-cum-'Sankgreal' *incipit*, it does not follow that Malory presents the Grail as a holy relic because of his 'personal devotion'.[7] I do not think we are justified in claiming a turn to religion over chivalry here. I would also emphasize once again that none of the religious terms in this colophon are rubricated, only the author, his characters and the object those characters will soon seek.

If Malory truly intended either 'The Sankgreal' or the *Morte* to reflect his own supposed piety, or wanted readers to reject chivalry in favour of religion, we might expect there to be fewer battles and tournaments, a more obvious Chaucer-like retraction of events and greater *mise-en-page* emphasis on religious language. We might expect, for instance, that phrases such as 'for Crystes love of Hevyn' would appear in frequent rubricated prayers; but this is not so.[8] In fact, this exact phrase appears only once in the *Morte Darthur*, in the very non-religious context of the war council which opens Tale II, when Arthur 'for Crystes love of hevyn' seeks the necessary 'counceyle' that will enable him to fight a just but bloody war against Rome, thereby mimicking the feats of his ancestors – in Winchester, his rubricated ancestors – **Belyne**, **Bryne** and **Constantyne** (71ᵛ; 147.17–21). The single instance of the phrase 'for thy Kynges love of Hevyn' is likewise not a religious or rubricated maxim, but an exclamation of martial fellowship uttered by Pryamus in requiring Gawayne's true identity (90ʳ; 179.2).

The similar phrase 'Oure Lady of Hevyn' likewise occurs only once, albeit in a moment of both sacred and secular sentiment when Malory records how Trystram's mother 'by myracle of Oure Lady of hevyn ... was delyverde' of her child (149ʳ; 290.11–12). Significantly, the Blessed Virgin is not rubricated, whereas

---

Vinaver, Commentary to 375.12–29 and 682.26–683.4; and my 'Inks and Hands and Fingers in the Manuscript of Malory's *Morte Darthur*', *Speculum* (forthcoming).

[7] *Contra* P. J. C. Field, 'Malory and the Grail', in *The Grail, the Quest and the World of Arthur*, ed. Norris J. Lacy (Cambridge, 2008), pp. 141–55.

[8] For the frequency of the phrases that follow I have benefitted from Kato's *Concordance*, s.v.

Melyodas, **Elyzabeth** and **Trystrams** are so highlighted. Likewise, the expression 'Fayre Lorde of Hevyn' occurs just once in the *Morte Darthur*, in the prayer 'Fayre Lorde of Hevyn, helpe and save Thy new-made knyght!' (358^r; 684.31–2). The prayer, significantly, is again for success and safety in battle, and follows Melyas's entreaty to Galahad, 'I pray you lette me have that adventure' (357^v; 684.17). It is the names **Melyas** and **Galahad** that are repeatedly rubricated on this folio (eight and six times respectively, plus a marginalium), not the Lord, and the prayer is unanswered. Melyas's injury no doubt reflects the fact that he sinned by ignoring the warnings of the inscribed cross and Sir Galahad, but the rubrication and marginalium still foreground earthly knights and earthly adventures more than orthodox piety. Launcelot's 'avision' denouncing his own sin during the Grail Quest is likewise bookmarked by one of Winchester's marginalia, but when the 'man [wyth] a crowne of golde' and his fellows kneel, lift up their hands to heaven and pray 'Swete Fadir of Hevyn, ... yelde unto everych of us as we have deserved', what is rubricated is the name and person of **Launcelot**, not the prayer or our Sweet Lord (373^r; 717.6–24). The same thematic and bibliographic emphasis on plot and character is found in the heartfelt prayer of thanks Bors makes to celebrate his escape from the trap of the suicidal (and lusty) ladies: having 'blyssed hys body and hys vysayge' between the deaths of the ladies and the disappearance of the tower, Bors then raises both hands to Heaven to pray, 'Fayre swete lorde, Fadir and God in hevyn, I am grevously ascaped!' (384^v–385^r; 740.28–35). This is a significant moment in Bors's Grail adventures, but whilst there is no doubting the sincerity of his prayer, it is, as always, Malory's characters who are rubricated, not God. In these and other ways, Malory foregrounds human character and deed, sacralizing secular adventure.

Although the preceding discussion does not cite every prayer in the Arthuriad, my examples are representative of the whole. Malory's language and themes consistently foreground Arthurian knighthood and earthly *worshyp*. Accordingly, the Winchester manuscript consistently rubricates human names, but not divine ones; prayers and religious language are not typically rubricated. In fact, only two prayers in 484 folios receive red ink: one closes Tale VI, and one introduces the final tale, Tale VIII. Malory concludes the 'Tale of the Sankgreal' with the following passage:

> Thus endith the Tale of the **Sankgreal**, that was breffly drawyn oute of Freynshe into Englysshe – which ys a tale cronycled for one of the trewyst and of the holyest that ys in thys worlde – by Sir **Thomas Maleorré, knyght. O Blessed Jesu, helpe hym thorow hys myght! Amen.** (409^r; 789.14–18)

As with the transition between Tales V and VI quoted above, the *explicit* to Tale VII morphs into the *incipit* for Tale VIII. Malory introduces the final tale by noting how he will 'overlepe grete bookis of Sir **Launcelot**' and his adventures as the Knight of the Cart. Claiming that he has 'loste the very mater of le Shevalere de Charyot', Malory therefore promises to

> departe frome the tale of Sir **Launcelot**; and here I go unto the Morte **Arthur**, and that caused Sir **Aggravayne**. And here on the othir syde folowyth 'The Moste Pyteuous Tale of the Morte **Arthure saunz Gwerdon**,' par

le Shyvalere Sir Thomas Malleorré, Knyght. Jesu, ayedé ly pur voutre mercy! Amen. (449^r; 869.1–17)

For Hanks, these colophons and their red-ink prayers exemplify 'Explicitly Christian' devices by which 'Malory signals his own presence as author, and moreover his presence as a Christian author engaging in a Christian act'.[9] Taken out of context, the red ink in these two passages does appear to emphasize prayer, but it equally obviously emphasizes Malory as author and knight. I thus agree about the authorial self-identification in these *explicits*. Given, however, that many of Malory's prayers are formulaic, that his characters' prayers are even more frequently perfunctory and that prayers in general are not rubricated in the *Morte* as a whole, including the prayer which closes the opening tale (70^v), I cannot accept the remainder of Hanks's argument.

Interestingly, in Winchester as it stands today, Malory's announcement that the final tale will start 'here on the othir syde' is ignored. Instead of beginning on the verso, Tale VIII starts a mere two blank lines below the colophon, still on the recto. The Caxton, in contrast, does leave nearly half a blank page after the *explicit*, beginning the final tale on a new page.[10] The fact that Caxton was willing to waste valuable paper in this way suggests perhaps that the exemplar did start Tale VIII on a new page. Even in Winchester, both the promised layout and the actual one are significant. Despite some critical debate about the precise number and location of narrative divisions in *Morte Darthur*, there is a clear narrative break in folio 449^r's *explicit*-cum-*incipit*, a break that occurs on both the bibliographic and textual levels. Part of that break is announced by the fact that the entire opening line of the promised 'Morte Arthure saunz Gwerdon' is rubricated and written in a slightly larger script. (See Plate XIII.) The red ink of the *explicit*'s prayer is thus simply a prelude to more red ink (in the *incipit*) rather than a stand-alone item of religious importance. Nor does Tale VIII's famous opening sentence, with its rubricated 'In May, whan every harte floryshyth and burgenyth', have anything to do with religion. Whether Malory wished particularly to highlight the final tale and its destruction of the worshipful Round Table, the fact that the May topos will now lead to hatred and slaughter rather than love, or perhaps both, this is the only tale in Winchester where the entire opening line is rubricated.[11] Given Malory's concern to establish narrative links between the tales, especially the early tales and later ones,[12] it is I think significant for Winchester's *ordinatio*

---

[9] Hanks, '"All maner of good love"', in *Malory and Christianity*, pp. 10–11.

[10] I am indebted to the Morgan Library for allowing me to examine their incunable directly, but the page break is readily viewable in the facsimile *Le Morte D'Arthur Printed by William Caxton*, 1485, intro. Paul Needham (London, 1976), sigs aa5^v–6^r. The only other half-page blank in the Caxton occurs between Caxton's Preface and his contents-rubric (sig. iiii^{r-v}). Quarter-page textual blanks occur between the 'Gareth' and 'Trystram' and Chapters 16–17 of the 'Sankgreal' (sigs p7^v–p8^r and R7^v). A single third of a page is blank between the Grail adventures of Percyval and Launcelot at C XIV.14–15 (sig. P7^r). All other pages are as full as possible.

[11] The openings of 'The Weddyng' (35^r), the episode of post-wedding adventures (45^r), Tale VI (349^r) and Tale VII (409^v) emphasize their first lines with more pronounced ascenders, a more elaborate or slightly larger script, and a larger Lombard initial. 'The Sankgreal' is further offset for having the only blue Lombard in Winchester.

[12] For narrative links across the *Morte Darthur*, see especially Murray J. Evans, 'Ordinatio and Narrative Links', in *Studies*, pp. 29–52.

that the only other tale that rubricates most of its opening line is the Roman War (Tale II at 71ʳ). Arthur's moment of greatest triumph in his defeat of Rome early in the *Morte* is thereby visually linked to – and contrasted with – his moment of death and the destruction of all he loved in the 'Morte Arthure' proper.

In light of all the ways in which neither Malory's Arthuriad nor its manuscript *ordinatio* prioritize prayer, there are two further personal and secular elements to consider regarding 'The Sankgreal' *explicit*. First is Helen Cooper's astute observation that, in Winchester, 'the last thirteen words are written in [slightly] larger letters, and may be intended to be read as a rhyming tag:

> By Sir Thomas Malory, knight.
> O blessed Jesu, help him through His might.[13]

The rhyme may be doggerel, but it nevertheless effectively and noticeably draws attention to Malory himself. In terms of the overall continuity or coherence of the *Morte Darthur*, it is significant that the entire Arthuriad closes with an extension of the same rhyme:[14]

> by Sir Thomas Maleoré, knyght,
> as Jesu helpe hym for Hys grete myght,
> as he is the servaunt of Jesu bothe day and nyght. (C XXI.13; 940.28–30)

Malory here invokes Jesus and asks readers to pray for his 'soule', but he also asks for 'good delyveraunce' (940.23–5). As Amy S. Kaufman notes, the 'knight-prisoner, far from expressing guilt or repentance, seems resigned but not necessarily contrite, as though his imprisonment is subject to conditions beyond his control'.[15]

This practical element of Malory's prayer is my second point. The two rhyming tags in the sixth and last colophons each reinforce the very utilitarian nature of Malory's prayers. Malory prays for, and asks readers to pray for, his physical release. Such prayers were no doubt genuine, but Malory's desire to escape from prison was equally genuine, for we know from biographical details that Malory was not afraid to work his own earthly and physical actions to gain such freedom, repeatedly escaping from gaol under his own auspices, or failing to return from legitimate but short-term releases.[16] Equally, as we have seen, Malory's colophons and prayers, including the Grail *explicit*, act as self-reflexive nods to Malory's authorship and the artistic merits of his Arthuriad. The secular and sacred often intertwine in the Middle Ages, and Malory puts faith in both his own actions and readers' prayers. The authorial self-reflection of Malory's *explicits* is all the more pronounced if the earlier abbreviations of 'M' in the opening 'Tale of

---

[13] Helen Cooper, ed., *Le Morte Darthur* (Oxford, 1998), p. 556, note to p. 402 of her edition. I quote Cooper's layout as well as language, including that she does not bold-rubricate the phrase in question.

[14] I evoke Brewer's notion of the *Morte*'s overall 'cohesion': D. S. Brewer, '"the hoole book"', in *Essays*, pp. 41–63 (esp. p. 42). See also n. 12, above. W breaks off before the final colophon.

[15] Amy S. Kaufman, '"For This was Drawyn by a Knyght Presoner', in *Prison Narratives from Boethius to Zana*, ed. Philip Edward Phillips (New York and Basingstoke, 2014), pp. 35–55 (p. 36).

[16] On Malory's imprisonments and sundry escapes, see P. J. C. Field, *The Life and Times of Sir Thomas Malory* (Cambridge, 1993), pp. 105–25.

King Arthur' do indeed stand for 'Malory' as well as 'Merlin'.[17] According to Seth Lerer, Chaucer in the fifteenth century becomes part of an historicized '"laureate" poetics'.[18] Malory is one fifteenth-century reader and writer who almost certainly knew Chaucer's work, and it is just possible that, whilst being less involved with authorial self-fashioning than was Chaucer, Malory too possessed a keen artistic purpose and sense of his own Arthuriad and his own literary reputation.[19] We might well connect this authorial awareness to Edward Donald Kennedy's argument that the prayer-*explicits* in Malory's Arthuriad, *explicits* excised by Caxton, function as 'pleas for help' indicative of Malory's 'hope for release from prison', possibly by writing a text that would find favour with the king.[20]

Caxton's excision of Malory's *explicits* is the most immediately obvious of his changes to the text of Malory's *Morte Darthur*, though even a brief perusal of the Roman War narrative quickly reveals that Caxton reduced that portion of the narrative – Caxton's fifth tale, Vinaver's (and now Field's) Tale II – by more than half. It is generally held that Caxton's narrative divisions of Malory's *Morte Darthur* add to the story's unity. Vinaver famously insisted that these divisions were an imposition on Malory's 'eight separate romances', but Vinaver's complaint necessarily sees the divisions as unifying what Vinaver considered to be Malory's disparate works.[21] Sally Shaw concurs that Caxton's book and chapter divisions make a more 'coherent whole' out of Malory's 'eight separate romances found in the Winchester MS'.[22] N. F. Blake similarly argues that Caxton's 'modifications' to Malory's text 'tended towards unity and order', an increased focus on Arthur, and a moralistic emphasis on chivalry and Christianity.[23] Indeed, for all of the disagreement amongst critics regarding the exact relationship between Winchester and the Caxton and who may or may not have modified the Roman War narrative, it is a commonplace to read that Caxton's changes to the overall story emphasize chivalry, Arthur and Christianity. It is one of my central contentions in this study that the physical layout of the Winchester manuscript, especially its consistent rubrication of characters' names throughout the *Morte Darthur*, likewise provides just such a unity by consistently drawing attention to certain important thematic strands in the narrative. The crucial difference, however, is that Winchester's *ordinatio* draws attention to Arthur and the Round Table Fellowship in ways that emphasize, celebrate and elegize their earthly characters, deeds and loves. The focus is thus on secular knighthood, secular

---

[17] See Chapter Two, pp. 61, 88–9. Merlin's name is abbreviated to 'M' at W fols 10^r; 15^v; 17^v; 18^{r-v}; 20^{r-v}; 21^r; 26^v; 27^{r-v}; 28^{r-v}; 34^r; 35^v; 36^r; 37^{r-v}; 39^v; 41^v; 44^r; 45^{r-v}; 49^r.
[18] Seth Lerer, *Chaucer and His Readers* (Princeton, 1993).
[19] On Malory's familiarity with Chaucer see Earl R. Anderson, 'Malory's "Fair Maid of Ascolat"', *Neuphilologische Mitteilungen* 87.2 (1986): 237–54 (243–4); P. J. C. Field, 'Malory's Minor Sources', in his *Texts and Sources*, pp. 27–31 (29–30); and especially Ralph Norris's careful articulation of Malory's minor sources in *Malory's Library* (Cambridge, 2008), pp. 6, 10, 36–9, 104–5, 124–6, 130–6, 156, 162–5.
[20] Edward Donald Kennedy, 'Malory's Use of Hardyng's *Chronicle*: A Reconsideration', *West Virginia University Philological Papers* 54 (2011): 8–15 (10).
[21] Vinaver, pp. xxxv–li (quotation from p. xxxix; repeated at p. xlii).
[22] Sally Shaw, 'Caxton and Malory', in *Essays*, pp. 114–45 (pp. 118 and 142–3).
[23] N. F. Blake, *Caxton and His World* (London, 1969), pp. 109–13 (p. 109).

deeds and secular living, not religion.²⁴ This is also the real focus, I hope to show, of Malory himself, but – significantly – Winchester visually reinforces the principal thematic strands and chivalric display that the text narrates.

Secular vs Sacred Grail Readings

For over a generation now the dominant scholarly reading of Malory's *Morte Darthur* considers 'The Tale of the Sankgreal' (Caxton's Books XIII–XVII; Vinaver's Tale VI) to be the turning point in the narrative, one which seems to confirm and condemn the failures and weaknesses supposedly hinted at by the factionalism that rears its head in the 'Boke off Syr Trystram'. 'The Tale of the Sankgreal', so it is said, thus emphasizes the Round Table's sins and failures, forecasting the ultimate collapse of the earthly Arthurian fellowship, and the possible transformation of those few individuals who are able to redeem themselves. In light of the Grail's associations with Christ, such sins, however much they vary in nature and number from one scholarly argument to the next, nevertheless are clearly defined by Christian ethics and doctrine. Vinaver had argued contrariwise, stating categorically that Malory's purpose in 'The Sankgreal' was 'to secularize the Grail theme as much as the story will allow'.²⁵ Vinaver's position eventually garnered qualified support from Larry D. Benson, and largely unqualified and highly detailed support from Sandra Ness Ihle.²⁶ Vinaver's position could easily be undermined, however, by his own insistence on the *Morte*'s lack of unity, an argument that could isolate 'The Sankgreal' and much of its meaning – whatever that meaning might be – from the remainder of the Arthuriad as a whole. It is, moreover, the curse of scholarly giants – and Vinaver was certainly such a figure – that those critics coming in the giant's wake attempt to topple the giant, or at least highlight those important factors overlooked by the giant. Consequently, in the years following the publication of Vinaver's *The Works of Sir Thomas Malory*, Malory scholars challenged, amongst much else, Vinaver's views on Malory's Grail Quest. So it is that the predominant scholarly interpretations of the *Morte* today run counter to Vinaver's claims for this tale. My aim in this chapter is to continue Vinaver's secular reading of the 'Tale of the Sankgreal', but to do so in ways which highlight 'The Sankgreal's' continuities with the rest of the *Morte Darthur* rather than its isolation or dissimilarities. But first we must remind ourselves of the opposing perspective.

An early, persuasive but amicable challenge to the notion of a more earthly *Morte Darthur* was mounted by C. S. Lewis, who argued that the entire *Morte* expects knights to act, and judges knights, by strong Christian ethics.²⁷ It remained, however, for the contributors to the deservedly influential *Malory's Originality* to

---

²⁴ Throughout this study I use 'secular' in the sense of 'Belonging to the world and its affairs' or 'belonging to the present or visible world as distinguished from the eternal or spiritual world': see *OED*, secular, adj. and n., 2a and 3a. I do not use 'secular' to mean 'irreligious'.
²⁵ Vinaver, Commentary, p. 1535.
²⁶ Larry D. Benson, *Malory's Morte Darthur* (Cambridge, Mass., 1976); Sandra Ness Ihle, *Malory's Grail Quest* (Madison, Wis., 1983).
²⁷ C. S. Lewis, 'The English Prose *Morte*', in *Essays*, pp. 7–28 (esp. pp. 16–17).

give particular prominence to the sinful failures of Malory's knights, an argument which recurs in various guises and essays throughout the collection.[28] This essentially moralistic and Christian interpretation of the *Morte* seemingly gains support by comparison with the Vulgate and Post-Vulgate Cycles, which *do* link Arthur's downfall to sin, failure and punishment. As the Post-Vulgate Arthur himself admits, 'Our Lord shows me clearly that it pleases Him to make me live this little time I have left in grief and sadness, for just as He wished – and was able – to raise me up through many beautiful adventures and without my deserving it, so is he now able to bring me down through cruel and evil adventures *because of my deserving and my sin.*'[29] This view of Arthurian chivalry being destroyed by sin and Christian failure has accordingly been repeatedly applied to Malory's *Morte Darthur* and reiterated over the years by scholars from a wide array of theoretical persuasions. The corollary of this argument is that Malory and his text ultimately espouse Christian over earthly or chivalric concerns. Thus Hanks unequivocally states that, 'From the Grail Quest on, Malory's work is heavily Christian.'[30] Corinne Saunders aptly summarizes this way of thinking when she similarly insists that, by the tragic close of the *Morte*, 'Only individual spirituality can redeem the sense of waste and loss. The final pages of the *Morte* … return to a firmly Christian perspective.'[31]

Chivalry itself is likewise still often – if not entirely accurately – considered automatically deeply Christian,[32] but usually this emphasis on the religiosity of the *Morte* is used to buttress the view that Malory is interrogating or condemning earthly chivalry. At the very least, so the argument goes, we are meant to see a new set of values in place for the conclusion of the *Morte*. By such accounts as these, Malory mimics the Vulgate or *Lancelot-Graal* Cycle in ultimately rejecting Arthurian chivalry in favour of God and religion. Thus, for Charles Moorman, the Grail announces and symbolizes the many sinful failures of earthly Arthurian chivalry and society (see note 28, above). Edmund Reiss similarly argues for a

---

[28] Most relevant here is Charles Moorman, '"The Tale of the Sankgreall"', in *Originality*, pp. 184–204. Moorman's chapter is a revision of his 'Malory's Treatment of The Sankgreall', *PMLA* 71.3 (1956): 496–509, and it appears again in slightly different form but with the same thesis and essential argument in Moorman's *The Book of Kyng Arthur* (Lexington, 1965), pp. 28–48. I cite the version from *Originality* because of the influence of the collection as a whole, including that of Moorman.

[29] 'Nosso Senhor, que praz que vi[v]a en doo e en tristeza este pouco que ey de viver, e bem mo mostra: que asi como el quis e foy poderoso de me erguer per muy fremossas aventuras e sen meu merecimento, bem assi e poderoso de me dirribar per aventuras feas e mas, *per meu mericimento e per meu pecado*': cited from Fanni Bogdanow, 'The Changing Vision of Arthur's Death', in *Dies Illa*, ed. Jane H. M. Taylor (Liverpool, 1984), pp. 107–23 (pp. 121–2, n. 68); translation from *The Post-Vulgate, Part III: The Death of Arthur*, trans. Martha Asher in *Lancelot-Grail*, ed. Norris J. Lacy, 5 vols (New York and London, 1993–96), Vol. V, ch. 156, p. 304; my emphasis.

[30] D. Thomas Hanks Jr, '"A Far Green Country Under a Swift Sunrise"', *Fifteenth-Century Studies* 36 (2011): 49–64 (55). Cf. Charles W. Whitworth, 'The Sacred and the Secular in Malory's *Tale of the Sankgreal*', *Yearbook of English Studies* 5 (1975): 19–29 (28–9).

[31] Corinne Saunders, 'Religion and Magic', in *The Cambridge Companion to the Arthurian Legend*, ed. Elizabeth Archibald and Ad Putter (Cambridge, 2009), pp. 201–17 (p. 214). Cf. Wilfred L. Guerin, '"The Tale of the Death of Arthur"', in *Originality*, pp. 233–74 (233 and 269–74). This view is problematized by Saunders's preceding argument (p. 213), that the supernatural elements surrounding Arthur's death are firmly non-Christian.

[32] For a detailed rejoinder see Richard W. Kaeuper, *Holy Warriors* (Philadelphia, 2009).

disconnect between Malory's 'Sankgreal' and what has gone before, so that previous Arthurian values and actions 'are not only negated but shown as wrong'; the lesson, urges Reiss, is to emulate Galahad by turning away from 'earthly things' in favour of 'Heavenly Jerusalem'.[33] Lawrence Besserman tackles the subject from a different angle, but his analysis of 'biblical analogies' and their significance to the *Morte* likewise rests upon the belief that 'Malory's most "secular" theme is illicit, adulterous love'.[34] Even Larry D. Benson, who does much to elucidate the secular nature of Malory's 'Sankgreal' as well as the complexity of Malory's art, nevertheless states categorically that Malory's *Morte Darthur* is partly 'a tragedy' brought about by 'Arthur and his knights suffering the just consequences of their own sins'.[35] Dorsey Armstrong, approaching the Grail and the *Morte* from different theoretical paradigms than these earlier critics, nonetheless likewise accepts that Malory's Grail Quest offers a spiritual test of secular chivalry, a test that most of the community fails.[36] As a final example of this view, consider Hanks and Janet Jesmok's bold claim that 'Christianity is omnipresent in the *Morte*', or Besserman's sustained argument that 'the *Morte* is pervaded by biblical analogies' that intertwine religious and chivalric codes in Malory's narrative to 'problematize the chivalric ethos of the *Morte*'.[37] This argument that Christianity ultimately supersedes chivalry in the *Morte Darthur*, however, ignores Malory's consistent emphasis on the human honour and human tragedy attendant upon Arthurian knighthood. Winchester's rubrication and marginalia, I contend, help to foreground and memorialize Malory's narrative and thematic focus on the enduring value of earthly chivalry.

A long-standing variation on the religious reading of the *Morte Darthur*, one which is given slightly different emphases depending on which critic one reads, is the argument that Malory's 'Tale of the Sankgreal' is less ascetic and condemnatory than its source, but that it remains a 'spiritual' tale in which Launcelot is depicted as a great knight but still a sinner, and thus 'not as good a knight as he should be'.[38] Building on this alternative reading, a recurring theme of recent criticism posits that the *Morte* is both secular and religious. The notion that the Middle Ages often blends the sacred with the secular (or vice versa) has much to recommend it, not only because of the prominence of the Church in mediaeval society but because various examples from chivalry, from the Church itself or

---

[33] Edmund Reiss, *Sir Thomas Malory* (New York, 1966), pp. 122 and 151.
[34] Lawrence Besserman, *Biblical Paradigms in Medieval English Literature from Cædmon to Malory* (New York and London, 2012), pp. 113–14. See also Besserman, pp. 123 and 125.
[35] Benson, *Malory's Morte Darthur*, p. 208. This tragic arc is what Benson sees as the *Morte*'s 'historical structure'; but, for Benson, Malory conjoins this historical thread with a 'thematic "comic" narrative ... that leads to the vindication of Arthurian chivalry' (p. 209).
[36] Dorsey Armstrong, *Gender and the Chivalric Community in Malory's Morte d'Arthur* (Gainesville, 2003), pp. 144–72. This argument is reiterated in her 'The (Non-)Christian Knight in Malory', *Arthuriana* 16.2 (2006): 30–4.
[37] D. Thomas Hanks Jr and Janet Jesmok, 'Introduction', in *Malory and Christianity*, pp. 1–8 (p. 1); Besserman, *Biblical Paradigms*, pp. 113 and 122. On biblical and Malorian parallels see also Kevin T. Grimm, 'Sir Thomas Malory's Narrative of Faith', *Arthuriana* 16.2 (2006):16–20.
[38] See (for the first quotation) Whitworth, 'Sacred and Secular', 20; (for the second quotation) Mary Hynes-Berry, 'Malory's Translation of Meaning', *Studies in Philology* 74 (1977): 243–57 (245). See also Lewis, 'The English Prose *Morte*', in *Essays*, pp. 14–20.

from literature, all reveal a complex synthesis of the sacred and profane.[39] This synthesis is even apparent in funerary monuments.[40] The problem with many of the current 'both ... and' approaches to Malory, however, is not the duality of the argument but the fact that many critics inevitably contradict themselves by privileging either earthly or celestial chivalry over the alternative; invariably it is celestial chivalry that wins out. Hence Kenneth Hodges's belief that the episodes of the Poisoned Apple and Healing of Sir Urry 'potentially' offer an *alternative* vision of *Christian* knighthood'.[41] Hence, too, Mahoney's statement about success in celestial matters being 'fully achievable only by withdrawal from the world'.[42] Likewise Raluca L. Radulescu forcefully but unsuccessfully tries to marry both views, claiming first that the 'Tale of the Sankgreal' reveals 'Malory's orthodox view of religion', followed immediately by the claim that 'Malory subordinates religious values to chivalric ones.'[43] Radulescu also argues that worshipful knights must subordinate themselves 'to both an earthly lord and God', that Malory seems to suggest that 'being the best knight of the world requires some degree of sinfulness' and – tellingly – that 'the phrase "best knight of the world" does not refer to religious perfection, but ... to the field of chivalric prowess'.[44] Hanks similarly argues (in part) that Malory presents the love of Launcelot and Gwenyvere as noble but adulterous and sinful, therefore requiring the lovers' penance and God's forgiveness. But because the lovers do repent and because God accordingly does grant grace and forgiveness, what Hanks and others consider to be Malory's tragedy of sinful failure is ultimately transformed into a tale of divine love, 'Christian redemption' and 'a Christian comedy'.[45]

As I hope to illustrate, however, Malory and his text consistently reveal that actions that Malory or his characters deem to be noble or worshipful should not necessarily be repented. Such actions frequently do have good and bad consequences, and they do in fact help to secure tragedy. But neither the tragedy nor the characters are sinful in Malory's eyes. Nor is Arthurian knighthood a failure. My claims are not always true of the sources; it is important to remember, however, that the fact that a plot event or scholarly interpretation holds true of the sources does not make it axiomatically true of Malory's *Morte Darthur*. Source-study, for all the manifest benefits it brings to the interpretation of Malory's Arthuriad, can occasionally lead readers astray. I thus intend to show that Malory's principal

---

[39] For some examples, see Maurice Keen, *Chivalry* (New Haven, 1984); Kaeuper, *Holy Warriors*; R. W. Southern, *Western Society and the Church in the Middle Ages* (London, 1970); Eamon Duffy, *The Stripping of the Altars*, 2nd edn (New Haven, 2005); Nicole R. Rice, *Lay Piety and Religious Discipline in Middle English Literature* (Cambridge, 2008).

[40] See Nigel Saul, *English Church Monuments in the Middle Ages* (Oxford, 2009); idem, *For Honour and Fame* (London, 2011), pp. 283–304.

[41] Kenneth Hodges, 'Haunting Pieties', *Arthuriana* 17.2 (2007): 28–48 (28; my emphases).

[42] Dhira B. Mahoney, 'The Truest and Holiest Tale', in *Studies*, pp. 109–28 (p. 123).

[43] Raluca L. Radulescu, 'Malory and the Quest for the Holy Grail', in *A Companion to Arthurian Literature*, ed. Helen Fulton (Oxford and Malden, 2009), pp. 326–39 (pp. 327–8, 333–4).

[44] Raluca L. Radulescu, 'Malory's Lancelot and the Key to Salvation', *Arthurian Literature* 25 (2008): 93–118 (at 93, 98 and 111).

[45] Hanks, '"All maner of good love"', in *Malory and Christianity*, pp. 9–28. Cf. the similar thesis (with different evidence) of Corey Olsen, 'Adulterated Love', also in *Malory and Christianity*, pp. 29–55. Besserman, *Biblical Paradigms*, pp. 124–7 and 132–3, also subscribes to this view of the *Morte* as a sort of divine comedy.

secular subject and theme is not adultery (*contra* Besserman), nor sinful failure (*contra* Moorman et al.), but the entirely laudable winning of earthly *worshyp*. This includes a focus on the kinds of characters and deeds interested in and deserving of worship. The tragic pathos and power of Malory's *Morte Darthur* rest precisely on the fact that Malory's greatest characters are tragic yet worshipful. The *Morte Darthur* is not a testament to sinful failure, but an illustration that heroic glory, tragedy and destruction are very often intricately bound together. It is for these reasons, I contend, that the rubrication and marginalia in the Winchester manuscript help to emphasize key themes and narrative movements in the *Morte* in ways that memorialize secular heroic knighthood and human greatness.

Malory's personal piety is hard to pin down: he may uphold the ingrained and knowingly devout Christian piety typical of late mediaeval England, or he may typify those members of the knightly class or gentry who used religion to their own purposes. Edward Hicks long ago suggested that Malory had Lollard sympathies, though Hicks felt that these sympathies were 'political rather than doctrinal'. Nevertheless, Hicks can justifiably note Malory's attacks on Coombe Abbey, as well as Newbold Revel's close proximity to such militantly Lollard 'hot-beds' as Coventry and Lutterworth, the latter of which housed Wycliffe himself (c. 1330–84), to support his position.[46] But the evidence is very circumstantial, and since Malory's uncle was Prior of the Hospitallers, and since Malory's grandfather seems to have built a small chapel at the Newbold Revel manor, Christina Hardyment equally justifiably argues that Malory came from a pious and anti-Lollard family.[47] Sons don't always follow in their grandfather's or uncle's footsteps, and authors don't always write what they intend, so all of this contradictory evidence is taunting and none of it is certain. What is less open to debate is the very Eucharistic properties afforded Malory's Grail. In the *Morte Darthur*, the Grail is explicitly described as 'the holy vessell and the sygnyfycacion of the Blyssed Bloode off Oure Lorde Jesu Cryste' (346ᵛ; 664.14–15). Two of the Grail's subsequent appearances in the *Morte* continue this Eucharistic idea: at Corbenic Launcelot witnesses 'the holy vessell' and 'thre men, whereof the too put the yongyste by lyknes betwene the prystes hondis' (401ʳ⁻ᵛ; 773–4); and later Joseph of Arimathea and the Grail appear to Galahad at Corbenic, where Joseph's 'obley' is 'smote' by 'a chylde' and transformed into 'a flesyshely man' (405ᵛ; 782–3). Since one of the central tenets of Lollard belief was a refusal to accept transubstantiation, Malory's association of the Grail with Christ's blood and body suggests that it is best to dismiss the notion of Malory as an out and out Lollard.

Malory's not being a Lollard, however, does not mean that he was deeply devout or that his literary interests were religious. Indeed, whatever his personal faith, and whatever one or two scenes in isolation may suggest, Malory's emphases in the *Morte Darthur* as a whole are firmly human and earthly. Winchester's rubrication of each and every character's name, I maintain, reinforces this earthly outlook by visually emphasizing Malory's human characters. The marginalia

---

[46] Edward Hicks, *Sir Thomas Malory* (Cambridge, Mass., 1928), especially pp. 22, 40, 44–51. Hicks's suggestion is endorsed by T. J. Lustig, *Knight Prisoner* (Brighton, 2013), p. 70.

[47] Christina Hardyment, *Malory* (London, 2005), p. 66.

and their record of these characters' earthly deeds function in the same way. Much scholarship on Malory's text that argues for a religious Arthuriad and a religious author tends to examine 'The Sankgreal' in isolation from the rest of the *Morte*; my argument is best illustrated by focusing on a number of crucial scenes from throughout the text, especially scenes which modern critics argue reveal Malory's or the *Morte*'s religious convictions. As Karen Cherewatuk justly observes, prior to 'The Tale of the Sangreal' 'Malory happily ignores the strictures of Christian asceticism.'[48] I will argue that he continues to do so again after the Grail Quest, returning to the secular and chivalric themes that have always been his true focus. For that matter, I shall also argue that even within 'The Sangreal' Malory balances celestial chivalry and religion with a concerted focus on secular fellowship and secular chivalry that elevates rather than castigates the earthly Arthurian way of life. Such a synthesis of sacred and secular is entirely consonant with certain aspects of mediaeval thought, but Malory's balance in 'The Sankgreal' is misleading. Far from moving towards celestial chivalry, Malory throughout the *Morte* presents Arthurian knighthood and its human exemplars as entirely worthy of respect and admiration, thereby sacralizing secular or earthly chivalry.

Swords, Sex and Questions of Sin

In light of my preceding argument, there are two significant scenes from the opening 'Tale of King Arthur' that I wish to focus on. One is Arthur's sexual liaison with his half-sister. The other is the founding of the Round Table. According to Malory's colophon, the *Morte Darthur*'s first tale is actually titled 'Fro the maryage of Kynge Uther unto Kynge Arthure' (W 70^v). This title is important for it foregrounds Arthur and his parents, foregrounds all the human agency and action between Uther's and Igrayne's marriage and Arthur's securing of his kingship. Within that broad outline neither of the scenes I wish to focus on should be used to condemn Arthur.

Malory introduces Morgawse as 'Kynge Lottis wyff', telling us further that she was sent as a spy to Arthur's court and that she was accompanied by 'hir foure sonnes'; he also emphasizes that Arthur 'caste grete love unto hir and desired to ly by her; and so they were agreed' (16^v–17^r; 33.30–34.2). It is thus made explicit that Morgawse and Arthur will be committing adultery, but there is no remark by either Malory or the lovers about any violation of the Commandments. Once the affair is over, Malory is equally explicit that 'Kynge Arthure knew nat that Kynge Lottis wyff was his sister' (34.7–8), a remark that, again, partly exculpates the lovers. It is unclear from Malory's wording whether Arthur's unknowing but incestuous union with Morgawse is a one-night or one-month affair (17^r; 34.1–5). What is certain is that critics often cite the incest as an early example of the kind of sinful behaviour that destroys the Round Table, especially since Merlin

---

[48] Karen Cherewatuk, *Marriage, Adultery, and Inheritance in Malory's Morte Darthur* (Cambridge, 2006), p. 90. See also Terence McCarthy, *An Introduction to Malory* (Cambridge, 1991), p. 14, who observes that Malory happily and regularly conflates the religious with the profane.

subsequently informs Arthur that God is angry with him (17ᵛ–18ʳ; 36.14–25). Thus, for Thomas C. Rumble, 'Arthur's incestuous begetting of Mordred … set[s] in motion a chain of events which … provide a dominant and carefully planned underplot for the entire *Le Morte Darthur*.'⁴⁹ Reiss is similarly scathing, arguing that the opening 'Tale of Kynge Uther and King Arthur' establishes not only the possible ideal merits of Arthurian kingship, but also 'the sins and troubles that menace Arthur and his realm and that will ultimately be instrumental in causing the destruction of his new order': Arthur's incestuous union with Morgawse is consequently only the most egregious of his sins.⁵⁰ Such expounding of sin, I suggest, is not the only way of reading things.

After the incest, in an attempt to avoid dying at Mordred's hands as prophesied by Merlin, Arthur has 'all the children that were borne in May Day, begotyn of lordis and borne of ladyes', set adrift in a ship at sea (22ʳ; 46.7–23). Besserman exemplifies a critical tendency to emphasize the analogies between Arthur's incest and May Day slaughter with biblical narratives to argue that the biblical contexts highlight and condemn Arthurian and indeed earthly sins and failures.⁵¹ Such arguments are, however, far truer of Malory's French source for this tale than they are of his English adaptation. The source in question is the Post-Vulgate *Suite du Merlin*, and as the leading authority on the Post-Vulgate Cycle insists, 'Only the Post-Vulgate [*Roman du Graal*] establishes a *direct connection* between the sin of Arthur and his death.'⁵² Although I am not suggesting that either God or Merlin condones incest, Malory's Merlin says explicitly that God is angry because the union with Morgawse will destroy the kingdom (17ᵛ–18ʳ; 36.15–17). Merlin does reiterate God's anger and desire to punish Arthur for his 'fowle dedis', but even this is much less condemnatory than the *Suite*'s castigation of Arthur as 'devil and enemy of Christ'.⁵³ Malory devotes more attention to suggesting that it is the actions of the son, not the sins of the father, which secure Arthur's death.

We must, moreover, be careful of the biblical analogy: if the May Day slaughter of young children makes Arthur resemble Herod, it follows that Mordred becomes not only a holy innocent, but Christ-like, for Christ is the future king Herod is hoping to destroy in his massacre of new-born males, just as Arthur hopes to remove the future threat posed by Mordred.⁵⁴ This Mordred-Christ parallel, of course, is nonsense: the 'unhappy' (923.15) Mordred is hardly the poster-child for divine agency, however commonplace it might be to see the wicked working God's will despite themselves. In fact, as Cooper points out, in all the stories of an innocent hero or heroine being cast adrift by an enemy or villain and rescued by God, the only other 'survivor … apart from Mordred who

---

⁴⁹ Thomas C. Rumble, '"The Tale of Tristram"', in *Originality*, pp. 118–83 (167–70 and 183; quoting 167). Cf. Moorman, '"Tale of the Sankgreall"', also in *Originality*, pp. 189–93.

⁵⁰ Reiss, *Thomas Malory*, pp. 36 and 42–3. See also Beverly Kennedy, *Knighthood in the Morte Darthur*, 2ⁿᵈ edn (Cambridge, 1992), pp. 6–8.

⁵¹ Besserman, *Biblical Paradigms*, pp. 130–1.

⁵² Fanni Bogdanow, 'La chute du royaume d'Arthur', *Romania* 107 (1986): 504–19 (511): 'Seule la Post-Vulgate [*Roman*] établit un rapport direct entre le péché d'Arthur et sa mort.'

⁵³ *La suite du roman de Merlin*, vol. 1, §11, p. 8: 'dyables et anemis Jhesucrist'.

⁵⁴ Lustig, *Knight Prisoner*, p. 24.

brings disaster on his community ... is Judas'.⁵⁵ What Malory's version of this episode reveals, then, is that critics cannot simply apply biblical echoes to the *Morte Darthur* in a straight 1:1 ratio; the supposed symbolism is often, as here, quite misleading. Certainly neither Malory as narrator nor his characters, including Merlin, mention God's wrath after Arthur and Morgawse's affair. On the contrary, Merlin emphasizes that Arthur shall have 'a worshypfull dethe' (18^r; 36.25), implying that readers or listeners – and God – continue to read him as a great hero. As for the notion that the Grail imposes a new set of values or a dogmatic interpretive key by which retrospectively to judge things, it is important to remember that what Malory tells us of the Grail and the Quest is often inconsistent. In this opening Tale 'of King Uther and King Arthur', for instance, Malory claims that there are four Grail elect (70^v; 143.23–4) when it later turns out in the actual Quest that there are only three. He also claims that one of them is Galaad the Hawte Prynce who also heals the maimed King Pellam (31^r; 68.15–17) when in fact it is Lancelot's son Galahad; and he promises that the fourth Grail knight is Sir Pelleas (143.23–4), but Pelleas does not achieve the Grail at all. As P. J. C. Field puts it, Malory's Grail pronouncements are 'not only unforthcoming and enigmatic, but self-contradictory'.⁵⁶ Malory is also famously contradictory in other parts of the *Morte*, but he is consistent in the value and worship of Arthurian knighthood and fellowship. The Grail and what we are told of it, in other words, are not the best keys to interpreting Malory's text.

I suggest, then, that Arthur's fame and honour in Tale I encourage readers or listeners to focus on values different from doctrinal teaching or biblical echoes. The same lack of concern with religious values occurs in Malory's account of the origins of the Round Table. As Thomas L. Wright observes, in the Post-Vulgate *Suite du Merlin* the Round Table is explicitly presented as a religious institution whose establishment and code recall the Table of the Last Supper and adumbrate the Holy Grail and celestial values.⁵⁷ Malory, significantly, rejects all this religious aura, and his table, with its fellowship and code, is clearly an earthly and human institution, not a religious allegory. Malory likewise later deletes from his adaptation of the Vulgate *Queste* a comparison between the Round Table, the Table of the Last Supper and the Grail Table at Corbenic.⁵⁸ Instead, Malory emphasizes that the Round Table betokens the 'rowndnes of the worlde', as well as 'ryght', 'felyshyp' and – crucially – 'worship' (365^{r-v}; 700.17–27). Mary Hynes-Berry concludes that Malory thus 'directs us to the religious commitment implicit in chivalry'. Given the focus on earthly Arthurian fellowship and worship here

---

⁵⁵ Helen Cooper, 'Counter-Romance', in *The Long Fifteenth Century*, ed. Cooper and Sally Mapstone (Oxford, 1997), pp. 141–62 (p. 153).

⁵⁶ Field, 'Malory and the Grail', in *The Grail, the Quest and the World of Arthur*, p. 146. Galahad is even given the sobriquet 'the Hawte Prynce' in the letters that appear on the Siege Perilous in 'The Tale of the Sankgreal' itself (670.5–8; at W 351^r, both **Galahad** and **Syege Perelous** are rubricated).

⁵⁷ Thomas L. Wright, '"The Tale of King Arthur"', in *Originality*, pp. 9–66 (pp. 10–12 and 36–9). This is the case even in some manuscripts of Hardyng's *Chronicle*, where marginal rubrics record 'How the kynge [Uther] bigan the Rounde Table in sign of the ordour of the saint grale that Josephe made at Avalon in Bretagne'. I cite London, BL Lansdowne MS 204, folio 66^v.

⁵⁸ Ihle, *Malory's Grail Quest*, pp. 112–13; Hynes-Berry, 'Malory's Translation', 246; *Queste*, pp. 74.20–78.2.

and throughout the *Morte*, however, it seems more likely that Malory is instead emphasizing the essential worth and worship of the Round Table and its knights *in their own right*, not because the knights 'are worthy to be the heavenly elect'. They are worthy to be knights of the earthly and Arthurian Round Table and that, for Malory, is sufficient. Malory's Round Table is from the outset a symbol of Arthurian worship and fellowship, an honour towards which all men of prowess, from Gawayne to Launcelot to Trystram, strive. As Pellynore reasons when he advises Arthur to promote Gawayne and Kay to the Round Table, Gawayne 'is as good a knyght of his tyme as is ony in this londe', and Kay 'many tymes ... hath done full worshipfully. And now at youre laste batayle he dud full honorably for to undirtake to sle too kynges' (48ʳ; 104.32–105.4). For Malory, at least within the *Morte Darthur*, the values worthy of reverence and devotion are the earthly and chivalric ones of worship and prowess, love and fellowship.

Here, again, it is important to note that Malory 'often reduced the connection between Christianity and chivalry that he found in many of his sources', including, in this instance, both the origins and parallels of the Round Table as well as in the Pentecostal Oath sworn annually by the Round Table Knights.[59] The Oath, which is essentially original to Malory, enjoins knights

> never to do outerage nothir mourthir, and allwayes to fle treson, and to gyff mercy unto hym that askith mercy, uppon payne of forfiture of theire worship and lordship of Kynge **Arthure** for evir more; and allwayes to do ladyes, damesels, and jantilwomen and wydowes soccoour, strengthe hem in hir ryghtes, and never to enforce them uppon payne of dethe. Also that no man take no batayles in a wrongefull quarell for no love ne for no worldis goodis. (44ʳ⁻ᵛ; 97.28–35)

As the fourth item or clause makes clear, Malory's Round Table Oath is essentially a feudal contract centred around the maintenance of worship, with a threat of dishonour and lost fealty to those who violate its precepts.[60] The Oath and its focus on how to behave worshipfully is reinforced in the Winchester manuscript, which likewise glorifies the deeds of Arthur and his knights, as well as Arthur and Gwenyvere's earthly love. Winchester does this partly through the rubricated **Arthure** in the middle of the Oath, which foregrounds the central authority of the Fellowship, and partly through this episode which concludes (at folio 44ᵛ) with two blank lines prefacing a rubricated '**Explicit the Weddyng of Kyng Arthur**', followed by three-quarters of a blank page. Often Malory's *explicits* mark a change of source as much as a new story or episode, but in this instance, as Cooper remarks, the *explicit* and page break seem to emphasize the titular

---

[59] Norris, *Malory's Library*, p. 21. Norris, pp. 20–2, supports Barber's suggestion that Malory's Round Table Oath is adapted from the actual oath sworn by the Knights of the Bath: Richard Barber, 'Malory's *Le Morte Darthur* and Court Culture under Edward IV', *Arthurian Literature* 12 (1993): 133–55 (148–9).
[60] On the military and political aspects of the Oath see further Robert L. Kelly, 'Royal Policy and Malory's Round Table', *Arthuriana* 14.1 (2004): 43–71. Kelly provides a valuable historicization, but I believe he goes too far in denying the Oath's chivalric and interpretative value.

wedding, as well as the material original to Malory that accompanies that wedding.[61] In this case, that original material is the Round Table Oath and, I would add, all that the Oath signifies, notably the deeds and motives and fellowship of earthly Arthurian knights. It is dangerous to put overmuch stock on Winchester's blank pages because they may just be scribal mistakes. Nevertheless, rubrication and manuscript *ordinatio* as a whole reinforce the textual and authorial focus on earthly characters and their earthly deeds, and do so in a fashion that celebrates rather than condemns Arthurian chivalry. Winchester's reinforcement of authorial theme is as true of the Oath as other moments in Malory's Arthuriad.

I noted above that Caxton's changes to Malory's text are generally thought to emphasize religion as well as Arthur and chivalry. Malory, I suggest, is more interested in the latter two elements than the first. A telling example of Caxton's tinkering with Malory's text occurs early in the narrative, in the much-contested Roman War story, alternatively titled by Malory 'The Tale of the Noble Kynge **Arthure** that was Emperor hymself thorow the Dygnyté of his Hondys', and '**The Noble Tale betwyxt Kynge Arthure and Lucius the Emperour of Rome**' (96ʳ; 189.18–22). Only the second title is fully rubricated, but I cite both titles partly to avoid confusing readers who prefer one over the other, and partly to draw attention to the fact that Malory's first title emphasizes Arthur's achievements and prowess as *earthly* king and warrior, he who won the imperial crown through 'dygnyté of his hondys'. This is a significant signposting, and it is one Caxton partially ignores. Caxton ignores Malory's signposting in a number of ways. The *incipit*s and *explicit*s that Caxton uses at the appropriate points throughout the entire *Morte* are usually straightforward numbers, such as 'Incipit liber quintus' or 'Explicit liber quartus', rather than '**Explycit the noble tale…**'.[62] Although Caxton's closing words to the Roman War story echo his chapter title and seem indebted to Malory's title commemorating Arthur's martial exploits, the book title he gives this section is simply 'The fyfthe book treateth of the conquest of Lucius th'emperour'. The more various and descriptive chapter titles for the entire *Morte*, what Caxton calls the 'rubrysshe of the contente of chapytres', including for Book V, are buried at the close of the Prologue. Finally, as noted, Caxton reduces the Roman War by half, partly by removing much of the combat details. Most of these changes actually minimize the emphases on Arthur and his fighting prowess that are created by Malory's one title, by the plot details that Caxton cuts, and by Winchester's rubrication.

Caxton's excisions to the Roman War story include, amongst much else, cutting the running joke between Arthur, Kay and Bedwere about the Giant of Seynte Mychaels Mounte being a saint. Caxton, argues Shaw, may have felt that the jokes

---

[61] Helen Cooper, 'Opening Up the Malory Manuscript', in *Debate*, pp. 255–84 (p. 261). Although not visible in the black-and-white or colour facsimiles, there are in fact three blank stubs after fol. 44. These stubs likely represent mistakes in quire estimation, not major narrative divisions.

[62] An exception is the transition between Malory's seventh and eighth tales, modified in the *incipit* to Book XX, where Caxton deletes Malory's 'on the other syde' promise of a page break that Winchester ignores, and instead inserts the page division. Caxton adopts most of Malory's wording of the *explicit-incipit* tale division: 'And here after foloweth the moost pytous history of the morte of kynge Arthur, the whiche is the xx book', but leaves nearly a half page blank: cf. W 449ʳ against C aa5ᵛ.

were 'blasphemous as well as irrelevant', especially since he does not modify Arthur's statement after the battle that thanks are due to God for the victory (78^v; 159.1; C-text in *Works* 205.5).[63] For Shaw, changes like these suggest that Caxton's revisions were designed in part to promote Christian and chivalric values; Blake makes a similar argument.[64] P. J. C. Field, pointing out the difficulties of identifying the reviser of the Caxton version of the Roman War, questions (amongst other things) Shaw's argument about Caxton's changes emphasizing Christianity and chivalry. Field accepts that these themes are present in the revised narrative, but argues that religion and chivalry are both 'cultural [and] literary commonplaces' in the late fifteenth century, meaning that Caxton or Malory or practically any other literary-minded person could be responsible for such changes.[65]

Field goes on to identify with considerable persuasion just who did and did not revise the Roman War. The distinction he raises between religious and literary persons, however, is important. One of the great challenges for mediaevals (as for moderns) was reconciling the challenges and temptations of daily living with the teachings and proscriptions of the Church. By the late Middle Ages, Christian belief had long 'shaped' and 'defined' social institutions and identities: the Christian calendar dictated daily routine whether in labour or leisure, and the material evidence of wills, tombs, inscriptions, effigies, brasses and wall paintings all bespeak, in Eamon Duffy's terms, 'enthusiastic and widespread conformity'.[66] Yet even Duffy admits that *individual* attitudes are difficult to determine. A good number of mediaeval literary texts and authors support orthodox religion; but a good many do not.[67] It is my contention that the rubrication of names in the Winchester manuscript helps to emphasize ways in which, whatever his *personal* faith or attitude to God and the Church may have been, Malory in *literary* matters runs firmly against what has been termed this commonplace cultural Christianity.[68] Most feast days in the *Morte Darthur*, for instance, are not rubricated, including Pentecost. On several occasions, however, **Penetecoste** is rubricated; in each break from the otherwise non-rubricated pattern, the rubrication helps to highlight a key narrative moment that in one way or another highlights the earthly heroic stature of one or more of Arthur's knights or the importance of the earthly Fellowship of the Round Table.[69]

In this literary lack of concern with religious matters Malory was hardly unique. As Colin Richmond attests, many of the gentry and aristocracy in

---

[63] Shaw, 'Caxton and Malory', in *Essays*, pp. 132 and 137. Caxton's text of the Roman War is given by Vinaver at the bottom of each page in his edition; I cite it here as 'C-text in *Works*', with page and line numbers.

[64] See above, n. 23.

[65] P. J. C. Field, 'Caxton's Roman War', in *Debate*, pp. 127–67 (p. 131). Field establishes that the changes to the *Morte Darthur* are indeed Caxton's, but that both witnesses, Winchester and the Caxton, are deficient in their openings of this Tale.

[66] Eamon Duffy, 'Religious Belief', in *A Social History of England, 1200–1500*, ed. Rosemary Horrox and W. Mark Ormrod (Cambridge, 2006), 293–339 (pp. 293–6).

[67] To take just one illustrative genre, romance alone reveals a plurality of attitudes to Christianity. See, e.g., *Christianity and Romance in Medieval England*, ed. Rosalind Field, Phillipa Hardman and Michelle Sweeney (Cambridge, 2010).

[68] I adopt this phrase from Fiona Tolhurst, 'Slouching towards Bethlehem', in *Malory and Christianity*, pp. 127–56 (130–2).

[69] See above, Chapter Two, Appendix II.

fifteenth-century England were in fact quite complacent in religious matters.[70] Elsewhere sacred and secular were more seamlessly integrated, yet David Aers influentially argues that the *Gawain*-poet not only 'thoroughly assimilated' but actively 'subordinate[d]' religion to more 'courtly forms of life'.[71] Malory, I suggest, does something similar, prioritizing earthly knighthood and love and fellowship over religion and penance. These latter qualities are of course present in the *Morte*, but they are consistently subordinated to human chivalric concerns, including human tragedy. As noted, Malory was no Lollard, but his two separate attacks on Coombe Abbey hardly bespeak devout faith in the Church and its ministers.[72] Malory's independence of thought is I think one reason for the *Morte Darthur*'s artistic merit and post-mediaeval success. Certainly 'great art is [often] located at the confluence of culturally imposed artistic means and objectives' coupled with 'a subjectively psychological realism', if not also a fair degree of subjective independence.[73] And the *Morte* is undoubtedly a great work of art, even if Malory nods a little more frequently than does Homer. Winchester's rubrication and marginalia highlighting human names and deeds consequently merely augment what is already present in the text itself.

It is worth remembering that Field himself raises substantial and convincing evidence against Malory being the reviser of the Roman War story in the *Morte Darthur* (Caxton's Book V; Vinaver's Tale II).[74] If we therefore accept that Caxton revised this tale, cutting material that he felt might grate on religious nerves, then it follows that in placing such material there in the first place, Malory himself had no such compunctions, especially since he incorporates the joke about the giant from the alliterative *Morte Arthure* when, like Caxton, he could easily have excised it.[75] Malory's Arthur explicitly claims that he is going on pilgrimage, telling Kay and Bedwere: 'Loke that ye too aftir evynsonge be surely armed, and your beste horsis, for *I woll ryde on pylgrymage prevayly* ... to Seynte **Mychaels Mounte** where mervayles ar shewed' (76ᵛ; 155.8–12; my emphasis). Once at the Mounte, Arthur pretends that he 'woll seche this seynte' (76ᵛ; 155.22), and once he has killed the Giant but nearly been crushed to death in the process, admits that 'This seynte have I sought nyghe unto my grete daungere' (78ʳ; 158.14–15). Similarly, when the combatants roll to the ground near Kay and Bedwere, and Kay announces his fear that Arthur has been killed, the king remarks that he is alive and has 'this corseynte ... clegged oute of the yondir clowys' (78ʳ; 158.6–7). 'Corseynte', naturally enough, means 'body of a saint', but also implies that said body is a religious relic. It is a word carried over from the alliterative *Morte* but

---

[70] Colin Richmond, 'Religion', in *Fifteenth-Century Attitudes*, ed. Rosemary Horrox (Cambridge, 1994), pp. 183–201.
[71] David Aers, 'Christianity for Courtly Subjects', in *A Companion to the Gawain-Poet*, ed. Derek Brewer and Jonathan Gibson (Cambridge 1997), pp. 91–101 (pp. 95–9).
[72] Neither are the attacks all that unusual for the time. Richard of York, Edward IV and Richard III all displayed a willingness to violate religious sanctuary to secure their enemies. See Charles Ross, *Richard III* (Berkeley and Los Angeles, 1981), pp. 86–7.
[73] George Devereux, *Dreams in Greek Tragedy* (Berkeley and Los Angeles, 1976), p. xi.
[74] Field, 'Caxton's Roman War', in *Debate*.
[75] The alliterative *Morte Arthure* is Malory's principal source for this tale, augmented by the Vulgate *Suite de Merlin* and Hardyng's *Chronicle*. For the giant episode see *Morte Arthure*, ed. Mary Hamel (New York and London, 1984), vv. 840–1221.

used in slightly different context by Malory; and it is repeated by Malory in the next sentence when he narrates how Bedwere 'caughte the corseynte oute of the kynges armys'. All of these saint phrases and jokes are cut by Caxton, who also excises Bedwere's caustic reflection: 'I have mykyll wondir, and **Mychael** be of suche a makyng, that ever God wolde suffir hym to abyde in hevyn. And if seyntis be suche that servys Jesu, I woll never seke for none, be the fayth of my body!' (78^r; 158.10–13). This, too, is a speech that Malory carries over straight from the poem. In both Malory and the source the joke relieves the considerable tension created by Arthur's mortal combat with a gigantic enemy. It is still noteworthy, though, that Malory was happy to keep the joke and that Caxton disliked it and took care to excise it.[76] In both texts, too, the fact that Arthur chooses only Kay and Bedwere as his companions testifies to the comradeship and bond between these three characters, reminding us of the importance of chivalric brotherhood to both the alliterative and prose *Morte*. More significantly, at this point in the Winchester manuscript, the names **Arthure**, **Kay**, **Bedwere** and even **Mychael** are all rubricated, but 'God' and 'Jesu' are not (folio 78^r). Nor is 'heaven'. Malory's scene and its manuscript rubrication thus emphasize human character, human bonds and human action.

There are other episodes throughout the *Morte* that likewise reveal Malory's greater concern with human character and action over religious strictures. One such scene is what Kathleen Coyne Kelly wittily terms 'the case of the circumvented consummation',[77] the well-known episode in which the young lovers Gareth and Lyonesse are twice violently prevented from their would-be sexual liaison by the illuminated, automaton knight with the reattachable head (133^v–135^r; 260.25–263.17). On the one hand, Gareth and Lyonesse's attempts at premarital sex might be condoned by society on the basis that they have in effect pledged marriage vows to one another. Nevertheless, their attempted physical union is clearly a lusty one and – however understandable – premarital sex was a sin in religious terms. Malory, moreover, is quite explicit that Gareth and Lyonesse turn to physical sex in an attempt to satisfy their 'hoote ... brennynge love' (262.24–5; cf. 260.27–8). Sex for pleasure likewise contravenes standard mediaeval Church doctrine. Although Lyonett insists that she prevents the sex to save the young lovers' *worshyp*, as well as her family's (262.20–1), and Malory tells us that 'Lynet was a lytyll dysplesed' and considered her sister 'a lytyll overhasty that she myght nat abyde hir tyme of maryage', the objections are based on the very secular concepts of honour and family reputation.[78] Given the prominence of earthly reputation and magic in this scene, we cannot take the sorcerous Lyonett and her unkillable knight as reputable spokespersons for the religious virtue of chastity, especially since the illuminated knight is silent. Malory as narrator, on the other hand, never condemns the lovers, and in fact the tone of the entire episode is

---

[76] I thus support the argument of Marc Ricciardi, '"Se what I shall do as for my trew parte"', *Arthuriana* 11.2 (2001): 20–31 (23–5), that Caxton's changes, amongst other things, reduce Malory's focus on Arthur's 'humanity' and his concern for and role within Round Table fellowship.
[77] Kathleen Coyne Kelly, 'Malory's Multiple Virgins', *Arthuriana* 9.2 (1999): 21–9 (22).
[78] For Malory's reflections of gentry attitudes to marriage, stable bloodlines and social order in the 'Tale of Sir Gareth', see Cherewatuk, *Marriage, Adultery, and Inheritance*, pp. 1–23.

humorous and sympathetic, implying that Malory supports the lovers rather than Lyonett or the Church. Critics are divided on whether Malory invented the 'Tale of Sir Gareth' as a Fair Unknown-Younger Brother type or adapted it from a French or English source. Regardless of the precise source or originality of the tale, Malory clearly chose to invent or incorporate this episode of sexual passion. This choice is significant, since the twofold attempt at sex shows that Malory had no qualms about flouting doctrinal convention.

Although in the 'Boke off Syr Trystram' Malory obviously inherited the adulterous love story of Trystram and Isode from the sources and tradition, he considerably and consistently downplays the love potion and thus the preternatural justification for that adultery being out of the lovers' control. Instead, Malory's Trystram and Isode are drawn to one another naturally, displaying 'grete love' and 'grete fantasy' for each other (155^v; 302.10–13; cf. 156^v–158^r; 304.11–306.27) even before they drink the famous and fatal cocktail. Indeed, when he first leaves the Irish court Trystram swears service to Isode both publicly before the court and privately to his lady, whereupon they exchange rings (159^{r-v}; 308.19–309.8). Such public pledging of troth and private exchanging of rings goes some way to fulfilling mediaeval marriage conventions. If Mark does not consider Trystram betrothed to Isode, he at least seems to think him in love; considering how best to spite and perhaps kill Trystram, Mark decides to wed Isode himself, sending Trystram to Ireland for a bride partly because of Trystram's praise 'for hir beauté and hir goodnesse' (165^r; 319.5–11). When Trystram returns to claim Isode as Mark's bride, but before he makes his purpose known, Malory tells us that 'the joy that La Beale Isode made of Sir Trystrames there myght no tunge telle, for of all men erthely she loved hym moste' (169^r; 326.28–30). Isode's father, King Angwyshe, is even more explicit in his wish that Trystram were marrying Isode himself (169^r; 327.3–4). All of these emphases condone the lovers' relationship.

Vinaver argues that much of the supposed inequities of Malory's 'Boke off Syr Trystram' stem from Malory's rather uninspired fidelity to an equally uninspired prose version of the more powerful verse tradition of Tristan and Iseult; 'Malory', claims Vinaver, 'knew no other version' and failed to grasp the subject's tragedy, turning the Tristan and Iseult story instead into a celebration of knighthood with a happy ending.[79] But Rumble illustrates with considerable care and evidence the general similarities between Malory's version of the story and some of the continental prose redactions.[80] Rumble also ably illustrates Malory's originality in terms of the characterization of Isode, the greater emphasis on chance or Fortune, and the reduction of the love potion as a motivating factor in favour of an 'early love' between his Trystram and Isode. As with Gareth and Lyonesse, Malory's handling of Trystram and Isode's love story suggests a specific artistic vision, one that downplays any notion of sin to support rather than condemn the lovers.

Accordingly, I do not share Rumble's accompanying conviction that Malory's greater tragic vision in the Arthuriad as opposed to its sources reflects Malory's conception of 'a *moral* tragedy' in which the 'Boke off Syr Trystram' helps clarify

---

[79] Vinaver, pp. lxxxii–lxxxix (quoting p. lxxxv) and 1443–7.
[80] Rumble, '"The Tale of Tristram"', in *Originality*, pp. 136–43 and 149–51.

and emphasize the sinful moral 'excesses' that 'weaken and crumble' the Round Table in *Le Morte Darthur*.[81] The textual evidence reveals just the opposite: Malory's narrative achieves its powerful tragic effect precisely because of the essential worshipfulness of his characters, and Malory's changes to his sources help to reinforce this nobility and effect. This pathos is as true of Trystram and Isode as other characters in the *Morte*. Those changes likewise emphasize Malory's human and non-religious focus since Mark's pettiness, Trystram's ranking as one of the best and most worshipful knights in the world, and the mutual and natural love between the lovers all endorse their affair. Thus, Trystram and Isode's unhappy deaths are – *contra* Vinaver – all the more pathetic (in the tragic, not belittling sense) for coming so late in the narrative, long after it appears that Malory has allowed them to escape their fatal destiny. In the *Morte*, Malory ends the 'Boke off Syr Trystram' with the lovers happily ensconced in Joyous Garde and even reconciled with the newly baptized Palomydes (345^v–346^v; 663–4). Although this happy ending is temporary, it is noteworthy. Malory's Mark is a villain, and his subsequent treacherous and cowardly backstabbing of Trystram 'as he sate harpynge afore hys lady' (447^r; 865.6–7), recounted to us late in the Arthuriad during the catalogue of names in the Healing of Sir Urry, shatters the lovers' blissful ever-after. Their deaths do not, however, function as a sign of divine morality or even a commonplace event which due reflection reveals to be Providential. On the contrary, Mark's cowardly treachery and scheming show that Malory's Trystram and Isode are brought low by an all-too-human villain with obvious earthly motivations. But at the end of the 'Boke off Syr Trystram', those deaths are still some distance away, and in this sense their temporary happy ending is, as noted, significant. Far from imposing a moral and religious message on the story, Malory closes his main book of Trystram and Isode by leaving the lovers in domestic bliss at Joyous Garde; however temporary, this loving domesticity actively endorses what is technically an adulterous and incestuous love.[82] Malory's focus is thus once again clearly secular and human, not religious; for if the Church used incest stories to emphasize humanity's sins and divine grace, Malory ignores the incestuous elements of Trystram and Isode's love, and mitigates the treasonous elements by consistently defaming Mark's character. Malory's originality and artistry put the focus squarely on Trystram and Isode's sympathetic human love and even more sympathetic tragedy.

Of Grails and Goodness

All of these scenes and others like them must be kept in mind when assessing Christian dogma and the potential message of Malory's version of the Grail Quest. As noted above, critics are often quick to see Malory's 'Tale of the Sankgreal' as a turning point in the narrative, one which highlights the so-called sinful failures

---

[81] Rumble, '"The Tale of Tristram"', in *Originality*, pp. 145–7; my emphasis. Vinaver, p. 1446, roundly, and to my mind justly, condemns this interpretation.

[82] Incestuous because Mark is Trystram's uncle and mediaeval incest laws defined the crime more tightly than modern ones. On mediaeval incest, see Elizabeth Archibald, *Incest and the Medieval Imagination* (Oxford, 2001).

of the Round Table, including the sins of lechery that are supposedly exemplified by such actions as Uther's pursuit of Igrayne, Arthur's liaison with Morgawse, Gareth and Lyonesse's youthful burning for one another, Trystram and Isode's love for one another, or Launcelot's affair with Gwenyvere (regardless of when precisely that affair is consummated). It seems to me that this debate over the religiousness of Malory's Arthuriad, like the debate over which text best represents Malory's final intentions for Le Morte Darthur, benefits from relating the lexical narrative that we read in modern editions to the material or bibliographic version of the text as it appears in the Winchester manuscript. Scholars have tried to use the manuscript to support the religious view. Nicole Eddy tentatively suggests that the relatively large number of marginalia accompanying 'The Sankgreal' in the manuscript, together with the relative paucity of marginalia in the subsequent concluding tales, might reflect what she terms the 'annotator's' sense that the Grail Quest marks 'the true climax of the *Morte*'.[83]

The marginalia are not part of the text of the *Morte*. I argued in the previous chapter that the marginalia and rubrication both derive from Malory, but even if one prefers the position of Cooper, Eddy and Wade that the marginalia represent an early reader response by the scribes or an annotator, they still provide a useful interpretative roadmap.[84] As Eddy herself acknowledges, all but one of the marginalia accompanying 'The Tale of the Sankgreal' actually have nothing to do with the holy vessel itself.[85] This is a telling silence. As is the case with the majority of marginalia throughout the manuscript, the main focus here is on the deeds of sundry knights: characters, swords, battles and death dominate. The marginalia record several visions as well, but these, too, are related to one of the knights. Although the marginalia throughout the 'Tale of the Sankgreal' may (as is claimed) give more notice to the knights' encounters with the marvellous than is common elsewhere in the manuscript, such marvellous marginalia are dominated by visions, and visions simply occur more frequently around the Grail than elsewhere in the *Morte*. More importantly for a secular *Morte Darthur*, the marvels are seen by Eddy's 'annotator', as Eddy herself rightly claims, as 'measure[s] of chivalric worth and attainment'.[86] In other words, even those marginalia which highlight Grail wonders are principally highlighting the earthly and knightly deeds of the most prominent members of the earthly Arthurian fellowship. Such 'chivalric ... attainment' is no different from what motivates action throughout

---

[83] Nicole Eddy, 'Annotating the Winchester Malory', *Viator* 42.2 (2011): 283–305 (297–9; quoting 298, n. 73). For a fuller account of the provenance and significance of the marginalia, see above, Chapter Two.

[84] Cf. Cooper, 'Opening Up', in *Debate*, p. 269.

[85] The exception is the marginalium at fol. 401ᵛ: 'The significacion of þe Sankgreal that ys called the holy vessel the whiche appered to Sir Launcelot'. An earlier 'pronostication of the Sank Greall' occurs in the 'Tale of Balyn', at fol. 31ʳ, after Balyn strikes the Dolorous Stroke.

[86] Eddy, 'Annotating the Winchester Malory', 299. Cooper, 'Opening Up', in *Debate*, pp. 269–70, argues that Scribe A is more interested than Scribe B in things like 'dreams, visions and prophecies'. However, P. J. C. Field, 'Malory's Own Marginalia', *Medium Ævum* 70 (2001): 226–39 (228–30), convincingly demonstrates that prophecies in the *Morte* are most common in those parts of the narrative copied by Scribe A, including Tale VI. The seeming differences in the content of the marginalia and the scribes' interests, then, is probably due purely to the 'varying' subject matter each scribe copied.

the *Morte*'s more earthly or human moments, meaning 'The Sankgreal' is a continuation, neither the climax nor the turning point, of the narrative.

Looking at the text of the *Morte Darthur* rather than its manuscript and scribes, scholars regularly remark that Malory shuts down magic and the supernatural as the *Morte* progresses through Arthur's reign towards the tragic collapse of his kingdom. Anna Caughey argues instead that the prominence of mysticism in 'The Sankgreal' provides a return of the marvellous, just as the repeated focus on the Grail knights' virginity ironically serves to foreground sex.[87] This strikes me as something of an exaggeration: women and sex, as both the *Morte* and its feminist and gender critics remind us, have always been central to Malory's Arthuriad. Hence Uther and Igrayne; hence Arthur and Morgawse and Arthur and Gwenyvere; hence Launcelot and Gwenyvere; hence Gareth and Lyonesse; hence Trystram and Isode and even Palomydes as Isode's would-be lover; hence Lamorak and Morgawse or any other number of heterosexual liaisons in the text. The same is true of magic. Marvellous figures and magic users such as Merlin, Morgan or Nenyve may become less prominent after the opening 'Tale of Kynge Uther and Kynge Arthure', but they or their actions never fully recede from memory or from significance. Even after Merlin is sealed away, his prophecies, perrons, tombs, sieges and floating swords continue to pervade the narrative, at times in the background, at times – as in the opening of 'The Sankgreal' when Galahad achieves the Siege Perilous or the Sword in the Floating Stone (349^v–352^r; 667.9–671.34) – suddenly bursting to the foreground and dominating if not dictating the action. It is true that the sundry miracles and mysticism of the Grail and its Quest are evocative of the marvellous, but really magic has never gone entirely away. As Corinne Saunders makes clear in her correction of the typical scholarly view of magic's decline in the *Morte*, magic occurs and recurs throughout the entirety of the *Morte Darthur*, including in the very landscape of Arthurian adventure, a landscape which is largely but not entirely familiar, into which the supernatural might at any moment intrude.[88] As Merlin's inscriptions of names on the Round Table attests, however, magic of whatever kind is firmly given a back seat to human character, to human deeds and to human fellowship. The rubrication of names in Winchester, like the names inscribed on the Round Table (sometimes in gold), consistently enact this human focus. The material text and the narrative text thus mirror one another in their thematic emphases.

The recurrence of magic in 'The Sankgreal', moreover, is yet another way in which Malory contains the apparent change of values that the Quest story brings with it, reminding readers of the continuities rather than the differences between his Grail world and the world of earthly adventure comprising most of the *Morte Darthur*. The manuscript marginalia in 'The Sankgreal' may well point to several visions, and most of these visions do have a Christian element, but the Grail per se is only mentioned in two (of eighty) marginalia throughout the manuscript as a whole, and any Christian message inherent in the scenes accompanying the

---

[87] Anna Caughey, 'Virginity, Sexuality, Repression and Return in the "Tale of the Sankgreal"', *Arthurian Literature 28: Blood, Sex, Malory* (2011): 155–79.
[88] Corinne Saunders, *Magic and the Supernatural in Medieval English Romance* (Cambridge, 2010), pp. 234–60.

Quest visions is firmly allegorical.[89] Furthermore, Malory's version of the Quest, as is often observed, has far fewer ubiquitous hermits to explain such allegories. The reason for this lack of exegesis is because Malory's interests lie elsewhere than in allegory and Christian doctrine. Indeed, as Larry D. Benson justifiably insists, Malory's reduction of the eremitical haranguing and allegorizing 'shifts the source of coherence from the hermits to the knights, especially Lancelot, the one knight who appears throughout the entire tale'.[90]

There are, nevertheless, four such Grail Quest 'avision[s]' denoted by manuscript marginalia: Launcelot's vision of his ancestors and his chastisement for living 'as a warryoure ... with vayneglory for the pleasure of the worlde' (373^r; 717.14–24); Gawayne's vision of the meadow full of 'proude and black' bulls, 'save thre of hem was all whyght, and one had a blacke spotte' (376^v; 724.3–16); Bors's vision of two birds, white and black, with a second vision of a chapel with a sick tree and two fair flowers (and whatever the allegory might be, there is no Grail sighting here (381^r; 733.24–734.18)); finally, Launcelot's second vision sends him to the Grail ship (399^v; 770.1–8). Almost all of these visions foreground knightly fellowship, and whilst the white vs black bulls and colouring are meant to castigate the majority of the Round Table in this particular adventure, Malory's excision of the majority of eremitical exegesis from this scene in the source greatly lessens such moral or religious lessons. In the French *Queste del Saint Graal* earthly and celestial glory are, in Hynes-Berry's phrase, 'profoundly incompatible' since the *Queste* is an allegorical exegesis of Eucharistic mysteries.[91] None of this, I contend, is true of Malory's 'Tale of the Sankgreal'.

As is frequently remarked, Malory allows Launcelot to get much closer to the Grail than the adultery with Gwenyvere or the version of the story inherited from the sources should allow. Thus, even with Launcelot's visions it is notable that the hermit who explicates his dream states that, 'for ... a synner erthely thou hast no pere as in knyghthode nother never shall have' (374^r; 718.32–3). This phrase epitomizes the many statements Malory inserted into his version of the Grail Quest that emphasize Launcelot's superior but sinful status. Vinaver points out that this clause emphasizing Launcelot's earthly superiority is original with Malory.[92] Although such statements are taken by some critics as proof of a schism between earthly chivalry and celestial chivalry, this is not necessarily the case. Nacien the hermit explains to Gawayne, while his companion Ector seems to ride away, that 'God knowith [Launcelot's] thought and hys unstablenesse. And yett shall he dye ryght an holy man, and no doute he hath no felow of none erthly synfull man lyvyng' (379^v; 729.35–730.2). For P. E. Tucker, Hynes-Berry and Radulescu this speech epitomizes Launcelot's sin of 'instability', revealing how much better a knight he could and should still be.[93] I disagree. The speech is

---

[89] As noted, the two Grail marginalia are 31^r (shortly after Balyn strikes the Dolorous Stroke): 'Here ys a pronosticacion of the Sank Greall'; and 401^r (Launcelot's partial Grail vision, during the Quest): 'The significacion of þe Sankgreal that ys called the holy vessell the whiche appered to Sir Launcelot'.
[90] Benson, *Malory's Morte Darthur*, p. 217.
[91] Hynes-Berry, 'Malory's Translation', 244.
[92] Vinaver, Commentary on *Works* 930.14–18.
[93] P. E. Tucker, 'The Place of the "Quest of the Holy Grail" in the *Morte Darthur*', *MLR* 48.4 (1953): 391–7; Hynes-Berry, 'Malory's Translation', 243–57, esp. 248–9; and Radulescu,

original to Malory and it is important, but not because it highlights Launcelot's failings and 'unstablenesse'. Rather, Nacien's words clearly elucidate the extent to which God rewards Launcelot *despite* his love of the queen. Far from illustrating the extent to which Launcelot 'ys nat stable' (379ᵛ; 729.33), Gawayne's interview with Nacien once again reminds listeners and readers just how constant and stable are Launcelot's motivations throughout *Le Morte Darthur*.

Launcelot is repeatedly humiliated in the Grail Quest, but a defining feature of his character even in the Quest remains his love of the queen. Malory approves of that love, even in 'The Sankgreal'. Consequently, the hermit-priest to whom Launcelot confesses his adultery enjoins Launcelot only to avoid 'that quenys felyship *as much as ye may forbere*' (364ʳ; 696.26–8) before sending him on his way with instructions to do 'suche penaunce *as hy myght* do and *to sew knyghthode*' (364ᵛ; 698.3–4). My first two emphases in these quotations highlight notable, realistic and very human qualifications of Launcelot's ability to avoid the queen, while the departing instruction (and my third emphasis) suggests that knighthood and penance are interrelated and that Launcelot even when repentant is to 'sew' ('pursue' or 'perform') deeds of chivalry. Malory thus partly conflates any distinctions between chivalry and Christianity, a point also made by Cherewatuk; but in adding that the final tragic destruction of the Round Table occurs because 'the grail quest touches so few knights and that Launcelot so quickly shakes off that touch', Cherewatuk typifies scholarly attitudes to 'The Tale of the Sankgreal' by implying that its chivalric ideology is different from that governing other movements in the *Morte*.[94] This is not entirely true, as Launcelot's simultaneous success and failure in the Quest illustrates.

As early as 'The Noble Tale of Sir Launcelot' Malory remarks how Launcelot 'loved the quene ... aboven all other ladyes dayes of his lyff, and for hir he dud many dedys of armys' (96ᵛ; 190.16–17), and the most obvious facet of Launcelot's character throughout the *Morte Darthur* is how absolutely stable he is in this love and chivalric motivation. In 'The Boke off Syr Trystram', Isode sends the defeated Palomydes to Gwenyvere with the message that Launcelot and Gwenyvere are, together with Trystram and Isode, the four great lovers of the realm (176ᵛ; 340.1–5), and Elayne of Corbyn and Dame Brusen twice use Launcelot's love of Gwenyvere to trick Launcelot into Elayne's bed (323ᵛ–324ᵛ; 622.32–624.33; and 328ʳ–329ʳ; 631.13–632.23). Launcelot continues to love Gwenyvere during the Grail Quest, and he loves her again in the tale that Vinaver named after them (Tale VII), the same tale in which Malory allows the one explicit consummation of their physical love during the Knight of the Cart episode: 'So, to passe upon thys tale, Sir Launcelot wente to bedde with the quene and toke no force of hys hurte honde, but toke hys pleasaunce and hys lykynge untyll hit was the dawnyng of the day; for wyte you well he slept nat, but wacched' (441ʳ; 852.21–4). Malory's prose here is laconic, probably also very male, yet telling, highlighting that nothing could be

'Malory and the Quest', in *Companion to Arthurian Literature*, p. 336. See also Lewis, 'English Prose *Morte*', in *Essays*, pp. 17–19. This view of Launcelot's instability is perhaps influenced by Vinaver, pp. 1536–7 (pp. 1522–4 in *O1*).

[94] Karen Cherewatuk, 'Sir Thomas Malory's "Grete Booke"', in *The Social and Literary Contexts of Malory's Morte Darthur*, ed. D. Thomas Hanks Jr and Jessica Gentry Brogdon (Cambridge, 2000), pp. 42–67 (pp. 61–3).

more natural than this joyous union between the lovers. Likewise at the close of the *Morte* Launcelot is motivated by love of Gwenyvere and love of Arthur, and sorrow at separation from them both, to become a hermit.[95] Far from being 'nat stable', then, Launcelot is constantly motivated by love of Gwenyvere and love of worship: this is the case before, during and after the Grail Quest.

In Launcelot's eyes, as in Malory's, knightly *worshyp* is paramount, and Launcelot's earthly worship is bound up with his earthly love of Gwenyvere. Nacien's speech tells us that God 'knowith' this, accepts it and partly rewards Launcelot for it: hence Launcelot's reputation as the greatest of earthly knights, hence his partial success in the Quest and hence too (we shall see in the next chapter) his ability to heal Sir Urry. By strict doctrinal standards, Malory's Launcelot would be a better Christian if he could rise above his feelings for the queen; but he is a more realistic and compelling and human character precisely because he cannot turn away from her.

The point, then, is not that earthly prowess is superseded by celestial prowess in Malory's 'Tale of the Sankgreal', but rather that there are, briefly and only within this section of the overall Arthuriad, two value systems and two sets of knights, one epitomized by Galahad and one epitomized by Launcelot.[96] The two values are juxtaposed in a discordant contradiction, and it is not at all clear in Malory's version that celestial chivalry negates earthly chivalry. Field makes much of Malory's fidelity to his source in this tale, and nearly as much of the relic-like presentation of the Grail, concluding that Malory himself was religiously faithful, especially devoted to Christ's blood.[97] I contend that Malory follows the letter more than the spirit of his source. As Field himself admits, Malory 'seems to have felt uncomfortable with [the *Queste*'s] thoroughgoing condemnation of secular life'. In adapting the Vulgate *Queste del Saint Graal* Malory cannot avoid seeming to have two different value systems, for the *Queste* not only distinguishes between earthly and celestial chivalry, its overarching *sens* reflects much Cistercian religious thought – though scholars no longer suggest that a Cistercian authored the French romance.[98] Unlike his source, Malory minimizes as much as possible the differences between celestial and earthly chivalry. Indeed, Galahad's celestial chivalry is, outside 'The Sankgreal', as ephemeral as the Grail floating past the Round Table Fellowship (353r; 674.2–8). When placed in the context of the *Morte Darthur* in its entirety, the consistent theme and standard is the earthly one championed by Launcelot. Launcelot's status as 'the best knyght ... of ony synfull man of the worlde' (352r; 672.14–19) is not, then, either

---

[95] See further Benson, *Malory's Morte Darthur*, pp. 243–5, who notes that what Benson considers to be Launcelot's tragic fall, as well as his corresponding comic rise, are both dependent upon consistent loyalty to Arthur and to Gwenyvere, even during the civil wars that help to destroy the kingdom.

[96] Whitworth, 'Sacred and Secular', 25 also argues for two narrative levels in 'The Sankgreal', but my argument and conclusions differ significantly from his.

[97] Field, Headnote to 'The Sankgreal', II:549; Field, 'Malory and the Grail', in *The Grail, the Quest and the World of Arthur*, pp. 149–51.

[98] For a lucid review of the issue see Karen Pratt, 'The Cistercians and the *Queste del Saint Graal*', *Reading Medieval Studies* 21 (1995): 69–96.

his or Malory's 'albatross'; it is the whole point.[99] Malory's focus is earthly, certainly not Cistercian and not even spiritual.

Neither Launcelot nor Malory wholeheartedly subscribe to religious goals. The nuns escorting Galaad to Lancelot at the beginning of the French *Queste* emphasize that 'No finer man, it seems to us, could receive the order of chivalry from you', thereby prioritizing Galaad's greatness and the reasons behind it:[100] his religious and virginal purity. Malory, in contrast, has his nuns pay tribute to *Launcelot*'s prestige: 'we pray you to make hym knyght, *for of a more worthyer mannes honde* may he nat resceyve the order of knyghthode' (349^v; 666.21–3; my emphasis). Malory thus emphasizes the father's chivalric priority, not the son's purity. Likewise in the *Queste* Lancelot 'had the young man keep a vigil in the chapel' the night before he is given his spurs; Malory's Launcelot, in contrast, spends the night in 'passyng good chere', and there is no mention of any vigil imposed on Galahad.[101] By excising the vigil, Malory limits the religious overtones of his brand of chivalry. The emphasis in the *Morte* is firmly on Galahad's suitability for knighthood and, more so, on Launcelot's stature as the pinnacle of Arthurian chivalry, the fount of Galahad's own innate virtues. Indeed, as Radulescu points out, Malory drops connections between Galahad and the biblical David that are manifest in the French tradition; even Gwenyvere's account of Galahad's and Launcelot's genealogy emphasizes not only descent from Christ, but, perhaps more importantly for Malory, their status as exemplars of the secular knightly class, noble or gentry: father and son are 'comyn of the beste *knyghtes* of the worlde and ... the grettist *jantillmen* of the worlde' (352^v; 673.20–5; my emphases).[102] The dichotomy between celestial and secular chivalry is further lessened by the fellowship and affection which marks Galahad and Launcelot's relationship in their time together near the close of the Quest (399^v–400^r; 770.28–772.21).[103] As Hynes-Berry remarks in an observation that effectively counters her central thesis about Launcelot being less than he ought to be, 'Malory was not really concerned with distinctions in spiritual character such as were developed through the [Vulgate] *Queste*'s treatment of Bors and Perceval. But he was concerned with a chivalric quest.'[104]

Malory's many minor additions to the Grail Quest all emphasize this earthly heroism; we accordingly see which set of values most interests him. To reinforce

---

[99] *Contra* Whitworth, 'Sacred and Secular', 20–1 (whose phrase this is), or Tucker, 'The Place of the "Quest"', 393.

[100] *La Queste del Saint Graal: Roman du XIIIe siècle*, ed. Albert Pauphilet (Paris, 1923), p. 2: 'Car de nul plus preudome de vos ne porroit il, a nostre cuidier, recevoir l'ordre de chevalerie.' The translation is from E. Jane Burns, *The Quest for the Holy Grail*, in *Lancelot-Grail*, gen. ed. Norris J. Lacy (New York and London, 1995), Vol. IV, pp. 1–87 (p. 3).

[101] Cf. and *contra Queste*, p. 3, 'fist toute la nuit veillier le vaslet au mostier' (trans. *Quest*, p. 3 [sic]) with *Morte Darthur*, 666.31–3. I am indebted to Ian Brunton, one of my Master's students, for reminding me of this contrast, but see further Raluca L. Radulescu, *Romance and Its Contexts in Fifteenth-Century England* (Cambridge, 2013), pp. 166–8.

[102] Radulescu, *Romance and Its Contexts*, pp. 169–72. I go further than Radulescu does in pursuing the secular implications of this scene.

[103] See Stephen C. B. Atkinson, "Malory's Lancelot and the Quest of the Grail," in *Studies*, pp. 129–52 (pp. 142–4); also Kenneth Hodges, *Forging Chivalric Communities in Malory's Le Morte Darthur* (New York and Basingstoke, 2005), pp. 120–2.

[104] Hynes-Berry, 'Malory's Translation', 253–4.

this anthropocentric focus, the appearances of 'God' in the hermit's speech and Nacien's (718.31–4 and 729.35) are, as always, not rubricated in the manuscript (W, 374^r and 379^v). In contrast, all of the earthly and chivalric characters' names *are* so highlighted, both here and throughout. A similar continuity is found in Gawayne's vision, since the companionship amongst both the black bulls and the white bulls attests Malory's emphasis on human fellowship – even if, in this instance, that fellowship is deemed sinful. As Field observes, Malory sometimes reproduces material from the sources because it is part of the authorized story, not necessarily because he endorses it.[105] His famous hedging of the adultery in his refusal through most of the *Morte* to acknowledge exactly when or how Launcelot and Gwenyvere's love begins and is consummated is one well-known consequence of this authorized inclusiveness. Rather less acknowledged by scholars is the likelihood that the Grail Quest is also such an inheritance, one Malory is reproducing for the completeness of his Arthuriad, not because he agrees with the allegorical castigation of earthly chivalry found in the source. I am thus in complete agreement with Larry D. Benson, who makes the judicious argument that, by the time Malory is writing his Arthuriad, the Grail Quest had become so 'popular' and 'essential' a component of the Arthurian legend that it had to be incorporated into any serious Arthurian narrative: after all, 'even ... so brief an account of Arthur's career as appears in Hardyng's *Chronicle*' required a Grail Quest. Consequently 'Malory had little choice; he *had* to include the story of the Grail quest' in what his invocations of authority make clear he intended to be an 'auctorysed' (C XXI.13; 940.10) account of 'The Hoole Book' (C XXI.13; 940.17) of Arthur's entire reign.[106]

I noted earlier that even the Grail marginalia denote primarily chivalric achievements, and emphasized (with Hynes-Berry) Malory's greater interest in quests over spirituality. Bors's assessment of the Grail Quest is precisely the same: that 'he shall have much erthly worship that may bryng hit to an ende' (380^r; 731.9–10). Launcelot views the Quest in a similar light, promising Gwenyvere that he shall return from this new adventure 'as sone as I may with my worship' (354^v; 677.9–10). Bors is more successful in fulfilling his goal than is Launcelot. Bors's Grail achievements are nonetheless typically ignored by scholars, whereas the question of Launcelot's worship or dishonour in the Grail Quest has become one of the more convoluted threads in Malory scholarship. What should be less open to debate is the kind of worship the cousins hope to achieve. Throughout the *Morte Darthur*, *worshyp* is an entirely secular goal and ideal, combining earthly fame, glory and honour, and is accordingly something sought by all knights and, as we shall see, by at least one lady. But just in case we miss the secular nature of winning worship, Bors adds the qualifier 'erthly' in his reaction to the Quest. Even the hermit with whom Bors is speaking accepts this conclusion.

Moorman, on the other hand, does disagree, claiming that 'Vinaver ... objects to Malory's secularized rendering' of the French here.[107] According to Moorman, 'the point is that Bors' is clearly in error and Malory is thus charting 'the begin-

---

[105] Field, *Life and Times*, pp. 171–2.
[106] Benson, *Malory's Morte Darthur*, p. 207.
[107] Moorman, '"Tale of the Sangreall"', in *Originality*, pp. 197–200 (p. 197).

nings of Bors' character development' from secular to celestial knight. Unlike Launcelot, so the argument goes, Bors begins as a secular knight but will soon and successfully become celestial. Vinaver does not, however, 'object' to Malory's version of events; rather, Vinaver highlights what he believes to be the marked contrast between Malory's version and the source, notably that 'Nothing is more alien to the [French] *Queste* than the phrase "earthly worship" as used here'.[108] Even Lewis concedes the possible evidentiary nature of this addition for a secular reading of the *Morte*.[109] Although Moorman misrepresents Vinaver, Field offers what looks like a more compelling objection, arguing that Vinaver's reasoning is faulty since the phrase 'tant d'oneur terriens' appears in the fragmentary MS Udine, Biblioteca Archivescovile 177 and – it is implied – in the complete British Library Add. MS 10294, the latter used by H. Oskar Sommer in his edition of the complete Vulgate Cycle.[110] Field concludes that since Udine and Sommer 'both' agree against Malory, 'it would be unreasonable to write that agreement off as coincidence'. This is sound, except that while Sommer's *edition* does indeed read 'tant donor [terriene]', the key word, *terriene*, is in square brackets. In the prefatory Note to his edition Sommer records that he collated his text against Paris, BN MS 342. Although it is not recorded in the relevant footnotes, I assume that *terriene* was emended from here: I have not seen this manuscript. I have examined other manuscripts, and they support Vinaver: BL Add. MS 10294 itself clearly reads only 'tant donor' (fol. 132^f), as does the late thirteenth- or early fourteenth-century manuscript British Library Royal MS 20.C.vi (fol. 136^a). British Library Additional MS 17443, of the second half of the thirteenth century, also reads 'tant danor' (fol. 33^d). Add. 17443 contains a *Queste* and *Mort Artu*, each of which begins with an elaborate miniature (respectively fols 1^r and 62^r), and each text is punctuated by various red or blue flourished initials of varying sizes; but there is no hint of 'terriene' in the passage in question. The *de luxe* British Library Royal MS 14.E.iii (early fourteenth century) similarly reads only 'tant donour' (fol. 118^c), as does the considerably plainer manuscript of the second quarter of the thirteenth century, British Library Royal MS 19.C.xiii (fol. 305^a). The same reading of 'tant honor' – without the qualifier 'terriene' – occurs in Pauphilet, based on Lyons, Palais des Arts 77. The late thirteenth-century *de luxe* manuscript Yale Beinecke 229, containing the final section of the *Lancelot*, a complete *Queste* and a complete *Mort Artu*, likewise reads only 'tant denor' (fol. 238^{r-b}).[111]

We will never know precisely which manuscript of the *Queste* Malory used, but even if his source did provide Bors's sentiment – and Field may well overestimate the prominence of that variant *terriens* – it remains important that

---

[108] Vinaver, Commentary on *Works* 955.9–10, 12, but see also pp. 1535–7. I cite O^3; Moorman would have been using O^1, but on this issue Vinaver's argument is identical across his editions; only the page numbers are different. Even in O^1, the passage is still Commentary to 955.9–10, 12.

[109] Lewis, 'English Prose *Morte*', in *Essays*, p. 15.

[110] Field, Headnote to 'The Sankgreal' and Commentary on 731.9–10. For the alternative French reading, see *The Vulgate Version of the Arthurian Romances: Volume VI*, ed. H. Oskar Sommer (Washington, 1913), p. 116.26.

[111] Yale 229 is available online at brbl-dl.library.yale.edu/vufind/Record/3433279. See also *La Queste del Saint Graal (The Quest of the Holy Grail) from the Old French Lancelot of Yale 229*, gen. ed. Elizabeth Moore Willingham (Turnhout, 2012), p. 135.

Malory adopted the phrase, just as it is important that this contrast between earthly and celestial knighthood continues through the hermit's response (paraphrased above), that whoever achieves the Quest 'shall be the beste knyght of the worlde and the fayryst of the felyship' (380^r; 731.12–13). Further, as Vinaver and Moorman both note, the language and stress in the Vulgate *Queste* are slightly but significantly different: Boort believes that the Quest 'is the loftiest quest ever undertaken[.] ... Whoever succeeds at it will receive the greatest honor imaginable to mortal men', whilst the hermit declaims the successful quester to be 'the most loyal soldier and the truest of all those participating in the quest'.[112] Far from denoting how much Bors has to change in order to achieve the Grail, then, Malory's alterations to his source material in fact bespeak the relative continuity of the adventure ethos. Indeed, just as Bors views the Grail Quest as a place to win worship, so he had earlier assayed – against Pelles's advice – the adventures of Corbyn Castle, adventures likewise instigated by the Grail's appearance and in which Bors likewise wins earthly worship (326^r–327^r; 627.5–629.15).

Notable in this light is Jill Mann's insistence that Malory's Grail Quest is *not* 'a radical change in the nature of adventure and the knight's relation to it', but rather a deepening and intensification of pre-existing themes through the imposition of a 'religious dimension'.[113] I am thus in complete agreement with Sandra Ness Ihle, who argues in different but convincing ways that, in contrast to the source, Malory's version of the Grail Quest 'becomes a chivalric adventure – special, to be sure, but distinguished from other adventures more in prominence than in kind'.[114] Such critical accounts of the continuity of adventure in the *Morte* are entirely accurate and compelling, but it is not so much that Malory adds religion to adventure as the other way around: like mediaeval chivalry itself, Malory adapts the Christian background of his source, creating, only during 'The Sankgreal', a twofold narrative that partly valorizes Galahad and the white bulls, but which – crucially – equally valorizes traditional earthly chivalry as epitomized by Launcelot. The bridge between the two thematic strands is secular human fellowship.[115] Hence the emphasis on fellowship in the 'Trystram', at the beginning, middle and end of Malory's Grail Quest, and in the final two tales.

This prominence of earthly fellowship in 'The Tale of the Sankgreal' is again made clear by Bors's encounter with the hermit, since Bors 'wellcomme[s]' any of his fellows who will also manage to achieve the Quest (380^r; 731.24–6). Likewise, Percyval when separated from Galahad longs to be reunited with him (404^v; 780.30–1). The concerns of Bors and Malory with the validity and importance of

---

[112] *Queste del Saint Graal*, p. 162: respectively 'la plus haute queste qui onques fust comenciee, ... ou cil avra tant honor, qui a fin la porra mener, que cuer d'ome mortel nel porroit penser', and 'li plus loiax serjanz et li plus verais de toute la Queste'; translation from Burns, trans., *Quest for the Holy Grail*, p. 52.

[113] Jill Mann, 'The Narrative of Distance, The Distance of Narrative in Malory's *Morte d'Arthur*', in her *Life in Words* (Toronto, 2014), pp. 275–311 (p. 287). Cf. Mann's 'Malory and the Grail Legend', also in *Life in Words*, pp. 312–31 (p. 319). Molly Martin uses gaze and gender theory to reach a similar conclusion: see Martin, *Vision and Gender in Malory's Morte Darthur* (Cambridge, 2010), pp. 118–47.

[114] Ihle, *Malory's Grail Quest*, p. 162.

[115] On the importance of earthly chivalric fellowship to Malory's conception of the Grail Quest, see further Ihle, *Malory's Grail Quest*, pp. 132–41.

earthly fellowship are even more apparent in Malory's conclusion to the Grail Quest, where Malory invents a scene in which Launcelot and Bors each vow lasting fellowship to the other: 'Cousyn, ye ar ryght wellcom to me' exclaims Launcelot when they are reunited, concluding with an oath to 'never departe in sundir whylis oure lyvys may laste'. To which Bors replies simply and movingly, 'Sir, ... as ye woll, so woll I' (409ʳ; 789.10–13).[116] We are thus reminded that while Galahad dies having renounced 'this wrecched worlde', and Percyval 'yelded hym to an ermytage ... and toke religious clothyng' whilst awaiting death, Bors refuses to renounce 'seculer clothyng, for that he purposed hym to go agayne into the realme of Logrus' (408ʳ⁻ᵛ; 787.16–788.17). Bors pursues and achieves the Grail, but having done so Bors also, no less than Launcelot, turns his back on Corbyn and Sarras and returns to Camelot. In other words, he seeks the traditional Malorian values of earthly adventure, earthly worship and earthly human fellowship.

Arthurian Heroism, Rubricated Names and Malorian Tragedy

In both Malory's Grail Quest and its source there is a contrast between Bors's success in the Quest and Launcelot's failure or qualified failure. For obvious reasons much scholarship on Malory's treatment of the Grail story is tied to Launcelot and the question of his success or failure in the Quest, and to the related question of the success or failure of Arthurian chivalry itself. Tucker, Moorman, Atkinson and Radulescu all focus, albeit in different ways, on potential divisions within Launcelot's character as alternatively best earthly knight and paragon of chivalry, or overly secular and failed knight and lover.[117] Taken as a whole, modern scholars offer a sliding scale of condemnation of Launcelot, with Moorman at the most severe, Lewis and Hynes-Berry in the middle, emphasizing Launcelot's success and failure, and Atkinson and Radulescu similarly emphasizing both failure and qualified success, adding that Launcelot's penance and self-knowledge make him a good role model for others. Although my position shares some beliefs with this middle ground, I argue that Launcelot remains heroic precisely because Malory is not ultimately concerned with religion.

According to Moorman, Launcelot is the 'tragic hero' of the *Morte Darthur* brought low by the ubiquitous 'tragic flaw': in Launcelot's case, his sins of pruriency, adultery and inconstancy.[118] The whole notion of the so-called tragic flaw

---

[116] Launcelot's sentiments in the Caxton are even more emphatic, the vow of fellowship including a promise of service for 'all that ever I may do for you and for yours, ... I promise you feythfully, and never to fayle. And wete ye well, gentyl cousyn sir Bors, ye and I shall never departe in sundir whylis oure lyvys may laste' (*Works* 1037.1–6). Vinaver accepts the Caxton additions as genuine. Field reads them as 'compositorial expansion' and rejects them accordingly (Commentary to 789.10 and 789.11). Tellingly, both versions emphasize secular chivalric fellowship.

[117] See Tucker, 'The Place of the "Quest"'; Moorman, '"Tale of the Sankgreal"', in *Originality*; Atkinson, 'Malory's Lancelot and the Quest' in *Studies*; and Radulescu, 'Malory and the Quest', in *Companion to Arthurian Literature*. See further (including for my next sentence) Hynes-Berry, 'Malory's Translation', and Lewis, 'English Prose *Morte*', in *Essays*.

[118] Moorman, '"Tale of the Sangreall"', in *Originality*, p. 192.

which brings low so many heroes from the Greek stage onwards, however, is misleading and simplistic. This is true, I maintain, of heroism in general, just as it is true of Malory's heroes in particular. For one thing, 'flaw' implies that the hero is broken or false, if not also morally wrongheaded and worthy of punishment. Malory's Launcelot *is* repeatedly castigated in 'The Sankgreal' for his 'synne' (363^r–364^v; 695.4–698.10 or 372^v; 716.7) and 'vayneglory' and worldly living (373^{r-v}; 717.14–23 or 375^v; 721.23–722.8), but he is also regularly hailed as a peerless knight (352^r; 672.8–19; 374^r; 718.32–4; 376^r; 722.9–11). Despite his failings, he is also granted a clear vision of the Grail whilst dining with King Pelles just before the conception of Galahad (323^{r-v}; 622.9–30), and two partial visions during the Quest proper: once when he is unable to enter the 'olde chapell' and so must witness the Grail procession from outside, 'half wakyng and half slepynge' (362^{r-v}; 693.5–694.8); and once after leaving the ship and Galahad and coming to a castle chamber, where he is allowed to see the Grail from the threshold but is forbidden entry to the room, only to be struck down when he does enter thinking to help the old priest (400^v–402^v; 772.22–775.35). Partial visions these may be, but even with the twenty-four-day coma they still constitute a considerable success, however qualified in comparison to the achievements of the three Grail elect. Even Launcelot's unparalleled failure in the tournament of white and black knights is greatly qualified by the standard praise that all who witness Launcelot's chivalric prowess 'mervayled that ever one knyght myght do so grete dedis of armys' (374^v; 720.4–5). Although Launcelot is then uncharacteristically defeated and captured, his defeat is explained as a natural consequence of the combat reality that 'a man may nat ever endure' (720.7–8; from C XV.5), an idea given repeated emphasis in the very earthly realm and values of 'The Boke off Syr Trystram'.[119] By such devices as these, Malory establishes earthly and knightly continuities between the values and themes of 'The Sankgreal' and the remainder of the *Morte Darthur*. He also establishes that Launcelot is not irreparably flawed, but glorious and heroic, even in defeat. Significantly, Launcelot's success and heroism are foregrounded by his voice and experience being added to Bors in the 'grete bookes' Arthur compiles to record and memorialize the Grail adventures undertaken by knights of his court (408^v–409^r; 788.28–35).

The other problem with the idea of a morally flawed or broken tragic hero is that it actually reduces the tragic effect or plot. The tragedy of a situation, narrative or hero is all the more poignant and powerful if the tragedy stems from a complex blend of good and bad motivations which, taken together, form an integral part of the hero's character. Such a combination of good and bad motives and actions, of character, fate and free will drives the tragic plot of the (heroic) alliterative *Morte Arthure*, but is equally responsible for the tragic elements of the (tragic-romance hybrids) stanzaic *Morte Arthur* and Malory's *Morte Darthur*.[120] Nor can we invoke Aristotle to support the tragic-flaw idea, contrary to a good

---

[119] See 178^v; 343.32–3, 197^r; 379.5–8, and 212^v; 408.4–7, and my 'Weeping, Wounds and *Worshyp* in Malory's *Morte* Darthur', *Arthurian Literature* 31 (2014): 61–82 (65–6).

[120] On the different ways in which tragedy is manifested in the three English *Mortes*, see my 'The Stanzaic *Morte Arthur* and Medieval Tragedy', *Reading Medieval Studies* 28 (2002): 87–111; *Understanding Genre and Medieval Romance* (Aldershot, 2008) especially pp. 99–149; and 'Genre as Context in the Alliterative *Morte Arthure*', *Arthuriana* 20.2 (2010): 45–65.

many authorities since the Victorians, since the word he uses, *hamartia*, strictly speaking translates as 'mistake' or 'error', often one made in ignorance. As E. R. Dodds observes, the commonplace view that Aristotle defined the hero as possessing a 'tragic flaw' actually stems from a seventeenth-century French misinterpretation of Aristotle, one inspired in part by misplaced faith in poetic justice and the notion, 'completely foreign' to a good many tragedies, that the bad are always punished whilst the good will always be rewarded.[121]

Moorman's complaint that Malory's Launcelot cannot abandon the 'secular chivalric way of life' without also forsaking his very identity, and that his chivalry is the source of both his 'greatest strength' and his 'greatest weakness', is thus entirely true.[122] But Launcelot's so-called weaknesses do not reflect his tragic flaw and sins: the whole point of his tragedy is precisely that the good and bad parts of his character are so intricately bound together. He is the greatest knight of the Round Table *because* of his love for Gwenyvere, not despite that love, and it is his love of honour, chivalry and fellowship that causes him to refuse to slay Arthur or Gawayne during their civil war.[123] Not to love Gwenyvere or *worshyp* or chivalry or Arthur would be to not be Launcelot. The tragedy stems precisely from this interplay of strength and weakness; but the two strands of character and indeed of heroism can never be completely disentangled. This is equally true, I maintain, of Malory's other tragic figures, including Balyn, Gawayne and Arthur himself. Malory's Balyn, for instance, can draw the sword-damsel's blade only because he is the best knight of the world, without treason or felony (22^v; 47.30–48.5; 22^v; 48.18–21; 23^r; 49.25–32), yet his first action with the sword is to behead the Lady of the Lake (24^{r-v}; 51.9–52.11), and his last is to kill his brother, who in turn mortally wounds Balyn (C II.17–19; 71.1–74.1, prophesied at 23^v; 50.2–4). Gawayne 'knows' what will come of a split between his family and Launcelot's, and on the basis of fellowship with Launcelot and this knowledge, he denounces Aggravayne and Mordred's plotting (449^v–450^r; 870.24–872.3); yet neither can Gawayne forgive the death of Gareth, and he subsequently swears a blood-feud against Launcelot (459^v; 888.23–33), a feud he does not let go until he lies on his deathbed (476^v–477^v; 917.27–919.18). Arthur is a good knight and better king who is nevertheless powerless to prevent, and partly responsible for, the destruction of his kingdom.[124] This complex combination in a hero's character of strength and nobility, weakness and error, explains the success and failure – and underlies the tragic paradox – of the consummate hero. This heroic paradox, I maintain, partly explains the greatness as well as the downfall of the Round Table. All of these elements are more profound in Malory's Arthuriad than in his sources. This is why the tragedy of Malory's characters is so moving and why

---

[121] E. R. Dodds, 'On Misunderstanding the *Oedipus Rex*', *Greece & Rome* SS 13.1 (1966): 37–49 (38–40). See further the excellent explication in D. W. Lucas, introduction, commentary and appendixes, *Aristotle: Poetics* (Oxford, 1968), App. IV, pp. 299–307.
[122] Moorman, '"Tale of the Sangreall"', in *Originality*, p. 192.
[123] See especially *Morte Darthur* 462^v–463^v; 894.5–895.30; 470^{r-v}; 906.14–907.18; 473^r; 911.30–2; 474^v; 914.13–25.
[124] For further explanation of the tragedy of these characters see my 'On Misunderstanding Malory's Balyn', in *Re-Viewing Le Morte Darthur*, pp. 149–62; *Understanding Genre*, pp. 137–42; and 'Characterization in Malory and Bonnie', *Arthuriana* 19.3 (2009): 123–35.

Malory designs his narrative and his manuscript so as to create a remembrance or calling to mind of past Arthurian chivalry.

If Aristotle did not proclaim a tragic flaw, he did insist upon the tragic hero's recognition or *anagnorisis*. In Malory's *Morte Darthur*, too, the tragedy is all the greater because each of the principals has some awareness of what is going on. One of several moments of recognition for Launcelot occurs in the Grail Quest when he laments that:

> My synne and my wyckednes hath brought me unto grete dishonoure. For whan I sought worldly adventures for worldely desyres I ever encheved them and had the bettir in every place, and never was I discomfite in no quarrell, were hit ryght were hit wronge. And now I take uppon me the adventures to seke of holy thynges, now I se and undirstonde that myn olde synne hyndryth me and shamyth me. (363ʳ; 695.7–13)

This speech is variously cited by critics as proof of Launcelot's sin, proof of his wasted potential, proof of his redemption, or a combination of all of these possibilities. As Vinaver points out, the corresponding scene in the Vulgate *Queste* stresses only Lancelot's 'pechié mortel' ('deadly sin'), with no mention of prior successes in 'worldly adventures'.[125] Moorman tries to read the changes and the speech as examples of Malory's condemnation of Launcelot,[126] but the opposite is the case: admittedly Malory's Launcelot is cognizant of his past sins and their hindering of his current success, but the marked emphasis in his speech on his considerable honour and success in 'worldly adventures' alerts us to another possibility. Malory's version of the Grail Quest is not only less dogmatic than the Vulgate's, but he also raises the possibility that the new rules of adventure are so markedly different as to negate all that has gone before and supersede all that follows. This negation of traditional Arthurian chivalry probably *is* true of the Vulgate *Queste*, a text, as Derek Brewer observes, that is largely 'anti-chivalric', at least in terms of traditional chivalry.[127] But a negation of chivalry is emphatically not true of the *Morte Darthur*, where neither Malory nor his characters reject traditional martial knighthood and the winning of *worshyp*. Indeed, as Brewer rightly insists, chivalric prowess, for Malory and his characters, is itself a 'moral quality'. The real issue with Launcelot's speech is not his supposed moral failure, but the ways in which his words highlight the collision of Malory's twofold narrative in 'The Tale of the Sankgreal'.

In Malory's version of events, unlike in the Vulgate *Lancelot-Graal* Cycle, the Grail is not the moral yardstick which measures and condemns the majority of the Round Table but an aberration from the usual realm of adventure. Hence Malory's emphasis on the adventurous elements of even the Grail Quest, hence his emphasis on earthly fellowship during the Quest, and hence the emphasis on Launcelot's past successes and worldly honour. Indeed, the overlap between sacred and secular values in the *Morte* is announced by Kay as long ago as the

---

[125] Vinaver, Commentary on *Works* 896.1–9; *Queste*, p. 62.5–6.
[126] Moorman, '"Tale of the Sankgreall"', in *Originality*, pp. 194–6.
[127] Derek Brewer, 'The Paradoxes of Honour in Malory', in *New Directions in Arthurian Studies*, ed. Alan Lupack (Cambridge, 2002), pp. 33–47 (p. 43 and, for the 'moral quality' quotation at the end of my paragraph, p. 38).

conclusion of 'The Noble Tale of Sir Launcelot du Lake'. There Kay recounts how 'Sir **Launcelot** toke my harneyse and leffte me his, and I rode in Goddys pece and no man wolde have ado with me' (113^r; 221.26–8). It was – and is – a familiar theological axiom that if human beings acted as they ought to, divinely endorsed benefits would eventually follow, whether on Earth or in Heaven. But as Malory makes perfectly clear, on this occasion, Kay enjoys 'God's peace' because of Launcelot's earthly reputation as a great knight: Kay is able to ride scot-free because of Launcelot's publicly recognized martial prowess. Even the placement of 'The Sankgreal' within the *Morte* as a whole is significant, for one thing that we learn from Malory's account of the Roman War is that he was not enslaved by his sources. The Roman War traditionally comes near the end of Arthur's life and reign, a final moment of greatness before the inevitable destruction of the realm. But Malory clearly had no qualms about radically altering this traditional narrative arc and moving the Roman War to an earlier moment in Arthur's career. In doing so he emphasizes the glory and success of Arthur and the Round Table fellowship by making the war an entirely successful endeavour rather than an abortive victory preceding Mordred's fatal rebellion. This rearrangement of the traditional Arthurian *matière* needs to be kept in mind when we look at the placement of the Grail Quest after the lengthy 'Boke off Syr Trystram' in the *Morte Darthur*, for one point of this arrangement is not merely to pave the way, at the end of the 'Trystram', for the beginning of the Quest, it is also to emphasize (repeatedly) the propensity of earthly adventure and love in the Arthurian universe.

The 'Boke off Syr Trystram' is the stereotypical realm of adventure, and a notable feature of adventure in this tale is the priority of chivalry, romantic love and reputation, as well as the connections between these values. It is in this tale especially that each of Trystram, Palomydes and Lamerok establishes himself as one of the top knights in or near Arthur's realm, and each loves a woman with whom he perhaps should not, by strict moral concerns, be involved. But heroism and morality are rarely appropriate bedfellows, whether in classical epic, mediaeval heroic literature or even in chivalric literature. The point is, the 'Trystram' repeatedly reinforces the priority and interconnectedness of earthly Arthurian knighthood, earthly *worshyp* and earthly love. Hence the fact that, in the Camelot league pools, the best or most proficient knights are also the most notable lovers: Launcelot is inspired by and loves Gwenyvere; Gareth is inspired by and loves Lyonesse; both Trystram and Palomydes are inspired by love of Isode, though Palomydes's love is unrequited; and Lamorak is inspired by and loves Morgawse.[128] Gawayne is an exception to this equation between knights and lovers, but only partially: although he is associated with no single woman in the *Morte Darthur*, or even with a series of women as he is in other texts, Gawayne's ghost does appear to Arthur before the final battle at Salisbury accompanied by the many 'fayre ladyes' he championed throughout his career to compensate for the one woman he accidentally decapitated as a young knight – and that woman throws herself in front of Gawayne's sword to protect the knight

---

[128] Lamorak's inspiration is less well known than his fellows', but see especially 197^v–198^v; 380.22–381.31 and 237^r; 456.4–13.

she loves.[129] Significantly, the beginning of 'The Book of Sir Launcelot and Queen Guinevere' reiterates the value of these same secular concerns and activities: love and adventure and worship are again central and defining elements of Arthurian chivalry and society. The vow of renewed comradeship between Launcelot and Bors that closes 'The Sankgreal' also brings the narrative and its principal themes full circle by recalling and allaying, as much as possible, Arthur's fears of the severing of fellowship (352^{r-v}; 672.25–35; 353^{r-v}; 674.24–675.14; 354^v; 677.16–18) by re-establishing earthly chivalric bonds. The same reintegration of fellowship occurs at the end of Tale VII with the magnificent catalogue of names in the Healing of Sir Urry episode (445^v–447^v; 862.25–866.8). Thus, by enveloping 'The Sankgreal' within the very secular concerns of the tales of 'Trystram' and 'Launcelot and Guinevere', Malory manages to keep the Quest aligned as much as possible with the rest of the *Morte Darthur*. In consequence, even within 'The Sankgreal' Malory focusses as much as possible on Launcelot, keeping him more centre-stage than does the Vulgate *Queste*.[130]

I contend that Winchester's rubrication of names mimics this alignment of secular values and adventures; for what the rubrication does, over and over for more than 484 folios, is reiterate Launcelot as one of the most recurring names, and thus one of the most important characters, in Malory's Arthuriad. Importance does not guarantee a lack of failure and condemnation, and Winchester's rubrication of all names reminds us of each of the principal players in the narrative, but taken in context of the *Morte* as a whole, the consistent rubrication of names, including Launcelot's, emphasizes the earthly deeds and lives and loves of the Round Table Fellowship. To reinforce this secular focus, the names of 'God' or 'Jesu' are, with one exception noted below, never rubricated during 'The Tale of the Sankgreal'. One might debate whether 'God' is a proper name at all, or is even subject to the same grammatical rules as other names, but it is notable that 'God' is never rubricated in Winchester.[131] 'Jesus' is a proper name, but unlike the names of Arthur and the Round Table knights, 'Jesu' is rubricated only once in the text proper, and there seem to be extenuating circumstances for that exception (see Chapter Two, App. II). Given the prominent rubrication of characters' name, the rubrication of the name **Sankgreal** itself serves as a partial levelling device, putting it temporarily on the same plane as the knights who seek it. The mere rubrication of **Sankgreal** does not change the Grail's status as 'an holy vessell' containing 'a parte of the bloode of Oure Lorde Jesu Cryste' (334^v; 643.15–17). But the notable thing about the Grail, after its holiness, is that it does not belong in this world.

---

[129] See 478^{r-v}; 920.30–921.18 and 38^v; 84.19–85.10. The women who accompany the dead Gawayne are Malory's invention: in the French *Mort Artu* Gauvain is accompanied by 'a crowd of poor people' (*La Mort le roi Artu*, ed. Jean Frappier, 3rd edn (Geneva and Paris, 1964), §176.11), and in the stanzaic *Morte* Gawayne's escort are 'angellys' comprising the 'Lordys ... and ladyes' he had championed (*Le Morte Arthur*, ed. P. F. Hissiger (The Hague, 1975), vv. 3196–212). On Gawain as lover, see Cory James Rushton, 'The Lady's Man', in *The Erotic in the Literature of Medieval Britain*, ed. Cory James Rushton and Amanda Hopkins (Cambridge, 2007), pp. 27–37.

[130] See further Benson, *Malory's Morte Darthur*, p. 217; Brewer, 'Paradoxes', in *New Directions*, p. 43.

[131] My reasoning here owes much to a conversation with P. J. C. Field, though I alone am responsible for any errors of thought or prose.

Although the Grail brings healing to some, and transformation or salvation to Galahad and Percyval, it does not, in marked contrast to the blood of Christ, bring redemption or salvation to all.[132] Galahad is also the perfect Grail knight because he is already perfect when the Quest begins, virginal and virtuous, so perfect that he cannot live in this world for long. Unlike most other rubricated places or objects or characters encountered by the Round Table knights throughout the narrative, neither the Grail nor Galahad truly belongs in Camelot. Hence the unusual twofold narrative of 'The Tale of the Sankgreal' versus the normal narrative and values of the rest of the *Morte Darthur* as a whole.

For many modern readers the Grail is a perfect symbol of human sin and the sinful tragedy of the majority of Round Table knights. This is not, I think, Malory's perspective. Hence Bors's view of the Quest as an opportunity for winning glory, hence the worshipful Launcelot's qualified success and hence Bors's return to Camelot (a name which is frequently rubricated, as (sometimes) is Sarras and Salysbury, and (always) Excalybur). The rubrication of **Sankgreal** and **Galahad** and **Percyval** visually foregrounds the fact that the Grail and its principal knights both belong to and are separate from the earthly Arthurian realm. But all the other rubricated knights are of a kind, as Malory proclaims by his repeated emphasis on the fellowship between, and worship of, the Round Table knights. And Arthurian fellowship and Arthurian glory are emphasized by the rubrication of each and every character's name. Collectively, the Winchester manuscript text of the *Morte Darthur* enshrines Arthurian chivalry with a rubricated memorial foregrounding the glory and tragedy of the Round Table knights.

Nor does it follow from Galahad's perfection and the fact that he does and does not belong to Camelot nor hold with its values that the other knights must be failures. Galahad is both insider and outsider, just like the Grail's values are antithetical – not necessarily superior – to traditional Arthurian chivalry. This belonging and not belonging is mirrored by many of the more curious or contradictory elements of 'The Tale of the Sankgreal'. There is, for one thing, Elayne of Corbyn's entrapment and violation of Launcelot, abetted by magic and deception. As Catherine Batt observes, Launcelot's insistence, once to Gwenyvere (327^v; 630.16–17) and once to Elayne (339^r; 651.2), that he was 'made to lye' by Elayne against his will, thinking her another, evokes 'the idiom of rape to mark the abuse done to his body, and denies consent in the fathering of Galahad'.[133] Even without Launcelot's remarks, it is clear from Brusen's words and actions that Launcelot is duped and drugged (323^v–324^v; 623.5–624.33; and 328^r–329^r;

---

[132] The Grail heals Percyval and Ector after they fail to recognize one another and nearly kill each other in armed combat (334^{r-v}; 642.2–643.11); it heals Launcelot of his madness and boar-wound (336^v–338^v; 646.31–650.20); and it heals the lame man called upon by Galahad to help the Grail elect carry the Grail table into Sarras (407^{r-v}; 785.33–786.8). Galahad's healing of the Maimed King is achieved with the blood from the spear, the blood of Christ, so this healing is Grail-related, but is not, strictly speaking, effected by the Grail per se (406^v; 784.14–21).

[133] Catherine Batt, *Malory's Morte Darthur: Remaking Arthurian Tradition* (New York and Basingstoke, 2002), p. 122. In light of such trickery and violation, it is hard to accept Lumiansky's argument that Launcelot is purified by the Grail's appearance in Pelles's castle prior to the ruse of Galahad's conception: R. M. Lumiansky, 'Malory's Steadfast Bors', *Tulane Studies in English* 8 (1958): 5–20 (11).

631.13–632.23). Needless to say, this sexual and sorcerous chicanery qualifies as a very curious, not to say dubious, manner of engendering the Christian knight *par excellence*. The Bible itself is likewise full of curious incidents, including the drunkenness of Noah (Genesis 9:20–6) or Lot and his daughters (Genesis 19), but the context and purpose of the Bible as a whole suggest a higher plane and higher purpose. The *Morte Darthur*, however, is not the Bible, and if we measure the significance of scenes in the *Morte Darthur* by their local context as well as the context of the Arthuriad in its entirety, it is clear that what Malory and almost all of his characters prioritize most is earthly fellowship, earthly love and earthly reputation. I noted earlier that Malory seems sympathetic to Gareth and Lyonesse, that their passion for one another is very human and realistic, but that it violates Church doctrine. Malory is equally sympathetic to Trystram and Isode and Launcelot and Gwenyvere, despite the treacherous and adulterous nature of both their loves. On the other hand, Lyonette is emphatic that her objections to her sister's attempted premarital sex reflect standard gentry attitudes to stable bloodlines and family honour (134^v; 262.20–1). Much later, the father of Elayne the Fair Maid of Ascolat is equally emphatic that his daughter not take the always promiscuous Gawayne to her bedchamber unsupervised (422^{r-v}; 815.32–816.2). In contrast, King Pelles, the father of Elayne of Corbyn, 'fayne wolde … have found the meane that Sir **Launcelot** sholde have leyne by his doughter' (323^v; 622.32–3). Elayne is equally 'glad' when she subsequently gets Launcelot 'in her armys' (324^r; 624.1–2). However much God brings good out of human misbehaviour, then, events in Malory's *Morte* may not be as straightforward as they seem. As Cherewatuk rightly notes, the actions of Pelles and his daughter violate 'the gentry's generally held expectation of a daughter's virginity as well as the grail's requirement of chastity for those who seek it'; consequently, 'the tale's moral compass swings in several directions'.[134] All of which means that the Grail is not the moral yardstick many critics would have us believe it is meant to be.

Moorman, for instance, argues that Malory 'elevates and dehumanizes Galahad' in order to emphasize the sinful failures of Arthurian chivalry in general and Launcelot in particular.[135] Elizabeth S. Sklar deservedly draws attention to Galahad's 'unpropitious beginning', yet she too subsequently argues for the supposed 'spiritual counter-code' inaugurated by the Grail as a solution to the failures of earthly Arthurian chivalry, including 'the potentially disastrous effects of sexuality in general and of female sexuality in particular'.[136] But this supposed sanctification is belied by Galahad's extremely earthly origins, origins that recall the equally deceptive conception of Arthur at the beginning of the *Morte*. In both cases the supernaturally abetted conception fulfils the requisite marvellous birth common to the heroic archetype, and in both cases the archetypal birth alerts readers that the hero is marked for greatness.[137] But since Galahad's conception

---

[134] Cherewatuk, *Marriage, Adultery, and Inheritance*, p. 66.
[135] Moorman, '"Tale of the Sankgreall"', in *Originality*, p. 196.
[136] Elizabeth S. Sklar, 'Malory's "Lancelot and Elaine"', *Arthurian Yearbook* 3 (1993): 127–40 (quoting 129, 136, 133).
[137] Uther's appearing before Igrayne in the guise of her husband, for instance, is an Arthurian trope that goes back to Geoffrey of Monmouth but which also echoes some classical myths of the conception of Herakles. Geoffrey's version is especially close to Plautus' *Amphitryon*,

hinges upon Launcelot's passion for Gwenyvere, the episode also foregrounds Launcelot's greatness, including the strength of his love for Gwenyvere. It is therefore misleading to contrast Launcelot's supposedly sinful love or the supposed perils of sexuality against Galahad's supposed superiority, for without Launcelot and Gwenyvere's all-too-human, earthly and adulterous love for one another, including a desire on at least his part to consummate or re-consummate the affair, Galahad would never have been born. Remove the sin or the sex and you remove the supposed new order of chivalry. As Brusen reminds Pelles, '**Launcelot** lovyth no lady in the worlde but all only Quene **Gwenyvere**. And therefore ... I shall make hym to lye wyth youre doughter, and he shall nat wyte but that he lyeth by Quene **Gwenyvere**' (323^v; 623.6–9). In Malory's eyes, there is no sin, nor any sexual peril. Ironically, and brilliantly, Malory even uses Elayne's second sexual deception of Launcelot as a way of emphasizing the naturalness of Launcelot's love for, and sex with, the queen. In Launcelot's mind, he is having sex with his beloved, and this impression is reinforced by placing Elayne's second encounter with Launcelot just after Gwenyvere arranges their sleeping chambers so that she and Launcelot can meet 'that nyght', and just before she genuinely sends for him, only to have her plans scuppered by Brusen's false summons (328^v–329^r; 631.26–632.29). Once again Malory's language is telling, for he emphasizes first that Launcelot 'wende that he had had another in hys armys' (that is, Gwenyvere), before describing their 'kyssynge and clyppynge' as 'a kyndely thynge' – that is, 'natural'. As with the narrator's sympathy for Gareth and Lyonesse or the attempt to leave Trystram and Isode in adulterous but domestic harmony, Malory's diction and narrative details endorse Launcelot and Gwenyvere's love, even at the very moment that Launcelot is, through no fault of his own, flouting that love.

The similarities between Galahad's and Arthur's origins suggest that, in some key respects, Galahad resembles key Arthurian heroes. The same suggestion is made by Galahad's sword and its acquisition. Galahad draws a sword from a floating stone, a sword formerly carried by Balyn and used in his blood-feud with the Lady of the Lake (23^v–24^v; 50.33–52.11), as well as his other often disastrous but clearly secular adventures (C II.19; 74.4–30; and 351^v–352^r; 671.3–34). Although critics often remark that Galahad is a foil to Balyn, there are only three heroes in all of Malory's Arthuriad who draw swords from enchanted locations: Arthur himself (repeatedly from C I.3–5 to 7; 6.27–10.32), Balyn (22^r–23^r; 47.20–49.28) and Galahad (351^v–352^r; 671.3–34). Like his magically abetted conception, then, Galahad's marvellous sword and the manner of its acquisition place him firmly within a select coterie of the *secular* Arthurian fellowship. Significantly, the marginalia in the Winchester manuscript echo and reinforce Galahad's similarity to his fellows, recording 'Here Galahad was made knyght' (349^v), and 'How Sir Galahad pulled the swerde out of the peron' or floating stone (351^v), but not his achievement of the Grail. Even Galahad's sitting in the Siege Perilous, a deed also recorded by marginalium (351^r), announces both Galahad's difference and sameness, for while no one else can attain the Siege, it is, nonetheless, a seat

in which Jupiter visits Alcmena in the guise of her husband Amphitryon, who is away at battle; Jupiter is accompanied by Mercury in the guise of the slave Sosia.

reserved for a key (if short-lived) member of the Round Table fellowship. As Benson justly points out, Galahad's adventures also follow the typical chivalric pattern for young heroes of knighthood, proving oneself in tourney, and proving oneself by successfully achieving a quest.[138] Like the Grail, then, Galahad does and does not belong in the Arthurian realm, but his chivalric signifiers of birth, weapon and seat at the Round Table are all typically secular. In other words, adventure, earthly love and fellowship remain key values, even in a character who participates mostly in adventures separate from the earthly realm. Malory thus continually reinforces these values, both in the overarching narrative themes of the *Morte Darthur*, and in the ways in which those themes are reflected in the *Morte*'s manuscript *ordinatio*.

There are consequently problems with seeing 'The Tale of the Sankgreal' as the imposition of a new, better and less sinful way of life. Benson characterizes the Grail adventures as 'the realm of miracles, with the motifs and thematic patterns reminiscent more of the life of Christ than of Arthurian knights'.[139] I would argue, in contrast, that Malory balances the sacred and secular much more closely than has been recognized. Donald L. Hoffman correctly argues that the most Christ-like act of all in Malory's *Morte Darthur*, the one act in which a person willingly dies to save another, is performed not by a Christ-like knight, but by a woman.[140] For Hoffman and others, the *imitatio Christi* of Percyval's Sister, enacted as it is by a woman in the masculine world of chivalry, is problematic, interrogating or even rebuking traditional models of gender and knighthood.[141] To my mind, however, the prominence of Percyval's Sister highlights further continuities between the Grail world and the more typical world of earthly Arthurian adventure. Throughout the *Morte Darthur*, as indeed throughout romance as a genre, women are central to the plot, announcing or instigating adventure, inspiring knights to deeds of arms and sometimes undergoing their own adventures. So it is in 'The Tale of the Sankgreal' that, for grief at their lovers' departure, 'many ... ladyes that loved knyghtes wolde have gone with hir lovis. And so had they done, had nat an olde knyght com amonge them in relygious clothynge' to deliver Nacien's message forbidding women from the Quest (353^v; 675.20–30). Female exclusion from the Grail Quest, like Launcelot's being struck down for his twenty-four years of sinful loving (401^v–402^r; 774.9–775.6), could both be taken as signs that this section of Malory's Arthuriad functions by different values. This is only partly true: female exclusion is belied by the centrality of Percyval's Sister and the damsels who accompany, foreshadow or even carry the Grail (e.g. 323^v;

---

[138] Benson, *Malory's Morte Darthur*, p. 211.
[139] Benson, *Malory's Morte Darthur*, p. 215.
[140] Donald L. Hoffman, 'Perceval's Sister', *Arthuriana* 6.4 (1996): 72–83 (73). Given the importance of character and name to Malory, I follow the example of Batt, *Remaking Arthurian Tradition*, in capitalizing Sister.
[141] In addition to Hoffman, 'Perceval's Sister', 73 and 78, see Caughey, 'Virginity, Sexuality and Return', 169, and especially Batt, *Remaking Arthurian Tradition*, pp. 138–46. Batt offers a thorough critical overview in the course of her own often stimulating interpretation. Caughey is explicit about her debt to Hoffman, quoting his 'Perceval's Sister', 73, but she misattributes the quotation to Hoffman's 'Malory's Tragic Merlin', originally published in *Arthurian Interpretations* 1.2 (1991): 15–31, and reprinted in *Merlin: A Casebook*, ed. Peter H. Goodrich and Raymond H. Thompson (New York and London, 2003), pp. 332–41.

622.23–30; 325^v; 626.31; 352^r; 671.35–672.24). Just as Galahad does and does not belong to Camelot, women do and do not belong in the Grail Quest.

Percyval's Sister is especially notable for guiding the Grail elect, promising to 'shew [Galahad] within … thre dayes the hyghest adventure that ever ony knyght saw' before bringing him to join Percyval and Bors, then expounding to them the mysteries of the Ship of Faith and its bed, sword and girdle, and spindles; eventually she prophesies her own posthumous fellowship with them (389^v–395^r; 750.30–761.25 and 398^v; 768.6–14).[142] To some extent, as Percyval's Sister herself claims, she even completes Galahad's knighthood by girding him with the Sword of the Strange Girdles, the most recent girdle being made from her own hair (394^v–395^r; 760.21–761.22). Most famously, she also sacrifices herself to save a leper lady, but one who is especially unworthy of the sacrifice due to the shameful custom that results in the Sister's death and 'the vengeaunce of Oure Lorde', who strikes down half the castle and all of its inhabitants to avenge the sixty maidens killed up to this point to satisfy the castle's evil custom (398^v–399^r; 768.27–769.24).[143] The role of guide seems to continue even in death, in a scene that Erin Kissick argues presents Percyval's Sister as a virgin saint-cum-relic whose uncorrupted body and purity help to sustain Launcelot:[144] for Launcelot is guided by a vision to travel in her boat (399^v; 770.1–27), a boat that brings him after 'a moneth and more' to Galahad, and after six months to Corbyn and the Sankgreal. Percyval's Sister is also the only questor apart from the three elect to reach Sarras (406^r; 784.1–4 and 407^r; 785.27–32), and although she sails there in death, her importance and success are marked by another of the *Morte Darthur*'s memorializing tombs. Like Balyn and Balan or Arthur and Gwenyvere, Percyval's Sister is buried next to those she loves, in her case, next to Galahad and Percyval 'in the spirituall palyse' (398^v; 768.12–14; 407^v; 786.11–13; 408^v; 788.19–20). Her prophecy of this reunion echoes the earlier prophecies and earthly markers (stones, tombs, tables) enacted by Merlin to denote sundry worshipful earthly deeds or warriors, just as her burial with beloved friends and fellow questors recalls and reinforces the thematic concern with secular fellowship that runs throughout the narrative. As Hoffman notes, the graveyard of the sixty maids, together with Percyval's Sister's sacrifice, is itself 'a memorial to the martyred ladies'.[145] I would add that the Sister's grave and narrative significance are marked by the marginalium on 'The dethe of Sir Percavalls Syster' (398^v), and even, albeit less obviously, by the marginalium about Launcelot's 'avisione' (399^v).

---

[142] These same actions are performed by Perceval's sister in the Vulgate *Queste*, and examined by Janina P. Traxler, 'Dying to Get to Sarras', in (an original contribution to) *The Grail*, ed. Dhira B. Mahoney (New York and London, 2000), pp. 261–78. Although we reach different conclusions, several of my points about Perceval's Sister in Malory were anticipated by Traxler in her discussion of the French original.

[143] Like God, Balyn and the three Grail knights all agree that the custom of bleeding maidens is shameful, deserving of violent opposition and correction: see *MD* 29^v–30^r; 65.7–23 and 397^{r-v}; 765.30–766.30. Cf. further the destruction of the Arthurian leper lady's castle to the earthquake and splitting of the temple following Christ's Crucifixion (Matthew 27:51).

[144] Erin Kissick, 'Mirroring Masculinities', *Arthurian Literature* 31 (2014): 101–30 (at 120–7).

[145] Hoffman, 'Perceval's Sister', 82, n. 11.

In addition to reinforcing secular fellowship and relations between men and women in the *Morte*, relations that in all other tales within the Arthuriad are firmly earthly, Percyval's Sister also reinforces the central theme and importance of *worshyp*. Although Galahad warns her that consenting to give up a dish of blood as is the custom of the castle will no doubt secure her death, Percyval's Sister is willing to risk death in order to prevent the bloodshed attendant upon the Grail knights' continued defence of her. In addition to this laudable concern with the safety of her fellows, she displays a notable concern for fame, remarking, 'Truly, ... and I dye for the helth of her I shall gete me grete *worship* and soule helthe, and *worship* to my lynayge' (398^r; 767.23-4; my emphasis). As Andrew Lynch and Lisa Robeson each convincingly argue in their different but equally perceptive accounts of this scene, Percyval's Sister effectively hazards her blood and body to win worship, the same sort of action regularly undertaken by male knights in the course of countless secular adventures throughout the *Morte Darthur*.[146] Indeed, Percyval's Sister's explicit desire for earthly worship on the eve of the climax of the Grail Quest recalls and reaffirms' Bors's attitude to the Quest at its outset. Most of what I argue about Percyval's Sister is equally applicable to the Vulgate *Queste*, but it is even more true of Malory's version since, for all of his oft-remarked fidelity to his source in this tale, he generally adopts the wording of the French *Queste* without adopting the many scenes of doctrinal exegesis. This reduction includes omitting or minimizing the parallels between biblical history and Arthurian history in his version of the Quest. Malory also gives Percyval's Sister more agency and explicatory power than does the source, having her speak knowledgably of marvellous matters that the French relegates to the narrator's authority.[147] Since the majority of Winchester's marginalia celebrate chivalric deeds and death, it is significant that Malory honours Percyval's Sister's worshipful sacrifice with a marginalium recording 'The deth of Sir Percevalls Syster' (W, fol. 398^v). The person and deeds of Percyval's Sister thus alert us to the fact that Christian values are not the only goal of the Grail narrative in Malory's version, where a woman is just as willing as a knight to die for fellowship and glory.

Fellowship, Worship and lacrimæ rerum

I emphasized at the start of this chapter the importance of studying 'The Sankgreal' in the context of the *Morte Darthur* as a whole rather than in isolation. It is equally problematic to read this one section as a final sweep of Tales VI–VIII. In addition to qualifying the supposed religious turn of Malory's narrative, a contextualization reminds us of the continued importance even in 'The Sankgreal' of earthly adventure, earthly fellowship and earthly worship. But there are

---

[146] Andrew Lynch, 'Gesture and Gender in Malory's *Le Morte Darthur*', in *Arthurian Romance and Gender*, ed. Friedrich Wolfzettel (Amsterdam and Atlanta, 1995), pp. 285–95 (p. 291); and Lisa Robeson, 'Women's Worship', in *Re-Viewing Le Morte Darthur*, pp. 107–18 (pp. 115–18). Hodges overlooks this aspect of Percyval's Sister's motivation in his attempted dismissal of female glory (*Forging Chivalric Communities*, p. 125).

[147] See Batt, *Remaking Arthurian Tradition*, pp. 141–6. I do not accept Batt's conclusion, that Malory is anxious about narrative stability or the 'legitimization of violence'.

also, as Kenneth Hodges points out, the extra-textual, socio-political contexts, notably the concern in fifteenth-century England with 'the potential threats of private religious fervor' and 'the consequences to society when a severe form of piety becomes popular'.[148] Certainly Arthur and Gwenyvere lament the loss of fellowship and disruption of unity that the Grail Quest will bring. For all the differences in their motivation, both Arthur and Gwenyvere view the beginning of the Grail Quest as a treacherous act, with Arthur complaining 'A, **Gawayne, Gawayne**! Ye have betrayed me' (354^r; 676.14), and Gwenyvere complaining 'A, **Launcelot, Launcelot**! Ye have betrayde me and putte me to the deth, for to leve thus my lorde!' (354^v; 677.7–8). Gwenyvere no doubt has an unvoiced personal motive in lamenting the absence of her lover, but her love of Launcelot in no way detracts from her love of Arthur and the Round Table as a whole, and we can justifiably take her concern for Arthur's safety and worship as genuine. The primacy of human character and human relationships is once again emphatically illustrated by the Winchester manuscript, where the rubrication of **Arthur, Galahad, Grayle, Camelot** and especially **Gawayne** and **Launcelot** during these speeches leaps out from the folio page. For Lydia Fletcher, the similarity in Arthur and Gwenyvere's language is a deliberate echo on Malory's part, adumbrating the final tragedy.[149] This foreshadowing is certainly present, but the reiteration in their language and their equally plangent reactions to the Quest also alert us to a *secular* or human reading of 'The Sankgreal' and ways in which values represented by Galahad are emphatically not endorsed by the majority of his fellows – especially his king and queen. Admittedly 'the moste party' of Round Table knights swear to seek the Grail, but the notable thing about the beginning of the Quest is that the knights follow and endorse the always-earthly Gawayne, not the celestial Galahad: 'So whan they of the Table Rounde harde Sir **Gawayne** sey so, they arose up the moste party and made such avowes as Sir **Gawayne** hadde made' (353^r; 674.24–6). Adventure and fellowship are driving forces, not spirituality.

Arthur is even more plangent about the destruction the Grail will bring in its wake when Nacien's damsel-messenger first announces the Quest. Far from rejoicing in any religious ecstasy or the proof of God's grace, Arthur bitterly laments how,

> Now ... I am sure at this quest of the **Sankegreall** shall *all ye* of the Rownde Table departe, and *nevyr shall I se you agayne holé togydirs*. Therefore ones shall I se you *togydir* in the medow, *all holé togydirs!* – therefore *I woll se you all holé*

---

[148] Hodges, *Forging Chivalric Communities*, pp. 110 and 111. See also Batt, *Remaking Arthurian Tradition*, pp. 133–5. The most severe threat to the late mediaeval English Church was Lollardy, a movement aided in some part by a handful of sympathetic 'Lollard knights', but as noted earlier, Malory was no doctrinal Lollard. See further K. B. McFarlane, *Lancastrian Kings and Lollard Knights* (Oxford, 1972), and Duffy, 'Religious Belief', in *A Social History of England*, pp. 323–9, who concludes that 'Lollardy was undoubtedly the greatest single challenge the English Church faced in this period', but qualifies that 'the importance of Lollardy in determining the agenda of fifteenth-century English Christianity has been grossly exaggerated'. Duffy's view is arguably an unspoken reprise of the tradition McFarlane challenged.

[149] Lydia Fletcher, '"Traytoures" and "Treson"', *Arthurian Literature 28: Blood, Sex, Malory* (2011): 75–88 (82).

togydir in the medow of **Camelot** – to juste and to turney, that aftir youre dethe men may speke of hit that such good knyghtes were here, such a day, *holé togydirs*. (W 352^{r-v}; *Works* 864.5–12; my emphases, and with a slight punctuation change; cf. *MD* 672.25–30)

Readers will notice that I return to the wording of Winchester (and Vinaver's edition) in this citation. I do so because Field argues on textual-critical grounds that the first 'therefore ... holé togydirs' clause is a scribal improvisation, and that the Caxton, which does not include this superfluous error, more accurately 'preserves what M[alory] wrote'.[150] Field's position is sensible, but since romance as a genre and Malory as an author are both fond of repetition, and since Malory is prone to flashes of psychological brilliance, Arthur's emotional state here might well result in some realistic and very human repetition. Exact verbal repetition, as noted a moment ago, is also part of Malory's form of lamentation. Nor can Field print the Caxton wording (at sig. N5^r) without some minor emendation. I therefore accept Winchester's reading as awkward but justified and authentic, foregrounding human fellowship and human emotion.

Certainly fellowship, worship and knighthood are the three palmary values and ideas throughout the *Morte Darthur*, and Arthur is clear that the Grail Quest will irrevocably sunder the worshipful fellowship of the Round Table which the previous tales and adventures in the *Morte* have seen come to fruition and glory.[151] Winchester's version of Arthur's lament is accordingly even more mournful precisely because of its recapitulation, reinforcing Arthur's character and his emotionally fraught state. As Mann emphasizes, the 'fourfold repetition of "holé togydir(s)" is Malory's own intensification of the single word "ensemble" in the [Vulgate] *Queste*'.[152] It is, for all intents and purposes, a significantly original modification of the source. As Moorman and Ihle perceptively observe in otherwise markedly different theses, the corresponding passage in the French book completely lacks Malory's profound sense of tragic waste and loss; this pathos and regret are achieved in large measure through the reiteration of 'holé togydirs'.[153] Significantly, Winchester's rubrication of characters' names and scattered marginalia recording various deeds by earthly heroes visually enacts and reinforces this human focus of knights wholly together.

Moorman argues further that the peace and comeliness which the Grail's subsequent arrival immediately casts over the Arthurian company (at 352^v–353^r;

---

[150] Field, Commentary on 672.27.

[151] On the importance of fellowship to Malory and the *Morte*, see especially Elizabeth Archibald, 'Malory's Ideal of Fellowship', *Review of English Studies* n.s. 43 (1992): 311–28; and my 'Malory's Secular Arthuriad', in *Malory and Christianity*, pp. 157–79. Although I do not accept all of their conclusions, both Mark Lambert and Kathleen Coyne Kelly testify, in very different ways, to the importance of the 'holé togydir' ideal in the *Morte*: see Mark Lambert, *Malory: Style and Vision in Le Morte Darthur* (New Haven and London, 1975), pp. 56–65; and Kathleen Coyne Kelly, 'Malory's Body Chivalric', *Arthuriana* 6.4 (1996): 52–71 (61–2), and eadem, 'Menaced Masculinity and Imperiled Virginity in the *Morte Darthur*', *Menacing Virgins*, ed. Kathleen Coyne Kelly and Marina Leslie (Cranbury, NJ, 1999), pp. 97–114 (pp. 107–8).

[152] Mann, 'Malory and the Grail', in her *Life in Words*, p. 320. For the single appearance of 'ensemble' in the corresponding scene in the source, see *Queste*, p. 13.

[153] Compare and contrast Moorman, '"Tale of the Sankgreall"', in *Originality*, pp. 203–4, with Ihle, *Malory's Grail Quest*, pp. 140–1.

673.26–674.10) is proof of the superiority of the celestial themes which, he claims, Malory shares with his source. Malory's ascetic renunciation of earthly institutions in this scene, however, is far from self-evident. On the contrary, while in the *Queste*, as Ihle illustrates, 'earthly attachments must give way to spiritual demands', Malory consistently emphasizes the earthly brotherhood that bonds knights together, and the Grail light that causes 'every knyght to beholde other ... fayrer than ever they were before' (673.33–4) intensifies rather than negates this bond, thereby 'link[ing] the initial appearance of the Grail to the idea of [secular human] brotherhood'.[154] Hence the considerable and repeated 'wepyng' when the one hundred and fifty knights of the Round Table depart for the Quest and, in another departure from the source, the fact that 'the kynge [too] turned away and myght nat speke for wepyng' (354^{r-v}; 676.33–677.18). Hence too the prominence of the word 'felyshyp' and its cognates throughout this tale; indeed, 'felyshyp' appears most frequently in the *Morte Darthur* in 'The Tale of the Sankgreal', and in that tale of countless human adventures, 'The Boke of Syr Trystram'.[155] Consequently, Malory's very human memorializing of the earthly chivalric fellowship is actively explicit in Arthur's concern that 'men may speke of' the Round Table company after the knights' deaths. The memorializing nature of this speech is not only reinforced but physically enabled by the manuscript, where Winchester's rubrication of knightly names renders the entire manuscript (and its narrative) into an elegiac monument to the glory and loss of 'such good knyghtes [as] were here, such a day, holé togydirs'. The manuscript itself becomes the knights' tomb, and the tomb celebrates, not castigates, its rubricated characters.

Many of Malory's small additions to his source material in 'The Sankgreal' thus have the effect of destabilizing the monologic asceticism of the Vulgate *Queste*. So, too, does the retrospective commentary which prefaces the tale of 'Sir Launcelot and Queen Guenivere' immediately upon the Quest's completion: 'for, as the booke seyth, had not sir **Launcelot** bene in his prevy thoughtes and in hys myndis so sette inwardly to the quene ... there had no knyght passed hym in the queste of the **Sankgreall**' (409^v; 790.12–15). Neither the French nor English book says any such thing, and the sentiment is original to Malory. Far from condemning Launcelot,[156] these words are further proof of the extent to which Malory mitigates Launcelot's failure in the Grail Quest, rendering the unqualified failure of the source into a qualified success in Malory's version. As B. J. Whiting notes in his classic study of Gawain, the Grail tradition and its condemnation of Gawain is one of the key factors contributing to the decline in Gawain's heroic reputation; Lancelot, in contrast, is granted a 'pious sophistry' that enables him much greater access to the Grail than he should by rights receive.[157] This enablement is even truer of Malory's Launcelot than of his French counterpart in the Vulgate *Queste*.

---

[154] Ihle, *Malory's Grail Quest*, pp. 132–3.
[155] Archibald, 'Malory's Ideal', 318; and Tomomi Kato, ed., *A Concordance to the Works of Sir Thomas Malory* (Tokyo, 1974), s.v. 'felyshep', 'felyship', felyshipped', 'felyshyp', 'felyshyppe', 'felyshyppyd', 'felysship'. Significantly, there are too many citations of 'felyshyp' to list here.
[156] *Contra* Charles Moorman, 'Caxton's *Morte Darthur*', *Fifteenth-Century Studies* 12 (1987): 99–113.
[157] B. J. Whiting, 'Gawain', *Mediaeval Studies* 9 (1947): 189–234 (215).

Tellingly, Winchester's rubrication at the opening of 'Sir Launcelot and Queen Guenivere' (Tale VII) similarly foregrounds Malory's focus on human character and human action.

As noted, the light from the Grail as it flits through the court illuminates each knight to his fellow. Throughout Winchester, the rubrication similarly highlights each knight for Malory's readers. Crucially, the rubricated names that leap off the page as one turns from the Grail Quest back to Camelot are the triad of Sankgreal–Gwenyvere–Launcelot.[158] The triad, however, is decidedly lopsided: '**Sankgreal**' occurs twice in the first four lines, the first appearance in the larger script of the opening line, and twice more over roughly the first half of the folio, for a total of four appearances (409^v; 790). Even when 'Sankgreal' does occur, however, it is always juxtaposed with, and quickly overshadowed by, rubricated references to **Arthur** (once), **Gwenyvere** (three times), **Launcelot** (seven times) and **Bors** (once), as well as one non-rubricated 'King' and four non-rubricated mentions of 'Queen', together with one rubricated appearance of '**Aggravayne** Sir **Gawayne's** brothir'. Both aurally and visually, the Grail quickly disappears as one works down the opening folio of the penultimate tale; what dominates instead are the names **Gwenyvere** and – even more so – **Launcelot**, and their names are so prominent because Malory is reintroducing and reprioritizing the lovers' passionate relationship. The mention and appearance of **Aggravayne** likewise emphasizes their imminent human tragedy by foregrounding one of their principal opponents of the closing tales. Given the thematic consistency of the Arthuriad as a whole and Malory's concern to establish various echoes and links forward and backward across the *Morte Darthur*, it is no doubt deliberate and significant that this same aural and visual dominance of **Launcelot** is found at the opening of the 'Tale of the Sankgreal' (349^r; 665), where his name appears rubricated eleven times, more than anyone else on this folio. Once again, Malory and Winchester emphasize thematic and narrative unity, a unity focussed on chivalric excellence epitomized by Launcelot and his Round Table fellows.

Although the majority of Caxton's major changes to the *Morte Darthur* occur in Tale II, Caxton also interferes with the closing tales at times, including in Tale VII, where he downplays Malory's emphasis on human character and human love. Caxton does this in the Fair Maid story by modifying Elayne of Ascolat's insistence that her very human love of Launcelot is divinely sanctioned. In Elayne's speech – 'my belyve ys that I do none offence, though I love an erthely man, *unto God, for He fourmed me thereto, and all maner of good love commyth of God.* ... And I take God to recorde, I ... had no myght to withstonde the fervent love, wherefore I have my deth' (428^{r-v}; 827.19–828.2) – the italicized phrase in my quotation was cut by Caxton. For Shaw, this excision, like some of Caxton's earlier modifications to the Roman War, stems from Caxton's concern with the possibly irreligious nature of Malory's text.[159] I argued earlier that Malory's willingness to carry over from the alliterative *Morte* the joke about the giant being

---

[158] My thinking here was inspired by conversations with Thomas H. Crofts and Megan G. Leitch, to each of whom I am much indebted.

[159] Shaw, 'Caxton and Malory', in *Essays*, pp. 129–30. Duffy characterizes Caxton as 'religiously conservative': *Stripping of the Altars*, p. 78.

a saint displays Malory's secular and human focus by revealing the extent to which he is unconcerned with religious controversy. Elayne's speech has the same implication since she uses it to rebut her priest's injunction to 'leve such thoughtes', thoughts that are 'ever ... unto Sir Launcelot' to the extent that 'she never slepte, ete, nother dranke, ... so that she muste nedis passe oute of thys worlde' (428^r; 827.12–19). According to Elayne's priest, her excessive love and suicidal despair for Launcelot are sinful; according to Elayne, her feelings and actions are not only human, they are divinely sanctioned. Since Elayne's argument is original to Malory, Malory's secular and human focus is arguably even more apparent here than in the Roman War.[160] Admittedly Elayne also expresses hope that the 'unnumerable paynys' that she suffers as a result of her love and her death might alleviate her sufferings in Purgatory (428^{r-v}; 827.27–31), a view that partly reflects orthodox religious belief as well as the widespread late mediaeval lay anxiety about Purgatory.[161] Elayne's speech thus shows that intermingling of secular and sacred that occurs now and again throughout the Arthuriad; but her primary focus, much to Caxton's evident consternation, is more earthly and human than heavenly or theological. Elayne does not repent her love and do penance, but dies for unrequited love, rebuffing her priest and appropriating her earthly suffering for earthly love as hopefully fulfilling some aspect of her Purgatorial pains. Such holds true for Malory's whole book.

Elayne's (and Malory's) human focus is reinforced by the *ordinatio* or rubrication in Winchester, since the rubricated name **Launcelot** appears seven times on folio 428^r prior to her speech, and another three times during the remainder of the speech at the bottom of this folio and once more near the top of the next. Neither 'God' nor any divine pronouns are so rubricated in this scene. This foregrounding of Launcelot is but one example of the marked intersection of the codicological and lexical texts of Malory's *Morte Darthur*. In this instance, the Winchester text of the *Morte* both aurally and visually prepares the reader for the prominence of Launcelot in Elayne's thoughts – and ours. Textual theme, authorial originality and treatment of sources, and manuscript layout all suggest that Malory and his characters are sympathetic to Elayne's love, behaviour and fate. The Maid's rich and worshipful burial, with the Requiem Mass implied by the 'masse-peny' offered on her behalf by Launcelot and his Round Table fellows (429^r; 830.17–24), bears this out.

The post-Grail valorization of Launcelot that occurs in Malory's text is partly the case even in the Vulgate *Mort le roi Artu*, where Lancelot after the Grail Quest is presented as once again honourable and chivalric, the best the world has to offer, even – paradoxically – as he is partly responsible for the Arthurian world's imminent destruction. But Malory follows and expands this favourable portrait of Launcelot, and he does so partly by increasing the poignancy and the emotion, as well as the tragedy, at the climax of the Arthurian story. Malory also downplays the religious elements. Critics often stress that Gwenyvere dies an abbess

---

[160] On the originality of the speech see Vinaver's Commentary on *Works* 1092.9–1095.14. On the thematic implications of the speech, see my 'Love and Death in Arthurian Romance', in *The Arthurian Way of Death*, ed. Karen Cherewatuk and K. S. Whetter (Cambridge, 2010), pp. 94–114 (pp. 110–12).

[161] On lay concerns with 'the pains of Purgatory' see Duffy, *Stripping of the Altars*, pp. 338–76.

(482^v–483^r; 928.33–930.2 and C XXI.10; 935.21–35) and Launcelot dies a monk (or even saint) in a religious community, sung to heaven by angels (C XXI.10; 934.10–25; and C XXI.12; 938.9–19). This is all quite true, but Malory juxtaposes these religious deaths with some extremely earthly and human emotions. The secular emotion is palpable in Launcelot and Gwenyvere's moving farewell. Originally in *La Mort Artu* there was no final meeting between Lancelot and Guinevere; the Palatinus Latinus manuscript version which does place the lovers together is a later interpolation that Malory did not know. Instead, as he does throughout his final tales, he turns to the stanzaic *Morte Arthur* for his source here. In the original *Mort Artu*, Guenievre dies before meeting Lancelot, and the author praises her penance and prayers for forgiveness.[162] It is the English stanzaic-poet who is generally credited with creating what Elizabeth Archibald justly describes as 'the powerful and emotional' meeting between Launcelot and Gaynor in the abbey.[163] The stanzaic *Morte*'s version of events greatly increases the pathos and emotion of the story's close; but Malory once again goes further than his source.

In the stanzaic *Morte*, Gaynor swoons when she learns of Launcelot's approach to the abbey where she has retired; waking, she explains to the Abbess and nuns how she and Launcelot are responsible for the kingdom's destruction, and explicitly states that she will seek her 'sowle hele' by 'amend[ing]' her sins and hopefully winning God's grace (vv. 3622–61). She then prays Launcelot to leave her, return to his lands and take a wife. Still loving her, he swears to follow her example, begs a parting kiss which she refuses, and then rides off, to the consternation of both (vv. 3662–741). Malory follows the stanzaic *Morte*'s basic plotline, but he makes a number of subtle yet effective adjustments. In both texts Launcelot hears that Gwenyvere has fled, no one knows where, and in both texts he rides alone in search of her; in both texts, too, he just happens, whether by chance or Fortune, eventually to arrive at Gwenyvere's abbey, instigating her swoon. In the poem, however, it is the nuns who decide to bring Launcelot before the queen (vv. 3634–56); in Malory, Gwenyvere herself asks her fellows to 'calle hym hyddir to me' (484^r; 932.23–7). Malory's Gwenyvere also speaks directly to Launcelot more than does her stanzaic counterpart; she tells the nuns of her and Launcelot's guilt, but addresses Launcelot directly concerning her intention 'to get [her] soule hele' and her hope that 'thorow Goddis grace and thorow Hys Passion ... I may have a syght of the blyssed face of Cryste Jesu, and on Doomesday to sytte on Hys ryght syde; for as synfull as ever I was, now ar seyntes in hevyn' (484^v; 932.28–933.2). Just prior to this meeting Malory also emphasizes Gwenyvere's 'grete penaunce' (482^v–483^r; 929.1–6). Since the notions of God's grace, Christ's Passion and human penance securing redemption are all straightforwardly orthodox (at least in the Middle Ages), we once again see Malory blending the secular with the sacred.

Nevertheless, although Gwenyvere's penance is at least partially genuine, Malory introduces into this religious orthodoxy his usual emphasis on human

---

[162] *Mort le roi Artu*, §197.10–17, p. 254. Frappier includes the Palatinus scene as an appendix.
[163] Elizabeth Archibald, 'Lancelot as Lover in the English Tradition before Malory', in *Arthurian Studies in Honour of P. J. C. Field*, ed. Bonnie Wheeler (Cambridge, 2004), pp. 199–216 (pp. 214–15).

fellowship, human love, and knighthood. One way this happens is by having Gwenyvere express her hope of grace directly to Launcelot rather than to the Abbess, as in the stanzaic *Morte*. Amy S. Kaufman argues for the continued potency of Gwenyvere's passion in the *Morte Darthur*, proposing that Gwenyvere has simply evolved from loving Arthur to loving Launcelot to loving God: a 'logical' progression in the queen's 'journey to subjectivity'.[164] Gwenyvere's passion, however, seems directed to all three: she becomes religious only when Arthur is dead, she then turns to loving God and acts accordingly, but her words and actions in this final meeting reveal that she also still loves Launcelot – so much so that she dare not kiss him for fear of a relapse (C XXI.10; 934.1–9). Reconciling the temptations and hardships of daily life with the proscriptions of the Church was a major concern for mediaeval Christians. Gwenyvere's pain in letting go of earthly attachments thus bespeaks Malory's realism and characterization at this point. The fact remains, however, that Launcelot is as much in the foreground here as is God. And as with everything Gwenyvere and Launcelot do, Arthur's shade hovers in the background.

The prominence of Launcelot and earthly love are mirrored and magnified by the Winchester manuscript, for what quite literally stands out in Gwenyvere's speech is the rubricated name of her lover: 'Cryste Jesu' and 'God' are never rubricated and so disappear amidst all the other dark brown text, but four red **Launcelot**s over three-quarters of the page figure quite prominently, especially since his is the only name appearing in, and so rubricated during, her speech (folio 484ᵛ). There are two red **Sankgreall**s at the bottom of the page, but since they appear during Launcelot's admission that his love for Gwenyvere caused him not to achieve the Grail, the effect of this, too, is to reinforce human love and earthly concerns by reiterating the prominence and power of Launcelot and Gwenyvere's very real passion. By happenstance this is the final surviving folio of the manuscript, meaning that the loss of the final gathering accidentally but tellingly foregrounds all the more Gwenyvere's and Malory's human focus: **Launcelot** and the knightly deeds and chivalric fellowship he epitomized.

The prominence of human emotion is even more apparent in Launcelot's reasons for becoming religious. Launcelot is still in France when Arthur and Mordred meet on Salisbury Plain. Arriving in the wake of the destruction of the Round Table Fellowship and the deaths of Gawayne and Arthur, Launcelot seeks out Gwenyvere with express intention: 'yf I had founden you now so dysposed, I had caste me to have had you into myn owne royame' (C XXI.9; 933.32–3). In this same speech Launcelot admits that he would have achieved the Grail and surpassed all Grail questers except Galahad 'had nat youre love bene' (484ᵛ; 933.27–9), and vows to mimic Gwenyvere's 'perfeccion'. What Launcelot does, in other words, is promise to undertake one last quest for his lover's sake, insisting that, 'sythen I fynde you thus desposed, I ensure you faythfully, I wyl ever take me to penaunce and praye[.] … Whefore, madame, I praye you kysse me' (C XXI.10; 933.33–934.2). No such speech occurs in the French source; even in the final meeting between the lovers in the stanzaic *Morte* there is no mention of their living together (vv. 3638–737). F. Whitehead argues that there are

---

[164] Amy S. Kaufman, 'Guenevere Burning', *Arthuriana* 20.1 (2010): 76–94 (at 78–9).

two remarkable and original features of Malory's version of events, neither of which is religious or even particularly penitential.[165] The first, it is claimed, is Launcelot's acknowledgement, simple fact rather than criticism, that he has partially 'sacrificed his renown on her behalf, counting this world (and the next) well lost for love'. Whitehead's claim is somewhat misleading since Launcelot categorically states that he would have achieved the Grail were it not for love of Gwenyvere (484^v; 933.25–9). Indeed, Launcelot and Malory both make the same point back at the beginning of Tale VII (respectively 410^r; 791.10–13; and 409^v; 790.10–15). Nonetheless, Launcelot equally categorically returns to that love immediately after the Grail Quest's completion, with Malory explicitly mentioning that 'they loved togydirs more hotter than they dud toforehonde' (409^v; 790.16–17). Launcelot does take pains to champion other ladies because, as he says to Gwenyvere, the mysteries of the Grail 'may nat be yet lyghtly forgotyn' (410^r; 791.13–15); but Malory takes pains to tell readers, and Launcelot takes pains to tell Gwenyvere, that the actions she objects to are also undertaken expressly 'for to eschew the slawndir' and keep their adulterous love secret (790.18–791.29). Thus, by the interview in the abbey, if Launcelot's vow to 'ever take me to penaunce and praye' sounds sincere, the phrase *'sythen ye* have taken you to perfeccion, *I must nedys* take me to perfection, *of ryght'* sounds designedly resigned rather than hopeful or penitent (my emphases). The secular and the sacred spectacularly collide here, but human emotions and concerns dominate. It is, after all, his lover more than his Creator that Launcelot hopes to appease.

Whitehead's second and even more remarkable point is the notion that with Arthur's demise, Launcelot and Gwenyvere, whilst genuinely mourning Arthur, can at least now pursue their love openly; retiring to Launcelot's 'owne royame', the lovers might even be able to enjoy the sort of domestic bliss temporarily won by Malory's Trystram and Isode at Joyous Garde. Such a prospect is, as Whitehead admits, somewhat 'indecent', and yet there it is, and it is an original and probably deliberate addition by Malory. Authors don't always write what they intend, of course, and scholarship has made much of Malory's inconsistencies and errors; but since Launcelot prefaces his desire to live with Gwenyvere by appealing to God's witness (C XXI.9; 933.31–3), the whole passage is granted a solemnity that endorses Launcelot's intentions as well as Malory's words. The idea of living happily with Gwenyvere, however strange, or even, to use Whitehead's term, 'profane', is clearly genuine. Once again Malory conjoins the secular with the sacred, and once again the secular ultimately prevails. Despite his Grail humiliations, Launcelot is unrepentant. He quite clearly only becomes religious out of love for Gwenyvere now that Arthur and the fellowship are 'disparbeled' (450^r; 872.3) and slain, and now that Gwenyvere denies herself to him.

Even this denial is dominated by human feeling and characters, for Gwenyvere laments how,

> Thorow thys same man and me hath all thys warre be wrought, and the deth of the moste nobelest knyghtes of the worlde, for thorow oure love that we have loved togydir ys my moste noble lorde slayne. … [A]nd I commaunde the, on

[165] F. Whitehead, 'Lancelot's Penance', in *Essays*, pp. 104–13 (pp. 111–12). The quotations that follow are from pp. 111 and 112.

Goddis behalff, that thou forsake my company. And to thy kyngedom loke thou turne agayne, and kepe well thy realme frome warre and wrake, for as well as I have loved the heretofore, myne harte woll nat serve me now to se the; for thorow the and me ys the floure of kyngis and knyghtes destroyed. (484^{r-v}; 932.29–933.10)

Gwenyvere gives notably more attention here to earthly than spiritual matters. As C. David Benson judiciously remarks, Jesus 'seems decidedly secondary' to human concerns; Gwenyvere's focus is instead on the injuries done 'her earthly not heavenly lord'.[166] She is equally focussed, we might add, on a very prosaic and secular concern with the welfare of Launcelot's earthly realm and happiness, and the memory of the Round Table Fellowship.

The final meeting between Malory's lovers also helps to demonstrate once again the fallacy of the modern critical notion that Launcelot is unstable. On the contrary, the concluding pages of Malory's *Morte Darthur* repeatedly demonstrate the absolute consistency of Launcelot's actions and motivations. I have already mentioned Launcelot's own admission of Gwenyvere's continued influence even during the Grail Quest, and we have just seen how he undertakes one final adventure out of love for her once she denies herself to him and he accordingly swears 'the same desteny that ye have takyn you to, I woll take me to' (484v; 933.17–18). Appropriately enough, Launcelot's final actions in the *Morte* also display the consistency of his love for Gawayne and Arthur. The importance and role of each of Launcelot, Gwenyvere, Arthur and Gawayne in the destruction of the realm are reinforced by the fact that the lovers' farewell meeting is enveloped between Launcelot's visit to Gawayne's tomb and Launcelot's arrival at Arthur's tomb. The arrival at Gawayne's tomb is deliberate and that at Arthur's fortunate or fated, but the two scenes conclude the same way. Displaying the consistency of his motivation and loves, Launcelot spends 'too nyghtes upon [Gawayne's] tumbe in prayers and in dolefull wepynge' (483^v–484^r; 931.32–3). Then he rides to find Gwenyvere in the hope of taking her to Benwick. And when she rebuffs him, he rides, 'wepyng' again, until he happens upon the hermitage where Bedwere and the former Archbishop are hearing mass and attending Arthur's grave (C XXI.10; 934.10–23). Launcelot's initial reaction on hearing Bedwere's news is to exclaim, 'Alas! Who may truste thys world?', a statement that might be thought to indicate an appropriately pious and penitential response to earthly suffering in anticipation of a *contemptus mundi* turn to more heavenly concerns on the part of Malory and his characters. But such is not the case. Instead, first Launcelot, then Bors, then, some time later, Galyhud, Galyhodyn, Blamour, Bleoberis, Wyllyars, Clarrus and Gahallantyne ask to join Bedwere and the Archbishop at Arthur's tomb in a macabre and sorrowful attempt to recreate the once glorious earthly fellowship of knights that is now destroyed. Just as the Round Table Fellowship was dominated by Arthur's kingship and the Oath he made all knights swear, so this fragmentary fellowship is dominated by Arthur's tomb and the attempt, by Bors and Launcelot, to remain by Arthur's side even if Arthur is dead. Likewise

---

[166] See C. David Benson, 'The Ending of the *Morte Darthur*', in *Companion*, pp. 221–38 (p. 236). Cf. my *Understanding Genre*, p. 144; Benson, *Malory's Morte Darthur*, pp. 244–5; and Vinaver, pp. xcviii and 1621–2.

the remnant of the Fellowship wish to join Launcelot and the dead Arthur. This company of mourners, as Archibald perceptively notes, is repeatedly described in terms of 'felowes' or 'felyshyp', thereby 'remind[ing] us of the value of this Arthurian and Malorian ideal'.[167] Fellowship is hardly exclusively secular, and Psalm 132/133 speaks of the pleasures of religious brethren dwelling together. This company of mourners at Arthur's grave, however, is not a monastic fellowship celebrating Christ. It is a sorrowful secular company who have lost their earthly leader (Arthur), and who join their earthly exemplar (Launcelot) in a new purpose: to render themselves into a memorializing tribute to Arthurian kingship and knighthood that emphasizes all the more the tragic sense of waste and loss generated by all those who fell to the earth at Salisbury Plain.[168] Just as Arthur's defeat of Lott and the rebel kings in the battle that cements his kingship is marked by a memorializing tomb and marginalium early in the *Morte Darthur* (28^v; 61.31–62.11), so now Arthur's death is marked by his own tomb, complete with rubricated inscription (482^v) and company of mourners.

Launcelot is consistent in his love of both Gwenyvere and Arthur; so too is Malory. Malory's love of his characters is evident throughout the lexical text of the *Morte Darthur*, through the thematic emphases of his Arthuriad and through the care he takes to name characters unnamed in the sources. Character is also highlighted by the rubrication and marginalia in Winchester, where manuscript *ordinatio* visually reinforces Malory's focus on earthly character and (by association) earthly themes associated with these characters. Despite the claims of many modern critics about the religiousness of Malory or his text, the orthodox elements of the *Morte Darthur* are cultural more than conclusive.[169] Malory was, on the other hand, even more concerned than his printer with character, fellowship and combat, themes that are constantly and explicitly reiterated throughout the entirety of the narrative, from Arthur's conception through to his death and the deaths of his last remaining followers. Malory's human focus and secular themes are consistently reiterated by Winchester's rubrication of names and memorialization of knightly deeds. Combat, fellowship and chivalric memorialization are accordingly the subjects of my next chapter.

---

[167] Archibald, 'Malory's Ideal', 325–6.
[168] On the centrality of waste and loss to the creation of tragic effect see Stephen Halliwell, 'Plato's Repudiation of the Tragic', in *Tragedy and the Tragic*, ed. M. S. Silk (Oxford, 1996), pp. 332–49.
[169] The Vulgate *Queste* is dominated by theological doctrine, and Moorman, '"Tale of the Sankgreall"', in *Originality*, p. 187, epitomizes the scholarly view that Malory faithfully 'preserves the core of the French book's doctrinal statements' during the Grail Quest, with all that this means for the remainder of the Arthuriad. Besserman, *Biblical Paradigms*, pp. 113–34, argues for parallels throughout the *Morte Darthur* with biblical narrative, adding that such biblical echoes would be easily recognized by Malory's contemporary audiences, and that such biblical analogues shape and ultimately transcend Malory's more secular moments. Vinaver, looking at 'The Sankgreal' in isolation, argues that 'Malory has little use' for this doctrine (see pp. lxxxix–xc and xciii–xciv). I am firmly in the Vinaverian camp.

4
Rubricated Elegy

One of my principal contentions in this book is that the Winchester manuscript of Sir Thomas Malory's *Le Morte Darthur*, London, British Library Additional MS 59678, serves not only as a textual witness, but also functions figuratively as a tomb and memorial to the knights of the Round Table Fellowship and the ladies who inspire, threaten or instigate chivalric adventure. The close interaction of material manuscript and lexical narrative for which I am arguing is mirrored by the various memorials and tombs erected by Merlin and others within the narrative, whilst the manuscript and its rubrication function as a memorializing tomb for the tragic narrative and its earthly characters. Since Merlin (or Merlin with Blaise as amanuensis) also regularly records the major deeds and events of the Round Table, there is perhaps a self-referential and slightly tongue-in-cheek doubling on Malory's part of his authorial identity with Merlin's.[1] Even without Merlin's efforts to memorialize the deeds of the Round Table Fellowship, Malory's Arthur is careful to ensure that his knights regularly testify to and record their adventures.[2] Thus, to take a few notable instances, Gawayne, Torre and Pellynore are each made by Merlin and Arthur to 'telle of hys adventure(s)' during the three quests celebrating Arthur and Gwenyvere's wedding (respectively 39ᵛ; 86.33–4; and 41ᵛ; 91.28–9; and, with different wording, 44ʳ; 96.34–5); so too do Uwayne, Gawayne and Marhaus 'telle [the kynge] all theire adventures' (70ʳ; 143.1–3) in the parallel set of quests that close the adventurous episode that follows the wedding and the establishment of the Round Table Oath (97.27–98.3); and Arthur has 'grete clerkes … cronycle … the adventures of the **Sangreall**' as related by Bors and Launcelot and 'made in grete bookes' (408ᵛ; 788.28–35). This recording of knightly deeds within the narrative is matched in the codex that contains the Arthuriad by the Winchester manuscript's rubrication of names. Winchester's rubrication accordingly signifies the importance of Arthurian knighthood and achievement.

The close interaction between manuscript and narrative, in conjunction with the elegiac function of the manuscript's rubrication of names, corresponds well

---

[1] On Merlin as scribe or author see further the intriguing suggestion by Carolyne Larrington, 'The Enchantress, the Knight and the Cleric', *Arthurian Literature* 25 (2008): 43–65. On possible associations between Merlin and Malory in Winchester's occasional abbreviated but rubricated instances of 'M', see above, Chapter Two, pp. 60–1, 88–9.

[2] All parenthetical references to the *Morte Darthur* are to Winchester's folio number and the relevant page of Field's edition. Caxton cross-references are used where Winchester is wanting. For the benefit of readers reading only one chapter, I repeat that I have put all names quoted from the *Morte* in bold type in an attempt to match Winchester's rubrication. My capitalization of Fellowship in 'Round Table Fellowship' is similarly meant to convey the importance of chivalric companionship within the *Morte*.

with mediaeval ideas of symbolism and memory. About symbols St Augustine writes, 'a sign is a thing which of itself makes some other thing come to mind, besides the impression that it presents to the senses'.[3] Augustine's purposes in so defining signs were no doubt religious, perhaps also allegorical, but the idea can fruitfully be applied to my conception of the Winchester manuscript and its relation to the narrative and principal secular themes of *Le Morte Darthur*. Similarly, on memory, Mary Carruthers influentially observes how visual stimuli played a key role in mediaeval recall. This is the case even in the late Middle Ages, when oral and aural memory clearly helped transmit stories to a wider audience than just the literate elite. Indeed, both Carruthers and Donald R. Howard conceive of mediaeval memory functioning, in Howard's phrase, like 'a set of "places"' or book of passages, each of which might be gained or remembered with the help of a memorial key – including specific words or images.[4] In this light we might consider the well-established comparison of late mediaeval literature to Gothic architecture to be partly memorial as well as structural. In this chapter I wish more specifically to explore the multiple ways in which memory, narrative and manuscript form interact in Malory's *Morte Darthur*, paying particular attention to the ways in which the rubrication of names in the Winchester manuscript text of the *Morte Darthur* effectively renders the entire Arthuriad a memorial to the earthly deeds and tragic fates of Arthur, Gwenyvere, Launcelot, Gawayne and the other Knights of the Round Table.

Obviously one method of memorializing the Round Table Fellowship, including Arthur and including the many women who interact with the knights, is via the lexical words on the page. The most obvious and consistent type of wording here is the narrative proper of the *Morte Darthur*, the story as it is recorded by the words on the manuscript page, but we also have the marginalia scattered throughout the manuscript. Perhaps most significant for my argument about the probable authorial provenance of Winchester's rubrication and marginalia is William Matthews's observation that Caxton's chapter headings 'serve as a very useful index to Malory's work'.[5] This, I agree, is quite true but the very usefulness and fullness of Caxton's chapter headings in this regard reveal just how impractical is the similar suggestion by Carol M. Meale that the rubrication of names in Winchester acts as a sort of 'signposting' or reader's aid.[6] Undoubtedly the names are highlighted by the red ink, but the red names are simply too ubiquitous to be of much use as a textual index. Glancing at any page, most readers are probably not going to be able to contextualize the phrase 'Sir **Launcelot** was wroth at hys grymme wordys and gurde to hym with his swerde', for instance, regardless

---

[3] Augustine, *De Doctrina Christiana*, ed. and trans. R. P. H. Green (Oxford, 1995), II.i, pp. 56–7: 'Signum est enim res praeter speciem quam ingerit sensibus aliud aliquid ex se faciens in cogitationem venire.'

[4] Donald R. Howard, *The Idea of the Canterbury Tales* (Berkeley and Los Angeles, 1976), p. 188; and Mary Carruthers, *The Book of Memory*, 2nd edn (Cambridge, 2008).

[5] William Matthews, 'The Besieged Printer', in *Debate*, pp. 35–64 (p. 64, n. 48).

[6] Carol M. Meale, '"The Hoole Book"', in *Companion* (1996), pp. 3–17 (p. 10). This claim has recently been supported by Jonathan Passaro, 'Malory's Text of the *Suite du Merlin*', *Arthurian Literature* 26 (2009): 39–75 (61). For a rebuttal of both Meale and Passaro, see my 'Malory, Hardyng, and the Winchester Manuscript', *Arthuriana* 22.4 (2012): 167–89 (at 170–4).

of the rubrication.⁷ Some names and scenes would become more recognizable on a second or subsequent reading or hearing, of course, but the combination of formulaic scenes and language in the *Morte*, including the propensity for armed combat to erupt at any moment, means that names alone are rarely going to identify a scene. On the other hand, we might well make this 'signposting' claim about Winchester's eighty *marginalia*, textual précis or bookmarks which *do* help index a number of major events and characters and themes throughout the *Morte Darthur*. In this sense, though not in others, I am in complete agreement with Nicole Eddy, who quite rightly concludes that Winchester's marginal annotations serve 'as a guide by which contemporary readers could more easily understand the *Morte*', though she sees such understanding happening *in situ* as readers work through the text, not as an index or means of jumping from one episode to the next and not as a type of thematic patterning.⁸ As we shall see, I strongly disagree with Eddy's conclusions about the marginalia lacking thematic context within Malory's Arthuriad as a whole.

Certainly many of Winchester's marginalia, like Caxton's chapter headings, denote action or important events. James Wade, however, advancing Cooper's position about the scribal origin of the marginalia, claims that several marginalia are 'in the wrong place'.⁹ One example, argues Wade, is the death of Columbe, where the marginal note demarking her suicide occurs next to the tomb built for Columbe and Lanceor by Mark at folio 26ᵛ, rather than immediately adjacent to her actual death at folio 25ᵛ (*MD* 54.22–56.32). The obvious explanation for this dislocation, urges Wade, is that Columbe is not named till the inscription on the tomb and thus Scribe A, not Malory, must be responsible for this marginal gloss; Malory would know the character's name, but the scribe had to wait. The marginalia, it is said, are thus scribal, not authorial.

I hopefully established that Winchester's marginalia derive ultimately from Malory in my discussion of Winchester's origins and *ordinatio* in Chapter Two. What I wish to emphasize in the current chapter is just how precisely the manuscript marginalium and textual tomb mirror one another here, even to the extent of the marginalium coming later than we might expect. As Wade himself acknowledges, 'the annotation paraphrases what is already a retrospective passage'.¹⁰ This mirroring, I suggest, is the real crux of the matter, for thematically it makes as much sense to place the Columbe marginalium next to her tomb as next to her death. Such placement is especially the case if the marginalia originate with Malory, for Malory would see the death and the tomb, the text and the

---

⁷ The phrase was chosen at random; it occurs in Tale II's Roman War (86ᵛ; 172.25–6).
⁸ Nicole Eddy, 'Annotating the Winchester Malory', *Viator* 42.2 (2011): 283–305 (305). Cf. James Wade, 'Malory's Marginalia Reconsidered', *Arthuriana* 21.3 (2011): 70–86, who does consider the marginalia to possess 'an indexical function' (78), but who also notes (72–4) that sometimes Caxton's chapter headings are more useful or successful 'indexical markers' than the marginalia. Wade's overarching thesis is, like that of Helen Cooper, that the marginalia reflect scribal engagement with the text. Eddy believes that the marginalia are probably scribal, but is equally willing to attribute them to an early reader. For Cooper's view of the marginalia, see Cooper, 'Opening Up the Malory Manuscript', in *Debate*, pp. 268–71.
⁹ Wade, 'Malory's Marginalia', 75.
¹⁰ Wade, 'Malory's Marginalia', 75.

marginalium, as interconnected elements of narrative plot and theme in ways the scribes would not: Malory would recognize, as his scribes might not, that the late marginalium memorializes the activities of the Round Table knights and their opponents. Malory would be even more likely to recognize that this slightly tardy correlation between text and marginalium actually reinforces the elegiac quality of the *Morte* in both its lexical and its codicological forms, including the marginalia. The tomb, after all, marks the 'grete sorow' caused by Launceor and Columbe's deaths, as well as memorializing their 'trew love' (26^r; 56.22–3). Even more significantly given the damning criticism often levelled against Balyn by modern scholars, the tomb's inscription exculpates Balyn of any wrongdoing, emphasizing that Launceor died by Balyn's hand 'at hys owne rekeyste', and that Columbe 'slew hirself with hys swerde for dole and sorow' (26^v; 56.29–32). Significantly for Balyn's reputation, the emphasis on Launceor's responsibility for his own death is original to Malory.[11] Balyn is thus exonerated, but not saved: as Alan Lupack justly observes, the tomb's 'inscription ... makes evident the tragic nature of the events. ... Even though Lanceor sought and initiated the combat with Balin and Columbe slew herself, Balin will suffer the consequences. Such is the tragic nature of the Arthurian world.'[12]

Elizabeth Edwards argues that tombstone writing has an especial authority in the *Morte Darthur*, and that 'writing on tombs has a particular credibility in the early books and on the Grail Quest'.[13] There are in fact a good many such memorializing monuments and inscriptions scattered in Balyn's wake, and much the same thing could be said about them. Merlin, for instance, soon arrives at Lanceor and Columbe's memorial where, 'with lettirs of golde', he prophesies 'the grettist bateyle betwyxte too knyghtes that ever was or ever shall be, and the trewyst lovers' (26^v; 56.33–57.4). Although the abbreviation pattern is inconsistent, Merlin's arrival here is one of those occasions in Winchester where his identity is unknown and his name appears as an abbreviated but rubricated '**M**', but also in full as **Merlion**.[14] His prophecy of Launcelot and Trystram's battle, moreover, is much more specific in Malory's version than the source, a fact which

---

[11] On the originality of the claim, see Vinaver, Commentary on *Works* 71.30–1. Kenneth Tiller, 'En-graving Chivalry', *Arthuriana* 14.2 (2004): 37–53 (41), makes the same point about Balyn being exonerated by the tomb. My argument overlaps with Tiller's in places, but we come to quite different conclusions: in particular, I disagree with Tiller's claim that without such tombs chivalric violence in the *Morte* is meaningless, and I disagree that Malory simultaneously uses tombs to undermine and 'problematize the code of chivalry' (49).

[12] Alan Lupack, 'Malory's Intratexts', in *Romance and Rhetoric*, ed. Georgina Donovain and Anita Obermeier (Turnhout, 2010), pp. 249–68 (p. 264). For a detailed account of Balyn's tragedy and a further defence of his actions, see my 'On Misunderstanding Malory's Balyn', in *Re-Viewing Le Morte Darthur*, ed. Whetter and Raluca L. Radulescu (Cambridge, 2005), pp. 149–62.

[13] Elizabeth Edwards, *The Genesis of Narrative in Malory's Morte Darthur* (Cambridge, 2001), pp. 177 and 167. Edwards's remarks are rather more convincing than Alan J. Fletcher's contention that 'the *Morte Darthur*'s numerous inscriptions, letters, and, especially, tomb memorializations' signify Malory's and his text's anxiety with the stability and reliability of authority: see Fletcher, *The Presence of Medieval English Literature* (Turnhout, 2012), pp. 219–20. In either case we might link such patterning to the well-established fact that Malory takes particular care in the early books of the *Morte* to establish connections with later events.

[14] On the abbreviation of Merlin's name see above, Chapter Two, pp. 59–60, 88–9, including the references to Cooper's discussion of the abbreviation.

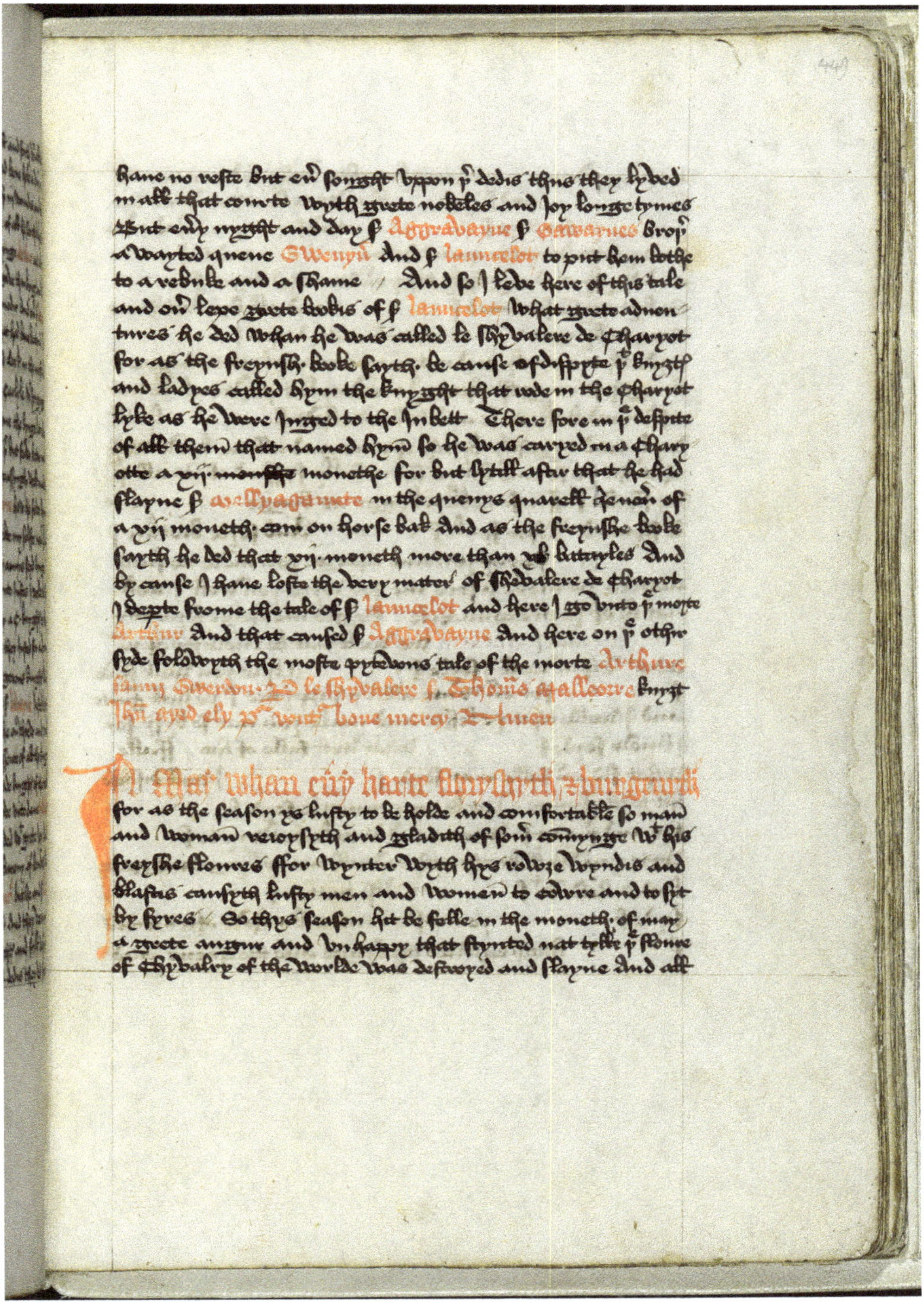

have no reste but euer sought uppon dedis thus they lyved in all that cowrte wyth grete nobeles and joy longe tymes. But every nyght and day sir Aggravayne sir Gawaynes brother awayted quene Gwenyvir and sir launcelot to put hem bothe to a rebuke and a shame. And so I leve here of this tale and ovir lepe grete bokis of sir launcelot what grete adven tures he ded whan he was called le shyvalere de charyot for as the frenysshe booke saythe be cause of dispyte that knyghtis and ladyes called hym the knyght that rode in the charyot lyke as he were juged to the jubett. There fore in dispite of all them that named hym so he was cawsed in a charyotte a xij moneths monethe for but lytyll after that he had slayne sir Mellyagraunte in the quenys quarell kened of a xij monethys. on horse bak And as the frensshe boke sayth he ded that xij moneth more than xl batayles. And by cause I have loste the very mater of shyvalere de charyot I departe from the tale of sir launcelot and here I go unto the morte Arthur And that caused sir Aggravayne And here on the other syde folowyth the moste pytewous tale of the morte Arthure saunz Guerdon: le shyvalere sir Thomas Malleorre knyght Jhu and ely us wyth love mercy & Amen

In May whan euery harte floryshyth & burgenyth for as the season ys lusty to be holde and comfortable so man and woman reioysyth and gladith of som commynge. With his fresshe flowrys. ffor Wynter wyth hys rowghe wyndis and blastys causyth lusty men and women to cowre and to sytt by feres So thys season hit be falle in the moneth of may a grete angur and vn happy that stynted nat tylle the floure of chyvalry of the worlde was destroyed and slayne And all

Plate XIII: The Tale VII *explicit*–Tale VIII *incipit*: Winchester, fol. 449ʳ.

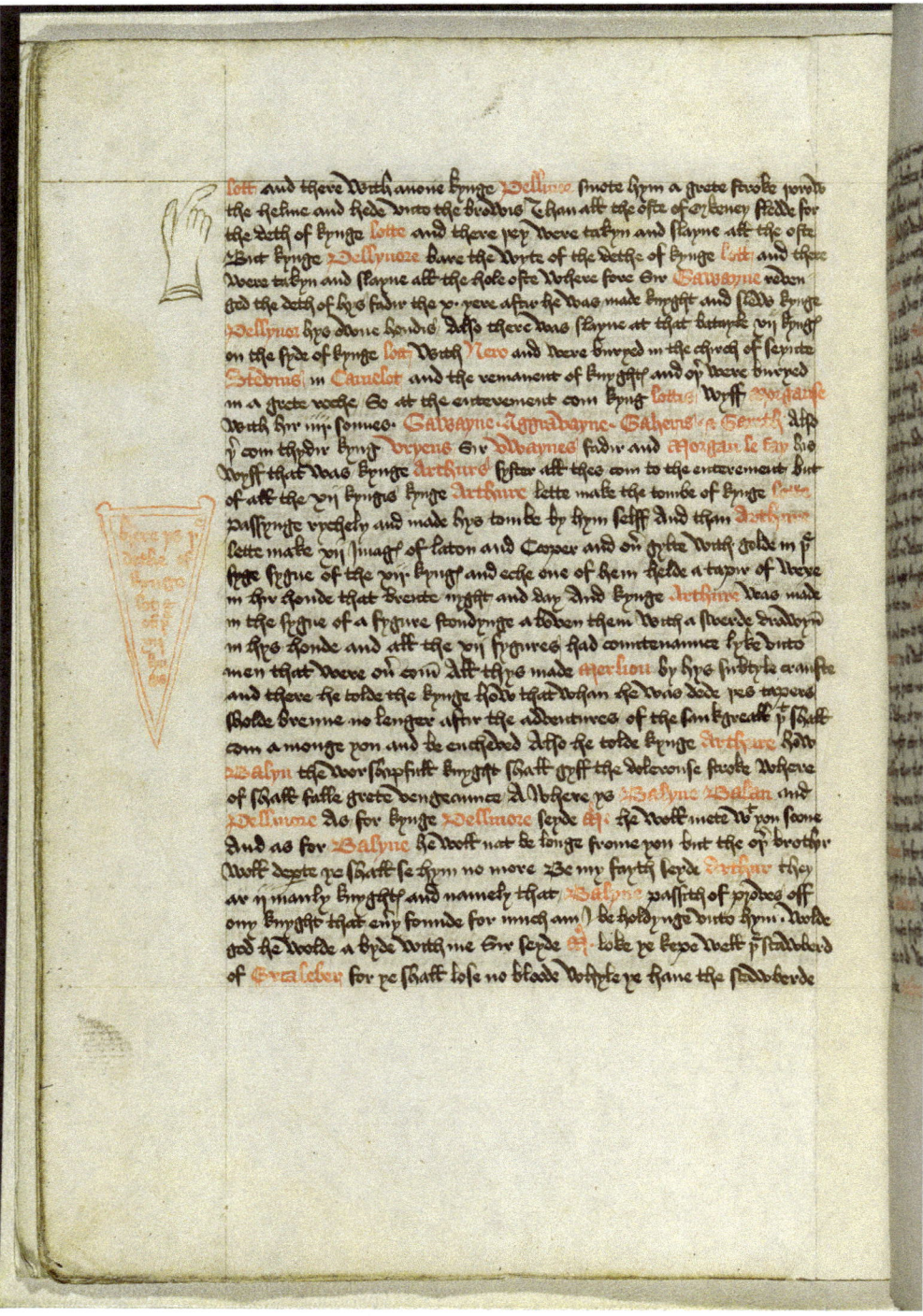

Plate XIV: Marginalium recording the deaths of Lott and the rebels and memorializing Arthur's victory: Winchester, fol. 28ᵛ.

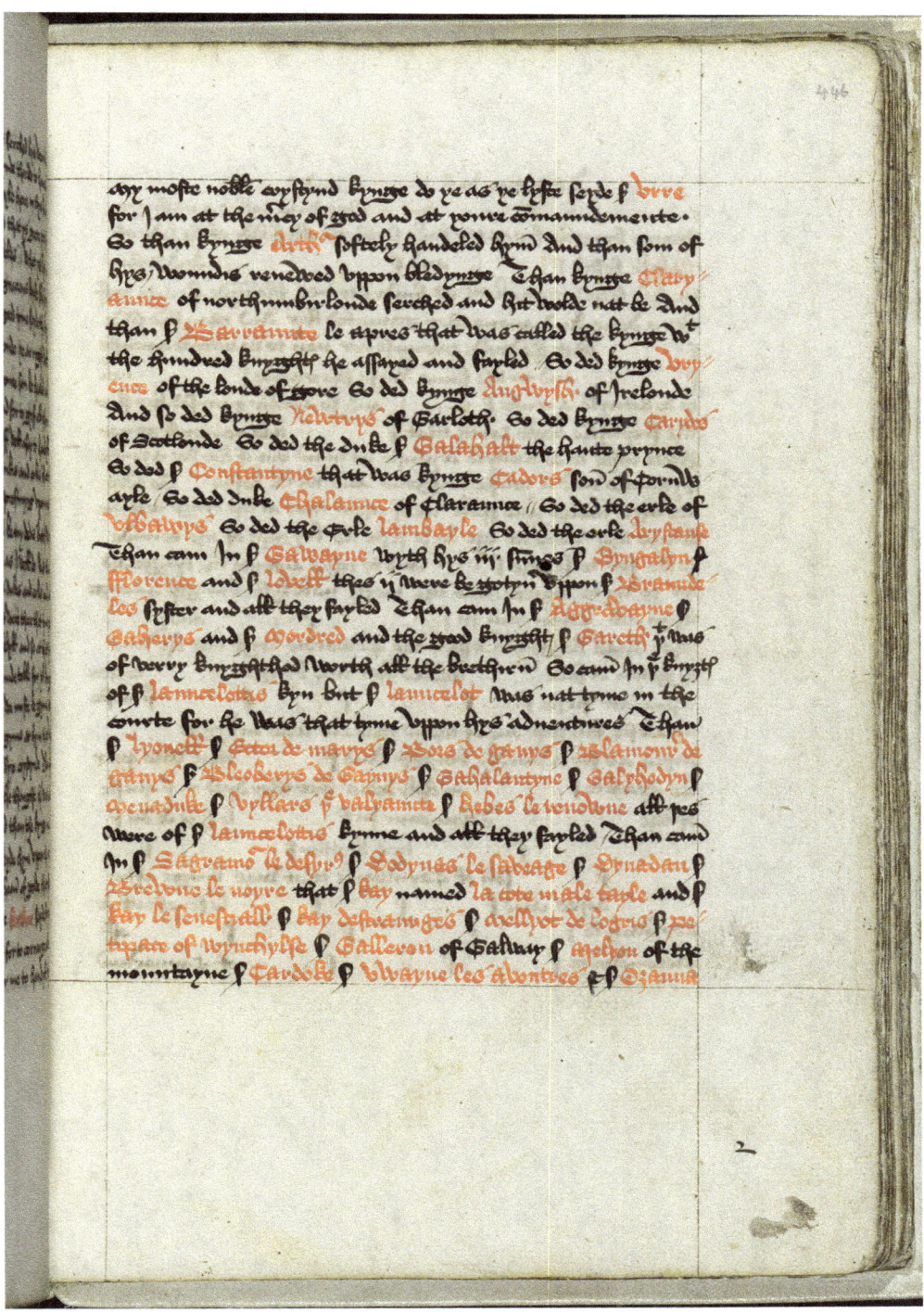

ay moste noble crystynd kynge do ye as ye hve seyde *Urre*
for I am at the mercy of god and at yowre commaundemente.
So than kynge *Arthur* sofftely handeled hym and than som of
hys woundis renewed uppon bledynge · Than kynge *Clary-*
aunce of northumbirlonde serched and hit wolde nat be · And
than *S Barraunte* le apres that was called the kynge wt
the hundred knyghtys he assayed and fayled · So ded kynge *Uri-*
ens of the londe of Gore · So ded kynge *Anguysh* of Irelonde
And so ded kynge *Nentrys* of Garloth · So ded kynge *Carados*
of Scotlonde · So ded the duke *S Galahalt* the haute prynce
So ded *S Constantyne* that was kynge *Cadors* son of Cornay-
ayle · So ded duke *Chalaunce* of Claraunce · So ded the erle of
Ulbawys · So ded the erle *lambayle* · So ded the erle *Aryftause*
Than cam in *S Gawayne* wyth hys iij sunys *S Gyngalyn S*
fflorence and *S lovell* thes ij were be gotyn uppon *S Braundi-*
les syster · and all they fayled · Than cam in *S Aggravayne S*
Gaherys and *S Mordred* and the good knyght *S Gareth* þt was
of verry knyghthod worth all the brethern · So cam in þe knyghts
of *S launcelottis* kyn but *S launcelot* was nat tyme in the
courte for he was that tyme uppon hys adventures · Than
S Lyonell S Ector de marys S Bors de Ganys S Blamour de
Ganys S Bleoberys de Ganys S Bahalauntyne S Galyhodyn
Menaduke S Vyllars S Hebes le renowne all þes
were of *S launcelottis* kynne · and all they fayled · Than cam
in *S Sagramor le desyr S Dodynas le sabeage S Dynadan S*
Bredone le noyre that *S kay* named *la cote male tayle* and *S*
kay le seneschall S kay destraunges S Mellyot de logris S pre-
tyvate of Wynchylsee S Galleron of Galway S Melyon of the
mountayne S Cardoke S Uwayne les Avoutres et S Ozanna

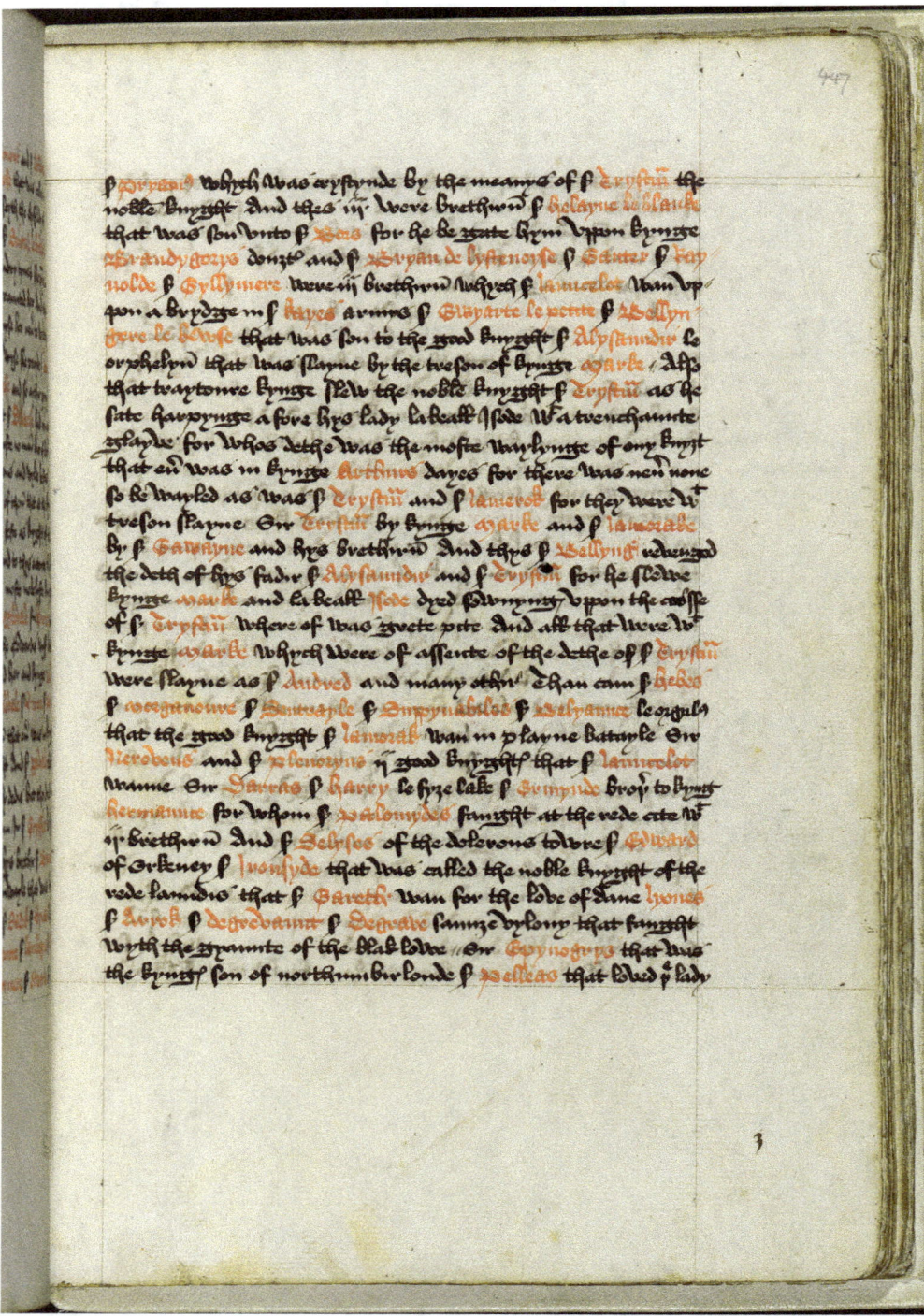

Plate XVI: The middle section of the great Urry catalogue: Winchester, fol. 447ʳ.

may well increase the connections between Malory's artistry, his Arthuriad and the manuscript that houses that story.[15]

As noted in Chapter Two, the deaths of first Harleuse le Berbeus and then Peryne de Mounte Belyarde at the hands of the invisible villain Garlon (*Garlonde* in W) are each marked with a marginalium (both on folio 29ᵛ), and both dead knights are memorialized with rich tombs (64.15–65.6). Harleuse's tomb records 'by whom the trechory [of his death] was done', but 'on the morne' Peryne's tomb is discovered to be marked by 'letters of golde' prophesying how 'Sir **Gawayne** shall revenge his fadirs dethe Kynge **Lot** on Kynge **Pellynore**'. There are likewise 'letters of gold' inscribed on the cross presaging Balyn's own doom (C II.17; 70.22–5), as well as on the single piteous tomb shared by Balyn and Balan (C II.18–19; 73.12–74.1). Merlin places more writing (we are not told the colour this time) around the reset pommel of Balyn's sword prophesying Gawayne's death at Launcelot's hands and by Balyn's old sword (34ʳ; 74.4–14). Not all of the *Morte*'s monuments are proleptic, of course, and much later in the Arthuriad Launcelot is careful to ensure that the tomb of the poisoned knight Patryse exculpates Gwenyvere of any responsibility for the man's death. This is done by inscribing the truth and her innocence on the tomb (416ʳ⁻ᵛ; 803.14–24). Many tombs and inscriptions in the *Morte* are thus linked to some of the most important events or themes in the narrative. What is particularly important for my purposes is the ways in which the Winchester manuscript and its rubrication of names and marginalia recording deeds and death mirror such narrative monuments; the manuscript is itself a commemorative tomb to Arthurian chivalry.

I am not, of course, claiming any originality in arguing for the importance of the material aspects of mediaeval literature. It has long been recognized that the *mise-en-page* of a text in its manuscript form can provide insight into narrative meaning and interpretation. Nor do I wish to downplay the importance of Meale's and Cooper's observations about ways in which the layout of the *Morte Darthur* in Winchester occasionally creates a markedly different reading experience, and even a different set of themes, than those foregrounded by Vinaver's presentation of the text. As Earl R. Anderson, Kevin T. Grimm, Meale and Cooper each observe in different ways, there is no manuscript justification for Vinaver's major narrative divisions between the episodes of the Fair Maid, the Great Tournament and the Knight of the Cart, the three middle stories of the tale entitled 'The Book of Sir Launcelot and Queen Guinevere' by Vinaver, and simply 'Sir Launcelot and Queen Guenivere' by Field.[16]

On the one hand, the famous May passage that Vinaver and Field each use to preface the Knight of the Cart episode obviously does emphasize the stable love of Launcelot and Gwenyvere, just as it – ironically, in context – introduces and attempts to whitewash the one scene in the entire *Morte Darthur* where

---

[15] For Malory's changes, see Vinaver, Commentary on *Works* 72.5–8.
[16] Contrast *Works* 1113–20 with *Winchester* fols 434ʳ–435ᵛ, and see Earl R. Anderson, 'Malory's "Fair Maid of Ascolat"', *Neuphilologische Mitteilungen* 87.2 (1986): 237–54 (esp. 251–2); Kevin T. Grimm, 'Knightly Love and the Narrative Structure of Malory's Tale Seven', *Arthurian Interpretations* 3.2 (1989): 76–95 (85–7), and idem, 'Editing Malory', *Arthuriana* 5.2 (1995): 5–14 (7–8); Meale, '"The Hoole Book"', in *Companion*, pp. 15–16; and Cooper, 'Opening Up', in *Debate*, pp. 262–3.

they do consummate their love (W, fols 434^v–435^r; *Works* 1119.1–1120.13; *MD* 841.1–842.11). On the other hand, Vinaver's narrative divisions with their page and section breaks, (sub)title pages and the relevant portion of Caxton's chapter headings clearly ignore and misrepresent the Arthuriad's more unified layout in Winchester. In Winchester, unlike in *Works*, the May passage follows *immediately* after Arthur's praise of Gareth's worshipful behaviour towards Launcelot in the Great Tournament. Since there are no major *explicits*, initials, spaces or even virgules denoting narrative divisions here (contrast *Works* 1114–19 with W, fols 434^v–435^r), Winchester's layout *connects* rather than severs love and chivalry. As Meale rightly says, 'to read the section unbroken [as in Winchester] is to gain a sense of the relation between the secular and the military, between love and loyalty and physical prowess and achievement'.[17] In its manuscript context, then, Malory's famous May passage partly celebrates the love and fellowship (or homosocial bond) amongst male companion-knights, a love that Gareth epitomizes in the 'grete turnemente and justis' held 'besydes Westemynster uppon Candylmasse day' (430^r; 832.1–13). Concomitantly and more obviously, the May passage also serves to encapsulate the heterosexual love of Launcelot and Gwenyvere in the Knight of the Cart episode. In this sense, it is the logical opening of the Cart sequence, and although Field removes Vinaver's distracting editorial divisions, he maintains the same location for the passage. It is clearer in Field's layout than in Vinaver's, and clearer still in Winchester, that the 'celebration of love', as Cooper perceptively notes, 'is continuous with the celebration of chivalry', just as 'Gareth's love for Lancelot … is of a piece with Guinevere and Lancelot's love for each other'.[18] In the case of both knightly fellowship and male–female relations, Malory seems to say in Winchester's version of events, stability and faithfulness are worshipful acts worthy of reward. In terms of Malory's focus on memorializing his characters, Winchester's emphasis on both knights and lovers reminds us of the dual aspects of Launcelot's own character, that he is the paragon of knights and lovers.

I am thus in complete agreement with Andrew Lynch, who persuasively suggests that 'the manuscript or printed page functions as a public arena where [knightly] exploits are enacted and witnessed'.[19] I would add that Winchester's *ordinatio* quite literally announces and enshrines the characters involved in the events of the narrative arena. The prominence of knightly (or homosocial) bonds within tournaments is hardly surprising given that Malory's version of the Arthur story begins with the civil war between Uther and the Duke of Tyntagil, and ends with the few knights who survived the final destruction of the Round Table fighting and dying in the Holy Land. This narrative bookending of violence is only natural since the 'technique of fighting, and more particularly of single combat, is Malory's favourite topic'.[20] Fighting in the *Morte*, moreover, remains significant throughout the narrative because fighting is always tied to *worshyp*. The connection between combat and worship remains true even when a particu-

---

[17] Meale, '"The Hoole Book"', in *Companion*, p. 16.
[18] Cooper, 'Opening Up', in *Debate*, p. 263.
[19] Andrew Lynch, *Malory's Book of Arms* (Cambridge, 1997), p. 53.
[20] Vinaver, p. xxxiii.

lar character in fact does not behave worshipfully in a particular fight: such a knight may be denounced as unworthy, but worship is still a primary valuation and motivation, a means of judging good or bad behaviour and a reward for the good. Lynch masterfully illustrates the prominence of fighting in the *Morte Darthur*, and my own views on Malorian combat owe much to his learning and example. Nevertheless, he also argues that fighting sometimes descends into mere theatricality or that Malory sometimes critiques violence.[21] I would respectfully offer an opposing interpretation, one based on the continual prominence of worship *throughout* the *Morte* and the repeated connections drawn between worship and fighting. For me, combat in the *Morte* is acceptable as the primary means of establishing *worshyp*, and worship, character and knightly deeds are all encoded and elegized by the consistent rubrication of names in Winchester.

Just as the *Morte Darthur* begins and ends in warfare, so too does Arthur's kingship. Furthermore, Arthur's own career as king and hero is announced and enveloped by inscriptions. At the beginning of Arthur's reign the sword he pulls from the stone is inscribed with golden letters that read 'Whoso pulleth oute this swerd of this stone and anvyld is rightwys kynge borne of all Englond' (C I.3–5; 7.14–16). Equally, at the end of his reign, having died of wounds received in the battle of Salisbury Plain, Arthur is buried in a tomb with the inscription **'Hic iacet Arthurus, Rex quondam Rexque futurus'** (928.28). Malory's version of the inscription, this exact phrase and this language, are original, though John Withrington shows that the idea and some form of the phrase about Arthur's return were in the air by the late fifteenth century.[22] Withrington's trenchant analysis of the contexts of Arthur's epitaph helps to reveal the full extent of 'Malory's skill and compassion as narrator'. I am arguing that Malory's artistry and skill encompass not merely the narrative content, but even the manuscript layout of his Arthuriad. (The tomb inscription appears on my cover image.)

The opening gathering of the Winchester manuscript is sadly lost, and the lacuna includes the sword-from-the-stone scene. But Arthur's tomb *is* recorded in Winchester, and the inscription, tellingly, is rubricated (482ᵛ). So, too, perhaps, would have been the gold letters on the sword. Between acquiring this sword and returning its successor to the lake, one of Arthur's weightiest actions is the defeat of Lott and the rebel kings and dukes. Not only is this victory signalled with a marginalium in Winchester (28ᵛ), the lexical text records a series of tombs built by Arthur and Merlin. These tombs for the dead rebels honour the noble rank and knightly prowess of Arthur's enemies. But the tombs also emphasize the prominence of worship and prowess in the *Morte* by revealing how occasionally, and Lott is a notable example, a knight might be recognized as a man of *worshyp* and yet fight against Arthur. The worship of Arthur's enemies is significant, for if his enemies are worthy opponents and yet insufficient to stand against him at length, then Arthur's own glory is accordingly all the greater. These tombs consequently honour Arthur's own prowess and victory, both by the very nature of the

---

[21] Lynch, *Book of Arms*; idem, '"Thou woll never have done"', in *The Social and Literary Contexts of Malory's Morte Darthur*, ed. D. Thomas Hanks Jr and Jessica G. Brogdon (Cambridge, 2000), pp. 24–41.

[22] John Withrington, 'The Arthurian Epitaph in Malory's "Morte Darthur"', *Arthurian Literature* 7 (1987): 103–44. The quotation that follows is from p. 144.

tombs themselves housing Arthur's dead foes, and in the fact that Merlin erects 'a fygure stondynge aboven [the rebels] with a swerde drawyn in hys honde' (28ᵛ; 62.2–11). Lott and the rebels may be men of worship, but they are no match for Arthur: Hector cannot stand against Achilles. As Kenneth Tiller points out, 'the monument [thus] stands for [Arthur's] sovereignty over all of England'.[23]

As part of his argument for the scribal provenance of Winchester's marginalia, Wade claims that this marginalium about 'þe dethe of Kynge Lot & þe xij kyngis' (28ᵛ) is again not precisely in the correct location, since it is several lines below Lott's actual death and one of the manuscript's pointing hands or *maniculae*; Wade argues that this placement reveals 'Scribe A's idiosyncratic use of both gloss and pointing hand'.[24] Since, however, folio 28ᵛ records Lott's death and the end of a major battle, the twelve rebel burials and their mourners and monuments, and then moves to a discussion between Arthur and Merlin about Balyn and Balan and Pellynore, as well as Excalibur, the page is quite heavily rubricated: almost every line of this page, in fact, shouts out one or more red names. (See Plate XIV.) The longest section of folio 28ᵛ not dominated by rubrication is in fact Malory's description of the rebels' tombs and the mention of Arthur's victorious image. And it is precisely here, in the middle of the folio, that the marginalium devoted to the rebels' deaths is located. As with Columbe's marginalium discussed above, the marginalium denoting Lott's death thus strikes me as being in precisely the right place, for it and the brown-ink narrative emphasize all the more the significance of Arthur's achievement. Wade's reliance on the *maniculae*, moreover, is problematic: unlike the marginalia proper (the written notes), the fingers only occur in the early portion of the manuscript (fols 9ᵛ–42ᵛ), and to my eye the pen and ink and hand are different from the main text and main scribal hands.[25] The *maniculae* were likely drawn very close to the time of Winchester's copying, and they represent an early reader response or reflect some sort of annotation from the copy-text. Whatever importance these fingers possess, however, they certainly violate the Winchester scribes' obvious preference for clean margins; Hilton Kelliher even concludes that they 'may be rather later than the copying'.[26] All told, the pointing fingers are less reliable than the rubrication and marginalia, at least until more is known of their origin and purpose. Consequently, since Wade's argument for the scribes placing the marginalium here is dubious, then we might look to the author for such a layout, particularly when codex and narrative context so tellingly and trenchantly interact.

Cooper sagaciously suggests that certain features of Winchester's layout 'may' be authorial.[27] As I argued in Chapter Two, there is evidence for going further than this claim. After all, Meale illustrates how 'the arrangement of the text in the manuscript and [Caxton's] print, and the high level of coincidence between the

---

[23] Tiller, 'En-graving Chivalry', 45. See further Lupack, 'Malory's Intratexts', in *Romance and Rhetoric*, p. 251, n. 4.
[24] Wade, 'Malory's Marginalia', 76.
[25] On the hand and significance of Winchester's *maniculae* see my 'Inks and Hands and Fingers in the Manuscript of Malory's Morte Darthur', *Speculum* (forthcoming 2017).
[26] Hilton Kelliher, 'The Early History of the Malory Manuscript', in *Aspects*, pp. 143–58 (p. 146). For the scribes' heavy preference for clean margins see P. J. C. Field, 'Malory's Own Marginalia', *Medium Ævum* 70 (2001): 226–39 (226–7).
[27] Cooper, 'Opening Up', in *Debate*, pp. 273 and 277.

divisions marked within each', allow scholars to discern which elements most likely derive from Malory.[28] In this chapter I wish to build on the work of Lynch, Cooper, Meale and Crofts to suggest ways in which the manuscript layout of the *Morte Darthur* also celebrates and elegizes earthly Arthurian chivalry. Such a thematically focussed *ordinatio*, I am further suggesting, is most likely an authorial innovation. Taken as a whole, the rubrication of names throughout the Arthuriad is the codicological equivalent to these lexical inscriptions within the text, rendering the Winchester manuscript itself into a physical monument that celebrates and memorializes the deeds of the Round Table Fellowship. The rubrication functions as the manuscript and narrative equivalent to what Nigel Saul styles the commemorative 'signifiers' of English burial monuments.[29]

In her analysis of *Roman de la Rose* manuscripts, Sylvia Huot highlights the didactic aspects of rubrication, the ways in which it not only announces the importance of a text, but also clarifies.[30] Rubrication also, claims Huot, reveals the mediaeval concern with voice and authorship. In *Roman de la Rose* manuscripts, for instance, rubrication 'has a double significance': it emphasizes generic conventions of encyclopaedia and romance that are conjoined in the *Rose*, and it reveals a deep interest in 'the poetics of first-person narrative'.[31] This association between rubrication and change in speaker during dialogue is relatively commonplace, occurring in manuscripts of various languages, particularly in breviaries and in parts of some Bibles. Music manuscripts in the fourteenth and fifteenth centuries likewise often place red notes at changes in metre.[32] Something similar seems to occur in some manuscripts of *Piers Plowman*, including Huntingdon Library MS 137, folios 16–17, where the names 'Mede', 'Reson' and 'Conscience' are rubricated.[33] An Arthurian example of rubricated speakers is said to be found in the Red Book of Hergest copy of *The Dream of Rhonabwy* in Oxford, Jesus College MS 111, folios 134ᵛ–138ᵛ. Here, it is suggested, 'in the absence of identification tags, the copyist often uses a rubricated capital to mark the new speaker's words'.[34] My own examination of the Red Book *Rhonabwy*, however, suggests that this is not the case. Rather, these so-called 'rubricated capital[s]' are in fact black with red tracing, and the red-touched letters are not confined to names or speech: instead, we have a variation on the common practice (observed in Chapter One) of touching the opening initials of most sentences and many names with red,

---

[28] Meale, '"The Hoole Book"', in *Companion*, p. 11.
[29] Nigel Saul, *English Church Monuments in the Middle Ages* (Oxford, 2009), p. 121. As Tiller, 'En-graving Chivalry', 38, observes, 'Malory sees the efficacy of chivalry not only through the deeds of Arthur's knights, but also through the inscription of them in topographic markers, in tombs'.
[30] Sylvia Huot, '"Ci parle l'aucteur"', *SubStance* 17.2 (1988): 42–8.
[31] Huot, '"Ci parle"', 45.
[32] I am indebted to Jennifer Bain for this insight.
[33] I am indebted to Jaclyn Rajsic for this example. I have not been able to examine the manuscript myself beyond seeing a few online images from the Digital Scriptorium Database. For a thorough overview of rubrication in *Piers* manuscripts, see C. David Benson and Lynne S. Blanchfield, *The Manuscripts of Piers Plowman* (Cambridge, 1997).
[34] Sioned Davies, 'Performing *Culhwch and Olwen*', *Arthurian Literature* 21 (2004): 29–51 (48, n. 60 for the quotation). My conclusions are based on examination of the digital facsimile of Jesus College 111, available via the Oxford Digital Library (image.ox.ac.uk). My thanks to Daniel Helbert for help with the Welsh.

regardless of whether or not dialogue is involved. My point, then, is simple: as is the case with the different uses of rubrication in chronicle and romance and Bible manuscripts discussed in Chapter One, none of these examples (covering various genres and languages) looks or functions exactly like Winchester. The markedly close connection between manuscript layout and narrative theme and actions, together with the uniqueness of Winchester's design and the ways in which the rubrication enhances Malory's artistry, suggest to me that Winchester's layout is textually significant: so significant, in fact, that the most likely source is Malory himself. I argued this authorial origin in detail in Chapter Two. But one aspect of Malory's artistry and manuscript layout that I have not yet discussed, one which relates to codicological contexts and visual cues to memory, is the fashion in which the *Morte*'s rubrication and marginalia function as both distinct from and corollary to the lexical narrative.

The rubrication in the Winchester manuscript of Malory's *Morte Darthur* serves in part to announce the importance of the story by visually valorizing the human characters whose names are rubricated and whose deeds comprise the plot. On the whole, however, Winchester's rubrication functions in a fashion different from the norm. Instead of announcing gloss or voice or didactic *sens*, Winchester's rubrication emphasizes and enshrines the entire narrative and its characters, turning the manuscript itself into a tomb of elegy and commemoration. Such memorialization also helps clarify Malory's focus on earthly and human rather than spiritual matters. There are even places where Malory's glorification of Arthurian chivalry results in the red manuscript letters mirroring what we are told are gold letters in the lexical words of the narrative. Thus, after Galahad's knighting at the beginning of 'The Tale of the Sankgreal', the court reassembles at the Round Table where, once again, they see 'the segys of the Rounde Table all aboute wretyn with golde lettirs' (349^v; 667.9–16). Similar 'lettirs of golde' are inscribed in the pommel of the floating sword (350^r; 668.11–12). In cases such as these, the gold letters of the narrative are not actually rubricated: the inscriptions and letters recorded by Malory are copied in Winchester in the same dark brown ink as the rest of the lexical text. But since the described gold letters of Round Table named seats or sword inscriptions are meant to aggrandize the individual knight who holds a Table seat or fulfils a significant deed, it is noteworthy how the rubrication of names in Winchester visually performs the same celebratory and memorializing effect as the lexical text recounts.

For all of the critical debate about possible divisions between earthly and celestial knighthood in the *Morte Darthur*, the notable thing about these narrative inscriptions is the ways in which they announce typical earthly Arthurian adventures: Galahad's name at the Round Table is but the same as that for each of the other members of the Fellowship, just as the arrival of the floating sword exemplifies the sort of marvel that accompanies Arthur's 'olde custom' of not sitting down to feast till he has heard or 'sene some adventure' (350^r; 667.30–668.8). Swords in magical resting places, especially floating stones, certainly qualify as marvellous adventures. Tellingly, then, there is in these important introductory Grail scenes no break with pre-existing Arthurian or chivalric values. Indeed, the authorial and textual focus on human character and chivalric deed is reinforced by the layout of the story in Winchester. The marginalia for this part of the story, for instance, celebrate Galahad being made knight (fol. 349ᵛ), sitting in the Siege Perilous (fol. 351ʳ) and pulling of the sword from the floating stone (fol. 351ᵛ).[35] Winchester's consistent rubrication of each and every knight's and lady's name likewise highlights and valorizes human characters and human deeds. This is especially so since the inscription on the sword reads (naturally) that it will only be drawn by 'the beste *knyght* of the *worlde*' (350ʳ; 668.9–15; my emphases).

Another notable textual and codicological symmetry in 'The Sankgreal' is visible with the marginalium recording Gawayne's accidental slaying of his cousin Uwayne. Once again the marginalium echoes lexical narrative events, for, in terms of plot, Gawayne builds a tomb and has his name recorded on it as the slayer of his cousin. The death and the tomb memorialize Uwayne, but also Gawayne's grief and guilt: 'Than began Sir Gawayne to wepe, and also Sir Ector. ... Than Sir Gawayne and Sir Ector buryed hym as them ought to bury a kynges sonne and made hit be wrytyn uppon hys tombe what was hys name and by whom he was slayne' (727.1–6). To reinforce the pathos of this scene as well as to emphasize connections between manuscript and narrative text, Malory marks Uwayne's death with a manuscript marginalium located almost midway between the fatal joust and the burial: 'Here Sir Gawayne slew Sir Uwayne his cousyn germayne' (378ʳ).

Significantly, then, the memorializing nature of Winchester's rubrication and the way it reinforces Malory's emphasis on knights of this world rather than God or Heaven or religious values is evident both in 'The Sankgreal' and at sundry points throughout *Morte Darthur*. The most notable example is the catalogue of knights who attempt the healing of Sir Urry, where the knights' names are consistently rubricated, whereas 'God' or 'Jhesu' are never rubricated (445ᵛ–448ᵛ; 862.25–868.5). The title 'Pope' is likewise not rubricated during the account of the Pope's injunction that Launcelot return Gwenyvere and that Arthur and Launcelot cease their civil war (463ᵛ–464ᵛ; 895.34–897.10). The characters' names, in contrast, kings and queens, lords and ladies, and especially knights, are consistently rubricated. Within the narrative, combat is Malory's most beloved and frequently occurring topic, but fighting, especially between a king of such 'grete goodnes' as Arthur and a knight of such 'hygh proues' and nobility as Launcelot, is not beloved by the Pope, who accordingly demands an accord (895.34–896.9). Outside the narrative, many readers and editors over the ages have likewise not shared Malory's fondness for martial achievement, even if their objections differ from those of the *Morte*'s Pope. Caxton thus frequently abridges the *Morte Darthur*'s many martial details, especially in the Roman War of Tale II.[36] Understandably, many modern editors of the *Morte* likewise sacrifice or at least greatly compress Malory's focus on fighting in order to make the *Morte* more

---

[35] To the best of my knowledge I was the first critic to draw attention to ways in which Winchester's marginalia highlight Galahad's status as knight; Radulescu now makes a similar observation. See, respectively, my 'Characterization in Malory and Bonnie', *Arthuriana* 19.3 (2009): 123–35 (124–5); Raluca L. Radulescu, *Romance and Its Contexts in Fifteenth-Century England* (Cambridge, 2013), pp. 168, 172. Radulescu and I reach quite different conclusions.

[36] On which see Sally Shaw, 'Caxton and Malory', in *Essays*, pp. 114–45 (pp. 132–5).

manageable and marketable.[37] Given Malory's penchant for stories of combat, however, much fighting obviously remains even in Caxton's version, even in the greatly reduced Roman War; but much fighting is cut and lost, including arming scenes which are, in epic-heroic tradition and in many romances, just as important as the combat which the arming scenes preface. Malory's martial details are important to his narrative, his characters and his principal themes. Significantly, fighting and its consequences are strikingly highlighted in Winchester by the rubrication of combatants' names and marginal records of sundry victories and deaths.

In light of Arthur's 'holé togydirs' lament (352^{r-v}; 672.25–30) discussed in my previous chapter, a notable feature of the opening episodes of Malory's tale of 'Sir Launcelot and Queen Guenivere' is just how frequently Arthur calls knights 'togyders' for a great joust or tournament: twice in the Fair Maid episode, immediately again in the Westminster or Great Tournament. The Urry episode that closes this penultimate tale of the Arthuriad likewise assembles most of the knights of the Round Table for a tourney. The Grail Quest had sundered most of the Round Table Fellowship and put a temporary end to tournaments and fighting for earthly glory. Hence Arthur's lament. Consequently, Arthur – and, for that matter, Malory – are quick to reintroduce and re-establish the validity of such martial practice and themes once the Grail Quest is a thing of the past. Robert L. Kelly argues for the continued influence of 'The Sankgreal' throughout Tale VII, an argument also made, albeit in different guise, by Stephen C. B. Atkinson and Raluca L. Radulescu in their views of the Healing of Sir Urry as a sort of Grail coda.[38] Elizabeth Scala takes a different tack, making overmuch of the lack of explicit arming scenes in the *Morte* to argue that Launcelot is frequently unarmed and thus rendered vulnerable and potentially less heroic throughout Tale VII.[39] I argue, in contrast to all of these scholars, that the immediate and renewed focus on Launcelot's championing of various women that opens Tale VII, together with the renewed prominence of real fighting and tournaments rather than the Grail Quest's allegorical fighting, reinforces the continued priority of earthly adventure and *worshyp* in the *Morte Darthur*. Codicology, I suggest, supports this contention.

It is noteworthy, for instance, how the rubrication of names in Winchester consistently and explicitly draws attention to the names of knights, and thus by association draws attention to the deeds of knights, including their deeds in combat. As I remarked above, the marginalia, too, display a marked martial interest, consistently emphasizing the deeds and deaths caused by some of Arthur's greatest knights. In what seems another instance of Caxton mimicking

---

[37] See, e.g., the condensed *Le Morte D'Arthur*, trans. and adapt. Joseph Glaser (Indianapolis, 2015); Peter Ackroyd's retelling, *The Death of King Arthur* (London, 2010); or *Le Morte Darthur*, ed. Helen Cooper (Oxford, 1998), where Cooper is explicit about 'generously' abbreviating combat sequences because of differences between Malorian and modern taste (p. xxv).

[38] Robert L. Kelly, 'Wounds, Healing, and Knighthood in Malory's Tale of Lancelot and Guenevere', in *Studies*, pp. 173–97; Stephen C. B. Atkinson, 'Malory's "Healing of Sir Urry"', *Studies in Philology* 78.4 (1981): 341–52; Raluca L. Radulescu, 'Malory's Lancelot and the Key to Salvation', *Arthurian Literature* 25 (2008): 93–118.

[39] Elizabeth Scala, 'Disarming Lancelot', *Studies in Philology* 99.4 (2002): 380–403.

Winchester, 'lists of names' in the Caxton print are often marked by punctuation strokes.[40] Needless to say, the rubricated names of Winchester are especially striking and emphatic during lists. Many such lists (in either textual witness) are found in tournaments or combat, as in the unhorsing combat during the rebellion of the eleven kings and dukes in the opening tale (W, fols 11^v–12^v), entitled 'The Tale of King Arthur' by Vinaver and retitled 'King Uther and King Arthur' by Field.[41] The most visually striking such list in Winchester, however, is undoubtedly the great catalogue of the 111 knights attempting the healing of Sir Urry (445^v–448^v; see Plates XV and XVI).[42]

The episode of the Healing of Sir Urry is Malory's addition to his sources and has long been recognized, in C. S. Lewis's phrase, as 'perhaps the greatest of all passages peculiar to Malory'.[43] It is also, according to Mark Lambert, 'the most purely Malorian episode in *Le Morte Darthur*'.[44] Certainly the centrality of names in the magnificent catalogue of knights who attempt the healing typifies Malory's approach to character. As Robert H. Wilson observes, Malory is especially prone to providing names for unnamed characters during catalogues, with the result that the *Morte* is unified (amongst other things) by the fact that the narrative is inhabited by recognizable characters with recognizable histories; this is especially true in Tales VII and VIII, where Malory tends to add more names than in earlier sections of the *Morte*.[45] As Field puts it, Wilson's evidence reveals how Malory's cataloguing of names 'create[s] complicated consistent action in tournaments and other ceremonial occasions'.[46] This consistency is one of the many effects Malory creates in the lexical text of the Urry episode, and the characterization and formality and history (re)created by the Urry catalogue are all reinforced both by the aural nature of the *Morte Darthur* and visually by the rubrication. Field notes further that there are 454 named characters in *Morte Darthur*,[47] to which I would add that fully a quarter of them appear in this scene; or at least this is what Malory claims when he informs us that, 'All thes hondred knyghtes and ten serched Sir **Urryes** woundis' (447^v; 366.7). All of this artistry, from the originality of the Urry episode to the emphasis on named individuals

---

[40] Shaw, 'Caxton and Malory', in *Essays*, p. 123. Cf., e.g., W, 11^v–12^r with C, b2^{r-v} or W, 446^r–447^r with C, aa2^v-aa4^r.

[41] Carol Kaske, 'Malory's Critique of Violence Before and Just After the Oath of the Round Table', in *Beowulf and Beyond*, ed. Hans Sauer and Renate Bauer (Frankfurt, 2007), pp. 259–70 (at p. 263), wittily styles this combat 'the game of musical horses'.

[42] I say 111 because Malory claims there are 110 knights who attempt the healing before Launcelot arrives, so 110 + Launcelot = 111. Despite Malory's claims, there are not quite 110 names listed: the Caxton records 102 or 103, with Winchester recording what amounts to 103: for textual-critical details, see Field, Commentary on 866.7.

[43] C. S. Lewis, 'The English Prose *Morte*', in *Essays*, pp. 7–28 (p. 20). With the possible exception of Gareth's adventures in Tale IV, which may or (more likely) may not be Malory's invention, the Healing of Sir Urry is also the longest example of Malory's originality in his Arthuriad. For a thorough overview of the scholarly positions on the originality of 'The Tale of Sir Gareth', see Ralph Norris, *Malory's Library* (Cambridge, 2008), pp. 81–94.

[44] Mark Lambert, *Malory: Style and Vision in Le Morte Darthur* (New Haven and London, 1975), p. 56.

[45] Robert H. Wilson, 'Addenda on Malory's Minor Characters', *Journal of English and Germanic Philology* 55 (1956): 563–87 (569–75).

[46] P. J. C. Field, 'Author, Scribe and Reader in Malory', in his *Texts and Sources*, pp. 72–88 (pp. 81–2).

[47] Field, 'Author, Scribe and Reader', in his *Texts and Sources*, p. 82.

and Malory's concerns with character and completeness, bespeaks and partly explains the episode's significance. What I especially wish to emphasize is that Malory's detailed care with names and characters is markedly mirrored, announced and reinforced by Winchester's rubrication.

Despite the fame of the Urry episode, there is very little scholarly agreement about its precise meaning. Critics agree that the episode is one of the most moving in the entire Arthuriad. Beyond that, though, there is considerably less consensus. Indeed, Catherine Batt argues that the Healing of Sir Urry exemplifies the *Morte*'s 'hermeneutic difficulties', difficulties (I would add) ably illustrated by the fact that Radulescu, a fine scholar of Malory and his contexts, offers three different interpretations of Launcelot's tears in nine pages![48] Earl R. Anderson similarly argues for the psychoanalytical difficulties of the scene, concluding that 'Lancelot's weeping points to an open-ended chain of signifiers that indicate the existence of knowledge that is inaccessible to us.'[49] Freud and Lacan (amongst other theorists) would no doubt support such a thesis, but Anderson's explication does little to advance our understanding of a key scene in Malory's Arthuriad. Atkinson tries in part to solve the issue by arguing for an interpretive disconnect within this episode between Arthur's chivalric approach to the Urry adventure and Launcelot's 'strictly spiritual' approach.[50] It seems to me, however, that such a conflict of opinion and such opposing values really typify scholarly preoccupations, not the views of the author or characters involved.

I observed in the previous chapter the predilection amongst Malorians to judge 'The Tale of the Sankgreal' and its knights by Christian doctrine. By such ethical and patristic standards Launcelot and his Round Table fellows, excepting the three Grail elect, are manifestly found wanting. No doubt as a result of what might be termed this Christian reading of Malory's Grail Quest, a similar commonality runs through various threads of scholarship devoted to the episode of the Healing of Sir Urry. Although there is less consensus here than elsewhere in the *Morte*, there is nonetheless a recurring insistence that Malory's text is dominated by Christian ethics or dogma or both. The earliest and perhaps most influential critics in this camp are P. E. Tucker and C. S. Lewis. Tucker argues that Launcelot's ability to heal Urry reveals that, despite his sins of pride and adultery, Launcelot can still be great provided he remembers humility and divine grace.[51] Lewis focusses on Launcelot's tears to argue, with characteristic grace and conviction, that Launcelot weeps because of his awareness of his own sin and lack of worth, and thus of the sinful inadequacies undermining the Round Table.[52]

---

[48] Respectively Catherine Batt, *Malory's Morte Darthur: Remaking Arthurian Tradition* (New York and Basingstoke, 2002), p. 158, and Radulescu, 'Malory's Lancelot', 106–14. Edmund Reiss, *Sir Thomas Malory* (New York, 1966), pp. 169–72, also highlights the supposed narrative inconsistencies and interpretive difficulties of the Urry episode and accordingly offers two opposing conclusions, one of seeming approbation and one of Launcelot's punishment.

[49] Earl R. Anderson, '"Ein Kind wird geschlagen"', *Literature and Psychology* 49.3 (2003): 45–74 (at 68).

[50] Atkinson, 'Malory's "Healing of Sir Urry"', *passim* (quotation from 343).

[51] P. E. Tucker, 'The Place of the "Quest of the Holy Grail" in the *Morte Darthur*', *MLR* 48.4 (1953): 391–7 (396). Cf. Tucker's 'Chivalry in the *Morte*', in *Essays*, pp. 64–103 (pp. 98–9).

[52] Lewis, 'English Prose *Morte*', in *Essays*, p. 20.

This view of Launcelot's ultimate lack of worth has been echoed or endorsed or expanded by a good many scholars, including R. M. Lumiansky, Robert L. Kelly and John Michael Walsh.[53] Judson B. Allen argues that the healing and tears denote both Launcelot's 'punishment and his vindication at the same time', but for Allen, Malory's point is that ultimately chivalry and holiness are incompatible and Camelot is a tragic but dismal failure.[54] According to Elizabeth Pochoda, Atkinson and Radulescu, even the impressive Urry catalogue that prefaces the healing is an indictment. Far from symbolizing a paean to Arthurian greatness, the catalogue, they each claim, is in fact a list of individual and collective Round Table disgrace and failure; Launcelot is, again, both partly successful and partly a failure.[55] The most avowedly Christian interpretations of the scene are offered by D. Thomas Hanks Jr, Corey Olsen and Sue Ellen Holbrook, each of whom looks for – or perhaps *imposes* – deeply religious contexts and significance on the episode. Thus Olsen argues that the episode reveals 'Lancelot's spiritual crisis', whilst Hanks claims that 'Lancelot's healing of Sir Urry is the most straightforwardly Christian event in the *Morte*', one enabled by prayer.[56] Holbrook, too, emphasizes the importance of prayer in the scene, especially Trinitarian prayer and a corresponding awareness of Trinitarian mysteries.[57]

Much modern scholarship, then, argues for a Christian Malory whose text is said to be consistently imbued with Christian thought and symbolism. Such a view seemingly gains support from the laying on of hands in the healing of Urry, an act which does have obvious parallels in religious tradition. It is worth remembering, though, that there is an even longer tradition of warrior heroes who are also known for their skills in healing as well as fighting. This heroic tradition includes Malory's Launcelot and Pryamus, as well as Pryamus in the alliterative *Morte Arthure* and Walewein in the Middle Dutch Arthurian tradition.[58] It also includes Homer's Achilles and Patroclus. I am not suggesting that Malory read Homer – though fruitful comparisons have been made between the *Iliad* and the Arthuriad.[59] The point is, as Lewis remarks, 'We partly make what we read.'[60] Thus, where I associate Launcelot's ability to heal with a select

---

[53] R. M. Lumiansky, '"The Tale of Lancelot and Guenevere"', in *Originality*, pp. 205–32 (p. 231); Kelly, 'Wounds, Healing, and Knighthood', in *Studies*, p. 178; and John Michael Walsh, 'Malory's "Very Mater of La Cheualer du Charyot", also in *Studies*, pp. 199–226 (pp. 216–22).

[54] Judson B. Allen, 'Malory's Diptych *Distinctio*', in *Studies*, pp. 237–55 (p. 246). Cf. Reiss, *Thomas Malory*, pp. 169–72.

[55] Elizabeth T. Pochoda, *Arthurian Propaganda* (Chapel Hill, 1971), pp. 129–30; Atkinson, 'Malory's "Healing of Sir Urry"', 344–6; Radulescu, 'Malory's Lancelot', 109–12.

[56] Corey Olsen, 'Adulterated Love', in *Malory and Christianity*, pp. 29–55 (p. 47); D. Thomas Hanks Jr, '"All maner of good love comyth of God"', also in *Malory and Christianity*, pp. 9–28 (pp. 16–17). William Matthews, *The Ill-Framed Knight* (Berkeley and Los Angeles, 1966), p. 49, likewise says that 'the tale of Sir Urry … seems nothing but holy', but his remark was seemingly buried by the authorship controversy which Matthews himself instigated.

[57] Sue Ellen Holbrook, 'Endless Virtue and Trinitarian Prayer in Lancelot's Healing of Urry', in *Malory and Christianity*, pp. 56–76.

[58] On Walewein, see David F. Johnson '"Men hadde niet Arsatere vonden alsoe goet"', *Arthuriana* 11.4 (2001): 39–52.

[59] See Sir Edward Strachey, ed., *Le Morte Darthur* (London, 1897), pp. ix–x and xiii–xiv; Andrew Lang, 'Le Morte Darthur', in *Le Morte Darthur*, ed. H. Oskar Sommer (London, 1891), III:xiii–xxv; Thomas H. Crofts, *Malory's Contemporary Audience* (Cambridge, 2006).

[60] Lewis, 'English Prose *Morte*', in *Essays*, p. 22.

group of healing warrior heroes, Holbrook emphasizes John Cassian's influence on Benedictine thought, and thus the influence of Cassian and Benedictine prayer upon Malory's Launcelot.[61] Cassian, however, was a real monk's monk, and his influence on Malory is even less likely than Homer's: certainly neither Homer nor Cassian has been suggested as a direct or indirect source in over a century of source study. Eamon Duffy argues for the late mediaeval laity's wide-ranging knowledge of and interest in the basic tenets of Christianity,[62] but Duffy himself acknowledges the variegated nature of late mediaeval religion, and for all of his erudition not everyone accepts all of Duffy's conclusions. Batt, for instance, warns that 'one cannot make a priori assumptions about Malory's religion on the basis of social placing', and in fact his handling of his sources for the Grail story 'suggest[s] little interest in interpreting scripture, or in other areas in lay spirituality's development'.[63] Even if one were to object to Batt's reading on the premise that it depends on an overly Protestant equation of mediaeval lay spirituality with the interpretation of scripture, as did one of the referees of this monograph, there is simply no evidence in the *Morte* that Malory was informed about or even interested in Augustine or Cassian or patristic philosophy. There isn't even any evidence that he read (or listened to others read or lecture or discuss) such Christian Platonists as William of Conches, Bernard Silvestris or Alan of Lille, each of whom might have appealed to Malory's secular eye because each advocated 'the importance of earthly understanding as the base of all human knowledge'.[64]

On the other hand, many historians emphasize the less homogenized, more diverse nature of late mediaeval religion in England, ranging from the genuinely – and at times generously – pious to the rather casual, lukewarm or 'even calculating' attitude evident amongst some of the gentry and aristocracy.[65] There are thus sufficient textual and socio-historical reasons to doubt that Malory's purposes in the healing of Sir Urry or elsewhere in the *Morte* are deeply religious or even typically moral. I argued in the previous chapter that reading the *Morte Darthur* in its entirety reveals Malory's primary values and themes to be human rather than divine. My claims are supported not only by the less homogenized view of English religion at the close of the Middle Ages, but also by a wide-ranging study of Wars of the Roses literature by Megan Leitch. Leitch argues that much fifteenth-century prose romance is predicated upon a 'distinctive secularity' whereby many literary authors writing under the threats of the Wars of the Roses 'eschewed expressing faith in providence and instead expressed a

---

[61] Holbrook, 'Endless Virtue', in *Malory and Christianity*, p. 64.
[62] Eamon Duffy, *The Stripping of the Altars*, 2nd edn (New Haven and London, 2005).
[63] Batt, *Remaking Arthurian Tradition*, p. 134.
[64] Roberta Frank, 'The *Beowulf* Poet's Sense of History', in *The Wisdom of Poetry*, ed. Larry D. Benson and Siegfried Wenzel (Kalamazoo, 1982), pp. 53–65 (p. 56).
[65] See especially Colin Richmond, 'Religion', in *Fifteenth-Century Attitudes*, ed. Rosemary Horrox (Cambridge, 1994), pp. 183–201; Richard G. Davies, 'The Church and the Wars of the Roses', in *The Wars of the Roses*, ed. A. J. Pollard (New York, 1995), pp. 134–61; Andrew Brown, *Church and Society in England, 1000–1500* (Basingstoke, 2003). I quote Richmond p. 191.

heightened degree of pragmatism and insistent focus on human affairs'.⁶⁶ Malory is one such writer concerned with secular issues.

Many mediaeval institutions and much mediaeval thought depend upon or at least include a synthesis of secular and sacred. Karen Cherewatuk argues compellingly for a similar balance in the *Morte Darthur*.⁶⁷ Whether Malory in matters of personal faith was one of the gentry's more orthodox, casual or dissenting representatives, however, strikes me as ultimately less important than the cumulative weight of the *Morte Darthur* in its entirety. I am not suggesting that Malory or the *Morte* completely ignores religion: to take two notable examples to the contrary, Elayne of Ascolat is granted a Requiem Mass (429ᵛ–430ʳ; 830.17–24), and Gwenyvere is concerned with the health of her immortal soul (482ᵛ–483ʳ; 928.33–929.6 and 484ʳ⁻ᵛ; 932.29–933.2). Various characters also invoke God or Christ, sometimes, as I outlined in Chapter Three, devoutly, sometimes formulaically, and sometimes in a blend of values or motives, as when King Angwysshaunce vows 'unto mylde **Mary** and unto **Jesu Cryste** … [to] be avenged uppon the **Romayns**' (72ʳ; 147.27–148.2), Launcelot invokes God's blessing on the maker of his spear (108ᵛ; 213.13–14) or Arthur swears to be so 'avengid' on Morgan le Fay 'that all Crystendom shall speke of hit' (58ʳ; 121.28–9). Angwysshaunce's vow is the one occasion in all the *Morte*'s nearly 400,000 words that 'Jesu' or 'Cryste' are rubricated, and his motives, tellingly, are far from Christian, despite the language involved.⁶⁸ It is worth noting further that Arthur instructs Launcelot to bury Elayne 'worshypfully', a term which has secular connotations in the *Morte*, and that Gwenyvere is remarkably silent about her soul's health until *after* Arthur's death and the destruction of the Round Table. The deaths of Elayne and Gwenyvere, in other words, are strictly orthodox only when taken out of context in the former case, and when focussing exclusively on eleventh-hour actions in the latter. Gwenyvere's focus on 'Goddis grace', penance and 'Hys Passsion' as means of saving her soul (932.33–933.2) does typify late mediaeval deathbed ritual,⁶⁹ but it must not blind us to Malory's overarching concern with knightly deed and chivalric fellowship.

Arguably the dominant tenor of much modern criticism presents Malory's knights, excepting the Grail elect, as sinful failures, and Malory himself as sooner or later rejecting earthly chivalry in favour of more doctrinal values. The reality, both in the *Morte Darthur* and in life, is more complicated, and my examples in the previous paragraph merge sacred and secular language, ideals or both. Nevertheless, this scholarly refrain emphasizing Malorian sin risks blinding readers to the dominant melodies in the *Morte*. It seems to me that the *Morte*'s principal themes and Malory's artistry – his handling of his sources, his characterization, his thematic and narrative emphases – bespeak an obvious and abiding affection for earthly knights and human deeds. As Saul judiciously insists, Malory's conception of chivalry is 'practical' and 'purely secular', and this secular conception of knighthood is entirely in keeping with much late mediaeval

---

⁶⁶ Megan G. Leitch, *Romancing Treason* (Oxford, 2015), pp. 9, 65–73, 81–4, 122–30. I quote p. 9.
⁶⁷ Karen Cherewatuk, 'Christian Rituals in Malory', in *Malory and Christianity*, pp. 77–91 (pp. 77–8).
⁶⁸ On this issue see further Chapter Two, Appendix II.
⁶⁹ Cherewatuk, 'Christian Rituals in Malory', in *Malory and Christianity*, pp. 84–5.

thought and action, particularly amongst the armigerous classes, where brave deeds and prowess were performed in service both to one's own chivalric genealogy and to one's lord or king.[70] A similar ideology, Saul reveals, runs like a refrain through the deeds and writings of Anthony Wydeville, Lord Scales and second Earl Rivers, a favoured candidate amongst scholars for Caxton's possible patron for Malory's book, as he was certainly a patron for other of Caxton's enterprises.[71]

Secular chivalric concerns are conspicuous in the *Morte Darthur* in the prominence and narrative detail devoted to fighting, but also in Malory's praise of Trystram as the fount of hunting 'tearmys':

> And therefore the booke of venery, of hawkynge and huntynge is called *The Booke of Sir* **Trystrams**.
>
> Wherefore, as me semyth, all jantyllmen that beryth olde armys ought of ryght to honoure Sir **Trystrams** for the goodly tearmys that jantylmen have and use and shall do unto the Day of Dome, that thereby in a maner all men of worshyp may discover a jantyllman frome a yoman and a yoman from a vylayne. For he that jantyll is woll drawe hym to jantyl tacchis and to folow the noble customys of jantylmen. (150^v; 293.17–25)

My point, then, is that while Malory recognizes final judgement in the Day of Doom, he is more concerned throughout the *Morte Darthur* with chivalric pastimes, principally fighting in earnest or play, but also with hunting, hawking and chivalric adventure.[72] The emphasis on the fellowship amongst earthly Round Table knights is part of Malory's focus on chivalry, for the Fellowship symbolizes secular chivalric brotherhood and activity.[73] This focus on earthly knighthood is, I suggest, manifestly announced and reinforced by the *material* context of the *Morte*: the rubrication and marginalia in the Winchester manuscript.

Structurally the Healing of Sir Urry is, like the *Morte* itself, bookended by martial display and competition. Malory introduces Urry as 'an adventurys knyght, and in all placis where he myght here of ony dedis of worshyp, there wold he be', including at the critical tournament in Spain where Urry is injured (444^v–445^r; 861.2–20). Malory closes the episode by holding a joust in which 'Sir **Urré** and Sir **Lavayne** justed beste', wherefore by common consent they 'were made knyghtes of the Table Rounde' (448^v; 868.18–22). I especially wish to note here the ways in which the structural and thematic emphases of Malory's Urry story poignantly reiterate and celebrate earthly fellowship, human adventure and chivalry. It is humanity, not spirituality, which drives Malory's narrative. Batt claims that the 'Urry episode … reconceptualizes chivalric violence' and that Urry himself

---

[70] Nigel Saul, *For Honour and Fame* (London, 2011), pp. 314–16 and 334–8. On secular tropes in fifteenth-century romance more broadly, see Leitch, *Romancing Treason*.

[71] On Wydeville's relationship with Caxton and possible dealings with Malory, see above, Chapter Two, pp. 64–5, 68–72.

[72] On ways in which Winchester's layout emphasizes the *Morte Darthur*'s focus on hunting and fighting, see further my 'Inks and Hands and Fingers in the Manuscript of Malory's *Morte Darthur*'.

[73] On fellowship in the *Morte* see Archibald's characteristically excellent study: Elizabeth Archibald, 'Malory's Ideal of Fellowship', *Review of English Studies*, n.s. 43 (1992): 311–28.

'painfully embodies the effects of violence'.[74] A movement away from traditional martial values or an ideological unrest with chivalric display, if present in the *Morte*, would indeed justify the emergence of a new set of values antithetical to Malory's favourite topic. There is, however, no change in the perception and significance of either violence or knighthood in this episode; just the opposite. Urry is maimed because the mother of a man he killed in combat curses his injuries so that they will not be healed 'untyll the beste knyght of the worlde had serched hys woundis' (445ʳ; 861.18). The wounds stay fresh and festering (the nature of the curse) for seven years. Then Urry arrives at Arthur's court where, 111 attempts later, he is healed by Launcelot. And as soon as he is healed, Arthur celebrates the cure and the knights by holding another tournament, thereby reminding the audience of the pre-eminent importance of martial endeavours and the winning of *worshyp* throughout the *Morte Darthur*.

For all of these reasons I am in complete agreement with Vinaver, D. S. Brewer, Larry D. Benson and C. David Benson in reading the Healing as an episode designed to valorize Launcelot.[75] After all, from a purely narrative point of view, were Malory advocating a cessation of violence or martial worship, Urry could have been left maimed or even left out of the story altogether. He is not. Nor is Malory condemning or qualifying Launcelot. Just the opposite: as Cooper astutely asserts, 'Lancelot's adultery may worry the hermits on the Grail quest, but Malory, in a passage without parallel in the Vulgate [Cycle], has God express His approval of Lancelot on his return to court by allowing him his own personal miracle, the healing of Sir Urry.'[76] Once again Malory sacralizes secular concerns, and he does so in both the lexical words of the text proper and the manuscript layout. From a codicological point of view, had Malory or his scribes wished to emphasize Christian rather than chivalric values, then the several references to 'God' or 'Jhesu' or the 'Trynyté' in the Urry scene might have been rubricated or marked by a marginalium in ways similar to the 'Testament' which prefaces Lydgate's *Troy Book* in London, British Library Royal MS 18.D.ii, a declaration in which only the name *Jhesu* is rubricated (against an otherwise brownish-black text).[77] In light of the cultural Christianity of late-mediaeval England, the religious poem in the Lydgate manuscript offers a telling example of the sort of thing we might justifiably expect from Malory or the manuscript of his text. But despite the weight given to prayer by some Malory scholars, such manuscript emphasis on religion is the exception rather than the rule in Winchester: knights, ladies and other proper nouns receive rubrication, but never God or the Trinity; even '**Jesu Cryste**' is rubricated only once in the narrative proper (72ʳ), and that exception is part of an heroic vow of vengeance, not a declaration of orthodox

---

[74] Batt, *Remaking Arthurian Tradition*, pp. 153–4.

[75] Vinaver, p. 1591; D. S. Brewer, '"the hole book"', in *Essays*, pp. 41–63 (p. 60); Larry D. Benson, *Malory's Morte Darthur* (Cambridge, Mass., 1976), pp. 227–30; and C. David Benson, 'The Ending of the *Morte Darthur*', in *Companion*, pp. 221–38 (pp. 228–9). Vinaver differs from myself and these other critics by explicitly denying any connection between the Healing and events elsewhere in the *Morte* (p. 1591, n. 2).

[76] Helen Cooper, 'Counter-Romance', in *The Long Fifteenth Century*, ed. Cooper and Sally Mapstone (Oxford, 1997), pp. 141–62 (p. 154).

[77] London, BL Royal MS 18.D.ii, fols 2ᵛ–3ᵛ. The MS, which the BL dates to 1457–c. 1530, is available online from the British Library's Digital Catalogue of Illuminated Manuscripts.

piety.[78] Two of the *explicits*, that for 'The Tale of the Sankgreal' (409ʳ) and that for the *explicit*-cum-*incipit* between the final two tales (449ʳ and Plate XIII), also rubricate **Jesu** during prayers, but these rubricated prayers are, as discussed in Chapter Three, unusual occurrences whose purpose seems at least as much artistic and pragmatic as pious.[79]

Likewise, although Launcelot himself prays partly for God's succour in healing Urry, he also, equally importantly and more in line with the values of the *Morte* as a whole, prays for continued public recognition of his earthly glory: 'Now, Blyssed Fadir and Son and Holy Goste, I beseche The of Thy mercy *that my symple worshyp and honesté be saved*, and Thou Blyssed Trynyté, Thou mayste yeff me power to hele thys syke knyght' (448ʳ; 867.22–5; my emphasis). The diction employed by Launcelot – and Malory – matters greatly here, for throughout the *Morte Darthur* worship is typically a secular concern. In Launcelot's prayer it is both secular and sacred, yet what is being saved is not Launcelot's soul, but his knightly reputation and glory. *Worshyp* has been repeatedly awarded to Launcelot by his peers since he began to prove himself in adventure in Tales II and III, and he seeks continual recognition – saving – of that reputation now. Furthermore, the peers who recognize Launcelot's worship, like Launcelot himself, consistently have their names rubricated across nearly four complete folios in the Urry catalogue (fols 445ᵛ–448ᵛ); none of the names for God is so highlighted. (See Plates XV and XVI.) In other words, as Brewer rightly insists, *worshyp* is not only the cornerstone of Malory's Arthurian society,[80] it is a preeminent human motivation and objective.

It is thus entirely appropriate that Arthur celebrates Urry's healing with yet another tournament, thereby reiterating and aggrandizing Arthurian chivalry, human martial prowess and fellowship. As Lambert perceptively insists, Urry 'does not exist except in relation to chivalric activities'.[81] The focus on names evident in the Urry catalogue and the rubricated manuscript reminds us of Malory's concern with knightly character and how the Round Table, both as a physical object and as a secular fellowship of 150 knights, is the true omphalos of Arthur's vision and kingdom.[82] So it is that the healing of Sir Urry marks the final occasion in the *Morte Darthur* when the Round Table knights are unified in a single mission and it serves, as Elizabeth Archibald lucidly affirms, 'as a final celebration of the Round Table fellowship'.[83] Significantly, Arthur himself explicitly states that he will attempt the healing first; not because he presumes success, but rather to unify and participate in the fellowship of the court (445ᵛ; 862.18–31).[84] And

---

[78] See above, Chapter Two, Appendix II, and p. 175.
[79] See above, Chapter Three, pp. 105–12.
[80] D. S. Brewer, ed., *The Morte Darthur: Parts Seven and Eight* (London, 1968), p. 25. See also Tucker, 'Chivalry in the *Morte*', in *Essays*.
[81] Lambert, *Style and Vision*, p. 58. See further Lynch, *Book of Arms*, p. 45.
[82] See further Cory James Rushton, '"Layde to the Colde Erthe"', in *The Arthurian Way of Death*, pp. 151–66, who goes so far as to claim that the Round Table as a collective body is the true centre and protagonist of the English Arthurian tradition, including the *Morte Darthur* (pp. 152–4).
[83] Archibald, 'Malory's Ideal', 326. See further Lambert, *Style and Vision*, pp. 56–65.
[84] Note here the consistency of character and theme across the *Morte*: Arthur's willingness to attempt the healing, not with the expectation of success but rather to inspire others, echoes

when all the 110 knights have tried and failed, Arthur similarly and explicitly commands Launcelot to attempt the healing, 'nat ... for no presumpcion, but for to beare us *felyshyp*, insomuche as ye be a *felow* of the Rounde Table' (447ᵛ–448ʳ; 866.25–867.8; my emphases).

There remains, though, the spectre of Launcelot's tears. Certainly it seems a curious response to what I have called a celebration of earthly Arthurian chivalry that Launcelot should himself continually weep 'as he had bene a chylde that had bene beatyn', whilst all around him praise the healing of Urry (448ᵛ; 868.1–2). At first glance, the tears might seem to undermine Launcelot's achievement and thus undermine the worshipful chivalry Launcelot epitomizes. Diction and imagery, some critics claim, suggest a wayward and severely chastised child, not a great hero. Batt in fact argues that 'fifteenth-century language of human–divine relations ... illuminates Launcelot's condition as a special child whom God chastises'.[85] Launcelot's chastisement would thus be 'an act of love' and a 'redemptive' experience. Olsen supports and adapts Batt's idea of Launcelot as a 'beloved' but wayward 'child of God', concluding that a religious connection and meaning seem 'inevitable'.[86] For Olsen, and perhaps Batt, the tears thus signify divine judgement and grace, but also Launcelot's awareness of his lack of worth. The notion that the healing and tears somehow highlight Launcelot's failure or tarnished worth is a common critical refrain, though critics differ as to whether the lack of worth is primarily a failure of chivalry or spirituality (or both). It is also, I respectfully suggest, a critical refrain that misses the mark.

After all, in light of the very public revelation of Launcelot's worship that is enacted through the healing, as well as the restoration of bodily wholeness to a knight long injured and suffering with a septic wound, it seems oddly gratuitous to interpret the episode as a chastisement of Launcelot. Literary scholars cannot ignore diction and imagery, but neither can they ignore logic or symbolism. Thus, if image-based readings of Launcelot's success create odd conclusions here, then it is necessary to reconsider the evidence. Doing so provides a simple and obvious solution: knighthood and glory and diction, not confusing imagery and religious allegory, provide the answer and the *sens* for Malory's narrative. If only the 'best knyght of the worlde' can heal Urry, and Launcelot heals him, then Launcelot must remain the best knight of the world and paragon of the Round Table Fellowship. There is always the possibility that this assessment of who or what is the best knight is ironic, but unlike what some critics say of Chaucer, Malory is not famous for saying one thing and meaning another. The whole nature of the Healing is, moreover, designed to showcase Launcelot's – and Arthur's – greatness. The tears are consequently not tears of religious joy or even contrition, but rather tears of earthly emotion, principally relief and gratitude. The relief is not, however, what Lumiansky would have us believe: that Launcelot is relieved to pass the test which Arthur has somehow cleverly contrived out of Urry's situation to discern whether or not Launcelot and Gwenyvere have been

---

a similar speech and action in the face of the sword-damsel's adventure back at the beginning of the 'Tale of Balyn' (22ᵛ; 48.8–12).

[85] Batt, *Remaking Arthurian Tradition*, p. 157.

[86] Olsen, 'Adulterated Love', in *Malory and Christianity*, p. 47.

unfaithful to him, and which Launcelot has somehow equally cleverly realized is a ruse.[87] There is no such test. Nor can I accept that Launcelot feels gratitude for being divinely chastised but nonetheless loved, or that being allowed to heal Urry after all others have failed and after the one episode in the entire *Morte* where Launcelot and Gwenyvere do explicitly consummate their relationship somehow signifies failure. On the contrary, the narrative emphasis on knighthood, on fellowship and on Launcelot's miraculous achievement actively reinforces Launcelot's heroic stature. Consequently, he must feel relief and gratitude precisely because he is still the pre-eminent knight of the world and still the yardstick of Round Table chivalric excellence. As noted above, there is a long and respectable tradition of heroes who are both warriors and healers, a tradition that includes Achilles outside Arthurian tradition and Gawayne and Pryamus within Arthurian legend. Chaucer taps into this tradition in the *Squire's Tale* with the gift of the magic sword that 'wole kerve and byte' and inflict wounds that can only be remedied by the sword itself.[88] The healing of Urry accordingly reinforces Launcelot's place within this tradition of select heroes. Some of these warrior-healers even weep in sympathy with their patients.[89]

The fact that human chivalric fellowship and values are still paramount at this late juncture in the Arthuriad is even more apparent in the response of Urry himself to the healing. For Urry, who might understandably be thought to have endured sufficient injury in combat, is happy to celebrate his own healing by risking himself in yet another tournament. As Jill Mann observes, the knightly body is repeatedly a 'testing ground' used to establish *worshyp*, *felyship* and – though Mann claims contrariwise – even character.[90] To reinforce the priority of chivalric prowess and human identity, Malory makes Urry one of the two victors of this celebratory tourney. As a result of their prowess in this tourney Urry and Lavayne, the other victor, are elevated to the ranks of the Round Table Fellowship. Neither Arthur's proposed tourney nor Urry's willingness to participate immediately after being healed should surprise us. As Percyval insists, 'hit ys [a knyghtes] kynde to haunte armys and noble dedys' (331^r; 637.8), a sentiment accepted equally by Malory's characters and his contemporaries.

Crucially, Winchester's rubrication reinforces this emphasis on human character and earthly deeds. Wilson judiciously observes that since 'the roll of knights failing to heal Sir Urre includes representatives of every one of the previous tales', Malory was clearly employing the catalogue and his character additions as means of unifying the *Morte*.[91] I would only add to this remark that,

---

[87] Lumiansky, '"The Tale of Lancelot and Guenevere"', in *Originality*, pp. 229–31.
[88] Geoffrey Chaucer, *The Squire's Tale*, lines 156–67, in *The Riverside Chaucer*, ed. Larry D. Benson, 3rd edn (Boston, 1987). Achilles is in fact mentioned by the Squire at lines 236–42.
[89] See Anderson, 'Malory's "Fair Maid of Ascolat"', 249, n. 24. Malory may even be varying the romance trope, evident in *Erec et Enide* and *Generides* and discussed by Hibbard, of a hero being awakened by tears. See Laura A. Hibbard, *Mediaeval Romance in England* (New York, 1924), p. 234. Lancelot and Urry are not lovers, and Urry is awake when Launcelot attempts the healing, but Urry's wholeness and thus his reawakened knighthood are certainly announced by Launcelot's tears.
[90] Jill Mann, 'Knightly Combat in Malory's *Morte d'Arthur*', in her *Life in Words*, ed. Mark David Rasmussen (Toronto, 2014), pp. 235–42 (quoting p. 242).
[91] Robert H. Wilson, 'How Many Books Did Malory Write?' *Studies in English* 30 (1951): 1–23 (23).

since the catalogue also includes most of the main characters as they occur across the Arthuriad in its entirety, Malory also clearly employs it for elegiac purposes. Both the fellowship and the elegy are rendered all the more pronounced by the rubrication of names in the Winchester manuscript. Thus, 'From the reader's point of view, [Launcelot's] tears foreshadow all the weeping that will accompany the destruction of the fellowship in the near future.'[92] By so emphatically and repeatedly highlighting the names of the knights comprising the Fellowship the rubrication manifestly reinforces this sense of loss. The marginalia and their record of knightly achievement and death have the same emphatic effect, albeit less consistently since there are only eighty marginalia scattered across the manuscript's 484 extant folios. Winchester today is missing its opening and closing gatherings, so originally there would have been more folios and, perhaps, a few more marginalia: but even as it stands, manuscript matter and narrative meaning in Malory's *Morte Darthur* are remarkably closely connected.

Another equally notable and even more poignant example of this lexical and codicological memorialization of lost chivalry comes at the end of the Arthuriad in the series of final, doleful battles. The last surviving marginalium, for instance, is arguably the most plangent of all the side-notes, recording 'How Sir Gawayn wrote a letter to Sir Launcelot at the tyme of his debe' (fol. 477^r). Although Gawayne dies helping to establish a beachhead against Mordred's army, his death wound comes as a result of a blow upon the old head-injury given him by Launcelot. Gawayne accordingly attributes his death to his friend, not his half-brother, insisting that he could not die of a 'more nobelar' man's hand (476^v–477^r; 918.5–919.2). Gawayne also informs Launcelot that his letter is 'wrytten with myne owne honde and subscrybed with parte of my harte blood' (477^v; 919.16–17). The entire scene is original to Malory, and it is one of profound sorrow, a sympathetic portrait of shattered friendship and heroism. As this scene well illustrates, Malory's artistry and originality peak in the closing tales of his Arthuriad, where he adapts his sources very freely indeed. Since the only names appearing on folio 477^r of the manuscript, which also has the final sorrowful marginalium, are the repeated triad of **Launcelot**, **Gawayne**, **Arthur**, Winchester's rubrication visually foregrounds the personal ties between these three men, forcefully announcing their importance to the plot and one another.

The visual impression of togetherness and import are confirmed by the lexical text when Arthur laments that

> here now thou lyghest, the man in the worlde that I loved moste. And now ys my joy gone! For now, my newev, Sir **Gawayne**, I woll discover me unto you, that in youre person and in Sir **Launcelot** I moste had my joy and myne affyaunce. And now have I lost my joy of you bothe, wherefore all myne erthely joy ys gone fro me! (476^v; 917.34–918.4)

In the stanzaic *Morte*, Arthur is sorrowful but silent, so that, as Vinaver notes, Malory adapts the wording of the French *Mort Artu* for Arthur's lament; but whereas 'in the French Arthur dwells on the vicissitudes of Fortune and the

---

[92] Muriel Whitaker, *Arthur's Kingdom of Adventure* (Cambridge and Totowa, 1984), p. 50. Cf. Benson, *Malory's Morte Darthur*, p. 229.

blind cruelty of Fate ... , in [*Morte Darthur*] he is acutely conscious of a sense of irretrievable personal loss'.[93] The French Artus also temporarily blames Gauvain for his role in separating Artus from Lancelot, as well as from Gauvain himself. No such blame is uttered by Malory's Arthur; furthermore, Malory adds to Arthur's lament Gawayne's letter, equal parts self-reproach, praise for Launcelot and appeal for aid. Whether due to codicological or scribal chance, or scribal fidelity to authorial design, the marginalium about Gawayne's letter begins on the very same line where Gawayne asks for 'paupir, penne, and inke'. Since the eighty main marginalia are also rubricated, the red ink of this final marginalium allows readers of Winchester – though not audience members listening to a reading – to visualize Gawayne's red blood. The placement of this final side-note, whoever planned it, draws attention to Malory's artistry and originality. The sense of personal loss and tragic waste pervading this scene is cleverly – and, I contend, deliberately – magnified by Winchester's rubrication and marginalia. Such a close intersection of manuscript layout and narrative event and theme is most likely to be authorial rather than scribal.

The way in which the rubrication draws attention to Malory's narrative and thematic concerns with human character, human suffering and tragic human heroism is continued at the battle on Salisbury Plain. Especially striking is folio 479^r and the description of the attempted peace treaty, for the only names on this folio are those of Mordred (eight times) and Arthur (six times): the repeated rubricated contrast of these two names (and only these names) emphatically underscores Arthur and Mordred's conflicting claims to kingship. Although Malory mostly downplays Mordred's paternity throughout the *Morte Darthur*, the rubricated juxtaposition of **Mordred** and **Arthur** also reminds us that the rival kings are son and father, thereby increasing the personal and human element whilst simultaneously paving the way for their imminent mutual slaughter.[94] In the ensuing battle, Winchester's rubrication again emphasizes Arthur, Mordred and Arthur's few remaining knights, but not God. At the end of 'thys doleful day' and this unhappy battle, Arthur gazes around the battlefield to see only Lucan and Bedwere left alive. The names of these knights are of course rubricated, as is Arthur's name. Significantly, however, the 'Jesu' of Arthur's invocation 'Jesu mercy! ... where ar all my noble knyghtes becom' is not rubricated, nor is the 'God' of Arthur's subsequent wish 'wolde to God ... that I wyste now where were that traytoure Sir **Mordred** that hath caused all thys mychyff' (479^v; 923.4–8). Arthur's focus, like Malory's and that of the sympathetic reader or listener, is firmly and appropriately placed on the dead and living knights and, especially in this final battle, on the principal figures of Arthur and Mordred themselves. Hence the emphasis on Arthur's and Mordred's individual prowess during the battle, where 'ever Kynge **Arthure** rode thorowoute the batayle of Sir **Mordred**

---

[93] Vinaver, Commentary on *Works* 1230.11–1232.17; *Le Morte Arthur*, ed. P. F. Hissiger (The Hague, 1975), vv. 3132–43; *La Mort le roi Artu*, ed. Jean Frappier, 3rd edn (Geneva, 1964), §§165–7, 172–3.

[94] On questions of legitimacy and dynasty at the close of the *Morte* see especially Karen Cherewatuk, *Marriage, Adultery, and Inheritance in Malory's Morte Darthur* (Cambridge, 2006), pp. 109–26, and Lisa Robeson, 'Malory and the Death of Kings', in *Arthurian Way of Death*, pp. 136–50.

many tymys and ded full nobely', and where 'Sir **Mordred** ded hys devoure that day and put hymselffe in grete perell' (479ᵛ; 922.22–9). The exchange between Lucan, Bedwere and Arthur before the iconic and grisly encounter between Arthur and Mordred that completes the battle and secures the tragic close of the Arthuriad is likewise dominated by the rubricated names of knights; visually, at least, the several unrubricated references to God are all but lost in the shuffle.

This rubrication of knightly names rather than divine ones strengthens my suggestion that most of the oft-invoked Christian register of Le Morte Darthur is formulaic, a reflection of social mores rather than narrative *sens*. Certainly Malory's focus at this moment emphasizes earthly emotions and human actions:

> Than Kynge **Arthur** loked aboute and was ware where stood Sir **Mordred** leanyng uppon hys swerde amonge a grete hepe of dede men. ...
> 'Sir, latte hym be', seyde Sir **Lucan**, ... 'And, good lorde, remember ye of your nyghtes dreme and what the spyryte of Sir **Gawayne** tolde you tonyght, and yet God of Hys grete goodnes hath preserved you hyddirto. And for Goddes sake, my lorde, leve of thys, for, blyssed be God, ye have won the fylde: for yet we ben here thre on lyve, and with Sir **Mordred** ys nat one on lyve.' ...
> 'Now tyde me dethe, tyde me lyff', seyde the kyng, ... 'he shall never ascape myne hondes!' ...
> 'God spyede you well!', seyde Sir **Bedyvere**.
> Than the kynge gate his speare in bothe hys hondis, and ran towarde Sir **Mordred**, cryyng and saying, 'Traytoure, now ys thy dethe-day com!'
> And whan Sir **Mordred** saw Kynge **Arthur** he ran untyll hym with hys swerde drawyn in hys honde; and there Kyng **Arthur** smote Sir **Mordred** undir the shylde, with a foyne of hys speare, thorowoute the body more than a fadom. And whan Sir **Mordred** felte that he had hys dethys wounde he threste hymselff with the myght that he had up to the burre of Kyng **Arthurs** speare, and ryght so he smote hys fadir, Kynge **Arthure**, with hys swerde holdynge in both hys hondys, upon the syde of the hede, that the swerde perced the helmet and the tay of the brayne. And therewith Mordred dayssshed downe starke dede to the erthe.
> And noble Kynge **Arthure** felle in a swoughe to the erthe, ... and Sir **Lucan** and Sir **Bedwere** offtetymys hove hym up. (479ᵛ–480ʳ; 923.9–924.8)

I quote this passage at length partly to reinforce what has already been said by Cooper, Crofts and myself about its powerful and macabre details, what Crofts pithily refers to as the 'tragic (and, to some degree, transcendent) power' of the scene, with its 'cathartic shuffling-off of mortalities and hatreds'.[95] But I also quote the scene at length to reveal how the *human* element, and thus the secular tragedy, are so effectively and emphatically announced by the rubrication – including the rubrication of the revenant Gawayne. As Cooper observes, Malory's version of the final battle is largely one massive mêlée. Uncharacteristically for Malory given his tendency to name characters, the tumult is anonymous; in contrast, the French *Mort Artu* presents 'a series of long-drawn-out individual combats'.[96]

---

[95] See Cooper, 'Counter-Romance', in *Long Fifteenth Century*, p. 155, and Helen Cooper, *The English Romance in Time* (Oxford, 2004), p. 403; Crofts, *Malory's Contemporary Audience*, pp. 147–8; and my *Understanding Genre and Medieval Romance* (Aldershot, 2008), pp. 145–6.
[96] Cooper, *Romance in Time*, p. 402 and n. 63; *Mort Artu*, §180.1–§191.2

Significantly for my purposes, this change to the source is one of several features of Malory's denouement that draws attention to Arthur and Mordred's individual combat, as well as to Fate. Cooper points out further that Malory employs the lexical juxtaposition 'hys fadir, Kynge **Arthure**' only on this occasion in all of the *Morte Darthur* and that, crucially, 'he holds [the phrase] back until the stroke that cuts down the whole Arthurian world'.[97]

Like Achilles' return to battle at the close of the *Iliad*, Arthur's return to battle to face Mordred is, as Crofts astutely observes, without hope: 'Like Achilles in *Iliad* XXI, Arthur has no plans for the future; we hear this in his [full] speech in this passage, where "now" is repeated six times. The moment in which Mordred and Arthur close is also amplified by certain details, at turns quotidian and nasty, of Malory's own invention.'[98] I would add to Crofts's assessment that the moment of their close in the Winchester manuscript is also amplified by the rubrication, where (ignoring the first two names of the page) there is a steady 2–4 fluctuation of **Mordred-Mordred**, **Arthur-Arthur**, **Mordred-Mordred**, **Arthurs-Arthure**, Mordred, **Arthure**. As in poetry or music, the climactic moment modifies the beat: as they each fall to the ground, the names suddenly appear only once each rather than twice: Mordred, **Arthure**. The syncopation is reinforced in two further ways. First, the standard rhythm of two names followed by the opposing two names is initially fairly even: there is one line of dark brown text between the first and second **Mordred** at the start of the battle, then the double-beat or collocation occurs steadily for four lines, followed by one more line of brown text before the final rubricated Arthur doubling. At that point, there is suddenly a delay of two lines before Mordred's final appearance, with Arthur closing out the exchange in the next line – almost as if the imagery and rhythm slow down just before the combatants collapse. And in a brilliant accidental – both codicological and musical – one of the scribes' few rubrication errors occurs here, where Mordred's final offbeat name as he falls to the ground is not actually rubricated. Given the care and consistency with which names are rubricated throughout Winchester, this non-rubricated Mordred is no doubt a mistake; but it is, in context, quite an effective one. Particularly in scenes like this, the rubrication becomes a memorial aid, a kind of anamnestic commentary on and visual reinforcement of the narrative, elegizing and eulogizing the human characters, human deeds and human deaths of the Round Table Fellowship. The rubrication error also visualizes how, in terms of glory and heroic kingship, it is not Mordred but Arthur whom one ought to remember.

Malory accordingly reiterates the finality of Arthur's death, and thus the need for elegiac commemoration, when Gwenyvere subsequently dies and Launcelot and his fellows collect her body in order to bury it beside Arthur's. I argued in the previous chapter that Launcelot's motivation and character are entirely consistent

---

[97] Cooper, 'Counter-Romance', in *Long Fifteenth Century*, p. 155. See also Felicity Riddy, *Sir Thomas Malory* (Leiden, 1987), pp. 152–3. Cooper is typically astute, but a similar collocation does occur slightly later as well, when Malory notes how Launcelot heard that '**Mordred** ... made warre ayenst Kyng **Arthur,** hys owne fadir' (483ʳ; 930.6–7). As Cherewatuk points out, Malory prepares for this conjunction with Mordred's earlier attempt to wed 'hys unclys wyff and hys fadirs wyff' (475ʳ; 915.10: *Marriage, Adultery, and Inheritance*, pp. 124–5).

[98] Crofts, *Malory's Contemporary Audience*, p. 147.

throughout the *Morte Darthur*. I addressed especially his love for Gwenyvere, but the consistency of Launcelot's human emotions and outlook, including his tendency (seen at Gawayne's grave) to mount tombs or (in Urry's healing) to shed tears, are again evident in his reaction to Arthur's and Gwenyvere's interment. For once the king and queen are buried, Launcelot swoons so much that the former Archbishop castigates Launcelot for his excessive grief, urging him to leave such love behind. Malory, however, not only emphasizes Launcelot's loving focus and distraught emotion, he creates a speech in which Launcelot justifies his actions and mourns the loss of both Gwenyvere and Arthur, lover and friend:

> 'Truly,' sayd Syr **Launcelot**, 'I trust I do not dysplese God, for He knoweth myn entente, for my sorow was not, nor is not, for ony rejoysyng of synne. But my sorow may never have ende, for whan I remembre of hir beaulté and of hir noblesse, that was bothe wyth hyr kyng and wyth hyr, so whan I sawe his corps and hir corps so lye togyders, truly myn herte wold not serve to susteyne my careful body. Also whan I remembere me how by my defaute and myn orgule and my pryde that they were bothe layed full lowe, ... wyt you wel, ... sanke so ... myn herte that I myght not susteyne myself'. (C XXI.11; 936.29–937.5)

Having thus defended his loves and grief, Launcelot prepares himself for death. But whereas in the Vulgate *Mort Artu* Lancelot eventually dies because he falls ill after 'four years' of fasting and ascetic discomfort, and even in the stanzaic *Morte Arthur* Launcelot dies after 'sevyn yerys' of 'penance and ... dyverse prayers', Malory's version is considerably different, both more human and more secular in focus.[99] Malory's Launcelot dies of excessive sorrow:

> Thenne Syr **Launcelot** never after ete but lytel mete, nor dranke, tyl he was dede, for than he seekened more and more[.] ... For the bysshop nor none of his felowes myght not make hym to ete, and lytel he dranke[.] ... For evermore, day and nyght, he prayed, *but somtyme he slombred a broken slepe. Ever he was lyeng grovelyng on the tombe of Kyng* Arthur *and Quene* Guenever, *and there was no comforte that the bysshop, nor Syr* **Bors**, *nor none of his felowes coude make hym.* (C XXI.12; 937.6–14; my emphasis)[100]

Here is no happy ending of the romance genre, nor even the happy ending of the orthodox penitent.

Launcelot does pray regularly, which obviously depicts sacred concerns and piety, as does his admission of his 'defaute and ... orgule and ... pryde'. But Launcelot's actions and words equally obviously depict secular motivations

---

[99] *Mort Artu*, §201.44–§202.10, pp. 260–1; *Morte Arthur*, vv. 3826–89. Another crucial difference is that in the stanzaic *Morte*, Launcelot predeceases Gaynor. Launcelot dies at vv. 3834–89, whilst Gaynor's death at 3954–61 comprises the final scene and penultimate stanza of the poem.

[100] Winchester breaks off at folio 484ᵛ, during the final meeting between Launcelot and Gwenyvere. Consequently, my Malory citation cross-references are to Caxton's book and chapter numbers, as well as Field's pages. The consistency of Winchester's rubrication of names, however, makes it certain that the opening and closing leaves, now lost and with the accompanying text necessarily supplied only by the Caxton print, would also rubricate names. I have therefore continued to bold-rubricate names in quoting the final pages of the *Morte*.

and earthly love, particularly since he had promised his beloved Gwenyvere in their final meeting together that he would always pray for her (484^v; 933.16–19). Similarly, although broken sleep is common for repentant saints, it is an equally commonplace condition of many an earthly romance lover, especially when one lover is separated from the other, as Launcelot is now permanently severed from Gwenyvere. Equally Janus-faced is Launcelot's own death: the Archbishop's vision of Launcelot being heaved 'unto heven' by 'angellys' (C XXI.12; 938.9–12) implies that Launcelot has managed to bypass the sufferings of Purgatory, sufferings which every late mediaeval Catholic feared yet expected. But as Duffy points out, 'only the saints could hope to go [to Heaven] directly', and Launcelot's words and actions hardly bespeak the sort of 'patiently borne' trials that the living could endure to speed one's soul through torment.[101] There are, as Cherewatuk observes, elements of hagiography here,[102] but there are also elements of pure romance mixed with secular tragedy. Once again, then, Malory reflects the mingling of sacred and secular that often defines late mediaeval culture. But sometimes, both in mediaeval culture and in mediaeval literature, one side of the sacred–secular scale weighs heavier. As Launcelot's grovelling and starving and lamentation make clear, his sorrow is earthly and all-consuming, secular and excessive, not sacred, patient or hagiographic. His lament for both Arthur and Gwenyvere also foregrounds their tomb, their dead bodies, and their now-departed nobility and *worshyp*. In prostrating himself grovelling on the tomb, Launcelot, in his sorrow, becomes temporarily *part* of the tomb, rendering himself into a weeping monument for the now-irrevocably lost glory and honour of Arthur and Gwenyvere: lost because the king and queen are now deceased.[103] Launcelot, no less than Malory himself, demands recognition of that lost worship, a recognition provided equally emphatically by Launcelot's words and actions within the narrative text, as well as by the rubricated elegy of the Winchester manuscript that records that text.

Crucially, Malory's Launcelot starves himself to death grovelling on the tomb of his lover and her husband, his beloved queen and king. Far from anticipating or embracing 'the perfect peace and felicity of eternal life with God' which, for Augustine, characterizes the 'true Christian' death,[104] Launcelot instead forcefully laments the loss of and pays tribute to both Gwenyvere *and* Arthur, invoking 'his corps and hir corps'. It is a strikingly original treatment of the burial and of Launcelot's own death; and it is human love, human sorrow and human tragedy,

---

[101] Duffy, *Stripping of the Altars*, pp. 341 and 342.

[102] Karen Cherewatuk, 'The Saint's Life of Sir Launcelot', *Arthuriana* 5.1 (1995): 62–78, and eadem, 'Malory's Launcelot and the Language of Sin and Confession', *Arthuriana* 16.2 (2006): 68–72. Cherewatuk's reading is cited as 'standard' by Virginia Blanton, '". . . the quene in Amysbery, a nunne in whyght clothys and blak . . ."', *Arthuriana* 20.1 (2010): 52–75 (68, n. 1).

[103] My thinking here is inspired by Scodel's trenchant comments on Homer's Andromache and memory, but Batt makes some similar arguments about Malory: see, respectively, Ruth Scodel, 'Inscription, Absence and Memory', *Studi italiani di filologia classica* 10 (1992): 57–76 (64); and Batt, *Remaking Arthurian Tradition*, pp. 174–81. As Batt herself admits, Launcelot's reaction to the burial of Arthur and Gwenyvere undermines Batt's claim that Gwenyvere is 'efface[d]' by her burial.

[104] Herbert A. Deane, *The Political and Social Ideas of St. Augustine* (New York, 1963), p. 67.

not divine love or grace, which dominate the scene and the imagination.[105] Launcelot lying grovelling and wilfully wasting away on the tomb of Arthur and Gwenyvere is, to my mind, one of the two most prominent and powerful images dominating the close of Malory's Arthuriad, the other being Arthur's martial pursuit of Mordred and the son hanging impaled upon the father's spear. Both images are human, both are memorable and both are tragic.

Launcelot's sorrow at being separated from Gwenyvere and Arthur is adumbrated by Launcelot's actions subsequent to his madness when, exiled from the court and living at Joyous Isle as Le Shyvalere Mafete, he would 'every day onys, for ony myrthis that all the ladyes myght make hym, he wolde onys every day loke towarde the realme of Logrys, where Kynge **Arthure** and Quene **Gwenyvere** was, and than wolde he falle uppon a wepyng as hys harte shulde to-braste' (339^v; 652.16–20). Significantly, Launcelot's relationship to the king and queen, his status as paragon of earthly knights and lovers, is announced and celebrated by three of Winchester's final four marginalia. Those marginalia read: 'How Quene Gwenyver besouȝt Sir Bors to fight for her' (412^v); 'How Sir Launcelot recowed Quene Gwenyvere from þe deth' (414^v); and 'He[re] Sir Launcelot felle into a depe pytte by þe treson off Sir Mellyaunte [sic] ten fadum' (442^v).

An obvious feature of Malory's plot in Tales VII and VIII, one remarked upon by a good many scholars, is the way in which the narrative unfolds in a series of crises in which Gwenyvere is in trouble, frequently accused of treason and equally frequently rescued by Launcelot. Equally often remarked by critics is that Malory inherits this plot structure from the sources, but that he adds many touches to make it distinctly his own. What has so far not been recognized is the way in which Winchester's closing marginalia echo this plot progression and artistry. I have already mentioned that the final marginalium marks Gawayne's deathbed letter to Launcelot (477^r; 918.17–23). One of the requests Gawayne makes in this letter is that Launcelot return to England to 'rescow that noble kynge that made the knyght' from Mordred's rebellion (477^{r-v}; 919.3–8). One of the facts that Arthur acknowledges whilst Gawayne lies dying is Arthur's love of and reliance upon both Gawayne and Launcelot. Appropriately, then, Winchester's other closing marginalia all emphasize Launcelot's status as what Arthur himself acknowledges as 'the moste man of worship in thys worlde' (412^v; 796.12–13) and the queen's undisputed champion. In the Poisoned Apple episode, for instance, Gwenyvere is 'appeled ... of treson' by Sir Mador for the death of his cousin Patryse (411^v; 794.1–26). Launcelot just prior to the dinner where the poisoning occurs is banished by Gwenyvere for championing other women, meaning that he is initially not present to defend her. None of the knights at the feast, including Gawayne and Bors, can honourably defend her because the circumstantial evidence makes her look guilty, and Bors is further unwilling to defend Gwenyvere because he is angry about Launcelot's exile. Nor can Arthur honourably defend her because as king he must oversee the trial by combat that will determine her fate. Gwenyvere thus desperately requires a champion, and Arthur recommends she appeal to Bors – an encounter marked by the fourth-last marginalium:

---

[105] Cf. Vinaver, pp. xciii–xcix, 1622–3, and Commentary on *Works* 1255.14–1257.11; see further my *Understanding Genre*, pp. 144–6.

'How Quene Gwenyver besou3t Sir Bors to fight for her' (412ᵛ; 796.16–20). This note bookmarks Launcelot's status as the queen's defender because, as Arthur explains, Bors is sought expressly as stand-in for his cousin (795.26–796.15), and because readers or listeners can guess and Malory as author of the marginalium would know, that Launcelot himself will arrive to defend Gwenyvere. In the meantime, though, Bors finally agrees to fight 'for my lorde Sir **Launcelottis** sake and for [Arthur's] sake'; the underlying fellowship and love that binds them all together is reinforced by the rubrication of **Bors, Arthure, Bors, Bors, Bors, Launcelottis, Bors, Bors, Launcelot** (413ʳ; 796.33–797.23). Textual sense and comparison of this passage to the Caxton suggest that Winchester is actually missing one 'Bors' and one 'Launcelot' due to scribal error, and Field emends accordingly; but even so, the rubrication as it stands markedly reinforces the narrative text and character interaction.

The corresponding visual and textual emphasis and human effect are compounded by the next marginalium, the third-from-last, celebrating Launcelot's last-minute arrival and the actual battle: 'How Sir Launcelot recowed Quene Gwenyvere from þe deth' (414ᵛ; 800.15–19). That morality – and thus religion – is not necessarily the driving force in Malory's *Morte* is apparent in Launcelot's retrospective comment on the battle, that because the queen had done him 'worshyp' on the day of his knighting, he would always 'be her knyght in ryght othir in wronge' (415ᵛ; 802.13–23). I observed in the previous chapter that heroism and morality do not necessarily coexist: a prime example of this heroic curiosity comes in Launcelot's admission here. For Launcelot admits, and audiences or readers realize, that in championing Gwenyvere 'in ryght othir in wronge', he violates the final precept of the Round Table Oath, 'that no man take no batayles in a wrongfefull quarell for no love ne no worldis goodis' (44ᵛ; 97.34–5). Notwithstanding his willingness to violate the Oath or the adulterous nature of his love, Launcelot remains the greatest knight of the Arthuriad, a favourite of critics. Indeed, scholars regularly claim that Launcelot is Malory's own favourite.[106] In this light it is important to remember Malory's concern to relate the 'auctorysed' story of 'The Hoole Book of Kyng Arthur and of His Noble Knyghtes of the Rounde Table' (C XXI.13; 940.10, 17–18), important to remember, that is, that Malory is concerned with peopling his narrative with a recognizable cast of characters dominated by the Fellowship of the Round Table. It is equally important to remember, though, that Malory goes out of his way to minimize Launcelot's and Gwenyvere's guilt, despite their treasonous and adulterous love. He does the same with Trystram and Isode. *Worshyp*, in the *Morte Darthur*, trumps morality. Consequently, for Malory and most readers, Launcelot's adultery and acting contrary to the Oath simply does not matter. The Poisoned Apple episode accordingly closes with the king thanking Launcelot for his 'goodnesse', and 'all the Knyghtes of the Table Rounde that were there' welcoming him (415ᵛ–416ʳ; 802.24–32). Their response primes the audience's response.

This notion of earthly worship not being contingent upon moral ethics, like that of human bonds being a more primary focus than religion in the *Morte*, is

---

[106] The earliest critic I can think of to make this claim is E. K. Chambers, *English Literature at the Close of the Middle Ages* (Oxford, 1945), pp. 197–8.

equally evident in the episode marked by Winchester's penultimate marginalium, that recording how 'He[re] Sir Launcelot felle into a depe pytte by þe treson off Sir Mellyaunte [sic] ten fadum' (442ᵛ; 855.27–35). Here, in the Knight of the Cart adventure, Gwenyvere is again appealed of treason, this time when her kidnapper Mellyagaunt discovers blood on her sheets and accuses her of sleeping with one of the injured knights sharing her chambers. In reality, of course, the blood comes from the injury Launcelot sustained to his hand when he 'braste' the bars out of the window to enjoy 'hys pleasaunce' with the queen in the one occasion in the entire *Morte Darthur* when Malory admits that Launcelot and Gwenyvere's relationship is physical as well as emotional (440ᵛ–441ʳ; 852.5–853.14). Hoping to use the queen's guilt to hide his own treason (441ᵛ; 853.27–9), Mellyagaunt warns Launcelot not to interfere: 'beware what ye do; for thoughe ye ar never so good a knyght, ... yet shude ye be avysed to do batayle in a wronge quarell, for God woll have a stroke in every batayle' (441ᵛ; 854.7–17). Launcelot admits that 'God ys to be drad!', but insists on defending the queen's innocence, swearing that 'thys nyght there lay none of thes ten wounded knyghtes with my lady Quene **Gwenyvere**. And that woll I prove with myne hondys' (441ᵛ; 854.18–21). As the invocations of 'God', charges of treason and exchanging of gloves establish, the ensuing battle between Launcelot and Mellyagaunt is the clearest instance of formal trial by combat in all of the *Morte*. The idea of trial by combat overseen by God is a common trope in mediaeval literature and society; the whole point of the exercise is that God will secure victory for the righteous rather than the strong. This higher justice should include God seeing through any legal technicalities. Launcelot's falling prey to Mellyagaunt's treachery, with its accompanying manuscript marginalium, happens immediately after this formal combat is established. The marginalium thus reinforces Mellyagaunt's villainy and Launcelot's earthly reasons for championing Gwenyvere, but also the divinely sanctioned battle Launcelot's entrapment is designed to avoid. Malory, however, arranges matters so that it is precisely by a technicality that Gwenyvere is innocent: she had extramarital sex with Launcelot, but contrary to what Mellyagaunt charges, not with any of the ten wounded knights. Despite the technicality, Launcelot is victorious. Indeed, when he arrives at the last minute to face the queen's accuser, Gwenyvere is released from her place of punishment 'and sette by the kynge in the grete truste of hir champion' (443ʳ⁻ᵛ; 857.13–858.16). As Keith Swanson points out, 'any notion of divine intervention' securing 'absolute justice is severely attenuated' by Launcelot's victory.[107] The fact that earthly love, human combat and worshipful prowess in the *Morte* trump morality or divine supervision is mirrored by Winchester's rubrication, which highlights the human element, but not the divine: 'God' is not rubricated in this episode (or elsewhere), whereas **Mellyagaunt, Launcelot, Lavayne, Arthur** and **Gwenyvere** all are. As Jacqueline Stuhmiller justly observes, 'Malory takes care to secularize the theoretically sacred process of the trial by battle.'[108] He does so, I suggest, because morality is not necessarily the standard for being a worshipful knight in

---

[107] Keith Swanson, '"God Woll Have a Stroke"', *Bulletin of the John Rylands University Library of Manchester* 74 (1992): 155–73 (167).
[108] Jacqueline Stuhmiller, '*Iudicium Dei, iudicium fortunae*', *Speculum* 81.2 (2006): 427–62 (435).

Malory's world any more than it is for being an honourable and respected warrior in Homer's. Malory's focus, like that of most of his characters, is on martial worship and love.

Malory's emphasis on human character, on knights and ladies and their human loves, lives and concerns, helps to explicate the closing relationship between Launcelot and Gwenyvere and the secular focus of the close of the *Morte Darthur*. Not only does Launcelot die starving and grovelling upon Arthur's and Gwenyvere's tomb, but he repents his vow to be buried at Joyous Garde. At the end, after six weeks of sorrow-making, Launcelot falls ill, asks for and receives his last rites in accordance with a Christian burial, and then 'prayed the bysshop that his felowes myght bere his body to Joyous Garde'. The last rites and prayers are sacred, but Launcelot's motives remain secular, especially concerning his own interment: '"Howbeit", sayd Syr **Launcelot**, "me repenteth sore, but I made myn avowe somtyme that in Joyous Garde I wold be buryed. And bycause of brekyng of myne avowe, I praye you al, lede me thyder"' (C XXI.12; 937.16–33). The clear regret about burial places implies that he would rather be buried near his beloved king and even more beloved queen than far away in his own castle, but because of an earthly oath, he is compelled to rest instead at Joyous Garde. Malory manages still to link the lovers even in death, for the former Archbishop and Bors and the other knights transport Launcelot to Joyous Garde 'in the same hors-bere that Quene **Guenevere** was layed in tofore that she was buryed' (C XXI.12; 938.23–5) when Launcelot and his fellows brought her corpse from Almysbury back to Glastonbury. As Vinaver notes, 'Several details of the description of Lancelot's burial are peculiar to M[alory]'s rendering', adding in passing the astute but unelaborated observation that the 'mention of Guinevere who was "layed in" "the same hors-bere" as Lancelot … is in keeping with [Malory]'s interpretation of the story as a whole'.[109] Indeed they are, and the details and the interpretation all emphasize the crucial fact that, in Malory's vision of the Arthuriad, the focus is not on God or the afterlife or repenting of a sinful love, but on the earthly celebration and memorialization of the lives, loves, deeds and bodies of the Round Table Fellowship, knights and ladies, kings and queens.

So it is that the figural conjoining of Launcelot and Gwenyvere even after death is continued in the two burial scenes: for the burial party at first Gwenyvere's and then Launcelot's funeral place 'an hondred torches brennyng aboute' each body (cf. C XXI.11; 936.12–13 with C XXI.12; 938.27). For Cherewatuk, the associations of Gwenyvere's body with Launcelot's work on 'two registers, the secular-romantic and the sacred-religious'; Malory's text is accordingly both 'heroic and religious'.[110] This conclusion has much to recommend it, but the same textual evidence can be used to suggest that Malory is hereby recalling and reinforcing the lovers' consistently earthly and physical love even more than their, or their author's, orthodox piety. After all, notwithstanding the mixture of chivalric and Christian language here, Launcelot's funeral is, as Cherewatuk admits, 'secular rather than monastic'. In this calling together of the two bodies through the same descriptive language, Malory may be thinking of the stanzaic *Morte Arthur*, where

---

[109] Vinaver, Commentary on *Works* 1258.20–33.
[110] Cherewatuk, 'Christian Rituals in Malory', in *Malory and Christianity*, p. 88.

the lovers' union is likewise recalled by the description of each dead body as 'Rede and fayer' and 'feyre and rede'.[111] Malory's version of the lovers' deaths is a particularly characteristic elaboration of the source-text, one that ably reflects the emphasis on martial achievement and chivalric genealogy that dominates gentry and aristocratic tombs in the late Middle Ages.[112] Even more importantly for my overarching thesis is the way in which Malory's themes are similarly invoked in the Winchester manuscript. The rubrication of each and every character's name in Winchester renders this memorialization of earthly human love and earthly and human accomplishment all the more pronounced. Or it would, if this part of Winchester survived. But the consistency of the rubrication throughout the manuscript makes it certain that the same *ordinatio* would occur here as elsewhere; that *ordinatio* would, as in the scenes of Gwenyvere's penance or death, foreground rubricated Arthurian names, especially, in Launcelot's burial, the continued highlighting of **Launcelot**, as well as those he leaves behind, especially **Bors**, the companion with whom he vowed lasting fellowship (409ʳ; 789.10–13). Even without its closing leaves, Winchester's consistent name rubrication prepares for the same memorializing effect.

In another example of the textual and codicological symmetry of the *Morte Darthur*, both Malory's interest in characterization and secular themes, as well as the consistency of Launcelot's own character and actions, are confirmed one final time in the *Morte* in what is the final speech-act in the entire text: Ector's words over Launcelot's dead body. This finality is in itself important, but the speech in question is also original to Malory. It is not in either the French *Mort Artu* or the stanzaic *Morte Arthur*, the two principal sources for Tale VIII. Instead, Malory seems to have adopted and adapted the speech from the equally moving threnody given by Mordred over the slain Gawayne in the alliterative *Morte Arthure*, a poem dominated by epic-heroic and martial values, not religious ones.[113] In Malory's case, Launcelot's brother Ector arrives just as Launcelot is being buried and delivers his own threnody, one as moving and elegiac as is the alliterative source and whose importance demands quoting at length:

> 'A, **Launcelot**!' he sayd, 'thou were hede of al Crysten *knyghtes*! And now I dare say', sayd Syr **Ector**, 'thou Sir **Launcelot**, there thou lyest, that thou were never matched of erthely *knyghtes* hande. And thou were the curtest *knyght* that ever bare shelde! And thou were the truest frende to thy lovar that ever bestrade hors, and thou were the trewest lover, of a synful man, that ever loved woman, and thou were the kyndest man that ever strake wyth swerde. And thou were the godelyest persone that ever cam emonge prees of *knyghtes*, and thou was the mekest man and the jentyllest that ever ete in halle emonge ladyes, and thou were the sternest *knyght* to thy mortal foo that ever put spere in the reest.'
> (C XXI.13; 939.12–23. My emphases.)

---

[111] *Morte Arthur*, vv. 3888 and 3956. All of this conjoining of the lovers' physical bodies further emphasizes the idea that their true focus even in religious settings remains one another.

[112] On chivalry and posthumous fame, see Saul, *For Honour and Fame*, pp. 283–304.

[113] For the scene in question see *Morte Arthure*, vv. 3875–85. For the alliterative *Morte*'s genre, see my 'Genre as Context in the Alliterative *Morte Arthure*', *Arthuriana* 20.2 (2010): 45–65.

Ector's lament is the last speech in the *Morte*, is original to Malory, and constitutes Malory's last word on Launcelot and the values of the Round Table and Arthurian chivalry. As the repetition of the word *knyght* indicates, it is a judgement that celebrates and memorializes Launcelot's secular and chivalric talents.[114] In this sense the appearance of 'synful man' in the speech's centre is not a religious note sounding *contemptus mundi*, but rather a corroboration that Launcelot is the best knight of the Round Table precisely because he is a sinful human knight and lover rather than a celestial cipher such as Galahad. As Michael W. Twomey reveals in his exemplary stylistic analysis of this passage, Ector's entire refrain 'is enclosed in an envelope structure based on the word "knight"[.] ... Between these unequivocal statements of Lancelot's prowess in combat, the speech depends heavily on a series of striking antitheses focusing on Lancelot's secular and chivalric virtues.'[115]

But the threnody does not just memorialize Launcelot. By reminding us of his chivalric achievements and of his profound effect on the Round Table Fellowship as a whole, Ector's speech takes on a synecdochical quality which deliberately calls to mind and elegizes all the other knights for whom Launcelot was the yardstick: Trystram, his only equal in love or combat, who is slain by the villainous Mark and whose death is recalled in the Urry catalogue (447^r; 865.6–15); Gareth, knighted by Launcelot's own hand (116^{r-v}; 228.15–229.17), just as he is later slain by the same hand (457^v; 885.4–11); Gawayne, slain in part through a wound given by Launcelot (cf. 473^r; 911.30–2; 474^v; 914.13–17; 476^v; 918.5–10; 477^r; 918.34–919.2); Lionel, slain whilst vainly seeking to rejoin Launcelot (C XXI.10; 934.26–8); and all the remnant, surpassed by Launcelot from Tale III till the Healing of Sir Urry in Tale VII, and then subsequently slain on a 'wycked' and 'unhappy day' in a doleful battle that 'never stynted tylle [all] the noble knyghtes were layde to the colde erthe' (479^r–480^r; 922.19–923.23). What we see and hear consistently throughout the close of the *Morte Darthur* are Malory's celebration of, and lament for, the glory and tragedy of Arthur and the Round Table knights as a worthwhile human ideal. The repeated deaths of the principals, like the repeated rubrication of their names, serve to foreground Malory's characters. The 'affective' aspect of memory is 'sensorily derived and emotionally charged': Launcelot's association with other knights, and the deaths of the entire Round Table Fellowship, are thus rendered all the more memorable because '[s]uccessful memory schemes all acknowledge the importance of tagging material emotionally ... , making each memory ... into a personal occasion'.[116]

The memorialization and glorification of Malory's characters is further announced through repeated diction. As Elizabeth Archibald perspicaciously observes, 'It is striking that the few survivors of the Götterdämmerung, Lancelot and his friends, are frequently described as "felowes" during their life as

---

[114] I make a similar point in my *Understanding Genre*, pp. 106–8, as does Elizabeth Archibald, 'Malory's Lancelot and Guenevere', in *A Companion to Arthurian Literature*, ed. Helen Fulton (Oxford and Malden, 2009), pp. 312–25 (p. 324).

[115] Michael W. Twomey, 'The Voice of Aurality in the *Morte Darthur*', *Arthuriana* 13.4 (2003): 103–18 (112–14). See also Brewer, ed., *Morte Darthur: Parts Seven and Eight*, pp. 13–14, and Benson, *Malory's Morte Darthur*, p. 246.

[116] Carruthers, *Book of Memory*, pp. 75–6.

hermits.' This repeated use of 'felowes' and 'felyshyp' at the end of the Arthuriad as in its beginning and middle is no doubt a deliberate repetition of the terms and ideas consistently employed by Malory to epitomize and memorialize 'the value of this Arthurian and Malorian ideal'.[117] Malory's final *explicit* and title for the whole book appropriately enough reminds us of the glory of that fellowship 'whan they were holé togyders': 'Here is the ende of The Hoole Book of Kyng **Arthur** and of His Noble Knyghtes of the Rounde Table, that whan they were holé togyders there was ever an Hondred and Fyfty' (C XXI.13; 940.17–19).[118] At this endpoint in the narrative, those 150 names and (depending on if the name is, say, **Trystram** or **Breunys**) the names of their friends, foes and lovers have all been consistently and repeatedly valorized or vilified across nearly five hundred folios. The rubricated elegy provided by the *ordinatio* of the *Morte Darthur* in the Winchester manuscript thus markedly reinforces the pathos of the tragic collapse of the Round Table. Part of the tragedy and pathos stems from the finality of Arthur's death and the way that finality carries over into other deaths.

In her stimulating account of narrative style in Malory's *Morte Darthur*, Mann emphasizes the interplay of obfuscation and nonsensical explanation, self-discovery and alienation whereby the 'themes of distance and wholeness are ... constantly played out in the routine activities of the knightly life: adventure, quest, combat', any or all of which, it must be remembered, might be linked to love and ladies.[119] This obfuscation in the face of explanation is reflected in the *Morte*'s very landscape, a landscape, in Mann's terms, 'littered with ... the residue of narrative – tombs, wounded knights, grieving women – bearing witness to a vanished story'.[120] What I hope to have revealed throughout this chapter and indeed this book as a whole are the many ways in which Winchester's *ordinatio* helps to elucidate the complexities and contradictions of Malory's narrative, spectacularly and repeatedly illustrating that it is precisely the knightly life in all of its earthly violence and human vagaries that is important to Malory and his characters. To adopt Mann's rhetoric, Winchester's rubrication and marginalia reduce the distance between narrative and audience, acting as a sort of visual hermeneutic key by which we are constantly shown and reminded that named characters and their deeds and loves and deaths are what is truly important, not the seeming gaps in narrative logic or the occasional prayer or moral quandary. In the world of the *Morte Darthur*, earthly *worshyp*, earthly characters and earthly fellowship are paramount. Patristic doctrine or even lay spirituality occur at times throughout the text, especially in 'The Tale of the Sankgreal' and in masses for the dead; but overall, it is the secular and chivalric, not the sacred and celestial, that most interests Malory and typifies the actions of the majority of his characters.

[117] Archibald, 'Malory's Ideal', 325–6.
[118] The final *explicit* famously records 140 knights, but as Field points out, that number is manifestly wrong, whether the error be scribal or authorial: Field, 'Author, Scribe and Reader', in *Texts and Sources*, p. 88. Field accordingly emends to 150 in his edition (Commentary on 940.19). Given the importance of the number and its probable titular role, I have capitalized 'Hondred and Fyfty'.
[119] Jill Mann, 'The Narrative of Distance, The Distance of Narrative in Malory's *Morte d'Arthur*', in her *Life in Words*, pp. 275–311 (quoting p. 283).
[120] Mann, 'Narrative of Distance, The Distance of Narrative', in her *Life in Words*, p. 299.

Mann argues forcefully that Malory's focus on taking the adventure reflects a late mediaeval concern with questions of chance and destiny that scholars usually associate more with Chaucer than with Malory; for Mann, Malory's solution is to emphasize the randomness of chance or adventure.[121] In such a universe, Mann suggests, *worshyp* becomes both the only quasi-logical motivation for narrative events and meaning, and a defining feature of knightly identity. I agree with Mann that Malory is deeply concerned with human interaction with chance, Fate and adventure, but I do not accept her accompanying assertion that in surrendering themselves to adventure Malory's knights perforce surrender their free will. Nor does it follow that Malory is uninterested in characterization. D. W. Robertson Jr insists that such an (essentially dramatic) engagement with character and plot over moral or allegorical significance is a modern, not mediaeval, manner of reading.[122] Few critics today read the *Morte Darthur* in strictly Robertsonian terms, yet Mann is not alone in downplaying the role or agency of character in the Arthuriad.[123] Malory, however, frequently engages with his characters as characters, not merely abstract types, and there is considerable reason to think that he was not all that unusual in his time for doing so. Certainly Roger Ascham's concerns about who was reading the *Morte* did not involve the moral or allegorical qualities of the text, but rather what Ascham perceived as the morally bankrupt behaviour of the protagonists.

Robertson further insists that mediaeval narratives cannot be tragic because of Catholic belief in the Resurrection and divine Providence. Nor is he alone in such thinking. Erich Auerbach argues that Christianity focusses all worldly tragedy on the Crucifixion, with the result that 'worldly grief has lost its independent value and has no further claim to tragedy'.[124] Religious salvation and the promise of a redemptive Christian afterlife, it is consequently upheld, ultimately supersede and negate earthly tragedy.[125] Although the mediaeval idea of the Wheel of Fortune is often associated with Boethius's *De Consolatione Philosophiae*, Boethius ultimately argues that Fortune is but one aspect of divine Providence. Accordingly, earthly suffering, tragic or otherwise, is really unimportant since living a good life will bring one closer to God whether or not one enjoys earthly happiness and riches and prosperity – whether or not one evades seeming tragedy. Boethius does, however, give more import to human history and deeds than does Augustine, a fact which necessitates and validates a certain anthropocentrism.[126] Nevertheless, for Robertson (and others) mediaeval thought allowed no

---

[121] Jill Mann, '"Taking the Adventure"', in her *Life in Words*, pp. 243–74 (esp. pp. 266–71), and eadem, 'Knightly Combat', likewise in *Life in Words*, pp. 235–9.

[122] D. W. Roberston Jr, *A Preface to Chaucer* (Princeton, 1962), esp. pp. 33–51 and 247–77.

[123] Her position is cautiously accepted by no less a scholar than Lupack, 'Malory's Intratexts', in *Romance and Rhetoric*, p. 250, n. 3. Even Brewer concludes that Malory is interested in types, not characters: Derek Brewer, 'The Presentation of the Character of Lancelot', *Arthurian Literature* 3 (1983): 26–52 (esp. 47–51).

[124] Erich Auerbach, *Literary Language and Its Public in Late Latin Antiquity and in the Middle Ages*, trans. Ralph Manheim (Princeton, 1965), p. 305.

[125] See, e.g., Laurence Michel, 'The Possibility of a Christian Tragedy', *Thought* 31 (1956): 403–28. Cf. I. A. Richards, *Principles of Literary Criticism* (London, 1926), p. 246.

[126] See F. P. Pickering, *Literature and Art in the Middle Ages* (Berlin, 1966; Florida, 1970), pp. 168–222. Boethius's greater human element may also explain why the Wheel of Fortune became a commonplace mediaeval trope that sometimes (as in Boethius or parts of Chaucer) had

meaningful distinction between secular and religious. Since earthly tragedy in part requires a sympathetic response from the audience as well as an inscrutable and perhaps uncaring universe, tragedy as a literary genre or theme ceased to have any meaning.[127] These conclusions seem rather naïve, especially when so baldly summarized; they are nevertheless conclusions advocated by some very influential scholars. The shadow of these scholars still looms large in some attitudes to mediaeval literary tragedy. Even Barbara Newman's nuanced investigation of secular and sacred crossovers in the Middle Ages opens by recounting how 'purely secular comedy (or tragedy) cannot exist in a medieval frame of reference' because the mediaeval reference always included both sacred and secular. Newman in her reading of Malory's Arthuriad both contrasts and doubles Arthur's 'secular tragedy' against Gwenyvere and Launcelot's 'Christian hagiography', concluding that Malory chooses to uphold 'both' 'sacred and secular values'.[128]

As so often, however, Malory seems not to be doing what he should, or not doing what modern readers expect. Certainly the narrative and codicological emphases on rubricated character and adventure, Fate and free will, strongly suggest that what gives life meaning in Malory's Arthuriad is not God as the unseen power behind fickle Fortune, but rather human endeavour in the face of Fate and adventure and free will. *Worshyp*, as Brewer quite rightly points out, is the palmary virtue, motivation and goal in the *Morte*.[129] The chance of winning such *worshyp* most often takes the form of earthly adventure, and *worshyp* is repeatedly gained or lost in the *Morte* on the basis of human chivalric activities. In this earthly and human focus Malory is different from Boethius or even, in the end, Chaucer's Troilus. It is worth recalling in this context that whatever his personal piety may have been, Malory had no scruples about twice relieving Coombe Abbey of some of its more readily transportable worldly possessions. Larceny does not negate Malory's own piety or the religiousness of much late mediaeval thought, but neither does late mediaeval Christian ideology necessarily dictate Malory's literary artistry and interests. Placing the *Morte Darthur* in its manuscript context reveals just how precisely and constantly Malory's narrative valorization of human adventure, human character and human achievement is matched and strengthened by the consistent rubrication of human characters' names throughout the Winchester manuscript. The rubrication of each and every character's name in Winchester, together with the less consistent but equally visual marginalia and their record of human deeds, turns the manuscript context of the *Morte*, turns the manuscript itself, into a special sort of monument to earthly Arthurian worship. Since, as Ruth Scodel observes of Homeric epitaphs, special monuments stress 'the special status of those with claims to memory',[130]

---

a Providential component and sometimes (as in other parts of Chaucer or much English Arthuriana) had a more independent and fickle agency akin to Chance or Fate.

[127] Robertson, *Preface*, pp. 473–4. For a thorough overview of Robertson's scholarship and the critical school of thought that followed from his beliefs, see Kathy Cawsey, *Twentieth-Century Chaucer Criticism* (Farnham and Burlington, Vt., 2011), pp. 85–108.

[128] Barbara Newman, *Medieval Crossover* (Notre Dame, 2013), pp. vii, 94, 101, 109.

[129] Brewer, ed., *Morte Darthur: Parts Seven and Eight*, p. 25.

[130] Scodel, 'Inscription, Absence and Memory', 68. *Contra* Tiller, 'En-graving Chivalry', 48–9.

Winchester quite spectacularly enshrines and elegizes the glory and honour of Arthur and his fellows. At the same time, Winchester helps to clarify the *sens* of Malory's Arthuriad: Malory is not interrogating Arthurian chivalry, he is praising its capacity for glory and lamenting its tragic passing.

Malory's principal focus throughout his Arthuriad is the nobility, deeds, fellowship and ultimate demise of the knights and ladies who comprise Arthurian society. To read Vinaver's magisterial Commentary is to be struck again and again by the realization that Malory had an attitude towards and vision of his materials distinct from his sources. One obvious example of this attitude is Malory's continual unweaving of the *entrelacement* of the French books. An equally important but more subtle example of Malory's human vision is evident in the way Malory opens his Arthuriad by transforming his French sources, the Vulgate prose *Merlin* and Post-Vulgate *Suite du Merlin*, from a history of the great magician into an account of the greatness of the young king, Arthur.[131] The first two of Malory's tales accordingly elaborate why Arthur can justifiably be considered the paragon of kings and knights; unlike his French counterpart, Malory's Arthur is worthy leader of a worthy host. Marc Ricciardi makes a compelling case that the Winchester-text of the Roman War promotes the Round Table ideal of fellowship, whereas the Caxton Malory portrays a king who is a more solitary hero; certainly it is true that Malory's Arthur is presented as both king and knight, one worthy of both titles and one who does his best to model knightly and kingly behaviour, tempering prowess with virtue.[132] As Dhira B. Mahoney observes, in these opening sections of the *Morte* Malory is careful to style Arthur 'Sir' more often than in later sections; such 'Sir Arthur' appearances, moreover, occur most typically during combat.[133] Malory thus emphasizes different aspects of Arthur's character, as well as Arthur's own prowess as a warrior. Here again Malory has his narrative finger on the pulse of the age since one of the givens of fifteenth-century English politics was that 'Upon the effective exercise of good lordship ... depended in part "worship".'[134] What I wish particularly to attend to is that this focus on Arthur's own heroic prowess, this focus on Arthur as part of the Fellowship of knights, is enhanced not merely by the lexical text of Winchester, but also by the manuscript's *ordinatio*.

Despite the readiness of many modern scholars to take Launcelot as Malory's chief focus, it is noteworthy that it is only after Arthur has secured his reign and empire that Malory turns his narrative to the adventures of the leading knights of the Fellowship in the Tales devoted to Launcelot, Gareth, Trystram and Galahad. Equally noteworthy is the extent to which Arthur's presence and importance, sometimes in the background and sometimes in the foreground, is constantly evoked even in these middle tales of the Arthuriad. Similarly, each of the knights

---

[131] Vinaver, p. 1279.

[132] Marc Ricciardi, '"Se what I shall do as for my trew parte"', *Arthuriana* 11.2 (2001): 20–31. *Contra* Beverly Kennedy, *Knighthood in the Morte Darthur*, 2nd edn (Cambridge, 1992), pp. 6–8.

[133] Dhira B. Mahoney, 'Narrative Treatment of Name in Malory's *Morte D'Arthur*', *ELH* 47.4 (1980): 646–56.

[134] A. J. Pollard, 'Introduction', in *The Wars of the Roses*, ed. Pollard (New York, 1995), pp. 1–19 (p. 7).

granted his own tale nonetheless interacts regularly with most of the other principal characters in the *Morte Darthur*. We are thus meant, in contrast to much French Arthuriana, to consider the knights' worship and adventures and their desire to be members of Arthur's Round Table as extensions of Arthur's own worth and heroic stature. So it is that both theme and structure dictate Arthur's return to relative prominence in the final two tales.[135] So it is too that Malory's accounts of the deaths of his principals, Arthur and Gwenyvere and Launcelot, as well as Gawayne and even Gareth and Trystram, are dominated by his originality or departures from his sources. As I argued in Chapter Three, although Trystram's death occurs offstage in the *Morte Darthur*, recounted in passing in the great Urry catalogue (447ʳ; 865.6–17) rather than at the close of 'The Boke off Syr Trystram', Malory's version of Trystram's death actually generates more sorrow and pathos for coming where and when it does than Vinaver allowed.[136] Gawayne's deathbed letter to Launcelot is likewise original and is further marked out by one of Winchester's marginalia (477ʳ; 918.17–919.18), just as – in the ways noted above – Malory's version of Arthur's death is also original.

As Wilson reveals in his sensitive studies of characterization in Malory, Malory was quite capable of rearranging, enhancing or ignoring his sources in order not only to people his Arthuriad with a recognizable cast, but also to give some of his cast certain distinguishing human traits.[137] Malory was not writing a novel, and modern readers of the *Morte* should not impose novelistic criteria and consistent psychological realism on the narrative. But to go too far the other way and deny that the *Morte* lacks recognizable characters or a unifying vision and artistry is to ignore the considerable evidence of Malory's handling of his sources, of the Unity Debate, and especially of Malory's handling of theme and character. Part of the artistry of works like *Chevalier de la Charrete*, *Troilus and Criseyde* or *Le Morte Darthur* is their authors' successes in fledgling characterization. We can predict Launcelot's or Gawayne's actions not only on the basis of genre and formulae, but also individuality. Like characters on the Greek stage, characters in Malory and certain other mediaeval works are defined – albeit loosely – by what they say and do, and by what others say about and do to them.[138] Malory's focus on recognizable characters is enhanced by the rubrication of names in the Winchester manuscript, where the red names initially emphasize the identity, and eventually or cumulatively emphasize the history and deeds, of the Arthurian characters so literally flagged for attention. The eighty marginalia bookmarking various knightly deeds, deaths or visions serve the same purpose. Seeing and reading the red names in the manuscript reinforce whose story is being told and reminds

---

[135] *Contra* Ruth Lexton, *Contested Language in Malory's Morte Darthur* (New York and Basingstoke, 2014).

[136] In fact, Vinaver argues that Malory 'failed above all to grasp and bring out the tragic theme' of the Trystram and Isode story (p. lxxxviii), and that Malory renders Trystram and Isode 'uniformly happy' (p. 1445). See above, pp. 126–7.

[137] Robert Henry Wilson, *Characterization in Malory* (Chicago, 1934); Robert H. Wilson, 'Malory's Naming of Minor Characters', *Journal of English and Germanic Philology* 42 (1943): 364–85; idem, 'Addenda'.

[138] See, for comparison, P. E. Easterling, 'Character in Sophocles', *Greece and Rome* SS 24.2 (1977): 121–9.

us that, for Malory, it is the earthly lives, deeds and deaths of the Round Table Fellowship that are paramount.[139]

In marked contrast, neither penitence nor religion nor God are so foregrounded by manuscript *ordinatio*. Fletcher contends that the *Morte*'s final colophon and its apostrophe to 'all jentylmen and jentylwymmen that redeth this book' (C XXI.13; 940.21) reveal Malory's 'final moment of authorial self-fashioning' in which he also memorializes himself within his elegiac Arthuriad.[140] This self-aggrandizement is no doubt partly correct, and it is equally noteworthy that Malory's final colophon asks his readers to pray for his deliverance; but even in these contexts Malory subordinates his own presence to prioritize his characters and their story, appealing specifically to those 'jentylmen and jentylwymmen that *redeth this book of Arthur and his knyghtes from the begynnyng to the endynge*' (my emphasis). As noted in Chapter One, Crofts observes how 'turning from' reading the *Morte* in its manuscript form 'back to the typographical text' of a modern (or even black-letter) edition, 'one feels as if the lights had gone out'.[141] This darkening is emphatically true at any point throughout the manuscript and its text, but it is – or would be, if we had the final folios – especially true of the close of the Arthuriad. Back near the beginning of 'The Hoole Book', after another major victory during the War with the Five Kings, Arthur 'kneled downe and thanked God mekely' (47ᵛ; 103.30–1); he then founds an abbey to memorialize the battle and the knightly deeds shown by both his own warriors and their enemies. The abbey by definition honours God and Christ, but it is also built explicitly to honour the dead knights, and its name foregrounds knightly deeds since the abbey is called 'the Abbay of **La Beale Adventure**' (104.5–10). To reinforce the memorializing nature of chivalric adventure, the abbey's name is rubricated in Winchester (47ᵛ). By 'the endynge' of the *Morte Darthur*, in contrast, the Round Table Fellowship is 'disparbled' and the Fellowship and the rubricated elegy alike are both extinguished by the closing of the manuscript. But the effect and the memory of the elegy and rubrication and knightly deeds remain. Ultimately, Malory presents the fall of the Round Table as a sorrowful – not sinful – tragedy, a tragedy secured precisely because the honour and greatness and very human contradictions of the principal characters leave the sympathetic reader with a sense of waste and loss. This is, however, only part of Malory's artistry. It seems equally likely that Malory's artistic vision extended to the manuscript layout of his tragic Arthuriad, a layout which enhances Malory's focus on human characters and human *worshyp* and which, in the end, provides a rubricated and elegiac monument for earthly Arthurian achievement. Matter and meaning in the *Morte Darthur* are remarkably closely connected.

---

[139] I am arguing for a material foregrounding of character and theme by the Winchester manuscript, but Lupack's notion of intratextual emphases within the *Morte* that bolster theme and character, including Launcelot and Gwenyvere's love, further reveals Malory's focus on character and his attempts to emphasize character. See Lupack, 'Malory's Intratexts', in *Romance and Rhetoric*, pp. 249–68.

[140] Fletcher, *Presence of Medieval English Literature*, pp. 255–8.

[141] Crofts, *Malory's Contemporary Audience*, p. 66.

Conclusion: The Red and the Black

Karen Cherewatuk, in her influential reading of Launcelot's death, follows 'fifteenth-century bishop and theologian Reginald Pecock' in emphasizing 'that a [mediaeval] Christian learns the stories of the saints "bi calling in to mynde what he hath bifore thilk day red or herd red in book, or herd prechid, or seen peinted"'.[1] This is quite true, and Cherewatuk is justified to claim that Malory and his contemporaries would have assimilated doctrinal and hagiographic knowledge alike when sitting in church. It is equally true, however, that a mediaeval lay person could likewise read, hear and see the deeds of more secular and chivalric exemplars and that this chivalric engagement occurred equally in churches, cathedrals and abbeys as in castles and manor houses. Indeed, the iconography of mediaeval religious buildings regularly juxtaposed Christian with chivalric images, sacred with secular; even stained glass might commemorate knightly status or genealogy.[2] The tombs and effigies of the armigerous classes, gentry and nobility, likewise visually emphasize knightly deeds, brotherhood-in-arms and chivalric pedigree. Chivalric culture and chivalric memory were thus closely imbricated, more so even than chivalry and Christianity. As Nigel Saul illustrates, chivalry accordingly

> generated a rich repertory of contemporary witness: tombstones and tomb effigies, funerary armour, objects associated with legendary heroes, armorials on walls and in windows, rolls of arms, biographies and family chronicles. Chivalry was found in the landscape, in churches, in baronial halls, even in abbey refectories. ... The memory of chivalry lived on in the culture which it created, and that culture was at once visual, physical and literary.[3]

Caxton utilizes this expectation that a mediaeval person would see and value chivalric trappings in the justification he puts in the mouths of his 'noble and dyvers gentylmen' in the preface to the *Morte Darthur*, where Arthur's historicity is said to be verifiable on the basis of considerable tangible evidence. Caxton's – or his interlocutors' – evidence includes Arthur's 'sepulture in the monasterye of Glastyngburye', and the 'many remembraunces ... of hym' that may yet and will forever be seen in England, including Arthur's seal at Westminster

---

[1] Karen Cherewatuk, 'The Saint's Life of Sir Launcelot', *Arthuriana* 5.1 (1995): 62–78 (64); Reginald Pecock, *The Repressor of Over Much Blaming of the Clergy*, ed. Churchill Babington (London, 1860), pp. 213–14.

[2] As a notable example, see the depiction of Malory's heirs and a family shield from two windows from a church in Stanford, near the Malory house at Swinford, discovered and reproduced by Christina Hardyment in her *Malory* (London, 2005), the first two plates on the second page of (unnumbered) colour plates between pp. 204–5.

[3] Nigel Saul, *For Honour and Fame* (London, 2011), pp. 283–304 (quoting p. 304).

Abbey, Gawayne's skull at Dover Castle, the Round Table at Winchester, and 'Launcelottes swerde and many other thynges'.[4]

Chivalry and religion sat cheek by jowl in the Middle Ages, but it is secular chivalric culture with which Malory associates himself and which he is memorializing in *Le Morte Darthur*. As P. J. C. Field justly observes of Malory's narrative voice, what most strikes an audience about Malory's narrative personae is the extent to which it is 'wholly focused on Arthur and his knights'.[5] One of the more compelling pieces of evidence in the authorship debate is the simple but significant fact that the Warwickshire Malory is the only one of the handful of possible candidates alive in the right time and place who was both a Malory and a knight.[6] Malory firmly and regularly associates himself with chivalric culture in the many self-references to 'Sir Thomas Malleorré, knyght' scattered across the *Morte*'s various *explicits* (346^v; 664.10–11; cf. 70^v; 144.2–3; 409^r; 789.17; 449^r; 869.15–16; C XXI.13; 940.28). Malory's fondness for knightly *worshyp*, for battle sequences, and for hunting and hawking all likewise bespeak his secular chivalric interests. In fact, Malory's familiarity with such matters and their sometimes specialized vocabulary occasionally caused grief for his scribes, who appear not to have shared such knightly insights.[7]

Malory's *Le Morte Darthur* is a strikingly original treatment of what was, even in his day, a well-known story. Part of Malory's originality resides in the fashion by which he glorifies and memorializes Arthurian chivalry. Furthermore, 'To remember Arthurian society and its achievements is, for Malory's purposes, to perceive and trace kinds of interconnectedness between stories.'[8] Throughout this study I have attempted to show that there is also a marked interconnectedness between Malory's lexical narrative and its themes on the one hand, and the physical *ordinatio* of that story in its manuscript context – the Winchester manuscript – on the other. A number of recent, and frequently stimulating, critics of the *Morte Darthur* argue, in different ways, that Malory and the *Morte* display considerable anxiety about the Arthuriad's logical if tragic ending, about its textual stability or even, in Catherine Batt's rendition of the idea, about the loss of '[m]aterial access to memory'.[9] I contend that the narrative and thematic evidence of the *Morte*, together with the close intersection of these themes and the visual layout of the *Morte* in its material manuscript context, suggest otherwise: Malory *is* concerned with memory and telos, but not due to any anxiety about textual or memorial instability. Rather, the function of 'The Hoole Book of Kyng

---

[4] 'Caxton's Prologue to *Le Morte Darthur*', *MD* II:854–7 (quoting from 854 and 855).

[5] P. J. C. Field, 'Malory and His Audience', in *New Directions in Arthurian Studies*, ed. Alan Lupack (Cambridge, 2002), pp. 21–32 (p. 29).

[6] Not all scholars accept this; for the weighty evidence, see P. J. C. Field, *The Life and Times of Sir Thomas Malory* (Cambridge, 1993), and the less speculative parts of Hardyment, *Malory*.

[7] See P. J. C. Field, 'Hunting, Hawking and Textual Criticism in Malory's *Morte Darthur*', in his *Texts and Sources*, pp. 103–13.

[8] Nick Davis, 'Narrative Composition and the Spatial Memory', in *Narrative*, ed. J. Hawthorne (London, 1985), pp. 24–39 (31).

[9] See, e.g., Felicity Riddy, *Sir Thomas Malory* (Leiden, 1987), pp. 140–3; Elizabeth Edwards, *The Genesis of Narrative in Malory's Morte Darthur* (Cambridge, 2001); Catherine Batt, *Malory's Morte Darthur: Remaking Arthurian Tradition* (New York and Basingstoke, 2002); and Thomas H. Crofts, *Malory's Contemporary Audience* (Cambridge, 2006), pp. 121–58. I quote Batt, p. xv, but cf. her p. 181 and throughout.

Arthur and of His Noble Knyghtes of the Round Table' (C XXI.13; 940.17–18) is to valorize and memorialize the lives and loves, deeds and *worshyp* of the Arthurian Fellowship during their earthly adventures.

As Murray J. Evans perceptively concluded in his careful elucidation of narrative links in the *Morte Darthur*, Malory subtly but consistently organizes his story and dialogue in such a way as to encourage his audience 'to remember, praise, and be drawn into emotional empathy with his exemplary characters, to see our "nowadays" in the light of the virtuous love and noble deeds of a better, and lost, historical Arthurian past'.[10] It is partly this combination of empathy and exemplarity that generates the increased pathos and tragedy of Malory's version of the Arthuriad over that of his sources. What I hope to have demonstrated in the current study is just how consistently and marvellously – and, I think, deliberately – this memorialization within the narrative structure of the *Morte Darthur* is mirrored and magnified by the rubrication and marginalia throughout the Winchester manuscript text of the *Morte*: London, British Library, Additional MS 59678. Winchester's rubrication of characters' names foregrounds precisely, strikingly and continuously just who and what Malory's readers are supposed to remember.

In one of the more potent scenes in the *Iliad*, in the build-up to the Viewing from the Walls (or *Teichoskopia*), Homer recounts how Helen is found in her chamber

> weaving a great web,
> a red folding robe, and working into it the numerous struggles
> of Trojans, breakers of horses, and bronze-armoured Achaians,
> struggles that they endured for her sake at the hands of the war god.[11]

Iris then sends Helen to the walls to watch the single combat between Menelaos and Paris to determine who will win her, whereupon Helen meets Priam and other Trojan elders already assembled near the Skaian Gates. At Priam's request, Helen identifies for the Trojans several of the Greek leaders and warriors, including Agamemnon, Odysseus and the larger Ajax. Although this scene in Helen's room and atop Troy's walls is not as famous in English literature as is the forging of Achilles' shield, it is a powerful moment in the poem and one of several key ekphrastic descriptions which serve to highlight the importance of Helen or Achilles to the narrative. Part of the poignancy of the episode lies in the ways in which it reveals Helen's awareness not only of her role in the Trojan War, but, more acutely, of the reputation forged by her actions, including and especially by the ways in which others interpret those actions. Something similar occurs in Malory's *Morte Darthur*, in a speech original to Malory, as Launcelot prepares for his banishment (468^{r-v}; 903.22–9). As Jon Whitman remarks, Launcelot's concern that 'aftir my dayes ... men shall cronycle uppon me that I was fleamed oute of

---

[10] Murray J. Evans, '*Ordinatio* and Narrative Links', in *Studies*, pp. 29–52 (p. 46). Further evidence of such textual engagement on Malory's part is supplied by Alan J. Fletcher, *The Presence of Medieval English Literature* (Turnhout, 2012), pp. 213–58. I am indebted to Megan G. Leitch for bringing Fletcher's study to my attention.

[11] Homer, *The Iliad of Homer*, trans. Richmond Lattimore (Chicago, 1951), III.125–8; cf. Helen at VI.357–8, and Andromache at XXII.437–48.

thys londe' reveals a concern about public reputation and 'anxiety' over how he will be remembered.[12] It is further notable that Launcelot's immediate response when first told of his banishment is to invoke a comparison of himself to 'noble Ector of Troy' (467^v; 902.9), a response again original to Malory. Launcelot's self-perception, his reputational awareness, centres around the idea that Hector was a great but seemingly ill-treated hero brought low by the fickleness of Fortune. Lancelot's reference thus evokes heroism and tragic defeat, a telling allusion on the eve of further civil war.[13] Human actions, especially when coupled with or conflicted by Fate, Helen and Launcelot each seem to say, have both synchronic and diachronic memorial consequences.

Although Hector is sympathetic and heroic in Homer's account of the Trojan War, and although Homer does not share Virgil's penchant for praising only one nation of heroes (Turnus, after all, is still Italian and thus Trojan-Roman), Achilles is nevertheless quite obviously *the* heroic exemplar of Homer's poem. But mediaeval accounts of the Trojan War are (like Virgil) much more partisan, with Hector and the Trojans presented in a more favourable light than the Greeks. No doubt this pro-Trojan partiality reflects mediaeval European myths of origin in which many European states traced their foundations back to the Trojans. One such aetiology is found in the Galfridian and *Brut* traditions in which Aeneas' descendants found and name the various parts of Britain. No doubt partly because of this Trojan paternity, manuscript illustrations of Lydgate's *Troy Book* (1420) give considerable emphasis to Hector's tomb, often displaying Hector's embalmed body 'stondynge as vp-riȝt, / By sotil crafte, as he were lyvynge'.[14] In effect, as Martha W. Driver notes, Hector's body is transformed into 'a work of art, a memorial object with the appearance of life placed beside a golden statue[.] ... In this case, however, the hero himself is the artifact, his tomb a perpetual shrine, a notion ... related to actual royal burial practice in the Middle Ages, though with classical underpinings.'[15] We see an exaggerated form of this sort of burial practice in Geoffrey of Monmouth's *Historia regum Britannie* where Geoffrey records how Stonehenge is erected by Merlin for Aurelius as a memorial to dead Britons.[16] As in literature, so in life: in mediaeval England 'the churches of the gentry were replete with artefacts and imagery', including '[t]ombs, brasses, donor panels,

---

[12] Jon Whitman, 'Posthumous Messages', in *The Making of Memory in the Middle Ages*, ed. Lucie Doležalová (Leiden, 2010), pp. 241–52 (p. 244). I do not consider such instances of a character's concern with public reputation in the same light as those critics who argue for Malory's supposed authorial anxieties about textual stability and closure.

[13] See further Mark Lambert, *Malory: Style and Vision in Le Morte Darthur* (New Haven and London, 1975), pp. 134–5, and my *Understanding Genre and Medieval Romance* (Aldershot, 2008), pp. 134–5.

[14] *Lydgate's Troy Book, A.D. 1412–20*, ed. Henry Bergen, EETS ES 103 (London, 1908), III, 5656–7. For detailed description, examples and analysis of the pictures, see Martha W. Driver, 'Medievalizing the Classical Past in Pierpont Morgan MS M 876', in *Middle English Poetry*, ed. A. J. Minnis (York, 2001), pp. 211–39. The relevant picture in Morgan M. 876, fol. 59^r, was pencilled in, but not coloured. It can now also be viewed via the Morgan's Medieval and Renaissance Manuscripts page, online at ica.themorgan.org[.]

[15] Driver, 'Medievalizing the Classical Past', in *Middle English Poetry*, p. 235. For Iliadic examples of Hector's self-memorialization, see Ruth Scodel, 'Inscription, Absence and Memory', *Studi italiani di filologia classica* 10 (1992): 57–76.

[16] Geoffrey of Monmouth, *The History of the Kings of Britain*, ed. Michael D. Reeve and trans. Neil Wright (Woodbridge, 2007), pp. 170–5, chapters 127–30.

dedicatory inscriptions, funerary armour, [and] the ubiquitous heraldic displays' designed to attest and proclaim secular deeds and identity as much as secure intercessory prayer for a celestial afterlife.[17]

I have tried to establish in the preceding chapters that the rubrication of names in the Winchester manuscript text of *Le Morte Darthur* has the same sort of enshrining and memorializing effect, emphasizing the celebratory and elegiac aspects of Malory's Arthuriad together with the glory and chivalric heroism attained by Arthur and his Round Table champions. Winchester's memorialization occurs on multiple levels: visually as one opens any folio and is immediately confronted by the striking effect of the rubrication; synchronically as one encounters the narrative text via reading or listening; and analeptically and diachronically as one reflects back on the 'Hoole Book' in either its lexical or codicological form. Each of these levels evokes and reinforces its fellows in an intratextual fashion. The memorializing effect is particularly strong, if somewhat random in appearance, in the case of the rubricated marginalia because of the way in which they bookmark and précis eighty specific deeds or events associated with Arthur and his knights. I am arguing, though, that text and manuscript interconnect with and reinforce one another. An appropriately Janus-faced textual case in point occurs with Malory's famous May passages. The first May passage, as we saw in Chapter Four, links the brotherly love of knights for one another to Launcelot's and Gwenyvere's heterosexual love for one another (434^v–435^v; 841.1–842.11). The second May passage destroys the traditional May-and-love topos to announce instead the May-time success of Aggravayne's and Mordred's all-too-earthly and wicked machinations, machinations that bring to a bloody end both the love of knights for their Round Table fellows and the love of knights for their ladies (449^{r-v}; 870.1–15). As Mark Lambert perceptively emphasizes, it is telling that in the first May passage Malory asks us not only to bring to mind beauty and passion and love, but also to recollect 'olde jantylnes and olde servyse, and many kynde dedes that was forgotyn' (435^r; 841.12–13).[18] In this way, the love-and-May topos becomes, for Malory, another means of earthly memorialization.

A recurring refrain amongst some of the best Malory criticism of the last fifty years is to point out the considerable tragic elements of Malory's version of the destruction of the Round Table, only to conclude that such tragedy is ultimately mitigated or even superseded by the increasing focus on religion and penance which, these critics claim, dominates the close of the *Morte Darthur*. Hence, to take only the most noteworthy examples, Wilfred L. Guerin's conclusion in the influential *Malory's Originality* that the 'tragedy occurs in the material world only' and that such suffering is relieved by 'salvation' and 'spiritual catharsis'; hence D. S. Brewer in the now classic introduction to his classroom edition of Tales VII and VIII, who concludes that 'Lancelot's and Guenevere's ... saintliness repudiates honour and shame', thereby securing a transcendent 'romance in a tragic mode'; hence P. J. C. Field in his contribution to the authoritative account of mediaeval English Arthuriana, who likewise advocates that the 'lovers' life

---

[17] Saul, *For Honour and Fame*, pp. 292–3.
[18] Lambert, *Style and Vision*, pp. 145–7.

of penance' contributes to redemption and a romance happy ending.[19] A similar assumption underlies Larry D. Benson's thesis that the *Morte* is simultaneously marked by an historical and tragic plot, but also by a corresponding thematic and comic plot; Barbara Newman recently entered the debate by relating the issue to her illustration of the sustained mediaeval mingling of sacred and secular, contesting that Malory wilfully conjoins a secular tragedy with a sacred comedy.[20]

One significant moment of religious comedy, for Benson, comes with Arthur's death and the inscription on his tomb. Although it is sometimes said that the inscription and even the very idea of 'Rex quondam Rexque futurus' (482^v; 928.28) is original to Malory, this is only partly true. It is true, in Elizabeth Edwards's words, that the 'sources never provide so much as a hint that there is any doubt about Arthur's death'.[21] Edwards argues – not entirely convincingly – that Malory is anxious about closure, but she rightly points out that the writing which ironically records this oral rumour of Arthur's return is 'in Latin, the very language of authority'. Yet John Withrington convincingly argues that the idea and even versions of the Latin tag about Arthur's possible return were much in the air by the time Malory composed his Arthuriad, both in manuscript and in oral forms.[22]

Malory thus, for Edwards and others, presents his audience with at least the hope of a revenant Arthur. One thematic consequence of this hope, so it is said by Benson, is that the idea of the king's return deliberately 'undercut[s] the tragedy' of his fall by suggesting that Arthur's supposed return must be a sign of divine approval and forgiveness; Field likewise argues that 'Arthur's mysterious end', like the 'lovers' life of penance', helps to qualify the tragedy.[23] Robert L. Kelly offers two variations on this tragic amelioration: that the penance undermines the tragedy but, for Kelly, the penance comes from the warriors, not the lovers; and that Malory's 'double view of Lancelot' as alternately a great knight who also heals, and a failed sinful knight who gives and receives wounds, 'considerably' lessens any tragic effect of the *Morte Darthur* by reducing the sense of wasted potential necessary for tragic pathos.[24] Recently D. Thomas Hanks Jr claimed that Malory 'transform[ed] his tale of chivalry and noble love', including the tragic death of Arthur, into a redemptive 'Christian comedy'.[25] For many readers, then,

---

[19] Wilfred L. Guerin, '"The Tale of the Death of Arthur"', in *Originality*, pp. 233–74 (at pp. 233 and 269); D. S. Brewer, ed., *The Morte Darthur: Parts Seven and Eight* (London, 1968), pp. 23–35 (at pp. 32–3); P. J. C. Field, 'Sir Thomas Malory's Le Morte Darthur', in *The Arthur of the English*, ed. W. R. J. Barron (Cardiff, 1999), pp. 224–46 (p. 246).
[20] Larry D. Benson, *Malory's Morte Darthur* (Cambridge, Mass., 1976); Barbara Newman, *Medieval Crossover* (Notre Dame, 2013), pp. 92–109.
[21] Edwards, *Genesis of Narrative*, pp. 175–7.
[22] John Withrington, 'The Arthurian Epitaph in Malory's "Morte Darthur"', *Arthurian Literature* 7 (1987): 103–44.
[23] Benson, *Malory's Morte Darthur*, pp. 240–1; Field, 'Sir Thomas Malory's Le Morte Darthur', in *Arthur of the English*, p. 246.
[24] Respectively, Robert L. Kelly, 'Penitence as a Remedy for War in Malory's "Tale of the Death of Arthur"', *Studies in Philology* 91 (1994): 111–35; and Kelly, 'Wounds, Healing, and Knighthood in Malory's Tale of Lancelot and Guenevere', in *Studies*, pp. 173–97 (pp. 191–2).
[25] D. Thomas Hanks Jr, '"All manner of good love comyth of God"', in *Malory and Christianity*, ed. D. Thomas Hanks Jr and Janet Jesmok (Kalamazoo, 2013), pp. 9–28. Cf. Fletcher, *Presence of Medieval English Literature*, pp. 230 and 237, who argues that Arthur's death is final but

divine forgiveness, or sin, or the penance which secures forgiveness (or a combination thereof) supersede any secular tragedy in the *Morte Darthur*.

I suggest, however, that Malory raises this possibility of Arthur's return only to quash it. The Latin authority here is thus as fictitious as, for Malory, the much more typical appeal to the French book, an appeal that sometimes genuinely intimates Malory's sources and which other times obfuscates his originality. In the case of Arthur's tomb, the whole notion of Arthur's resurrection is a red herring in Malory's Arthuriad. Far from confirming a hope and transcendence that negate sorrow, Malory's account of the king's tomb with its authoritative inscription of Arthur's possible return, serves – like so much else in the *Morte Darthur* – only to emphasize the human and tragic elements of his narrative.[26] Malory will have no truck with the mystical notion of Arthur's resurgence.

This sceptical finality may, as Marilyn Corrie partly observes, be a pessimistic reflection of the civil strife and bloodshed of Malory's day.[27] After all, Malory lived through and occasionally fought in the bloodiest period in England's history, a history that included invasions and deprivations by the Romans, the Angles and Saxons and Jutes, the Vikings and the Normans, as well as the national and civil wars of Malory's own age. Those civil wars in fifteenth-century England produced a real and violent game of thrones, one in which Malory served powerful magnates loyal first to York and eventually, in a reversal of favours, to Lancaster.[28] In light of these historical and political contexts, it is logical and justifiable to trace the influence of real people and real events in Malory's vision of the Arthurian story. Felicity Riddy therefore links the collapse of the Round Table in Malory's Arthuriad to the real-life collapse of England's imperial ambitions with the loss of French territories under Henry VI, just as Vinaver considered Arthur's martial successes and itinerary in the Roman War to be a tribute to Henry V.[29] Notwithstanding the *Morte*'s historical affinities, however, Malory is ultimately writing fiction, not history; his naming of characters unnamed in his sources, his wilful selection, rearrangement and modification of his sources, and his rubrication of individual names all indicate what is real and important in the *Morte Darthur*: the characters and story of Arthur and the Fellowship of Round Table knights and their stature as chivalric exemplars. The nation is secondary to the Fellowship, and the Fellowship is made possible by individual knights, including Arthur himself. Malory's goal of producing a complete but fictional life of Arthur would certainly allow him to present Arthur's death in mystical or transcendent terms as suggested by the once and future idea; he does not choose to avail himself of this option.

---

also Christian: he is once and future in the same way that all Christians will return in the future life to come.

[26] See further Vinaver, pp. xcix and 1626.

[27] Marilyn Corrie, 'Self-Determination in the Post-Vulgate *Suite du Merlin* and Malory's *Le Morte Darthur*', *Medium Ævum* 73.2 (2004): 273–89 (283). Corrie seems to see Malory as both accepting and rejecting the idea of Arthur's return.

[28] The best account of Malory's political affinities and misfortunes remains Field, *Life and Times*.

[29] Felicity Riddy, 'Contextualizing *Le Morte Darthur*', in *Companion*, pp. 55–73 (esp. pp. 66–73); Vinaver, pp. 1367–8 and Commentary on *Works* 227.4–5.

Arthur's importance, for Malory, does not mean his death can be sidestepped, and his heroic stature does not enable him to return from death. Malory's fifteenth-century audience would be all too aware of the bloody and sometimes fatal consequences of armed combat.[30] Malory uses his and his audience's knowledge of warfare to punch up the verisimilitude and heroism of Arthur's end by having him end the story as he began – as an active knight engaged in knightly pursuits, including fighting. As Andrew Lynch puts it, by obfuscating the precise time and circumstances of Arthur's death, Malory gives the king 'the obscure end of a wounded "poor knight" of the age, taken in haste from the battlefield and privately buried with little state'.[31] Arthur is wounded and dies – as, eventually, occurs with any warrior, whether knight, hero or king. I would only dispute Lynch's conclusion, that Arthur is 'remembered [only] by a loyal few'. For me, Winchester's rubrication and marginalia provide precisely the sort of visual and aggrandizing public monument that Lynch argues is lacking here.

Thematically, Malory is obviously preparing for the certainty and finality of Arthur's end with all of the tragic threads running throughout the entirety of the *Morte Darthur*. He also alerts us to the lack of promised return or religious consolation back on Salisbury Plain. As is often commented upon, when the ghost of Gawayne appears in a dream to warn Arthur not to fight Mordred, Malory's Arthur does everything in his power to attempt to avoid the final battle. The French Arthur, in contrast, does no such thing.[32] Here, for a moment, Malory gestures towards an alternate telos; but it is, and was no doubt intended to be, an empty gesture. Arthur's vow in the final battle to slay Mordred or die trying is one of the more epic-heroic elements of the *Morte*, and such epic-heroic elements alert us to the hero's tragedy, a tragedy that often follows such an heroic vow.[33] In this sense it is noteworthy that the vow itself allows for no continuance beyond revenge: '"Now tyde me dethe, tyde me lyff", seyde the kyng, "now I se hym yondir alone, he shall never ascape myne hondes!" … Than the kynge gate his speare in bothe hys hondis, and ran towarde Sir **Mordred**, crying and saying, "Traytoure, now ys thy dethe-day com!"' (480^r; 923.24–30). As noted in Chapter Four, Crofts rightly compares Arthur's return to battle in his final pursuit of Mordred to the return of Achilles in that both heroes are entirely without hope: 'Like Achilles in *Iliad* XXI, Arthur has no plans for the future; we hear this in his speech in this passage [in its entirety], where "now" is repeated six times.'[34] If Achilles slaughters Hector, his own death is doomed to follow; Achilles knows this as much as does Homer's audience.[35] The same is true in *Morte Darthur* of Arthur and Mordred, and the grim and original details of Malory's version of the father–son mutual slaying reinforce the reality and certainty of death. So it is, I suggest, that Malory's final comment

---

[30] See further Stephen C. B. Atkinson, '"They … toke their shyldys before them and drew oute their sweryds…"', in *Wounds and Wound Repair in Medieval Culture*, ed. Larissa Tracy and Kelly DeVries (Leiden, 2015), pp. 519–43.

[31] Andrew Lynch, ' … "If Indeed I Go"', *Arthurian Literature* 27 (2010): 19–31 (24).

[32] *La Mort le roi Artu*, ed. Jean Frappier, 3rd edn (Geneva, 1964), §§176–9, pp. 225–30.

[33] See my 'Warfare and Combat in *Le Morte Darthur*', in *Writing War*, ed. Corinne Saunders, Françoise Le Saux and Neil Thomas (Cambridge, 2004), pp. 169–86 (pp. 175–6).

[34] Crofts, *Malory's Contemporary Audience*, p. 147.

[35] On Achilles' awareness of his destiny, see especially *Iliad* IX, 405–16, XVIII.79–126 and XIX.420–3.

on the rumours of Arthur's return is to say not only 'I woll nat say that hit shall be so', but also, tellingly, 'here in thys worlde he chaunged hys lyff' (482ᵛ; 928.25–6). The crucial word is 'chaunged'. This statement seems, in context, an emphatic announcement of the finality of Arthur's exit. Malory uses the same phrase earlier in the *Morte* for Percyval's acceptance of his mother's death on the grounds that 'all we muste change the lyff' (365ʳ; 700.10). Chaucer likewise uses the word to denote the death of Arcite: 'His spirit chaunged hous and wente ther / As I cam nevere, I kan nat tellen wher'.³⁶ The point of the phrase in Malory's apostrophe on Arthur's return is thus to negate that return: Arthur's life has 'chaunged' because he no longer has a life. The grave, the tomb, the Latin inscription and especially the community of mourning knights who assemble around it all serve together to foreground Arthur's dead body, especially his heroic qualities and the merits of his chivalric kingship.³⁷

Significantly, the Latin epitaph on Arthur's grave is rubricated in the Winchester manuscript (482ᵛ; also the cover of this book). The rubricated epitaph mirrors the names engraved – often in gold letters – on the Round Table, the Siege Perilous or the many other monuments erected by Merlin throughout the early years of the Round Table. This echo of inscriptions of other knights serves in part to remind Malory's audience that, for Malory, Arthur is just as important as Launcelot, maybe even more important. Withrington argues that Malory must refuse to confirm or deny Arthur's death because, artistically, an irredeemably deceased Arthur would render the subsequent religious redemption of Launcelot and Gwenyvere anticlimactic.³⁸ To my mind this Arthurian focus is the whole point: Malory asks us to remember the glory and lament the tragic fall of Launcelot and Gwenyvere and Gawayne and Gareth and all the remnant of the Round Table, but Malory also asks us to remember and lament *Arthur's* glory and destruction. The other characters are who they are because of Arthur. They are parts – important parts, but parts nevertheless – of the whole Arthurian collective, a Fellowship whose greatness, as Arthur notes on the eve of the Grail Quest, stems in large part from its being 'holé togydirs' (352ʳ⁻ᵛ; 672.25–30).³⁹ As a result, even if one insists on the literalness of the inscription on the tomb – and I myself do not think we are meant to do so – arguably the sliver of hope it generates makes the loss all the worse by emphasizing the present shattered Fellowship, whatever might happen in some mystical future.

I noted in Chapter Four how Merlin and Arthur take steps to ensure that the adventures of Arthur and his knights are recounted and recorded for posterity.

---

[36] Geoffrey Chaucer, *The Knight's Tale*, in *The Riverside Chaucer*, ed. Larry D. Benson, 3rd edn (Boston, 1987), vv. 2809–10. Ralph Norris, *Malory's Library* (Cambridge, 2008), makes a compelling case for Malory's familiarity with Chaucer.

[37] *Contra* Elizabeth T. Pochoda, *Arthurian Propaganda* (Chapel Hill, 1971), pp. 130–40, who argues that Arthur's failures as king destroy the Round Table; and Ruth Lexton, *Contested Language in Malory's Morte Darthur* (New York and Basingstoke, 2014), whose thesis is that Malory persistently undercuts Arthurian kingship.

[38] Withrington, 'The Arthurian Epitaph in Malory', 139–44. Cf. Lambert, *Style and Vision*, p. 129, n. 7.

[39] Given the socio-political turmoil of Malory's day and career, he may well have thought that a great realm depended equally on a great collection of knights as well as a great king: see Saul, *For Honour and Fame*, pp. 312–17.

Now, at the end, when both Merlin and Arthur are gone, 'Sir Bedwere, a Knyght of the Table Rounde, made hit to be wrytten' (482^v; 928.21–2). Assuming that 'thys tale' which Malory attributes to Bedwere refers backward and forward both, then Bedwere creates the factual story of Arthur's being 'lad away in a shyp wherein were thre quenys' plus Dame Nynyve (482^{r-v}; 928.7–10), confirms the certainty of Arthur's burial (481^v–482^r; 927.12–928.1) and, it seems, also makes the rumour of Arthur's possible return. Bedwere's making, that is, encompasses the identification of the body in the ground, but also the final stories and rumours about that body.[40] In contrast to his evocations of the 'auctorysed' French book that is his preferred source citation, though, Malory here emphasizes the rumour and hearsay surrounding Arthur's supposed return: '*som* men say ... that Kynge Arthure ys nat dede' and '*many* men say that there ys wrytten' on his tomb the prophesied return (482^v; 928.21–8). As Lynch, from whom I adopt this idea of Malory's scepticism, observes, Malory is far from certain about the legitimacy of these rumours.[41] Lynch astutely adds that Malory cuts the scenes of Arthur praying that prepare for the king's death in the French *Mort Artu* and stanzaic *Morte Arthur* (Malory's principal sources for Tale VIII), and that he also downplays the visual splendour that should (and did) accompany a fifteenth-century royal burial. Lynch concludes that the unobtrusive fashion of Arthur's death connects him all the more to the Fellowship of the Round Table, reminding us one last time that the 'special character' of Arthur's leadership resides not in religious piety or personal airs or material possessions, but rather in the secular knightly skills and concerns he shares with his affinity: the 'human, bodily, this-worldly qualities of loyalty, courage[, prowess] and endurance'.[42]

Malory's and Bedwere's Arthurian memorialization is consequently instigated and achieved precisely by slowing the narrative pace to focus on the inescapable fact of Arthur's death. Everything that happens in the wake of that death happens precisely because Arthur is decidedly gone, 'chaunged' from this life and this world. Only because he knows Arthur is dead and buried does Bedwere join the former archbishop at Arthur's tomb (482^r; 927.32). Only because Arthur is dead can Launcelot hope that Gwenyvere might at last retire with him to live together in his native France (C XXI.9; 933.32–3). Precisely because Arthur is dead there is no more hope, and partly because she is 'a trew lover' (435^v; 842.11),[43] Gwenyvere can no longer sustain her affair with Launcelot. What was acceptable in the halcyon glory days of Arthur and the Round Table Fellowship is no longer tenable in the tragic face of 'an hondred thousande leyde dede uppon the downe' (479^v; 922.32). Consequently, Malory's narrative, diction and principal themes all work to decry any idea of Arthur as *Rex futurus*. The subsequent burial of Gwenyvere next to Arthur in his grave reinforces this finality. For Alan J. Fletcher, 'things

---

[40] The Middle English word *maken* can mean 'To write or compose (a book, poem, song, prayer, letter, etc.); compile'. See *Middle English Dictionary*, ed. Hans Kurath et al. (Ann Arbor, 1952–2001), online edn, s.v. 'maken, 5a'.

[41] Lynch, ' ... "If Indeed I Go"', 20–1.

[42] Lynch, ' ... "If Indeed I Go"', 21–4; *Mort le roi Artu*, §§191.24–192.2, p. 246; stanzaic *Le Morte Arthur*, ed. P. F. Hissiger (The Hague, 1975), vv. 3404–15.

[43] Significantly, this striking sentiment is original to Malory, as is Launcelot's later hope for domestic harmony at long last, however sorrowful its contributing factor.

achieve authority as reliable points of reference in [*Morte Darthur*] the moment that they cease to be'.⁴⁴ This is too teleological, too focussed on finitude. Endings are significant, but so, for Malory, are beginnings and middles. As Lambert rightly insists, the audience finds the tragedy of the final tales more effective and pathetic for having lived through the flowering of Arthurian chivalry in the earlier tales.⁴⁵ As Malory's title makes clear, he is glorifying and elegizing the 'Hoole Book', not merely the death of Arthur or Launcelot or Gwenyvere or Gawayne. Although Fletcher is mistaken to emphasize the ends as more meaningful than earlier moments in the *Morte*, he is correct that Malory accentuates the 'disparbling', the dissolution of the Round Table and its leader: Malory continually foregrounds the secular tragedy of the fall of the Round Table, a tragedy rendered all the worse by the inescapability of Arthur's end.

While the rubricated inscription on Arthur's grave does not support belief in Arthur's return, nor the validity of a supposed turn to religious expiation in the *Morte Darthur*, it does remind us of the connections between rubrication and name, and thus between name and character and worshipful but earthly deeds and loves. As Lynch perspicaciously observes, 'the manuscript or printed page [consequently] functions as a public arena where exploits are enacted and witnessed'.⁴⁶ Names and naming, as everyone from the ancient Greeks to philologists to modern theorists tell us, are important for establishing personal identity.⁴⁷ In this sense, Winchester's rubrication of names and marginalia necessarily highlight the character and deeds performed by those various names throughout the entirety of the *Morte Darthur*. The rare and erroneous instance in the *Morte* of a reasonably lengthy Latin tag thus serves to remind us that Malory is not writing a history or chronicle or vita, but a tragic-romance hybrid focussed on various individual heroes.⁴⁸ Consequently, the inscription which *does* venerate such a worshipful story and such a cast of characters is not the Latin inscription on Arthur's tomb, nor even the many inscriptions or prophecies of Merlin, but rather the manuscript rubrication itself. Winchester's rubrication, that is, affords an unusual and powerful correlation of thematic, lexical and bibliographic movements, rendering the entire manuscript text of the *Morte* into a celebratory but elegiac tomb for the 'Hoole Book of Kyng Arthur'. Just as Stonehenge is erected by Merlin for Aurelius as a memorial to dead Britons in Geoffrey's *Historia*, so Winchester's rubrication and marginalia are used in the manuscript text of the *Morte Darthur* to create a visual remembrance of past action, a recalling of secular Arthurian chivalry, secular Arthurian love and secular Arthurian adventures. My overarching argument is not adversely affected if the rubrication or marginalia are eventually proven to be a particularly striking innovation of scribe or patron; but the rarity of Winchester's pattern of rubrication of names and the unusual congruence of physical manuscript layout with lexical thematic text make it much more likely that the source for the rubrication idea is Malory himself. The same holds true of the marginalia, especially given the awareness

---

[44] Fletcher, *Presence of Medieval English Literature*, p. 253.
[45] Lambert, *Style and Vision*, p. 124.
[46] Andrew Lynch, *Malory's Book of Arms* (Cambridge, 1997), p. 53.
[47] On names in literature, see Alastair Fowler, *Literary Names* (Oxford, 2012).
[48] On the genre of the *Morte Darthur*, see my *Understanding Genre*, pp. 99–159.

they reveal of the text of the *Morte Darthur* as a 'hoole book'.[49] Malory's art and artistry are thus grander and more self-aware than is typically acknowledged (or even allowed). It has, however, recently been suggested that Merlin and Malory share memorial knowledge of Arthur's past and future.[50] This claim supports the possibility that Malory uses the abbreviation of 'M' for Merlin in the opening tale of the Arthuriad to refer to himself as both author and rubricated elegy-maker.

M. B. Parkes, writing of the advent of written versus oral literature, asserts that 'the written word' and written texts created the possibility for words to speak 'directly to the mind through the eye'.[51] Often enough for the student of pre-modern (classical, mediaeval or Renaissance) literature, the written word and its punctuation as we encounter it in modern texts is partially editorial, however closely indebted to a source manuscript. It is the task of the manuscript scholar, like the textual scholar, to recapture and re-enable what John Scattergood calls these manuscript 'ghosts from the past' and their *'voces paginarum'*.[52] It is my contention that Winchester's rubrication and marginalia reinforce this ability of the text to speak in certain visual and memorable ways. Mediaeval scholars, or at least those devoted to codicology, recognize and argue that 'Medieval reading … included looking, in a non-linear, holistic way, at all the components of the page', that letters and symbols, for the mediaeval mind, possessed both figural and literal elements, 'the non-verbal and the verbal, … the graphic and the textual'.[53] Hence the influential notion of the mediaeval book of memory.[54] The rubrication of names and marginalia in Winchester is, for me, a specific case in point of this sort of bibliographic, visual and memorial emphasis.

I established in Chapter One the uniqueness of the style and consistency of the rubrication of names found in the Winchester manuscript text of *Le Morte Darthur*. Some names, or at least some opening initials of some names, are given rubrication in some parts of some Bibles. Some names are rubricated or underlined in red in some chronicle manuscripts. In some romances, scribes touch the opening letters of names or other words in red; such is the case in Cambridge University Library Additional MS 7071, the manuscript of the Post-Vulgate *Suite du Merlin*, where the scribes sometimes touch the opening letters of sentences or names with red. But no manuscript of which I am aware looks precisely like Winchester. The closest analogue to Winchester's *mise-en-page* is the copy of *Generides* in New York, Pierpont Morgan Library MS M.876, but contrary to Carol M. Meale's claim, the Morgan *Generides* looks almost nothing like Winchester.[55] There are admittedly several instances of the hero's name or heroine's name

---

[49] See P. J. C. Field, 'Malory's Own Marginalia', *Medium Ævum* 70 (2001): 226–39.
[50] Jamie McKinstry, *Middle English Romance and the Craft of Memory* (Cambridge, 2015), pp. 194 and 199. McKinstry and I share a concern with Malory and memory, but we have very different methods and conclusions.
[51] M. B. Parkes, *Pause and Effect* (Berkeley and Los Angeles, 1993), p. 1.
[52] John Scattergood, 'Preface', in his *Manuscripts and Ghosts* (Dublin, 2006), pp. 15–19 (p. 18).
[53] As two recent examples, I quote Maidie Hilmo, 'The Power of Images in the Auchinleck, Vernon, Pearl, and Two *Piers Plowman* Manuscripts', in *Opening Up Middle English Manuscripts*, Kathryn Kerby-Fulton, Maidie Hilmo and Linda Olsen (Ithaca and London, 2012), pp. 153–205 (p. 153); and Mary Franklin-Brown, *Reading the World* (Chicago and London, 2012), p. 43.
[54] See here Mary Carruthers, *The Book of Memory*, 2nd edn (Cambridge, 2008).
[55] *Contra* Carol M. Meale, '"The Hoole Book"', in *Companion*, pp. 3–17 (p. 10 and n. 21).

being rubricated in the Morgan manuscript, but the rubrication is confined to the two lead characters, not to all characters as in Winchester. In another contrast to Winchester, the names that are rubricated in the Morgan *Generides* were obviously decorated in the usual fashion of leaving blank spaces and coming back later with the new pen and ink: some names are cramped, others have too much space around them, and the vast majority were never executed at all (see Plates II, III and IV). Although the Morgan rubrication, such as it is, was never finished, there is enough of a pattern in place to establish that the rubrication of names would never be extended to all characters. Neither the planned decoration nor the execution of the Morgan *Generides* is the same as the Winchester *Morte Darthur*. Winchester's *ordinatio*, far from being typical of fifteenth-century manuscripts, is, to all extents and purposes, unique.

This uniqueness of the style and consistency of rubrication found in Winchester raises the question of the purpose and provenance of the manuscript's design. It is my contention that the manuscript layout mirrors and visually emphasizes the principal themes of the lexical text of the *Morte Darthur*. I argued in Chapter Two that the most likely originator of Winchester's rubrication pattern is Malory himself. Malory is also, I suggested, the source for the marginalia. Winchester's *ordinatio* was devised by Malory, and then, whether through written or visual cues, verbal instructions or some other manner, copied through the various transmission stages between the holograph and Winchester and the Caxton. The evidence, after all, indicates that Caxton's copy-text shared a similar layout to Winchester, and that Winchester's marginalia, rubrication, double virgules and coloured initials influenced Caxton's design of the 1485 incunable edition of *Le Morte Darthur*. My contention that manuscript layout as well as textual matter could be – and was – transmitted through several possible stages is entirely in keeping with Doyle and Parkes's account of scribal copying practice.[56] Winchester's *mise-en-page*, moreover, memorializes Arthur and the Round Table knights and their lives and deeds, loves and losses and tragic ends, and it does so in ways which minimize what Donald R. Howard terms the chance distortions of memory.[57] The layout of the *Morte Darthur* in its material manuscript serves not only to help readers remember the glory and tragedy of Malory's 'Hoole Book of Kyng Arthur and of His Noble Knyghtes of the Rounde Table', but also directs us to remember that not all secular deeds are vain; that occasionally, especially perhaps in an age as troubled as Malory's, humanity might do well to value and foster *earthly* fellowship, love and deeds.

Since *worshyp* is acquired and maintained in the *Morte Darthur* primarily through public (or publicized) combat, reputation is as much communal as individual. Heroes can control their own actions to a certain extent, but not necessarily the tongues of the wider public. As a result, 'Praise, blame, and memory

---

[56] A. I. Doyle and M. B. Parkes, 'The Production of Copies of the *Canterbury Tales* and the *Confessio Amantis* in the Early Fifteenth Century', in *Medieval Scribes, Manuscripts and Libraries*, ed. Parkes and Andrew G. Watson (London, 1978), pp. 163–210 (p. 165).

[57] Donald R. Howard, *The Idea of the Canterbury Tales* (Berkeley and Los Angeles, 1976), p. 189. Contrary to McKinstry, *Romance and the Craft of Memory*, p. 199, Winchester's memorializing effect also ensures that 'Malory's characters' and sympathies have not in fact 'disappeared' from view.

itself', as Scodel says of Homeric memory, 'are perpetuated' as much by common opinion as by individual heroic action,[58] even if, as with Arthur's drawing of the sword from the stone (C I.3–5; 8.10–11.9), public opinion (the voice of the commons) endorses individual action (the drawing of the sword). Malory did not read Homer, but his tumultuous career as knight and retainer, including having his services sought – and his time in prison maintained – by both Lancastrians and Yorkists, would have made him overly familiar with the vagaries of public opinion during the endgame of the Wars of the Roses. Consequently, various memorials within Malory's *Morte Darthur* attempt to control public reputation, clarifying, for instance, that Balyn is not responsible for Launceor's death or that Gwenyvere is innocent of Patryse's poisoning. The rubrication of names and marginalia recording various deeds in the Winchester manuscript continue and magnify Malory's focus on the worshipful nature of his protagonists.

As a result of Malory's human and secular focus, a focus evident in both narrative text and manuscript layout, I argue in Chapter Three that readers of the *Morte Darthur* should reconsider the long-standing critical commonplaces that the Round Table is destroyed by sin and that Malory sooner or later rejects chivalry and fellowship. Despite the scholarly penchant for reading the *Morte Darthur* as a Christian text whose principal actions and values reveal the limitations of earthly chivalry, I urge instead that critics give credit to the many ways in which Malory and his text privilege character, action and secular tragedy. Far from denouncing the sinful collapse of Arthurian chivalry or ushering in a new and superior set of values, Malory's 'Tale of the Sankgreal' functions as a sort of celestial but temporary comic relief: this is not a divine comedy of the sacred happy ending, merely the calm before the storm. 'The Sankgreal' offers a glimpse of what might-have-been, including of an alternate set of laws and values reflecting a careful juggling of the sacred and secular. But the following tales of 'Sir Launcelot and Queen Guenivere' and the 'Morte Arthure' proper reveal just how emphatically these alternate values are not operative in the *Morte Darthur* as a whole. Malory's human focus is quite apparent in the sympathy his text displays towards his lovers, particularly Gareth and Lyonesse, Trystram and Isode, and Launcelot and Gwenyvere. Malory's sympathy extends to what Cherewatuk pointedly terms a 'relaxed attitude toward sex' considerably at odds with fifteenth-century orthodox teaching but quite prominent in *Le Morte Darthur*.[59] Malory's anthropomorphic focus is not a failing in the Arthurian universe, just a difference. Secular chivalric values secured the establishment and glory of Arthur and his knights before the Quest for the Holy Grail, and these same earthly chivalric values secure the destruction of Arthur and his knights after the Grail. Such doubling of success and failure creates the tragic paradox of *Le Morte Darthur*. Hence Launcelot's completely successful violation of the notion that 'God woll have a stroke in every batayle' (441ᵛ; 854.16–17) by first committing adultery with and then saving Gwenyvere in the Knight of the Cart episode. Hence, spectacularly, the episode of the Healing of Sir Urry, another

---

[58] Scodel, 'Inscription, Absence and Memory', 63.
[59] Karen Cherewatuk, *Marriage, Adultery, and Inheritance in Malory's Morte Darthur* (Cambridge, 2006), p. 78.

seemingly divine approbation of Launcelot's prowess and reputation, as well as his abiding and physical love of Gwenyvere.

A number of critics draw attention to Malory's emphasis on treason in the Knight of the Cart and elsewhere in the *Morte*, often linking this textual theme to Malory's awareness of and engagement with late mediaeval treason laws.[60] Treason and the law are certainly present in the *Morte Darthur*, but the real connection between Malory and his age, and the real point of the relapse into post-Grail adultery, is perhaps precisely the inability of even the best kings and knights to evade destruction. In this sense Malory is not (or not merely) lamenting lost empire, as Riddy claims, or glorifying Henry V, as Vinaver claims.[61] Rather, he is reflecting upon an age of success and failure, wisdom and folly. Late mediaeval cathedrals were built to celebrate God, but also the bishops, architects and craftsmen who built them and whose faces occasionally found their way onto the visages of gargoyles and statues adorning the stone. Late mediaeval England could conquer and lose France, the Crusades could not capture and keep Jerusalem, and England could descend into civil war. Similar secular achievements, obstinacies and sorrows are (*mutatis mutandis*) invariably the producers of great heroic poetry in earlier ages, and even, in poems like the alliterative *Morte Arthure*, in days closer to Malory's own. But we must also acknowledge the connections between ages of unrest and heroic prose, notably the *Morte Darthur*, a book whose manuscript rubrication and marginalia glorify and lament the magnificent rise and tragic fall of the Round Table. This memorializing effect and the considered intersection of narrative theme with manuscript *ordinatio* are explored fully in my fourth and final chapter.

English prose romance was rare in England before Malory, meaning that English prose romance *ordinatio* was likewise rare. Meale asserts that 'there was virtually no precedent amongst copies of secular works which could have suggested ways of arranging a narrative and presenting it in material form'.[62] This paucity of prose romance precedents makes it at least possible that Malory himself is responsible for the decision to rubricate names in Winchester and record some of his rubricated characters' notable deeds with marginalia; my illustration in Chapter Four of the thematic effectiveness of the rubrication and marginalia greatly strengthens that possibility. Winchester's rubrication of each and every name throughout the *Morte Darthur* repeatedly draws attention to the awesome and at times terrible presence and actions of human character and human heroics. The rubrication, as Cooper puts it, is the 'visible equivalent to Malory's presentation of a shame culture, his insistence on a knightliness that consists in "worship"'.[63] Together with the marginalia recording knightly deeds and the emphasis on martial adventure within the narrative, the rubrication of knightly names in the manuscript also, I would add, render public action in the *Morte* nearly as much lexical as physical: the actions of Arthur and his knights are

---

[60] See, e.g., Edwards, *Genesis of Narrative*, pp. 153–66 and the critics cited therein; Lexton, *Contested Language*, pp. 139–71; and especially Megan G. Leitch, *Romancing Treason* (Oxford, 2015), pp. 92–137 and the critics cited therein.
[61] See n. 29, above.
[62] Meale, '"The Hoole Book"', in *Companion*, p. 13.
[63] Helen Cooper, 'Opening Up the Malory Manuscript', in *Debate*, pp. 255–84 (p. 273).

continuously emphasized and memorialized by manuscript layout and authorial theme alike. It is, consistently, great and tragic human endeavour and *worshyp* that the manuscript layout emphasizes, not God or religion or even moderation.

Jill Mann makes a characteristically convincing case for there being a multiplicity of religious voices in mediaeval literature and that, by way of two examples, Chaucer is more interested in human matters than is Dante, whose focus in the *Commedia* is more divine than human.[64] I would add that Malory's focus is at least as human as Chaucer's. Malory lived in an age marked by piety and violence; whatever his personal religiousness, however, his focus in the *Morte Darthur* is secular chivalry and the glory and tragedy of heroic endeavour. The uniqueness of Winchester's style of rubrication, together with the ways in which the rubrication and marginalia reinforce Malory's focus on character and deed, suggest that Malory himself is responsible for Winchester's striking *ordinatio*. Certainly other late mediaeval authors seem to have taken some pains to oversee their work, including appearance and illustration. Gower went some way to doing this.[65] Chaucer shows leanings this way in his complaints about scribal contamination at the close of *Troilus* or in his missive to his scribe Adam.[66] Chaucer's parody of romance conventions and metre includes a visual component in the *ordinatio* of *Thopas* in the Ellesmere, Hengwrt and Cambridge Dd.4.24, Gg.4.27 and Ii.3.26 manuscripts, meaning that the layout of *Thopas* is probably authorial.[67] Phillipa Hardman is thus no doubt correct to contend 'that Chaucer, like Gower, might also have planned to use illustrations as part of the presentation of his framed narratives'.[68] I argued in Chapter One that John Hardyng himself is likewise the reason why several prominent manuscripts of Hardyng's *Chronicle* employ decorative or emphatic strategies in the Arthurian section of the *Chronicle* to aggrandize Arthur. There are, then, several prominent precedents to support my conclusion that Malory himself is responsible for Winchester's *mise-en-page*. What I hope to have established further is the fact that the cumulative and forceful effect of narrative plot and style, Malory's authorial artistry – in particular his characterization and handling of sources – and manuscript layout all emphasize the very human and tragic dissolution of the glorious Round Table Fellowship. Throughout the Winchester manuscript Malory's characters are brought to life and light not only by what they say and do and by what Malory says about them, but by the rubrication of each and every name. The consistent rubrication glorifies and elegizes, and the manuscript itself ultimately enshrines, the 150 members of the Round Table and their lady-loves and king, a king who, 'thurgh the noble prowesse of hymself and his Knyghtes of the Rounde Table' (C I.7; II.24–5) deserves our admiration and lamentation.

---

[64] Jill Mann, 'Chaucer and Atheism', *Studies in the Age of Chaucer* 17 (1995): 5–19 (16–17).

[65] Derek Pearsall, 'The Ellesmere Chaucer and Contemporary English Literary Manuscripts', in *The Ellesmere Chaucer*, ed. Martin Stevens and Daniel Woodward (San Marino and Tokyo, 1997), pp. 263–80 (pp. 268–9).

[66] Geoffrey Chaucer, *Troilus and Criseyde*, V.1793–8, and 'Chaucers wordes unto Adam, his owne scriveyn'; I cite *The Riverside Chaucer*, ed. Larry D. Benson, 3rd edn (Boston, 1987).

[67] Helen Cooper, *The Canterbury Tales*, 2nd edn (Oxford, 1996), p. 300.

[68] Phillipa Hardman, 'Presenting the Text', in *Chaucer Illustrated*, ed. William K. Finley and Joseph Rosenblum (New Castle, Del. and London, 2003), pp. 37–72 (pp. 38–9).

Bibliography

Manuscripts

Cambridge, Mass.
   Harvard University MS Eng 1054
Cambridge, UK
   Cambridge University Library Additional MS 7071
   Cambridge University Library MS Ii.3.26
   Fitzwilliam Museum MS McClean 181
   Trinity College MS O.5.2
   Trinity College MS R.3.3
   Trinity College MS R.3.15
Edinburgh
   National Library of Scotland, Advocates 19.2.1 (Auchinleck)
Lincoln
   Lincoln Cathedral Library MS 91 (Thornton)
London
   British Library
      Additional MS 5474
      Additional MS 10292–4
      Additional MS 17443
      Additional MS 23929
      Additional MS 38117 (Huth)
      Additional MS 59678 (Winchester)
      Cotton MS Otho C.xiii (Otho Laȝamon)
      Egerton MS 989
      Egerton MS 1992
      Harley MS 49
      Harley MS 53
      Harley MS 661
      Harley MS 1896
      Harley MS 2252
      Harley MS 2417
      Harley MS 6342
      Lansdowne MS 204
      Royal MS 1.E.ix
      Royal MS 14.E.iii
      Royal MS 18.C.ii
      Royal MS 18.C.xxvi
      Royal MS 19.B.vii
      Royal MS 19.C.xiii
      Royal MS 20.A.ii

Royal MS 20.C.vi
Royal MS 20.D.ii
Royal MS 20.D.iv
Sloane MS 1686

New Haven
Yale University Beinecke MS 229 (Yale 229)

New York
Pierpont Morgan Library MS B.5
Pierpont Morgan Library MS M.41
Pierpont Morgan Library MS M.372
Pierpont Morgan Library MS M.503
Pierpont Morgan Library MSS M.805, M.806, M.807
Pierpont Morgan Library MS M.876

Oxford
Bodleian Library MS 414
Bodleian Library MS Arch Selden B.10
Bodleian Library MS Ashmole 34
Bodleian Library MS Douce 189
Bodleian Library MS Douce 199
Bodleian Library MS Douce 345
Bodleian Library MS Rawlinson C.86
Jesus College MS 111 (Red Book of Hergest)

Paris
Bibliothèque nationale de France, fr. 16999

Primary Sources

Ackroyd, Peter. *The Death of King Arthur: Thomas Malory's Le Morte d'Arthur*. London: Penguin, 2010.Ascham, Roger. *The Scholemaster*. *The English Works of Roger Ascham*. Ed. William Aldis Wright. Cambridge: Cambridge University Press, 1904. 171–302.

Ascham, Roger. *The Scholemaster*. *The English Works of Roger Ascham*. Ed. William Aldis Wright. Cambridge: Cambridge University Press, 1904. 171–302.

The Auchinleck Manuscript. Ed. David Burnley and Alison Wiggins. National Library of Scotland Digital Library. http://auchinleck.nls.uk/[.]

Augustine. *De Doctrina Christiana*. Ed. and Trans. R. P. H. Green. Oxford: Clarendon, 1995.

Boke of St Albans, see *English Hunting and Hawking*.

Brut, see *Oldest Anglo-Norman*.

Caxton's Malory: A New Edition of Sir Thomas Malory's Le Morte Darthur Based on the Pierpont Morgan Copy of William Caxton's Edition of 1485. Ed. James W. Spisak. 2 vols. Berkeley: University of California Press, 1983.

Chaucer, Geoffrey. *The Knight's Tale*. In *The Riverside Chaucer*. Ed. Larry D. Benson. 3rd edn. Boston: Houghton Mifflin, 1987.

——. *The Parson's Tale*. In *The Riverside Chaucer*. Ed. Larry D. Benson. 3rd edn. Boston: Houghton Mifflin, 1987. 288–328.

——. *The Squire's Tale*. In *The Riverside Chaucer*. Ed. Larry D. Benson. 3rd edn. Boston: Houghton Mifflin, 1987. 169–77.

——. *Troilus and Criseyde*. In *The Riverside Chaucer*. Ed. Larry D. Benson. 3rd edn. Boston: Houghton Mifflin, 1987. 471–585.

English Hunting and Hawking in The Boke of St. Albans: A Facsimile Edition of sigs. a2–f8 of The Boke of St. Albans (1486). Ed. Rachel Hands. Oxford: Oxford University Press, 1975.

Foxe, John. *The Unabridged Acts and Monuments Online or TAMO*, 1583 edition. HRI Online Publications, Sheffield, 2011.

Generides, see *A Royal Historie of...*

Geoffrey of Monmouth. *The History of the Kings of Britain: An Edition and Translation of De gestis Britonum [Historia Regum Britanniae]*. Ed. Michael Reeve. Trans. Neil Wright. Woodbridge: Boydell, 2007.

Hardyng, John. *The Chronicle of John Hardyng . . . together with the Continuation by Richard Grafton*. Ed. Henry Ellis. London, 1812; rpr. New York: AMS Press, 1974.

—. 'John Hardyng's Arthur: A Critical Edition', unpublished PhD dissertation, Christine Marie Harker, University of California, Riverside, 1996.

Homer. *The Iliad of Homer*. Trans. Richmond Lattimore. Chicago: University of Chicago Press, 1951.

Lancelot: roman en prose du XIIIe siècle. Ed. Alexandre Micha. 9 vols. Geneva: Librarie Droz, 1979–83.

Lancelot-Grail: The Old French Arthurian Vulgate and Post-Vulgate in Translation. Gen. Ed. Norris J. Lacy. 5 vols. New York and London: Garland, 1993–96.

The Life of St Cuthbert in English Verse, c. A.D. 1450. Ed. J. T. Fowler. Publications of the Surtees Society 87. Durham, 1891.

Lydgate, John. *Lydgate's Troy Book*. Ed. Henry Bergen. 4 vols. EETS ES 97, 103, 106, 126. London: Kegan Paul, Trench, Trübner & Co, 1906–35.

Malory, Sir Thomas. *Le Morte Darthur*. Ed. P. J. C. Field. 2 vols. Cambridge: D. S. Brewer, 2013.

—. *Le Morte Darthur: or The Hoole Book of Kyng Arthur and of His Noble Knyghtes of the Rounde Table*. Ed. Stephen H. A. Shepherd. New York: Norton, 2004.

—. *Le Morte Darthur: The Winchester Manuscript*. Ed. Helen Cooper. Oxford: Oxford University Press, 1998.

—. *Le Morte D'Arthur: Condensed and Modernized*. Trans. and Adapt. Joseph Glaser. Indianapolis: Hackett, 2015.

—. *The Works of Sir Thomas Malory*. Ed. Eugène Vinaver. 3rd edn. Rev. P. J. C. Field. Oxford: Clarendon, 1990.

La Mort le roi Artu: roman du XIIIe siècle. Ed. Jean Frappier. 3rd edn. Geneva: Librarie Droz, 1964.

Le Morte Arthur: A Critical Edition. Ed. P. F. Hissiger. The Hague: Mouton, 1975.

Morte Arthure: A Critical Edition. Ed. Mary Hamel. New York and London: Garland, 1984.

Le Morte D'Arthur Printed by William Caxton, 1485. Intro Paul Needham. London: Scolar Press, 1976.

The Oldest Anglo-Norman Prose Brut Chronicle: An Edition and Translation. Ed. and Trans. Julia Marvin. Woodbridge: Boydell, 2006.

Pecock, Reginald. *The Repressor of Over Much Blaming of the Clergy*. Ed. Churchill Babington. London: Longman, 1860.

The Post-Vulgate, Part III: The Death of Arthur. Trans. Martha Asher. *Lancelot-Grail: The Old French Arthurian Vulgate and Post-Vulgate in Translation*. Gen. Ed. Norris J. Lacy. New York and London: Garland, 1993–96. Vol. V: 291–312.

The Quest for the Holy Grail. Trans. E. Jane Burns. *Lancelot-Grail: The Old French Arthurian Vulgate and Post-Vulgate in Translation*. Gen. Ed. Norris J. Lacy. New York and London: Garland, 1993–96. Vol. IV: 1–87.

La Queste del Saint Graal: roman du XIIIe siècle. Ed. Albert Pauphilet. Paris: Champion, 1923.
La Queste del Saint Graal (The Quest of the Holy Grail) from the Old French Lancelot of Yale 229, with Essays, Glossaries, and Note to the Text. Gen. Ed. Elizabeth Moore Willingham. Turnhout: Brepols, 2012.
A Royal Historie of the Excellent Knight Generides. Ed. Frederick J. Furnivall. Roxburghe Club. Hertford: Stephen Austin, 1865.
The Thornton Manuscript (Lincoln Cathedral MS. 91). Intro. D. S. Brewer and A. E. B. Owen. Rev. edn. London: Scolar, 1977.
The Vulgate Version of the Arthurian Romances, Volume VI: *Les Aventures ou La Queste del Saint Graal, La Mort Le Roi Artu*. Ed. H. Oskar Sommer. Washington: Carnegie Insititute, 1913.
The Winchester Malory: A Facsimile. Intro. N. R. Ker. EETS SS 4. London: Oxford University Press, 1976.

Secondary Sources

Aers, David. 'Christianity for Courtly Subjects: Reflections on the *Gawain*-Poet'. *A Companion to the Gawain-Poet*. Ed. Derek Brewer and Jonathan Gibson. Cambridge: D. S. Brewer, 1997. 91–101.
Allen, Judson B. 'Malory's Diptych *Distinctio*: The Closing Books of His Work'. *Studies in Malory*. Ed. James W. Spisak. Kalamazoo: Medieval Institute Publications, 1985. 237–55.
Anderson, Earl R. '"Ein Kind wird geschlagen": The Meaning of Malory's Tale of the Healing of Sir Urry'. *Literature and Psychology* 49.3 (2003): 45–74.
——. 'Malory's "Fair Maid of Ascolat"'. *Neuphilologische Mitteilungen* 87.2 (1986): 237–54.
Archibald, Elizabeth. *Incest and the Medieval Imagination*. Oxford: Clarendon, 2001.
——. 'Lancelot as Lover in the English Tradition before Malory'. *Arthurian Studies in Honour of P. J. C. Field*. Ed. Bonnie Wheeler. Cambridge: D. S. Brewer, 2004. 199–216.
——. 'Malory's Ideal of Fellowship'. *Review of English Studies* n.s. 43 (1992): 311–28.
——. 'Malory's Lancelot and Guenevere'. *A Companion to Arthurian Literature*. Ed. Helen Fulton. Oxford and Malden: Wiley-Blackwell, 2009. 312–25.
Archibald, Elizabeth and A. S. G. Edwards, eds. *A Companion to Malory*. Cambridge: D. S. Brewer, 1996.
Armstrong, Dorsey. *Gender and the Chivalric Community in Malory's Morte d'Arthur*. Gainesville: University Press of Florida, 2003.
——. 'The (Non-)Christian Knight in Malory: A Contradiction in Terms?' *Arthuriana* 16.2 (2006): 30–4.
——. 'Postcolonial Palomides: Malory's Saracen Knight and the Unmaking of Arthurian Community'. *Exemplaria* 18 (2006): 175–203.
Atkin, Tamara and A. S. G. Edwards. 'Printers, Publishers and Promoters to 1558'. *A Companion to the Early Printed Book in Britain 1476–1558*. Ed. Vincent Gillespie and Susan Powell. Cambridge: D. S. Brewer, 2014. 27–44.
Atkinson, Stephen C. B. 'Malory's "Healing of Sir Urry": Lancelot, the Earthly Fellowship, and the World of the Grail'. *Studies in Philology* 78.4 (1981): 341–52.
——. 'Malory's Lancelot and the Quest of the Grail.' *Studies in Malory*. Ed. James W. Spisak. Kalamazoo: Medieval Institute Publications, 1985. 129–52.
——. '"They ... toke their shyldys before them and drew oute their sweryds...": Inflicting and Healing Wounds in Malory's *Morte Darthur*'. *Wounds and Wound Repair in Medieval Culture*. Ed. Larissa Tracy and Kelly DeVries. Leiden: Brill, 2015. 519–43.

Aurner, Nellie Slayton. *Caxton, Mirror of Fifteenth-Century Letters: A Study of the Literature of the First English Press*. London, 1926; New York: Russell, 1965.
Barber, Richard. 'Malory's *Le Morte Darthur* and Court Culture under Edward IV'. *Arthurian Literature* 12 (1993): 133–55.
Batt, Catherine. *Malory's Morte Darthur: Remaking Arthurian Tradition*. New York and Basingstoke: Palgrave, 2002.
Beal, Peter, compiler. *Index of English Literary Manuscripts*, Volume 1: *1450–1625*. London: Mansell; New York: R. R. Bowker, 1980.
Benson, C. David. 'The Ending of the *Morte Darthur*.' *A Companion to Malory*. Ed. Elizabeth Archibald and A. S. G. Edwards. Cambridge: D. S. Brewer, 1996. 221–38.
Benson, C. David and Lynne S. Blanchfield. *The Manuscripts of Piers Plowman: The B-Version*. Cambridge: D. S. Brewer, 1997.
Benson, Larry D. *Malory's Morte Darthur*. Cambridge, Mass.: Harvard University Press, 1976.
Bergen, Henry, ed. *Lydgate's Troy Book*. EETS ES 126. Vol. IV. London: Kegan Paul, 1935.
Besserman, Lawrence. *Biblical Paradigms in Medieval English Literature from Cædmon to Malory*. New York and London: Routledge, 2012.
Blades, William. *The Life and Typography of William Caxton, England's First Printer, with Evidence of his Typographical Connection with Colard Mansion, the Printer at Bruges*. Volume II. London: Joseph Lilly, 1863.
Blake, N. F. *Caxton and His World*. London: Andre Deutsch, 1969.
——. 'Caxton at Work: A Reconsideration'. *The Malory Debate: Essays on the Texts of Le Morte Darthur*. Ed. Bonnie Wheeler, Robert L. Kindrick and Michael N. Salda. Cambridge: D. S. Brewer, 2000. 233–53.
——. 'Caxton Prepares His Edition of the *Morte Darthur*'. *Journal of Librarianship* 8.4 (1976): 272–85.
Blanton, Virginia. '"... the quene in Amysbery, a nunne in whyght clothys and blak ...": Guinevere's Asceticism and Penance in Malory's *Le Morte Darthur*', *Arthuriana* 20.1 (2010): 52–75.
Boffey, Julia. *Manuscript and Print in London c. 1475–1530*. London: British Library, 2012.
Bogdanow, Fanni. 'The Changing Vision of Arthur's Death'. *Dies Illa: Death in the Middle Ages: Proceedings of the 1983 Manchester Colloquium*. Ed. Jane H. M. Taylor. Liverpool: Francis Cairns, 1984. 107–23.
——. 'La chute du royaume d'Arthur: Évolution du thème'. *Romania* 107 (1986): 504–19.
——. 'The Post-Vulgate *Roman du Graal*'. *The Arthur of the French: The Arthurian Legend in Medieval French and Occitan Literature*. Ed. Glyn S. Burgess and Karen Pratt. Cardiff: University of Wales Press, 2006. 342–52.
——. *The Romance of the Grail: A Study of the Structure and Genesis of a Thirteenth-Century Arthurian Prose Romance*. Manchester: Manchester University Press; New York: Barnes & Noble, 1966.
Brewer, D. S. "Form in the *Morte Darthur*." *Medium Ævum* 21 (1952): 14–24.
——. '"the hoole book"'. *Essays on Malory*. Ed. J. A. W. Bennett. Oxford: Clarendon, 1963. 41–63.
——. ed. *The Morte Darthur: Parts Seven and Eight*. By Sir Thomas Malory. London: Arnold, 1968.
Brewer, Derek. 'The Paradoxes of Honour in Malory'. *New Directions in Arthurian Studies*. Ed. Alan Lupack. Cambridge: D. S. Brewer, 2002. 33–47.
——. 'The Presentation of the Character of Lancelot: Chrétien to Malory'. *Arthurian Literature* 3 (1983): 26–52.

The British Library Catalogue of Additions to the Manuscripts, New Series 1976–80. Part I: Descriptions. London: British Library, 1995.

Brown, Andrew. *Church and Society in England, 1000–1500*. New York and Basingstoke: Palgrave, 2003.

Bryan, Elizabeth J. *Collaborative Meaning in Medieval Scribal Culture: The Otho Laȝamon*. Ann Arbor: University of Michigan Press, 1999.

Bühler, Curt F. *The Fifteenth-Century Book: The Scribes, the Printers, the Decorators*. Philadelphia: University of Pennsylvania Press, 1960.

Busby, Keith. *Codex and Context: Reading Old French Verse Narrative in Manuscript*. 2 vols. Amsterdam: Rodopi, 2002.

Camille, Michael. *Image on the Edge: The Margins of Medieval Art*. London: Reaktion, 1992.

Cannon, Christopher. *Middle English Literature: A Cultural History*. Cambridge and Malden: Polity, 2008.

Carruthers, Mary. *The Book of Memory: A Study of Memory in Medieval Culture*. 2nd edn. Cambridge: Cambridge University Press, 2008.

Caughey, Anna. 'Virginity, Sexuality, Repression and Return in the "Tale of the Sankgreal"'. *Arthurian Literature 28: Blood, Sex, Malory* (2011): 155–79.

Cawsey, Kathy. *Twentieth-Century Chaucer Criticism: Reading Audiences*. Farnham and Burlington, Vt.: Ashgate, 2011.

Chambers, E. K. *English Literature at the Close of the Middle Ages*. Oxford: Clarendon, 1945.

Chase, Carol J. 'Un manuscrit mesconnëu de l'*Estoire del Saint Graal*: Bourg-en-Bresse, Médiathèque Vailland 55. Le programme paratextuel'. *Journal of the International Arthurian Society* 3.1 (2015): 72–101.

Cherewatuk, Karen. 'Born-Again Virgins and Holy Bastards: Bors and Elayne and Lancelot and Galahad'. *Arthuriana* 11.2 (2001): 52–63.

——. 'Christian Rituals in Malory: The Evidence of Funerals'. *Malory and Christianity: Essays on Sir Thomas Malory's Morte Darthur*. Ed. D. Thomas Hanks Jr and Janet Jesmok. Kalamazoo: Medieval Institute Publications, 2013. 77–91.

——. '"Gentyl" Audiences and "Grete Bookes": Chivalric Manuals and the *Morte Darthur*'. *Arthurian Literature* 15 (1997): 205–16.

——. 'Malory's Launcelot and the Language of Sin and Confession.' *Arthuriana* 16.2 (2006): 68–72.

——. *Marriage, Adultery, and Inheritance in Malory's Morte Darthur*. Cambridge: D. S. Brewer, 2006.

——. 'The Saint's Life of Sir Launcelot: Hagiography and the Conclusion of Malory's *Morte Darthur*'. *Arthuriana* 5.1 (1995): 62–78.

——. 'Sir Thomas Malory's "Grete Booke"'. *The Social and Literary Contexts of Malory's Morte Darthur*. Ed. D. Thomas Hanks Jr and Jessica Gentry Brogdon. Cambridge: D. S. Brewer, 2000. 42–67.

Christianson, C. Paul. 'The Rise of London's Book-Trade'. *The Cambridge History of the Book in Britain*, Volume III: *1400–1557*. Ed. Lotte Hellinga and J. B. Trapp. Cambridge: Cambridge University Press, 1999. 128–47.

Clark, David Eugene. 'Hearing and Reading Narrative Divisions in the *Morte Darthur*'. *Arthuriana* 24.2 (2014): 92–125.

——. 'Scribal Modifications to Concluding Formulae in the Winchester Manuscript'. *Arthurian Literature* 32 (2015): 123–54.

Cooper, Helen. 'The Book of Sir Tristram de Lyones'. *A Companion to Malory*. Ed. Elizabeth Archibald and A. S. G. Edwards. Cambridge: D. S. Brewer, 1996. 183–201.

——. *The Canterbury Tales*. 2nd edn. Oxford: Oxford University Press, 1996.

——. 'Counter-Romance: Civil Strife and Father-Killing in the Prose Romances'. *The Long Fifteenth Century: Essays for Douglas Gray*. Ed. Helen Cooper and Sally Mapstone. Oxford: Clarendon, 1997. 141–62.

——. *The English Romance in Time: Transforming Motifs from Geoffrey of Monmouth to the Death of Shakespeare*. Oxford: Clarendon, 2004.

——. 'M for Merlin: The Case of the Winchester Manuscript'. *Medieval Heritage: Essays in Honour of Tadahiro Ikegami*. Ed. Masahiko Kanno et al. Tokyo: Yushodo Press, 1997. 93–107.

——. 'Opening Up the Malory Manuscript'. *The Malory Debate: Essays on the Texts of Le Morte Darthur*. Ed. Bonnie Wheeler, Robert L. Kindrick and Michael N. Salda. Cambridge: D. S. Brewer, 2000. 255–84.

Cooper, Helen, ed. *Le Morte Darthur*. See under Primary Sources.

Corrie, Marilyn. 'Self-Determination in the Post-Vulgate *Suite du Merlin* and Malory's *Le Morte Darthur*'. *Medium Ævum* 73.2 (2004): 273–89.

Crofts, Thomas H. 'Death in the Margins: Dying and Scribal Performance in the Winchester Manuscript'. *The Arthurian Way of Death. The English Tradition*. Ed. Karen Cherewatuk and K. S. Whetter. Cambridge: D. S. Brewer, 2009. 115–23.

——. *Malory's Contemporary Audience: The Social Reading of Romance in Late Medieval England*. Cambridge: D. S. Brewer, 2006.

——. 'The Occasion of the *Morte Arthure*: Textual History and Marginal Decoration in the Thornton MS'. *Arthuriana* 20.2 (2010): 5–27.

Davies, Richard G. 'The Church and the Wars of the Roses'. *The Wars of the Roses*. Ed. A. J. Pollard. New York: St Martin's, 1995. 134–61.

Davies, Sioned. 'Performing *Culhwch and Olwen*.' *Arthurian Literature* 21: Celtic Arthurian Material (2004): 29–51.

Davis, Nick. 'Narrative Composition and the Spatial Memory'. *Narrative: From Malory to Motion Pictures*. Ed. J. Hawthorne. London: Arnold, 1985. 24–39.

De Hamel, Christopher. *The British Library Guide to Manuscript Illumination: History and Techniques*. London: The British Library, 2001.

Devereux, George. *Dreams in Greek Tragedy: An Ethno-Psycho-Analytical Study*. Berkeley and Los Angeles: University of California Press, 1976.

Dodds, E. R. 'On Misunderstanding the *Oedipus Rex*'. *Greece & Rome* SS 13.1 (1966): 37–49.

Doyle, A. I. and M. B. Parkes. 'The Production of Copies of the *Canterbury Tales* and the *Confessio Amantis* in the Early Fifteenth Century'. *Medieval Scribes, Manuscripts and Libraries: Essays Presented to N. R. Ker*. Ed. M. B. Parkes and Andrew G. Watson. London: Scolar, 1978. 163–210.

Driver, Martha W. 'Medievalizing the Classical Past in Pierpont Morgan MS M 876'. *Middle English Poetry: Texts and Traditions. Essays in Honour of Derek Pearsall*. Ed. A. J. Minnis. York: York Medieval Press, 2001. 211–39.

Duffy, Eamon. 'Religious Belief'. *A Social History of England, 1200–1500*. Ed. Rosemary Horrox and W. Mark Ormrod. Cambridge: Cambridge University Press, 2006. 293–339.

——. *The Stripping of the Altars: Traditional Religion in England c. 1400–c. 1580*. 2nd edn. New Haven: Yale University Press, 2005.

Easterling, P. E. 'Character in Sophocles.' *Greece and Rome* SS 24.2 (1977): 121–9.

Eckhardt, Caroline D. 'Reconsidering Malory'. *The Fortunes of King Arthur*. Ed. Norris J. Lacy. Cambridge: D. S. Brewer, 2005. 195–208.

Eddy, Nicole. 'Annotating the Winchester Malory: A Fifteenth-Century Guide to the Martialism, the Marvels, and the Narrative Structure of the *Morte Darthur*'. *Viator* 42.2 (2011): 283–305.

Edwards, A. S. G. 'Decorated Caxtons'. *Incunabla: Studies in Fifteenth-Century Printed Books Presented to Lotte Hellinga*. Ed. Martin Davies. London: British Library, 1999. 493–506.

——. 'The Manuscript: British Library MS Cotton Nero A.x'. *A Companion to the Gawain-Poet*. Ed. Derek Brewer and Jonathan Gibson. Cambridge: D. S. Brewer, 1997. 197–219.

——. 'The Manuscripts and Texts of the Second Version of John Hardyng's *Chronicle*'. *England in the Fifteenth Century: Proceedings of the 1986 Harlaxton Symposium*. Ed. Daniel Williams. Woodbridge: Boydell, 1987. 75–84.

Edwards, A. S. G. and Derek Pearsall. 'The Manuscripts of the Major English Poetic Texts'. *Book Production and Publishing in Britain 1375–1475*. Ed. Jeremy Griffiths and Derek Pearsall. Cambridge: Cambridge University Press, 1989. 257–78.

Edwards, Elizabeth. *The Genesis of Narrative in Malory's Morte Darthur*. Cambridge: D. S. Brewer, 2001.

Evans, Murray J. 'Camelot or Corbenic?: Malory's New Blend of Secular and Religious Chivalry in the "Tale of the Holy Grail"'. *English Studies in Canada* 8 (1982): 249–61.

——. 'The Explicits and Narrative Division in the Winchester MS: A Critique of Vinaver's Malory'. *Philological Quarterly* 58.3 (1979): 263–81.

——. '*Ordinatio* and Narrative Links: The Impact of Malory's Tales as a "hoole book"'. *Studies in Malory*. Ed. James W. Spisak. Kalamazoo: Medieval Institute Publications, 1985. 29–52.

——. *Rereading Middle English Romance: Manuscript Layout, Decoration, and the Rhetoric of Composite Structure*. Montreal and Kingston: McGill-Queen's University Press, 1995.

——. 'The Two Scribes in the Winchester MS: The Ninth *Explicit* and Malory's "Hoole Book"'. *Manuscripta* 27 (1983): 38–44.

Field, P. J. C. 'Author, Scribe and Reader in Malory: The Case of Harleuse and Peryne'. *Malory: Texts and Sources*. 72–88.

——. 'Caxton's Roman War'. *The Malory Debate: Essays on the Texts of Le Morte Darthur*. Ed. Bonnie Wheeler, Robert L. Kindrick and Michael N. Salda. Cambridge: D. S. Brewer, 2000. 127–67.

——. 'The Choice of Text for Malory's *Morte Darthur*'. *Malory: Texts and Sources*. 14–26.

——. 'The Earliest Texts of Malory's *Morte Darthur*'. *Malory: Texts and Sources*. 1–13.

——. 'Fifteenth-Century History in Malory's *Morte Darthur*'. *Malory: Texts and Sources*. 47–71.

——. 'Hunting, Hawking and Textual Criticism in Malory's *Morte Darthur*.' *Malory: Texts and Sources*. 103–13.

——. *The Life and Times of Sir Thomas Malory*. Cambridge: D. S. Brewer, 1993.

——. *Malory: Texts and Sources*. Cambridge: D. S. Brewer, 1998.

——. 'Malory and His Audience.' *New Directions in Arthurian Studies*. Ed. Alan Lupack. Cambridge: D. S. Brewer, 2002. 21–32.

——. 'Malory and His Scribes'. *Arthuriana* 14.1 (2004): 31–42.

——. 'Malory and the Grail: The Importance of Detail'. *The Grail, the Quest and the World of Arthur*. Ed. Norris J. Lacy. Cambridge, D. S. Brewer, 2008. 141–55.

——. 'Malory and *The Wedding of Sir Gawain and Dame Ragnell*'. *Malory: Texts and Sources*. 284–94.

——. 'Malory's Minor Sources.' *Malory: Texts and Sources*. 27–31.

——. 'Malory's Own Marginalia'. *Medium Ævum* 70 (2001): 226–39.

——. 'Malory's Source-Manuscript for the First Tale of *Le Morte Darthur*'. *Arthurian Literature* 29 (2012): 111–19.

——. *Romance and Chronicle: A Study of Malory's Prose Style*. London: Barrie, 1971.

———. 'Sir Thomas Malory's *Le Morte Darthur*'. *The Arthur of the English: The Arthurian Legend in Medieval English Life and Literature*. Ed. W. R. J. Barron. Cardiff: University of Wales Press, 1999. 225–46.
Field, Rosalind, Phillipa Hardman and Michelle Sweeney, eds. *Christianity and Romance in Medieval England*. Cambridge: D. S. Brewer, 2010.
Finlayson, John. 'Reading Romances in Their Manuscript: Lincoln Cathedral Manuscript 91 ("Thornton")'. *Anglia* 123.4 (2006): 632–66.
Fletcher, Alan J. *The Presence of Medieval English Literature: Studies at the Interface of History, Author, and Text in a Selection of Middle English Literary Landmarks*. Turnhout: Brepols, 2012.
Fletcher, Lydia. '"Traytoures" and "Treson": The Language of Treason in the Works of Sir Thomas Malory'. *Arthurian Literature 28: Blood, Sex, Malory* (2011): 75–88.
Fowler, Alastair. *Literary Names: Personal Names in English Literature*. Oxford: Oxford University Press, 2012.
Frank, Roberta. 'The *Beowulf* Poet's Sense of History'. *The Wisdom of Poetry: Essays in Early English Literature in Honor of Morton W. Bloomfield*. Ed. Larry D. Benson and Siegfried Wenzel. Kalamazoo: Medieval Institute Publications, 1982. 53–65.
Franklin-Brown, Mary. *Reading the World: Encyclopedic Writing in the Scholastic Age*. Chicago and London: University of Chicago Press, 2012.
Frappier, Jean. 'The Vulgate Cycle'. *Arthurian Literature in the Middle Ages: A Collaborative History*. Ed. Roger Sherman Loomis. Oxford: Clarendon, 1959. 295–318.
Gillespie, Alexandra. 'The History of the Book'. *New Medieval Literatures* 9 (2007): 245–86.
Griffith, Richard R. 'Arthur's Author: The Mystery of Sir Thomas Malory'. *Ventures in Research* 1 (1972): 7–43.
———. 'The Authorship Question Reconsidered: A Case for Thomas Malory of Papworth St Agnes, Cambridgeshire'. *Aspects of Malory*. Ed. Toshiyuki Takamiya and Derek Brewer. Cambridge: D. S. Brewer; Totowa: Rowman & Littlefield, 1981. 159–77.
———. 'Caxton's Copy-Text for *Le Morte Darthur*: Tracing the Provenance'. *Traditions and Innovations: Essays on British Literature of the Middle Ages and the Renaissance*. Ed. David G. Allen and Robert A. White. Newark: University of Delaware Press, 1990. 75–87.
Grimbert, Joan Tasker. 'Tristan and Iseult at the Cathedral of Santiago de Compostela'. *Arthurian Literature* 31 (2014): 131–64.
Grimm, Kevin T. 'Editing Malory: What's at (the) Stake?' *Arthuriana* 5.2 (1995): 5–14.
———. 'Knightly Love and the Narrative Structure of Malory's Tale Seven'. *Arthurian Interpretations* 3.2 (1989): 76–95.
———. 'Sir Thomas Malory's Narrative of Faith'. *Arthuriana* 16.2 (2006): 16–20.
Guddat-Figge, Gisela. *Catalogue of Manuscripts Containing Middle English Romances*. Munich: Wilhelm Fink, 1976.
Guerin, Wilfred L. '"The Tale of the Death of Arthur": Catastrophe and Resolution'. *Malory's Originality: A Critical Study of Le Morte Darthur*. Ed. R. M. Lumiansky. Baltimore: Johns Hopkins Press, 1964. 233–74.
Gumbert, J. P. '"Typography" in the Manuscript Book'. *Journal of the Printing Historical Society* 22 (1993): 5–28.
Halliwell, Stephen. 'Plato's Repudiation of the Tragic'. *Tragedy and the Tragic: Greek Theatre and Beyond*. Ed. M. S. Silk. Oxford: Clarendon, 1996. 332–49.
Hanks, D. Thomas, Jr. '"A Far Green Country Under a Swift Sunrise" – Tolkien's Eucatastrophe and Malory's *Morte Darthur*'. *Fifteenth-Century Studies* 36 (2011): 49–64.

———. '"All maner of good love comyth of God"': Malory, God's Grace, and Noble Love'. *Malory and Christianity: Essays on Sir Thomas Malory's Morte Darthur*. Ed. D. Thomas Hanks Jr and Janet Jesmok. Kalamazoo: Medieval Institute Publications, 2013. 9–28.

———. 'Back to the Past: Editing Malory's *Le Morte Darthur*'. *The Malory Debate: Essays on the Texts of Le Morte Darthur*. Ed. Bonnie Wheeler, Robert L. Kindrick and Michael N. Salda. Cambridge: D. S. Brewer, 2000. 285–300.

———. 'Textual Harassment: Caxton, de Worde and Malory's *Morte Darthur*'. *Re-Viewing Le Morte Darthur: Texts and Contexts, Characters and Themes*. Ed. K. S. Whetter and Raluca L. Radulescu. Cambridge: D. S. Brewer, 2005. 27–47.

Hanna, Ralph III. 'Middle English Manuscripts and the Study of Literature'. *New Medieval Literatures* 4 (2004): 243–63.

Hardman, Phillipa. 'Fitt Divisions in Middle English Romances: A Consideration of the Evidence'. *Yearbook of English Studies* 22 (1992): 63–82.

———. 'Presenting the Text: Pictorial Tradition in Fifteenth-Century Manuscripts of the *Canterbury Tales*'. *Chaucer Illustrated: Five Hundred Years of The Canterbury Tales in Pictures*. Ed. William K. Finley and Joseph Rosenblum. New Castle, Del.: Oak Knell Press, and London: British Library, 2003. 37–72.

———. 'The Unity of the Ireland Manuscript'. *Reading Medieval Studies* 2 (1976): 45–62.

Hardyment, Christina. *Malory: The Life and Times of King Arthur's Chronicler*. London: HarperCollins, 2005.

Hellinga, Lotte. *Caxton in Focus: The Beginning of Printing in England*. London: British Library, 1982.

———. 'The Malory Manuscript and Caxton'. *Aspects of Malory*. Ed. Toshiyuki Takamiya and Derek Brewer. Cambridge and Totowa: D. S. Brewer, 1981. 127–41.

———. 'Sale Advertisements for Books Printed in the Fifteenth Century'. *Books for Sale: The Advertising and Promotion of Print since the Fifteenth Century*. Ed. Robin Myers, Michael Harris and Giles Mandelbrote. New Castle, Del. and London: Oak Knoll and British Library, 2009. 1–25.

Hibbard, Laura A. *Mediaeval Romance in England: A Study of the Sources and Analogues of the Non-Cyclic Metrical Romances*. Oxford: Oxford University Press, 1924.

Hicks, Edward. *Sir Thomas Malory: His Turbulent Career*. Cambridge, Mass.: Harvard University Press, 1928.

Hilmo, Maidie. 'The Power of Images in the Auchinleck, Vernon, Pearl, and Two *Piers Plowman* Manuscripts'. *Opening Up Middle English Manuscripts: Literary and Visual Approaches*. Kathryn Kerby-Fulton, Maidie Hilmo and Linda Olsen. Ithaca and London: Cornell University Press, 2012. 153–205.

Hodges, Kenneth. *Forging Chivalric Communities in Malory's Le Morte Darthur*. New York and Basingstoke: Palgrave, 2005.

———. 'Haunting Pieties: Malory's Use of Chivalric Christian *Exempla* after the Grail'. *Arthuriana* 17.2 (2007): 28–48.

Hoffman, Donald L. 'Malory's Tragic Merlin'. *Arthurian Interpretations* 1.2 (1991): 15–31.

———. 'Perceval's Sister: Malory's "Rejected" Masculinities'. *Arthuriana* 6.4 (1996): 72–83.

Holbrook, Sue Ellen. 'Endless Virtue and Trinitarian Prayer in Lancelot's Healing of Urry'. *Malory and Christianity: Essays on Sir Thomas Malory's Morte Darthur*. Ed. D. Thomas Hanks Jr and Janet Jesmok. Kalamazoo: Medieval Institute Publications, 2013. 56–76.

———. 'On the Attractions of the Malory Incunable and the Malory Manuscript'. *The Malory Debate: Essays on the Texts of Le Morte Darthur*. Ed. Bonnie Wheeler, Robert L. Kindrick and Michael N. Salda. Cambridge: D. S. Brewer, 2000. 323–65.

Howard, Donald R. *The Idea of the Canterbury Tales*. Berkeley and Los Angeles: University of California Press, 1976.
Hudson, Harriet. 'Middle English Popular Romances: The Manuscript Evidence'. *Manuscripta* 28 (1984): 67–78.
Huot, Sylvia. '"Ci parle l'aucteur": The Rubrication of Voice and Authorship in *Roman de la Rose* Manuscripts'. *SubStance* 17.2 (1988): 42–8.
Hynes-Berry, Mary. 'Malory's Translation of Meaning: *The Tale of the Sankgreal*'. *Studies in Philology* 74 (1977): 243–57.
Ihle, Sandra Ness. *Malory's Grail Quest: Invention and Adaptation in Medieval Prose Romance*. Madison, Wis.: University of Wisconsin Press, 1983.
Index of English Literary Manuscripts. Volume 1: *1450–1625*. Compiled Peter Beal. London and New York: Mansell, 1980.
Johnson, David F. '"Men hadde niet Arsatere vonden alsoe goet": Walewein as Healer in the Middle Dutch Arthurian Tradition'. *Arthuriana* 11.4 (2001): 39–52.
Johnston, Michael. *Romance and Gentry in Late Medieval England*. Oxford: Oxford University Press, 2014.
Kaeuper, Richard W. *Chivalry and Violence in Medieval Europe*. Oxford: Oxford University Press, 1999.
——. *Holy Warriors: The Religious Ideology of Chivalry*. Philadelphia: University of Pennsylvania Press, 2009.
Kato, Takako. *Caxton's Morte Darthur: The Printing Process and the Authenticity of the Text*. Oxford: Society for the Study of Medieval Languages and Literature, 2002.
——. 'Corrected Mistakes in the Winchester Manuscript'. *Re-Viewing Le Morte Darthur: Texts and Contexts, Characters and Themes*. Ed. K. S. Whetter and Raluca L. Radulescu. Cambridge: D. S. Brewer, 2005. 9–25.
Kato, Tomomi, ed. *A Concordance to the Works of Sir Thomas Malory*. Tokyo: University of Tokyo Press, 1974.
Kaufman, Amy S. '"For This was Drawyn by a Knyght Presoner": Sir Thomas Malory and *Le Morte Darthur*'. *Prison Narratives from Boethius to Zana*. Ed. Philip Edward Phillips. New York and Basingstoke: Palgrave, 2014. 35–55.
——. 'Guenevere Burning.' *Arthuriana* 20.1 (2010): 76–94.
Keen, Maurice. *Chivalry*. New Haven: Yale University Press, 1984.
Kelliher, Hilton. 'The Early History of the Malory Manuscript'. *Aspects of Malory*. Ed. Toshiyuki Takamiya and Derek Brewer. Cambridge and Totowa: D. S. Brewer, 1981. 143–58.
Kelly, Kathleen Coyne. 'Malory's Body Chivalric'. *Arthuriana* 6.4 (1996): 52–71.
——. 'Malory's Multiple Virgins'. *Arthuriana* 9.2 (1999): 21–9.
——. 'Menaced Masculinity and Imperiled Virginity in the *Morte Darthur*'. *Menacing Virgins: Representing Virginity in the Middle Ages and Renaissance*. Ed. Kathleen Coyne Kelly and Marina Leslie. Cranbury, NJ: University of Delaware Press, 1999. 97–114.
Kelly, Robert L. 'Penitence as a Remedy for War in Malory's "Tale of the Death of Arthur"'. *Studies in Philology* 91 (1994): 111–35.
——. 'Royal Policy and Malory's Round Table'. *Arthuriana* 14.1 (2004): 43–71.
——. 'Wounds, Healing, and Knighthood in Malory's Tale of Lancelot and Guenevere'. *Studies in Malory*. Ed. James W. Spisak. Kalamazoo: Medieval Institute Publications, 1985. 173–97.
Kennedy, Beverly. *Knighthood in the Morte Darthur*. 2nd edn. Cambridge: D. S. Brewer, 1992.
Kennedy, Edward Donald. 'Caxton, Malory, and the "Noble Tale of King Arthur and the Emperor Lucius"'. *The Malory Debate: Essays on the Texts of Le Morte Darthur*.

Ed. Bonnie Wheeler, Robert L. Kindrick and Michael N. Salda. Cambridge: D. S. Brewer, 2000. 217–32.

——. 'Malory and His English Sources'. *Aspects of Malory*. Ed. Toshiyuki Takamiya and Derek Brewer. Cambridge and Totowa: D. S. Brewer, 1981. 27–55.

——. 'Malory's Use of Hardyng's *Chronicle*'. *N&Q* ns 16 (1969): 167–70.

——. 'Malory's Use of Hardyng's *Chronicle*: A Reconsideration'. *West Virginia University Philological Papers* 54 (2011): 8–15.

——. 'Sir Thomas Malory's (French) Romance and (English) Chronicle'. *Arthurian Studies in Honour of P. J. C. Field*. Ed. Bonnie Wheeler. Cambridge: D. S. Brewer, 2004. 223–34.

Kennedy, Elspeth et al. 'Lancelot with and without the Grail: *Lancelot do Lac* and the Vulgate Cycle'. *The Arthur of the French: The Arthurian Legend in Medieval French and Occitan Literature*. Ed. Glyn S. Burgess and Karen Pratt. Cardiff: University of Wales Press, 2006. 274–324.

Ker, N. R. See under Primary Sources: *The Winchester Malory*.

Kindrick, Robert L. 'Introduction: Caxton, Malory, and an Authentic Arthurian Text'. *The Malory Debate: Essays on the Texts of Le Morte Darthur*. Ed. Bonnie Wheeler, Robert L. Kindrick and Michael N. Salda. Cambridge: D. S. Brewer, 2000. xv–xxxii.

Kingsford, C. L. 'The First Version of Hardyng's *Chronicle*'. *EHR* 27.107 (1912): 462–82.

Kingsford, Charles Lethbridge. *English Historical Literature in the Fifteenth Century*. Oxford: Clarendon, 1913.

Kissick, Erin. 'Mirroring Masculinities: Transformative Female Corpses in Malory's *Morte Darthur*'. *Arthurian Literature* 31 (2014): 101–30.

Kuskin, William. *Symbolic Caxton: Literary Culture and Print Capitalism*. Notre Dame, Ind.: University of Notre Dame Press, 2008.

Lambert, Mark. *Malory: Style and Vision in Le Morte Darthur*. New Haven and London: Yale University Press, 1975.

Lang, Andrew. 'Le Morte Darthur'. *Le Morte Darthur*. By Sir Thomas Malory. Ed. H. Oskar Sommer. Volume 3: *Studies on the Sources*. London: Nutt, 1891. xiii–xxv.

Larrington, Carolyne. 'The Enchantress, the Knight and the Cleric: Authorial Surrogates in Arthurian Romance'. *Arthurian Literature* 25 (2008): 43–65.

Leitch, Megan G. *Romancing Treason: The Literature of the Wars of the Roses*. Oxford: Oxford University Press, 2015.

Lerer, Seth. *Chaucer and His Readers: Imagining the Author in Late-Medieval England*. Princeton: Princeton University Press, 1993.

Lester, G. A. *Sir John Paston's 'Grete Boke': A Descriptive Catalogue, with an Introduction, of British Library MS Lansdowne 285*. Cambridge and Totowa: D. S. Brewer, 1984.

Lewis, C. S. 'The English Prose *Morte*'. *Essays on Malory*. Ed. J. A. W. Bennett. Oxford: Clarendon, 1963. 7–28.

Lexton, Ruth. *Contested Language in Malory's Morte Darthur: The Politics of Romance in Fifteenth-Century England*. New York and Basingstoke: Palgrave Macmillan, 2014.

Lloyd-Morgan, Ceridwen. 'Medieval Welsh Tales or Romances?: Problems of Genre and Terminology'. *Cambrian Medieval Celtic Studies* 47 (2004): 41–58.

Lucas, D. W., introduction, commentary and appendixes, *Aristotle: Poetics*. Oxford: Clarendon, 1968.

Lumiansky, R. M., ed. *Malory's Originality: A Critical Study of Le Morte Darthur*. Baltimore: Johns Hopkins Press, 1964.

——. 'Malory's Steadfast Bors'. *Tulane Studies in English* 8 (1958): 5–20.

——. 'Sir Thomas Malory's *Le Morte Darthur*, 1947–1987: Author, Title, Text'. *Speculum* 62.4 (1987): 878–97.

———. '"The Tale of Lancelot and Guenevere": Suspense'. *Malory's Originality: A Critical Study of Le Morte Darthur*. Ed. Lumiansky. Baltimore: Johns Hopkins Press, 1964. 205–32.

Lupack, Alan. 'Malory's Intratexts'. *Romance and Rhetoric: Essays in Honour of Dhira B. Mahoney*. Ed. Georgina Donovain and Anita Obermeier. Turnhout: Brepols, 2010. 249–68.

Lustig, T. J. *Knight Prisoner: Thomas Malory Then and Now*. Brighton: Sussex Academic Press, 2013.

Lynch, Andrew. 'Gesture and Gender in Malory's *Le Morte Darthur*'. *Arthurian Romance and Gender: Selected Proceedings of the XVII International Arthurian Congress*. Ed. Friedrich Wolfzettel. Amsterdam and Atlanta: Rodopi, 1995. 285–95.

———. '... "If Indeed I Go": Arthur's Uncertain End in Malory and Tennyson'. *Arthurian Literature* 27 (2010): 19–31.

———. *Malory's Book of Arms: The Narrative of Combat in Le Morte Darthur*. Cambridge: D. S. Brewer, 1997.

———. '"Thou woll never have done": Ideology, Context, and Excess in Malory's War'. *The Social and Literary Contexts of Malory's Morte Darthur*. Ed. D. Thomas Hanks Jr and Jessica G. Brogdon. Cambridge: D. S. Brewer, 2000. 24–41.

McCarthy, Terence. 'Caxton and the Text of Malory's Book 2'. *Modern Philology* 71 (1973): 144–52.

———. *An Introduction to Malory*. Cambridge: D. S. Brewer, 1991.

McFarlane, K. B. *Lancastrian Kings and Lollard Knights*. Oxford: Clarendon, 1972.

McKenzie, D. F. *Bibliography and the Sociology of Texts*. Cambridge: Cambridge University Press, 1999.

McKinstry, Jamie. *Middle English Romance and the Craft of Memory*. Cambridge: D. S. Brewer, 2015.

Mahoney, Dhira B. 'Narrative Treatment of Name in Malory's *Morte D'Arthur*'. *ELH* 47.4 (1980): 646–56.

———. 'The Truest and Holiest Tale: Malory's Transformation of *La Queste del Saint Graal*'. *Studies in Malory*. Ed. James W. Spisak. Kalamazoo: Medieval Institute Publications, 1985. 109–28.

Manly, John M. and Edith Rickert. *The Text of the Canterbury Tales, Studied on the Basis of All Known Manuscripts*, Vol. I: *Descriptions of the Manuscripts*. Chicago and London: University of Chicago Press, 1940.

Mann, Jill. 'Chaucer and Atheism'. *Studies in the Age of Chaucer* 17 (1995): 5–19.

———. 'Knightly Combat in Malory's *Morte d'Arthur*'. *Life in Words: Essays on Chaucer, the Gawain-Poet, and Malory*. Ed. Mark David Rasmussen. Toronto: University of Toronto Press, 2014. 235–42.

———. 'Malory and the Grail Legend'. *Life in Words*. 312–31.

———. 'The Narrative of Distance, The Distance of Narrative in Malory's *Morte d'Arthur*'. *Life in Words*. 275–311.

———. '"Taking the Adventure": Malory and the *Suite du Merlin*'. *Life in Words*. 243–74.

Markland, Murray F. 'The Role of William Caxton'. *Research Studies* 28.2 (1960): 47–60.

Martin, Molly. *Vision and Gender in Malory's Morte Darthur*. Cambridge: D. S. Brewer, 2010.

Marvin, Julia, ed. and trans. *The Oldest Anglo-Norman Prose Brut Chronicle: An Edition and Translation*. Woodbridge: Boydell, 2006.

Matthews, William. 'The Besieged Printer'. *The Malory Debate: Essays on the Texts of Le Morte Darthur*. Ed. Bonnie Wheeler et al. Cambridge: D. S. Brewer, 2000. 35–64.

———. 'Caxton and Chaucer: A Re-View'. *The Malory Debate: Essays on the Texts of Le Morte Darthur*. Ed. Bonnie Wheeler et al. Cambridge: D. S. Brewer, 2000. 1–34.

———. *The Ill-Framed Knight: A Skeptical Inquiry into the Identity of Sir Thomas Malory*. Berkeley and Los Angeles: University of California Press, 1966.

———. 'A Question of Texts'. *The Malory Debate: Essays on the Texts of Morte Darthur*. Ed. Bonnie Wheeler et al. Cambridge: D. S. Brewer, 2000. 65–107.

———. *The Tragedy of Arthur: A Study of the Alliterative 'Morte Arthure'*. Berkeley and Los Angeles: University of California Press, 1960.

Meale, Carol M. '"The Hoole Book": Editing and the Creation of Meaning in Malory's Text." *A Companion to Malory*. Ed. Elizabeth Archibald and A. S. G. Edwards. Cambridge: D. S. Brewer, 1996. 1–17.

———. 'The Manuscripts and Early Audience of the Middle English Prose *Merlin*'. *The Changing Face of Arthurian Romance: Essays on Arthurian Prose Romances in Memory of Cedric E. Pickford*. Ed. Alison Adams et al. Cambridge: D.S. Brewer, 1986. 92–111.

———. 'Manuscripts, Readers and Patrons in Fifteenth-Century England: Sir Thomas Malory and Arthurian Romance'. *Arthurian Literature* 4 (1985): 93–126.

———. 'The Morgan Library Copy of *Generides*'. *Romance in Medieval England*. Ed. Maldwyn Mills, Jennifer Fellows and Carol M. Meale. Cambridge: D. S. Brewer, 1991. 89–104.

Michel, Laurence. 'The Possibility of a Christian Tragedy'. *Thought* 31 (1956): 403–28.

Middleton, Roger. 'The Manuscripts'. *The Arthur of the French: The Arthurian Legend in Medieval French and Occitan Literature*. Ed. Glyn S. Burgess and Karen Pratt. Cardiff: University of Wales Press, 2006. 8–92.

———. 'Manuscripts of the *Lancelot-Grail Cycle* in England and Wales: Some Books and Their Owners'. *A Companion to the Lancelot-Grail Cycle*. Ed. Carol Dover. Cambridge: D. S. Brewer, 2003. 219–35.

Moll, Richard J. *Before Malory: Reading Arthur in Later Medieval England*. Toronto: University of Toronto Press, 2003.

Moorman, Charles. *The Book of Kyng Arthur: The Unity of Malory's Morte Darthur*. Lexington: University of Kentucky Press, 1965.

———. 'Caxton's *Morte Darthur*: Malory's Second Edition?' *Fifteenth-Century Studies* 12 (1987): 99–113.

———. 'Desperately Defending Winchester: Arguments from the Edge'. *The Malory Debate: Essays on the Texts of Le Morte Darthur*. Ed. Bonnie Wheeler, Robert L. Kindrick and Michael N. Salda. Cambridge: D. S. Brewer, 2000. 109–15.

———. 'Malory's Treatment of The Sankgreall'. *PMLA* 71.3 (1956): 496–509.

———. '"The Tale of the Sankgreall": Human Frailty'. *Malory's Originality: A Critical Study of Le Morte Darthur*. Ed. R. M. Lumiansky. Baltimore: Johns Hopkins Press, 1964. 184–204.

Mukai, Tsuyoshi. 'De Worde's 1498 *Morte Darthur* and Caxton's Copy-Text'. *Review of English Studies* n.s. 51 (2000): 24–40.

Nakao, Yuji. 'Does Malory Really Revise His Vocabulary? – Some Negative Evidence'. *Poetica* 25–6 (1987): 93–109.

———. 'Musings on the Reviser of Book V in Caxton's Malory'. *The Malory Debate: Essays on the Texts of Le Morte Darthur*. Ed. Bonnie Wheeler, Robert L. Kindrick and Michael N. Salda. Cambridge: D. S. Brewer, 2000. 191–216.

Newman, Barbara. *Medieval Crossover: Reading the Secular against the Sacred*. Notre Dame: University of Notre Dame Press, 2013.

Noguchi, Shunichi. 'Caxton's Malory'. *Poetica* 8 (1977): 72–84.

———. 'Caxton's Malory Again'. *Poetica* 24 (1986): 33–8.

———. 'The Winchester Malory'. *The Malory Debate: Essays on the Texts of Le Morte Darthur*. Ed. Bonnie Wheeler, Robert L. Kindrick and Michael N. Salda. Cambridge: D. S. Brewer, 2000. 117–25.

Norris, Ralph. 'Errors in the Malory Archetype: The Case of Vinaver's Wight and Balan's Curious Remark'. *Studies in Bibliography* 60 (forthcoming 2017).
———. *Malory's Library: The Sources of the Morte Darthur*. Cambridge: D. S. Brewer, 2008.
———. 'Once Again King Arthur and the Ambassadors: A Textual Crux in Malory's Morte Darthur'. *Journal of the International Arthurian Society* 3.1 (2015): 102–19.
———. 'Sir Thomas Malory and *The Wedding of Sir Gawain and Dame Ragnell* Reconsidered'. *Arthuriana* 19.2 (2009): 82–102.
Oakeshott, W. F. 'The Finding of the Manuscript'. *Essays on Malory*. Ed. J. A. W. Bennett. Oxford: Clarendon, 1963. 1–6.
Olsen, Corey. 'Adulterated Love: The Tragedy of Malory's Lancelot and Guinevere'. *Malory and Christianity: Essays on Sir Thomas Malory's Morte Darthur*. Ed. D. Thomas Hanks Jr and Janet Jesmok. Kalamazoo: Medieval Institute Publications, 2013. 29–55.
Parkes, M. B. 'The Influence of the Concepts of *Ordinatio* and *Compilatio* on the Development of The Book'. *Medieval Learning and Literature: Essays Presented to Richard William Hunt*. Ed. J. J. G. Alexander and M. T. Gibson. Oxford: Clarendon, 1976. 115–41.
———. *Pause and Effect: An Introduction to the History of Punctuation in the West*. Berkeley and Los Angeles: University of California Press, 1993.
Partridge, Stephen. 'Designing the Page'. *The Production of Books in England 1350–1500*. Ed. Alexandra Gillespie and Daniel Wakelin. Cambridge: Cambridge University Press, 2011. 79–103.
———. '"The Makere of this Boke": Chaucer's *Retraction* and the Author as Scribe'. *Author, Reader, Book: Medieval Authorship in Theory and Practice*. Ed. Stephen Partridge and Erik Kwakkel. Toronto: University of Toronto Press, 2012. 106–53.
Passaro, Jonathan. 'Malory's Text of the *Suite du Merlin*'. *Arthurian Literature* 26 (2009): 39–75.
Pearsall, Derek. *The Canterbury Tales*. London: Allen & Unwin, 1985.
———. 'The Ellesmere Chaucer and Contemporary English Literary Manuscripts'. *The Ellesmere Chaucer: Essays in Interpretation*. Ed. Martin Stevens and Daniel Woodward. San Marino: Huntington Library, and Tokyo: Yushodo, 1997. 263–80.
———. 'Texts, Textual Criticism, and Fifteenth Century Manuscript Production'. *Fifteenth-Century Studies: Recent Essays*. Ed. Robert F. Yeager. Hamden, Conn.: Archon, 1984. 121–36.
Perkins, Nicolas and Alison Wiggins. *The Romance of the Middle Ages*. Oxford: Bodleian Library, 2012.
Peverley, Sarah L. 'Dynasty and Division: The Depiction of King and Kingdom in John Hardyng's *Chronicle*'. *Medieval Chronicle* 3 (2004): 149–70.
———. 'Political Consciousness and the Literary Mind in Late Medieval England: Men "Brought up of nought" in Vale, Hardyng, *Mankind*, and Malory'. *Studies in Philology* 105 (Winter 2008): 1–29.
Phillips, Noelle. 'Seeing Red: Reading Rubrication in Oxford, Corpus Christi College MS 201's *Piers Plowman*'. *Chaucer Review* 47.4 (2013): 439–64.
Pickering, F. P. *Literature and Art in the Middle Ages*. Berlin, 1966; Florida: University of Miami Press, 1970.
Pochoda, Elizabeth T. *Arthurian Propaganda: Le Morte Darthur as an Historical Ideal of Life*. Chapel Hill: University of North Carolina Press, 1971.
Pollard, A. J. 'Introduction: Society, Politics and the Wars of the Roses'. *The Wars of the Roses*. Ed. A. J. Pollard. New York: St. Martin's, 1995. 1–19.
Pratt, Karen. 'The Cistercians and the *Queste del Saint Graal*.' *Reading Medieval Studies* 21 (1995): 69–96.

Purdie, Rhiannon. *Anglicising Romance: Tail-Rhyme and Genre in Medieval English Literature*. Cambridge: D. S. Brewer, 2008.
Radulescu, Raluca L. *The Gentry Context for Malory's Morte Darthur*. Cambridge: D. S. Brewer, 2003.
———. 'Malory and the Quest for the Holy Grail'. *A Companion to Arthurian Literature*. Ed. Helen Fulton. Oxford and Malden: Wiley-Blackwell, 2009. 326–39.
———. 'Malory's Lancelot and the Key to Salvation'. *Arthurian Literature* 25 (2008): 93–118.
———. *Romance and Its Contexts in Fifteenth-Century England: Politics, Piety and Penitence*. Cambridge: D. S. Brewer, 2013.
Rayner, Samantha. 'The Case of the "curious document": Thomas Malory, William Matthews and Eugène Vinaver'. *Journal of the International Arthurian Society* 3.1 (2015): 120–38.
Reiss, Edmund. *Sir Thomas Malory*. New York: Twayne, 1966.
Ricciardi, Marc. '"Se what I shall do as for my trew parte": Fellowship and Fortitude in Malory's *Noble Tale of King Arthur and the Emperor Lucius*'. *Arthuriana* 11.2 (2001): 20–31.
Rice, Nicole R. *Lay Piety and Religious Discipline in Middle English Literature*. Cambridge: Cambridge University Press, 2008.
Richmond, Colin. 'Religion'. *Fifteenth-Century Attitudes: Perceptions of Society in Late Medieval England*. Ed. Rosemary Horrox. Cambridge: Cambridge University Press, 1994. 183–201.
Riddy, Felicity. 'Contextualizing *Le Morte Darthur*: Empire and Civil War'. *A Companion to Malory*. Ed. Elizabeth Edwards and A. S. G. Edwards. Cambridge: D. S. Brewer, 1996. 55–73.
———. *Sir Thomas Malory*. Leiden: Brill, 1987.
Robertson, D. W., Jr. 'Historical Criticism'. *English Institute Essays* (1950): 3–31.
———. *A Preface to Chaucer: Studies in Medieval Perspectives*. Princeton: Princeton University Press, 1962.
Robeson, Lisa. 'Malory and the Death of Kings: The Politics of Regicide at Salisbury Plain'. *The Arthurian Way of Death: The English Tradition*. Ed. Karen Cherewatuk and K. S. Whetter. Cambridge: D. S. Brewer, 2009. 136–50.
———. 'Women's Worship: Female Versions of Chivalric Honour'. *Re-Viewing Le Morte Darthur: Texts and Contexts, Characters and Themes*. Ed. K. S. Whetter and Raluca L. Radulescu. Cambridge: D. S. Brewer, 2005. 107–18.
Rogers, Janine. *Unified Fields: Science and Literary Form*. Montreal and Kingston: McGill-Queen's University Press, 2014.
Roland, Meg. '"Alas! Who may truste thys world": The Malory Documents and a Parallel-Text Edition'. *The Book Unbound: Editing and Reading Medieval Manuscripts and Texts*. Ed. Siân Echard and Stephen Partridge. Toronto: University of Toronto Press, 2004. 37–57.
———. 'Malory's Roman War Episode: An Argument for a Parallel Text'. *The Malory Debate: Essays on the Texts of Le Morte Darthur*. Ed. Bonnie Wheeler et al. Cambridge: D. S. Brewer, 2000. 315–21.
Ross, Charles. *Edward IV*. Berkeley and Los Angeles: University of California Press, 1974.
———. *Richard III*. Berkeley and Los Angeles: University of California Press, 1981.
Rumble, Thomas C. '"The Tale of Tristram": Development by Analogy'. *Malory's Originality: A Critical Study of Le Morte Darthur*. Ed. R. M. Lumiansky. Baltimore: Johns Hopkins Press, 1964. 118–83.

Rushton, Cory James. 'The Lady's Man: Gawain as Lover in Middle English Literature'. *The Erotic in the Literature of Medieval Britain*. Ed. Cory James Rushton and Amanda Hopkins. Cambridge: D. S. Brewer, 2007. 27–37.

——. '"Layde to the Colde Erthe": Death, Arthur's Knights, and Narrative Closure'. *The Arthurian Way of Death: The English Tradition*. Ed. Karen Cherewatuk and K. S. Whetter. Cambridge: D. S. Brewer, 2009. 151–66.

Sandler, Lucy Freeman. *Illuminators and Patrons in Fourteenth-Century England: The Psalter and Hours of Humphrey de Bohun and the Manuscripts of the Bohun Family*. London: The British Library; Toronto: University of Toronto Press, 2014.

Saul, Nigel. *English Church Monuments in the Middle Ages: History and Representation*. Oxford: Oxford University Press, 2009.

——. *For Honour and Fame: Chivalry in England, 1066–1500*. London: Bodley Head, 2011.

Saunders, Corinne. *Magic and the Supernatural in Medieval English Romance*. Cambridge: D. S. Brewer, 2010.

——. 'Religion and Magic'. *The Cambridge Companion to the Arthurian Legend*. Ed. Elizabeth Archibald and Ad Putter. Cambridge: Cambridge University Press, 2009. 201–17.

Scala, Elizabeth. 'Disarming Lancelot.' *Studies in Philology* 99.4 (2002): 380–403.

Scattergood, John. *Manuscripts and Ghosts: Essays on the Transmission of Medieval and Early Renaissance Literature*. Dublin: Four Courts, 2006.

Scodel, Ruth. 'Inscription, Absence and Memory: Epic and Early Epitaph'. *Studi italiani di filologia classica* 10 (1992): 57–76.

Scott, Kathleen. '*Caveat Lector*: Ownership and Standardization in the Illustration of Fifteenth-Century English Manuscripts'. *English Manuscript Studies 1100–1700* 1 (1989): 19–63.

Shaw, Sally. 'Caxton and Malory'. *Essays on Malory*. Ed. J. A. W. Bennett. Oxford: Clarendon, 1963. 114–45.

Sklar, Elizabeth S. 'Malory's "Lancelot and Elaine": Prelude to a Quest'. *Arthurian Yearbook* 3 (1993): 127–40.

Smith, Jeremy J. 'Some Spellings in Caxton's Malory'. *Poetica* 24 (1986): 58–63.

Smith, Margaret M. 'Patterns of Incomplete Rubrication in Incunables and What They Suggest about Working Methods'. *Medieval Book Production: Assessing the Evidence*. Ed. Linda L. Brownrigg. Los Altos Hills, Calif.: Anderson-Lovelace, 1990. 133–46.

Southern, R. W. *The Making of the Middle Ages*. London: Hutchinson, 1953.

——. *Western Society and the Church in the Middle Ages*. London: Penguin, 1970.

Spisak, James W., ed. *Studies in Malory*. Kalamazoo: Medieval Institute Publications, 1985.

Stones, Alison. 'The Earliest Illustrated Prose *Lancelot* Manuscript?' *Reading Medieval Studies* 3 (1977): 12–44.

——. '"Mise en page" in the French *Lancelot-Grail*: The First 150 Years of the Illustrative Tradition'. *A Companion to the Lancelot-Grail Cycle*. Ed. Carol Dover. Cambridge: D. S. Brewer, 2003. 125–44.

Strachey, Sir Edward, ed. *Le Morte Darthur*. London: Macmillan, 1897.

Stubbings, Frank. 'A New Manuscript of *Generydes*'. *Transactions of the Cambridge Bibliographical Society* 10 (1993): 317–40.

Stuhmiller, Jacqueline. '*Iudicium Dei, iudicium fortunae*: Trial by Combat in Malory's *Le Morte Darthur*'. *Speculum* 81.2 (2006): 427–62.

Summers, Joanna. *Late-Medieval Prison Writing and the Politics of Autobiography*. Oxford: Clarendon, 2004.

Sutton, Anne F. 'Malory in Newgate: A New Document'. *The Library* 7th series 1.3 (2000): 243–62.

Swanson, Keith. '"God Woll Have a Stroke": Judicial Combat in the *Morte Darthur*'. *Bulletin of the John Rylands University Library of Manchester* 74 (1992): 155–73.

Takagi, Masako and Toshiyuki Takamiya. 'Caxton Edits the Roman War Episode: The *Chronicles of England* and Caxton's Book V'. *The Malory Debate: Essays on the Texts of Le Morte Darthur*. Ed. Bonnie Wheeler, Robert L. Kindrick and Michael N. Salda. Cambridge: D. S. Brewer, 2000. 169–90.

Takamiya, Toshiyuki. 'Editor/Compositor at Work: The Case of Caxton's Malory'. *Arthurian and Other Studies Presented to Shunichi Noguchi*. Ed. Takashi Suzuki and Tsuyoshi Mukai. Cambridge: D. S. Brewer, 1993. 143–51.

Takamiya, Toshiyuki, and Derek Brewer, ed. *Aspects of Malory*. Cambridge: D. S. Brewer, 1981.

Tieken-Boon van Ostade, Ingrid. *The Two Versions of Malory's Morte Darthur: Multiple Negation and the Editing of the Text*. Cambridge: D. S. Brewer, 1995.

Tiller, Kenneth. 'En-graving Chivalry: Tombs, Burial, and the Ideology of Knighthood in Malory's *Tale of King Arthur*'. *Arthuriana* 14.2 (2004): 37–53.

Tolhurst, Fiona. 'Slouching towards Bethlehem: Secularized Salvation in *Le Morte Darthur*'. *Malory and Christianity: Essays on Sir Thomas Malory's Morte Darthur*. Ed. D. Thomas Hanks Jr and Janet Jesmok. Kalamazoo: Medieval Institute Publications, 2013. 127–56.

Traxler, Janina P. 'Dying to Get to Sarras: Perceval's Sister and the Grail Quest'. *The Grail: A Casebook*. Ed. Dhira B. Mahoney. New York and London: Garland, 2000. 261–78.

Tucker, P. E. 'Chivalry in the *Morte*'. *Essays on Malory*. Ed. J. A. W. Bennett. Oxford: Clarendon, 1963. 64–103.

——. 'The Place of the "Quest of the Holy Grail" in the *Morte Darthur*'. *Modern Language Review* 48.4 (1953): 391–7.

Twomey, Michael W. 'The Voice of Aurality in the *Morte Darthur*'. *Arthuriana* 13.4 (2003): 103–18.

Vaughan, Richard. *Valois Burgundy*. London: Penguin, 1975.

Vinaver, see the apparatus to Malory, *Works*.

Wade, James. 'Malory's Marginalia Reconsidered'. *Arthuriana* 21.3 (2011): 70–86.

Walsh, John Michael. 'Malory's "Very Mater of La Cheualer du Charyot": Characterization and Structure'. *Studies in Malory*. Ed. James W. Spisak. Kalamazoo: Medieval Institute Publications, 1985. 199–226.

Walters, Lori. 'The Creation of a "Super Romance": Paris, Bibliothèque Nationale, fonds français, MS 1433'. *Arthurian Yearbook* 1 (1991): 3–25.

Ward, H. L. D. *Catalogue of Romances in the Department of Manuscripts in the British Museum*. 3 vols. London, 1883, 1893.

Wheeler, Bonnie and Michael N. Salda. 'Introduction: The Debate on Editing Malory's *Le Morte Darthur*'. *The Malory Debate: Essays on the Texts of Le Morte Darthur*. Ed. Bonnie Wheeler, Robert L. Kindrick and Michael N. Salda. Cambridge: D. S. Brewer, 2000. ix–xiii.

Whetter, K. S. 'Characterization in Malory and Bonnie'. *Arthuriana* 19.3 (2009): 123–35.

——. 'Genre as Context in the Alliterative *Morte Arthure*'. *Arthuriana* 20.2 (2010): 45–65.

——. 'The Historicity of Combat in *Le Morte Darthur*'. *Arthurian Studies in Honour of P. J. C. Field*. Ed. Bonnie Wheeler. Cambridge: D. S. Brewer, 2004. 261–70.

——. 'Inks and Hands and Fingers in the Manuscript of Malory's *Morte Darthur*'. *Speculum* (forthcoming, 2017).

——. 'Love and Death in Arthurian Romance'. *The Arthurian Way of Death: The English Tradition*. Ed. Karen Cherewatuk and K. S. Whetter. Cambridge: D. S. Brewer, 2010. 94–114.

———. 'Malory, Hardyng, and the Winchester Manuscript: Some Preliminary Conclusions'. *Arthuriana* 22.4 (2012): 167–89.
———. 'Malory's Secular Arthuriad'. *Malory and Christianity: Essays on Sir Thomas Malory's Morte Darthur*. Ed. D. Thomas Hanks Jr and Janet Jesmok. Kalamazoo: Medieval Institute Publications, 2013. 157–79.
———. 'On Misunderstanding Malory's Balyn'. *Re-Viewing Le Morte Darthur: Texts and Contexts, Characters and Themes*. Ed. K. S. Whetter and Raluca L. Radulescu. Cambridge: D. S. Brewer, 2005. 149–62.
———. 'The Stanzaic *Morte Arthur* and Medieval Tragedy'. *Reading Medieval Studies* 28 (2002): 87–111.
———. *Understanding Genre and Medieval Romance*. Aldershot: Ashgate, 2008.
———. 'Warfare and Combat in *Le Morte Darthur*'. *Writing War: Medieval Literary Responses to Warfare*. Ed. Corinne Saunders, Françoise Le Saux and Neil Thomas. Cambridge: D. S. Brewer, 2004. 169–86.
———. 'Weeping, Wounds and Worshyp in Malory's *Morte Darthur*'. *Arthurian Literature* 31 (2014): 61–82.
Whitaker, Muriel. *Arthur's Kingdom of Adventure: The World of Malory's Morte Darthur*. Cambridge and Totowa: D. S. Brewer, 1984.
Whitehead, F. 'Lancelot's Penance.' *Essays on Malory*. Ed. J. A. W. Bennett. Oxford: Clarendon, 1963. 104–13
Whiting, B. J. 'Gawain: His Reputation, His Courtesy and His Appearance in Chaucer's *Squire's Tale*'. *Mediaeval Studies* 9 (1947): 189–234.
Whitman, Jon. 'Posthumous Messages: Memory, Romance, and the *Morte Darthur*'. *The Making of Memory in the Middle Ages*. Ed. Lucie Doležalová. Leiden: Brill, 2010. 241–52.
Whitworth, Charles W. 'The Sacred and the Secular in Malory's *Tale of the Sankgreal*'. *Yearbook of English Studies* 5 (1975): 19–29.
Wilson, Robert H. 'Addenda on Malory's Minor Characters'. *Journal of English and Germanic Philology* 55 (1956): 563–87.
———. 'How Many Books Did Malory Write?' *Studies in English* 30 (1951): 1–23.
———. 'Malory's "French Book" Again'. *Comparative Literature* 2 (1950): 172–81.
———. 'Malory's Naming of Minor Characters'. *Journal of English and Germanic Philology* 42 (1943): 364–85.
Wilson, Robert Henry. *Characterization in Malory: A Comparison with His Sources*. Chicago: University of Chicago Libraries, 1934; n.p.: Folcroft Library, 1970.
Winks, Robin W., ed. *The Historian as Detective: Essays on Evidence*. New York: Harper & Row, 1968.
Withrington, John. 'The Arthurian Epitaph in Malory's "Morte Darthur"'. *Arthurian Literature* 7 (1987): 103–44
———. 'Caxton, Malory, and the Roman War in the *Morte Darthur*'. *Studies in Philology* 89.3 (1992): 350–66.
Wright, Thomas L. '"The Tale of King Arthur": Beginnings and Foreshadowings'. *Malory's Originality: A Critical Study of Le Morte Darthur*. Ed. R. M. Lumiansky. Baltimore: Johns Hopkins Press, 1964. 9–66.
Yeats-Edwards, Paul. 'The Winchester Malory Manuscript: An Attempted History'. *The Malory Debate: Essays on the Texts of Le Morte Darthur*. Ed. Bonnie Wheeler, Robert L. Kindrick and Michael N. Salda. Cambridge: D. S. Brewer, 2000. 367–89.

Index

The index itemizes the main topics and threads of my argument, including characters, but does not reference subjects or persons mentioned only in passing. In indexing the names and work of other scholars I have (for reasons of space) only listed those cited directly in the text, not any footnote references. Indexed Plate numbers appear in bold type and denote both the manuscript images and their captions.

Achilles 166, 173, 180, 184, 201–2, 206
Aetiology 202
Affect 192
Archibald, Elizabeth 154, 158, 178, 192–93
Armstrong, Dorsey 115
Ascham, Roger 2, 194
Astley, John 69, 74
Atkinson, Stephen C. B. 137, 170, 172–73
Auchinleck MS *see* Manuscripts, *under* Edinburgh
authorship debate (of *Morte Darthur*) 15–16, 23, 47 n. 83, 64–68, 200

Batt, Catherine 143, 172, 174, 176–77, 179, 200
Benson, C. David 52, 157, 177
Benson, Larry D. 113, 115, 130, 134, 146, 177, 204
Besserman, Lawrence 115, 117, 119
Bibles, decoration in 32, 41, 51, 53, 167, 210
  Bibles moralise 31
  Great Bible, the 32, 51, 52–3
  rubrication in 30, 31, 41, 51, 167–8, 210
Blake, N. F. 64, 72, 76, 112, 123
Boethius 194–5
Boffey, Julia 62
Bohun Psalter 62–3, 83
Boke of St Albans 75–6
book production and trade, early 4, 62–4, 66–7, 75–6, 91
breviaries 31, 167
Brewer, D. S., also Derek 140, 177–78, 195, 203
Brut 18, 32–4, 35, 36, 41, 46, 51, 53, 83, 84, 202
  Arthur story in 33
  Malory's knowledge of 33
  manuscript rubrication of 32–34, **Plates V–VII**, 53, 72, 84, 210

see also Chronicles of England
Bühler, Curt F. 62, 76
Burgundy 66–7
Busby, Keith 29

Caxton, William 2–11, 16–18, 20–21, 23–24, 33, 43, 57, 62, 64, 66–73 *et passim*
  the Caxton 2–3, 5–10, 16–21, 23–25, 57, 64, 71–80, 84–5 *et passim*
  copy-text for the *Morte* 8–10, 23–4, 57, 64, 69–70, 72–3, 75–81, 84, 91, 92, 110
  correlations in layout between the Caxton and Winchester 76–81, 84, 85, 170–71, 211
  Golden Legend 75
  patrons 64, 67, 68, 71, 176
  Prologue to the *Morte Darthur* 64, 122, 199–200
  Recueil des histoires de Troie 75
  Table of Contents for the *Morte Darthur* 30, 76, 122
  Use of colour 75–6
  Uses Winchester as correction copy 10, 70, 75, 76–7
Chambers, E. K. 90
Chase, Carol J. 42
Chaucer, Geoffrey 3, 14–15, 61, 63, 72, 105, 112, 179–80, 194–5, 197, 207, 214
  Canterbury Tales manuscripts of 32, 49–51, 52, 53, 63, 214
  Squire's Tale 180
  'The Retraction' 51 n. 97, 105
Cherewatuk, Karen 69, 89, 106, 118, 131, 144, 175, 186, 190, 199, 212
chivalry 1, 29, 31, 36, 64, 69, 105–23, 130–46, 163–64, 167–71, 175–81, 191–214, *see also* knighthood
Chrétien de Troyes 48, 197
  Chevalier de la Charrete 197

Chevalier au lion 48
Chronicle manuscripts *see Brut* and Hardyng
Chronicles of England 18, 33, 76
coloured incunables 75–6
Compilatio 5 n. 15
Coombe Abbey 117, 124, 195
Cooper, Helen 9–12, 14, 17, 26, 60–61, 73, 74, 80, 82–84, 88–9, 91, 111, 119–20, 121–22, 128, 161, 163–67, 177, 183–84, 213
Crofts, Thomas H. 10, 25, 26, 85, 167, 183–84, 198, 206

de Worde, Wynkyn 2–3, 23–24
Degrevant 74
Doyle, A. I. 3, 63, 74, 91, 211
Driver, Martha W. 202
Duffy, Eamon 90, 123, 174, 186
Dutch Arthuriana 173

Earl of Tolous 74
Eckhardt, Caroline D. 61
Eddy, Nicole 84–5, 88, 90, 128, 161
Edward IV 41, 64, 66, 68, 71, 205
Edwards, A. S. G. 3, 38, 40
Edwards, Elizabeth 162, 204
Emotion 84, 126–7, 144–5, 150, 153–56, 179–80, 183, 185, 192, 194–5, 198, 200–01
   See also Malory, *Morte Darthur*, under Pathos
Estoire del Saint Graal 41, 47, 69
Evans, Murray J. 10–14, 31–32, 201
Exeter Arthurian Congress 7, 8 n. 27
Eye-skip errors 9 n. 35, 16, 74 n. 88, 91, 98–103

Field, P. J. C. 6–9, 10, 12–14, 15, 16, 17, 18, 21, 24, 34, 54, 59, 65, 67–70, 73, 75, 77, 79, 81, 82–85, 88, 92, 107, 120, 123–24, 132, 134–35, 150, 163–64, 171, 188, 200, 203–04

Geoffrey of Monmouth 144 n. 137, 202, 209
Gower, John 72
Generides 26–28, **Plates II–IV**, 37, 53, 63, 180 n. 89, 210–11
Gillespie, Alexandra 3, 4
Greyfriars Abbey and Church 66–7
Griffith, Richard R. 65, 72
Grimm, Kevin T. 10, 11, 163
Guerin, Wilfred L. 203

Hanks, D. Thomas 12, 105, 110, 114–16, 173, 204

Hardyng, John, *Chronicle* (both versions) 34–41, 42, 46, 212
   manuscript layout 35–41, **Plates VIII–XI**, 45, 53, 210
   as source for Malory 34–36, 41, 53
Hector of Troy 202, 206
Helen of Troy 201–2
Hellinga, Lotte 4, 9, 57
Henry IV 51
Henry V 205, 213
Henry VI 205
Hicks, Edward 65–6, 117
history of the book 3–4
Hodges, Kenneth 116, 149
Holbrook, Sue Ellen 84, 173–4
Homer, *Iliad* 173, 184, 190, 195, 201–02, 206, 212
Homoeoteleuton 74 and n. 88, 91
Howard, Donald R. 160, 211
Huot, Sylvia 52, 167
Hynes-Berry, Mary 120, 130, 133–34, 137

Ihle, Sandra Ness 113, 136, 150–51
Isumbras 74

Johnston, Michael 63–4

Kaeuper, Richard W. 31
Kaufman, Amy S. 111, 155
Kato, Takako 17, 53, 73, 79–80
Keen, Maurice 31, 116 n. 39
Kelliher, Hilton 56, 57, 61, 64, 69, 81–82, 166
Kelly, Robert L. 170, 204
Kennedy, Edward Donald 18–19, 33, 34–5, 112
Ker, N. R. 25, 57, 61, 82
knighthood 64, 69, 87, 105, 175–76, 180, 191–93, 199, 212, 213
   see also chivalry *and* Malory, *Morte Darthur*, celebrates chivalry

Lambert, Mark 171, 178, 203, 209
Lancelot, prose 34, 41, 43, 46–47
Lancelot-Graal 41–3, 114, 140
   manuscript layout of **Plate XII**, 42–43, 44, 47–8, 58
   manuscripts 41–3, 46–7
   as source for Malory 41, 177
Leitch, Megan G. 174–5
Lewis, C. S. 7, 85 n. 123, 113, 135, 137, 171–73
Lupack, Alan 162
Lydgate's *Troy Book* 26, 28, 177, 202
Lynch, Andrew 26, 148, 164–65, 167, 206, 208–09

INDEX

Mahoney, Dhira 116, 196
Malory, Sir Thomas
  artistry 3, 19, 35, 53–5, 60–61, 81, 85, 88, 91–2, 111–12, 124–27, 141, 154, 162–63, 165–8, 171–2, 175, 181–2, 196–8, 207, 210, 214
  biographical details 2, 15–16, 57, 64–71, 91 n. 143, Appendix I: 94, Appendix II: 97, 107, 111–12, 117, 124, 195, 200, 212
  concern with character 35, 54–5, 61, 86–8, 107–09, 112, 117, 122, 125–27, 129, 139–40, 149–50, 152, 155, 158, 159–60, 168, 171–2, 175, 188, 191, 194, 197–8
  family 64, 70–1, 117
  French book of see under Malory, sources
  identity see under authorship debate
  influence on later story-tellers 2
  library for sources 53, 64–69
  narrative style 54–5, 150, 192–3, 200–1, 208
  originality 35, 54, 61, 88, 92, 107 n. 6, 121–2, 126–7, 130–1, 150–1, 153, 156, 162, 165, 171–2, 181–2, 184, 186–7, 191–2, 197, 200–06, 208 n. 43,
  patron 4, 53, 64, 68–72
  responsible for Winchester's layout 1, 5, 22, 31, 53–92, *et passim*
  sources 41, 53, 64–5, 89–90, 114, 116, 126–27, 130, 134–36, 148, 150–54, 162–63, 181–2, 187, 191, 196–7, 204, 205, 208
  Weddynge of Sir Gawen and Dame Ragnelle and 32
  writing of Morte Darthur 2, 4, 7–8, 14–20, 43, 54–55, 60–61, 64–6, 72–73, 91, 134, 159, 181–2

  Morte Darthur passim especially 105–98, 203–14
    Arthur 55, 59, 108, 112, 115, 118–25, 141–42, 149–50, 159–60, 165–66, 170, 172, 181–2, 187–8, 196–209
      Death of 106, 155, 157–58, 165, 181–87, 193, 197, 204–09
      Final battle with Mordred 182–4, 187
      Kingship 11, 34–41, 86, 118–19, 139, 157–58, 165, 187, 196–7, 207–8
      Marginalia 86, 87, 158, **Plate XIV**, 165–6
      Reaction to Grail Quest 142, 149–50
      Wedding 159
      Victories 21, 59–60, 84, 86, 89, 108, 122, 125, 141, 158, 165–6, 196, 198
    'Arthur and Lucius' see under Malory, Morte Darthur, 'King Arthur and the Emperor Lucius'
    Balyn 19–20, 85–6, 105–06, 139, 145, 162–63, 212
      Marginalia 85–6
    Bedwere 106, 122, 124–25, 157, 182–83, 208
    Blaise 89, 159
    'Book of Sir Launcelot and Queen Guinevere' see under Malory, Morte Darthur, 'Sir Launcelot and Queen Guenivere'
    'Book of Sir Tristram de Lyones' see under Malory, Morte Darthur, 'Sir Tristram de Lyones'
    Bors 106, 109, 134–37, 142–3, 157, 187–8, 191
      Marginalia 85, 130, 187–8
    Camelot Appendix I:93, 137, 141, 143, 147, 149–50, 152, 173
    celebrates chivalry 29–30, 105, 114–18, 122, 151, 159, 168, 175, 178–9, 190–2, 195–6, 209
    Columbe 85, 161–2, 166
    Corbynic, Corbyn, Corbin 117, 120, 131, 136–7, 147
    early readers 1–4, 14, 43, 81–3, 87–8, 107–08, 111
    Ector 130, 191–2
    Elayne of Ascolat 106, 144, 152–53, 175
    Elayne of Corbyn 100, 131, 143–45
    Excalybur 55, 59, Appendix I:94, 143, 166
    failure of chivalry in 29, 113–18, 137, 144, 172–3, 175
    feast days in 123
    Fellowship 31, 88, 105, 108, 112–13, 118, 120–25, 133–34, 136–44, 148–208
    fighting 60, 84, 89, Appendix II: 93, 95 and 97, 109, 128, 141, 158, 162, 164–5, 169–71, 173, 176–7, 181–84, 188, 192, 200, 206, 211
    fighters who heal 173–4, 180, 204
    Galahad 90, 106, 132–33, 136, 143–44, 149, 158–9, 196
      Marginalia 85, 87, 145, 169
    Galantyne Appendix I:94 and 98,
    Gareth 84–6, 125–26, 141, 144, 145, 164, 192, 196–7, 212
      Marginalia 86,
    Gawayne 20, 89, 130–31, 139, 141–42, 144, 149, 159, 187

Death of 139–40, 155, 157, 181–2, 187, 192, 197, 209
  Feud with Launcelot 139
  Friendship with Launcelot 86, 157, 181
  Marginalia 55, 86, 87, 130, 169, 181–2, 187, 197
genre 19–20
Giant of St Michael's Mount 122–25, 152–53
Grail 85, 90, 106, 117, 120, 142–4, 150–51
  Marginalia 85, 128–29, 134,
  Rubrication inconsistencies: see Appendix I and II; 142
Grail Quest 89, 115, 120, 128, 130–31, 133–37, 140, 146–50, 170, 212
  Marginalia 130
  See also Malory, Morte Darthur, 'The Sankgreal'
Great Tournament episode 163–64, 170
Gwenyvere 13, 54, 86, 87, 128, 129, 131, 133–34, 141, 143–45, 151–52, 175, 187–90, 212
  Death of 29, 106, 153–54, 184–7, 190–1, 197, 203–4, 208–9
  Final meeting with Launcelot 55, 153–57, 208
  Reaction to Grail Quest 149–50
  Wedding 159
Harleuse 85, 163
Healing of Urry (episode) 116, 142, 169, 170, 171–80, 212–13
  Catalogue 127, 142, **Plates XV–XVI**, 169, 171, 173, 178, 180–81, 192
Isode 87, 91, 126–7, 131, 141, 144–5, 156, 188, 212
  Rubrication errors with her name Appendix II: 99–100, 103
Joyous Garde 127, 156, 190
Kay 124–25, 141
'King Arthur and the Emperor Lucius' 108, 122–25, 141, 169
  Revision controversy see under Malory, Morte Darthur, Roman War, debate
'King Uther and King Arthur' 59, 107, 118–22
Knight of the Cart episode 131, 163–4, 189–90, 212–13
Knighthood in 105, 109, 141–42, 159–98
  See also celebrates chivalry
Lady of the Lake 85, 139
Lamorak 129, 141
Launcelot 19–20, 54, 87, 115, 141–42, 163–4, 170, 173–4, 177–8, 187–92, 196, 201–2, 212

Death of 106, 130, 132, 154, 186–7, 190–92, 197, 199, 203–4, 209
Ector's threnody for 191–2
Fathering of Galahad 143–5
Final meeting with Gwenyvere 55, 153–57, 208
Friendship with Arthur and Gawayne 86, 157–58, 181–2
Grail adventures 90, 130–40
Marginalia 55, 86, 87, 90, 109, 130, 181, 187–9
Tears 172–3, 179–81, 187
Launceor 85, 161–2
Love 54, 86–7, 105, 112, 121, 124, 126, 132, 141–45, 151–3, 163–4, 181, 185–93, 201, 203–4
Lott 86, 87, 89, 158, 165–66
Lucius, Emperor of Rome 86, 87
Lyonesse 125–26, 144, 145, 212
Lyonett 125–26, 144
Mador 54, 187
manuscript, see under Winchester
Marhalte (Marhaus) 87, 89, 159
Mark, King 126, 127, 161
May Day Slaughter 119–20
May Passage 163–64, 203
Mellyagaunt 189
Melyas 109
Memorialization in 89–90, 140, 143, 147, 151, 158–214
  see also Winchester, under memorializing function of
Merlin 59–61, 88–89, 92, 95–6, 118–19, 129, 147, 159, 162–63, 165–66, 207–10
  abbreviated name 44, 59–61, 88–9, 111–12
monuments in 54, 92, 116, 147, 151, 158–63, 165–9, 186, 191, 193, 195, 198, 203, 204–9, 212
Mordred 86, 182–4, 187, 203, 206
Morgawse 118–20, 128, 129, 141
'Morte Arthur' 109–11, 153–58, 171, 181–7, 203–9, 212
'Most Piteous Tale of the Morte Arthur saunz Guerdon' see under Malory, Morte Darthur, 'Morte Arthur'
narrative divisions in 11–15, **Plate I**, 56–8, 76–81, 105, 110, **Plate XIII**, 163–64
'Noble Tale of Sir Launcelot du Lake' see under Malory, Morte Darthur, 'Sir Launcelot du Lake'
Palomydes 131, 141
Pathos 117, 127, 150, 154, 169, 193, 197–8, 201, 204, 209

INDEX

Patryse 54, 163, 187, 212
Pellynore 89, 159
Pentecostal Oath *see under* Malory, *Morte Darthur*, Round Table
Percyval 90, 106, 136–37, 143, 147, 180, 207
Percyval's Sister 146–48
   Marginalium 147–48
Peryne 85, 163
Poisoned Apple episode 54, 116, 187–8
Prayer in 105–11, 173–4, 179, 185–6, 190, 193, 208
print history 23–4
Roman War, debate over revisions to 15–21, 25, 112, 122–24
Rome 34, 38, 60, Appendix II:97, 108, 111
Round Table 53–4, 85, Appendix II: 97, 110, 118, 120–22, 129, 139, 151, 159–60, 168, 172, 178, 188, 190, 192, 196–8, 207, 213
   Oath 121–22, 157, 159, 188; *see also* Malory, *Morte Darthur* Fellowship
Salisbury 55, 59, Appendix I:93, 143
Salisbury Plain Appendix II:104, 141, 155, 158, 165, 182, 206
'The Sankgreal' 105, 108, 109–11, 113–16, 118, 120–21, 127–52, 168–70, 172, 212
   Dual values in 132, 136, 140, 143, 212
Sarras 55, 59, Appendix I:93, 137, 143, 147
'Sir Gareth of Orkney' 86, 107, 126
'Sir Launcelot and Queen Guenivere' 142, 151–53, 170–71, 187–90, 212
'Sir Launcelot du Lake' 131, 140–41
'Sir Tristram de Lyones' [both books] 86–7, 90–91, 106–08, 126–27, 136, 141, 151
Supernatural in 128–29
Swords *see* weapons
'Tale of Balyn' 85
   Layout of 11–14, 56, 78, 85–6
'Tale of King Arthur' *see under* Malory, *Morte Darthur*, 'King Uther and King Arthur'
'Tale of King Arthur and the Emperor Lucius' *see under* Malory, *Morte Darthur*, 'King Arthur and the Emperor Lucius'
'Tale of Lancelot' *see under* Malory, *Morte Darthur*, 'Sir Launcelot du Lake'
'Tale of the Noble King Arthur that was Emperor Himself through Dignity of His Hands' *see under* Malory, *Morte Darthur*, 'King Arthur and the Emperor Lucius'
'Tale of the Sankgreal briefly drawn out of French' *see under* Malory, *Morte Darthur*, 'The Sankgreal'
'Tale of Sir Gareth of Orkney that was called Bewmaynes' *see under* Malory, *Morte Darthur*, 'Sir Gareth of Orkney'
textual debate 5–21, 122–24
titles 87–8, 118, 122, 193
Torre 89, 159
Treason 54, 127, 139, 187–9, 213
trial by combat in 54, 187, 189–90, 212
Trystram 86–7, 90–1, 107–09, 126–27, 141, 144, 156, 192, 196, 212
   Death of 126–7, 192, 197
   and hunting terms 176
   Marginalia 86–7, 90–1
Urry 176–80
   see also Malory, *Morte Darthur*, Healing of Urry
Uwayne 159, 169
Weapons 55, 84, 86, 87, Appendix I:94, Appendix II: 97 and 98, 106, 128, 129, 139, 141, 143 n. 132, 145, 147, 163, 165, 168–9, 175, 180, 183, 187, 191, 206, 212
'Weddyng of Kyng Arthur'
   Layout of 10–13
Winchester MS of *see under* Winchester
Women's centrality in 146–47
Worshyp 19, 90, 105, 108–09, 116, 132, 134, 141–44, 148–50, 164–6, 170, 175, 177–8, 188, 193–5, 201, 211–14
Written records in 89–90, 131, 159–63, 165, 168–9, 207–8
Ywayne 89

Manly and Rickert 32 n. 34, 50
Mann, Jill 87, 136, 150, 180, 193–4, 214
Manuscript-print crossover 2–4, 49 n. 92, 62, 75–6
Manuscript study 2–4, 210
Manuscripts
   Bourg-en-Bresse
      MS Médiathèque Vailland 55 42, 47
   Cambridge, MA
      Harvard University MS Eng 1054 40
   Cambridge, UK
      Cambridge University Library Additional MS 7071 43–46, 47–8, 210
      Cambridge University Library MS Dd.4.24 214

INDEX

Cambridge University Library MS
  Gg.4.27 214
Cambridge University Library MS
  Ff.1.6 (Findern) 63–4
Cambridge University Library MS
  Ii.3.26 50, 214
Fitzwilliam Museum MS McClean
  181 49–50
Trinity College MS O.5.2 28
Trinity College MS R.3.3 49–50
Trinity College MS R.3.15 49, 51
  Foliation of 51 n. 97
Edinburgh
  National Library of Scotland,
    Advocates 19.2.1
    (Auchinleck) 31–32, 49
Lincoln
  Lincoln Cathedral Library MS 91
    (Thornton) 48–49, 63–64, 69 n.
    66, 74
London, British Library
  Additional MS 5474 41
  Additional MS 38117 (Huth) 44
  Additional MS 59678
    (Winchester) 1–9, 21, **Plates I,
    XIII–XVI**, *et passim*
  Additional MS 10292–94 42, **Plate XII**,
    135
  Additional MS 17443 135
  Additional MS 23929 41 n. 66
  Cotton MS Caligula A.ix 52 n. 101
  Cotton MS Otho C.xiii (Otho
    Laȝamon) 38, 39 n. 60
  Egerton MS 989 41 n. 67
  Egerton MS 1992 36 n. 49, 39–40
  Egerton MS 3277 (Bohun
    Psalter) 62–3
  Harley MS 49 41 n. 66
  Harley MS 53 33
  Harley MS 661 38, 40
  Harley MS 1896 52 n. 99
  Harley MS 2252 32, 48, 69 n. 66
  Harley MS 6342 47
  Lansdowne MS 204 36–40, 45, 120 n.
    57, **Plates VIII–X**
    faulty foliation of 36 n. 51
  Lansdowne MS 285 74
  Royal MS 1.E.ix 51
  Royal MS 14.E.iii 47, 69, 135
  Royal MS 18.C.ii 50
  Royal MS 18.C.xxvi 52 n. 99
  Royal MS 18.D.ii 177
  Royal MS 19.B.vii 43
  Royal MS 19.C.xiii 135
  Royal MS 20.A.ii 34
  Royal MS 20.C.vi 46, 135
  Royal MS 20.D.ii 41 n. 67
  Royal MS 20.D.iv 47
  Sloane MS 1686 49–50
New Haven
  Yale University Beinecke MS 229 (Yale
    229) 135
New Jersey,
  Princeton, University Library, MS
    Taylor 9 (Ireland) 63
New York,
  Pierpont Morgan Library MS 775 74
  Pierpont Morgan Library MS B.5 36
    n. 49, 40
  Pierpont Morgan Library MS M.41 41
  Pierpont Morgan Library MS
    M.249 49–50
  Pierpont Morgan Library MS
    M.372 52
  Pierpont Morgan Library MS
    M.503 52
  Pierpont Morgan Library MSS M.805,
    M.806, M.807 43, 44 n. 76
  Pierpont Morgan Library MS
    M.876 26–28, **Plates II–IV**, 37, 53,
    202 n. 14, 210
Oxford,
  Bodleian Library MS 414 50 n. 95
  Bodleian Library MS Arch Selden
    B.10 38–39, **Plate XI**
  Bodleian Library MS Ashmole
    34 38–40
  Bodleian Library MS Bodley 840 33,
    Plate VI
  Bodleian Library MS Douce 189 41 n.
    67, 43
  Bodleian Library MS Douce 199 44
    n. 76
  Bodleian Library MS Douce 345 36 n.
    49, 38–40
  Bodleian Library MS Laud Miscellany
    550 33, **Plate VII**
  Bodleian Library MS Lyell 34 33
  Bodleian Library MS Rawlinson
    C.86 32 n. 36
  Corpus Christi College MS 201 52
  Jesus College MS 29 52 n. 101
  Jesus College MS 111 (Red Book of
    Hergest) 48, 167
Paris,
  Bibliothèque nationale de France, fr.
    1433 48
  Bibliothèque nationale de France, fr.
    16999 47
Margaret of York 66–7
Matthews, William 5–8, 10, 15–21, 24, 65–6,
  68, 75, 78, 79, 160, 173 n. 56

INDEX 241

Meale, Carol M. 11–12, 14, 26–28, 58, 68–70, 78, 82, 160, 163–64, 166–67, 210, 213
Merchant Adventurers 66
Middleton, Roger 69
Moorman, Charles 8, 18–19, 24, 114, 117, 134–36, 137–40, 144, 150–51, 158 n. 169
Mort le roi Artu 41, 43, 46, 47, 69, 181–2, 183, 185, 191, 208
Morte Darthur see under Malory, Sir Thomas
Morte Arthur, stanzaic 32, 35, 154, 181–2, 185, 190–1, 208
    manuscript layout of 32, 48–9
Morte Arthure, alliterative 17–18, 19–21, 35, 124, 173, 191, 213
    manuscript layout of 48–9

names and naming 88, 90, 209
    abbreviated 44–6
Neville, Richard, Earl of Warwick 70–1
Newgate Prison 16
Newman, Barbara 195, 204
Norris, Ralph 15 n. 58, 34

Oakeshott, Walter F. 24
ordinatio 5 n. 15, 20–2, 27–8, 31, 36–8, 40, 52–3, 63, 72–4, 81, 163
Owein 48

Parkes, M. B. 3, 5n15, 63, 74, 91, 210, 211
Passaro, Jonathan 43–6, 48
Paston, John 69, 74
Paternoster Row 66–7
Pearsall, Derek 3
Piers Plowman 52, 167
Phillips, Noelle 52
Post-Vulgate Cycle *see Roman du Graal*
Print culture 2–4

Queste del Saint Graal 34, **Plate XII**, 41, 46, 47, 69, 120, 130, 132–33, 135–36, 140, 142, 148, 150–51

Radulescu, Raluca L. 116, 130, 133, 137, 170, 172–73
Reiss, Edmund 114–15, 119
Religious attitudes 105–58
Rhonabwy, Dream of 52, 167
Richmond, Colin 123–24
Riddy, Felicity 205, 213
Robertson, D. W., Jr 194–5
Roland, Meg 17
Rolle, Richard 51
Roman de la Rose, rubrication in 52, 167
Roman du Graal 43, 114

manuscript layout in 43–6
manuscripts 43
romance (genre), manuscript layout 13–5, 26–32, 41–9, 53, 168, 210–1, 213
Rubrication, general 25–26, 30–53
    as dialogue markers 52, 167
    distinction between red letters and headings 31
    etymology 30
    in Bibles *see under* Bibles
    in Breviaries 31, 167
    in Calendars 31
    in drama 25
    in liturgical texts 25, 31, 51, 53
    in miniature captions 27–8, **Plates III, XII**, 41–4, 52
    in music 167
    in Winchester MS *see under* Winchester
    indexing function of 34, 36, 50–1, 52 n. 103, 63, 83–5
Rumble, Thomas C. 119, 126–27

Sandler, Lucy Freeman 83
Saunders, Corinne 114
Saul, Nigel 1, 64, 167, 175–76, 199
Scodel, Ruth 195, 212
Scribal copying practice 62–4, 73–4, 80, 91–2
Shaw, Sally 5, 7, 16, 112, 122–3, 152
Siege of Thebes 28
Suite du Merlin, Post-Vulgate 43–44, 119–20, 196
    manuscripts of 43–46, 47–8, 53, 210
Suite du Merlin, Vulgate 18, 41, 43, 196
Sutton, Anne F 16, 66–7

Thornton manuscript *see* Manuscripts, *under* Lincoln
Thornton, Robert 74
Tower of London 16, 64, 67–8
Tragic flaw 137–39
Tristan, prose 41
    manuscript layout of 41, 43, 126
    verse tradition of 126
Tucker, P. E. 130, 137, 172
Twomey, Michael W. 192

Vinaver, Eugène 5–17, 24, 29, 57, 73, 112, 113, 126–27, 130, 134–36, 140, 150, 158 n. 169, 163–64, 177, 181–82, 190, 196–97, 205, 213
Virgil 202
Vulgate Cycle *see Lancelot-Graal*

Wade, James 88, 128, 161, 166
Wars of the Roses 2, 71, 174–75, 205, 212, 213

literature of 174–75
Weddynge of Sir Gawen and Dame Ragnell 32
Whiting, B. J. 151
Whitman, Jon 201
Wilson, Robert H. 14, 35, 88, 171, 180, 197
Winchester manuscript 1–9, 21–2, 23–6,
　Plates I, XIII–XVI, *et passim*
　annotations (non-scribal) 58, 81–2
　blank pages 11–13, 56, 91–2
　corrections in 56, 58, 82
　date 56, 57, 70
　decorated initials 56, 57–8, 77–81, 91–2
　discovery 2, 5, 24
　explicits xiv, 10–14, 20, **Plate I**, 56–7, 58,
　　70, 77–8, 105, 107–12, 121–22, **Plate
　　XIII**, 164, 178, 193, 198, 200
　incipits **Plate I**, 56–7, 107–8, 109–10, 122,
　　Plate XIII, 178
　maniculae 53, 58, 61, 81, 82, 166
　marginalia 20, 22, 29–30, 53, 55, 58, 61,
　　73, 78–9, 81–8, 90, 128, 170, 181–8
　　as cross-referencing system 90
　　derive from Malory 55–6, 61, 79, 81,
　　　83–5, 87–8, 91
　　indexical function 161, 203
　　highlight character or deed 85–8, 90,
　　　128, 130, 159–66, 181, 195, 197, 203
　　thematic function 22, 83–8, 91, 105,
　　　128, 158–66, 160, 181, 195, 203
　memorializing function of 1, 21–2, 29–30,
　　54, 85, 92, 112, 115, 117, 143, 158–63,
　　et passim
　missing folios 56, 165, 181, 185 n. 100
　ordinatio passim, especially 21–2, 27,
　　29–31, 35–6, 54–104, 110–12, 153,
　　158, 167, 176, 191
　printer's ink on 9, 57, 62, 70, 75
　relation to exemplar 53, 60–1, 74–5,
　　79–82, 88

rubrication xiv, 1, 4, 20, 22, 25–30, *et
　passim*
　derived from Malory *passim*
　as emphasis on character 29, 31, 55,
　　59–61 *et passim*
　errors in pattern 55, 58–60, 80, 91–2,
　　Appendix II, 183
　lack of rubrication in divine
　　names 90, Appendix I: 92–3,
　　Appendix II: 97, 106–09, 125, 134,
　　153, 155, 169, 177–8, 181–3, 189
　method of execution 27, 53, 58–61,
　　72–5, 91–2
　place names 25, 28, 51, 55, 58–9,
　　Appendix I, Appendix II, 106
　secular emphasis 90, 105–88
　thematic function 1, 20, 22, 29, 31, 40,
　　61–2, 72, 83–8, 90–1 *et passim*
　as visual reading aid 26, 160–1, 168
　what is and is not rubricated 55–104,
　　106
　scribes 31, 53, 56, 60, 62–4, 72, 74–5, 80–2,
　　91–2, Appendix I and II, 128–9,
　　161, 166, 183, 188
　stemma 2, 8–10, 73, 84
　textual divisions *see Morte Darthur*
　　narrative divisions, *under* Malory
　watermarks 15, 57, 62, 75, 82
　uniqueness of rubrication 23–53, 55,
　　62–4, 72, 76, 81, 91, 105, 167–8, 210–1
Withrington, John 20–1, 165, 204, 207
Wydeville (or Woodville), Sir Anthony,
　　Lord Scales and second Earl
　　Rivers 64–65, 68–72, 176
Wydeville (or Woodville), Elizabeth,
　　Queen of England 70–1
Wydeville (or Woodville), Jacquetta,
　　Duchess of Bedford and Countess
　　Rivers 65, 68, 70

Addenda to the Paperback Edition

ADDENDA TO APPENDIX I (pp. 92–4):
CLASSIFICATIONS OF RUBRICATION

Place Names: although place names are certainly rubricated far less ubiquitously than are characters' names, there is comparatively more rubrication of places in the Roman War story in Tale II (fols 71^r–96^r) than elsewhere in W. Although the greater rubrication of place in the Roman War is misleading in comparison to the manuscript-text as a whole, the increased frequency does highlight both the extent of Rome's threat and Arthur's victory.

Other types of rubrication

Creyme is rubricated (88^v) in Arthur's boast before Metz that 'there shall never harlot have happe, by the helpe of oure Lord, to kylle a crowned kynge that with **creyme** is anoynted.' Again, the effect of the unusual rubrication is to valorize Arthur.

There is a faulty rubricated episode transition with **'Here levith the tale of Sir Launcelot and spekith of Sir** Launcelot**'** (376^r). This transition is unusual in two ways. First, frequently in such rubricated phrases the scribes will print character names in brown: see, e.g., 364^v. Second, the struck-out **Launcelot**, which occurs in abbreviated form at the end of the manuscript line, is obviously an error for 'Gawayne' but the scribes did not notice the mistake. The negation seems to be that of a later reader. See also Field, Commentary on 722.22–3.

ADDENDA TO APPENDIX II (PP. 94–104):
RUBRICATION ERRORS

Scribe A
–12^v (seven lines from the bottom) has another Kay error: failure to rubricate his name.
–15^v (at four lines from the bottom) has a failure to rubricate 'Merlyon' (in full).
–20^v (at line 11) also has a failure to rubricate an abbreviated 'M'.
–26^v also has a failure to rubricate a full 'Merlion' during his prophecy of Launcelot and Trystram's battle. The failure could be due to the difficulty caused by the switching back and forth between abbreviated and non-abbreviated Merlins, a difficulty exacerbated here by the scribe's attempt to fit the condensed name – 'Mlion' – in at the very end of a line (line 8).

–27ʳ has another failure to rubricate a full 'Merlion' when he is advising Balyn and Balan. The failure could again be due to the difficulty caused by the switching back and forth between abbreviated and non-abbreviated Merlins.

–28ʳ has a failure to rubricate 'Lotte' in the 'merveylous' fighting leading up to his death.

–35ᵛ has another failure to rubricate a full 'Merlion' when he finds the fifty knights necessary to fill the Round Table at Arthur and Gwenyvere's wedding. The explanation for the failure is likely the same as before: the difficulty of tracking Merlin's movements (plus, as always, the general difficulty of constantly switching pens and inks to implement the rubrication pattern).

Scribe B

–91ᵛ has a failure to rubricate the very minor character 'Florydas'.

Scribe A

–215ʳ has a failure to rubricate one appearance of 'Carados'.

–216ʳ has two instances of the relatively common failure to rubricate 'La Beall Isode'.

–217ʳ also has a failure to rubricate 'Brangwayne'.

–217ᵛ has a failure to rubricate one appearance of 'Trystram'.

–228ᵛ has a failure to rubricate 'Arthure' at the start of line 22, though his name is rubricated at the end of the same line.

–233ʳ has three instances of a failure to rubricate 'Governayle'.

–355ᵛ has a slight rubrication hangover at line 3, where the opening 's' of '**Bagdemagus s**quire' is red.

–377ʳ witnesses a failure to rubricate one appearance of 'Ector'.

–378ᵛ likewise sees a failure to rubricate one appearance of 'Ector'.

–475ʳ has a failure to rubricate one appearance of 'Gwenyvere'.

ARTHURIAN STUDIES

I ASPECTS OF MALORY, *edited by Toshiyuki Takamiya and Derek Brewer*

II THE ALLITERATIVE *MORTE ARTHURE*: A Reassessment of the Poem, *edited by Karl Heinz Göller*

III THE ARTHURIAN BIBLIOGRAPHY, I: Author Listing, *edited by C. E. Pickford and R. W. Last*

IV THE CHARACTER OF KING ARTHUR IN MEDIEVAL LITERATURE, *Rosemary Morris*

V PERCEVAL: The Story of the Grail, by Chrétien de Troyes, *translated by Nigel Bryant*

VI THE ARTHURIAN BIBLIOGRAPHY, II: Subject Index, *edited by C. E. Pickford and R. W. Last*

VII THE LEGEND OF ARTHUR IN THE MIDDLE AGES, *edited by P. B. Grout, R. A. Lodge, C. E. Pickford and E. K. C. Varty*

VIII THE ROMANCE OF YDER, *edited and translated by Alison Adams*

IX THE RETURN OF KING ARTHUR, *Beverly Taylor and Elisabeth Brewer*

X ARTHUR'S KINGDOM OF ADVENTURE: The World of Malory's *Morte Darthur*, *Muriel Whitaker*

XI KNIGHTHOOD IN THE *MORTE DARTHUR*, *Beverly Kennedy*

XII LE ROMAN DE TRISTAN EN PROSE, tome I, *edited by Renée L. Curtis*

XIII LE ROMAN DE TRISTAN EN PROSE, tome II, *edited by Renée L. Curtis*

XIV LE ROMAN DE TRISTAN EN PROSE, tome III, *edited by Renée L. Curtis*

XV LOVE'S MASKS: Identity, Intertextuality, and Meaning in the Old French Tristan Poems, *Merritt R. Blakeslee*

XVI THE CHANGING FACE OF ARTHURIAN ROMANCE: Essays on Arthurian Prose Romances in memory of Cedric E. Pickford, *edited by Alison Adams, Armel H. Diverres, Karen Stern and Kenneth Varty*

XVII REWARDS AND PUNISHMENTS IN THE ARTHURIAN ROMANCES AND LYRIC POETRY OF MEDIEVAL FRANCE: Essays presented to Kenneth Varty on the occasion of his sixtieth birthday, *edited by Peter V. Davies and Angus J. Kennedy*

XVIII CEI AND THE ARTHURIAN LEGEND, *Linda Gowans*

XIX LA3AMON'S *BRUT*: The Poem and its Sources, *Françoise H. M. Le Saux*

XX READING THE *MORTE DARTHUR*, *Terence McCarthy*, reprinted as *AN INTRODUCTION TO MALORY*

XXI CAMELOT REGAINED: The Arthurian Revival and Tennyson, 1800–1849, *Roger Simpson*

XXII THE LEGENDS OF KING ARTHUR IN ART, *Muriel Whitaker*

XXIII GOTTFRIED VON STRASSBURG AND THE MEDIEVAL TRISTAN LEGEND: Papers from an Anglo-North American symposium, *edited with an introduction by Adrian Stevens and Roy Wisbey*

XXIV ARTHURIAN POETS: CHARLES WILLIAMS, *edited and introduced by David Llewellyn Dodds*

XXV AN INDEX OF THEMES AND MOTIFS IN TWELFTH-CENTURY FRENCH ARTHURIAN POETRY, *E. H. Ruck*

XXVI CHRÉTIEN DE TROYES AND THE GERMAN MIDDLE AGES: Papers from an international symposium, *edited with an introduction by Martin H. Jones and Roy Wisbey*

XXVII SIR GAWAIN AND THE GREEN KNIGHT: Sources and Analogues, *compiled by Elisabeth Brewer*

XXVIII CLIGÉS by Chrétien de Troyes, *edited by Stewart Gregory and Claude Luttrell*

XXIX THE LIFE AND TIMES OF SIR THOMAS MALORY, *P. J. C. Field*

XXX T. H. WHITE'S *THE ONCE AND FUTURE KING*, *Elisabeth Brewer*

XXXI ARTHURIAN BIBLIOGRAPHY, III: 1978–1992, Author Listing and Subject Index, *compiled by Caroline Palmer*

XXXII ARTHURIAN POETS: JOHN MASEFIELD, *edited and introduced by David Llewellyn Dodds*

XXXIII THE TEXT AND TRADITION OF LA3AMON'S *BRUT*, *edited by Françoise Le Saux*

XXXIV CHIVALRY IN TWELFTH-CENTURY GERMANY: The Works of Hartmann von Aue, *W. H. Jackson*

XXXV THE TWO VERSIONS OF MALORY'S *MORTE DARTHUR*: Multiple Negation and the Editing of the Text, *Ingrid Tieken-Boon van Ostade*

XXXVI RECONSTRUCTING CAMELOT: French Romantic Medievalism and the Arthurian Tradition, *Michael Glencross*

XXXVII A COMPANION TO MALORY, *edited by Elizabeth Archibald and A. S. G. Edwards*

XXXVIII A COMPANION TO THE *GAWAIN*-POET, *edited by Derek Brewer and Jonathan Gibson*

XXXIX MALORY'S BOOK OF ARMS: The Narrative of Combat in *Le Morte Darthur*, *Andrew Lynch*

XL MALORY: TEXTS AND SOURCES, *P. J. C. Field*

XLI KING ARTHUR IN AMERICA, *Alan Lupack and Barbara Tepa Lupack*

XLII THE SOCIAL AND LITERARY CONTEXTS OF MALORY'S *MORTE DARTHUR*, *edited by D. Thomas Hanks Jr*

XLIII THE GENESIS OF NARRATIVE IN MALORY'S *MORTE DARTHUR*, *Elizabeth Edwards*

XLIV GLASTONBURY ABBEY AND THE ARTHURIAN TRADITION, *edited by James P. Carley*

XLV THE KNIGHT WITHOUT THE SWORD: A Social Landscape of Malorian Chivalry, *Hyonjin Kim*

XLVI ULRICH VON ZATZIKHOVEN'S *LANZELET*: Narrative Style and Entertainment, *Nicola McLelland*

XLVII THE MALORY DEBATE: Essays on the Texts of *Le Morte Darthur*, *edited by Bonnie Wheeler, Robert L. Kindrick and Michael N. Salda*

XLVIII MERLIN AND THE GRAIL: *Joseph of Arimathea, Merlin, Perceval*: The Trilogy of Arthurian romances attributed to Robert de Boron, *translated by Nigel Bryant*

XLIX ARTHURIAN BIBLIOGRAPHY IV: 1993–1998, Author Listing and Subject Index, *compiled by Elaine Barber*
L *DIU CRÔNE* AND THE MEDIEVAL ARTHURIAN CYCLE, *Neil Thomas*
LII KING ARTHUR IN MUSIC, *edited by Richard Barber*
LIII THE BOOK OF LANCELOT: The Middle Dutch *Lancelot* Compilation and the Medieval Tradition of Narrative Cycles, *Bart Besamusca*
LIV A COMPANION TO THE *LANCELOT-GRAIL* CYCLE, *edited by Carol Dover*
LV THE GENTRY CONTEXT FOR MALORY'S *MORTE DARTHUR*, *Raluca L. Radulescu*
LVI PARZIVAL: With *Titurel* and the *Love Lyrics*, by Wolfram von Eschenbach, *translated by Cyril Edwards*
LVII ARTHURIAN STUDIES IN HONOUR OF P. J. C. FIELD, *edited by Bonnie Wheeler*
LVIII THE LEGEND OF THE GRAIL, *translated by Nigel Bryant*
LIX THE GRAIL LEGEND IN MODERN LITERATURE, *John B. Marino*
LX RE-VIEWING *LE MORTE DARTHUR*: Texts and Contexts, Characters and Themes, *edited by K. S. Whetter and Raluca L. Radulescu*
LXI THE SCOTS AND MEDIEVAL ARTHURIAN LEGEND, *edited by Rhiannon Purdie and Nicola Royan*
LXII WIRNT VON GRAVENBERG'S *WIGALOIS*: Intertextuality and Interpretation, *Neil Thomas*
LXIII A COMPANION TO CHRÉTIEN DE TROYES, *edited by Norris J. Lacy and Joan Tasker Grimbert*
LXIV THE FORTUNES OF KING ARTHUR, *edited by Norris J. Lacy*
LXV A HISTORY OF ARTHURIAN SCHOLARSHIP, *edited by Norris J. Lacy*
LXVI MALORY'S CONTEMPORARY AUDIENCE: The Social Reading of Romance in Late Medieval England, *Thomas H. Crofts*
LXVII MARRIAGE, ADULTERY AND INHERITANCE IN MALORY'S *MORTE DARTHUR*, *Karen Cherewatuk*
LXVIII EDWARD III'S ROUND TABLE AT WINDSOR: The House of the Round Table and the Windsor Festival of 1344, *Julian Munby, Richard Barber and Richard Brown*
LXIX GEOFFREY OF MONMOUTH: *THE HISTORY OF THE KINGS OF BRITAIN*: An edition and translation of the *De gestis Britonum* [*Historia Regum Britanniae*], *edited by Michael D. Reeve, translated by Neil Wright*
LXX RADIO CAMELOT: Arthurian Legends on the BBC, 1922–2005, *Roger Simpson*
LXXI MALORY'S LIBRARY: The Sources of the *Morte Darthur*, *Ralph Norris*
LXXII THE GRAIL, THE QUEST, AND THE WORLD OF ARTHUR, *edited by Norris J. Lacy*
LXXIII ILLUSTRATING CAMELOT, *Barbara Tepa Lupack with Alan Lupack*
LXXIV THE ARTHURIAN WAY OF DEATH: The English Tradition, *edited by Karen Cherewatuk and K. S. Whetter*

LXXV VISION AND GENDER IN MALORY'S *MORTE DARTHUR*, Molly Martin

LXXVI THE INTERLACE STRUCTURE OF THE THIRD PART OF THE *PROSE LANCELOT*, Frank Brandsma

LXXVII *PERCEFOREST*: The Prehistory of King Arthur's Britain, *translated by Nigel Bryant*

LXXVIII CHRÉTIEN DE TROYES IN PROSE: The Burgundian *Erec* and *Cligés*, *translated by Joan Tasker Grimbert and Carol J. Chase*

LXXIX THE *CONTINUATIONS* OF CHRÉTIEN'S *PERCEVAL*: Content and Construction, Extension and Ending, *Leah Tether*

LXXX SIR THOMAS MALORY: *Le Morte Darthur, edited by P. J. C. Field*

LXXXI MALORY AND HIS EUROPEAN CONTEMPORARIES: Adapting Late Medieval Arthurian Romance Collections, *Miriam Edlich-Muth*

LXXXII THE COMPLETE STORY OF THE GRAIL: Chrétien de Troyes' *Perceval* and its continuations, *translated by Nigel Bryant*

LXXXIII EMOTIONS IN MEDIEVAL ARTHURIAN LITERATURE: Body, Mind, Voice, *edited by Frank Brandsma, Carolyne Larrington and Corinne Saunders*

www.ingramcontent.com/pod-product-compliance
Lightning Source LLC
Chambersburg PA
CBHW051606230426
43668CB00013B/1999